ALLEN COUNTY PUBLIC LIBRARY
ACPL ITEM
DISCARDED
Y0-BUC-408

HORROR and SCIENCE FICTION FILMS II

by Donald C. Willis

THE SCARECROW PRESS, INC.
Metuchen, N.J., & London 1982

Library of Congress Cataloging in Publication Data

Willis, Donald C.
Horror and science fiction films II.

1. Horror films--Catalogs. 2. Science fiction films--Catalogs. I. Title.
PN1995.9.H6W53 791.43'09'0916 81-23295
ISBN 0-8108-1517-6 AACR2

Manufactured in the United States of America

For Janet,
a book of her own

INTRODUCTION

Horror and Science Fiction Films II is a supplement, or sequel, to *Horror and Science Fiction Films: A Checklist* (1972). The main list this time is in effect three-lists-in-one: first, entries for films released in the decade since the completion of the earlier manuscript (October, 1971); second, selected titles not in the 1972 checklist, but released between 1899 and 1971; third, selected updatings and revisions of entries in the original checklist.

Animated and short films will now be found in the main list--this includes new entries as well as updatings of/transfers from the old "shorts-and-animated-films" sub-list. The stop-motion wonders of Ladislas Starevitch and the cartoon-animation classics of (principally) Winsor McCay, Max Fleischer, Tex Avery, and Walt Disney have convinced me that animated and short films can no longer conscionably be consigned to a sub-list.

Otherwise, qualifications for a film's inclusion in the main list--as science fiction or horror--remain much the same as for the first volume. One slight policy-change: those films described in reference sources as, vaguely, "futuristic," or set in a not-appreciably-different-or-distant-sounding future, will be found in this volume's peripheral-and-problem-films section (the untenably-titled "out" sub-list of the 1972 edition). "Appreciably different" is, of course, finally a subjective matter. But one example here of *science fiction* would be EMPTY SEA, in which a private company drains the Norwegian Sea; while FLYGNIVA 450 ("wanton terrorism" in Sweden "in the near future"), for a contrasting example, seems simply *fiction*, a narrative twist on contemporary phenomena.

In the last decade, the line between "suspense" and "horror" in film has become almost as badly blurred as that between science fiction and the cinema of more-or-less-current events. Alfred Hitchcock's PSYCHO (1960) and The BIRDS (1963)--two of the most influential movies of the last 20 years--are pretty clearly horror movies: they're not just out to make you jump--they evoke (and more successfully than most horror movies) a nightmare world, whether fantastic or psychological. But not all movies featuring psychopathic killers or animal menaces are horrific. The FAN, PLAY MISTY FOR ME, and ALL THE KIND STRANGERS seem closer to WAIT UNTIL DARK and suspense than to horror--they neither venture into nor conjure up new worlds. SWEET KILL is suspense according to one review, horror according to another. DOBERMAN PATROL sounds like a suspenser; TO KILL A CLOWN verges on horror. (The latter is near-nightmare--guard dogs as psychotic's enforcers.) Hitchcock's own Seventies thriller FRENZY seems more in the tradition of DIAL M FOR MURDER than that of PSYCHO, while John Carpenter's TV-movie SOMEONE'S WATCHING ME! recalls (faintly) REAR WINDOW. Hitchcock-clone Brian De Palma's DRESSED TO KILL plays like a suspenser with horrific sequences (i.e., the visualized nightmare/daydreams). In HALLOWEEN (Carpenter again) and TERROR TRAIN, the psychopathic menace seems to become a supernatural menace by film's end, handily solving classification problems. (The supernatural being, by definition, another, generally darker world.) A horror movie can also be defined--very simply--as one with a monster in it. (As anyone who grew up on "Famous Monsters" will tell you.) The only solution: MPAA genre-coding. ("H" for "horror," etc.)

If it's becoming more and more difficult to define and delimit "horror" and "science fiction" in films, it has become almost impossible to define and delimit "films." The "Battlestar Galactica" TV series became TV-movies in syndication. "The Martian Chronicles" was a TV miniseries here, a movie overseas. The "Planet of the Apes" TV series became "The New Planet of the Apes" TV-movie series. But, its title notwithstanding, the "CBS Late Movie" ("The New Avengers," "The Avengers," "The Night Stalker") is primarily a showcase for old TV series. (See peripheral and problem films for listings on the latter.)

Scattered throughout the main, alphabetical listing this volume are several extensive, informal, title-by-title "retrospectives." They include flashbacks to Universal (the 1931-to-1949 period), Val Lewton, Bela Lugosi, Hammer,and Dr. Jekyll and Mr. Hyde. Key titles: SON OF FRANKENSTEIN, BRIDE OF FRANKENSTEIN, The MAD GHOUL, The MUMMY'S CURSE, ISLE OF THE DEAD, CURSE OF THE CAT PEOPLE, The SEVENTH VICTIM, WHITE ZOMBIE, MURDERS IN THE RUE MORGUE (1932), The BLACK CAT (1934), DEVIL BAT, VAMPIRE CIRCUS, HORROR OF DRACULA, HOUSE OF FRIGHT, TESTAMENT OF DR. CORDELIER, and The NUTTY PROFESSOR.

The retrospective entries for Universal, Lewton, and Lugosi generally represent sixth-time-around personal impressions. The entries for Hammer films are more often one-time-only considerations. The more-contemporary Hammer has been one casualty of my continued preference for "the classics." I have tried (these past few years) to make up for my neglect by seeing as many Hammers as I could, yet HORROR OF DRACULA remains for me one of a very few re-viewable Hammer films--no second-time-around, for instance, for something like FRANKENSTEIN CREATED WOMAN, TASTE THE BLOOD OF DRACULA, or The MUMMY (1959), films which don't exactly cry out for one viewing. Notable exceptions to the once-is-enough rule for Hammer: VAMPIRE CIRCUS, FIVE MILLION YEARS TO EARTH, COUNTESS DRACULA.

I have, for this volume, indexed vampire, werewolf, and mummy films (as well as, again, Dracula and Frankenstein films). These sub-lists within the main list are not meant to replace similar sub-genre lists published elsewhere, but are intended only as addenda to established listings, and refer only to new material in this volume. I have also indexed a few subjects peculiar to the Seventies--Big Foot and the Bermuda Triangle.

There are approximately 2,350 titles in the main list. Of these, approximately half are features from the 1972-1981 period; 300, features from the 1913-1971 period (titles not listed in the first volume); 350, updatings (indicated by asterisks) of previous entries; 250, short films; and 250, TV-movies. Approximately 600 of the entries are critically annotated. The cut-off date for new entries was October 31, 1981.

Additions, corrections, and suggestions are welcomed.

For assistance in tracking down information on hard-to-track-down titles I warmly thank Bill Warren, whose interest in research (to paraphrase John Litel in RETURN OF DOCTOR X) almost equals my own. I would also like to thank Jim Shapiro--for notes on films and film music--Linda Artel and Nancy Goldman of the Pacific Film Archive library, Barbara Hill (for Lugosiana), Jill Mandrake (for making inquiries about a supplement), Gold Key Entertainment, Joe Dante, and Fred Olen Ray.

(Incidentally, there is no such movie as DANGEROUS PEOPLE--as far as I know--as mentioned in the original introduction. I meant DANGEROUS AFFAIR and/or STRANGE PEOPLE.)

The Seventies was the decade of JAWS, CLAWS, "Gnaws" (on "The New Avengers"), FROGS, DOGS, rats (WILLARD, BEN, FOOD OF THE GODS), bats (CHOSEN SURVIVORS, NIGHTWING), cats (NIGHT OF THE 1000 CATS), worms (SQUIRM), snakes (STANLEY, SSSSSS), ants (IT HAPPENED AT LAKEWOOD MANOR, EMPIRE OF THE ANTS). It was the best of times (SOLARIS, DARK STAR, VAMPIRE CIRCUS); it was the worst of times (ZOMBIE, The OTHER, CARRIE). Horror (HALLOWEEN & co.) and science fiction (STAR WARS & co.) became the reigning box-office genres, and regional film-production flourished--Florida, Georgia, Texas, etc. made their own monster and spaceman movies. A worst-list for these prolific Seventies could be composed only by someone stalwart enough to sit *all* the way through to the last, dying frames of the last recorded exploits of the third cousin of Big Foot; or to see *every* TV super-hero movie; or to watch *all* of TWISTED BRAIN (an esthetic impossibility). A best-list, however, is more feasible....

Twelve-Best (1971-1981)

1. SOLARIS
2. DARK STAR

3. VAMPIRE CIRCUS
4. TRILOGY OF TERROR ("Amelia")
5. NOSFERATU
6. CLOSE ENCOUNTERS OF THE THIRD KIND
7. MONTY PYTHON AND THE HOLY GRAIL
8. BEAUTY AND THE BEAST (1979)
9. ALLEGRO NON TROPPO
10. The ANDROMEDA STRAIN/The MANITOU/The CHANGELING (tie)

Runners-up: RECORDED LIVE/SCANNERS/The TENANT/The LAST WAVE/JAWS/EVOLUTION/PSYCHOMANIA/DUEL/YOUNG FRANKENSTEIN/The HILLS HAVE EYES/FLASH GORDON/MANIAC/The BROOD/COUNTESS DRACULA.

Twelve-Best (All-Time)

1. The MASCOT
2. BEAUTY AND THE BEAST (1946)
3. ORPHEUS
4. DEAD OF NIGHT (ventriloquist sequence)
5. The MAGIC CLOCK
6. NOSFERATU (1922)
7. FAUST (1926)
8. The PET
9. NIGHT OF THE HUNTER
10. The THING/SOLARIS/2001 (tie)

Runners-up: KING KONG (1933)/CURSE OF THE DEMON/DARK STAR/HOT WATER/ISLE OF THE DEAD (1945)/PSYCHO/VAMPIRE CIRCUS/REPULSION/FANTASIA ("The Sorcerer's Apprentice" & "Night on Bald Mountain").

(N.B. All holdovers here from 1972 I have since seen again. Others on the 1972 honor roll--but _not_ here--I unfortunately _haven't_ seen again. Still others I unfortunately _have_. All films in the above list--except The PET, which I'll take a chance on--I have seen more than once.)

Personal (Even Perverse) Favorites

MARK OF THE VAMPIRE (1935)
HORROR OF DRACULA
ARSENIC AND OLD LACE
BRIDE OF FRANKENSTEIN
SON OF FRANKENSTEIN
The UNINVITED
SIREN OF ATLANTIS
ABBOTT AND COSTELLO MEET FRANKENSTEIN
SON OF KONG
The MAD GHOUL

Also: GODZILLA VS.THE SMOG MONSTER/GAMERA VS.GUIRON/MASK OF FU MANCHU/PHANTASM/LEMORA/The HOWLING/WHITE ZOMBIE/CHANDU THE MAGICIAN/DOCTOR X (1932).
Perverser and Perverser: SECRET BEYOND THE DOOR.../POWER OF THE

WHISTLER/The PRESIDENT VANISHES/The CORPSE VANISHES/NIGHT OF TERROR (1933)/The RAVEN (1935)/DEVIL BAT/CURSE OF THE LIVING CORPSE/WHEN THE SCREAMING STOPS/ROBOT MONSTER/The LOST CITY/MESA OF LOST WOMEN/PLAN 9 FROM OUTER SPACE/The CREEPING TERROR. Perversest: The WHITE GORILLA.

Memorable Parts of Films

the "brainstorms" in The DEVIL COMMANDS
the kiln sequence in The CRIMINAL LIFE OF ARCHIBALDO DE LA CRUZ
the ghost sequences in UGETSU, A CHRISTMAS CAROL (1951), and The HAUNTING OF M.
the "opera" sequences in PSYCHIC KILLER and The TENANT
the "demon" sequences in WITCHCRAFT THROUGH THE AGES
the "flashback" sequence in INVADERS FROM MARS
the "history" sequence in The DEVIL'S HAND (1942)
the flight sequences in NON-STOP,NEW YORK
the newsreel in IT HAPPENED HERE
the climactic sequences of FACE BEHIND THE MASK, HANGOVER SQUARE, DRACULA (1979), PROVIDENCE, PHANTOM OF THE MOULIN ROUGE, and of course RED PLANET MARS
the effects sequences in The LOST WORLD (1925), The INVISIBLE RAY (1936), DEVIL DOLL (1936), METROPOLIS, The INVISIBLE MAN'S REVENGE, EARTH VS.THE FLYING SAUCERS, RUSLAN I LUDMILA (1973), STAR TREK, and The EMPIRE STRIKES BACK
the monsters in The MYSTERIOUS ISLAND (1929), The MONOLITH MONSTERS, FIEND WITHOUT A FACE, GODZILLA'S REVENGE, GARGOYLES, The ASPHYX, LITTLE SHOP OF HORRORS, INFRAMAN, BUG, SHOCK WAVES, KINGDOM OF THE SPIDERS, ERASERHEAD, ALIEN, DRAGONSLAYER, and of course The GIANT CLAW.

Memorable Performances

Peter Lorre in STRANGER ON THE THIRD FLOOR, BEAST WITH FIVE FINGERS, and ARSENIC AND OLD LACE
Lorre and Karloff in The BOOGIEMAN WILL GET YOU
Boris Karloff in MASK OF FU MANCHU, BRIDE OF FRANKENSTEIN, and BEDLAM
Bela Lugosi in MURDERS IN THE RUE MORGUE, SON OF FRANKENSTEIN
Charles Laughton in ISLAND OF LOST SOULS, The HUNCHBACK OF NOTRE DAME, and The STRANGE DOOR
Simone Simon in CAT PEOPLE, CURSE OF THE CAT PEOPLE
Jean Brooks in The SEVENTH VICTIM, The FALCON AND THE CO-EDS
John Barrymore, Fredric March, and Jean-Louis Barrault as Mr. Hyde, Mr. Hyde, and Opale, resp.
Michael Redgrave in DEAD OF NIGHT
Niall MacGinnis in CURSE OF THE DEMON
Robert Mitchum in NIGHT OF THE HUNTER
Alastair Sim in A CHRISTMAS CAROL (1951)
Anthony Perkins in PSYCHO
John Cassavetes in ROSEMARY'S BABY
Jack Nicholson in The SHINING.

Memorable Scores

Bernard Herrmann's for The GHOST AND MRS.MUIR, HANGOVER SQUARE, DAY THE EARTH STOOD STILL, PSYCHO
Franz Waxman's for BRIDE OF FRANKENSTEIN, The INVISIBLE RAY
Leigh Harline's for ISLE OF THE DEAD
James Bernard's for HORROR OF DRACULA
Roy Webb's for CAT PEOPLE, I WALKED WITH A ZOMBIE, STRANGER ON THE THIRD FLOOR
Max Steiner's for KING KONG, SON OF KONG, ARSENIC AND OLD LACE
Dimitri Tiomkin's for The THING
John Williams' for CLOSE ENCOUNTERS OF THE THIRD KIND, JAWS, RAIDERS OF THE LOST ARK
Jerry Goldsmith's for STAR TREK
Mario Castelnuovo-Tedesco's for AND THEN THERE WERE NONE
Frank Skinner and H.J.Salter's for SON OF FRANKENSTEIN.

That about does it for (introductory) lists....

TABLE OF CONTENTS

EXPLANATORY NOTES

The general order of information for entries in the main listing is as follows:

title/country of origin/distribution company (note: TV distributors of films originally released theatrically are listed first, in parentheses)/production companies/year/animation, color, scope indications/running time/alternate titles/director/script-writer/source, story-writer/photographer/music composer/art director/special effects/makeup/reference sources/cast/synopsis and comment.

* - refers to an entry in the 1972 main list.

** - refers to an entry in the 1972 out list.

*** - refers to an entry in the 1972 shorts-and-animated-films list.

_____ - underlined words indicate corrected material.

(A) - refers to an entry continued in the addenda.

(P) - refers to an entry in the peripheral-and-problem-films section.

(M) - refers to an entry in the main list.

Variety citations without page numbers generally refer to reviews in Variety's (indexed) Film Reviews sections.

ABBREVIATIONS

Arg - Argentine
B - British
Braz - Brazilian
Can - Canadian
Chin - Chinese
Cz - Czechoslovakian
Dan - Danish
Egy - Egyptian
F - French
G - German
H.K. - Hong Kong
Hung - Hungarian
I - Italian
J - Japanese
Sp - Spanish
W.G. - West German

AA - Allied Artists
AI - American International Pictures
BFI - British Film Institute
BV - Buena Vista
Biog - Biograph
Boxo Int'l - Boxoffice International
CFF - Children's Film Foundation
Col - Columbia
Educ - Educational
FN - First National
FVI - Film Ventures International
Fox - Twentieth Century-Fox
Indep.-Int'l. - Independent-International
Para - Paramount
UA - United Artists
Univ - Universal-International
WB - Warner Brothers

anim - cartoon animation
stopmo anim - stop-motion (or object or puppet) animation
m - minutes
c - circa or copyright
sfa - same film as
aka - also known as
orig t - original title
int t - intermediate title (title in-between original and release titles of a film)
alt t - alternate title
re-r t - re-release title

cr t - credits title (on the film itself)
tr t - translated title

D - director
SP - screenplay
Adap - adaptation
Add'l Dial - additional dialogue
Ph - photography
Mus - musical score
PD - production design
AD - art direction
SpFX - special effects
VisFX - visual effects
SpMkp - special makeup
Elec - electronic (music) or electrical (effects)
MechFX - mechanical effects
Opt - opticals
Min - miniatures
Roto - rotoscope
SdFX - sound effects
Cost - costumes
Exec P - executive producer
Narr - narration
Ed - editor
Sup - supervision
Assoc - associate
Cons - consultant
Adv - adviser
Asst - assistant

Ref - reference sources
pb - pressbook
pr - press release

AFI - American Film Institute Catalog
AMPAS - Academy of Motion Picture Arts and Sciences Annual Index
BFC - British Film Catalog
Boxo - Boxoffice
Cinef - Cinefantastique
FD - Film Daily
FFacts - Film Facts
FM - Famous Monsters
Glut/CMM - "Classic Movie Monsters"
Glut/TDB - "The Dracula Book"
Glut/TFL - "The Frankenstein Legend"
HR - Hollywood Reporter
HKFFest - Hong Kong Film Festival
IFG - International Film Guide
JFFJ - Japanese Fantasy Film Journal
LAT - Los Angeles Times
LC - Library of Congress (Motion Pictures)
Lee(p) - Lee(problems) (Reference Guide...)
MFB - Monthly Film Bulletin

MPH - Motion Picture Herald
Maltin/OMAM - "Of Mice and Magic"
Maltin/TVM - "TV Movies"
NYT - New York Times
PFA - Pacific Film Archive (Film Notes)
S&S - Sight and Sound
SFC - San Francisco Chronicle
SFE - San Francisco Examiner
screen - information directly from film's credits
TV - information directly from TV showing of film
TVFFSB - Television Feature Film Source Book
TVG - TV Guide
UFQ - Unijapan Film Quarterly
V - Variety(weekly)
V(d) - Variety(daily)
VV - The Village Voice
WorldF - World Filmography

HORROR AND SCIENCE FICTION FILMS II

A VENEZIA...UN DICEMBRE ROSSO SHOCKING see DON'T LOOK NOW

AARON'S ROD (B) 1923 20m. Ref: BFC. Lee. See also: Mystery of Dr. Fu-Manchu series.

*The ABOMINABLE DR. PHIBES 1971 Sets: Brian Eatwell. Mkp: Trevor Crole-Rees. Ref: Lee. Sequel: DR. PHIBES RISES AGAIN.

AAYIRAM JANMANGAL (India Tamil) Pallavi 1970 Color 128m. D: Durai. SP: M.O. Shanmugham. Mus: M.S. Viswanathan. Ref: Dharap. with Vijayakumar, Lata, Manorama.

Woman's spirit attempts to lure untrue lover to his death.

*ABBOTT AND COSTELLO MEET DR. JEKYLL AND MR. HYDE 1953 (DR. JEKYLL AND MRS. HYDE-orig t) Ref: TV. Glut/CMM.

Electrified wax model of Frankenstein monster seems to come to life; Lou turned into mouse; later, into "Hyde"; still later, he bites several cops, who become "Hydes." Three-movies-in-one, none very good: Abbott and Costello in London; Boris Karloff as Jekyll and Hyde; Craig Stevens and Women's Suffrage. A procession of stunts, effects, fantasy, and slapstick, only vaguely related to comedy, and featuring one of the screen's least interesting Hydes--Karloff and double Eddie Parker just skulk about a lot.

*ABBOTT AND COSTELLO MEET FRANKENSTEIN 1948 83m. (BUD ABBOTT AND LOU COSTELLO MEET FRANKENSTEIN-cr t) Mkp: also Jack Kevan. Ref: screen. V 6/30/48. Glut/CMM.

ABBOTT AND COSTELLO MEET FRANKENSTEIN is arguably the best of the classic Universal Draculas, certainly the best of their Forties Frankensteins, and constitutes the one right use of Larry Talbot/The Wolf Man (Lon Chaney Jr.)--comic foil. (He just takes himself too seriously.) Abbott and Costello are funnier, Universal's monsters scarier, juxtaposed. (Conversely, the movie drifts a bit when the monsters aren't on.) The grand-scale sets and convincing effects set off Abbott and Costello's deft, small-scale comedy. The one disappointment: Bela Lugosi as Dracula, in what amounts to little better than a bit part.

ABBY AI/Mid-America 1974 color 89m. (POSSESS MY SOUL-orig t) Story,D: William Girdler. Story,SP: G.C. Layne. Ph: William Asman. Mus: R.O. Ragland. PD: J. Patrick Kelly III. SpFX: Gene Grigg, Sam Price. Mkp: Joe Kenney. Ref: MFB'75: 171. V 1/1/75. 6/26/74:6(rated). B.Warren. with William Marshall, Carol Speed, Austin Stoker, Bob Holt(demon's voice), Casey Brown, Terry Carter.

"Eshu, god of sexuality and evil-doing," possesses young wife. (MFB)

ABERDEEN EXPERIMENT, The see SCARED TO DEATH(1980)

ACH JODEL MIR NOCH EINEN see 2069: A SEX ODYSSEY

ACT OF KINDNESS(by R.C.-Hayes) see FROM BEYOND THE GRAVE

ADDAMS FAMILY, The see HALLOWEEN WITH THE ADDAMS FAMILY

ADELA JESTE NEVECERELA or ADELE HASN'T HAD HER SUPPER YET see DINNER FOR ADELE

ADOLESCENTS IN THE UNIVERSE (Russ) 1976 Ref: V 7/28/76:32: "a happy vision of robots from out of space."

ADONDE MUERE EL VIENTO (Arg) Mural SCA 1976 D: F. Siro. Ref: IFG'76:89: "for the horror market." with John Russell, Tippi Hedren.

The ADULT VERSION OF JEKYLL AND HIDE Entertainment Ventures 1972 color 85m. D: B. Ron Elliot(aka L.Ray Monde?). From Stevenson's story, "The Strange Case of Dr. Jekyll and Mr. Hyde." Ref: Daisne. Lee. Glut/CMM: flashback to the original Hyde. with Jack Buddliner(Dr. Leader aka Dr. Jekyll), Jane Tsentas(Miss Hide), Rene Bond.

The ADVENTURES OF FLUTTERGUY (B) BFI 1978 anim color 20m. SP,D,Des: D. Holwill. Ref: Zagreb 78 cat.: factory makes "human beings from parts...."

The ADVENTURES OF GOOPY AND BAGHA (India-Bengali?) Purnima 1969 color & b&w 132m. (GOOPY GYNE BAGHA BYNE) SP,D,Mus, Cost: Satyajit Ray. Story: U.K. Roychowdhury. Ph: Soumendu Roy. AD: Bansi Chandragupta. Sequel: KINGDOM OF DIAMONDS. Ref: MFB'72:51-2. Lee. with Tapen Chatterjee, Robi Ghose, Santosh Dutt.

King of the Ghosts (with the tones of a "science-fiction creature") and dancing followers; demented wizard; musical spell that holds army in thrall. (MFB)

The ADVENTURES OF PIMPLE--TRILBY (B) Folly 1914 21m. (TRILBY BY PIMPLE & CO.) SP,D: Fred & Joe Evans. Ref: BFC. with F.Evans(Trilby), J. Evans(Svengali).

AGE OF PISCES Gold Key-TV("Zodiac" series) 1972 color 95m. Ref: TVFFSB: "world of black magic." with Mark Damon, Oliver Reed, Nancy Gates.

AI NO BOREI see EMPIRE OF PASSION

AILILIA (H.K.) Eng Wah 1975 color 115m. SP,D: Lung Kang. SP: also Pansy Mang Kwan. Ph: Chen Hung. Mus: Wong Tse Yan. Ref: V 9/3/75. with Chen Chen, Chen Siu Chow, Tong Ching.
"Spacegirl" from flying saucer warns mankind of impending doom.

AKAZA, THE GOD OF VENGEANCE see CRASH!

AKCE BORORO see OPERATION BORORO

ALABAMA'S GHOST Ellmann 1972 SP,D: Fredric Hobbs. Ref: P. LePage. Willis/SW. V 3/7/73:12. 10/18/72:5(rated). with Lani Freeman, Pierre LePage.
Vampiric rock group pursues its quarry on motorcycles.

ALASKA'S BIGFOOT Gold Key-TV 197-? Ref: V 2/13/80:51.

Los ALEGRES VAMPIROS DE VOGEL (Sp) Titanic 1974 D: J.P. Tabernero. Ref: V 5/8/74:214. 8/29/73:20: aka THOSE CRUEL AND BLOODY VAMPIRES. with Agata Lys.

ALF LAYLAH WA-LAYLAH see ARABIAN NIGHTS

ALICE SWEET ALICE AA/Harristown 1977 color 108m. (HOLY TERROR-'81 Dynamite Ent. reissue. COMMUNION-alt t) SP,D: Alfred Sole. SP: also Rosemary Ritvo. Ph: John Friberg. Mus: Stephen Lawrence. PD: John Lawless. SpFX: Illusions, Inc. Ref: screen. V(d) 9/28/77. V 9/21/77. 4/8/81:8. SFC 6/13/78. MFB'77:190. with Paula Sheppard, Linda Miller, Mildred Clinton, Brooke Shields, Lillian Roth, Alphonse De Noble, Rudolph Willrich, Niles McMaster.
Butcher-knife murders apparently committed by "evil" girl. A gallery of psychological grotesques in a very loud, crude slash-and-stab horror thriller. Gross and unpleasant.

ALICE'S ADVENTURES IN WONDERLAND (by L.Carroll) see FELIX THE CAT IN BLUNDERLAND

ALIEN (B) Fox/Brandywine(Shusett) 1979 color/scope 117m. (STARBEAST-orig t) D: Ridley Scott. SP,Story: Dan O'Bannon. Story: also Ronald Shusett. SP: also (uncredited) Walter Hill, David Giler. Ph: Derek Vanlint; (min) Denys Ayling. Mus: Jerry Goldsmith. Alien: (des) H.R. Giger; (head FX) Carlo Rambaldi. SpFX: (sup) Brian Johnson, Nick Allder; (coord) Clinton Cavers. Concept Art: Ron Cobb et al. Min: Roger Dicken. SpOptFX: Filmfex. SpGraphicFX: Bernard Lodge. Video: Dick Hewitt. Model Sup: Peter Boysey. Ref: screen. MFB'79:191. Cinef IX:1:10-39. V 5/23/79. with Tom Skerritt,

Sigourney Weaver, Veronica Cartwright, Harry Dean Stanton, John Hurt, Ian Holm(robot), Yaphet Kotto, Bolaji Badejo (alien), Helen Horton(voice of "Mother").

A private company sends a manned spaceship on a blind mission to bring back a "perfect form of life" from a distant planet--the life form turns out to be an ever-evolving octopus-shark-devil monster which subsists on other living things. A cold, hermetic, intermittently fascinating creature feature, ALIEN is a showcase for one (or several) of our more memorable movie monsters. It's actually six-monsters-in-one, each incarnation intent on killing (in movies like ALIEN variety is the spice of death)--the scientist on board admires the creature's "purity...and hostility." But if Ridley Scott's earlier film The DUELLISTS was thematically over-explicit, ALIEN is subtle to a fault. Its hide-and-go-seek substructure resolutely resists mining: the ship's crew searches for the monster (the irrational? the absolute? the unpleasant?) and finds the ship's cat (the feline?); it searches for the cat and finds the monster. The narrative patterns are more evocative of time-tested shock-and-suspense tactics than they are of meaning. And as impressive as the incarnations of the alien are, the best-sustained sequence is probably the winding-down of the epileptic robot.

ALIEN CONTAMINATION (I) Cannon 1980 (CONTAMINATION: ALIEN ON EARTH-orig t) D: Luigi Cozzi(aka Lewis Coates). Ref: FM 169:18-23. V 7/23/80: at Trieste. 5/6/81:4(rated).

1989. Eggs of aliens brought from Mars to Earth.

The ALIEN DEAD Firebird Int'l. 1980 80m. (IT FELL FROM THE SKY-orig t) SP,D,Ph: Fred Olen Ray. SP: also Martin Alan Nicholas. Ph: also Gary Singer. Mus: Franklin Sledge. SpFX,P: Ray, Chuck Sumner. SpMkp: Allen Duckworth. SpAnim FX: Bart J. Mixon. Ref: F.O.Ray: from script titled SWAMP OF THE BLOOD LEECHES. with Buster Crabbe, Raymond Roberts, Linda Lewis, Mike Bonavia(Miller Haze), John Leirier(Paisley), Rich Vogan(Krelboin).

Meteorite crashes into houseboat, turns its passengers into carnivorous ghouls; hommages to Roger Corman.

ALIEN ENCOUNTER see STARSHIP INVASIONS. UFOS ARE REAL.

The ALIEN ENCOUNTERS (Can.?) Gold Key-TV/Flocker 1979 color 90m. SP,D: James T. Flocker. Ph & SpFxSeqs: Holger Kasper. Mus: William Loose. Opt: Ray Mercer. SdFxEd: C.T. Welch. Ref: TV. V 5/24/78:6. with Augie Tribach, Matt Boston, Phil Catalli, Patricia Hunt, Bonnie Henry, Eugene Davis(man in black).

Killer-wolf's death, haunted hotel, etc., all explained as visitations by alien beings; "space probes," flying globes exploring Earth's surface. "Wally changed his mind about UFO's." Unwitting minimal cinema.

The ALIEN FACTOR (Gold Key-TV)/CVE 1979 color 80m. SP,D,P: Don Dohler. Ph: Britt McDonough. Mus & SdFX: Kenneth Walker. SpMkpDes: John Cosentino, Larry Schlechter. Anim & Titles: Ernest D. Farino. Logo: Tim Hammell. Ref: TV. V 2/14/79:71(ad). CineFan 2:8-9. with Don Leifert, Cosentino, Schlechter(aliens); Tom Griffith, Mary Mertens, Johnny Walker.

Three "zoological specimens" (including an "energy being" and a "cockroach beast") from a crash-landed spaceship terrorize a small town; alien-in-human-form. Sf/monster movie is generally dismayingly amateurish, but features some nice makeup and special effects and a surprisingly sophisticated score. One good shock scene (instant monster) in a dark cellar.

ALIEN LOVER ABC-TV/Fox-Lenjen 1975 color 74m. D: Lela Swift. Ref: TVFFSB: "television image from another dimension." with Kate Mulgrew, Pernell Roberts, Susan Brown, John Ventantonio.

ALIEN ZONE (Gold Key-TV)/Jupiter 1979 color 85m. Ref: V 10/25/78(rated). GKey: "deranged alien from another world." with John Ericson, Bernard Fox.

The ALIENS ARE COMING NBC-TV/Woodruff-QM 1980 color 94m. D: Harvey Hart. SP: Robert W. Lenski. Ph: Jacques Marquette. Mus: William Goldstein. AD: G. Chan, N. Newberry. Ref: TV. with Tom Mason, Eric Braeden, Caroline McWilliams, John Milford, Max Gail; John Huston(voice of alien)?

Emotionless aliens land on Earth, begin to possess bodies of humans. Elements from several dozen sf films (beginning with INVADERS FROM MARS and IT CAME FROM OUTER SPACE), not very well assimilated. "Cute" acting and dialogue; skimpy effects.

ALISON'S BIRTHDAY (Austral.) AFC-Fontana 1979 color 95m. SP,D: Ian Coughlan. Ph: Kevan Lind. Mus: Brian King, Alan Oloman. PD: Robert Hildritch. Ref: IFG'80:63. V 10/17/79: "reasonably average possession-by-another-spirit film." with Joanne Samuel, Lou Brown, Bunney Brooke, Margie McCrae, John Bluthal.

ALL WEEKEND LOVERS see KILLING GAME, The

ALLEGRO NON TROPPO (I) New Line/Bozzetto 1976 anim & live color 85m. (ALLEGRO MA NON TROPPO-orig t) SP,D,Anim: Bruno Bozzetto. SP: also Guido Manuli, M. Nichetti. Ph: Mario Masini; (anim) Luciano Marzetti. Mus: Ravel, Vivaldi, Dvorak, Debussy, Stravinsky, Sibelius. Ref: MFB'79:167. B.Warren. screen. Filmex. V 12/8/76. 5/7/75:139. UC Daily Cal 11/23/77. with M. Giovannini, N. Garay.

Hommage to and parody of Disney's FANTASIA (including "Bolero" Coke-bottle-creatures parody of the "Rite of Spring" sequence); "Fire Bird" seq. ending in chaos. More even a film than FANTASIA--if it doesn't quite hit peaks like "The Sorcerer's Apprentice," it also lacks the cupids-and-hippos valleys. The "Bolero" sequence--pure, obsessive forward movement--is (despite a limp ending) both the most ambitious and successful sequence. Generally, the film is droll, but quite unpretentious--as, perhaps, an inverted comment on the pretensions of FANTASIA.

L'ALLIANCE (F) CAPAC 1971 color 90m. D: Christian De Chalonge. SP & with: Jean-Claude Carriere, from his novel. Ph: Alain Derobe. Mus: Gilbert Amy. Sets: H. Monloup. Ref: Cinef F'73:39: "human-like insects" survive nuclear holocaust. Lee(V 9/16/70). with Anna Karina, Isabelle Sadoyan, Jean Wiener.

ALLIGATOR Group 1 1980 color 94m. D: Lewis Teague. SP: John Sayles; Frank Ray Perilli? Ph: Joseph Mangine. Ref: V 11/19/80. 10/15/80:17(ad). with Robert Forster, Robin Riker, Michael V. Gazzo, Perry Lang, Jack Carter, Henry Silva, Dean Jagger, Sue Lyon, Angel Tompkins.
Plot: see HUMANOIDS FROM THE DEEP; substitute dogs for salmon, and an alligator for coelacanths.

ALMOST HUMAN see SHOCK WAVES

The ALPHA INCIDENT Studio Film Int'l. 1978 color 95m. (GIFT FROM A RED PLANET-orig t) D,P,Ed: Bill Rebane. SP: Ingrid Neumayer. Ph: Bela St. Jon. Sets: Dale Kuipers. Ref: Boxo 8/6/79:25. FM 161:13. AMPAS. V 6/22/77:32. with Ralph Meeker, Stafford Morgan, John Goff, Carol Newell, John Alderman.
Strange virus strikes down travelers stranded at a remote train station.

ALRAUNE (Hung.) 1918 D: Michael Curtiz. Ref: Lee(FIR'70:538). Canham/THP(Vol.I).

ALTERED STATES WB 1980 color 102m. D: Ken Russell. SP: Paddy Chayefsky (aka Sidney Aaron), from his novel. Ph: Jordan Cronenweth; (time-lapse) Lou Schwartzberg; (macro) Oxford Scientific Films. Mus: John Corigliano. PD: Richard McDonald. SpFX: Chuck Gaspar; (asst) Larry Fuentes. SpVisFX: Bran Ferren. SpOptFX: R. Blalack, J. Shourt. SpMkp: Dick Smith; (asst) Carl Fullerton. Ref: screen. V 12/10/80. SF Exam. 1/23/81. with William Hurt, Blair Brown, Bob Balaban, Charles Haid, Miguel Godreau(primal man), Charles White Eagle (brujo), Drew Barrymore, George Gaynes.
A scientist attempting to unlock the "millions of years of memory in our minds" appears to regress genetically to primal man (and then to "reconstitute" himself) by means of sensory deprivation and Toltec drugs. A variation on "Dr. Jekyll and Mr. Hyde," with little resonance. Hurt at first seems to enjoy being an apeman. (Only later does he have to be rescued from "the pit.") And this scrappy, "hyper" "Hyde" is fun to watch as well as be. These sequences have another big plus:

we don't have to listen to the characters nag, nag, nag--others, themselves, the universe--in their "search for truth." Hurt is about as credible a seeker-after-truth as Lugosi is in The APEMAN.

ALUCARDA (Mex) Proa 1975 (ALUCARDA LA HIJA DE LAS TINIEBLAS) D: Juan L. Moctezuma. Ref: V 9/21/77:6: at Sitges. 2/2/77: 32: at Paris sf-fest. 11/3/76:36. 3/31/76:55,66. Daily American: witchcraft, exorcism. Trieste pr: Satan's daughter; de Sade. with Susana Kamini, Claudio Brook, Adriana Roel, David Silva, Betty Catania.

AMANTES DEL DIABLO see DIABOLICAL MEETINGS

The AMAZING CAPTAIN NEMO CBS-TV/WB-TV & Irwin Allen 1978 color 103m. D: Alex March. SP: Mann Rubin, Robert Bloch, et al. Based on the character in Jules Verne's "20,000 Leagues under the Sea." Ph: Lamar Boren. Mus: Richard LaSalle. AD: Eugene Lourie, D. Alt. SpPhFX: L.B. Abbott, Van Der Veer. Ref: MFB'78:151-2. V 3/15/78:73: from TV pilot series "The Return of Captain Nemo." with Jose Ferrer, Burgess Meredith, Tom Hallick, Burr DeBenning, Lynda Day George, Mel Ferrer, Horst Bucholz, Warren Stevens.

After a century in suspended animation, Capt. Nemo again searches for Atlantis; sub with robot crew.

AMAZING DR. JEKYLL see EROTIC DR. JECKYL

The AMAZING MR. BLUNDEN (B) Film Gems/Hemisphere 1972('74-U.S.) color 99m. SP,D: Lionel Jeffries. From the story "The Ghosts" by Antonia Barber. Ph: Gerry Fisher. Mus: Elmer Bernstein. PD: Wilfred Shingleton. SpFX: Pat Moore. Ref: MFB'73:3. V 9/11/74:7(rated). Willis/SW: '77 Goldstone reissue. with Laurence Naismith, Lynne Frederick, Garry Miller, Rosalyn Landor, Diana Dors.

The ghosts of two children inhabit an old country mansion; time travel.

AMAZING SPIDER-MAN, The see SPIDER-MAN. SPIDER-MAN STRIKES BACK. SPIDER-MAN: THE DRAGON'S CHALLENGE

AMAZING WORLD OF GHOSTS Gold Key-TV/Delineator 1978 color 94m. D & Exec P: Wheeler Dixon. SP: Christopher Sereni. Mus Sup: Jim Cookman. Anim: Granato. Narr: Sidney Paul. Ref: TV. TVG. GKey.

Speculation about the existence of ghosts and other fantastic creatures.

AMAZING WORLD OF PSYCHIC PHENOMENA Sunn 1976 color 95m. SP,D: Robert Guenette. Narr: Raymond Burr. Ref: TVFFSB. TVG 1/13/79. Willis/SW. with Uri Geller, Jeane Dixon.

Speculation re: telepathy, clairvoyance, precognition, psychic photography.

AMERICAN TICKLER, OR THE WINNER OF 10 ACADEMY AWARDS Spectrum 1976 color 77m. (DRAWS-B) D: Chuck Vincent. Ph: James McCalmont. Mus: Peter McKenzie. Ref: MFB'77:231. with Joan Sumner, W.P. Dremak, Marlow Ferguson, Jeff Alin.

Sketch: New York City terrorized by "giant, laboratory-produced penis, 'King Dong'"; JAWS parody.

An AMERICAN WEREWOLF IN LONDON Univ/PolyGram(American Werewolf) 1981 color 102m. SP,D: John Landis. Ph: Robert Paynter. Mus: Elmer Bernstein. AD: Leslie Dilley. SpMkpFX: Rick Baker; (asst) Elaine Baker, Doug Beswick, Joe Ross et al. SpFX: Effects Assoc. Opt: Camera FX. Ref: screen. Cinef XI:3. J.Willis. V 7/15/81:4(rated). 8/19/81. with David Naughton(werewolf), Jenny Agutter, Griffin Dunne(undead), John Woodvine, Frank Oz(with Miss Piggy & Kermit); "Carl La Fong."

Attack by werewolf leaves one young man "undead" corpse, the other a werewolf; dial. refs. to The WOLF MAN(1941), CURSE OF THE WEREWOLF; nightmare seqs. with monsters. Intermittently amusing horror-comedy. The pre-attack buildup is both engagingly suspenseful and funny, but the tone is less-carefully-controlled in the later shock and dramatic scenes. Dunne is a genial walking corpse; Naughton, a more conventional, doomed werewolf. The transformation effects are more elaborate (and sillier) than ever--they make Naughton look like an inflatable plastic werewolf.

AMERICATHON UA/Lorimar 1979 color 85m. Story,SP,D: Neil Israel. SP: also M. Mislove, M. Johnson. Story: also Peter Bergman, Phil Proctor. Ph: G. Hirschfield. Mus: Tom Scott. PD: Stan Jolley. Ref: V 8/15/79. 11/24/80:22. VV 8/20/79: "smiling androids." with Harvey Korman, Fred Willard, John Ritter, Chief Dan George, Terry McGovern, Meatloaf, Dorothy Stratten.

National telethon in the U.S., c.1998.

AMIR HAMZEH VA GOURE DELGIR (Iran.) 1977 anim color 28m. D: N. Zarrinkelk. Ref: Zagreb 78 cat.: demon turns princess into onager.

The AMITYVILLE HORROR AI/Cinema 77 1979 color 117m. D: Stuart Rosenberg. SP: Sandor Stern, from the book by Jay Anson. Ph: Fred J. Koenekamp. Mus: Lalo Schifrin. AD: Kim Swados. VisFxDes: William Cruse. SpFX: Delwyn Rheaume. Mkp: Steve Abrums. Ref: screen. V 8/1/79. MFB'80:3. with James Brolin, Margot Kidder, Rod Steiger, Don Stroud, Michael Sacks, Natasha Ryan, Val Avery, Murray Hamilton, John Larch.

Family moves into house built on site of reputed witch's haunt; plagues of flies and blood; erupting floorboards; hallucinations; man who resembles dead murderer and seems possessed by his spirit. A few decent scares, but mostly shameless false alarms, and occasionally risible manifestations of the evil house's power. (It drives a priest and a nun to spit up.) The drama boils down to the far-from-thrilling question: will the family move out before the visions of violence become a reality?

AMORE LIBERO--FREE LOVE see HOT DREAMS

AMOURS DE LA BELLE FERRONNIERE see FRANCIS THE FIRST

L'AMPELOPEDE (F) Nanou 1974 color 85m. SP,D: Rachel Weinberg. Ph: Claude Becogniee. Ref: V 5/8/74:140. 3/6/74: "a small Ampelopede is born" to a "missing-link monster" and the servant girl he loves. with Patricia Pierangeli, Isabelle Huppert, Jean Pignol(monster), J.M. Marguet.

AMY AND HER FRIEND see CURSE OF THE CAT PEOPLE

L'AN 01 (F) CA/Uz 1973 87m. D: Jacques Doilon. SP: Gebe. Ph: Renan Polles. Ref: V 3/21/73: worker-less alternate world; Alain Resnais segment.

ANANDHA BAIRAVI (India-Tamil) Srividhya 1978 144m. SP,D: Mohan Gandhiraman. Story: V.G. Govindan. Mus. R. Ramanujam. Ref: Dharap. with Ravichandran, V.S. Raghavan, K.D. Santhanam.

Spirit of dead woman possesses ex-lover's wife.

ANATOMY OF A HORROR (Can.) Horror Picture 1980? color 100m. (DEADLINE-orig t) SP,D: Mario Azzopardi. SP: also Dick Oleksiak. Ref: IFG'81:96: horror-movie writer finds horror in his own life. V 5/7/80:548. with Stephen Young, Sharon Masters.

ANATOMY OF TERROR (B) ABC-TV/ITC-TV 1974 color 75m. D: Peter Jefferies. SP: Brian Clemens. Mus: Laurie Johnson. Anim: Dolphin. Ref: TV. TVG. with Paul Burke, Polly Bergen, William Job, Basil Henson, Dinsdale Landen.

An American in London begins to assume the identity of an Englishman; he proves to have been brainwashed by the enemy during the Korean War, and accidentally programmed with the same ID as another man. Perfunctorily shot and acted. The hidden premise is so far-fetched, however, that it does make for a baffling (if still unsatisfying) mystery. Landen (as a detective) has some wry moments.

AND FRANKENSTEIN CREATED WOMAN see FRANKENSTEIN CREATED WOMAN

--AND NOW THE SCREAMING STARTS! (B) Cinerama/Amicus 1973 color 87m. (I HAVE NO MOUTH BUT I MUST SCREAM-orig t. FENGRIFFEN. BRIDE OF FENGRIFFEN. THEN THE SCREAMING STARTS-all int ts) D: Roy Ward Baker. SP: Roger Marshall, from the novel "Fengriffen" by David Case. Ph: Denys Coop. Mus: Douglas Gamley. AD: Tony Curtis. Mkp: Paul Rabiger. Ref: MFB'74:243. V 5/9/73. TV. Lee. Cinef W'73:42. Pirie/HOH. Willis/SW. with Stephanie Beacham, Herbert Lom, Geoffrey Whitehead(ghost), Peter Cushing, Patrick Magee, Ian Ogilvy,

Guy Rolfe, Rosalie Crutchley, Lloyd Lamble, Frank Forsyth.
Woodsman's curse on House of Fengriffen is fulfilled by his spectral hand and avenging ghost. Shrill, crude shocker, with one or two surprises. The heroine never stops screaming--one begins to fear for one's ears. The phantom, crawling hand materializes at will and sees to it that noone tampers with Fengriffen fate.

AND THE BONES CAME TOGETHER ABC-TV/Titus 1972 color 73m. Ref: TVFFSB. Cinef F'73:37: curse; "love beyond death." with Laurence Luckinbill, Robin Strasser, Herbert Berghof.

*AND THEN THERE WERE NONE 1945 See also: TEN LITTLE INDIANS (1975). Mus sc: Mario Castelnuovo-Tedesco. Ref: screen. V 7/11/45. Jim Shapiro.
There's an elusive, tantalizing sense of dread weaving through the comic fabric of this Rene Clair suspense-comedy. Even as the characters are ruling out the supernatural (Walter Huston: "I don't believe in the invisible man"), the photography, the atmospheric music, and the Dudley Nichols script (with its dining-table "Indians" snapped off, mysteriously, one by one) are suggesting it. In fact, Lucien Andriot's camera--which always seems to be jutting past the characters, locating dead bodies, and probing corners and ceilings--in effect "plays" the island's sinister, "invisible" host, U.N. Owen. It subtly evokes a sense of [illegible], the sense of an omnipresent host/force toying with the characters, and serves as chilly counterpoint to the bantering tone of much of the dialogue.

ANDERE, Der(by P. Lindau) see PROCUREUR HALLERS

ANDERE LAECHELN, Das SEE OTHER SMILE, The

*The ANDROMEDA STRAIN 1971 SpPhFX: Douglas Trumbull, James Shourt. Mkp: Bud Westmore. Ref: screen. TV. MFB'71:135. Lee. Cinef Smr'71:24-5. and with Richard O'Brien, Eric Christmas.
Scoop VII, an experimental satellite, returns to Earth bearing a deadly, crystalline microorganism. A generally engrossing updating of Fifties sf-mysteries like MAGNETIC MONSTER and (still the best) The THING. There are so many narrative details and twists, and there's so much scientific data, that at its best the story seems to tell itself--you don't notice the actors nudging it along. When you do notice the actors, they seem to be intruding--most of the dramatic inflections they provide seem false or strident, misguided attempts to inject the juice of "human interest" into the film. The lean, semi-documentary beauty of the Michael Crichton material stubbornly resists such melodramatic fattening.

ANDY WARHOL'S BAD New World/Warhol-Tornberg 1976 color 109m. (BAD-alt t) D: Jed Johnson. SP: Pat Hackett, George Abagnalo. Ph: Alan Metzger. Mus: Mike Bloomfield. AD: Eugene

Rudolf. Mkp: John Alese. Ref: screen. V 3/30/77. MFB'77: 63-4: "visceral and sanguinary excesses." with Carroll Baker, Perry King, Susan Tyrell, Lawrence Tierney, Gordon Oas-Heim, Barbara Allen.

Electrolysis parlor is front for home dial-a-murder organization. Flippant on the surface, BAD is surprisingly earnest beneath it. The script opposes the cold "money people" (who do anything for money or kicks) with the frustrated, "crazy" plain folk, who can't quite act on their festering hate, but who want "unwanted people" removed and are willing to pay for the service. One strain of character seems intended to comment on the other, but the two come off more like alternate diagnoses of contemporary horrors. In addition to the "crazies" and the "colds," there are the "humans"--Tyrell as the main one is a droll caricature of a hypersensitive, all-too-human mother, and her super-heated acting style is played amusingly off Baker's "cold," deadpan, anti-acting "style."

ANDY WARHOL'S DRACULA (U.S.-I-F) Bryanston/Warhol-CCC & 1-Ponti-Yanne & Rassam 1974 color 103m. (BLOOD FOR DRACULA-alt t. ANDY WARHOL'S YOUNG DRACULA-Central Park Films re-r t. DRACULA VUOLE VIVERE: CERCA SANGUE DI VERGINE! DRACULA CERCA SANGUE DI VERGINE...E MORI DI SETE!) SP,D: Paul Morrissey. Ph: Luigi Kuveiller. Mus: Claudio Gizzi. PD: Enrico Job. SpFX: Carlo Rambaldi. Mkp: Mario Di Salvio. SpSdFX: Roberto Arcangeli. Ref: screen. MFB'75:104. Willis/SW. Bianco #4/78. V 1/29/75:38. 2/27/74. with Joe Dallesandro, Udo Kier(Dracula), Maxime McKendry, Vittorio De Sica, Milena Vukotic, Roman Polanski, Arno Juerging(Anton).

Count Dracula abandons Rumania for Italy in his quest for virgin's blood. The first regurgitatory horror movie: this Dracula has a weak stomach--garlic and non-virgin's blood disagree with it. Very sick humor, and sicker than it is funny, but not without a certain morbid fascination. Hacked-off limbs and vomited-up blood are "punch lines" here, and they're "delivered" with an all-too-gleeful gracelessness. (The dialogue itself is also treated rather disdainfully.) Script and camera linger on Dracula's death throes, which in effect last the entire movie; and the aristocratic Kier's agonized writhings somehow evoke--if rather haphazardly--laughs, derision, _and_ pity.

ANDY WARHOL'S FRANKENSTEIN (U.S.-I-F) Bryanston/Warhol-CCC & 1-Ponti-Yanne & Rassam 1974 3-D/color/scope 95m. (FLESH FOR FRANKENSTEIN-alt t. CARNE PER FRANKENSTEIN. Il MOSTRO E IN TAVOLE...BARONE FRANKSTEIN(sic). DE LA CHAIR POUR FRANKENSTEIN) D: Antonio Margheriti. SP: Paul Morrissey, Tonino Guerra. Ph: Luigi Kuveiller. Mus: Claudio Gizzi. PD: Enrico Job. SpFX: Carlo Rambaldi. Mkp: Mario Di Salvio. SpSdFX: Roberto Arcangeli. Ref: screen. MFB'75:52. Bianco Index'75. Daisne. Willis/SW. V 4/10/74:4(rated, as The FRANKENSTEIN EXPERIMENT),30: WARHOL'S FRANKENSTEIN, UP FRANKENSTEIN, The DEVIL AND DR. FRANKENSTEIN-proposed ts. 2/27/74.

with Joe Dallesandro, Monique Van Vooren, Udo Kier, Carla Mancini(female monster), Srdjan Zelenovic(male monster), Arno Juerging(Otto).

Baron Frankenstein hopes to found a Serbian master race of zombies--but his male zombie is more interested in the hero than in his female zombie. A thin joke, the foundation of this most aimless of the Warhol horrors. (Not a recommendation.) Again, as in his DRACULA, the class struggle seems to yield only losers. Purposeless perverseness.

ANGELES Y QUERUBINES (Mex) Cine 1972 color 80m. D & Ph: Raphael Corkidi. SP: Carlos Illescas. Mus: Nacho Mendez. AD: Terre Corkidi. Ref: IFG'74:241-2: family of vampires. V 8/16/72: "eerie atmosphere." Murphy. with Ana Luisa Peluffo, Helena Rojo, R. Canedo, David Silva.

ANGOISSE, L'(by P.Mills & C.de Vylars) see HOUSE OF MYSTERY (1961). MEDIUM, The(1934)

ANIMA PERSA see FORBIDDEN ROOM(1977)

ANIMALES NO SE MIRAN AL ESPEJO, Los see BEASTS DON'T LOOK IN THE MIRROR

ANNO ZERO GUERRA NELLO SPAZIO see WAR IN SPACE(Nais, 1977)

ANTEFATTO see TWITCH OF THE DEATH NERVE

The ANTI-CHRIST (I) Avco Embassy/Capitolina 1974('78-U.S.) color 112m. (L'ANTICRISTO. The TEMPTER-orig U.S. t) SP,D: Alberto De Martino. SP: also G. Clerici, V. Mannino. Ph: A. Massaccesi; (mattes) Biamonte Cinegroup. Mus: Ennio Morricone, Bruno Nicolai. AD: Umberto Bertacca. Ref: MFB'76:75. TVFFSB. SFC. V 11/1/78. 7/17/74:26. Bianco Index '74. with Mel Ferrer, Arthur Kennedy, George Coulouris, Carla Gravina, Alida Valli, Anita Strindberg, Umberto Orsini.

Spirit of 15th-century witch possesses woman; birth of the anti-Christ prevented.

See also: OMEN, The.

ANTS see IT HAPPENED AT LAKEWOOD MANOR

ANY BODY...ANY WAY Distribpix/SHB 1968 color 79m. (ANYBODY, ANYWHERE. BEHIND LOCKED DOORS-'75 Boxo Int'l re-r t) SP,D: Charles Romine. SP: also S.H. Brasloff. Ph: Victor Petrashevic. Mus D: H.R. Kugler. AD: John Annus. Ref: AFI. MFB '73:71. Meyers. Willis/SW. Ind.Film Jnl 12/24/73:88(ad). V 8/1/73:25(rated). with Eve Reeves, Joyce Denner, Daniel Garth, Ivan Hagar.

Bodies of madman's female victims seem to return to life, attack him in his cellar dungeon.

*The APE 1940 From the play by A.H. Shirk. Ref: TV.

Sappy, morally "uplifting" parable which gives the phrase

"well-meaning" new meaning. The climax, in particular, is a richly ludicrous combination of shock and sentimentality, in which Boris Karloff's unscrupulous/beneficent (depending upon how you look at it) Dr. Adrian is simultaneously revealed as both killer and healer: "Walk! Walk!" he cries, encouraging the paralyzed girl whose cure--ah, ambivalence!--has cost so many lives. Below-average Monogram.

APE (U.S.-Kor.) Worldwide Entertainment-Jack Harris/Lee Ming 1976 3-D/color 87m. (The NEW KING KONG-orig t. A*P*E-alt t. SUPER KONG-I) D,Co-P: Paul Leder. SP: Joseph Morgan, W. Huber; Reuben Leder? Ph: Bruce Mackae? Mus: Bruce MacRae? Ref: Willis/SW. Glut/CMM. Bianco #5-6/77:228. V 4/14/76:36. (d) 12/17/76. Meyers. with Rod Arrants, Joanne De Verona, Alex Nicol.

Big, mean gorilla vs. Korean and U.S. armies.

*The APEMAN 1943 Ref: TV. Lennig/TC. V 3/17/43.

"Haunted" house; "televisor"; "ghost hunter" (Minerva Urecal) who records sounds of ghosts. Bela Lugosi is a scientist who has transformed himself into an apeman and who uses human spinal fluid to become human again. He's finally reduced to growling at and scaring his gorilla (Emil Van Horn). Sad, but a long way from Jean Marais and BEAUTY AND THE BEAST. Lugosi and the ape have an odd sort of rapport which recalls a similar teaming in MURDERS IN THE RUE MORGUE; but this is comedy material played straight. Arthur Lennig (not without reason) considers this Lugosi's worst Monogram, but surely he overrates RETURN OF THE APEMAN and The INVISIBLE GHOST.

APOCALIPSIS CANIBAL (Sp) Dara-Beatrice 1980 D: Vincent Darum. Ref: V 5/13/81:333. with Robert O'Neal, L. Fonoll.

The APPLE (U.S.-W.G.) Cannon/N.F. Geria III 1981? color 90m. SP,D: Menahem Golan. Mus: Coby Recht. PD: Jurgen Kiebach. Ref: Boxo 10/1/79:24. 12/31/79:20. V 5/7/80:17(ad). with Joss Ackland, Catherine Mary Stewart, Allan Love.

Sf-rock opera set at the end of this century.

The AQUARIAN Gold Key-TV("Zodiac" series) 1972? color 95m. Ref: TVFFSB. with Joan Collins, Richard Todd, Franco Nero.

A man finds himself able to "leave his body at will...."

AQUARIUS (F) Films 13-Ilio 1972 D: J.P. Pollet. Ref: V 5/3/72:93: "sci-fi tale of men forced to the sea like lemmings."

AQUELLA CASA EN LAS AFUERAS (Sp) Kalendar 1980 color 101m. SP,D: Eugenio Martin. SP: also A. Cuevas et al. Ph: Manuel Rojas. Mus: Carmelo Bernaola. AD: J.M. Alarcon. Ref: V 11/19/80: "sufficient terror." with Javier Escriva, Silvia Aguilar, Alida Valli, Carmen Maura.

Mysterious house of abortion; schizophrenic killer.

ARABIAN ADVENTURE (B) AFD/EMI/Badger 1979 color 98m. D: Kevin Connor. SP: Brian Hayles. Ph: Alan Hume. Mus: Ken Thorne. PD: Elliot Scott. SpFX:(sup) George Gibbs; Richard Conway, David Harris. Mkp: Robin Grantham, Yvonne Coppard. Ref: MFB'79:143. V 5/30/79. FM 161:23-27. AMPAS. with Milo O'Shea, Christopher Lee, Oliver Tobias, Emma Samms, Shane Rimmer, Milton Reid, Mickey Rooney, Peter Cushing, Capucine.
Dictator's double trapped in magic mirror; sacred rose of omnipotence; jinnee in bottle; "three fire-breathing mechanical monsters"; man turned into toad. (MFB)

ARABIAN NIGHTS (I-F) PEA-LPAA 1974('80-U.S.) color 130m. (Il FIORE DELLE MILLE E UNA NOTTE) SP,D: Pier Paolo Pasolini, from stories in "Alf Laylah Wa-Laylah." SP: also Dacia Maraini. Ph: G. Ruzzolini. Mus: Ennio Morricone. AD: Dante Ferretti. SpFX: Rank. Cost: Danilo Donati. Ref: MFB'75:79. V 5/29/74. Bianco Index'74. with Ninetto Davoli, Ines Pellegrina, Franco Citti(demon), Margaret Clementi, T. Bouche.
Demon who turns man into monkey; "premonitions, levitations, transmogrifications." (MFB)

ARCHE DE NOE, L' see NOAH'S ARK

The ARCHER: FUGITIVE FROM THE EMPIRE NBC-TV/Univ & Mad-Dog 1981 color 94m. SP,D,P: Nicholas Corea. Ph: John McPherson. Mus: Ian Underwood. AD: Lloyd S. Papez. SpFX: Bill Schirmer. Mkp: Mike McCracken et al. SdFxEd: B.J. Pincus. Ref: TV. V 4/22/81:44. with Lane Caudell, Belinda Bauer, Victor Campos, Kabir Bedi, Marc Alaimo, George Kennedy, Richard Dix, Tony Swartz.
Good against evil in the kingdom of Malveel(sp?); sorceress Estra and her monster ("Greetings, Goddess!"); oracle; snake people; magic bow.

ARE WE ALONE IN THE UNIVERSE? Gold Key-TV 1978 color 93m. D,P: George Gale. Narr: Hugh Douglas. Ref: TV. GKey. TVG.
Speculation on possible visitations by extraterrestrials.

The ARGONAUTS (I) Luce 1977 (Gli ARGONAUTI) D: Aldo d'Angelo. Ref: V 5/17/78:237: "sci-fi." 5/11/77:226. 10/20/76:84. with Alfredo Raino, Simona Gigliano.

The ARIES COMPUTER Gold Key-TV("Zodiac" series) 1972? color 92m. Ref: TVFFSB: "the year 2013...computer of superhuman intelligence...." with Vincent Price, Andrew Keir, Assaf Dayan, Stephanie Beacham.

ARMAGEDDON 1975 see DOOMSDAY MACHINE, The

ARNOLD Cinerama(Avco Embassy?)/Fenady-Bing Crosby 1973 color 95m. D: Georg Fenady. SP: Jameson Brewer, John F. Murray. Ph: W. Jurgenson. Mus: George Duning. AD: Monty Elliott. SpPhFX: Joe Mercurio. Mkp: Jack H. Young. Ref: MFB'75:255-6. V 10/24/73. with Stella Stevens, Roddy McDowall, Shani

Wallis, Elsa Lanchester, Farley Granger, Victor Buono, John McGiver, Bernard Fox, Patric Knowles.
Mysterious murders in old mansion; "fright devices." (MFB)

ARU MITTSU (J) Nihon 1967 73m. "Shikimu"(1 of 3 parts): SP, D: Shinya Yamamoto. Ref: WorldF'67. with Michiyo Mako.
Man who looks at "The Beauty" ("an incarnation of moon and rabbit") "dies covered with blood."

ASA-NISSE I AGENTFORM (Swed) Filmcenter 1967 97m. SP,D: Arne Stivell. SP: also Gits Olsson. Mus: L. Fors. Ref: World F'67. with John Elfstrom, C.-G. Lindstedt(Invisible Man).

ASAJI GA YADO see UGETSU

ASHES (B) Gainsborough/Balcon 1930 23m. D: Frank Birch. SP: Angus Macphail. Ref: BFC. with Ernest Thesiger, Herbert Mundin, Elsa Lanchester.
Cricket match begins in 1940 and ends in the year 2000.

The ASPHYX (B) (Group IV-TV)/Paragon/Glendale 1972 color/ scope 99m. D: Peter Newbrook. SP: Brian Comport. Story: Christina & Laurence Beers. Ph: Freddie Young. Mus: Bill McGuffie. AD: John Stoll. SpFX: Ted Samuels. Mkp: Jimmy Evans. Ref: TV. MFB'73:72. V 9/20/72. with Robert Stephens, Robert Powell, Jane Lapotaire, Alex Scott, Fiona Walker.
A scientist perfects a lantern which enables him to photograph and capture the death-spirit of living things, before it can claim their bodies--thus conferring immortality on them. The scenes concerning the interrupted asphyx, screeching and writhing like a ghostly ymir, are riveting, and fraught with suggestions of nether-world drama. But the asphyx turns out not to be the subject of the film, just the pretext. The asphyx is only an idea repeated several times rather than developed. The subject is really immortality, and the treatment of it is on the level of The UNEARTHLY. Piercing thoughts like "None of us was meant to be immortal" abound.

The ASTRONAUT ABC-TV/Univ-TV 1972 color 75m. D: Robert M. Lewis. SP: G. DiPego et al. Ph: Alric Edens. AD: George Webb. Ref: Lee(LAT 1/8/72). with Jackie Cooper, Monte Markham, Susan Clark, Robert Lansing, Richard Anderson, John Lupton.
First man on Mars dies mysteriously.

ASYLUM (B) Cinerama/Amicus-Harbor 1972 color 88m. (HOUSE OF CRAZIES-'80 re-r t) D: Roy Ward Baker. SP: Robert Bloch, from his stories "The Weird Tailor," "Lucy Comes To Stay," "Frozen Fear" & "Mannikins of Horror." Ph: Denys Coop. Mus: Douglas Gamley; Moussorgsky. AD: Tony Curtis. SpFX: Ernie Sullivan. Mkp: Roy Ashton. Ref: TV. V 1/30/80:5. 8/2/72. MFB'72:183. J.Shapiro. with Herbert Lom, Barry Morse, Britt Ekland, Richard Todd, Peter Cushing, Patrick Magee, Barbara

Parkins, Charlotte Rampling, Megs Jenkins, Frank Forsyth, Sylvia Sims, James Villiers.

Four stories, involving living parts of corpse (animated-by-ouanga), living tailor's dummy (animated-by-astrology), schizophrenia, doll-willed-to-life; told by asylum inmates. Zilch times four equals zilch. Faint echoes of BEAST WITH FIVE FINGERS, DEAD OF NIGHT('45), PSYCHO, DEVIL DOLL('36 and '64). But in and of itself, zilch.

ASYLUM EROTICA see SLAUGHTER HOTEL

ASYLUM OF SATAN United Film Corp./Bil-Ko 1975(1972) color 80m. SP,D,Mus: William Girdler. SP: also J.P. Kelley. Ph: William L. Asman. Ref: CineFan 2:28. Willis/SW. V 9/13/72: 26(rated). with Charles Kissinger, Carla Borelli, Nick Jolly, Sherry Stein.

Hell as a Satan-run asylum of lost souls (which disappears at the end of the film).

AT THE EARTH'S CORE (B) AI/Amicus 1976 color 90m. D: Kevin Connor. SP: Milton Subotsky, from Edgar Rice Burroughs' novel. See also: LAND THAT TIME FORGOT. PEOPLE THAT TIME FORGOT. Ph: Alan Hume; (process) Charles Staffell. Mus: Mike Vickers. PD: Maurice Carter. SpFX: Ian Wingrove. Mkp: Neville Smallwood, Robin Grantham. Ref: MFB'76:144. TV. V 6/23/76. CineFan 2:15-16. with Doug McClure, Peter Cushing, Caroline Munro, Keith Barron, Cy Grant(Ra), Bobby Parr(Sagoth chief).

Professor's "iron mole" burrows to the center of the Earth, to prehistoric Pellucidar; ape-like Sagoths; giant rhamphorincusi(sp?), or Mahars, who rule; man-eating plant; fire-breathing monster; waddling dinosaur. Tacky, engagingly silly sf-adventure. Cushing and McClure are genial guides; the Mahars-in-the-mist are half-imposing, half-ludicrous winged meanies; and Munro is must-see viewing. Nice music and sound effects.

AT ZIJI DUCHOVE! see LONG LIVE GHOSTS!

ATAQUE DE LOS MUERTOS SIN OJOS see RETURN OF THE EVIL DEAD

ATAQUE DE LOS ZOMBIES ATOMICOS see ZOMBIES ATOMICOS

ATRAPADOS Panorama 1981 b&w & color 91m. D,Ph,Co-P: Matthew Patrick. SP & with: Julio Torresoto. Mus: John Petersen, Daniel Licht. AD: Felix Cordero. Ref: V 7/15/81: post-nuclear holocaust; "outer space montages." with Sonia Vivas, Charlene Koh, Mark Massi.

ATTACK OF THE KILLER TOMATOES NAI/Four Square 1977 color 87m. SP,D,Ed: John De Bello. SP: also Costa Dillon, Steve Peace. Ph: John K. Culley. Mus: Paul Sundfor, Gordon Goodwin. SpFX: Greg Auer. Ref: screen. V 1/31/79. AMPAS. with David Miller, Sharon Taylor, Eric Christmas, Ron Shapiro, Al Sklar, Jack

Riley.

A meant-to-be-comic monster-movie, but not as funny as the accidental ones, as tomatoes grow big, attack humans, and are finally repulsed by music. This is not really even a parody since the plot doesn't follow the familiar (but endearing) patterns of its forebears, but veers off into "whacky" comedy and political satire. Love that title, though.

ATTACK OF THE PHANTOMS Avco Embassy/NBC-TV/Hanna-Barbera & Kiss 1978 color 93m. (KISS IN ATTACK OF THE PHANTOMS-alt t) D: Gordon Hessler. SP: Jan-Michael Sherman, Don Buday. Ph: A. Robert Caramico. Mus: Hoyt Curtain. PD: James G. Hulsey. SpFX: Don Courtney; Westheimer. Mkp: E.L. Bentley. SdFX: Horta. Props: W.L. Hudson. P: Terry Morse Jr. Ref: TV. MFB '80:207-8. V 5/9/79:76(ad). 1/16/80:39(ad). 5/2/79:38: TV premiere 10/28/78, as KISS MEETS THE PHANTOM OF THE PARK. with KISS, Anthony Zerbe, Deborah Ryan, Carmine Caridi, Don Steele.

Mad scientist's robots are actually abducted, reprogrammed humans; amusement park's Chamber of Thrills features the Frankenstein monster, Dracula, werewolf, mummy; KISS has super-powers....Well, it's better than Milton DeLugg.

AU RENDEZ-VOUS DE LA MORT JOYEUSE (F-I) Telecip-Artistes Associes/PEA 1972 color 82m. SP,D: Juan Bunuel. SP: also Pierre Maintigneux. Ph: Ghislain Cloquet. AD: Robert Clavel. SpFX: Pierre Durin. Ref: V 5/9/73:136. 1/17/73. Cinef F'73: 43: living house. with Francoise Fabian, Jean-Marc Bory, Yasmine Dahm, Claude Dauphin.

"Haunted house"; girl who can turn into "witchlike creature." (V)

AU SERVICE DU DIABLE see DEVIL'S NIGHTMARE

AUDREY ROSE UA/Wise 1977 color/scope 112m. D: Robert Wise. SP,Co-P: Frank De Felitta, from his novel. Ph: Victor J. Kemper. Mus: Michael Small. PD: Harry Horner. SpFX: Henry Millar Jr. Mkp: Frank Griffin. Ref: V(d) 4/6/77. MFB'77:188. TV. with Marsha Mason, Anthony Hopkins, John Beck, Susan Swift(Ivy/Audrey Rose), Norman Lloyd, John Hillerman.

Through metempsychosis, little Audrey Rose is reborn as Ivy Templeton; hypnotic regression. To the immediate horror of a child's burning to death in a car accident, AUDREY ROSE opposes the prospect of a happier reincarnation. This is an occasionally moving second-chance drama which, unfortunately, dwindles into a second-chance spiritual-tract, a mere plug for reincarnation. Hopkins is a very convincing hawker of same--his abrupt invocation of the name of Audrey Rose (during one of Ivy's nightmares reliving Audrey Rose's death) momentarily dissolves the didactic in the dramatic. But the script seems generally more interested in spiritual conversion than in dramatic immersion.

AUSSAAT UND KOSMOS(by E.von Daniken) see MYSTERIES OF THE GODS

AUSTRIA 1700 see MARK OF THE DEVIL

AUTO CLINIC Col 1938 anim 8m. (Krazy Kat) SP: Allen Rose. Anim: Harry Love. Ref: LC. screen: robots run car clinic.

AUTOPSY (I) Brenner/Clodio(Pescarolo) 1974('78-U.S.) color 125m. (MACCHIE SOLARI) SP,D: Armando Crispini. SP: also Lucio Battistrada. Ph: Carlo Carlini. Mus: Ennio Morricone. AD: Elia Balletti. Ref: Bianco Index'75. V 10/4/78. Willis/SW. with Mimsy Farmer, Barry Primus, Ray Lovelock, Angela Goodwin, Massimo Serato, Carlo Cattaneo.

Woman who works in morgue; mysterious suicides; "horror museum." (V)

AUTUMN CHILD see REFLECTION OF FEAR

The AWAKENING (U.S.-B?) WB/Orion-EMI/Solo 1980 color 102m. D: Mike Newell. SP: Allan Scott, Chris Bryant, Clive Exton, from Bram Stoker's book "The Jewel of Seven Stars." Ph: Jack Cardiff. Mus: Claude Bolling. PD: Michael Stringer. SpFxD: John Stears. Mkp: George Frost. Ref: screen. V 9/17/80. FM 170:39-41. MFB'80:208. with Charlton Heston, Susannah York, Jill Townsend, Stephanie Zimbalist(Margaret/Kara), Patrick Drury.

Thirty-one "darkenings of the sun" after 1800 B.C., the spirit of the Egyptian Queen Kara is transmigrated into the newborn daughter of an archaeologist. Or is it?--Kara (who died at age 18) has to wait until the present-day Margaret is 18 before she can *really* begin to awaken. Then there's an elaborate ceremony, and *finally*--the awakening. The movie, frustratingly, ends at the beginning. It's a long wait for one shot, which (although rather satisfying) hardly begins to justify the plot's confusion and disjointedness. (We're never quite sure *why* we're waiting, or what the Heston character's role is in Kara's scheme.) Punctuated by gratuitous, OMEN-style stunt-violence.

*The AWFUL DR. ORLOF 1962 Mus: J. Pagan, A.R. Angel. AD: A. Simont. Ref: AFI: "near robot." with F. Comejo.

Sequels: *The DIABOLICAL DR. Z? *DR. ORLOFF'S MONSTER. *ORGIES OF DR. ORLOFF. *ORLOFF AND THE INVISIBLE MAN. Los OJOS SINIESTROS DEL DR. ORLOFF.

BABA YAGA-THE DEVIL WITCH (I-F) 14 Luglio/Simone Allouche 1973 SP,D: Corrado Farina. Based on Guido Crepar's cartoon strip. Ph: A. Parolin. Mus: Piero Umiliana. AD: Giulia Mafai. Ref: MFB'74:268. V 7/25/73. with Carroll Baker(Baba Yaga), George Eastman, Isabelle de Funes, Ely Galleani, Angela Covello.

Lesbian witch casts hypnotic spells, brings doll to life; "bottomless pit." (MFB)

BABAING KIDLAT see LIGHTNING WOMAN

BABY KILLER see IT'S ALIVE(1973)

BABYSITTER MURDERS see HALLOWEEN

*BACK FROM THE DEAD Emirau 1957 scope OptFX: Jack Rabin, Louis DeWitt. Ref: TV.

Man's wife--possessed by spirit of his dead first wife--loses her unborn ("You'll have to make allowances if she's not herself for a few days"); black-arts master; aborted sacrificial ritual. Supernatural yarn with little bite--evil here is a lady with a rotten disposition and a satanist with a wooden eyeball for a door-knocker. Embarrassingly hokey horror score. The one eerie (almost incidental) note sounded: the second wife's displaced spirit is still around ("all alone in a cold, dark place"), at one point aiding her sister in fighting the evil spirit. For your memorable-moments-in-scope-TV-prints file: a scene which cuts the actresses off either side of the image, creating an effect of two invisible women chatting.

BACK TO THE PLANET OF THE APES see NEW PLANET OF THE APES, The

BACKSTAGE PHANTOM see HOUSE OF FEAR(1939)

BAD see ANDY WARHOL'S BAD

BAD RONALD ABC-TV/Lorimar 1974 color 74m. D: Buzz Kulik. SP: Andrew P. Marin, from the novel by Holbrook Vance. Ph: Charles F. Wheeler. Mus: Fred Karlin. Ref: TV. TVFFSB. with Kim Hunter, Scott Jacoby, Pippa Scott, Anita Corsaut, John Larch, Dabney Coleman, Cindy & Lisa Eilbacher.

Psychotic boy wanted for murder "haunts" house. Loose, limp variation on "Goldilocks and the Three Bears" ("Somebody's been trying to get into my diary"), with the standard shocks and psychology. An occasional ear-catching phrase (e.g., "sibling calamities").

BAFFLED! (B) ITC-TV/Arena 1971 color 90m. D,P: Philip Leacock. SP: Theodore Apstein. Ph: Ken Hodges. Mus: Richard Hill. AD: Harry Pottle. Ref: MFB'72:183: ESP & black magic. Maltin/TVM. with Leonard Nimoy, Susan Hampshire, Vera Miles, Rachel Roberts, Angharad Rees, Shane Rimmer.

BALLAD OF TAM LIN, The(by R.Burns) see TAM LIN

BAMYUDA NO NAZO see BERMUDA DEPTHS, The

BANANA MONSTER see SCHLOCK

BAND WAGGON (B) Gainsborough 1940 85m. D: Marcel Varnel. SP: M. Edgar, Val Guest, from the radio series. Ref: BFC. with Arthur Askey, Moore Marriott, Donald Calthrop.

Spies in "haunted" castle.

BANGALORE BHOOTHA (India-Kannada) SLC 1975 167m. Story,D: A.B. Jagan Mohan Rao. Story: also Srinivas. SP: M.D. Sundar. Mus: Guna Sinah. Ref: Dharap. with Dwarkish, Gangadhar, Dinesh, Balkrishna, Jaya Sree.

Scientist's experiments give person "ghost-like appearance."

BANKIET (Pol) 1976? anim cut-outs 8m. SP,D,Des: Z. Oraczewska. Ref: PFA(Trieste pr).

"Elaborate dishes" at banquet devour the guests.

BARBE-BLEUE see BLUEBEARD(1972)

The BARE BREASTED COUNTESS (Belg-F) Brux Int'l/Marc 1975 color/scope 101m. (La COMTESSE AUX SEINS NUS) SP,D,Ph,Ed: Jesus Franco. Mus: Daniel White. Ref: MFB'78:217. with Lina Romay(Irina, Countess of Karlstein), Alica Arno, Jack Taylor, Monica Swin.

Mysterious countess proves to be descended from a family of vampires.

BARN OF THE NAKED DEAD see TERROR CIRCUS

BARON BLOOD (I-W.G.) AI/Leone/Euro-America & Geissler 1972 color 90m. (Gli ORRORI DEL CASTELLO DI NORIMBERGA. CHAMBER OF TORTURES. The BLOOD BARON-both int ts. The THIRST OF BARON BLOOD-ad t. The TORTURE CHAMBER OF BARON BLOOD-alt t) SP,D: Mario Bava. SP: also Vincent Fotre; W. Eser? Adap: William A. Bairn. Ph: Emilio Varriani; Antonio Rinaldi? Mus: Les Baxter; S. Cipriani. AD: Enzo Bulgarelli. SpFX: Franco Tocci. Ref: TV. V 10/25/72. 7/19/72:5. Willis/SW. S Union 1/26/74. B.Warren. Lee. Bianco Index'73. with Joseph Cotten, Elke Sommer, Massimo Girotti, Alan Collins, A. Cantafora.

Young man returns to ancestral home (Castle of the Devils); with incantations raises corpse of sadistic Baron Otto Von Kleist, who has the "power to change his appearance" (to that of Joseph Cotten); witch (who cursed Baron to die horribly again and again) also raised; directs hero to amulet which revives corpses of Baron's victims, who torture and kill him. Apart from the gleefully Grand Guignol ending, this isn't nearly as amusing as it probably sounds, though Bava (never the subtlest of directors) milks every shock for all it's worth--at one point the camera zooms four times into the ghastly face of the walking corpse. (The word "superfluous" may apply here.) Sommer is quite decorative.

BARRACUDA Republic/American General 1978 color 96m. (The LUCIFER PROJECT-orig t) SP,D: Harry Kerwin. SP: also Wayne David Crawford. Ph: H.E. Gibson. Mus: Klaus Schulze. Ref: MFB'78:193-4. AMPAS. V 4/26/78:39(ad). CineFan 2:29. TVG. with Crawford, Jason Evers, Roberta Leighton, Bert Freed, William Kerwin, Cliff Emmich.

Florida. Chemicals in ocean turn barracuda into killers.

BARRY McKENZIE HOLDS HIS OWN (B-Austral.) EMI/Grundy 1974 color/scope 120m. SP,D,P: Bruce Beresford. SP: also Barry Humphries. Ph: Don McAlpine. Mus: Peter Best. PD: John Stoddart. SpFX: Cliff Robertson et al. Sequel to The ADVENTURES OF BARRY McKENZIE. Ref: CineFan 2:26. MFB'75:128. V 5/5/76:98. 1/1/75. with Barry Crocker, Humphries, Donald Pleasence(Erich, Count Plasma).

Count Plasma and vampire accomplice; "Christopher Lee Dracula spoof." (CineFan)

The BASHFUL BUZZARD WB 1945 anim color 7m. D: Bob Clampett. SP: Michael Sasanoff. Ref: TV. LC. Maltin/OMAM: Beaky Buzzard.

Ludicrously-shy buzzard brings giant, fanged, flying dragon home to Roseann-Roseannadanna-voiced ma, for dinner stew. Funny cartoon.

BAT, The see CHOSEN SURVIVORS

The BAT PEOPLE AI/Shaw 1974(1973) color 92m. (IT'S ALIVE-orig t. IT LIVES BY NIGHT-int t?) SP,P: Lou Shaw. D: Jerry Jameson. Ph: Matthew Leonetti. Mus: Artie Kane. Ref: V 11/7/73:27. TVFFSB. Scheuer/MOTV. Murphy. Meyers. Willis/SW. with Stewart Moss, Marianne McAndrew, Michael Pataki, Paul Carr, Arthur Space, Pat Delaney.

Bat-bitten man becomes huge bat, commits series of murders.

*The BAT WHISPERS Atlantic 1930 Ref: screen.

There are some elaborate tracking shots and tricks with shadows here, and an alarmingly queasy maid is good for laughs. But The BAT WHISPERS is not as inventive-of-kind as The LAST WARNING(1929) or The OLD DARK HOUSE(1932). The slim plot depends, simply, on whoever's nearest the light switch--or candle--at crucial moments. Chester Morris mugs peculiarly, and is shot crazily in hard close-ups, for reasons not hard to guess if you're familiar with the '59 remake.

*BATTLE BENEATH THE EARTH Reynolds-Vetter 1968 Ref: TV. and with Paula Li Shiu, Carl Jaffe, Bee Duffell.

Transportation tubes; solaric light for growing plants underground; brainwashing. Garish, klutzy, comic-book-style sf-adventure plays like an "underground" Sam Fuller movie. Inventive in weird, silly ways, this movie is informed, at its best, by a wild-eyed, loony charm; at its worst, by simple dullness. The on-beyond-irresponsible script yields the destined-to-become-classic-camp, "Condition: Silence" sequence, in which everyone and everything in the U.S. stops for a few minutes, so that some highly sensitive sound-detectors can get a fix on the location of the tunnels that the renegade Red Chinese are laser-boring beneath us. (Shhh!)

BATTLE BEYOND THE STARS New World & Orion 1980 color 104m. D: Jimmy T. Murakami. SP,Story: John Sayles. Story: also Anne Dyer. Ph: Daniel Lacambre. Mus: James Horner. AD: Jim

Cameron, C.Breen. Min: (ph fx) C.Comisky; (des) M.Shallock; (ph) G.Dodge, D.Skotak. SpDes: Robert Skotak. SpProps: Tim Duffy, Cuttlefish. SpSdFX: Alan S. Howarth. SpMkp: Steve Neill, Rick Stratton. SpThanx: Jack Rabin et al. Ref: MFB '80:209. screen. V 7/30/80. FM 170:20-25. with Richard Thomas, John Saxon, Robert Vaughn, Darlanne Fluegel, George Peppard, Sybil Danning, Sam Jaffe, Morgan Woodward, Lynn Carlin (ship's voice), Jeff Corey, Dick Davalos.

Defenseless planet enlists mercenaries in battle against villainous Sador (Saxon) and his Stellar Converter; reptilian alien; clone-like Nestor; androids, mutants; Dial-a-Date leftover rotting; Bible-like law Varda. Sf version of The SEVEN SAMURAI (by way of The MAGNIFICENT SEVEN) isn't quite funny enough for adults, but is probably fast and furious enough for kids. Peppard as a space cowboy representing Earth is--with his easy manner and grin--instant atmosphere. Out-of-place in space, he still looks perfectly at home, positively basking in incongruity. The effects are hardly innovative, but they don't let up.

BATTLE BEYOND THE STARS see GREEN SLIME, The

BATTLE FOR THE PLANET OF THE APES Fox/APJAC 1973 color/scope 86m. (COLONIZATION OF THE PLANET OF THE APES-orig t) D: J. Lee Thompson. SP: John W. & Joyce H. Corrington. Story: Paul Dehn. Sequel to PLANET OF THE APES. Ph: Richard H. Kline. Mus: Leonard Rosenman. AD: Dale Hennesy. SpMechFX: Gerald Endler. Mkp:(des) John Chambers;(sup) Joe Di Bella. Ref: MFB'73:163-4: "half-hearted confrontation between the apes and another colony of underground mutants...(radiation-scarred humans)." V 5/23/73. TV. with Roddy McDowall, Claude Akins, Natalie Trundy, Severn Darden, Lew Ayres, Paul Williams, Austin Stoker, France Nuyen, Paul Stevens, Pat Cardi, John Landis, John Huston.

Laws, rules, protocol, technicalities--all engendered by the unchecked proliferation of factions (apes, gorillas, humans, mutant-humans). The script must have been delivered to the set by Western Union apes--even the well-engineered climactic confrontation is marred by a message-in-a-line. A whole world playing foil to McDowall's twitches!

BATTLE OF THE STARS (I) Picturmedia-Cinema Int'l/Nais 1979 D: Alfonso Brescia(aka Al Bradley). Ref: V 5/7/80:345(ad). 10/26/79:29(ad): sf. 5/17/78:242. with John Richardson, Jason Palance, Yanti Somer.

BATTLESTAR GALACTICA ABC-TV/Univ-TV & Larson 1978 color 122m. D: Richard A. Colla. SP: Glen A. Larson. See also: CONQUEST OF THE EARTH. Ph: Ben Colman. Mus: Stu Phillips. AD: John E. Chilberg II. SpFX: Karl Miller, Joe Goss;(ph) Richard Edlund, Dennis Muren;(elec) John Peyser Jr. Anim Des: Harry Moreau. P: Jon Dykstra. Sup P: Leslie Stevens. Ref: TV. MFB'79:67. V 9/20/78:52. 7/18/79:33. with (regulars) Lorne

Greene, Richard L. Hatch, Dirk Benedict, Maren Jensen, John Colicos, Ed Begley Jr., Laurette Spang; Wilfrid Hyde-White, Jane Seymour, Lew Ayres.

TV-movie later shown theatrically in Sensurround; ff. titles 1978-79 series entries later shown as TV-movies. An sf-stew of STAR WARS, The CRAWLING EYE (menace-in-mist, kids in peril), WHEN WORLDS COLLIDE, ROOTS, etc. Good effects; nice score; tepid dramatics.

BATTLESTAR GALACTICA: CURSE OF THE CYLONS color 94m. D: Christian Nyby II. SP: Glen A. Larson, Jim Carlson, Terrence McDonnell. Story: Larson, Michael Sloan. Ph: H.J. Penner. Mus: Stu Phillips. SpFxCons: David H. Garber, Wayne Smith. Ref: TV: planet of pig-like creatures. TVG. and with Barry Nelson, Brett Somers, Dennis Fimple, William Bryant.

BATTLESTAR GALACTICA: EXPERIMENT IN TERROR Ref: KBHK-TV.

BATTLESTAR GALACTICA: GREETINGS FROM EARTH D: Rod Holcomb. SP: Glen A. Larson. Ph: Ben Colman. Ref: TV. and with Ray Bolger, Bobby Van, Lloyd Bochner, Curt Lowens, Randolph Mantooth.

BATTLESTAR GALACTICA: The GUN ON ICE PLANET ZERO D: Alan J. Levi. SP: Donald Bellisario. Ph: Enzo Martinelli. AD: Richard D. James. Ref: TV. TVG. and with Roy Thinnes, Denny Miller, Richard Lynch.

BATTLESTAR GALACTICA: The LIVING LEGEND D: Vince Edwards. SP, Story: Glen A. Larson. Story: also Ken Pettus. Ref: TV. TVG. MFB'80:113-14. 166: theatrical feature MISSION GALACTICA: The CYLON ATTACK from this and FIRE IN SPACE episode. and with Lloyd Bridges, Anne Lockhart.

The legendary commander Cain launches the long-lost Battlestar Pegasus into combat against two Cylon star bases. "Individual initiative" vs. "teamwork" in an updating of CEILING ZERO. Some stirring moments with Bridges and the effects, if you can navigate through a bewildering maze of battle strategies and tolerate the more syrupy scenes. "Rocky Jones," where are you?

BATTLESTAR GALACTICA: LOST PLANET OF THE GODS D: Christian Nyby II. SP: G.A. Larson, D. Bellisario. Ph: H.J. Penner. Ref: TV. TVG. and with Jane Seymour.

Magnetic sea, lost-planet pyramids in October '78 episode.

BATTLESTAR GALACTICA: MURDER IN SPACE SP,D: D. Bellisario. SP: also Michael Sloan et al. Ph: B. Colman, H.J. Penner. AD: Peters, Camden, James. Ref: TV. TVG. and with Brock Peters, Bruce Glover, Audrey Landers, Charles Bloom.

Overheard conversation solves all in this entry.

BATTLESTAR GALACTICA: PHANTOM IN SPACE Ref: KBHK-TV. J.Shapiro. and with Edward Mulhare.

BATTLESTAR GALACTICA: SPACE CASANOVA D: Daniel Haller, Christian Nyby II. SP: D.G. Phinney, J. Carlson, T. McDonnell, D. Bellisario. Ph: Colman, Penner. AD: Peters, Camden, James. Ref: TV. TVG. and with Paul Fix, Nick Holt, James Whitmore Jr., Sean McClory.

BATTLESTAR GALACTICA: SPACE PRISON D: Rod Holcomb, Winrich Kolbe, Daniel Haller. SP: Bellisario, Larson. Ph: Colman. AD: Peters, Camden, Murakami. Ref: TV. and with Fred Astaire, Anne Jeffreys, Ina Balin, Lloyd Bochner, John Hoyt.
Interstellar fugitive (Astaire); Cylon pilots; bolo-like "laser balls."

BATTLESTAR GALACTICA: WAR OF THE GODS D: Haller. SP: Larson. Ref: TV. TVG. and with John Williams.
Series entry accounts, allegorically, for angels, the soul, the Devil, and basketball. "Then we got caught in the war between good and evil?" Check.

BATWOMAN (Mex) Calderon 1968 color 80m. (La MUJER MURCIELAGO) D: Rene Cardona. SP: Alfredo Salazar. Ph: A. Jimenez. Mus: A.D. Conde. AD: J.T. Torija. Ref: WorldF'68. with Maura Monti, Roberto Canedo, Hector Godoy, David Silva, Crox Alvarado, Eric del Castillo, Armando Silvestre.
Batwoman and Interpol vs. Dr. Williams and some Black-Lagoonish creatures.

BAYTEKIN FEZADA CARPISANLAR see FLASH GORDON'S BATTLE IN SPACE

BE FOREVER, YAMATO (J) Toei 1980 anim color 145m. (YAMATO TOWA NI) D: Reiji Matsumoto. SP: Toshio Masuda. Sequel to SPACE CRUISER. Ref: V 8/20/80:45. 5/13/81:258.

The BEAST (F) J.Allen/Argos 1975('77-U.S.) color 102m. (La BETE) SP,D,Ed: Walerian Borowczyk. Ph: B. Daillencourt, M. Grignon. Mus: Domenico Scarlatti. AD: Jacques d'Ovidio. Mkp: Odette Berroyer. Ref: MFB'78:194-5. Meyers. V 5/4/77: 43(ad). 8/27/75. Willis/SW. with Sirpa Lane, Lisbeth Hummel, Elisabeth Kahson, Pierre Benedetti(beast).
Beast with tail and clawed hand; dream of beast ("cross between a bear and a wolf"). (MFB)

BEAST, The see KING KONG(1933)

The BEAST AND THE VIXENS Shermart 1973 D & Co-P: Ray Nadeau. Ref: Bill Warren. V 4/11/73:5(rated). with Jean Gibson, Uschi Digard, Joe Smith.
Bigfoot comedy.

*The BEAST FROM 20,000 FATHOMS 1953 From Bradbury's story "The Foghorn" or "Up from the Deep." Mkp: Louis Phillippi. Ref: TV. Satevepost. and with Steve Brodie, James Best.
A basic Fifties movie-monster script, complete with indispensable ingredients: a "documentary" opening (lots of

precise figures); peek-a-boo first glimpses of the monster (a 100-million-year-old rhedosaurus); scattered sightings; homey touches (in a lighthouse and a bathysphere) before disaster strikes; rampant skepticism before the convincer (the beast walking down Wall Street); romance in narrative pockets; scientists; a monster's-progress map; the military; useless weapons; a spectacular climax, and Kenneth Tobey. The script is competent-of-kind, neither too silly nor too absorbing, and neither the monster nor the people have much personality.

BEAST IN SPACE (I) Nais 1978 D: Alfonso Brescia(aka Al Bradley). Ref: V 5/17/78:242. with Sirpa Lane, Vassilli Caris, V. Venantini.

The BEAST MUST DIE (B) Cinerama/Amicus 1974 color 93m. D: Paul Annett. SP: Michael Winder, from the story "There Shall Be No Darkness" by James Blish. Ph: Jack Hildyard. Mus: Douglas Gamley. AD: John Stoll. SpFX: Ted Samuels. Mkp: Paul Rabiger. Ref: MFB'74:119-20. Willis/SW. V 4/24/74. 9/19/73:4. with Calvin Lockhart, Peter Cushing, Charles Gray, Anton Diffring, Marlene Clark, Michael Gambon(werewolf).

Big-game hunter employs electronic surveillance equipment to track down the biggest game--a werewolf.

BEAST OF BORNEO DuWorld 1934 65m. D,P: Harry Garson. SP: Alfred Hustwick, Frank J. Murray. Ref: Turner/Price. LC. with John Preston, Mae Stuart, Eugene Sigaloff(Dr. Boris Borodoff), Doris Brook.

Mad doctor obsessed with proving man's evolution from apes; huge killer-orangutang.

*The BEAST WITH FIVE FINGERS 1946 SpFX: William McGann, H. Koenekamp. Ref: screen. Jim Shapiro. Lee. Aranda/LB: ideas from Luis Bunuel. NYT 12/26/46. V 12/25/46. and with Belle Mitchell, Barbara Brown, John Alvin.

If you can make it through the rather deadly first hour of The BEAST..., your patience will be rewarded--by the bravura sequence in which Peter Lorre's Hilary finds himself at wit's end (and beyond) coping with a "living" severed hand. It lives of course solely in his guilt-wracked mind, but there it thrives. Key image: the charred hand emerging, implacably, from the fireplace. (Or, mind-over-matter.) Lorre is excellent as the obsessed secretary, his fury and his calm the two disturbing, complementary sides of his madness. You have, however, only Bach's "Chaconne" and the lighting effects to see you through the rest of the all-thumbs storytelling and characterization.

BEAST WITH TWO HEADS see THING WITH TWO HEADS, The

BEAUTY AND THE BEAST (B) Clarendon 1905 11m. D: Percy Stow. Ref: BFC.

Kiss turns beast into prince.

*BEAUTY AND THE BEAST 1946 From Mme. de Beaumont's fairy tale. SpMkp: C. Berard; Arakelian? Ref: screen. Sadoul/Morris. V 12/24/47.

Jean Cocteau's fairy tale is like a fantastic anagram of emotional reality--using only some simple, elegant conceits and effects, he evokes a world of fear, love, and terror. There are--for example--the stylized movements of Beauty (Josette Day) and the Beast (Jean Marais), who can hardly bear to look at each other (for different reasons); the constricting clothes and makeup of the Beast, which are suggestive of an entrapped soul (he is bound emotionally to her, physically to his nature); the Beast lapping water from a stream; his ears prickling at the sound of a deer. His body invariably betrays him--he's obviously a beast, but it's those details, those involuntary tics, that are so embarrassing, so pathetic--they're like nature's last, quick, unjust brush-strokes. The beast's animal instincts are too keen; they're inconsonant with his human feelings, and yet....Cocteau succeeds in making his beast, paradoxically, at once wholly inhuman and wholly human.

BEAUTY AND THE BEAST NBC-TV/Bridgepalm 1976 color 74m. D: Fielder Cook. SP: Sherman Yellen, from the Perrault fairy tale. Ph: Jack Hildyard, Paul Beeson. Mus: Ron Goodwin. AD: Eliott Scott. SpMkp: Del Acevedo; Wally Schneiderman? Ref: TVFFSB. TVG. MFB'78:194. TVSeason. V 12/8/76:59. with George C. Scott(the beast), Trish Van Devere, Bernard Lee, Virginia McKenna, Patricia Quinn.

Beast with magic powers; magic castle.

BEAUTY AND THE BEAST (Cz) CFP/Barrandov 1979 color 90m. (PANNA A NETVOR. The VIRGIN AND THE MONSTER-cr t) SP,D: Juraj Herz. Story: Ota Hofmann, F. Hrubin. Ph: Jiri Machane. Mus: Peter Hapka. AD: Vladimir Labsky. Mkp: Juri Huryah(sp?). Ref: screen. V 2/7/79. IFG'80:103. PFA notes 11/1/80. HKFFest. with Zdena Studenkova, Vlastimil Harapes(the beast), Vaclav Vosko, Jana Brejchova.

Savage, bird-like beast with human eyes and voice; enchanted forest; castle with strange "servants" and magic door to outer world. Cocteau brought genius to the "beauty and the beast" story; Herz brings skill and invention, and his version is satisfying in its own ways. Here, at first, it's simply boredom that makes beauty yearn for her unseen beast's company--then sympathy, and finally love move her. This strange romance, always bordering on the ludicrous, is emotionally engaging, until, at least, the bland, ENCHANTED COTTAGE ending. Herz even gives his unnamed beast schizophrenic duologues with himself, and they work better than one might expect. The loveliest moment: beauty catching--mystically, from afar--an echo of the piano theme which the beast is playing with his freshly-won human hands. (The latter seem at first simply a codicil to a curse since they're useless--at least for slaughtering game.)

*BEDLAM 1946 SP: C. Keith(aka Val Lewton). SpFX: Vernon L. Walker. Ref: TV. screen. MFB'74:260. Siegel/VL. V 4/24/46. and with Ellen Corby, John Ince, Skelton Knaggs.

This last of the Lewton thrillers is untypically upbeat and didactic, and--concerned as it is with the power of goodness--seems rather tangential to what's most interesting in Lewton. It's not a bad film, only basically uninteresting (Florence Nightingale _noir_), and is buoyed by occasional wit, wisdom, and even lyricism. Boris Karloff's callous Sims is even more obviously "wrong" here (and Anna Lee's Nell Bowen "right") than is his Pherides in ISLE OF THE DEAD--which fact doesn't leave much room for ambiguity. (Karloff's performance, however, is wittily "right.") Sims' "Because I _had_ to" does not quite square him or his actions dramatically. His motives seem rather less mixed than Pherides', less excusable.

BEDTIME WITH ROSIE (B) FPD 1974 color 76m. D,P: Wolf Rilla. SP: Ivor Burgoyne. Ph: Mark McDonald. Mus: Roger Webb. Ref: MFB'75:52. with Una Stubbs, Diana Dors, Johnny Briggs.

Nightmare sequence with vampire.

The BEES New World/Bee One-Panorama 1978 color 83m. SP,D,P: Alfredo Zacharias. Ph: Leon Sanchez. Mus: Richard Gillis. AD: J.R. Granada. SpFX: Jack Rabin. Ref: V 10/19/78:97. 11/15/78. TV. FM 165:73. with John Saxon, Angel Tompkins, John Carradine, Claudio Brook, Julio Cesar.

Killer bees threaten to take over "the entire Western Hemisphere." Golly!

*BEFORE I HANG _1940_ Story: Karl Brown, R.D. Andrews. Mus D: Morris Stoloff. Ref: TV. Lee.

One of the two outright duds in the 1939-1942 Karloff Columbia series. (The other: MAN WITH NINE LIVES.) Like The APE, BEFORE I HANG tries, rather foolishly, to be shocking and touching at the same time (e.g., Karloff's Dr. Garth crying "George, I don't want to hurt you! George!"--as he strangles George). And Karloff is always at his blandest playing the kindly old scientist straight. (His _comic_ nice old scientist in The BOOGIEMAN WILL GET YOU is very engaging.)

*BEGINNING OF THE END 1957 Ph: Jack Marta. Mus: Albert Glasser. AD: Walter Keller. SpPhFX: B.I. Gordon. Ref: TV. and with Than Wyenn, Thomas B. Henry, Richard Emory.

BEGINNING OF THE END is simply THEM! (or GODZILLA) with grasshoppers. But pathetic effects mar even the semi-ingenious climax, in which giant grasshoppers are lured through Chicago and into Lake Michigan. (Peter Graves: "Give me an oscillator and a fast boat.") Bonus: probably the only camera-as-giant-grasshopper subjective shot in films.

BEHIND LOCKED DOORS see ANY BODY...ANY WAY

BEHIND THE MASK OF TUTANKAMEN(by B.Wynne) see CURSE OF KING TUT'S TOMB, The

*BELA LUGOSI MEETS A BROOKLYN GORILLA Realart 1952 Add'l Dial: "Ukie" Sherin, Edmond G. Seward. AD: James Sullivan. Ref: V 9/10/52. Lee.

The BELL OF HELL (Sp-F) Hesperia/Boetie 1973 color 106m. (La CAMPANA DEL INFIERNO) D,P: Claudio Guerin Hill. SP: Santiago Moncada. Ph: Manuel Rojas. Mus: Adolfo Waitzman. AD: E.T. de la Fuente. SpFX: Manuel Baquero. Ref: MFB'74:94. V 5/8/74:207. 9/26/73. with Renaud Verley, Viveca Lindfors, Alfredo Mayo, Maribel Martin.

"Bizarre mansion"; "nauseating flashback" to slaughterhouse; woman "horribly swollen" after bee attack; man bricked up alive in old church. (MFB)

BELLMAN, The see SORCERER, The

The BELLS Sawyer's Features 1914 40m. Ref: Lee(MPW): all versions of The BELLS based on the play by Leopold Lewis, from the novel "Le Juif Polonais" by Erckmann-Chatrian.

The BELLS (B) BSFP 1931 trilingual 75m. D: O.M. Werndorff, H. Templeton. SP: C.H. Dand. Ref: BFC: the Mathias story. Chirat. with Donald Calthrop, Jane Welsh, O.B. Clarence.

See also: JUIF POLONAIS, Le(1931).

BEN Cinerama/Bing Crosby 1972 color 94m. D: Phil Karlson. SP: Gilbert Ralston. Sequel to WILLARD. Ph: Russell Metty. Mus: Walter Scharf. AD: R.M. Brooks. SpFX: Bud David. SpPhFX: Howard Anderson Co. Marionettes: Rene. Mkp: Jack H. Young. Ref: MFB'73:4: "be-kind-to-rats import." V 6/14/72. TV. with Lee Harcourt Montgomery(Danny), Joseph Campanella, Arthur O'Connell, Kaz Garas, Kenneth Tobey, Rosemary Murphy, Meredith Baxter, Norman Alden.

Ben and his killer-rats hole up in L.A.'s storm drains; befriend sickly boy. This is half routine-thriller material and half loony boy-and-his-rat story ("Some rats are okay"), with little Danny composing songs about his buddy Ben ("They don't see you as I do"), constructing a rat-marionette for his mini-stage show, and allowing Ben and pals to hop aboard his electric train for a run. At the end, the bedraggled Ben returns, half-rat and half-cinder, after almost being burned to death by some people who don't see him as Danny does.

BERGERE ET LE RAMONEUR, La see KING AND THE MOCKINGBIRD, The

The BERMUDA DEPTHS (U.S.-J) Jad-TV/ABC-TV/Rankin-Bass & Tsuburaya 1978 color 100m. (BAMYUDA NO NAZO) D: Tom Kotani. SP: William Overgard. Story: Arthur Rankin Jr. Ph: Jeri Sopanen;(underwater) Stanton Waterman. Mus: Maury Laws. SpFX: Mark Sagawa. SpProps: Gary Zeller et al. Ref: TVFFSB. TV. JFFJ 13:30. V 5/17/78:14(ad). Meyers. with Burl Ives, Leigh McCloskey, Connie Sellecca(Jennie), Carl Weathers.

The giant, prehistoric sea turtle/devil-god of the Bermuda triangle grants eternal life and beauty to a young woman,

Jennie, born in 1701. Imagine (if you can) PORTRAIT OF JENNIE crossed with GAMMERA-THE INVINCIBLE--the phantom gamin and the giant turtle. This balmy romantic-fantasy (played quite seriously) is camp in conception, stilted drama in execution. Jennie is a reluctant siren; her eternal life with the turtle, a curse--this is supposed to be high-romantic tragedy....One could die trying to suspend disbelief. Agreeably outlandish next-to-last shot.

The BERMUDA TRIANGLE Taft Int'l/Sunn 1978 color 94m. D: Richard Friedenberg. SP: Stephen Lord, from the book by Charles Berlitz. Ph: Henning Schellerup. Mus: John Cameron. SpFX: Doug Hubbard. Mkp: D. Marsh. SdFxSup: James Bryon. Ref: MFB'79:191-2: actors "assailed by nothing more frightening than a green camera filter or tacky matte effects." TV: flying saucers over Puerto Rico. V 1/17/79. with Donald Albee, Lin Berlitz, Warren Kemmerling, Fritz Leiber, Thalmus Rasulala, Vickery Turner.

The BERMUDA TRIANGLE (I-Mex) Nucleo/Conacine 1978 color 115m. (Il TRIANGOLO DELLE BERMUDE. El TRIANGULO DIABOLICO DE LAS BERMUDAS. TRIANGLE...THE BERMUDA MYSTERY-ad t. DEATH TRIANGLE-ad t) SP,D: Rene Cardona Jr. SP: also Carlos Valdemar. Ph: Leon Sanchez. Mus: Stelvio Cipriani. Ref: V 5/17/78:222. 3/1/78:32. 8/17/77:30. 3/30/77:32. 3/22/78:72(ad): "door to another world." IFG'78:228. Bianco #3/78:167. with John Huston, Gloria Guida, Marina Vlady, Claudine Auger, Hugo Stiglitz, Carlos East.

See also: BERMUDA DEPTHS, The. BEYOND THE BERMUDA TRIANGLE. CAYMAN TRIANGLE, The. DEVIL'S TRIANGLE. IN SEARCH OF DRACULA. ISLAND, The. LURE OF THE DEVIL'S TRIANGLE. MYSTERIES FROM BEYOND EARTH. MYSTERIES FROM BEYOND THE TRIANGLE. NEW, ORIGINAL WONDER WOMAN, The. OUTER SPACE CONNECTION, The. SATAN'S TRIANGLE. SECRETS OF THE BERMUDA TRIANGLE. SHARKS' CAVE, The. STALKER. STARSHIP INVASIONS.

BERMUDAS: LA CUEVA DE LOS TIBURONES see SHARKS' CAVE, The

BERMUDE: LA FOSSA MALEDETTA see SHARKS' CAVE, The

BESTIA UCCIDE A SANGUE FREDDO, La see SLAUGHTER HOTEL

BETE, La see BEAST, The

BETTY BOOP, M.D. Para 1932 anim 6m. D: Dave Fleischer. Anim: W. Bowsky, T. Goodson. Ref: TV. Glut/CMM. LC.

Betty Boop's elixir Jippo turns one taker into Fredric March's Mr. Hyde; turns old man young, thin man fat, etc. Sweet and lively.

BETTY BOOP'S MUSEUM (NTA-TV)/Para 1932 anim 5m. D: Dave Fleischer. Anim: W. Henning, R. Timinsky. Ref: TV. LC.

Museum with animal skeletons and 1,000-year-old mummy coming to life, skeleton-hand emerging from portrait.

BEWARE MY BRETHREN (B) Cinerama/World Arts Media 1972 color 98m. (The FIEND-B. BEWARE OF THE BRETHREN-cr t) D,P: Robert Hartford-Davis. SP: Brian Comport. Ph: Desmond Dickinson. Mus: Tony Osborne, Richard Kerr. AD: George Provis. Ref: TVFFSB: horror. MFB'72:94. Cinef III:2:30. FFacts: "eerie" house. with Ann Todd, Patrick Magee, Tony Beckley, Suzanna Leigh, Percy Herbert, Ronald Allen.
Young Londoner kills women for the good of their souls, records their screams; crucifixion.

BEWARE OF THE BLOB or BEWARE! THE BLOB see SON OF BLOB

BEYOND, The see ...E TU VIVRAI NEL TERRORE!

BEYOND ATLANTIS (Fili-U.S.) Dimension/Cohen-Woolner 1973 color 89m. (SEA CREATURES-orig t) D: Eddie Romero. SP: Charles Johnson. Story: Stephanie Rothman. Ph: Justo Paulino;(underwater) Michael J. Dugan. Mus: Ed Norton. PD: Billy Formosa. SpFX: Teofilo Hilario. Opt: Modern. Ref: screen. MFB'77:119. V 1/24/73:18. with Patrick Wayne, John Ashley, Sid Haig, Leigh Christian(Syrene), Lenore Stevens, George Nader, Vic Diaz, Eddie Garcia, Gil Arceo.
Tribe of amphibious semi-humans (some with big goggle-eyes) "may be descended from the Minoans...of the lost city of Atlantis." (MFB) Tired, tacky melo-adventure re: greed.

BEYOND EVIL IFI/Scope III 1980 color 94m. SP,D: Herb Freed. SP: also Paul Ross. Story: David Baugh(n). Ph: Ken Plotin. Ref: V 5/7/80. with John Saxon, Lynda Day George, Michael Dante, David Opatoshu, Mario Milano.
100-year-old spirit of woman attempts to possess man.

BEYOND TERROR (Sp) Cinevision 1980 color 80m. (MAS ALLA DEL TERROR) SP,D: Tomas Aznar. SP: also M. Lizondo, A. Casado. Ph: J. Bragado. Sets: G. Andres. SpFX: Francisco Garcia, Pablo Perez. Ref: V 9/17/80. 10/1/80:73(ad). with F.S. Grajera, Raquel Ramirez, Emilio Siegrist, David Forrest.
Youth-gang members haunted and killed by ghosts of their victims and by "some half-decomposed skeletons" from church's catacombs.

BEYOND THE BERMUDA TRIANGLE NBC-TV/Playboy 1975 color 75m. D: William A. Graham. SP: Charles A. McDaniel. Ph: Gayne Rescher. Mus: Harry Sukman. SdFX: Angel. Ref: TV Season. TV. TVFFSB. with Fred MacMurray, Sam Groom, Donna Mills, Woody Woodbury, Susanne Reed.
Mysterious disappearances off the Florida coast traced to psychic "doors" to another dimension; love transcends the dimensions. How sweet.

BEYOND THE DARKNESS (W.G.) Mid-Broadway/TV 13 1974('76-U.S.) color 84m. (MAGDALENA-POSSESSED BY THE DEVIL-B. MAGDELENA-VOM TEUFEL BESESSEN) D: Michael Walter. SP: J.C. Aurive. Ph: E.W. Kalinke. Mus: H.M. Majewski. AD: Peter Rothe.

Ref: MFB'75:157. Meyers. Bianco Index'76:40. with Dagmar Hedrich, Werner Bruhns, Elizabeth Volkmann, Eva Kinsky.
Woman "bedded by an (invisible) Beelzebub." (MFB)

BEYOND THE DOOR (I) FVI/Ro-As 1974('75-U.S.) color 109m. (CHI SEI? DEVIL WITHIN HER. WHO?-ad t) SP,D: Sonia Assonitis (aka Oliver Hellman), R. D'E. Piazzoli(aka R.Barrett). SP: also S. Molteni, A. Crudo et al. Ph: Piazzoli. Mus: Franco Micalizzi;(U.S.) Riz Ortolani. AD: Piero Filippone, F.P.-Velchi. SpFX: Donn Davison, Wally Gentleman. SdFX: Roberto Arcangeli. Ref: TV. Bianco Index'74. MFB'75:152-3. Willis/SW. V 8/6/75: U.S.-Ital. co-pro.? 7/17/74:26. with Juliet Mills, Richard Johnson, Gabriele Lavia, David Colin Jr., B. Fiorini.
Demonic possession; suspended time; Johnson as midwife to the Devil's progeny. The Devil makes a mess of his hostess's (Mills's) body here, and in general proves most un-urbane. (Post-EXORCIST devils are slobs, which makes for fun effects, but poor pr.) The jolliest effects occur in the children's room, where toy octopi and dolls spring creepily to life. The Devil plays more serious (and familiar) tricks in the master bedroom.

BEYOND THE DOOR II (I) FVI/Laser 1977('79-U.S.) color 95m. (SHOCK TRANSFERT-SUSPENCE-HYPNOS. SUSPENSE-ad t. SHOCK-B) D: Mario Bava. SP: L. Bava et al. Ph: Alberto Spagnoli. Mus: I Libra. AD: Francesco Vanorio. Ref: MFB'80:95. V 8/17/77:30. 5/11/77:288. SFC 5/9/79(ad). 5/12/79. with Daria Nicolodi, John Steiner, David Colin Jr., Ivan Rassimov.
Possessed boy ("a perverse little brute in Bermuda shorts"); nightmares; hallucinations; walled-up body. (MFB)

BID TIME RETURN(by R. Matheson) see SOMEWHERE IN TIME

The BIG BUS Para 1976 color/scope 89m. D: James Frawley. SP: Fred Freeman, Lawrence J. Cohen. Ph: Harry Stradling Jr. Mus: David Shire. PD: Joel Schiller. SpFX: Lee Vasque et al. Ref: MFB'76:228-9. V 6/23/76. TV. with Joseph Bologna, John Beck, Stockard Channing, Rene Auberjonois, Jose Ferrer, Ruth Gordon, Lynn Redgrave, Sally Kellerman, Larry Hagman.
The Cyclops, world's first nuclear-powered bus (launched to the strains of "Also Sprach Zarathustra"); story of previous bus disaster and cannibalism. Very broad disaster-movie spoof. Timing brings off a few of the gags. And there _is_ Sally Kellerman.

BIG CALIBRE Supreme 1934 54m. D: Robert N. Bradbury. SP: Perry Murdock. Ph: William Hyer. Ref: Turner/Price: "the weirdest Western ever made." FQ Smr'80:54. with Bob Steele, Peggy Campbell, Georgia O'Dell, Earl Dwire, Murdock(Zenz).
Zenz, a grotesquely-disguised, insane chemist, commits murders by hurling glass capsules of corrosive gas.

BIG FOOT--MAN OR BEAST? Gold Key-TV/American Nat'l 1975 color 92m. (cf. IN SEARCH OF BIGFOOT) SP,D: Lawrence Crowley et al.

Mus: Jeff Gilman. Narr: J. English Smith. Ref: TV. TVFFSB. GKey.
Interviews with those who claim to have encountered Big Foot; facts and figures on the Pacific Northwest.
See also: ALASKA'S BIGFOOT. BEAST AND THE VIXENS. *BIGFOOT. CAPTURE OF BIGFOOT, The. CURSE OF BIGFOOT. IN SEARCH OF BIGFOOT. LEGEND OF BIGFOOT. MYSTERIOUS MONSTERS. NIGHT OF THE DEMON. PANIC IN THE WILDERNESS. PROPHECY. REVENGE OF BIGFOOT. SASQUATCH. SCREAMS OF A WINTER NIGHT. SNOWBEAST. YETI.

The BIG GAME Gold Key-TV 1972 color 95m. D: Robert Day. Ref: TVG. TV. TVFFSB: "device that can control the thought patterns of tremendous populations...." with Stephen Boyd, France Nuyen, Ray Milland, Cameron Mitchell.

BIGFOOT see BIG FOOT--MAN OR BEAST?

BIGFOOT--THE MYSTERIOUS MONSTER see MYSTERIOUS MONSTERS

BILLION DOLLAR THREAT ABC-TV/Col-TV(Gerber) 1979 color 93m. D: Barry Shear. SP: Jimmy Sangster. Ph: J. Woolf. Mus: Richard Shores. AD: R.Bellah, D.Hennesy. SpFX: Joe Unsinn. Ref: V 4/18/79:156. MFB'79:192. with Dale Robinette, Ralph Bellamy, Keenan Wynn, Patrick MacNee, Harold Sakata, Beth & Karen Specht, Than Wyenn.
Threat to destroy Earth's ozone layer; steel-armed baddie; laser cigarettes; ignitable dental floss.

BIO-WOMAN (B) 1981? anim short D: Bob Godfrey. Ref: V 7/1/81:30: "woman created from chemicals."

*BITE ME, DARLING (W.G.) (Greenfield-TV)/Intent Int'l 1970 (LOVE: VAMPIRE STYLE-TV) Ref: TVFFSB. M/TVM 6/71. Murphy. and with B. Skay, B. Valentin, Herbert Fux.

BITRU(by A.Paraz) see NOAH'S ARK

BIXIE JINCHAI see GOLDEN HAIRPIN

BLACK AND WHITE (India) Mitra 1953 (SHADA KALO) D: Amal Bose. From R.L. Stevenson's "The Strange Case of Dr. Jekyll and Mr. Hyde." Ph: D. Ghose. Ref: Lee(Filmfare). with Sipra, Sisir, Gurudas.

BLACK ANGEL (B) Painted Lady 1980 color/scope 25m. SP,D,P: Roger Christian. Ph: R. Pratt. Mus: Trevor Jones. ElecFX: Paddy Kingsland. Ref: MFB'80:201. with Tony Vogel, J. Gibb.
Maiden in "thrall of the Black Angel," a phantom.

The BLACK BELLY OF THE TARANTULA (I-F) MGM/Danon-PAC 1972 color 88m. (La TARANTOLA DAL VENTRE NERO) D: Paolo Cavara. SP: Lucile Laks. Story,P: Marcello Danon. Ph: M. Gatti. Mus: Ennio Morricone. AD: Piero Poletto. Ref: MFB'72:196. Bianco Index'73. V 5/10/72. with Giancarlo Giannini,

Stefania Sandrelli, Claudine Auger, Barbara Bouchet, Barbara Bach, Annabella Incontrera.
Series of brutal murders ("modelled" on the "wasp-spider pattern"). (MFB)

*The BLACK CAT 1934 Story: Ruric, Ulmer. Mus:(d) Heinz Roemheld; Liszt, Schumann, Tchaikowsky. SpFX: John P. Fulton. Ref: TV. MFB'75:164. and with Harry Cording, Luis Alberni, Paul Weigel, Paul Panzer; John Carradine?
The BLACK CAT is one of the more puzzling passages in horror-movie history. It's a paean to the opaque, and while obviously "about" death--every character, set, and prop is associated with death ("Even the phone....")--it's almost impossible to refine its subject further; the actors run up and down this one metal stairway so often that _it_ begins to seem the crux of the film. ("This is a very tricky house.") The subject seems, finally, to be simply Karloff and Lugosi. In effect at least the film (badly cut before release) is a vehicle for these two actors, and both handle the portentousness of their material, well let's say, _interestingly_. At times they act quite strangely, like somnambulists or dazed ballet dancers, and Lugosi's slow, deliberate, agonized delivery of the line "_Many_..._have_..._gone_..._there_--_few_..._have_..._returned_" is the high point or the low point of the film. (It's difficult to say which.) The BLACK CAT is ridiculously somber and at the same time--thanks to the hypnotic effect of the staging, playing, and music--hard not to watch. It's _all_ portent, a lightning flash without the thunder.

The BLACK CAT (I-B) Selenia 1980? (Il GATTO DI PARK LANE) D: Lucio Fulci. Based on the story by Poe. Ref: V 10/15/80: 194. 5/13/81:166. with Patrick Magee, Mimsy Farmer, Al Cliver.
See also: EXCITE ME. SABBAT OF THE BLACK CAT. NOCHE DE LOS ASESINOS(P).

BLACK CHRISTMAS (Can.) Ambassador/Film Funding-Vision IV 1974 color 97m. (SILENT NIGHT, EVIL NIGHT-alt t? STRANGER IN THE HOUSE-TV) D,P: Robert Clark. SP: Roy Moore. Ph: Reginald Morris. Mus: Carl Zittrer. AD: Karen Bromley. Ref: MFB'75: 217. TVG. Willis/SW. V 10/16/74. with Olivia Hussey, Keir Dullea, Margot Kidder, Andrea Martin, John Saxon, Art Hindle.
Psychopathic killer in sorority-house attic.

*BLACK DRAGONS Banner 1942 Ref: TV. pr. and with Max Hoffman Jr., Edward Piel Sr., Bernard Gorcey.
With the aid of death masks, a Nazi plastic surgeon (Bela Lugosi) transforms six members of the Japanese Black Dragons into facsimiles of American businessmen. Now considered expendable, he hastily trades identities with another man, Colomb (also Lugosi), in order to escape to the U.S. and wreak revenge on the saboteurs--one of which (George Pembroke) he succeeds in turning into a "monster" (with serum and hypnosis). Another impossible Monogram screenplay, with an

"Oh, come on!" premise, featuring two of Hollywood's most famous voices--Lugosi's and "Lone Ranger" Clayton Moore's. Lugosi is given to wistful philosophizing ("One must not flirt with one's destiny") as Colomb/Melcher. (Though a dual role, his part as the "real" Colomb lasts only half a minute.) But his only really shining moment comes when he shoves a dying man to the ground and chuckles (wistfully). The "thrilling," "dramatic" musical accompaniment is quintessential "B" scoring. A hair's-breadth away from being Monogram's worst.

BLACK FRANKENSTEIN see BLACKENSTEIN

BLACK GODDESS (Braz-Nigerian) 1980 D: Ola Balogun. Ref: V 3/19/80:26: "ghost story down through the ages."

The BLACK HOLE BV 1979 color/Technovision 98m. D: Gary Nelson. SP: Jeb Rosebrook, Gerry Day. Story: Rosebrook, Bob Barbash, Richard Landau. Ph: Frank Phillips;(min) Art Cruickshank;(opt) Eustace Lycett. Mus: John Barry. PD & Min: Peter Ellenshaw. AnimSpFxSup: Joe Hale. MechFxSup: Danny Lee. Robot Des: George F. McGinnis. SpSdFX: Stephen Katz. Mattes: Harrison Ellenshaw. Ref: V 12/19/79. TV. MFB'80:19-20. with Maximilian Schell, Anthony Perkins, Robert Forster, Joseph Bottoms, Yvette Mimieux, Ernest Borgnine; Roddy McDowall and Slim Pickens(robots' voices).

A research spaceship discovers a lost survey ship in a "nullified gravity" field near a Black Hole; telepathy; surgically-created, humanoid "robot" slaves. Vapid-to-none story, dialogue, characters; watchable robots, spaceships, meteors, Black Holes. In fact the robots seem to get more footage than the humans--and deserve to. (They're funnier, and also better shots.)

*BLACK LIMELIGHT 1938 (FOOTSTEPS IN THE SAND-TV) SP: also Walter Summers. From Gordon Sherry's play. Ref: TV. BFC. MPH 7/8/39.

Light-sensitive "moon murderer" suffering from nyctalopia can see in the dark. Strained story, situations; risible dialogue. ("What are you going to do--put the moon in the witness box?") The movie is like the aftermath of a thriller or domestic drama; everyone talks about what happened, and nothing happens.

BLACK MAGIC (H.K.?) World Northal/Shaw 1975?('80-U.S.) color/scope SP,D: Calvin Moore. Ph: Antonio St. Martin. Mus: Ferrara. Ref: poster: "voodoo curse." SFC(ad). V 4/7/76:44: with Lotis Key, Ramon Zamora? shot in Manila? 5/14/75:86(ad): with Ti Lung, Tanny. with "Ty Young," "Lilly Leigh."

BLACK MAGIC 2 (H.K.) Shaw 1977 color 95m. (KOU-HUN CHIANG T'OU. The SOUL CATCHING BLACK MAGIC-tr t?) D: Ho Meng-hua. SP: Yi Kuang. Ph: Tsao Hui-chi. Mus: Chan Yang Yu. AD: Chen Ching-shen. Mkp: Wu Hsu-ching. Ref: V 12/14/77: not a sequel to Shaw's BLACK MAGIC. 5/12/76:392. IFG'77:179. with

Ti Lung, T'ien Ni(aka Tanny?), Lo Lieh, Terry Liu, Lily Li.
Madman resurrects army of corpses by driving long nails into their heads.

BLACK NOON CBS-TV/Screen Gems & Fenady 1971 color 73m. D: Bernard Kowalski. SP,P: Andrew J. Fenady. Ph: Keith Smith. Mus: George Duning. AD: Ross Bellah. Ref: TV. with Roy Thinnes, Yvette Mimieux, Gloria Grahame, Lyn Loring, Ray Milland, Henry Silva, Hank Worden, Joshua Bryant, B. Eilbacher.
Folks in Western town of San Melas (read: Salem) have covenant with Death and the Devil; legendary Lilith(Mimieux); black rites. Dullish, with formula uses of slow motion and distorting lenses. Odd stray line: "The Song of Solomon... our song."

*The BLACK RAVEN 1943 Ref: screen. TVFFSB: "horror film." V 6/30/43.
Glenn Strange's hilariously off-target attempts at comic relief break up the monotony of this thunderstorm mystery. George Zucco is dry and detached at first, but the script tries to make him over at the end into a nice old gent, beloved by all. (Doesn't work.) Unnecessary explanations dept.: (tough gangster) "I didn't get this way by being a cream puff!"

BLACK RIBBON FOR DEBORAH, A see DEBORAH

BLACK SUN (Cz) Barrandov 1979 color 135m. (CERNE SLUNCE. TEMNE SLUNCE) SP,D: Otakar Vavra. SP: also Jiri Sotola. From the novel "Krakatit" by Karel Capek. Ph: Miroslav Ondricek. Mus: Martin Kratochvili. AD: Karel Lior. Ref: IFG'80: 105. V 7/30/80. with Radoslav Hrzobohaty, Jiri Tomas.
Inventor discovers "form of matter" that is converted into neutron-type bomb. (V)

*BLACK SUNDAY 1960 D:(U.S.) Lee Kresel. SP: also Marcello Coscia. Ph & AD: also M. Bava. Ref: TV. AFI.
In BLACK SUNDAY, Mario Bava is not merely indiscriminate--he throws in <u>everything</u>: an exploding coffin, a vampire-witch and her double, visions in drinks, a piano key that strikes a sepulchral note, a slow-motion coach, scorpions in corpses' eyes, sound effects, shadows, fog, etc. And there are some exhilarating tracking shots up and into crypts and through cemeteries. But the bravura, Grand Guignol effects alternate with strictly conventional shock-scenes. And the macabre love story here seems, finally, merely a pretext for frissons (some imaginative, some not)--a pretext for Bava's zoom-lens circus.

BLACK THE RIPPER Dimension/FRSCO 1975 SP,P: Frank R. Saletri. Ref: Meyers. V 2/25/76:28. 5/8/74:53. with Hugh van Patten, Bole Nikoli, Renata Harmon.

BLACKENSTEIN (Greenfield-TV)/Exclusive Int'l/Frisco 1973 color (RETURN OF BLACKENSTEIN-orig t? BLACK FRANKENSTEIN-TV) D:

William A. Levey. SP,P: Frank R. Saletri. Ref: Willis/SW. B.Warren. TVFFSB. V 4/24/74:4. 12/19/73:11(ad). 1/3/73:60. 11/15/72:35. with John Hart, Ivory Stone, Andrea King, Liz Renay.

BLACKSNAKE Signal 166/Trident 1973 color/scope 82m. (SWEET SUZY-alt t. SLAVES-B) Story,SP,D,P,Ed: Russ Meyer. SP: also Len Neubauer. Story: also A.J. Ryan. Ph: Arthur Ornitz. Mus: Bill Loose, Al Teeter. AD: Rick Heatherly. Mkp: Bud Miller. Ref: MFB'78:54. Willis/SW. V 7/11/73. 3/7/73:4(rated). with Anouska Hempel, David Warbeck, Percy Herbert, Vikki Richards, Dave Prowse(Jonathan, the zombie), Bob Minor.

BLACULA AI/Power 1972 color 93m. D: William Crain. SP: Joan Torres, Raymond Koenig. Sequel: SCREAM BLACULA SCREAM. Ph: John Stevens. Mus: Gene Page. AD: Walter Herndon. SpFX: Roger George. Mkp: Fred Phillips. Ref: MFB'73:188-9. screen. Glut/TDB. with William Marshall(Blacula), Vonetta McGee, Denise Nicholas, Thalmus Rasulala, Gordon Pinsent, Ketty Lester, Elisha Cook.

While visiting Castle Dracula in Transylvania, African Prince Mamuwalde is vampirized by the Count (Charles Macaulay) and dubbed "Blacula." An awkward mixture of romance, vampire-pic cliches, and shocks (a few effective). Blacula--by turns flip, romantic, and menacing--is an unplayable role. The slow-motion attack of the vampiress is funny and frightening (whether or not it was meant to be).

BLACULA IS BEAUTIFUL, BLACULA LIVES AGAIN! or BLACULA II see SCREAM BLACULA SCREAM

BLADE AF SATANS BOG see LEAVES FROM SATAN'S BOOK

BLIND DEAD, The see TOMBS OF THE BLIND DEAD

BLINKER'S SPY SPOTTER (B) (JED-TV)/CFF/Eyeline 1971 color 58m. Story,D: Jack Stephens. SP: David Ash, Harold Orton. Mus: Harry Robinson. Ref: TVFFSB: spy-catching invention. MFB'72:131: "Pulsar Crystal X," "goal-repeller." with David Spooner, Sally-Ann Marlowe, Milton Reid, Bernard Bresslaw.

*The BLOB 1958 Sequel: SON OF BLOB. SpFX: Barton Sloane. Ref: Lee.

BLOEDVERWANTEN see BLOOD-RELATIONS

BLONDIE'S BIG DEAL Col 1949 66m. D: Edward Bernds. SP: L.W. Henley, from Chic Young's "Blondie" comic strip. Ph: Vincent Farrar. Mus D: M. Bakaleinikoff. AD: Perry Smith. Ref: TV. TVG. "Great Movie Series." V 3/16/49. with Penny Singleton, Arthur Lake, Jerome Cowan, Larry Simms, Stanley Andrews.

Dagwood invents a fire-repellent paint--any material treated with it will not burn. Broad, labored series comedy, with expected plot developments.

BLOOD (I-W.G.) TransEuropa/TV 13 1971 color 94m. (L'OCCHIO NEL LABIRINTO) SP,D: Mario Caiano. SP: also A. Saguera, H. Hachler. Ph: G. Ciarlo. Mus: R. Nicolosi. AD: F. Calabrese, O. Pischinger. SpFX: De Rossi Sforza. Ref: MFB'74:182-3. Bianco Index'73. with Rosemary Dexter, Adolfo Celi, Horst Frank, Alida Valli, F. Ressel.

Nightmares; "ruined house"; "bizarre characters"; "vampiristic elements." (MFB)

BLOOD Bryanston/Kent 1974 color 74m. SP,D: Andy Milligan. Ref: Murphy. Glut/TDB/CMM. Willis/SW. with Allen Berendt, Hope St(r)ansbury, Eve Crosby, Pamela Adams.

Dracula's daughter meets the Wolf Man/Larry Talbot.

BLOOD see MARTIN

*BLOOD AND LACE 1971 SpMkp: Dennis Marsh. Opt: Cinefx. Ref: TV. TVFFSB. MFB'73:5. Cinef Fall'71:37. and with Len Lesser, Vic Tayback, Dennis Christopher.

Hammer-wielding man in monster-mask; hammer and cleaver murders; bodies in cellar freezer. "I thought there was something fishy about that Mrs. Deere and her house." The script's gift for understatement goes no further than the above line--BLOOD AND LACE is generally far-from-backward about springing its corpses, cleavers, and severed hands on you. It so wants to be Grand Guignol, and it really tries, but too hard, with no sense of style. The acting, writing, and score are uniformly awful. The movie's only charm lies in its campy determination to shock.

BLOOD BARON see BARON BLOOD

BLOOD BEACH Gross/Shaw-Beckerman(Empress) 1980 color 90m. Story,SP,D: Jeffrey Bloom. Story,P: Steven Nalevansky. Ph: Steve Poster. Mus: Gil Melle. AD: William Sandell. SpFX: Dellwyn Rheaume. SpDesCons: Malcolm Lubliner. Opt: Howard Anderson. Mkp: Monty Westmore. Ref: screen. V 1/28/81. MFB '81:44. with David Huffman, Mariana Hill, John Saxon, Burt Young, Otis Young.

Huge, sucker-plant-like creature haunts sands of Southern California beach; at end, fragments of destroyed creature become new creatures. Unremarkable, low-key monster movie whose only idea--the people-sucking sands--is from INVADERS FROM MARS. The beast, at least, is kept under wraps until the last 10 minutes. Competently acted and dialogued, but dull, and very flimsily plotted.

BLOOD BRIDES see HATCHET FOR THE HONEYMOON

BLOOD CEREMONY see LEGEND OF BLOOD CASTLE

BLOOD CITY see WELCOME TO BLOOD CITY

BLOOD COUPLE see GANJA AND HESS

BLOOD CULT OF SHANGRI-LA see THIRSTY DEAD, The

BLOOD FOR DRACULA see ANDY WARHOL'S DRACULA

*BLOOD FROM THE MUMMY'S TOMB AI 1971 D: also Michael Carreras. Ref: screen. Lee: "crawling hand."
Spirit of Egyptian princess possesses woman. A hash of ideas from Stoker's "Jewel of Seven Stars." This Hammer version reduces it and its wealth of intriguing detail to a cat, a snake, and a ring. The lazy use of narration stifles all plot interest.

BLOOD LEGACY see LEGACY OF BLOOD(1971)

*BLOOD OF FRANKENSTEIN Indep.-Int'l. 1971 color 90m. (The BLOOD SEEKERS-orig t. SATAN'S BLOODY FREAKS-alt t) D: Al Adamson. SP: W. Pugsley, Samuel M. Sherman. Ph: Gary Graver, Paul Glickman. Mus: William Lava. AD: Ray Markham. ElecFX: Kenneth Strickfaden. SpMkp: George Barr. SpVisFX: Bob LeBar. Dracula Ring: Ruzi. Ref: TV. Lee. MFB'74:247-8. FM 161:81. Murphy. and with Regina Carol, Russ Tamblyn, Forrest J. Ackerman, Greydon Clark, Shelly Weiss(creature).
J. Carrol Naish runs a "creature emporium" in Venice, Ca., and Lon Chaney Jr. (as a thug of a creature) carries around an axe--he was perhaps also the editor of this semi-pro effort. Dracula whips Frankenstein (i.e., the Monster) in battle, but then stays out in the sun too long (two seconds); and Forry gets killed. (Not recommended for the more impressionable readers of Famous Monsters.)

*BLOOD OF GHASTLY HORROR (AA-TV) 1971 color/scope 87m. (MAN WITH THE SYNTHETIC BRAIN-TV) Story,D,P: Al Adamson. SP: Dick Poston, Chris Martino. Story: also Sam Sherman. Ph: L. Horvath, W. Zsigmond. Mus: Jimmy Roosa, Don McGinnis. Mkp: Lee James. Ref: Lee. TVFFSB. TVG. FIR'79:464: sfa FIEND WITH THE ELECTRONIC BRAIN? and with Regina Carol, Roy Morton, Tacey Robbins.
Doctor unleashes zombie to revenge son "destroyed by another doctor's artificial 'Brain Component'." (TVFFSB)

BLOOD ORGY see GORE GORE GIRLS

BLOOD ORGY OF THE SHE DEVILS Gemini/Occult 1972 color 73m. SP,D,P: Ted V. Mikels. Ph: Anthony Salinas. Mus: Carl Zittrer. SpFX: Lee James. Ref: TVFFSB. V 5/11/77:405(ad). 6/28/72:24(rated). Lee(p): sfa STRIGANZA? CineFan 2:29: spells, reincarnation. with Lila Zaborin, Tom Pace, Leslie McRae, Victor Izay, William Bagdad.
"Female witches practice black magic." (TVFFSB)

BLOOD PIE (Sp) Teide 1971 color/scope 89m. (PASTEL DE SANGRE) SP,D: J.M. Valles et al. Ph: L. Cuadrado. Mus: Juan Pineda. AD: Andres Vallve. Ref: Lee(SpCinema). IFG'73:295. with Marta May, Charo Lopez, Julian Ugarte, Romy, M. Paredes.

Four stories, involving phantoms, vampire Celts, and a beautiful Frankenstein monster.

BLOOD REINCARNATION (H.K.-Chinese) Fong Ming 1974 color 99m. (YIN-YANG CHIEH) SP,D: Ting Shan-Hsi. Ph: C. Ching-Chu. AD: Y. Shih-Cheng. Ref: MFB'76:119-120. with Shih Tien, Shirley Huang, Chiang Nan, Yang Chun.
Three stories: "The Treasure" (spirit possession); "The Wanton" (water spirit, exorcist); "Lau Tin Sok" (exorcists, ghost, reincarnation).

BLOOD-RELATIONS (Dutch-F) Jaap van Rij/CTIS 1977 color 97m. (BLOEDVERWANTEN. Les VAMPIRES EN ONT RAS DE BOL) D: Wim Lindner. SP: John Brasom, from Belcampo's short story. Ph: W. Bal. Mus: J.M. de Scarano. AD: Hans Oosterhuis. Ref: MFB '79:21. V 5/11/77:384. IFG'78:239. with Maxim Hamel, Eddie Constantine, Sophie Deschamps, Gregoire Aslan, Robert Dalban.
Group of vampires gets its blood from hospital's plasma bottles.

BLOOD RUBY see RUBY

BLOOD SEEKERS, The see BLOOD OF FRANKENSTEIN

BLOOD SISTERS see SISTERS

The BLOOD SPATTERED BRIDE (Sp) (Barry-TV)/Europix-Morgana 1972('74-U.S.) 83m.(102m.) (La NOVIA ENSANGRENTADA. 'TIL DEATH DO US PART-alt TV t) SP,D: Vicente Aranda. From the novella "Carmilla" by J.S. Le Fanu. Ph: F. Arribas. Mus: A. P. Olea. PD: J.A. Soler. SpFX: Antonio Molina. Ref: Lee. MFB'80:138. TVFFSB. Murphy. Willis/SW. with Simon Andreu, Maribel Martin, Alexandra Bastedo(vampire), R.M. Rodriguez.
Strange woman appears to be reincarnation of vampire.

BLOOD TELLS; OR, THE ANTI-FRIVOLITY LEAGUE (B) Ideal 1916 32m. D: E.J. Collins. SP: George Robey. Ref: BFC. with Robey, Harry Lofting.
Blood transfusion from burglar turns purity-league chairman into rake.

BLOOD TYPE: BLUE (J) Toho 1978 (BURU KURISUMASU) D: Kihachi Okamoto. Mus: Masaru Sato. Ref: JFFJ 13:33. with Tatsuya Nakadai.
Title phenomenon linked to "exposure to UFO's."

BLOOD VIRGIN, The see SYMPTOMS

BLOOD WATERS OF DR. Z Capital/Barton 1973 color 100m. (ZAAT-orig t) D,P: Don Barton. SP: Lee O. Larew, Ron Kivett. Ph: Jack McGowan. Mus: Jami DeFrates, Barry Hodgin. SpMkp: Ron Kivett. Ref: Meyers. V 5/11/77:205(ad). Lee. Cinef W'73:35. with Marshall Grauer, Wade Popwell(monster), Sanna Ringhaver.
Serum turns man into killer-catfish.

BLOOD WEDDING see HE KNOWS YOU'RE ALONE

BLOOD WILL HAVE BLOOD see DEMONS OF THE MIND

BLOODBATH see TWITCH OF THE DEATH NERVE

BLOODEATERS Parker Nat'l/CM 1980 color 84m. (FOREST OF FEAR-orig t) SP,D,P: Chuck McCrann. Ph: David Sperling. Mus: Ted Shapiro. Mkp: Craig Harris. Ref: V 10/29/80. with John Amplas, Charles Austin, Beverly Shapiro, Dennis Helfend.
Experimental herbicide sprayed on marijuana-crop harvesters turns them into "bloodthirsty, zombie-like monsters."

BLOODLUST (Swiss) Monarex 1976 color/scope 88m. (MOSQUITO DER SCHANDER. MOSQUITO-ad t) D: Marijan Vajda. SP: N. Supasi, M. D'Alcala. Ph: D. Khan. Mus: David Llywelyn. AD: R. Jacob. Ref: MFB'77:126. V 3/10/76:27(ad). with Werner Pochath, Ellen Umlauf, Peter Hamm, B. Zamula.
Brutalized young man takes to visiting mortuaries and mutilating and vampirizing corpses, "drawing blood with a pipette." (MFB)

BLOODSUCKING FREAKS Troma 1976(1981) color (The INCREDIBLE TORTURE SHOW-orig t) SP,D,P: Joel Reed. Mus: Michael Sahl. Ref: V 2/4/81:4(rated). 5/13/81:65(ad): "human dart boards, home-style brain surgery." 11/24/76:11. Willis/SW. with Lynette Sheldon, Karen Fraser, Michelle Craig, S. O'Brien.

BLOODTHIRSTY ROSES see EVIL OF DRACULA

BLUE DEMON EN PASAPORTE A LA MUERTE (Mex) Corsa/America 1968 color 85m. D: Alfredo B. Crevenna. SP: A. Ruanova, E.G. Muriel. Ref: WorldF'68. with Blue Demon, Ana Luisa Peluffo, Erich del Castillo, Maura Monti, Jose Galvez.
Group of scientists and spies fashions robot.

BLUE SUNSHINE Cinema Shares Int'l/Ellanby 1977 color 97m. SP,D: Jeff Lieberman. Ph: Don Knight. Mus: Charles Gross. AD: Ray Storey. Puppets: Paul Ashley. Ref: MFB'77:228. FM 165:11,73. AMPAS. with Zalman King, Robert Walden, Mark Goddard, Deborah Winters, Alice Ghostley, Argentina Brunetti.
Delayed reaction to rare strain of LSD causes Stanford grads to snap--10 years later--and become homicidal; ref.to RODAN.(A)

*BLUEBEARD 1944 PD: Eugene Schufftan. Mkp: Milburn Morante. Ref: TV. V 1/31/45. and with Emmett Lynn.
Parisian artist who strangles his "Maid of Orleans" model (for "defiling the image he made of her") repeats the process with each of his subsequent models; tries to curb his compulsion by designing marionettes for his production of Gounod's opera "Faust." An intriguing premise, wasted by a script which devotes more time to the surete than it does to Gaston Morel (John Carradine). Incessant and incessantly-bland music by Erdody. However, five points to director Edgar

Ulmer (or the writers) for coming up with the shot of Carradine and Jean Parker "in" the fireplace flames (paralleling a "hellfire" shot from a "Faust" performance), and six for the next-to-last shot: the camera pulling back and up from the Seine, as it carries away Morel's body--and carried away those of his victims. (Just the right photographic accent for jogging the visual memory.)

BLUEBEARD (U.S.-F-I-W.G.) Cinerama/Barnabe-Gloria-Geiselgasteig 1972 color 124m. (BARBE-BLEUE) SP,D: Edward Dmytryk. SP: also Ennio Di Concini, Maria Pia Fusco. Ph: Gabor Pogany. Mus: Ennio Morricone. AD: Tomas Vayer. Ref: MFB'73:72-73. screen. V 8/23/72. with Richard Burton, Raquel Welch, Joey Heatherton, Virna Lisi, Nathalie Delon, M. Tolo, A. Belli.

Impotent Nazi baron keeps bodies of his wives--or victims--in refrigerated vault. Horror! Drama! Comedy!--but the confused script and direction make it difficult, sometimes, to tell which is which. The Lisi episode is one-note, but a funny one. The rest are primarily dull reversals-of-expectations. Acting and Joey Heatherton have apparently never been introduced to one another.

*The BODY SNATCHER 1945 SP: Val Lewton(aka C. Keith). Ref: MFB'79:237. Siegel/VL. TV. V 2/21/45. and with Mary Gordon, Bill Williams.

The interplay between good and evil, schematized in an interesting but very uneven script. Russell Wade's Fettes is "kind"; Boris Karloff's John Gray is "bad." But--complication--Fettes at one point requires body-snatcher Gray's help, thus indirectly causing the death of a street singer (in a rather literal rendering of Hippocrates' darkness-and-light dialectic). The "lightening" of Gray's character is accomplished even more crudely than is the "darkening" of Fettes'--i.e., through an embarrassing explanation by Gray of his own perversity. The ingenious/idiotic payoff of this out-of-darkness-light schema: in order to see Gray's white horse, on the other side of a wall, the lame girl finally stands. Some of Karloff's best lines as Gray seem, strangely enough, to come straight from the Stevenson original. (Karloff only makes them <u>sound</u> as if they had been written expressly for him.)

BODY SNATCHERS, The(by J. Finney) see INVASION OF THE BODY SNATCHERS(1978)

BOG Marshall 1978 color 95m. D: Don Keeslar. SP: Carl Kitt. Ph: Jack Willoughby. Mus: Bill Walker. Ref: V 10/18/78:147 (ád). with Gloria De Haven, Aldo Ray, Marshall Thompson.

BOGY (Belg) 1971? anim 1 second D: Jules Vercammen. Ref: IFG'72:381: "terrifying face."

BOLD KING COLE Van Beuren 1936 anim color 6m. Ref: TV. LC.

Felix the Cat vs. castle-full of ghosts.

BOMBA ON PANTHER ISLAND Mono 1949 76m. (PANTHER ISLAND-alt t) SP,D: Ford Beebe. Based on the Roy Rockwood series of books. Ph: W. Sickner. Mus: Edward J. Kay. Ref: "Great Movie Series." TVFFSB. V 1/11/50. with Johnny Sheffield, Allene Roberts, Lita Baron, Charles Irwin, Smoki Whitfield.
Island natives "superstitiously believe that the black panther on the prowl is really a devil reincarnated." (GMS)

BOMBS OVER LONDON see MIDNIGHT MENACE

BON LIT, Un see MIDNIGHT EPISODE, A

BONECAS DIABOLICAS see DEVILISH DOLLS

The BOOGEY MAN Gross/IAF 1980 color 90m. SP,D,P: Ulli Lommel. SP: also Suzanna Love, David Herschel. Ph: David Sperling, Jochen Breitenstein. Mus: Tim Krog. AD: Robert Morgan. SpFX: Craig Harris. Ref: screen. V 11/19/80. with S. and Nicholas Love, Ron James, John Carradine, Llewelyn Thomas.
Murdered man's spirit released when mirror containing it breaks; its fragments unleash psychic powers which cause knives, scissors, pitchfork, hose to levitate and kill. After seeing The BOOGEY MAN, you may still not believe a pitchfork can fly. This is simply another vehicle for some elaborately-gross violence. (The two-on-a-knife trick is a particular delight.) It does, however, include one of the Ten Most Unlikely Images in films: a possessed woman levitating in her living room, while she croaks out post-EXORCIST noises, a mirror fragment perched in her eye (like a demon monocle) generates evil rays, and a priest desperately waves a cross up at her. "Wouldn't it be simpler," a character at one point naively asks, "to get another mirror?"

*The BOOGIEMAN WILL GET YOU 1942 Mus D: M.W. Stoloff. AD: Lionel Banks? Ref: TV. V 10/14/42.
Peter Lorre (as Dr. Lorencz) and Boris Karloff (as Dr. Billings) are a delightfully droll team in this horror spoof. They seem to be in--or from--another world; in their reciprocal balminess they're like a surreal vaudeville team. The script is at its best parodying horror movies, and worst imitating "Arsenic and Old Lace" with a zany old housekeeper and a handyman. Last and arguably best of Karloff's Columbia series, and one of Lorre's most endearing performances.

The BOOKWORM MGM 1939 anim color 7m. D: Friz Freleng. Ref: Glut/CMM: Dr. Jekyll and Mr. Hyde; sequel: The BOOKWORM TURNS. LC. Maltin/OMAM. Lee: "Macbeth," "The Raven."

The BOOKWORM TURNS MGM 1940 anim color 7m. Ref: Glut/CMM: sequel to above t. no Maltin/OMAM.

BORN OF THE WIND Film-makers' Coop 1961 20m. D: Mike Kuchar. Ref: Lee.
Scientist brings mummy to life.

BOTSCHAFT DER GOTTER see MYSTERIES OF THE GODS

*BOWERY AT MIDNIGHT Banner 1942 Ref: TV. V 11/11/42.
Secret formula for reviving dead; psychology professor who leads double life as gangster. The pointlessly convoluted plot of BOWERY AT MIDNIGHT seems an end in itself, as if the mere convolutions were an achievement. Stray winners, however, in the dialogue: (beleaguered police chief) "I can feel the hot breath of the outraged public on my neck!", or (Bela Lugosi's gangster-prof) "How often have I told you to stop that cat from desecrating my graves!" Not Monogram's finest hour.

BOWERY BOYS, The (aka The EAST SIDE KIDS) series
See: BLUES BUSTERS(P). *BOWERY BOYS MEET THE MONSTERS. *GHOST CHASERS. *GHOST CREEPS, The. GHOSTS ON THE LOOSE. *HOLD THAT LINE. *JALOPY. JUNGLE GENTS. JUNIOR G-MEN. *JUNIOR "G" MEN OF THE AIR. LOOSE IN LONDON. MASTER MINDS. *NO HOLDS BARRED. *PARIS PLAYBOYS. SPOOK BUSTERS. SPOOK CHASERS. *SPOOKS RUN WILD.

A BOY AND HIS DOG Films Inc./LQJ 1975 color/scope 87m. SP,D: L.Q. Jones, from the novella by Harlan Ellison. Ph: John A. Morrill. Mus: Tim McIntire; J. Mendoza-Nava. PD: Ray Boyle. SpFX: Frank Rowe. Mkp: Wes Dawn. SdFX: G.D. Marchant. Ref: V 3/26/75. screen. pr. with Don Johnson, Susanne Benton, "Tiger"("Blood"; voice: McIntire), Charles McGraw, Jason Robards, Alvy Moore.
2014 A.D., post WWIII: underground city; above-ground guerilla bands; hip, telepathic dog ("Oh, Jesus!"). The dog's wit certainly helps--his sarcasm is more varied and finely honed than that of his ancestor Cleo (in the old "People's Choice" TV series). But the movie seems skimpy dramatically, its vision of the future just an anagram of a dozen other filmic futures. The ending is cynical about women and sentimental about dogs.

The BOY WHO CRIED WEREWOLF Univ/RKF 1973 color 93m. D: Nathan Juran. SP: Bob Homel. Ph: M.P. Joyce. Mus: Ted Stovall. Mkp: Tom Burman. OptFX: James W. Elkin. Ref: TV. MFB'73: 244-45. V 8/1/73. with Kerwin Mathews(werewolf), Elaine Devry, Robert J. Wilke, Jack Lucas, Paul Baxley(werewolf).
Werewolf's bite turns family man into werewolf. Uneasy combination horror movie-soap opera. Mathews as "Dad," the werewolf, is comically hyper-active. Piquant dialogue: "Dad's gonna become a werewolf again--we _gotta_ do something!" "How many times do I have to tell you?--it's Dad. _He's_ the werewolf!"

The BOY WITH TWO HEADS (B) CFF/Eyeline 1974 color series of 7 (114m. total) D,Co-SP: Jonathan Ingrams. Ph: N. Binney. Mus: Harry Robinson. SpFX: Les Bowie. Ref: MFB'74:121-22. with Spencer Plumridge, Clive Revill(Chico's voice), L. Ash.
South American witch-doctor's living shrunken head conjures up rainstorm, turns into dove, etc.

The BOYS FROM BRAZIL Fox/ITC 1978 color/scope 125m. D: Franklin J. Schaffner. SP: Heywood Gould, from Ira Levin's novel. Ph: Henri Decae. Mus: Jerry Goldsmith. PD: Gil Parrondo. SpFX: Roy Whybrow. Mkp: B. Lodge, C. Tucker. Ref: V 9/27/78. TV. MFB'79:68-9: "Dr. Mengele, the infamous geneticist from Auschwitz, is alive and well in South America, and preparing to populate the globe with perfectly cloned reproductions of his Fuhrer...." with Gregory Peck, Laurence Olivier, James Mason, Lilli Palmer, Uta Hagen, Denholm Elliott, Rosemary Harris, John Dehner, Jeremy Black(clones), Bruno Ganz, Wolfgang Preiss, Michael Gough, Anne Meara.

"Wouldn't you want to live in a world full of Mozarts and Picassos?" A leading question (posed by a scientist in the course of the film), and one more interesting than that asked and answered by the film itself. It takes only one phrase ("You're *weird!*"), from one of the story's incipient Hitlers, to deflate Dr. Mengele and his grand designs for world conquest. This succinct squelch is meant to be a comic shock. (Imagine a horror movie in which the monster tells his creator, "You're *mad!*") But it's too little, way too late--the mad doctor's plans seem, from the beginning, rather unworkable and unwieldy; the behavior of the clones not necessarily as predictable as he assumes. Peck and Olivier give "polished" but essentially very hollow performances.

BOYS' SCHOOL see DISPARUS DE SAINT-AGIL, Les

BRACULA--THE TERROR OF THE LIVING DEAD! (Sp-I) Petruka/Prodimex 1972 color 97m. (La ORGIA DE LOS MUERTOS) SP,D: Jose Luis Merino. SP: also E. Columbo. Ph: M. Rizzolo. Mus: Francesco De Masi. AD: E. Torre, F. Di Stefano. Ref: MFB '78:118. V 5/9/73:144. with Stan Cooper(aka C. Quiney?), Dianik Zurakowska, Paul Naschy(Igor), Maria Pia Conte, Gerard Tichy(Dr.Bracula), Isarco Ravaioli, Aurora De Alba.

Doctor succeeds in harnessing "nebula electricity," creates "living corpses...beings controlled by capsules implanted in their brains"; black magic summons up missing count. (MFB)

*The BRAIN FROM PLANET AROUS 1957 Mkp: Jack Pierce. Ref: TV.

Prime moments: good, bare-brained alien Bal placating snarling Earth dog: "Good dog! Good dog!"; bad alien Gor (inside the hero's body) lasciviously describing the "strange elation" that the touch of the hero's girl friend produces in him. Key phrase: "the fissure of Rolando." Most distinctive feature: possessed hero John Agar's (terribly unconvincing) terrible laugh, practiced each time Gor scores a point off earthlings.

BRAM STOKER'S DRACULA see DRACULA(1974)

BRAVE NEW WORLD NBC-TV/Univ-TV 1980(1978) color 150m. D: Burt Brinckerhoff. SP: Robert E. Thompson, from Aldous Huxley's novel. Ph: Harry L. Wolf. Mus: Paul Chihara. AD: Tom H. John. Ref: TV. SFC 3/7/80. Cinef X:1:16-17. with Keir

Dullea, Bud Cort, Kristoffer Tabori, Julie Cobb, Ron O'Neal.
The world of constant pleasure in the year 632 A.F. A camp vision of a sterile future, or a sterile vision of a camp future--take your pick. An sf-sitcom, lacking only a laugh-track. The withering (or withered) irony is inescapable; it's in every gesture and line. ("We're going to be late for the senso-feelies," "I think you're _very_ pneumatic," etc.)

BREAKFAST AT THE MANCHESTER MORGUE see DON'T OPEN THE WINDOW

BRENDA STARR Wolper-TV 1976 color 74m. D: Mel Stuart. Ref: TVFFSB. Maltin/TVM: voodoo. with Jill St. John, Jed Allan, Victor Buono, Sorrell Booke, Barbara Luna, Torin Thatcher.

BRIDE, The see HERE COMES THE BRIDE

BRIDE OF FENGRIFFEN see --AND NOW THE SCREAMING STARTS!

*BRIDE OF FRANKENSTEIN 1935 Sequel to FRANKENSTEIN(1931). Sequel: SON OF FRANKENSTEIN. Ref: TV.
"The creation of life is enthralling!" cries Dr. Pretorius (Ernest Thesiger), who wants "no nonsense about being _good_." BRIDE OF FRANKENSTEIN makes such enthrallment comprehensible. The music (by Franz Waxman), sets, lighting, camerawork, and Thesiger's performance insure that you share his enthusiasm, his damn-the-consequences attitude toward scientific advancement. It helps of course that the "consequences" scenes (i.e., the man-made monster (Boris Karloff) finding no peace, in town or country) tend toward routine action and queasy pathos: _we_ pay for our enthrallment as surely as does the no-nonsense Pretorius. (Even the score goes temporarily treacly.) And Colin Clive as Dr. Frankenstein--the torn-one-way-then-the-other center of the piece--is far less proficient at expressing sourness and disgust with science than he is at expressing exultation in same. Karloff, however, is perhaps even more impressive--he has a more complex role--than Thesiger. And his last look of resigned anguish at his unwilling "bride" (Elsa Lanchester) before throwing the doomsday switch is probably the peak moment of the Universal series, the point at which its themes of creation, isolation, and alienation come most clearly and movingly into focus.

*BRIDE OF THE MONSTER Rolling M 1956 (The MONSTER OF THE MARSHES-orig t) Ph: William C. Thompson, Ted Allan. Mus: Frank Worth. SpFX: Pat Dinga. Ref: Pitts/HFS: sequel: NIGHT OF THE GHOULS? Lennig/TC. Lee. TV. and with Tony McCoy, George Becwar, Harvey Dunn.
A good line is worth repeating: "He tampered in God's domain."

BRIDEGROOM FOR TWO see LET'S LOVE AND LAUGH

BRIDEGROOM'S WIDOW, The(by F. Thompson and E. Paulton) see LET'S LOVE AND LAUGH

BRIDES (Showtime-TV)/Sharon Sachs 1978 3m. Ref: TV: "vampire weddings" and giant chickens are "in."

BRILLANTENSCHIFF, Das see DIAMOND SHIP, The

BRODERNA (Swed) 1914 D: Mauritz Stiller. Ref: screen. PFA.
Ray invention (which looks like a gramaphone), demonstrated, destroys ship at anchor.

The BROOD (Can.) New World/Mutual-Elgin Int'l. & CFDC 1979 color 91m. SP,D: David Cronenberg. Ph: Mark Irwin. Mus: Howard Shore. AD: Carol Spier. SpFX: Allan Kotter. SpMkp: Jack Young, Dennis Pike. Ref: screen. MFB'80:44-45. SFC 8/3/79. V 6/6/79. FC 3/80:36. with Oliver Reed, Samantha Eggar, Art Hindle, Cindy Hinds, Henry Beckerman, Susan Hogan.
Through "psychoplasmics," a woman (Eggar) bears a brood of deformed, homicidal dwarfs, "children of her rage"; these "mean widdle ids" let loose her wrath upon her mother and father and her other "enemies." A sometimes ingenious scrambling of INVADERS FROM MARS and FORBIDDEN PLANET themes, The BROOD is at once a black joke on psychoanalysis and a psychologically intriguing construction. ("These things--i.e., frustration, anger--tend to express themselves one way or another.") If it works a bit too neatly--here's the cause (warped psyche) and here's the effect (heads hammered in)--it also has the appeal of neatness, unity. And the scenes juxtaposing the woman's actual child with her mutant brothers and sisters are tinged with suggestions of inherited psychological horrors and odd emotional bonds (between mother and daughter, between child and dwarf-child).

**BROTHER JOHN Col 1971 color 94m. (KANE-orig t) D: James Goldstone. SP: Ernest Kinoy. Ph: G.P. Finnerman. Mus: Quincy Jones. AD: Al Brenner. SpFX: Geza Gaspar. SdFX: Edit-Int'l. Ref: TV. Lee. TVG. MFB'72:28. with Sidney Poitier(Kane), Will Geer, Bradford Dillman, Beverly Todd, Warren J. Kemmerling, Paul Winfield, Ramon Bieri.
Alien born to human parents judges Earth wanting and ripe for destruction. An sf version of Sodom and Gomorrah. Poitier as "God" finds people on Earth "like maggots on a rotten apple," and who's to argue with him? Still, this ground has been covered before in movies like PLAN 9 FROM OUTER SPACE, which had more laughs. Geer is engaging as the local doc.

BRRR! see UNCANNY, The

BRUKA, QUEEN OF EVIL see DEVIL WOMAN(1970)

*BRUTE FORCE 1914 (IN PREHISTORIC DAYS-orig t. sfa The PRIMITIVE MAN?) SP,D: D.W. Griffith. Sequel to MAN'S GENESIS. Ph: Billy Bitzer. SpFX: Howard Gaye. Ref: AF-Index. Lee: alligator-monster. "Films of DWG." Bianco #5-8/1975:238. with Robert Harron, Mae Marsh, Wilfred Lucas, Charles H. Mailes, Lionel Barrymore.

*The BRUTE MAN 1946 See also: PEARL OF DEATH. Ph: Maury Gertsman. AD: John B. Goodman, Abraham Grossman. Ref: FM 165:16. TV. V 10/23/46. and with Donald MacBride.

If it's hard to understand why Universal kept one "Creeper" movie (i.e., HOUSE OF HORRORS), it's easy to see why they let the other (i.e., The BRUTE MAN) go (to PRC). The latter movie is so flimsy that its three co-plots seem to be operating independently of one another. The shock scenes alternate between, (a) having the Creeper (Rondo Hatton) confront his victims (scream) and, (b) having the Creeper sneak up on his victims (no scream). The presence of a blind girl and an unfortunate, acid-disfigured "monster" means that there's as much play for sentiment as for shock. But this is only for those who scare and cry very easily.

BRUTES AND SAVAGES see DEATH TRAP

BUCHAMUKURE DAIHAKKEN see COMPUTER FREE-FOR-ALL

BUCHSE DER PANDORA(by F. Wedekind) see LULU

BUCK ROGERS IN THE 25TH CENTURY Univ 1979 color 89m. D: Daniel Haller. Sp & Exec P: Glen A. Larson. SP: also Leslie Stevens. Based on the Robert C. Dille characters. Ph: Frank Beascoechea; L.J. South. Mus: Stu Phillips. AD: Paul Peters. SpFX: Bud Ewing, Jack Faggard. VisFX: D.M. Garber, Wayne Smith. ComputerFX: Colin Cantwell. AnimDes: Harry Moreau. Ref: MFB'79:144-45. V 4/4/79. with Gil Gerard, Pamela Hensley, Erin Gray, Henry Silva, Tim O'Connor, Joseph Wiseman.

Suspended animation; robot; "disfigured humans"; self-programming computers. (MFB)

BUCK ROGERS IN THE 25TH CENTURY: FLIGHT OF THE WAR WITCH NBC-TV 1979? color 94m. D: Larry Stewart. SP: Robert W. Gilmer. Ref: TVG. TV: series episode shown on TV as 2-hour movie. with Gil Gerard, Erin Gray, Tim O'Connor, Felix Silla(robot), Pamela Hensley, Julie Newmar, Sam Jaffe, Michael Ansara, Vera Miles, Sid Haig.

Time warp, year 1987 to 2491; "vortex" or Black Hole, into another universe; energy shield; too-cute robot.

BUD ABBOTT AND LOU COSTELLO MEET FRANKENSTEIN see ABBOTT AND COSTELLO MEET FRANKENSTEIN

BUG Para 1975 color 101m. D: Jeannot Szwarc. SP,P: William Castle. SP: also Thomas Page, from his novel "The Hephaestus Plague." Ph: Michel Hugo;(insects) Ken Middleham. Elec Mus: Charles Fox. AD: Jack Martin Smith. SpFX: Phil Cory, Walter Dion. Mkp: Tom Miller, Jr. Ref: TV. MFB'75:257. V 6/11/75. TVG. with Bradford Dillman, Joanna Miles, Jesse Vint, Jamie Smith Jackson, Patty McCormack, Richard Gilliland.

Earthquake releases hordes of incendiary, carbon-eating "firebugs"; crossed with a cockroach, they become carnivores; finally, they get wings and cry, fry, fly. Entomologically intriguing sf plays like a sick Disney True-Life Adventure. These bugs don't miss one disgusting trick. Some of their more outre stunts might in fact qualify as surreal if they didn't seem simply gratuitously strange. Unfortunately, the people in the movie are taken as seriously as the insects, and all the characterizations seem rather weirdly miscalculated. At times it even seems as if the bugs must be figments of Dillman's imagination--or vice versa. It's a strange movie.

BULLDOG DRUMMOND UA/Goldwyn 1929 93m. D: F. Richard Jones. SP: Sidney Howard, Wallace Smith, based on the play by Gerald DuMaurier & the characters created by "Sapper." Ph: Gregg Toland, George Barnes. AD: William Cameron Menzies. Ref: FQ Spr'80:17-18: "mad doctor's torture room" or "central chamber." Everson/TDIF. AFI. screen: impregnable-electric-door invention ("Ingenious, isn't it?"); drugs for inducing consciousness, idiocy; thunderstorm. with Ronald Colman, Joan Bennett, Lawrence Grant, Montagu Love, Lilyan Tashman, Tetsu Komai, Claude Allister, Charles Sellon.

Colman's urbanity as Drummond is highly engaging--he strikes all the right, mocking notes--and Grant's measured vituperativeness as Dr. Lakington is a match for him. The stiltedness of the less colorful villains is also amusing, sometimes intentionally, sometimes not. But this was before heroine Bennett began to act, and her earnestness seems only accidentally amusing. Menzies' fairy tale/Gothic design--elaborate ceilings, fantastic facades and stairways, gigantic doors and skylights--sets the far-from-reality tone. The movie is pre-Hitchcock in its sense of adventure and romance as only harmless fun, entailing no real risks, and is jolly enough as such, thanks mainly to Colman and Menzies.

BUNKER'S PATENT BELLOWS 1910 (*BUNTER'S PATENT BELLOWS-t. error) Ref: BFC.

BUQUE MALDITO, El see HORROR OF THE ZOMBIES

BURIED ALIVE see DR. RENAULT'S SECRET

BURKE AND HARE (B) Shipman-Armitage 1971 color 91m. D: Vernon Sewell. SP: Ernie Bradford. Ph: Desmond Dickinson. Mus: Roger Webb. AD: Scott MacGregor. SpFX: Pat Moore. Ref: Lee. MFB'72:28. Pirie/HOH. Bianco #4/77:143. with Derren Nesbitt, Harry Andrews, Yootha Joyce, Robin Hawdon, Glynn Edwards, Yutte Stensgaard.

Body-snatching, Edinburgh, early 19th Century. See also: DR. JEKYLL AND SISTER HYDE.

The BURNING Filmways/Miramax 1981(1979?) color Story,D: Tony Maylam. SP: Peter Lawrence, Bob Weinstein. Story: also H. Weinstein, B. Grey. Ph: Harvey Harrison. Mus: Rick Wakeman. SpFX & Mkp: Tom Savini. Ref: V 12/26/79(rated): FVI. 3/25/81 (rated). 3/18/81:199(ad). 5/6/81: "disfigured cretin wields giant shears...." with Brian Matthews, Leah Ayres, Brian Backer, Larry Joshua.

BURNT OFFERINGS UA/PEA-Curtis 1976 color 115m. SP,D: Dan Curtis. SP: also William F. Nolan, from Robert Marasco's novel. Ph: Jacques Marquette; Stevan Larner. Mus: Robert Cobert. PD: Eugene Lourie. SpFX: Cliff Wenger. Opt: Howard Anderson. Portraits: John Dornes. Ref: MFB'77:94: country house "periodically restores itself by feeding on its tenants." V 8/25/76. TV. with Karen Black, Oliver Reed, Bette Davis, Burgess Meredith, Eileen Heckart, Lee H. Montgomery.

The old house that possesses people, making them act funny (and actors look silly), seems to be the new horror-story explanation for marital discord. (In Forties horror movies, the deceptively-personable maniac was the explanation.) It takes an eternity here for the characters to conclude, "I hate this place!" The house gobbles them up anyway. (It's not exclusive.)

BURU KURISUMASU see BLOOD TYPE: BLUE

The BUTTERFLY MURDERS (H.K.-Cant.) Seasonal 1979 color/scope 100m. (TIEH PIEN) Story & D: Tsui Hark. SP: L. Chi-Ming, L. Nung-kang. Ph: Fan Ching-Yu. Mus: C. Hsun-ch'i, K. Chia-hui. AD: C. Ching-sen. Ref: V 8/1/79. IFG'81:164-5. with Lau Siu-Ming, Wong Shih-Tong, Michelle Mee, Jo Jo Chan.

"Futuristic robot man"; "bizarre murders by a swarm of butterflies" (V); "vampiric butterflies." (IFG)

BY THE KAISER'S ORDERS (B) Barker 1914 48m. D: F. Thornton. SP: Rowland Talbot. Ref: BFC.

Chemist-spy attempts to ignite explosives with "stolen F-ray."

CACADOR DE FANTASMA see GHOST HUNTER, The

The CAFE L'EGYPTE (B) 1924 28m. See also: Further Mysteries of Dr. Fu-Manchu series. Ref: BFC.

CAGED VIRGINS see CRAZED VAMPIRE

CAGLIOSTRO (I) Rampart/Fox(Italy) 1974('77-U.S.) color 103m. SP,D: Daniele Pettinari. SP: also Pier Carpi, Enrico Bonaccorti, from Carpi's book "Cagliostro Il Taumaturgo." Ph: Giuseppe Pinori. Mus: Manuel De Sica. AD: Giorgio Desideri. Ref: TVFFSB. V 5/21/75:32. 3/19/75: "ESP and black magic." Bianco Index'75. Willis/SW. with Curt Jurgens, Bekim Fehmiu (Cagliostro), Robert Alda, Rosanna Schiaffino, Evelyn Stewart, Massimo Girotti, Luigi Pistilli.

See also: *BLACK MAGIC(1949). FRANCIS THE FIRST. The MUMMY(1932).

CALEB POWERS see WITCHING HOUR, The(1934)

The CALL OF SIVA (B) 1923 20m. See also: Mystery of Dr. Fu-Manchu series. Ref: BFC. Lee.

*CALLING DR. DEATH 1943 Ref: TV. V 12/15/43. and with Alec Craig, Charles Wagenheim, Patricia Morison, John Ellis.

Sadistic murderer; hypnosis. The first entry in Universal's "Inner Sanctum" series plays like a cross between a typical Universal "B" shocker and an experimental film: there are elaborate "subjective" tracking shots, odd camera angles, and whole sequences featuring a "subjective" soundtrack. And the climax is a (would-be) tour-de-force "flashback" via hypnosis, including one segment in which the hypnotizer is hypnotized--a trance within a trance. (It does get involved.) But the story, dialogue (interior and exterior), and acting are poor, and even J. Carrol Naish's inspector's Columbo-like relationship with suspect Lon Chaney Jr. lacks something (like Peter Falk's sense of humor).

CAMERA THAT KILLS BAD GUYS, The see MACHINE TO KILL BAD PEOPLE, The

CAMPANA DEL INFIERNO, La see BELL OF HELL, The

CANDLE FOR THE DEVIL, A see NIGHTMARE HOTEL

CANICHE see POODLE

CANNIBAL see LAST SURVIVOR, The

CANNIBAL GIRLS (Can.) AI/Scary Pictures 1972 color 84m. D, SP,Exec P: Ivan Reitman. SP,P: Robert Sandler. Ph: Robert Saad. Mus: Doug Riley. SpFX: Richard Whyte, Michael Lotosky. Ref: MFB'76:77-8. V 4/18/73. Aros. with Eugene Levy, Andrea Martin, Ronald Ulrich, Randall Carpenter.

"The legend of the Cannibal Girls--sisters...under the influence of a demonic preacher seduce men, kill them, and either eat them on the spot or have their servant Bunker butcher them...." (MFB)

CANNIBAL HOLOCAUST see LAST SURVIVOR, The

Les CANNIBALES (F) Eurocine 1979 D: Jesus Franco? Ref: V 5/13/81:283: horror. 5/7/80:475.

The CANTERVILLE GHOST Dynamic 1954 15m. From Oscar Wilde's story. Ref: Lee. no LC. with Monty Woolley.

See also: GHOST HUNTER, The. WORLD OF HORROR.

CAPITAN NEMO see MYSTERIOUS ISLAND(1972)

CAPTAIN AMERICA CBS-TV/Univ-TV 1979 color 94m. D: Rod Holcomb. SP: Don Ingalls, Chester Krumholz, based on the comic-book character created by Kirby & Simon. Ph: R.W. Browne. Mus: Mike Post, Pete Carpenter. AD: Lou Montejano. Ref: TV. V 1/24/79:70. with Reb Brown, Len Birman, Heather Menzies, Steve Forrest, Robin Mattson.

Injection of super-hormone FLAG (developed by his father from adrenal-gland cells) gives Steve Rogers (Brown) super-strength; detonation of neutron bomb linked to man's pulse rate. The script strains mightily to give its super-hero some individuality; in the end he seems just another super-hero, and the strain was for nothing.

CAPTAIN FUTURE (J) Toei-TV 1979 anim 24m. (KYAPUTEN FUYUCHA) D: S. Katsumata. Based on novels by Edmond Hamilton. Ref: JFFJ 13:35: TV-series episode shown theatrically; robot, android.

CAPTAIN KRONOS-VAMPIRE HUNTER (B) Para/Hammer 1972('74-U.S.) color 91m. (KRONOS-orig t. CAPTAIN KRONUS-VAMPIRE HUNTER. VAMPIRE CASTLE-int ts?) SP,D: Brian Clemens. Ph: Ian Wilson. Mus: Laurie Johnson. PD: Robert Jones. Mkp: Jim Evans. Ref: MFB'74:69-70. Lee. Murphy. Willis/SW. V 6/26/74. 6/14/72:22. with Horst Janson, John Carson(vampire), John Cater(hunchback), Shane Briant, Caroline Munro, Ian Hendry, W.Ventham(vampire).

Vampire, Lady Durward, and her resurrected husband; girls who die "of advanced old age"; "professional vampire hunters." (MFB)

CAPTIVE Gold Key-TV 1980 color 90m. Ref: GKey. with David Ladd, Cameron Mitchell, Lori Saunders.

2100 A.D. Earth vs. the planet Styrolia.

The CAPTURE OF BIGFOOT Studio Film Int'l. 1979 color 95m. SP,D: Bill Rebane. SP: also Ingrid Neumayer. Ref: Boxo 7/2/79:23. 2/25/80:32. V 7/25/79:37. 9/26/79:25(rated). Willis/SW. with Richard Kennedy, Katherine Hopkins, Stafford Morgan, John Goff, Otis Young.

Bigfoot runs amok in city.

CAPULINA VS. LOS MONSTRUOUS (Mex) Panorama 1973 color D: Miguel Morayta. Ref: V 5/8/74:238. Glut/TDB: sfa CAPULINA CONTRA LOS VAMPIROS (Zacarias, '73)?

The CAR Univ 1977 color/scope 98m. (WHEELS-orig t) D,Co-P: Elliot Silverstein. SP: Dennis Shryack, Michael Butler, Lane Slate. Ph: Gerald Hirschfeld. Mus: Leonard Rosenman. AD: Loyd S. Papez. SpFxPh: Albert Whitlock. Ref: V 3/3/76:30. (d) 5/11/77. M.Dempsey. MFB'77:164. with James Brolin, John Marley, Kathleen Lloyd, R.G. Armstrong, John Rubinstein, Kim Richards, Doris Dowling, Kyle Richards, Kate Murtagh.

Phantom car terrorizes small town.

CARMILLA(by J.S. Le Fanu) see BARE BREASTED COUNTESS, The. BLOOD SPATTERED BRIDE, The. DAUGHTER OF DRACULA. LUST FOR A VAMPIRE. TWINS OF EVIL.

CARNAGE see TWITCH OF THE DEATH NERVE

CARNAL ENCOUNTERS OF THE BAREST KIND Mustang/Beehive 1979 color 81m. D: Donald Bryce. SP: William Margold. Ref: Boxo 12/31/79:14. with Serena, Jamie Gillis, John Holmes, Margold.
"Alienologist" runs his class "films of alien/human encounters."

CARNE PER FRANKENSTEIN see ANDY WARHOL'S FRANKENSTEIN

CARRIE UA/Red Bank 1976 color 98m. D: Brian De Palma. SP: Lawrence D. Cohen, from the novel by Stephen King. See also: NIGHTS OF YASSMIN. Ph: Mario Tosi. Mus: Pino Donaggio. AD: William Kenney, Jack Fisk. SpFX: Greg Auer, Kenneth Pepiot. Ref: screen. MFB'77:3. V(d) 11/1/76. with Sissy Spacek(Carrie), Piper Laurie, Amy Irving, William Katt, John Travolta, Nancy Allen, P.J. Soles.
High-school girl uses puberty-linked, telekinetic powers to wreak revenge on her tormentors. The movie that confirmed the delusions of persecution of millions of ex-high-school students. But it's debatable who's meaner to Carrie--her fellow students or her director, who draws out their elaborate prank for 90 minutes, then lovingly shoots its penultimate moments--Carrie's queen-of-the-prom walk to the stage--in slow motion. Her stylistically extended moment of "glory" here is an emotional-fuse-blowing mixture of pseudo-lyricism (a mawkish dream-seemingly-coming-true) and pseudo-irony. (De Palma ungallantly prefaces Carrie's dream walk with a shot of the blood-bucket that's about to dampen her spirits.) Even Sissy Spacek's vibrance can't negate the De Palma effect. Later, when Carrie's repressive, hyper-religious mother (Laurie) is "crucified" by telekinetically-flung kitchen utensils (cut here to a shot of a crucifix, in case you're slow), the audience cheers, on cue--De Palma, the cheerleader at the crucifixion. (Nice work if you can get it.)

The CARS THAT ATE PEOPLE (Austral) New Line/AFD-RSPP/Crawford 1974 color/scope 88m. (The CARS THAT ATE PARIS-orig t) Story,SP,D: Peter Weir. Story: also Keith Gow, Piers Davies. Ph: John McLean. Mus: Bruce Smeaton. AD: David C. Copping. Ref: MFB'75:101. V 6/26/74. with Terry Camilleri, Melissa Jaffa, John Meillon, Kevin Miles.
Surgeon's experiments leave victims helpless "veggies."

CASA DELL'EXORCISMO see LISA AND THE DEVIL

CASE OF JONATHAN DREW, The see LODGER, The(1926)

The CASE OF THE FULL MOON MURDERS Seaburg(Sean S.Cunningham)/ Lobster & Dana 1973 color 74m. (SEX ON THE GROOVE TUBE--'77 Newport re-r t. The CASE OF THE SMILING STIFFS-B) D,P: Cunningham, Brud Talbot. SP: Jerry Hayling. Ph: Gus Graham. Mus: Bud Fanton. Ref: MFB'75:29-30. Willis/SW. V 11/28/73. with Fred Lincoln, Ron Browne, Cathy Walker(vampire), Harry

Reems, Jean Jennings.
The diagnosis in four bizarre, full-moon murders is "death by vampiristic fellatio." (MFB)

CASPER COMES TO CLOWN (Harvey Films-TV)/Para 1951 anim color 8m. D: I. Sparber. SP: I. Klein. Ref: TV. LC. Maltin/OMAM.
Fanged monster-gorilla in circus; "scare meter" for ghosts. See also: ONCE UPON A RHYME.

CASK OF AMONTILLADO, The(by E.A.Poe) see EVENING OF EDGAR ALLAN POE, An. SAVAGE CURSE, The.

CASSIOPEA (Russ) 1975? (MOSCOW-CASSIOPEA) D: Richard Victorov. PD: K. Zagorsky? Ref: V 7/30/75:28. 11/28/73:28. with Innokenti Smoktunovsky.
Story of 40-year voyage to distant star.

El CASTILLO DE LAS MOMIAS DE GUANAJATO (Mex) 1972 Sequel to Las MOMIAS DE GUANAJATO. Ref: Glut/CMM. with "Blue Angel," "Tinieblas," "Superzan."

CASTLE ROCK (Can.) CBS-TV/Movie Night 1981 color 60m. D: John Desmond. SP: Mel & Ethel Brez. Ph: Wayne Summers et al. Mus: Kerry Crawford, Jonathan Goldsmith. Ref: TV. TVG. with James C. Burge, Cindy Girling, Margaret Phillips, Lynda Green.
Isolated estate; cat demon? Tepid women's-Gothic which seems to end in the middle, as if it were originally part of a mini-series.

CASTLE SINISTER (B) Delta 1932 50m. D: Widgey R. Newman. Ref: BFC. with Haddon Mason, Eric Adeney, Wally Patch.
"Horror. Devon. Mad doctor tries to put girl's brain into apeman's head."

CAT see NIGHT CREATURE

The CAT AND THE CANARY (B) Quartet/Cinema Shares Int'l/Richard Gordon(Grenadier) 1978('81?-U.S.) SP,D: Radley Metzger. From John Willard's play. Ph: Alex Thom(p)son. Mus: Steven Cagan. AD: Anthony Pratt. Ref: V 11/22/78. 2/18/81:6(rated). MFB'81:45. with Honor Blackman, Michael Callan, Edward Fox, Wendy Hiller, Olivia Hussey, Carol Lynley, Peter McEnery, Wilfrid Hyde-White, Beatrix Lehmann, Daniel Massey.
Murder, mutilation, hooded killer, torture chamber, all at Glencliffe Manor, 1934.

The CAT CREATURE 1973 color 72m. D: Curtis Harrington. SP: Robert Bloch. Ref: TV. Maltin/TVM. TVG. with David Hedison, Meredith Baxter, Stuart Whitman, Gale Sondergaard, John Carradine, Kent Smith, Milton Parsons, Peter Lorre Jr., John Abbott, Renne Jarrett.
Mummy that comes to life when amulet is removed from it; blood-drinking cat? Undistinguished except for an amusingly outlandish climax, in which a bunch of snarling cats leaps on

the mummy. The script contains intentional narrative echoes of Forties horrors like CAT PEOPLE and HOUSE OF FRANKENSTEIN.

The CAT FROM OUTER SPACE BV 1978 color 103m. D: Norman Tokar. SP: Ted Key. Ph: C.F. Wheeler. Mus: Lalo Schifrin. AD: J.B. Mansbridge, P. Ames. Mattes: P.S. Ellenshaw. SpFX: Lycett, Cruickshank, Lee. Ref: MFB'78:215. V 6/21/78. with Sandy Duncan, Ken Berry, Harry Morgan, Roddy McDowall, McLean Stevenson, Jesse White, Alan Young, Hans Conreid, Ronnie Schell.
Telepathic cat needs human help to repair its crash-landed spaceship.

*CAT PEOPLE 1942 Sound: John L. Cass. Ref: screen. Siegel/VL. V 11/18/42. and with Elizabeth Dunne, Mary Halsey, Dot Farley.
Val Lewton may ultimately be remembered less for whole films than for the performances of certain of the actresses in them--Jean Brooks and Elizabeth Russell in The SEVENTH VICTIM, Ellen Drew in ISLE OF THE DEAD, Simone Simon in CAT PEOPLE. If his films seem, at their best, as affecting as they are chilling, it's due in large part to the presence of these women. There's an authentic sense of desolateness about them--in contrast to the air of inauthenticity about the more-happily-disposed Lewton characters. In CAT PEOPLE, Simone Simon's lycanthropic tendencies as Irena (she is a were-panther) isolate her from her husband (Kent Smith), and rarely has the plight of the solitary monster seemed as heartrending as *she* makes it. Simon conveys Irena's humanity, her sadness, with face, voice, and eyes. Her delicately-wrought, moving performance survives even in the context of the crudely-written dialogue given her, Smith, and Jane Randolph. (The latter's "definition of love" survives only as a shining moment in camp.)

CAT PEOPLE Univ 1982? D: Paul Schrader. SP: Alan Ormsby. Ref: V 7/22/81:28. with Nastassia Kinski, Malcolm McDowell.

The CAT THAT HATED PEOPLE MGM 1948 anim color 7m. D: Tex Avery. SP: Heck Allen. Anim: Walter Clinton et al. Ref: screen. LC. MFB'76:113.
Cat takes rocket to mad planet of live objects; "1938 PORKY IN WACKYLAND revisited." (MFB) Top-notch Avery.

CATACLYSM First Int'l. 1981 Co-D,P: Darryl Marshak. SP: Philip Yordan. Ref: B.Warren. V 3/18/81:4(rated).
Ex-Nazi proves to be the Devil's emissary.

CATALIN AND CATALINA (Rum.) Animafilm 1974 anim short? D: L. Sirbu. Ref: IFG'75:472: "wicked witch...conceived as a monstrous red owl."

CATHY'S CURSE (F-Can.) 21st Century/Makifilms & Agora 1976 ('80-U.S.) color 91m. (CAUCHEMARS) SP,D: Eddy Matalon. SP: also A. Sens-Cazenave, M. Clement. Ph: J.-J. Tarbes, R. Cuipka. Mus: Didier Vasseur. SpFX: Eurocitel. Ref: MFB'77: 229-30. Boxo 7/28/80:9. with Alan Scarfe, Randi Allen,

Beverley Murray, Roy Witham.
Spirit-possessed girl; medium; trance.

*The CATMAN OF PARIS (NTA-TV) 1946 Mus: Dale Butts. Mkp: Bob Marks? See also:*MONSTER STRIKES, The. Ref: TV. V 2/20/46. and with Tanis Chandler, Maurice Cass, Paul Marion.
"There have been cat people," according to the script, or at least there has been one catman, who appears every 300 years or so, when the conjunction of the stars is right--first in Rome, last in Paris ("the ninth life of a cat"). Douglas Dumbrille plays the "man," Robert Wilke the "cat" half of the creature (and the latter in one sequence only, and with Dumbrille's voice). The dry, humorless script exhausts all its ingenuity in making it look like hero Carl Esmond is the werecat. The cast makes this sound like Paris, Illinois. One good, belated shock when the killer is suddenly and incontrovertibly revealed to us as a catman.

CAUCHEMARS see CATHY'S CURSE

Il CAV. COSTANTE NICOSIA DEMONIACO OVVERO DRACULA IN BRIANZA (I) Titanus/Coralta 1975 color 100m. (DRACULA IN THE PROVINCES-ad t) SP,D: Lucio Fulci. SP: also Pupi Avati, Bruno Corbucci, M. Amendola. Ph: Sergio Salvati. Mus: Franco Bixio et al. AD: P. Basile. Ref: Bianco Index'75. V 9/17/75:32. 5/7/75:204: comedy. with Lando Buzzanca, Rossano Brazzi, Sylva Koscina, Valentina Cortese, Ciccio Ingrassia, Christa Linder, Moira Orfei, John Steiner(Dragulescu).

CAVE FULL OF GHOSTS IN THE WEST MOUNTAIN see LEGEND OF THE MOUNTAIN

CAVE OF THE SHARKS see SHARKS' CAVE, The

CAVEMAN UA/Turman-Foster 1981 color 91m. SP,D: Carl Gottlieb. SP: also Rudy De Luca. Ph: Alan Hume. Mus: Lalo Schifrin. PD: Philip M. Jefferies. SpVisFX: David Allen, Roy Arbogast. Ref: V 4/15/81. with Ringo Starr, Dennis Quaid, Shelley Long, Jack Gilford, John Matuszak, Barbara Bach.
Comedy set in prehistoric times; dizzy dinosaurs.

The CAYMAN TRIANGLE Hefalump 1977 color 92m. SP,D,P: Anderson Humphreys. SP: also Ralph Clemente. Ph: Ed Paveitti et al. Ref: V 12/7/77. with Reid Dennis, John Morgan, A.H.
Pirate curse; missing ships in the Bermuda Triangle.

CEMETERY GIRLS (Sp) MPM/Eva(Janus) 1973('79-U.S.) color 91m. (El GRAN AMOR DEL CONDE DRACULA. DRACULA'S VIRGIN LOVERS-B) SP,D: Javier Aguirre. SP: also Jacinto Molina, A. Insua. Ph: R.P. Cubero. Mus: Carmelo Belona. Ref: MFB'75:9. Willis/SW. V 1/16/74:26(rated, as DRACULA'S GREAT LOVE). with Paul Naschy(aka J.Molina)(Wendell Dracula), Haydee Politoff, Rossana Yanni, Vic Winner, Mista Miller, Ingrid Garbo.
Dracula needs willing virgin to revive long-dead daughter.

CEREMONIA SANGRIENTA see LEGEND OF BLOOD CASTLE

CERNE SLUNCE see BLACK SUN

CHABELO Y PEPITO... see PEPITO Y CHABELO...

CHAMBER OF HORRORS (B) Instructional 1929 silent 62m. SP,D: Walter Summers. Ref: BFC: "horror." with Frank Stanmore.
"Man dreams he murders his mistress and goes mad during night in Madame Tussaud's waxworks."

CHAMBER OF TORTURES see BARON BLOOD

CHANDANA (India-Telugu) Sridhar 1974 155m. SP,D,P: Giri Babu. Ph: N. Iyengar. Mus: Ramesh Naidu. Ref: Dharap. with Ranganath, R. Babu, Jayanthi.
Woman poses as ghost to frighten murderer of her sister into confessing.

*CHANDU THE MAGICIAN 1932 Mus D: Louis de Francesco. AD: Max Parker. Ref: screen.
The direction of the actors in CHANDU may be far from brilliant, but if the movie has little finesse, it has lots of energy. There are wild traveling shots, ray effects, shadow effects, crystal balls, statues that come to life--and the music *cascades*. Oddly, however, it's Herbert Mundin's generally-uncomic relief which rates the most convincing effects--e.g., a miniature conscience, a double. Villain Roxor's climactic speech is pretty silly, and he's shot from a strange angle, but Bela Lugosi's delivery overcomes all.

The CHANGELING (Can.) AFD/Pan-Canadian 1980 color/scope 107m. D: Peter Medak. SP: William Gray, Diana Maddox. Story: Russell Hunter. Ph: John Coquillon. Mus: Rick Wilkins; (music-box theme) Howard Blake. PD: Trevor Williams. SpFX: (coord) Gene Grigg;(asst) Michael Clifford, Barry Madden, William Orr. SdFX: Patrick & Dennis Drummond, Robert Grieve. Ref: screen. V 2/20/80. FM 165:28-35. CineFan 2:59(Duvoli). MFB'80:173. with George C. Scott, Trish Van Devere, Barry Morse, Melvin Douglas, John Colicos, Jean Marsh.
The ghost of a boy murdered many years ago attempts to communicate with the widower who leases the house he haunts. The CHANGELING is all surface, all show, but as such quite effective. A *deluxe* haunted-house movie, it's elaborately scored, and it's flooded with sophisticated effects--e.g., a necklace snaking up and out of the dirt at the bottom of a dry well; all the doors of said house slamming shut in quick succession; an unexpected voice coming through very faintly on a *tape recording* of a seance. The filmmakers themselves seem to have a sixth sense for divining sounds, notes, and images that tease the imagination. The film, however, is finally almost *too* rich in such details--they seem to crowd out characterization. The film's narrative integrity, ironically, falls victim to its cinematic ingenuity--stars Scott

and Van Devere are merely required to be in the right room at the right time for the right effect. The plot is similar to that of the (much inferior) 1970 TV-movie The HOUSE THAT WOULD NOT DIE.

CHANOC CONTRA EL TIGRE Y EL VAMPIRO (Mex) Azteca 1971 color D: Gilberto M. Solares. SP: Raul M. Solares, R.P. Grovas. Ref: Lee(poster). with Tin-Tan, Aurora Cavel, Victor Alcocer.

CHARLIE CHAN IN THE JADE MASK see JADE MASK, The

CHARLIE CHAN IN THE SCARLET CLUE see SCARLET CLUE, The

Les CHARLOTS CHEZ DRACULA JUNIOR (F) Belstar-Stephan-Films de la Tour 1980 color Ref: V 9/10/80:51. 5/13/81:285,283: aka Les CHARLOTS CONTRE DRACULA. 2/4/81:51: "vampire spoof." FM 174:10. with Andreas Voutsinas, Amelie Prevost.

CHARM, The see MASCOT, The

CHARMURTI (India-Bengali) Mokshada 1978 132m. SP,D: Umanath Bhattacharjee. Mus: Ajoy Das. Ref: Dharap. with Chinmoy Roy, Sivaji, Krishna Saha, R. Ghosh, Santosh Dutta.
Four children solve "haunted"-bungalow mystery.

CHATEAU DE LA TERREUR see QUELQU'UN A TUE

CHEMINS DE LA VIOLENCE see LIPS OF BLOOD

CHERE PE CHERA (India) 1979? D: Raj Tilak. Ref: IFG'80:181.
"A freestyle DR. JEKYLL AND MR. HYDE."

CHI SEI? see BEYOND THE DOOR

The CHILD Boxoffice Int'l./Panorama 1977 color 83m. D: Robert Voskanian. SP: Ralph Lucas. Ph: Mori Alavi. Mus: Rob Wallace. Ref: Meyers. AMPAS. V 12/22/76:7(rated). Willis/SW. with Richard Hanners, Laurel Barnett, Frank Janson, Rosalie Cole.
Little girl has supernatural control of cannibalistic ghouls in nearby cemetery.

The CHILDREN World Northal/Albright 1980 color 90m. D: Max Kalmanowicz. SP: Carlton J. Albright, Edward Terry. Ph: Barry Abrams. Mus: Harry Manfredini. Mkp: Carla White. Ref: V 7/9/80. with Martin Shakar, Gil Rogers, Gale Garnett, Jessie Abrams, Tracy Griswold, Joy Glaccum.
Radioactive cloud from nuclear power plant engulfs children in bus, turns them into "zombie-like terrors."

CHILDREN SHOULDN'T PLAY WITH DEAD THINGS (Gold Key-TV)/Europix/Geneni(Brandywine-Movie Arts) 1972(1974) color 101m. (ZREAKS-B) SP,D,Co-P: Benjamin Clark. Sp,SpMkp,with: Alan Ormsby. Ph: Jack McGowan. Mus: Carl Zittrer. AD: Forest Carpenter. Opt: Opt.House. Ref: TV. MFB'75:6-7.'77:179.

Willis/SW. V 5/24/72:6(rated). FFacts. with Anya Ormsby, Jane Daly, Bruce Solomon, Seth Sklarey("Orville," ghoul).

Living corpses (revived by incantations) wreak revenge on desecrators of their graves. Post-NIGHT OF THE LIVING DEAD motley zombies, annexed to a plot about a (stage? film?) director who has no respect for the dead. He not only gets his just desserts--he is just dessert. Lamely acted and dialogued, and rather weirdly didactic. (The lesson: don't tread on the dead.) However, even in someone else's movie, the Romero cannibal-ghoul is still a disturbing idea, just about the only one here.

A CHILD'S VOICE (Irish) BAC 1978 color 30m. D: Kieran Hickey. SP: David Thomson. Ph: Sean Corcoran. Narr: Valentine Dyall. Ref: MFB'80:100-101: "chilling little ghost story." with T.P. McKenna, Stephen Brennan.

CHILL FACTOR see COLD NIGHT'S DEATH, A

CHINATOWN NIGHTS (B) Col/Victory 1938 70m. D: Tony Frenguelli. SP: Nigel Byass. See also: DR. SIN FANG. Ref: BFC: "Silver Ray." with H. Agar Lyons(Dr.Sin Fang), Anne Grey, Robert Hobbs, Nell Emerald.

The CHINESE IN PARIS (F) Cine Qua Non(Yanne Rassam) & [illegible] 1974 color 115m. (Les CHINOIS A PARIS) SP,D: Jean Yanne. SP: also Gerard Sire, from Robert Beauvais' book. Ph: Jean Boffety. Ref: V 3/13/74:17(ad),34: satire; Red Chinese occupy Paris. 2/20/74. with Yanne, Michel Serrault, Nicole Calfan, Georges Wilson, Bernard Blier.

CHINESE MAGIC (B) Paul 1900 2m. (YELLOW PERIL-alt t?) D: Walter Booth. Ref: BFC.

Chinese conjurer turns himself into giant bat.

CHINESE RED (F) Les Films Elementaires 1977 color & b&w 75m. (Le ROUGE DE CHINE) SP,D,Ed,with: Jacques Richard. Ph: Pascal Laperrousaz. Ref: screen. PFA notes 4/7/80. with Agathe Vannier, Bernard Dubois.

A la Feuillade and Murnau--"a film then of vampires" (Michael Open). Or maybe not. There's a shot of a sailing ship pulling out of frame at one point that's probably an hommage to the '22 NOSFERATU. And the film opens with dirt being thrown on a coffin, and then someone emerging from a crypt. Plus: a few shots of (perhaps) Death personified. Minimal cinema at its most mercilessly minimal.

CHINK IN THE ARMOUR(by Mrs.Belloc Lowndes) see HOUSE OF PERIL

CHOMPS AI/Hanna-Barbera 1979 color 89m. D: Don Chaffey. SP: Joseph Barbera et al. Ph: C.F. Wheeler. Mus: Hoyt Curtin. Ref: V 12/26/79: powerful, mean "mechanical pooch." AMPAS: aka C.H.O.M.P.S. with Wesley Eure, Valerie Bertinelli, Chuck McCann, Regis Toomey, Jim Backus, Red Buttons.

The CHOSEN (I-B) AI/Embassy-Aston 1977 color/Technovision 102m. (HOLOCAUST 2000-orig t) SP,D: Alberto De Martino. SP: also Sergio Donati, Michael Robson. Ph: Erico Menczer. Mus: Ennio Morricone. AD: Uberto Bertacca. SpFX: Gino De Rossi. Mkp: Penny Steyne. Ref: MFB'78:47. Meyers. V 1/11/78. with Kirk Douglas, Simon Ward, Agostina Belli, Anthony Quayle, Virginia McKenna, Ivo Garrani, Alexander Knox, Adolfo Celi.
Design of thermonuclear plant corresponds to "7-headed beast" of Anti-Christ, end-of-the-world prophecy.

CHOSEN SURVIVORS (U.S.-Mex) Col/Metromedia/Alpine-Churubusco 1974 color 98m. (The BAT-orig t) D: Sutton Roley. SP: H.B. Cross, J.R. Moffly. Ph: Gabriel Torres. Mus: Fred Karlin. AD: J.R. Granada. SpFX: Federico Farfan. SpBatFX: Tony Urbano. SdFX: Paul Laune. Opt: Modern. Ref: MFB'74:270-1. V 5/29/74. Cinef Smr'72:46. with Jackie Cooper, Alex Cord, Richard Jaeckel, Bradford Dillman, Pedro Armendariz Jr., Diana Muldaur, Kelly Lange.
Ten people sheltered in underground complex during raging nuclear war are attacked by hordes of vampire bats.

A CHRISTMAS CAROL (B) Alpha 1960 28m. D,P: Robert Hartford-Davis. From the story by Charles Dickens. Ref: BFC. with John Hayter, Stewart Brown.
See also: PASSIONS OF CAROL, The.

CHRYSLER THEATRE see CODE NAME: HERACLITUS

CHUANG TAO CHENG see SPOOKY BUNCH, The

CINDERELLA 2000 Indep.-Int'l. 1977 color/scope 89m. D,P: Al Adamson. SP: Bud Donnelly. Ph: Louis Horvath. Mus: Sparky Sugarman. Titles: Bob LeBar. Ref: Meyers. V 5/17/78:210(ad). 5/11/77:177(ad). Boxo 7/30/79:21. Willis/SW. Cinef VI:3:24. with Catherine Erhardt, Rena Harmon, Eddie Garetti(robot).
In the year 2047, computers rule the world, and love is forbidden without their consent.

CINQ GARS POUR SINGAPOUR(by J.Bruce) see SINGAPORE, SINGAPORE

CINQUE BAMBOLE PER LA LUNA D'AGOSTO see FIVE DOLLS...

CINQUE MARINES PER SINGAPORE see SINGAPORE, SINGAPORE

CIRCLE OF IRON Avco Embassy/Volare 1979 color 102m. (The SILENT FLUTE-orig t) D: Richard Moore. SP: Stirling Silliphant, Stanley Mann. Story: Bruce Lee, James Coburn, Silliphant. Ph: Ronnie Taylor. Mus: Bruce Smeaton. PD: Johannes Larsen. Ref: V 1/24/79. MFB'78:247. with David Carradine, Jeff Cooper, Roddy McDowall, Eli Wallach, Christopher Lee, Erica Creer, Earl Maynard(black giant).
Demons, Death, monkey people, pantherman.

CITY OF LOST MEN see LOST CITY, The

*The CLAIRVOYANT Vogue-Gainsborough 1935 Ph: G. MacWilliams. Mus: Arthur Benjamin. AD: A. Junge. Ref: TV: TRANS-ATLANTIC TUNNEL footage? and with Athole Stewart.

The midway or meeting point between the 1933 INVISIBLE MAN (starring Claude Rains) and the 1957 CURSE OF THE DEMON (co-scripted by Charles Bennett), all three stories of mortals caught up in the novelty and excitement of their own super-natural or super-scientific powers. This version--uniting Rains and Bennett--isn't quite the character study it might have been. (Rains eventually gets sucked into a plot bog.) But it's not as silly as the similar NIGHT HAS A THOUSAND EYES. Rains is all boyish enthusiasm, vanity, doubt--natural reactions to his supernatural power of clairvoyance. He might be Young Karswell, the conjurer of demons in CURSE. (Rains: "It may be a gift from God." Fay Wray: "Or the Devil.")

CLAM FAIRY (H.K.) 1970? color (PANG HSIEN) Ref: Eberhard.

"Ghost" beckoning from cemetery; old house; "herd of demons, who are dead people."

CLASH OF THE TITANS (B) UA/MGM 1981 color 118m. D: Desmond Davis. SP: Beverley Cross. Ph: Ted Moore. Mus: Laurence Rosenthal. PD: Frank White. SpVisFX & Co-P: Ray Harryhausen. Ref: V 6/10/81. VV 6/10/81. with Laurence Olivier, Harry Hamlin, Claire Bloom, Judi Bowker, Maggie Smith, Burgess Meredith, Ursula Andress, Flora Robson(witch), Donald Houston, J.Gwillim.

Giant Kraken; skeleton-like Charon, ferryman to the Isle of the Dead (inhabited by Medusa and two-headed monster-dog). (A)

CLAWS Alaska 1977 color 90m. (DEVIL BEAR-orig t) D: Richard Bansbach, R.E. Pierson. SP,Ph,P: Chuck D. Keen. SP: also Brian Russell. Mus Sup: Gene Kauer, Doug Lackey. Ref: TV. V 7/30/75:7. 9/1/76:32. with Jason Evers, Leon Ames, Myron Healey, Anthony Caruso, Carla Layton, Glenn Sipes.

"Giant Grizzly Turns Rogue Killer" (teletype message)--or is it a Kush Ta Ka or devil-bear (a la Indian legend), "big as a house"? No matter. "A few well-placed slugs will turn him into a rug" (over-confident hunter). All this and pathos too. And Santa never shows up....

A CLOCKWORK ORANGE (B) WB/Hawk 1971 color 137m. SP,D,P: Stanley Kubrick. From the novel by Anthony Burgess. Ph: John Alcott. Elec Mus: Walter Carlos; Beethoven, Rossini et al. PD: John Barry. SpProps: H. Makkink, C. Kubrick. Ref: screen. V 12/15/71. MFB'72:28-9. Cinef Smr'72. Lee: vampire seq. with Malcolm McDowell, Patrick Magee, Michael Bates, Adrienne Corri, Sheila Raynor, Margaret Tyzack.

Scientific behavior-conditioning in the ultra-violent near-future. This looks, at first, like no movie you've ever seen. But Kubrick's one-point-a-scene method eventually palls, giving the viewer time to flash-forward and anticipate story twists and turns. (In the "homecoming" sequence, the point is made almost instantly, then merely held--the hard pedal--for several minutes.) The one fully successful sequence is the "Singin' in the Rain" one, in which the "choreography" emphasizes rather than softens or lyricizes the brutality. Engaging narration.

The CLONE MASTER NBC-TV/Para-TV 1978 color 94m. D: Don Medford. SP,P: John D.F. Black. Ph: Joe Biroc. Mus: Glenn Paxtone. SpFX: Joe Mercurio. Ref: TV. V 9/20/78:61. with Art Hindle(biochemist & clone), Robyn Douglass, Ralph Bellamy, John Van Dreelen, Ed Lauter.
Two scientists succeed in creating telepathic clones.

The CLONES Filmmakers Int'l./Hunt-Card 1973 color 94m. (DEAD MAN RUNNING-orig t. The CLONING OF DR.APPLEBY. The CLONING. The MINDSWEEPERS-all int ts. CLONES-B) Story,D: Paul Hunt, Lamar Card. SP: Steve Fisher. Ph: Gary Graver. Mus: Allen D. Allen. SpFX: Harry Woolman. Ref: MFB'74:172,211. Aros. TVFFSB. Les Otis. V 3/7/73:4(rated). 10/4/72:24. 8/2/72:12. Cinef W'73:42. with Michael Greene, Otis Young, Gregory Sierra, Susan Hunt, Alex Nicol, Stanley Adams, John Barrymore Jr., Noble "Kid" Chissell, Angelo Rossitto, Bruce Bennett.
Scientist encounters his clone, discovers plot to take over world "through control of the weather." (MFB)

The CLONES OF BRUCE LEE (H.K.) Newport/Wei Ling 1979? color 90m. (SHEN-WEI SAN MENG-LUNG) D: Chiang Hung. Ref: MFB'80: 221. V 7/16/80(rated). with Lu Hsiao-Lung, Kuo Shih-Chih, Chu Lung(clones).
Mad-professor-created Lee clones vs. "bronze men" (i.e., "drugged humans"); laser weapon. (MFB)

The CLONING OF CLIFFORD SWIMMER ABC-TV/Lefferts 1974 color 74m. D: Lela Swift. Ref: TVFFSB. with Peter Haskell, Lance Kerwin, Sheree North, Sharon Farrell.
Psychogeneticist creates clone of man.

CLONING, The or CLONING OF DR.APPLEBY, The see CLONES, The

CLONUS or CLONUS HORROR, The see PARTS THE CLONUS HORROR

CLOSE ENCOUNTERS OF THE THIRD KIND Col/EMI 1977/1980 color/scope 135m./125m. (The SPECIAL EDITION: CLOSE ENCOUNTERS OF THE THIRD KIND-'80 re-edited version) SP,D,VisFxConception: Steven Spielberg. Ph: Vilmos Zsigmond, William A. Fraker; (India) Douglas Slocombe;(add'l) John Alonzo, Laszlo Kovacs; ('80 footage) Alan Davian. Mus: John Williams. PD: Joe Alves. SpPhFX:(sup) Douglas Trumbull;(ph) Richard Yuricich. Alien Des: Carlo Rambaldi. Anim & VisFxSup: Robert Swarthe. Ship Ph: Dennis Muren. SpMechFX: Roy Arbogast. SupSdFxEd: Frank Warner. Ref: screen. MFB'78:63-4.'80:189. V 11/9/77. 8/6/80. with Richard Dreyfuss, Francois Truffaut, Teri Garr, Melinda Dillon, Bob Balaban, Roberts Blossom, Cary Guffey, Carl Weathers, Hal Barwood, Matthew Robbins, Bill Thurman, Warren Kemmerling, Lance Henrikson.
Alien beings arrange a rendezvous with humans at The Devil's

Tower, Wyoming. Science-fiction as spectacle, skillfully designed to provoke awe, wonder, "wow!"'s. CLOSE ENCOUNTERS is essentially two long, very-well-orchestrated set-pieces sandwiching fragments of a domestic drama. It's more a deluxe effects-showcase than narrative. The characters play straight to the special effects. They/we want to be amazed, and they/we are. We see through their eyes, through them, but not--the movie's weakness--into them. As long as the film stays on the surface--with the play of lights and shadows, sound and music--it's near-brilliant. When it attempts to describe the characters' dissatisfaction with things-as-they-are, to explain their need for answers, it falters. The shared vision of the sawed-off mountain is made to seem both the problem and the solution--to bear, that is, all the dramatic weight. Spielberg wants to evoke a sense of ongoing lives disrupted before he has evoked a sense of, simply, ongoing lives; and, almost exclusively, he attempts to evoke this sense through Roy Neary's (Dreyfuss') obsession with the image of the mountain. But if Spielberg seems, with characterization, to be stuck on one note, he is, in his conception of effects, almost symphonic. Even ostensibly-simple shots of the Indiana night-sky are so magical that they seem to be effects (some are)--"the heavens" are right at the characters' doorstep. In one sequence, the uproar of a frantic, country-road alien encounter gives way to the sound of a cricket: the magic here is not so much in the noise of the one or the other, but in the juxtaposition of the familiar and the unfamiliar. Spielberg's characters are looking for answers from above, from the sky; but, wisely, he doesn't spell those answers out for us. He doesn't have to. We've seen--and heard--miracles worked.

The CLUE OF THE PIGTAIL (B) 1923 22m. See also: Mystery of Dr. Fu-Manchu series. Ref: BFC. Lee.

CODE NAME: HERACLITUS Univ-TV/Jack Laird 1967 color 88m. D: James Goldstone. SP: Alvin Sapinsley. Ph: Bud Thackery. Mus: Johnny Mandel. AD: John J. Lloyd. Ref: TV. TVFFSB. TVG. Maltin/TVM: from 2 "Chrysler Theatre" TV shows. with Stanley Baker("zombie"), Leslie Nielsen, Jack Weston, Sheree North, Kurt Kasznar, Signe Hasso, Ricardo Montalban, Chuck Courtney.

Man's "brief death" of 7 minutes destroys parts of his brain controlling emotions, memory, and conscience, making him an ideal spy. By the end, however, he seems a good deal more "sensitive," ethically, than the "normal" people around him. ("Maybe I'm not such a zombie after all.") Check.

CODE NAME MINUS ONE see GEMINI MAN, The

CODE NAME: TRIXIE see CRAZIES, The

COLD BLOODED BEAST see SLAUGHTER HOTEL

A COLD NIGHT'S DEATH ABC-TV/Spelling-Goldberg 1973 color 73m. (CHILL FACTOR-alt t) D: Jerrold Freedman. SP: Christopher

Knopf. Ph: Leonard J. South. Elec Mus: Gil Melle. AD: Rolland M. Brooks. SdFxEd: Edward Rossi. Ref: TV. TVFFSB. with Robert Culp, Eli Wallach, Michael C. Gwynne.

Two scientists at an Arctic research station find themselves the subjects of experiments conducted by apes. The Culp and Wallach characters (the irrational vs. the rational man) make, in their incompatibility, too-ideal subjects for the apes' stress tests--their resistance is too easily lowered. But the Arctic environment--chattering chimps, wind, electronic music--is eerily barren, and the movie ends at just the right moment, with enough but not too much explanation. (Explanations would be difficult.) Strangely effective at times *despite* the unsubtle characterization and the outrageous premise.

The COLLECTOR (Yug) Zagreb 1972? anim short D: Milan Blazekovic. Ref: IFG'73:492.

Butterfly deposits collector in *its* collection.

The COLONEL AND THE WOLFMAN (Braz) Alcino Diniz-Embrafilme 1978 color 118m. (O CORONEL E O LOBISOMEM) SP,D: Diniz. Dial: J.C. de Carvalho, from his novel. Ph: Antonio Goncalves. Mus: H. Vilela, M. Versiani. Ref: IFG'80:80. V 5/30/79. with Mauricio do Valle, Maria Claudia, Tonico Pereira(werewolf).

Military man "dreams of sexpots and werewolves."

COLONIZATION OF THE PLANET OF THE APES see BATTLE FOR THE PLANET OF THE APES

The COLOR OF BLOOD ABC-TV 1973 color 74m. Ref: TVFFSB: "compulsive murderer," "lonely country house." with Norman Eshley, Katharine Schofield, Derek Smith.

COMA UA/MGM 1977 color 113m. SP,D: Michael Crichton, from Robin Cook's novel. Ph: Victor J. Kemper. Mus: Jerry Goldsmith. PD: Albert Brenner. SpFX: Joe Day, Ernie Smith. Ref: MFB'78:216-17. V 1/25/78. with Genevieve Bujold, Michael Douglas, Elizabeth Ashley, Rip Torn, Richard Widmark, Lois Chiles.

Bodies of coma victims from Boston Memorial Hospital are stored and maintained by computer at the Jefferson Institute, and then used internationally for "spare part" surgery. Pat medical-conspiracy material, padded out with superfluous suspense sequences. Predictable plot and character development. The two showpiece sequences--the bodies-hanging-in-bags and the coma-victims-on-wires--aren't really worth the narrative trip.

The COMEBACK (B) Lone Star/Heritage 1977('79-U.S.) color 100m. (The DAY THE SCREAMING STOPPED-orig t) D,P: Pete Walker. SP: Murray Smith; Michael Sloan. Ph: Peter Jessop. Mus: Stanley Myers. AD: Mike Pickwoad. Mkp: George Partleton. Ref: Boxo 2/25/80:20. MFB'78:155. V 6/1/77:26. Willis/SW. with Jack Jones, David Doyle, Pamela Stephenson, Richard Johnson, Bill Owen.

"Woman-creature" seems to haunt English country house.

COMEDIE FANTASTICA (Rum.) BFS 1975 color 88m. SP,D: I. Popescu Gopo. Ph: G. Ionescu, S. Horvath. Mus: D. Capoinu. Ref: V 8/6/75: comedy. with Cornel Coman, D. Radulescu.
Lab-created youth with "robot-like" "mother" and computer "father."

COMIC STRIP HERO see KILLING GAME, The

COMING OF DRACULA'S BRIDE, The see DRACULA'S BRIDE

COMMUNION see ALICE SWEET ALICE

COMPUTER FREE-FOR-ALL (J) Toho 1969 color 84m. (BUCHAMUKURE DAIHAKKEN) D: K. Furusawa. SP: Yasuo Tanami. Mus: N. Yamamoto. Ref: AFI: computer that revives murdered woman. with Hajime Hana, Kei Tani.

COMPUTER KILLERS see HORROR HOSPITAL

The COMPUTER SUPERMAN (Thai) Chaiyo 1977 color 120m. (Yod MANOOT COMPUTER) SP,D: Santa Pestonji. SP: also K. Boonchu. Story: Ratiporn. Ph: Tirapong. Mus: Mandarin Lab. SpFX: Toho Films. Ref: V 5/11/77:79: robot, "freaks." with Yodchai Megsuan, Poh Teng.

*The COMPUTER WORE TENNIS SHOES 1969 Sequels: NOW YOU SEE HIM, NOW YOU DON'T. The STRONGEST MAN IN THE WORLD. AD: John B. Mansbridge. Ref: Lee.

COMTESSE AUX SEINS NUS see BARE BREASTED COUNTESS, The

CONCERTO PER PISTOLA SOLISTA see WEEKEND MURDERS

CONDORMAN (B) BV 1981 color/scope 90m. D: Charles Jarrott. SP: Marc Stirdivant, from Robert Sheckley's novel, "The Game of X." Ph: C.F. Wheeler. Mus: Henry Mancini. PD: Albert Witherick. SpFX: Colin Chilvers. Ref: V 8/5/81. SFC 8/17/81. with Michael Crawford, Oliver Reed, Barbara Carrera, James Hampton, Jean-Pierre Kalfon, Dana Elcar.
Cartoonist who lives his strip's adventures; laser gun.

The CONFESSIONAL (B) Brandon/Heritage 1975('77-U.S., Atlas) color 104m. (HOUSE OF MORTAL SIN-B) Story,D,P: Pete Walker. SP: David McGillivray. Ph: Peter Jessop. Mus: Stanley Myers. AD: Chris Burke. Ref: MFB'76:53: man who dies of fright. Brandon: "Satanic priest." Bianco Index'76. Willis/SW. with Anthony Sharp, Susan Penhaligon, Stephanie Beacham, Mervyn Johns, Norman Eshley.

CONFESSIONS OF A MALE ESCORT (W.G.) Brummer-Farb 1974 color 88m. (OBSZONITATEN) D: Alois Brummer. Ph: Paco Joan. Ref: MFB'76:7-8. with Stefan Grey, Sandra Reni, Miriam Moor.
"Tiresomely spooky country house"; "projected penis transplant"; zombie; vampire.

CONNECTICUT YANKEE IN KING ARTHUR'S COURT, A(by M.Twain) see UNIDENTIFIED FLYING ODDBALL

*The CONQUEROR WORM 1968 (aka EDGAR ALLAN POE'S CONQUEROR WORM) SpFX: Roger Dicken. Ref: screen. Lee.

Formula revenge story, done with about as much ingenuity as it takes to wind a clock. "Style" here means brief zooms and reverse-zooms, slow and fast panning, and neatly-composed long shots; "content" means flurries of violence, and the witchfinder intoning, "We're doing God's work."

CONQUEST OF THE DEEPS see NEPTUNE FACTOR, The

CONQUEST OF THE EARTH ABC-TV/Univ-TV & Larson 1980 color 99m. D: Sidney Hayers, Sigmund Neufeld Jr., Barry Crane. SP: G.A. Larson. Adap: Francesca Turner. From the "Battlestar Galactica" TV series. Ph: Ben Colman et al. Mus: Stu Phillips. AD: F.T. Tuch et al. Min & SpPh:(sup) D.M. Garber, W. Smith; Universal Hartland. Ref: MFB'81:110-11. and with Kent McCord, Robert Reed, William Daniels, Lara Parker, Wolfman Jack, Richard Lynch, Sharon Acker, Peter Mark Richman, B. Van Dyke.

Android; "cerebral mutants"; Cylon secret weapon on Earth.

CONQUEST OF THE PLANET OF THE APES Fox/APJAC 1972 color/scope 85m. D: J. Lee Thompson. SP: Paul Dehn. Sequel to PLANET OF THE APES. Ph: Bruce Surtees. Mus: Tom Scott. AD: Philip Jeffries. MkpDes: John Chambers; Dan Striepeke. Ref: MFB'72: 157-58. V 6/14/72. TV. with Roddy McDowall, Don Murray, Hari Rhodes, Ricardo Montalban, Natalie Trundy, Severn Darden, H.M. Wynant, Joyce Haber, Lou Wagner, John Dennis, John Randolph.

1991. Apes, trained to replace now-extinct cats and dogs (killed by space virus), revolt against their human masters. Forgettable Spartacus plot, but McDowall in ape-makeup is still riveting--the makeup almost seems to make his face more rather than less expressive. (Makeup-as-characterization.) Non-apes Murray and Montalban are at best accessories to the plot.

CONTACT (Russ) 1979? anim short? (KOUMANI) D: V. Tarassov. Ref: IFG'80:373: alien encounter.

CONTAMINATION see ALIEN CONTAMINATION

CONTES IMMORAUX see IMMORAL TALES

CONTINUOUS KATHERINE MORTENHOE(by D.Compton) see DEATHWATCH

CONVIENE FAR BENE L'AMORE see SEX MACHINE

COPACABANA, MON AMOUR (Braz) Sganzerla 1973 color 85m. SP, D,Mus: Rogerio Sganzerla. Ph: R. Laclete. Mus: also G. Gil. Ref: Brasil. with Helena Ignez, O. Serra, Lilian Lemmertz.

Children possessed by demons; witch-doctor.

The COPS AND ROBIN ABC-TV 1978 color 95m. From the "Future Cop" TV series. Ref: TVG: "experimental android." with

Ernest Borgnine, Michael Shannon(robot), John Amos, Natasha Ryan, Carol Lynley, Elizabeth Farley.

CORONEL E O LOBISOMEM, O see COLONEL AND THE WOLFMAN, The

CORPI PRESENTANO TRACCE DI VIOLENZA CARNALE see TORSO

CORPSE, The see CRUCIBLE OF HORROR

CORPSE MANIA (H.K.-Cantonese) 1981 Ref: V 8/26/81:45: horror.

*The CORPSE VANISHES 1942 Ref: TV. LC. Lennig/TC.

Bela Lugosi as Dr. Lorenz is "peculiar, *strange*"--he's a horticulturist-hypnotist (yes) and he sleeps in a coffin (yes)--but he doesn't quite prepare one for his "family," which is a real menagerie: there's Elizabeth Russell (from the Lewton films) as the mad Countess; Angelo (as he's billed) as a sadistic dwarf; an unpleasant old woman (Minerva Urecal), and her idiot son (Frank Moran), a hair fetishist. And the whole family *skulks*. (Doctor: "I find it difficult to explain their peculiarities to some people.") Some of the script's more outre details (e.g., the idiot chewing on a chicken bone while he's chasing a woman) border on surreal comedy. Unfortunately, Bela and his friends are really the "supporting" players, and Luana Walters and Iris Coffin the stars, of a dull framing story. But Lugosi's campy glee seems just right for this movie, which is far from Monogram's worst.

CORRECTION, PLEASE or HOW WE GOT INTO PICTURES (B) Arts Council 1979 color & b&w 52m. D: Noel Burch. Ph: Les Young. Mus: John Buller. Ref: screen. PFA notes 3/4/80. with Alex McCrindle, Sue Lloyd.

Hypnotism seq. from DR.MABUSE(Part I,1922) recreated; hypnotic fumes; fantasy seqs. from EXPLOSION OF A MOTOR CAR & The INGENIOUS SOUBRETTE. Film supposedly suggests ways in which movies shape our perceptions, and does point up differences in film grammar between 1900 and the present. But one reading is as good as another.

The CORRUPTION OF CHRIS MILLER (Sp) Lanir-Armet 1973('75-U.S.) color/scope 115m. (La CORRUPTION DE CHRIS MILLER. SISTERS OF CORRUPTION-B) D: Juan A. Bardem. SP: Santiago Moncada. Ph: Juan Gelpi. Mus: Waldo de Los Rios. AD: R. Gomez. Ref: MFB'75:53. Willis/SW. V 9/25/74:23(ad). 8/8/73. with Jean Seberg, Marisol, Perla Cristal, Gerard Tichy, Bardem.

"Psychological thriller....mad slicker-clad sickle-murderer." (MFB)

COSMO 2000--PLANET WITHOUT A NAME see WAR IN SPACE(Nais, 1977)

COSMOS--WAR OF THE PLANETS (I) Pictumedia/Nais 1977 color 90m. (sfa COSMO 2000--L'INVASION DEGLI EXTRACORPI?) D: Alfonso Brescia(aka Al Bradley). Ref: TVFFSB. V 10/18/78:134. 8/17/77:30. with John Richardson, Yanti Somer, W. Buchanan,

Vasilli Kramensis, Gisella Hahn.
"Future journey" of a "starlost spaceship." (TVFFSB)

COUNT DOWNE see SON OF DRACULA(1974)

COUNT DRACULA AND HIS VAMPIRE BRIDE (B) Dynamite Ent./Hammer 1973('79-U.S.) color 88m. (The SATANIC RITES OF DRACULA-B. DRACULA IS DEAD AND WELL AND LIVING IN LONDON-orig t) D: Alan Gibson. SP: Don Houghton. Ph: Brian Probyn. Mus: John Cavacas. AD: Lionel Couch. SpFX: Les Bowie. Mkp: George Blackler. Ref: MFB'74:51. V 12/6/78. AMPAS. Glut/TDB. with Christopher Lee(Dracula), Peter Cushing, Michael Coles, William Franklyn, Joanna Lumley, Richard Vernon, Patrick Barr.
Dracula plots to impregnate occultist Prof. Lorrimer Van Helsing's granddaughter with "a plague virus which could wipe out mankind." (MFB)

COUNT DRACULA, THE TRUE STORY see VLAD TEPES

*COUNTESS DRACULA Fox/Rank 1970('72-U.S.) See also: WEREWOLF VS.THE VAMPIRE WOMAN, The. Ref: TV. Lee. and with Sandor Eles, Lesley-Anne Down, Nike Arrighi, Charles Farrell.
The aging Countess Elisabeth Nadasdy (Ingrid Pitt) discovers that applications of the blood of virgins temporarily rejuvenate her; she proceeds to impersonate her own daughter and takes a young lover, Imre (Eles). The vehicle may be blood, but COUNTESS DRACULA is closer, thematically, to "Dr.Jekyll and Mr.Hyde" than it is to "Dracula." Here, however, it's Jekyll (i.e., Elisabeth), and not Hyde (i.e., Elisabeth-as-Ilona) who gets uglier with each reversion. Old age is horror; youth and the guise of Ilona are liberation for the Countess--as Hydes are traditionally liberation for Jekylls. Pitt and the script make her sexual desperation seem quite immediate; surprisingly, perhaps, because she's such an unpleasant, unsympathetic character. Her motivations are selfish, but compelling. She's both callous and pathetic--more a tragic villainess than a heroine. Unfortunately, the only other character who is drawn as forcefully is that of her older lover, Captain Dobi (Nigel Green), who loves his Countess, young or old. (Yet has a possessive interest in keeping her old, and unattractive to others.) Otherwise, characterization is merely expedient.

COUNTESS DRACULA see DEVIL'S WEDDING NIGHT, The

CRACKING UP Comedy Jam 1977 color 74m. D: Rowby Goren, Chuck Staley. SP: The Ace Trucking Co. et al. Ph: Bob Collins. Mus: Ward Jewell. Ref: MFB'79:145. V 7/27/77. with Phil Proctor, Peter Bergman, Fred Willard, Neil Israel, The Credibility Gap.
California struck by earthquake and tidal wave.

CRASH! Group 1 1977 color/scope 80m. (AKAZA,THE GOD OF VENGEANCE-orig t) D: Charles Band. SP: Marc Marais. Ph: Tom

Cecato. Mus: Andrew Belling. Ref: Meyers. Bianco #5-6/77: 232: 1976? Willis/SW. Maltin/TVM. with Jose Ferrer, Sue Lyon, John Ericson, John Carradine, Leslie Parrish.
Supernatural power in old curio inhabits wheelchair, car.

The CRATER LAKE MONSTER (Gold Key-TV)/Crown Int'l. 1977 color 85m. SP,D,P: William Stromberg. SP: also Richard Cardella. Ph: Paul Gentry. PD: Roger Heisman. SpFX:(d) David Allen; Jon Berg, Phil Tippett. SpMechFX: Steve Neill. SpMinFX: Tom Scherman. SpOptFX: Van Der Veer. Ref: Meyers. V 5/11/77:120 (ad). GKey. Willis/SW. FFacts. with Cardella, Glenn Roberts, Mark Siegel, Kacey Cobb.
Monster hatches from meteorite-heated egg at bottom of lake.

CRAZE (B) WB/Harbor(Cohen) 1973 color 95m. D: Freddie Francis. SP: Aben Kandel, Herman Cohen. From the novel "Infernal Idol" by Henry Seymour. Ph: John Wilcox. Mus: John Scott. AD: George Provis. Ref: MFB'74:123. Willis/SW. V 6/12/74. with Jack Palance, Diana Dors, Julie Ege, Edith Evans, Hugh Griffith, Trevor Howard, Michael Jayston, Suzy Kendall, Percy Herbert, Martin Potter, Frank Forsyth.
Antique-shop owner's human sacrifices to African idol seem to bring him success.

CRAZED VAMPIRE (F) Boxoffice Int'l./Framo-ABC 1972 color 90m. (VIERGES ET VAMPIRES. REQUIEM POUR UN VAMPIRE. CAGED VIRGINS-alt t. SEX VAMPIRES-alt t?) D: Jean Rollin. Ph: Renan Pooes. Ref: Indep.Film Jnl. 12/24/73:88(ad). Meyers. Lee. Glut/TDB. Willis/SW. V 10/18/72:4(rated, as The VIRGINS AND THE VAMPIRES). Cinef F'73:38. with Phillip(p)e Gaste, Marie Pierre Castel, Louise Dhour, Mirielle D'Argent.
Old chateau houses sect of hypnotic vampires.

The CRAZIES Cambist/Pittsburgh 1973 103m. (CODE NAME: TRIXIE-alt t) SP,D,Ed: George Romero. Story: Paul McCollough. Ph: S.W. Hinzman. Mus: Bruce Roberts. SpFX: Regis Survinski, Tony Pantanello. Mkp: Bonnie Priore. Ref: screen. MFB'78:42-3. NYT 3/24/73. V 1/24/73. with Lane Carroll, W.G. McMillan, Harold Wayne Jones, Lynn Lowry, Lloyd Hollar.
Experimental vaccine in Pennsylvania town's water supply makes inhabitants go berserk. Ideas run through George Romero's films somewhat as the virus runs through the community in The CRAZIES--i.e., rather crazily. And here they seem rather incidental to the more sensationalistic elements. Blood billows up out of mouths, spatters walls, collects in pools; it sprays, gushes, cascades, and does everything but figure eights. The script is a hodge-podge of violence and abnormal psychology and sociology. Only once, briefly--when a mad girl exclaims "Oh!" as she dies--do the violence and quirky psychology lyrically fuse.

*The CRAZY RAY 1923 50m. Ref: screen.
Professor Crase's ray stops, starts, speeds up all Paris, as he and others turn the ray on, off, on again....TARGET

EARTH(1954) perhaps takes its deserted-city-streets opening from The CRAZY RAY, which in turn takes the notion of speeded-up time from ONESIME HORLOGER(1912), The TIMES ARE OUT OF JOINT (1910), and HOW TO MAKE TIME FLY(1906). This is a pleasant, but rather slight Rene Clair comedy, with the premise simply a pretext for a series of generally-amusing stunts (e.g., the hero encountering time-frozen Parisians).

CREATURE FROM BLACK LAKE (Cinema Shares Int'l-TV)/Howco Int'l./ McCullough 1976 color/scope 97m. D: Joy Houck Jr. SP: Jim McCullough Jr. Ph: Dean Cundey. Mus: Jaime Mendoza-Nava. AD: Roger Pancake. SpFX: Sterling Franck. Mkp: Charlene Cundey. Opt: CFI. Ref: TV. TVFFSB. TVG. Meyers. Willis/SW. with Jack Elam, Dub Taylor, John David Carson, Bill Thurman, Dennis Fimple, Roy Tatum(creature), Catherine McClenn.

Ape-man creature at large in Louisiana backwoods. Generally inconsequential, occasionally unconscionably serious, CREATURE is not quite comedy, and not really horror, but is at least marginally more bearable than the usual Legend of Boggyfoot perpetrations. Highlight: Elam's "_Nuthin'_!" story.

CREATURE OF THE DEVIL see DEAD MEN WALK

*CREATURE OF THE WALKING DEAD Alameda _1960_('65-U.S.) Footage from *MARK OF DEATH. PD: Luis De Leon. Mkp: Lester Andre? Ref: TV. Lee. TVFFSB. AFI. and with Lloyd Nelson.

Man resurrects his grandfather, a scientist, from the dead, keeps him alive with rejuvenating blood; scientist reverts to old-age (and looks like "vampire" to one witness) when grandson is late with his plasma supply; spiritualist "sees" vampire's captive. Another marvel of recycling from Jerry Warren--here, _new_ scenes (with dialogue in English) are spliced into _old_ footage, which is spookily accompanied by "narration" (and _a_ dubbed line or two), instead of the original dialogue. Two half-movies don't make a whole. Three-note music-track is a classic of its kind. (_Duh_-_duhh_-_duhhh_!)

The CREATURE WASN'T NICE Creature Feature 1981 Ref: V 9/9/81:4(rated).

CREATURES, The see FROM BEYOND THE GRAVE

CREEPER, The character see BRUTE MAN, The. HOUSE OF HORRORS. PEARL OF DEATH.

The CREEPING FLESH (B) Col/WFS-Tigon 1972 color 90m. D: Freddie Francis. SP: Peter Spenceley, Jonathan Rumbold. Ph: Norman Warwick. Mus: Paul Ferris. AD: George Provis. Mkp: Roy Ashton. Titles: GSE. Ref: TV. Lee. V 3/14/73. FM 165:40, 43-4. TVFFSB. MFB'73:25-6. Cinef IX:1:34. with Peter Cushing, Christopher Lee, Lorna Heilbron, George Benson, Kenneth J. Warren, Duncan Lamont, Michael Ripper, Jenny Runacre, H. Wallace.

"Evil is a disease"--the blood cells of violent insanity are extracted from the skeleton of a member of an ancient race of evil giants, and injected into a woman. *She* goes mad; *it* is revived by rain water. (Nice shots later of its cloaked, intimidating bulk....) "Absolute nonsense" (thank you, script) and incredibly contrived, to scant point except to provide a sort of cinematic display-case for the fearsome-looking skeleton (which was created by Roger Dicken). It has lain buried for several geologic eras, and seems to lie dormant on Dr. Cushing's table for about as long again before it finally, *finally* revives.

*The CREEPING TERROR (Gold Key-TV) 1964 (DANGEROUS CHARTER-alt TV t) D,P,Ed: A.J. Nelson. Ph: Andrew Janczak. Mus: Frederick Kopp. SpDes: Jon Lackey. Ref: TV. TVFFSB. AFI.

Creature from spaceship plods about scooping up and eating people. In the tacky tradition of ATTACK OF THE MAYAN MUMMY, the narrator here *tells* you the dialogue and action, and the actors' mouths just open and close. ("The monster next appeared in Lovers' Lane, and anyone who survived that catastrophe would never go there again.") The creature belches as it ingests its victims, and it waddles so slowly that they have to *wait* for it to come to them. A film illuminated by its own special ineptitude.

The CREMATORS New World/Arista 1972 color 75m. SP,D,P: Harry Essex. From the novelette "Dune Roller" by Judy Ditky. Ph: Robert Caramico. Mus: Albert Glasser. SpPhFX: Doug Beswick. Mkp: Ron Kinney. Ref: TV. Lee. with Maria Di Aragon, Marvin C. Howard, Eric Allison, Mason Caulfield, Al Ward.

Legendary "dune roller" is actually living meteorite that fell into lake 300 years ago and is gathering its lost fragments to itself; its rocks radiate to communicate with home base. Amateur-level production, though the scenes with the gigantic, incinerating head-fireball and its midget minions are loonily amusing. Glasser's blaring, cheesy score sets the sub-"B" tone.

CRESCENDO (B) WB/Hammer 1969('72-U.S.) color 95m. D: Alan Gibson. SP: Jimmy Sangster, Alfred Shaughnessy. Ph: Paul Beeson. Mus: Malcolm Williamson. AD: Scott MacGregor. Mkp: Stella Morris. Ref: Maltin/TVM: "chiller"; "crazy family." Lee: "horror: mad-twin-in-attic." TVFFSB. Willis/SW. V 11/1/72. with Stephanie Powers, James Olson, Jane Lapotaire, J.Ackland.

CRIES IN THE NIGHT (Can.) Incident/Barry Allen 1980 color D,P: Bill Fruet. SP: Ida Nelson. Mus: Jerry Fielding. Ref: V 5/7/80:106-7(ad): horror. 5/13/81:63. IFG'81:96. with Kay Hawtr(e)y, Barry Morse, Harvey Atkin.

Guests begin to disappear from guest home/ex-funeral parlor.

CRIME AND THE PENALTY (B) Martin 1916 57m. D: R.H. West. Ref: BFC. with Alesia Leon, Jack Lovatt, Louis Nanten.

"Crook hires scientist to kidnap cousin's wife with aid of chimpanzee that strangles when hypnotised."

CRIME DOCTOR'S MANHUNT Col 1946 64m. D: William Castle. SP: Leigh Brackett. Story: Eric Taylor. From Max Marcin's "Crime Doctor" radio show. Ph: P. Tannura. Mus D: M. Bakaleinikoff. Ref: V 9/18/46. LC. with Warner Baxter, Ellen Drew, William Frawley, Claire Carleton, Myron Healey, O.Howlin, F.Pierlot.

"Personality split" causes woman "to assume dead sister's stronger personality." (V) See also: SISTERS.

CRIME DOCTOR'S WARNING Col 1945 69m. D: William Castle. SP: Eric Taylor. Ph: L.W. O'Connell. Mus D: Paul Sawtell. Ref: V 12/19/45. LC. Maltin/TVM. with Warner Baxter, John Litel, Dusty Anderson, Miles Mander, John Abbott, J.M. Kerrigan, E. Ciannelli, Coulter Irwin.

"A strange corpse and a strange killer....model's dead body (found) in a plaster cast of a statue"; man who suffers from memory lapses. (V)

CRIME DOES NOT PAY (India-Hindustani) Ramsay 1972 color 141m. (Do GAZ JAMEEN KE NEECHE) D: R.T. Shyam. SP: Kumar Ramsay. Ph: G.& K. Ramsay. Mus: S.-Jagmohan. Ref: Dharap. with Surendra Kumar, Pooja, Shobhana.

Man seeking revenge returns from the grave "with the help of some chemical compound...."

*The CRIME OF DOCTOR CRESPI Liberty 1935 Story: J.H. Auer. Mus D: Milton Schwartzwald. AD: William Saulter. Mkp: Fred Ryle. Ref: screen. Turner/Price. with Harriet Russell.

CRIME OF DOCTOR CRESPI has to be one of the worst must-see movies ever made. Not that it's so bad it's good--most of it is just bad. (Or, as someone commented afterwards, in the Avenue's lobby, re: the rather threadbare hospital set: "One hall, one nurse, one door, one office, one desk....") But Erich von Stroheim as Andre Crespi commands your attention. He employs an alarming variety of bizarre tics and twitches, and acts with his fingers, scalp, eyebrows, eyes, lips, cigarette, and tongue. (He gives the latter crazed-anteater-like flicks before taking sips of his drink.) He creates the most vivid illusion of character. Poor Dwight Frye, however, is helpless in a David Manners-type role as a fellow doctor. (He stands around as if paralyzed by Stroheim's incredible display.)

CRIME OF VOODOO see OUANGA

*CRIMES AT THE DARK HOUSE Pennant 1940 SP: Edward Dryhurst, Frederick Hayward, H.F. Maltby. AD: Bernard Robinson. Ref: screen. W.K.Everson. BFC. and with Hilary Eaves, David Horne.

Old-fashioned melodrama amusingly punctuated by Tod Slaughter's horrendousness. His acts (and threats) of violence are so outrageous they're hilarious: (to Hay Petrie) "Betray that trust, and I'll feed your entrails to the pigs!"

CRIMES IN THE WAX MUSEUM see NIGHTMARE IN WAX

The CRIMES OF THE BLACK CAT (I) Peppercorn-Wormser/Capitolina 1972('76-U.S.) color/scope 108m. (SETTE SCIALLI DI SETA GIALLA) SP,D: Sergio Pastore. SP: also A.Continenza, G. Simonelli. Ph: G. Mancori. Mus: Manuel De Sica. AD: A. Boccianti. SpFX: Eugenio Ascani. Ref: MFB'76:88. V 4/21/76:7 (rated). Bianco Index'72. with Antonio De Teffe, Sylva Koscina, Giacomo Rossi Stuart, Umberto Raho, Shirley Corrigan.
Cat with curare on claws induced to kill; "sub-Bava effects." (MFB)

CRIMES OF THE FUTURE (Can.) Emergent 1970 color 70m. SP,D, P,Ph,Ed: David Cronenberg. Ref: Lee(MFB'71:217-18). FC 3/80: 37: "the awful Rogue's Malady." with Ronald Mlodzik, T.Zolty.
Genetic mutations.

**The CRIMINAL LIFE OF ARCHIBALDO DE LA CRUZ (Mex) Dan Talbot/ Alianza 1955('62-U.S.) 91m. (ENSAYO DE UN CRIMEN) SP,D: Luis Bunuel. SP: also Eduardo U. Pages. From Rodolfo Usigli's novel. Ph: Agustin Jimenez. Mus: J.P. Herrera. AD: Jesus Bracho. Ref: screen. Aranda/LB. FM 31:18. AFI. with Ernesto Alonso, Miroslava, Ariadna Welter, Rita Macedo, Carlos Riquelme, Rodolfo Acosta.
Surreal-psychological horror-comedy--a ceramist, unable to consummate his erotic desire to kill women, "cremates" a life-size dummy (a replica of his intended victim) in his kiln. Only in *his* eyes is the incinerating woman real--we, however, seem to be seeing *through his eyes* at this point: for him, fulfillment; for us, *horror*. ARCHIBALDO is a basically sharp, sporadically brilliant black comedy, slowed occasionally by "information" scenes. It's alternately unnerving and endearing and features an absurdly happy, absurdly satisfying ending.

The CRIMSON CANDLE (B) Mainwaring 1934 SP,D,P: Bernerd Mainwaring. Ref: BFC. with Eve Gray, Kynaston Reeves, E. Makeham.
"Doctor proves maid engineered ex-lover's death by curse."

*The CRIMSON PIRATE 1952 Ph: Otto Heller. Mus: William Alwyn. AD: Paul Sheriff. Mkp: Tony Sforzini. Ref: TV. V 8/27/52.
18th-century inventor aids pirate hero with "undersea boat," "liquid explosive," flame-thrower, hot-air balloon. Cult-favorite swashbuckler aspires to Douglas Fairbanks, but is closer in tone to Abbott and Costello. It's not sharp enough for comedy; too lightweight for drama; passes as a vehicle for stunts and acrobatics. The score, like the script, is occasionally stirring, generally too larky.

CROCODILE Cobra Media 1981 SpFX: S. Saengduenchai. Ref: V 5/9/79:297(ad): giant, man-eating crocodile. 6/24/81:4(rated).

CROSSROADS (B) Bartlett 1955 19m. D: John Fitchen. Ref: BFC: "dead man returns" to avenge murder. with Christopher Lee(ghost), Ferdy Mayne, Mercy Haystead.

CRUCIBLE OF HORROR (B) London Cannon/Abacus 1970 color 91m. (VELVET HOUSE-orig t. The CORPSE-B) D: Viktors Ritelis. SP:

Olaf Pooley. Ph: John Mackey. Mus: John Hotchkis. AD: Peter Hampton. Ref: MFB'72:158. Aros. Lee. BFC. with Michael Gough, Yvonne Mitchell, Simon Gough, David Butler, Sharon Gurney.
Family patriarch appears to return from the dead.

CRUCIBLE OF TERROR (B) (Official-TV)/Glendale 1971 color 91m. SP,D: Ted Hooker. SP: also Tom Parkinson. Ph & Exec P: Peter Newbrook. Mus: Paris Rutherford. AD: Arnold Chapkis. Mkp: Jimmy Evans. Ref: TV. TVFFSB. Lee(MFB'72:69). with Mike Raven, Mary Maude, James Bolam, Melissa Stribling, Ronald Lacey.
Artist who coats models in bronze to preserve their beauty; tin-mine-disaster site supposedly haunted by those who died there; supernatural kimono belonging to dead Japanese girl; wearer of it becomes instrument of her revenge. Interminable psychological-horror-fantasy, with transparent suspense ploys and unpleasant characters: (wife to husband) "I'll respect you when you stop making me sick!"; (painter to model) "Oh, you make me sick!"; (son to father) "You <u>are</u> mad. I have a good mind to have you certified." Sunnybrook Farm this isn't.

CRUISE INTO TERROR ABC-TV/Spelling-Cramer 1978 color 95m. D: Bruce Kessler. SP: Michael Braverman. Ref: TVFFSB. TV Season. TV: hokum. with Ray Milland, Hugh O'Brian, John Forsythe, Chris George, Lynda Day George, Frank Converse, Stella Stevens, Lee Meriwether, Marshall Thompson.
Egyptian sarcophagus unleashes evil forces on ship.

CRY DEMON see EVIL, The

A CRY IN THE NIGHT (B) New Agency 1915 20m. D: Ernest G. Batley. Ref: BFC. with James Russell(The Thing).
"Horror. Tec proves girl's father was killed by mad scientist's winged gorilla."

CRY WOLF (B) PPP 1980 31m. D: Leszek Burzynski. SP: Stan Hey. Ph: Robert Krasker. Music from WAR OF THE WORLDS(1953). PD: Don Taylor. Mkp: Tom Smith. Ref: MFB'80:201. with Paul Maxwell(werewolf), Rosalind Ayres, Stephen Greif.
"Canine serum" in tea turns doctor into werewolf.

The CRYING HOUSE (F) Richard 197-? 16m. (La MAISON QUI PLEURE) D: Jacques Richard, Jacques Robiolles. Ref: PFA notes 4/7/80.
Female hitchhiker turns out to be ghost.

CRYPT OF THE BLIND DEAD see TOMBS OF THE BLIND DEAD

CRYPT OF THE LIVING DEAD (U.S.-Sp) (AA-TV)/Atlas/Coast-Orbita 1973 color/scope 93m. (YOUNG HANNAH,QUEEN OF THE VAMPIRES-alt t. La TUMBA DE LA ISLA MALDITA. VAMPIRE WOMEN-B) D: Ray Danton; J.S. Valls? SP,P: Lou Shaw. Story: Lois Gibson. Ph: Juan Gelpi. Mus: Phillip Lambro. AD: Juan Alberto. SpFX: A. Molina. Mkp: M.G. Rey. Ref: MFB'76:259. V 5/9/73:137. 4/18/73:6(rated, as HANNAH, QUEEN OF THE VAMPIRES).B.Warren. TVG: werewolf? TVFFSB. Aros. with Andrew Prine, Mark Damon,

Patty Shepard, Teresa Gimpera, Jack La Rue Jr.
Vampire-bride of crusader Louis VII unearthed on Vampire Island.

The CUCKOO MURDER CASE MGM 1931 anim 7m. Ref: LC. Maltin/OMAM: Flip the Frog "flirts with Death in an old dark house."

Le CULTE DU VAMPIRE (F) 1971 color SP,D: Jean Rollin. Ref: Lee(Photon 21:44). with Willy Braque, Louise Dhour.

CULTE VAUDOU AU DAHOMEY, Le see VAUDOU, Le

CURIOUS ADVENTURES OF MR. WONDERBIRD see KING AND THE MOCKINGBIRD, The

The CURIOUS DR. HUMPP (Arg) Unicorn/PAA 1967?('70-U.S.) 85m. (La VENGANZA DEL SEXO) SP,D: Emilio Vieyra. Story: Raul Zorrilla. Ph: A.G. Paz. Mus: V. Buchino. Ref: AFI. with Ricardo Bauleo, Gloria Prat, Susana Beltran, Justin Martin.
Sex-crazed scientist--controlled by brain kept alive in lab--turns subjects into "robots."

CURSE (J) Toei 1977('80-U.S.) D: Shunya Ito. Ref: VV 5/5/80: 41. with Shunya Owada.
Community cursed by ancient dog-spirit; "communal exorcism."

CURSE OF BIGFOOT Gold Key-TV/Etiwanda 1972 color 87m. D: Don Fields. SP: J.T. Fields. Ref: TV. TVFFSB. with William Simonsen, Robert Clymire, Jan Swihart, Ken Kloepfer.
Mummified beast found in ancient Indian burial ground in California returns to life. Pathetic monster-movie-travelogue.

*The CURSE OF FRANKENSTEIN Hammer-Clarion 1957 Mkp: also Roy Ashton? Sequel: REVENGE OF FRANKENSTEIN. See also: HORROR OF FRANKENSTEIN. Ref: TV. Glut/TFL. Lee. and with Paul Hardtmuth, Melvyn Hayes(young Victor).
It would be tempting to dismiss this as the first and worst of Hammer's Frankensteins--but then what would one do with FRANKENSTEIN CREATED WOMAN? Jimmy Sangster's script presents Baron Victor (Peter Cushing) as a total heel, but, incomprehensibly, he doesn't make him an <u>amusing</u> heel. Victor is a murderer, a body snatcher, an egomaniac, and a cad with the ladies, and yet he's as flat a character as his queasy assistant Paul (Robert Urquhart), who's always eyeing Victor askance and calling his life-creating experiments "a revolt against nature." The actors all but carry tags: "unscrupulous," "voice of conscience," "foolish maid," etc. That dizzying excitement you feel is James Bernard's score.

The CURSE OF KING TUT'S TOMB NBC-TV/Stromberg-Kerby 1980 color 93m. D: Philip Leacock. SP: Herb Meadow, from Barry Wynne's book "Behind the Mask of Tutankhamen." Ph: Bob Edwards. Mus: Gil Melle. AD: John Biggs. SpFX: Effects Associates. Narr: Paul Scofield. Ref: TV. SFC 5/8/80. with Raymond Burr, Eva

Marie Saint, Robin Ellis, Harry Andrews, Wendy Hiller, Tom Baker, Barbara Murray, Angharad Rees, John Palmer.

Discoverers of royal Egyptian tomb seem to be under death curse; die by scorpion, snake, etc. Familiar melodramatic thriller ploys/characters/dialogue--what difference if it's the supernatural, human intrigue, or coincidence behind the tired melodrama?

CURSE OF THE BLACK WIDOW ABC-TV/Dan Curtis 1977 color 95m. (LOVE TRAP-alt TV t) D: Curtis. SP: Robert Blees, Earl W. Wallace. Ph: Paul Lohmann; Stevan Larner. Mus: Robert Cobert. AD: Phil Barber. SpFX: Roy Downey. Mkp: Richard Cobos, Mike Westmore. Ref: TV. TV Season. TVG. with Anthony Franciosa, Donna Mills, Patty Duke Astin, Roz Kelly, June Lockhart, June Allyson, Jeff Corey, Sid Caesar, Vic Morrow, Robert Burton.

According to Chinese (and also North-American Indian) legend, "the spider woman" turns into a giant black-widow spider during the cycle of the full moon, wraps her victims in webs, and drains them of blood. In present-day California, a schizophrenic woman (Astin), bitten by spiders as a baby, and a young girl bear the mark of the spider woman--a red hourglass on the stomach. Dan Curtis tames and domesticates the dreaded black widow, turning the subject into another of his mundane TV horrors. (The only actual spiders seen are of the hairy, large, rather nondescript variety.) Though there are a few fairly horrific moments and some good bits of acting, from Roz Kelly (especially), Astin, and Franciosa, Cobert's flip, tepid score pretty much sets the tone.

*The CURSE OF THE CAT PEOPLE 1944 Story: Val Lewton. Mkp: Mel Berns. Ref: TV. Siegel/VL. MFB'79:238. V 2/23/44.

CURSE OF THE CAT PEOPLE is a battleground--between child psychology and fantasy, between Lewton's projected AMY AND HER FRIEND and CAT PEOPLE, for which he had been assigned to make a sequel. There are small victories for both sides; bigger losses. CURSE tries to explain away the supernatural in its predecessor: Oliver (the continuing Kent Smith character) at one point says that his first wife, Irena (Simone Simon), "went completely mad." Are we to believe his words (in this movie) or Irena's talons (in the other)? CURSE attempts to re-create CAT PEOPLE in its own image: as the Irena of CURSE is only an illusion conjured up out of a photograph and a child's need for a companion, so the original's Irena became, it's suggested, a panther only in her mind. (Conversely, if CAT PEOPLE is considered the informing film, then it's the Oliver of CURSE who's trying to suppress reality--i.e., the unpleasant memory of a were-wife.) The irony is that, after cancelling the supernatural basis of the first film, CURSE replaces it with tantalizing supernatural overtones of its own. In fact, "Is Irena only an illusion?" is the most intriguing question posed by CURSE, since the script patly answers most of the strictly-psychological questions it poses. The Irena of the sequel seems, finally, a spiritual compromise, at once Amy's (Ann Carter's) invention and the original Irena's spirit.

In Irena's last shot, she (Irena) dissolves away, after Amy and her father go into the house, as if--her job done, and the bond between them of emotional exile broken--she can depart. Irena seems here to be directing her own actions, as if Amy had not so much created her as briefly brought her, by chance, back from limbo. Simon's Irena is the one character who escapes psychological pigeonholing, thanks in part to the confusing continuity between CAT and CURSE; in part to the actress's warmth of presence, and in part to the empathetic echoes of her CAT PEOPLE persona here--in both Irena II and in Amy.

*CURSE OF THE DEMON 1957 93m.(uncut vers.) SpPhFX: S.D. Onions. Ref: screen. Lee. Photon 26:31-41.

Niall MacGinnis's demonologist, Karswell, in CURSE OF THE DEMON is an elaboration on Claude Rains's clairvoyant in The CLAIRVOYANT(1935). Both films were co-authored by Charles Bennett; both are about ordinary men blessed/cursed with extraordinary powers, at first controlling, then controlled by same. Memorable, droll image from CURSE: Karswell at the outdoor party, shielding himself from the force of the storm which he himself has conjured up, both pleased with and rather embarrassed by the fury of it. (The human and the superhuman intersecting....) There's a hint here, already, that Karswell is not totally in control.

CURSE OF THE DEVIL (Sp-Mex) Goldstone/Lotus-Escorpion 1973('76-U.S.) color 87m. (El RETORNO DE WALPURGIS) D: Carlos Aured Alonso. SP: Jacinto Molina. Sequel to MARK OF THE WOLFMAN. Ph: Francisco Sanchez. SpFX: Paul Percy. Ref: MFB'76:218. Willis/SW. AMPAS. Meyers. V 11/17/76:12. 5/29/74:27. 5/8/74:207. with Paul Naschy(aka J.Molina), Fabiola Falcon, A.V. Molina, Maritza Olivares.

Satanist leader, Princess Bathory, curses knight's family; "a veritable population explosion of psychopathic killers, werewolves, and hysterically incanting gypsies." (MFB)

*CURSE OF THE FACELESS MAN 1958 Ph: Kenneth Peach. Mus: Gerald Fried. AD: William Glasgow. PD: Herman Schoenbrun. SpFX: Ira Anderson. SpMkpDes: Charles Gemora. Narr: Morris Ankrum. Ref: TV. Bill Warren. and with Bob Bryant(creature), J.Arvan.

Awkward reworking of the '32 MUMMY plot, featuring rather tortuous explanations of a rather ordinary menace. Flat narration, music.

CURSE OF THE HEADLESS HORSEMAN Kirt 1972(1974) color (VALLEY OF THE HEADLESS HORSEMAN-orig t) D: John Kirkland. Ref: Lee (V 5/12/71). Willis/SW. V 5/24/72:6(rated). with Ultra-Violet, Marland Proctor, Claudia Dean.

*The CURSE OF THE LIVING CORPSE Deal(Iselin-Tenney) 1964(1963) Dial: Alan Naidob. Mus: Bill Holcomb, George Burt. AD: Robert Verberkmoss(sp?). Ref: TV. AFI. and with Roy R. Scheider.

New England, 1892. A rich man who fears being buried alive--

he suffers from an "atrophy of the nervous system" which gives the appearance of death--curses members of his family to die the deaths they fear most if they break the terms of his will. Ridiculously florid, old-fashioned melodrama, with deep-purple prose and passions from the entire cast. Every line a prize: "Out here are the eyes of night, and in there (the crypt) no living eyes can see us." "To think that one man could kill so many people with such single-minded cunning!" And on and on!

CURSE OF THE MAYAN TEMPLE Gold Key-TV/Bill Burrud 1977 color 92m. D,P: John Burrud, Milas Hinshaw. SP: Hinshaw, Miriam Bird. Ph: Wolfgang Obst et al. Mus Sup: Gene Kauer, Douglas Lackey. Ref: TV. V 3/1/78:100(ad). GKey. TVG. with W. and Sharon Obst.

Human sacrifice (200 A.D.); cursed medallion, "foreboding" forest (1937); cave bats and storm (1977). Semi-documentary minimal cinema.

The CURSE OF THE MOON CHILD Gold Key-TV 1972 color 95m. Ref: TVFFSB. with Adam West, Jeremy Slate, Sherry Jackson.

Necromancy and witchcraft in Victorian England.

CURSE OF THE MUMMY (B) Taffner-TV/Thames-TV 1971 color 90m. Based on Bram Stoker's novel "The Jewel of Seven Stars." Ref: TVFFSB. with Isobel Black, Patrick Mower, Donald Churchill.

Egyptologist attempts to reincarnate cursed queen Tera.

CURSE OF THE PHARAOH see PHARAOH'S CURSE, The

CYBORG see SIX MILLION DOLLAR MAN, The

CYBORG 009 (J) Toei 1980 anim 130m. (SAIBOOGU 009) D: Yasuhiro Yamaguchi. SP: Takazo Nakanishi. Based on the TV series. Ref: V 5/13/81:258.

CYBORG 009--LEGEND OF SUPER GALAXY (J) Toei 1981 anim feature D: Masayuki Akehi. Ref: JFFJ 13:35: based on the "Cyborg 009" TV series; nine "super robots."

CYCLOPS (Bulg.) Bulgarian Film 1976 color 100m. (TSEKLOPUT or CYKLOPAT) SP,D,AD: Christo Christov. From the novel by Gencho Stoyev. Ph: Vanets Dimitrov. Mus: Kiril Chiboulka. Ref: V 11/10/76. Bianco #4/77:71-2. with Michail Moutafov, Penka Citselkova, Nevena Kokanova, Penko Penkov.

"Scifi pic....a resurfaced Atlantis....commander of the last surviving individuals on this planet." (V)

DAFFY DUCK AND THE DINOSAUR WB 1939 anim 7m. D: Chuck Jones. SP: Dave Monahan. Mus: C.W. Stalling. Voices: Mel Blanc. Ref: Maltin/OMAM. LC. Lee. TV

Jack Benny-voiced caveman and dinosaur-pet hunt Daffy (his

semi-hysterical, put-one-over-on-'em laugh already perfected).

DAIKAIJU NO KAITEI NIMAN MARU see GODZILLA

DAITETSUJIN WANSEBUN see GIANT IRON MAN ONE-SEVEN

DAITOKYO YOTSUYA KAIDAN (J) Toei-TV 1978 D: Y. Harada. Ref: JFFJ 13:34: TV-movie; ghost story.

DALLA NUBE ALLA RESISTENZA see FROM THE CLOUD TO THE RESISTANCE

DAMA DUENDA, La see GHOST LADY, The

DAMIEN--OMEN II Fox/Bernhard 1978 color/scope 109m. D: Don Taylor. SP: Stanley Mann, Michael Hodges. Story,P: Harvey Bernhard. Sequel to The OMEN. Ph: Bill Butler;(Israel) Gil Taylor;(min) Stanley Cortez. Mus: Jerry Goldsmith. PD: Philip M. Jefferies, Fred Harpman. SpFX: Ira Anderson Jr. Ref: MFB'78:237-8. V 6/7/78. with William Holden, Lee Grant, Robert Foxworth, Jonathan Scott-Taylor(Damien), Lew Ayres, Sylvia Sidney, Alan Arbus, Lance Henriksen, Leo McKern, Ian Hendry.
Face of the Anti-Christ found on ancient wall is identified with that of orphan, Damien.

DAMNATION ALLEY Fox 1977(1976) color 91m. D: Jack Smight. SP: Alan Sharp, Lukas Heller, from Roger Zelazny's novel. Ph: Harry Stradling Jr. Mus: Jerry Goldsmith. PD: Preston Ames. SpFX: Milt Rice. Laser Anim: Mimi Gramatki. MicroPh: Ken Middleham. Ref: MFB'78:196. V 10/26/77. with Jan-Michael Vincent, George Peppard, Dominique Sanda, Paul Winfield, Robert Donner, Seamon Glass.
Post-WWIII. Giant scorpions, carnivorous cockroaches, etc.

DAMNED IN VENICE see VENETIAN BLACK

DANDY DICK OF BISHOPSGATE (B) Natural Colour 1911 11m. D: Theo Bouwmeester. Ref: BFC.
"Insane man locks dead fiancee's room for 40 years and dies after seeing vision of her."

DANGEROUS CHARTER see CREEPING TERROR, The

DANS LES GRIFFES DE L'ARAIGNEE see IN THE SPIDER'S GRIP

DANSE MACABRE(by E.A.Poe) see WEB OF THE SPIDER

DARINDA (India-Hindustani) Bunty 1977 color 146m. SP,D: Kaushal Bharati. Mus: K. Anandji. Ref: Dharap. with Sunil Dutt, Feroz Khan, Parveen Babi, Premnath, Raj Mehra.
Youth uses "supernatural powers" to wreak revenge on parents' killers.

The DARK FVI/Montoro-Clark 1979 color/scope 92m. D: John "Bud" Cardos. SP: Stanford Whitmore. Ph: John Morrill. Mus:

Roger Kellaway. AD: Rusty Rosene. SpFX: Robby Knot(t). Sp MkpFX: Steve Neill. SpAnimFX: Harry Moreau, Peter Kuran. Ref: screen. V 5/2/79. with William Devane, Cathy Lee Crosby, Richard Jaeckel, Keenan Wynn, Casey Kasem, Vivian Blaine, Biff Elliot, Warren Kemmerling, Jay Lawrence, John Bloom(The Dark), Erik Howell; Angelo Rossitto?

Santa Monica, Calif. "Mangler"/"zombie" at large proves to be "werewolf in blue jeans from outer space" (V) that knocks out electricity, murders with laser-like rays from eyes, and grows more powerful each night; psychic, visions. Uneasy mixture of hokum and seriousness. The monster's ultra-monstrousness is amusing, but the themes of violence and guilt lose out to lines like "I've got your mangler cornered in the old monastery on 24th Street." Devane, Crosby, and Wynn have their persuasive moments, but what is it that the alien is always so deafeningly whispering?

DARK AUGUST Raffia 1975 (The HANT-orig t) D,Co-P: Martin Goldman. Mus: William Fischer. Ref: Bill Warren. V 9/4/74: 30. with Kim Hunter, William Robertson.

"Psychic forces at work in a small town." (BW)

*DARK INTRUDER Shamley 1965 Mus: Lalo Schifrin. Mkp: Bud Westmore. Opt: Pacific Title. Ref: screen. NYT 7/22/65. TV. V 7/28/65. AFI. MFB'80:211-12: aka SOMETHING WITH CLAWS. and with Charles Bolender(Nikola), Peter Brocco.

Characterization in DARK INTRUDER may be expedient, but the plot is involved and engaging, an archaeological mystery the clues to which--certain birth dates, a pint-sized mummy, a gargoylish figurine, a "professor" with claws--constitute key elements in the mythology of a lost civilization (Sumer). Barre Lyndon's script provides intriguing narrative answers as well as questions and is like effective, minor Lovecraft. Its premise concerns expelled demons trying to reenter the world--The Shadow over San Francisco, as it were. "Evidently Lyndon was exposed to such films as The LODGER...." (V) See: LODGER, The(1944, SP: Barre Lyndon).

DARK PLACES (B) (AI-TV)/Cinerama/Sedgled-Glenbeigh 1972('74-U.S.) color 91m. D & Adap: Don Sharp. SP: Ed Brennan, Joseph Van Winkle. Adap: also James Hannah Jr. Ph: Ernest Steward. Mus: Wilfred Josephs. AD: Geoffrey Tozer. Ref: MFB'75:132. TVFFSB. Willis/SW. V 5/22/74. Bianco Index'75. with Christopher Lee, Joan Collins, Robert Hardy, Herbert Lom, Jane Birkin, Jean Marsh, Linda Gray.

House reputedly haunted by murdered family members; trance; spirit possession.

The DARK SECRET OF HARVEST HOME NBC-TV/Univ-TV 1978 color 200m. D: Leo Penn. SP: Jack Guss, Charles E. Israel. Adap: Jennifer & James Miller. From the novel "Harvest Home" by Thomas Tryon. Ph: Charles Correll, J. Dickson, F.V. Phillips. Mus: Paul Chihara. AD: Philip Barber. SdFxEd: Jeff Bushelman. Ref: TV. TVFFSB. V 2/1/78:61. with Bette Davis, David Ackroyd,

Joanna Miles, John Calvin, Laurie Prange, Rene Auberjonois, Norman Lloyd, Donald Pleasence(voice).

Women of secluded New England village of Cornwall Coombe perform ancient pagan rites, sacrifice man for the good of the crops. The script takes forever to unburden itself of its few "secrets," and even with all its dawdling never really makes sense of a profusion of strange incidents and details--e.g., the "ghost," the acromegalic girl, the false pregnancy, the neighbor-woman's suicide, the weird-kid's presence. An unending pageant of odd local customs and rituals ("The Ways") seems intended to foster an air of Menacing Innocuousness. The film's dark, Utopian vision is a cross between The WICKER MAN (the retreat to paganism) and The STEPFORD WIVES (the happy community that's a conformist scheme by members of one sex). Three hours of "atmosphere."

DARK STAR (Gold Key-TV)/Atlantic & Bryanston/Jack Harris/USC 1974(1972) color 83m.(45m.) (DARK STAR: A SCIENCE FICTION ADVENTURE-orig t) SP,D,Mus: John Carpenter. SP,PD,SpFxPh,Ed: Dan O'Bannon. Ph: Douglas Knapp. Anim: Bob Greenberg;(sp) John Wash. OptFX & Lyrics: Bill Taylor. Art: Jim Danforth. SpFX: Greg Jein, Harry Walter. ShipDes: Ron Cobb. Ref: MFB '78:22-3. screen. V 5/1/74. Lee. Boxo 3/10/80:5. Willis/SW. Cinef W'73:4-7. with Brian Narelle, Dre Pahich, O'Bannon, Cookie Knapp(computer voice).

Droll, good-natured existential, or mock-existential, outer-space comedy, with style, wit, and a beautifully controlled tone of genial absurdity, as astronauts on a mission to destroy "unstable planets" confront a ridiculously perverse universe. There's a beach-ball creature/mascot that's as bored as they are and resorts to games of violence for fun; a bomb that argues with the ship's computer and captain and threatens to become, rather arbitrarily, God; and so forth. The film's humor depends on the near-lost arts of timing, staging, and pacing and seems related to both the Buster Keaton cliffhanging comedy and Kubrick's 2001. Lives here hang, hilariously, by slowly-unravelling threads. One of the funniest sequences: a monologue by Pinback (O'Bannon), as he records, for posterity, his deep personal dissatisfaction ("I *hate* these men!") with life in space. The resulting, videotaped montage of his moods, over time, becomes in effect a witty (yet strangely touching) cross-section of character. The movie is as deft verbally as it is visually.

The DARKER SIDE OF TERROR CBS-TV/Banner 1979 color 94m. D: Gus Trikonis. Sp,P: John H. Shaner, Al Ramrus. Ph: Donald M. Morgan. Mus: Paul Chihara. AD: William Sandell. SpFX: Sandler. SpPhFX: Jack Rabin. Ref: TV. TVG. with Robert Forster, Adrienne Barbeau, Ray Milland, David Sheiner.

Professor's cloning of his best student goes awry when the clone (Forster) becomes temporarily homicidal, starts to take over the cloned man's life and wife. Over-serious, deliberate, semi-kinky. A black comedy was perhaps indicated. As in CODE NAME: HERACLITUS the quasi-human is more human than the humans.

**DARNA AT ANG PLANETMAN (Fili) Uni-Art 1969? D: M.D. Navarro. Ref: FJA. Lee(Borst). no WF. with Vic Vargas, Gina Pareno.
Flying saucers, ray guns, aliens.

DARNA VS. PLANET WOMEN (Fili) 1978? Ref: SFC 11/24/78. with Vilma Santos, Ben Tot Jr.

DARTMOUTH MURDERS, The(by C.Orr) see SHOT IN THE DARK, A(1935)

DARWAZA (India-Hindustani) Kiran Ramsay 1978 color 133m. D: Tulsi & Shyam Ramsay. SP: Kumar Ramsay. Mus: Sapan Jagmohan. Ref: Dharap. with Anil Dhawan, Shamlee, Bhagwan.
A Thakur who kills a worshipper of Kali is cursed and becomes "an animal which kills people"; to save his son he sends him to the city.

*DAUGHTER OF DR. JEKYLL Film Venturers 1957 SpPhFX: Jack Rabin, Louis DeWitt. Mkp: Louis Philippi. Ref: TV. Glut/CMM: clip from FRANKENSTEIN 1970. and with Mollie McCard.
Prologue with Dr.J/Mr.H; Dr.J's daughter (Gloria Talbott) sees hypnotically-induced-nightmare images of herself as wolf woman. Closer plot-wise (and quality-wise) to SHE-WOLF OF LONDON than to most other Jekyll-and-Hyde movies. The dialogue plays beautifully into your Z-movie expectations: Janet Jekyll to George (John Agar), her fiance: "If you love me, please kill me!" George to Janet (later): "It's the doctor--he's mad!--worse than that--he turns into some sort of creature!" The eeriest (unintentional) effect: the "fog," which seems to move when the camera moves.

The DAUGHTER OF DRACULA (F-Sp-Port.) CFdF 1972 color (La FILLE DE DRACULA. La HIJA DE DRACULA) D: Jesus Franco. Ref: Glut/TDB. Murphy: from "Carmilla" by Le Fanu. Daisne. with Howard Vernon(Count Karnstein), Britt Nichols, Dennis Price, Soledad Miranda, Alberto Dalbes, Anne Libert, Paul Muller.

DAUGHTERS OF DRACULA see VAMPYRES

DAUGHTERS OF FIRE (Braz) 1978 color (As FILHAS DO FOGO) SP, D: Walter Khouri. Ph: G. Gabriel. Mus: R. Duprat. AD: M. Weinstock. Ref: IFG'80:79. with Paola Morra, Maria Rosa.
"A horror film about anxiety, the Evil One, tragic love, death, and the supernatural, with strong symbolic overtones."

DAUGHTERS OF SATAN (U.S.-Fili) UA/A&S 1972 color 90m. D: Hollingsworth Morse. SP: John C. Higgins. Story: John Bushelman. Ph: Nonong Rasca. Mus: Richard LaSalle. AD: H. Balon. Mkp: F.C. Blau Jr. Ref: V 10/4/72. FFacts. MFB'73:50. Scheuer/MOTV. with Tom Selleck, Barra Grant, T.P. Guthrie, Vic Diaz.
Witch in painting resembles man's wife; "coven of reincarnated witches"; "ghostly apparition." (MFB)

DAWN OF THE DEAD UFDC/Laurel-Cuomo-Argento 1978 color 125m. (ZOMBIES-Eur.t. DAWN OF THE LIVING DEAD-orig t) SP,D: George

Romero. Sequel to NIGHT OF THE LIVING DEAD. Ph: Michael Gornick. Mus & Cons: Dario Argento. AD: Josie Caruso, Barbara Lifsher. SpFX & Mkp: Tom Savini. OptFX: Exceptional. Ref: screen. V 4/18/79. 10/11/78:44. FM 161:81. MFB'80:33. with David Emge, Ken Foree, Scott H. Reininger, Gaylen Ross.

Four people take refuge in a huge shopping complex, as cannibalistic zombies overrun the U.S. George Romero does to shopping centers what Jerry Lewis used to do to Hollywood studios (The ERRAND BOY), hotels (The BELLBOY), etc. And like Lewis, he displays no sense of selection, comic or dramatic: he uses all the department-store gags, all the grocery-store gags, and he would seem by now to have exhausted the subject of zombies too. The connections he makes here between consumerism and cannibalism seem too obvious, too explicit ("They're us"), the ghouls' gravitation to the shopping mall too thematically accommodating. ("It was a very important place to them.") DAWN OF THE DEAD is existential low comedy/horror, by turns hokily funny, hokily gory, and bathetic, though there is one solid characterization--Reininger as Roger. His character is developed up out of the situation; it's simply a series of logical responses to a siege of bumbling-but-dangerous zombies: contempt, fear, disgust, etc. But a sense of senselessness generally comes too easily to Romero. There's no sense of meaning draining here as the narrative progresses--it's gone at the beginning, where Romero places the most downbeat, horrific scenes of cannibalism. The latter might even be disturbing if audiences didn't get such a kick out of them. (They are not intrinsically amusing.)

DAWN OF THE MUMMY Harmony Gold 1981? D: Armand Weston. SP: Daria Price, Ronald Dobrin. Ref: FM 176. V 5/7/80:289(ad).

DAY AFTER TOMORROW, The see STRANGE HOLIDAY

The DAY IT CAME TO EARTH Howco Int'l. 1977 color D & Exec P: Harry Z. Thomason. SP: Paul Fisk. Ph: Mike Varner. Mus: Joe Southerland. Ref: Willis/SW. V 11/30/77:22(rated). with Wink Roberts, Roger Manning, Bob Ginnaven, Delight DeBruine.

A DAY OF JUDGMENT Maverick(Earl Owensby) 1980 color 92m. D: C.D.H. Reynolds. SP: Tom McIntyre. Ph: Irl Dixon. Mus: Arthur & Clay Smith. Ref: V 8/27/80:27(ad): "the night he came to collect his own." Boxo 8/25/80:29: "horror-suspense." with William T. Hicks, Harris Bloodworth, Helene Tryon, R. Dedmon.

DAY OF THE ANIMALS FVI 1977 color/scope 95m. D: William Girdler. SP: William & Eleanor E. Norton. Story,P: Edward L. Montoro. Ph: Robert Sorrentino. Mus: Lalo Schifrin. SpFX: Sam Burney. SpPhFX: Howard Anderson Co. SdFX: Fred Brown. Ref: MFB'77:166-67. V(d) 6/6/77. TV. with Christopher George, Leslie Nielsen, Lynda Day George, Richard Jaeckel, Michael Ansara, Ruth Roman, Jon Cedar, Paul Mantee, A. Stevens, G. Lamb.

Aerosol-spray damage to the Earth's ozone layer proves to be behind animal attacks on hiking party; sun also seems to get to one man (Nielsen's Jenson) before the atmosphere rights itself. Every bird, bear, rat, wildcat, rattler, and dog here has his day. Rote suspense melodrama--one wild scene with the berserk Nielsen, a bear, and thunder and lightning suggests that a "Day of the Humans" might have been more frightening.

DAY OF THE WOMAN see I SPIT ON YOUR GRAVE

The DAY THE EARTH GOT STONED Int'l Harmony/Secret World War 1980 (1978) 80m. (J-MEN FOREVER-orig t) D: Richard Patterson. SP & with: Phil Proctor, Peter Bergman. Ph: Bruce Logan. Mus: Richard Theiss. AD: Galen Longfellow.SdFX: Alan Splet. Ref: V 2/13/80. poster. screen: superhero parody employing excerpts from Republic serials, including ADVENTURES OF CAPTAIN MARVEL, The BLACK WIDOW, CAPTAIN AMERICA, DARKEST AFRICA, FIGHTING DEVIL DOGS, The MYSTERIOUS DR.SATAN, SPY SMASHER, UNDERSEA KINGDOM, ZOMBIES OF THE STRATOSPHERE--and of course DELUGE, Republic's stock source. with(stock footage) Lionel Atwill(voice: "Bela Lugosi"), Rod Cameron, John Hamilton, Tom Tyler, John Wayne, Theodore Gottlieb, L. Nimoy; (voice) Michael Gwynne.

From his base on the moon, The Lightning Bug attempts to enslave and destroy humanity with rock 'n' roll. Packaged camp. Proctor and Bergman aren't as inventive with their invented dialogue and interior monologue as your average ROCKY HORROR PICTURE SHOW audience. The graft of the hip dialogue to the square Republic visuals doesn't quite take--they remain two separate worlds, except at odd moments when the dialogue seems to be in exact psychological-inverse-synch with the faces. Perhaps if the voices had been "straight" too....The hip words are hardly surprising coming from hip voices. Still and all, the subversion is intermittently irresistible.

DAY THE EARTH MOVED ABC-TV/ABC Circle 1974 color 74m. D: Robert M. Lewis. SP: Jack Turley, Max Jack. Ref: TV Season. TVFFSB: " new method of predicting earthquakes." with Jackie Cooper, Stella Stevens, Cleavon Little, William Windom, Sid Melton, Beverly Garland.

DAY THE SCREAMING STOPPED see COMEBACK, The

The DAY TIME ENDED Compass Int'l./Manson Int'l. 1980 color/scope 80m. (VORTEX-orig t? TIMEWARP-int t?) D: John "Bud" Cardos. SP,P,SpFxCoord: Wayne Schmidt. SP,P: also Steve Neill, Paul Gentry. SP: also J.L. Carroll, David Schmoeller. Ph: John Morrill. Mus: Richard Band. AD: Rusty Rosene;(sp fx) Dave Carson. SpFX: Rich Bennette, Jim Danforth, David Allen et al. AnimFX: (sup) Peter Kuran;(stopmo) Lyle Conway. Models:(des) Lain Liska;(exec) Greg Jein. Ref: FM 161:58-61. V 10/17/79:121(ad). 11/19/80. MFB'80:128. with Dorothy Malone, Chris Mitchum, Jim Davis, Marcy Lafferty, Scott Kolden.

"Radiation effects from a trinary supernova" create "cosmic disturbance"; alien beings; dinosaurs; abolition of time. (MFB)

DE LA CHAIR POUR FRANKENSTEIN see ANDY WARHOL'S FRANKENSTEIN

DEAD AND BURIED Avco Embassy/Shusett 1981 color 92m. D: Gary A. Sherman. SP: Ronald Shusett, Dan O'Bannon. Story: Jeff Millar, Alex Stern. Mus: Joe Renzetti. MkpFX: Stan Winston. Ref: V 6/3/81: living dead? with James Farentino, Melody Anderson, Jack Albertson, Dennis Redfield, Lisa Blount.

The DEAD ARE ALIVE (Yug-W.G.-I) Nat'l Gen'l/Inex-CCC-Mondial TeFi 1972 color/scope 104m. (L'ETRUSCO UCCIDI ANCORA. The ETRUSCAN KILLS AGAIN-ad t) SP,D: Armando Crispino. SP: also L. Battistrada. Ph: E. Menczer, S. Banovic. Mus: Riz Ortolani. AD: G. Burchiellaro. Ref: Bianco Index'73. Lee. Willis/SW. V 7/12/72. with Samantha Eggar, Alex Cord, John Marley, Nadja Tiller, Horst Frank.

Etruscan demon apparently behind gory murders.

The DEAD DON'T DIE NBC-TV/Cramer & Baumes 1975 color 74m. D: Curtis Harrington. SP: Robert Bloch. Ph: James Crabe. Mus: Robert Prince. Ref: TV. TVFFSB. with George Hamilton, Ray Milland(Varek), Linda Cristal, Joan Blondell, Ralph Meeker, Reggie Nalder(zombie), James McEachin, Milton Parsons, Yvette Vickers; Chauncey Haines?

1934. The mad Varek ("a voice that speaks through the mouths of corpses") leads an army of voodoo-controlled zombies; one of them (Cristal) with independent will; all vanish at end. Rather agreeably bad, old-fashioned horror thriller combines WHITE ZOMBIE with INVADERS FROM MARS (zombies who fail die by remote control). Monogram and PRC don't die!

DEAD KIDS (Austral-N.Z.) Hemdale-Richwhite/South Street 1981 color/scope 105m. SP,D: Michael Laughlin. SP,P: William Condon. Ph: Louis Horvath. PD: Susanna Moore. SpFxMkp: Craig Reardon. Ref: V 9/2/81: "suspense-horror....bizarre stabbings." with Michael Murphy, Louise Fletcher, Scott Brady, Fiona Lewis.

DEAD MAN RUNNING see CLONES, The

*DEAD MAN'S EYES 1944 Ref: TV.

Generally vapid "Inner Sanctum" mystery livens up only when Lon Chaney Jr. and Acquanetta are vying for worst-actor honors. Amazingly, she wins. Hear her try to say, with emotion, "I don't know what it is! I don't!" Also, hear Thomas Gomez say "He wouldn't be the first man to be driven mad by studying the processes of the mind" and (in the same movie!) "Blindness is a serious thing to have happen to an artist."

*DEAD MEN WALK 1942 (CREATURE OF THE DEVIL-alt t) Ref: TV. LC. V 4/7/43. Lee.

Vampire Lore 1-A, with whole scenes lifted complete from other vampire movies. A leading candidate for dullest horror movie of the Forties. (See also SHE-WOLF OF LONDON.) George Zucco's vampire talks a lot, has an odd laugh, and likes to vanish suddenly.

DEAD OF NIGHT NBC-TV/Dan Curtis 1977(1974) color 74m. D: Curtis. SP: Richard Matheson. See also: TRILOGY OF TERROR(1975).

Mus: Robert Cobert. AD: Trevor Williams. Ref: TV Season. Cinef III:2:17: orig.shot for TV series. with Horst Bucholz, Ed Begley Jr., Joan Hackett, Patrick Macnee, Lee Montgomery, Anjanette Comer, Elisha Cook, Ann Doran.

Three stories: "Second Chance," from Jack Finney's story; "No Such Thing as a Vampire," from Matheson's story; "Bobby."

DEAD OF NIGHT see DEATHDREAM

DEADLINE see ANATOMY OF A HORROR

DEADLY BLESSING UA/PolyGram/Inter Planetary 1981 color 100m. SP,D: Wes Craven. SP: also Glenn M. Benest, Matthew Barr. Ph: Robert C. Jessup. Mus: James Horner. PD: Jock Marty. SpFX: Jack Bennett. Mkp: Jimi White. OptFX: Modern. SdFxEd: Bill Phillips. Ref: screen. V 8/19/81. with Maren Jensen, Susan Buckner, Sharon Stone, Jeff East, Lisa Hartman, Lois Nettleton, Ernest Borgnine, Annabelle Weenick.

Woman claimed by Satanic forces; psychic girl belonging to Hittites, religious sect; transvestite killer; snake and spider scares. Hollow shocker will at least keep you jumping (whether you want to or not). The it's-not-who-you-thought-it-was resolution is limply ironic. (The forces of repression simply strike from another, unexpected source.) It's also very confusing--in it, a woman turns out to be a man, a psychic turns out to be a red herring, a ghost floats in, and a demon pops up through the floorboards. But if you like to jump....

The DEADLY ODOR (Cz) Brandon 1970? anim color 11m. D: Vaclav Bedrich. SP: V. Vasut. Anim: B. Sramek. Mus: L. Fiser. Ref: Brandon: 5 horror-movie spoofs. See also: GETTING CLEAN. SPOILED WEDDING, The. SUNKEN SUBMARINE. UNFINISHED WEEKEND.

The DEADLY VISITOR ABC-TV/Titus 1973 color 73m. Ref: TVFFSB: "vicious and invisible female presence." with Gwen Verdon, Perry King, Stephen Macht, Ann Miles.

DEAFULA Signscope/Holstrom 1975 SP,D: Peter Wechsburg. Ref: Murphy: Dracula's illegitimate son. Glut/TDB: for the deaf. Willis/SW.

A DEAL WITH THE DEVIL (B) Hepworth 1916 17m. D: Frank Wilson. Ref: BFC: chemist trades soul for youth.

DEAR, DEAD DELILAH Avco Embassy/Southern Star 1972 color 90m. SP,D: John Farris. Ph: W.R. Johnson. Mus: Bill Justis. AD: James Tilton. Ref: FFacts. Lee. TVFFSB. TVG. Bianco Index'76. with Agnes Moorehead, Will Geer, Michael Ansara, Dennis Patrick.

Axe murders in old Southern mansion.

DEATH BY INVITATION Paragon/Kirt 1971 color 88m. SP,D: Ken Friedman. Ph: Alec Hirschfeld. Mus: Sonny Kohl. Mkp: Thomas Brumberger. Ref: screen. Lee. no FFacts. with Shelby Levering-

ton, Aaron Phillips, Norman Paige.
Witch's curse haunts family. Slightly different but pretty shoddy. "Highlight": the witch's incredibly vicious monologue.

DEATH CAR ON THE FREEWAY CBS-TV/Shpetner 1979 color 94m. D: Hal Needham. SP: William Wood. Ph: Bobby Byrne. Mus: Richard Markowitz. AD: Hilyard Brown. SpFX: Cliff Wenger. Ref: TV. with Shelley Hack, George Hamilton, Frank Gorshin, Peter Graves, Barbara Rush, Dinah Shore, Harriet Nelson, Abe Vigoda, Sid Haig, Robert F. Lyons.
DUEL, with a van as the "demon" vehicle (it even self-destructs in slow motion); its driver, the bluegrass-playing "Fiddler," preys on lone women in cars and is, in effect, invisible--his windshield is one-way glass. And he is, the script more-than-hints, male chauvinism gone berserk. Our heroine (Hack) is not *supposed* to be paranoid, but her world seems only one-step-removed from REPULSION (even dogs snarl at her)--objective social comment becomes scrambled with subjective psychology, as "suspense" takes over, and *all* males begin to seem threatening to her. Some of the lethal-bumper-car stunts are unnerving, but so is rush-hour traffic.

DEATH CORPS see SHOCK WAVES

DEATH DIMENSION Movietime/Spectacular 1978 color 91m. D: Al Adamson. Ref: Boxo 2/25/80:20: "bomb that could freeze the entire planet." V 10/19/77:48. with Jim Kelly, George Lazenby, Harold Sakata, Myron Lee.

DEATH DIVE see FER DE LANCE

DEATH IS A NUMBER (B) Delman 1951 50m. D: Horace Shepherd. SP: Charles K. Shaw. Ref: BFC. with T. Alexander, L. Osmond.
"Racing driver's death in crash fulfils 300-year-old curse."

DEATH IS CHILD'S PLAY see WOULD YOU KILL A CHILD?

DEATH LINE see RAW MEAT

DEATH MAGAZINE, or HOW TO BECOME A FLOWERPOT (W.G.) Filmwelt 1979 color & b&w 73m. (TODESMAGAZIN order WIE WERDE ICH EIN BLUMENTOPF?) SP,D,P,Ph: Rosa Von Praunheim. Ref: V 12/5/79.
"Macabre" punk-documentary: interview with "rock pop vampire woman Anja"; images of corpses.

DEATH MOON CBS-TV/EMI-TV & Gimbel 1978 color 93m. (DEATHMOON-end cr t) D: Bruce Kessler. SP: George Schenk. Mus: Paul Chihara. AD: Herman Zimmerman. Mkp: Bob Dawn, Michael Westmore. Ref: TV. Jim Shapiro. TVG. TV Season. with Robert Foxworth(werewolf), Barbara Trentham, France Nuyen, Dolph Sweet, Debralee Scott, Joan Freeman.
"Polynesian folklore": man inherits lycanthropic curse, turns into homicidal werewolf. Film adds nothing to Hollywood

folklore except a Hawaiian setting. Vapid as mystery/shocker/suspenser/romantic drama.

The DEATH OF THE FLEA CIRCUS DIRECTOR, or OTTOCARO WEISS REFORMS HIS FIRM (Swiss) Koerfer & Filmverlag der Autoren 1972 111m. (Der TOD DES FLOHZIRKUSDIREKTORS oder OTTOCARO WEISS REFORMIERT SIENE FIRMA) D,P: Thomas Koerfer. SP: Dieter Feldhausen. Ph: R. Berta. Mus: Ernst Kolz. AD: T. von Goldschmidt. Ref: MFB'76:258-9. V 8/22/73. with Francois Simon.
Dr. Moosbruger develops a new plague-virus.

DEATH RACE 2000 New World 1975 color 79m. D: Paul Bartel. SP: Robert Thom, Charles Griffith, from Ib Melchior's story "The Racer." Ph: Tak Fujimoto. Mus: Paul Chihara. AD: R. Royce, B.B. Neel. SpOptFX: Jack Rabin. SpFX: Richard MacLean. Car Des: James Powers. Mkp: Pat Hutchence. Ref: screen. MFB '76:26-7. V 5/7/75. with David Carradine(Frankenstein), Simone Griffeth, Sylvester Stallone, Mary Woronov, Joyce Jameson, John Landis, Roberta Collins, Don Steele.
"In the year 2000, the citizens of the United Provinces of America...gather for the annual Trans-continental Death Race." (MFB) The star driver, Frankenstein, supposedly the artificially-reconstructed survivor and winner of previous races, is actually just another in a series of "Frankensteins," government-bred for the annual event. DEATH RACE 2000 is at least not afflicted with over-seriousness, that bane of filmic future-visions; it, however, has its own problem--it's just not that funny, and a movie in which point-hungry race-car drivers go gunning for hapless pedestrians is hilarious or it's nothing. The idea is more outrageous than the execution--a more documentary-like approach might better have set off the outrageousness. As is, the movie at times almost comes off as a have-the-cake-and-eat-it-too joke, as it both roundly condemns and eagerly exploits violence-as-spectacle, skirting a saving, self-conscious hypocrisy.

The DEATH SCOUTS NBC-TV/Solow 1977 color 94m. D: Marc Daniels. Sequel to The MAN FROM ATLANTIS. Ref: TVFFSB. with Patrick Duffy, Belinda Montgomery, Tiffany Bolling.
"Water-breathing aliens from another planet" scout Earth.

DEATH SHIP (Can.-B) Avco Embassy/ABP-Bloodstar 1980 color 91m. D: Alvin Rakoff. SP: John Robins. Story: Jack Hill, David P. Lewis. Ph: Rene Verzier. AD: C. Burke, M. Proulx. SpFX: Mike Albrechtsen, Peter Hughes. SdFxEd: Bill Trent. Mkp: Joan Isaacson. Ref: V 4/16/80. 8/22/79:39(ad). MFB'80:212. with George Kennedy, Richard Crenna, Nick Mancuso, Sally Ann Howes, Kate Reid, Victoria Burgoyne.
Nazi torture ship "set on killing its inhabitants." (V)

DEATH SMILES ON A MURDERER (I?) Avco Embassy 1973? color D: Aristide Massaccesi. Ref: TVFFSB. with Ewa Aulin, Klaus Kinski, Angela Bo.
Man tries to revive the dead.

*DEATH TAKES A HOLIDAY 1934 From A. Casella's play "La Morte in Vacanza" (as adapted by W.Ferris). AD: Hans Dreier. Ref: screen. Lee. with O. Hoffmann.

Death (Fredric March) takes a three-day vacation as a mere mortal, falls in love, takes his beloved (Evelyn Venable) back with him. As Sirki, he makes bad double entendres about his other self and inspires others to muse about "the mystery that's just beyond sight and sound." (Films and Filming?) Predictable dramatic discoveries (e.g., love is as great as Death); vacuous dialogue. Nice translucent-shadow/cloak effect for Death-as-Death. A metaphysical con job.

DEATH: THE ULTIMATE MYSTERY (Gold Key-TV)/Sandler Institutional 1975? color 94m. SP,D,P: Robert Emenegger, Allan Sandler. Ph: Hans Beimler. Mus: Emenegger. Ref: TV. TVG. V 3/26/75: 58: sfa LIFE AFTER DEATH? 2/13/80:51. with Cameron Mitchell, Gloria Prince, Dr. Maurice Rawlings.

Docu-drama in which the (generally unseen) narrator/protagonist visits the mummies of Egypt and Guanajato, Mexico, a swami in India, etc., and ruminates about reincarnation, hypnotic regression, life-after-death--and Parisians. ("These people know how to live!")

DEATH TRAP Virgo Int'l./Mars 1976 color 89m. (EATEN ALIVE-orig t. BRUTES AND SAVAGES-int t?) Story,D,Mus: Tobe Hooper. SP: Alvin L. Fast, Mardi Rustam. Adap: Kim Henkel. Ph: Robert Caramico. Mus:also Wayne Bell. AD: Marshall Reed. SpFX: A&A. MechFX: Bob Mattey. Ref: MFB'78:217-18. '79:60. V 10/13/76:4(rated, as STARLIGHT SLAUGHTER). Bianco #4/77:142. Willis/SW. with Neville Brand, Mel Ferrer, Carolyn Jones, Marilyn Burns, William Finley, Stuart Whitman, Roberta Collins.

Mad hotel-proprietor feeds victims to pet crocodile.

DEATH TRIANGLE see BERMUDA TRIANGLE, The (I-Mex,1978)

DEATH WATCH see DEATHWATCH

DEATH WEEKEND see HOUSE BY THE LAKE

DEATHDAY see MADHOUSE

DEATHDREAM (Can.?) (Gold Key-TV)/Europix Int'l/Impact Quadrant 1972(1974) color 90m. (The NIGHT WALK-orig t. The NIGHT ANDY CAME HOME-int t. DEAD OF NIGHT-B) D,P: Bob Clark. SP: Alan Ormsby. Ph: Jack McGowan. Mus: Carl Zittrer. AD: Forest Carpenter. Ref: MFB'77:230. Ecran 6/75:22. Willis/SW. FC 3/80:30. TVFFSB. Lee(p). with John Marley, Lynn Carlin, Richard Backus(zombie-vampire), Anya Ormsby, H. Forsythe.

U.S. soldier who reportedly died in action returns, a "walking corpse" dependent on blood.

DEATHMASTER AI/RF-WP 1972 color 88m. (KHORDA-orig t) D: Ray Danton. SP: R.L. Grove. Ph: Wilmer C. Butler. Mus: Bill Marx. SpFX: John Oliver. Mkp: Mark Bussan. Assoc P & with:

Robert Quarry. Ref: TV. MFB'76:231. Lee. with Bill Ewing, Brenda Dickson, Betty Anne Rees, Le Sesne Hilton(Barbado).
Topanga Canyon, Calif. Vampire who commands the elements and heals wounds becomes guru to hippie commune, turns its members into vampires. The vampire guru Khorda (Quarry) certainly seems to have the answers. He counters the hippies' "Wow, man!" exclamations with phrases like "the infinity of the night" and "the ecstasy of eternity." But is he a savior or a sinister con artist? This ambiguity is rather dissipated in liberal displays of fangs and stakes. And the delineation of both hippie and vampire worlds could have used more comedy. (Or more-intentional comedy.)

DEATHSPORT New World 1978 color 83m. SP,D: Henry Suso. D: also Allan Arkush. SP: also Donald Stewart. Story: F. Doel. Ph: Gary Graver. Mus: Andrew Stein. AD: S. Compton. SpFxPh: H. Stockert. SpPhFX: Jack Rabin. Opt: Philip Huff. Ref: TV. MFB'79:119-120. V 4/26/78. with David Carradine, Claudia Jennings, Richard Lynch, W. Smithers, Jesse Vint.
1000 years from now: the post-holocaust world is made up of Mutants, Statemen, and Range Guides; "hand-blasters" (ray guns); "death machines" (motorcycles); psychic healing; force field; mystical-psychoanalytic dialogue; noise, noise, noise. If there's a ringing in your ears afterwards, it may be the effect of the last 37 explosions. Bronson Canyon lives!

DEATHWATCH (F-W.G.) Selta-Little Bear-Antenne 2-Sara-Gaumont/TV 13 1980 color/scope 128m. (La MORT EN DIRECT. DEATH WATCH) SP,D: Bertrand Tavernier. SP: also David Rayfiel(sp?). From the novel "The Unsleeping Eye" or "The Continuous Katherine Mortenhoe" by David Compton. Ph: P.-W. Glenn. Mus: Antoine Duhamel. PD: Tony Pratt. Ref: MFB'81:52-3. V 2/6/80. 5/9/79:422(ad). FM 161:12. with Romy Schneider, Harvey Keitel, Harry Dean Stanton, Max Von Sydow.
In a future society, death and disease have been almost completely banished.

DEBORAH (I) (AA-TV)/Paola 1974 color 107m. (Un FIOCCO NERO PER DEBORAH. A BLACK RIBBON FOR DEBORAH-ad t) D: Marcello Andrei. Ph: Claudio Racca. Mus: Albert Verrecchia. PD: E.R. Poccetto. Ref: TVFFSB: woman with psychic powers. TVG. TV. V 1/22/75:35(ad). 7/17/74:26. with Gig Young, Bradford Dillman, Marina Malfatti, Lucretia Love, Delia Boccardo.
Psychic forces shatter wine glasses, choke medium.

DECOY FOR TERROR Hemisphere 1971? color 90m. (PLAYGIRL KILLER-alt t) Ref: TVFFSB. Medved/TGTA. no AFI. with Neil Sedaka, William Kirwin.
Artist murders his models, stores bodies in meat locker.

DEEP RED (I) Group IV & Mahler/Seda Spettacoli-S.Argento 1975 color 98m. (PROFONDO ROSSO. The HATCHET MURDERS-'80 re-r t) SP,D: Dario Argento. SP: also Bernardino Zapponi, G. Bassan. Ph: Luigi Kuveiller. Mus: Giorgio Gaslini. AD: Bassan. SpFX:

Germano Natali, Carlo Rambaldi. Ref: TV. TVG. SFC 8/1/80(ad). V 10/27/76:5. 6/23/76. 9/18/74:30: aka The SABRE TOOTH TIGER? FFacts: aka DRIPPING DEEP RED. with David Hemmings, Daria Nicolodi, Gabriele Lavia, Macha Meril, G. Mauri, F. Meniconi.

Mind reader who picks up thoughts of homicidal schizophrenic; "haunted" villa harboring mouldering corpse in walled-up room; ambulatory dummy? Slight mystery, embellished with ingeniously nasty murders, "pulsating" music, and quirky, fetishistic camerawork. (At critical moments the camera will, in extreme close-up, virtually nuzzle selected, odd objects.) The mystery plot hinges on the fact that the hero has seen the killer's face but doesn't realize it until the climactic scene. Mere cleverness stretched very, very thin.

DEER--GOLDEN ANTLERS (Russ) Gorky 1972 SP,D: Alexander Row. SP: also Lev Potyomkin? Ph: Y. Dyakonov, V. Okunev. Mus: Anatoli Filippenko. AD: Arseni Klopotovsky. Ref: Soviet Film #2/72. with Georgi Millyar(Baba-Yaga the witch), Ira & Lena Chigrinova, Raisa Ryazanova.

"Wicked goblins"; cap of invisibility; "forest come to life."

The DEGENERATES JER 1967 73m. D,P: Andy Milligan. Ref: AFI. with Bryarly Lee, Marcia Howard, Hope Stansbury, Robert Burgos.

Year 2000, post-nuclear holocaust.

DEJEUNER SUR L'HERBE see PICNIC ON THE GRASS

DELITTO DEL DIAVOLO see QUEENS OF EVIL

DEMAIN LES MOMES (F) Unite Trois 1976 color 95m. SP,D: Jean Pourtale. SP: also F. Vialle, R. Lepoutre. Ph: J.-J. Rochut. Mus: Eric De Marsan. Sets: Michel Farge. Ref: V(d) 11/9/76. with Niels Arestrug, Michel Esposito, Brigitte Rouan.

End-of-civilization story.

DEMON! New World/Larco 1976 color 87m. (GOD TOLD ME TO-alt t) SP,D,P: Larry Cohen. Ph: Paul Glickman. Mus: Frank Cordell. SpMkp: Steve Neill. Ref: screen. Willis/SW. MFB'81: 46-7. V(d) 12/3/76. with Tony Lo Bianco, Sandy Dennis, Sam Levene, Sylvia Sidney, Robert Drivas, Mike Kellin, Richard Lynch(Bernard), Deborah Raffin, Harry Bellaver, W. Roerick.

A psychological-religious-sf-horror-mystery in which people suddenly go berserk and start killing. Offbeat, sensationalistic, and, above all, bizarre. Apparently, "God" will keep making "Christs" until He gets Him right.

DEMON, DEMON! ABC-TV 1975 color 75m. Ref: TVFFSB. TVG: possessed woman? with Bradford Dillman, Juliet Mills, R. Symonds.

The DEMON LOVER Wolf Lore 1976 color SP,D: Donald G. Jackson, Jerry Younkins. Ref: Meyers. Willis/SW. V 5/26/76:4(rated). with Gunnar Hanse, Val Mayerik, Christmas Robbins, Tom Hutton.

Occultist conjures up horned demon. See also: DEMON LOVER DIARY(P).

DEMON POND (J) Shochiku 1980 color 124m. (YASHAGA IKE) D: Masahiro Shinoda. SP: H. Minura, T. Tamura. Story: Kyoka Izumi. Ph: Masao Kosugi. Mus: Isao Tomita. AD: Kiyoshi Awazu et al. SpVisFX: Nobuo Yajima. Ref: V 3/26/80. JFFJ 13: 6. SFC 9/5/80. with Tamasaburo Bando(demon), Go Kato.

Ghosts and monsters of "demon pond...lie dormant as long as couple rings a magic bell"; tidal wave; demon princess. (V).

DEMON SEED UA/MGM/Jaffe 1977 color/scope 95m. D: Donald Cammell. SP: Robert Jaffe, Roger O. Hirson, from Dean R. Koontz's novel. Ph: Bill Butler. Mus: Jerry Fielding. PD: Edward Carfagno. Synthavision: Bo Gehring. ElecAnim: R.L. Froman; (des) Ron Hays. SpPh: Jordan Belson. SpFX: Tom Fisher;(mech) Glen Robinson. SpMkp: Frank Griffin. Titles: Mary Meacham. Ref: MFB'77:209. CineFan 2:59. V 3/30/77. TV. with Julie Christie, Fritz Weaver, Gerrit Graham, Felix Silla(baby), Berry Kroeger, Lisa Lu, Alfred Dennis, Robert Vaughn(Proteus' voice).

Thinking computer (with "synthetic cortex") impregnates woman with "synthetic spermatozoa"; operates house's mechanical systems, laser ray, pyramidal all-purpose weapon. Or, "Rosemary: A Baby Odyssey." _It_ has a monstrous shell, but a human kernel. Is its computer-father fiend or savior? Is its child the solution, or just an aggravation of the problem (i.e., science amok)? The ambiguity is nice, but it's mainly frosting. The cake: suspense, some wit, and lots of effects. The script shrewdly exploits HAL-o-phobia, or fear-of-machines, as it simultaneously exploits the technology it questions. (The latter irony seems frosting too.)

DEMON WITCH CHILD (Sp) Coliseum/Richard 1975?('76-U.S.) color (sfa El PODER DE LAS TINIEBLAS?) D: Amando De Ossorio. Ref: Meyers. V 5/7/75. Willis/SW. with Julian Mateos, Fernando Sancho, Lone Fleming, Marian Salgado, Angel del Pozo.

Dead satanist possesses little girl.

DEMONOID American Panorama 1981 color (MACABRA-orig t) Ref: FM 170:12-14. V 6/10/81:4(rated). "Sneak Previews"(Dog of the Week). with Stuart Whitman, Samantha Eggar.

Mummified hand possesses man's body.

The DEMONS (Port.-F) Hemisphere/Interfilme-CFDF 1972('74-U.S.) color 97m. (Os DEMONIOS. Les DEMONS) SP,D: Jesus Franco. From David Khunne's novel. Ph: R. Artigot. Mus: Jean-Bernard Raiteux. Ref: MFB'74:173. V 5/22/74:11. Bianco Index'73. with Anne Libert, Britt Nichols, Howard Vernon, Albert Dalbes.

Witch's curse; torture; ghost; "bride of Satan"; bride's kiss turns victims into skeletons.

DEMONS OF THE MIND (B) Cinemation/Hammer-Godwin(EMI) 1971('76-U.S.) color 89m. (BLOOD WILL HAVE BLOOD-orig t) D: Peter Sykes. Story,SP: Christopher Wicking. Story,P: Frank Godwin. Ph: Arthur Grant. Mus: Harry Robinson. AD: Michael Stringer. Mkp: Trevor Crole-Rees. Ref: MFB'72:229-30. SFC 4/11/80: sfa DEMONS OF THE NIGHT? Lee(V 9/8/71). Willis/SW. TV. with Paul

Jones, Gillian Hills, Robert Hardy, Michael Hordern, Patrick Magee, Shane Briant, Yvonne Mitchell, Kenneth J. Warren, Robert Brown, Virginia Wetherell, Sheila Raynor.
1830. "Bleak mansion," hereditary insanity, "unknown murderer," hypnosis, "willed" death. (MFB)

DENSHI SENTAI DENJIMAN (J) Toei-TV 1980 46m. D: K. Takemoto. SP: S. Uehara. Ref: V 5/13/81:258. JFFJ 13:36: from the "Denjiman" TV series; robot, lasers, monsters.

DERANGED AI/Karr Int'l. 1974 color 82m. D: Jeff Gillen, Alan Ormsby. SP: Ormsby. Based on the same material as PSYCHO. Ph: Jack McGowan. Mus: Carl Zittrer. AD: Albert Fischer. Ref: MFB'76:51. Willis/SW. V 2/27/74. with Roberts Blossom, Cosette Lee, Robert Warner, Marcia Diamond.
Middle-aged man studies embalming and taxidermy in effort to restore dead mother's beauty; seance, murder.

DES FRISSONS PARTOUT see JEFF GORDON STRIKES AGAIN

DES MORTS (Belg.-F) Zeno/Losange 1979 color 103m. (OF THE DEAD-alt t. Les RITES DES MORTS) SP,D,Ph: Thierry Zeno. SP, D: also Dominique Garny, Jean-Pol Ferbus. Ph: also T. Stogner. Mus: Alain Pierre. Ref: PFA notes 5/20/80. FC 3/80:78-9: "a horrifying, liberating feature documentary" on the physical fact of death. V 5/7/80:476. 2/7/79: "a truly repulsive film."

DESCUARTIZADOR DE BINBROOK, El see NECROPHAGUS

DESIRE (B) B&C 1920 54m. (The MAGIC SKIN-alt t) SP,D: G.E. Hall. From "La Peau de Chagrin" or "The Wild Ass's Skin" by Balzac. Ref: BFC. with Dennis Neilson-Terry, Yvonne Arnaud.
Dream: "ass's skin grants author's wishes...."

*DESTINATION MOON 1950 SpFX: Lee Zavitz. Anim: Walter Lantz. Ref: TV. LC. Lee. V 6/28/50. and with Joe Sawyer.
Dramatically, not much of an improvement on the earlier and similar GIRL IN THE MOON(Fritz Lang, 1929). The music and effects are--perhaps predictably--far superior to story, acting, and dialogue. George Pal's first sf feature shows a proper respect for outer space, but not for the intelligence of the viewer, as the script piles on superfluous suspense and comedy. The sequences on the moon are elegantly "framed" by, a) a nice, long, leisurely first-men-on-the-moon panning shot (their point-of-view) and, b) a final trio-of-shots: of the receding moon, the spaceship, and the approaching Earth.

DESTINATION NIGHTMARE Medallion-TV/Roach 1958 94m. D: Paul Landers. Ref: TV. TVFFSB. with Boris Karloff, Whit Bissell, Tod Andrews, Myron Healey, Jean Del Val.
Four stories of "the unexplainable"; from the unsold TV series "The Veil."

DEVATHALARA DEEVINCHANDI (India-Telugu) Jayabhari Art 1977 164m. SP,D: Kommineni. Dial: Jandyala. Mus: Chakravarthy.

Ref: Dharap. with Ranganath, Prabha, Chandra Mohan, Giribabu.
Snake goddess takes the form of a woman to kill four men. Tamil version: NAGAM EN DEIVAM RMS Cine 1978 scope 145m. D: Seshagiri Rao. Dial: K.A.V. Govindan. Mus: Chakravarthi. with Giri Babu, Ranganathan, Prabha.
See also: NAGIN.

DEVIL AND DR. FRANKENSTEIN, The see ANDY WARHOL'S FRANKENSTEIN

The DEVIL AND MISS SARAH ABC-TV/Univ-TV 1971 color 73m. D: Michael Caffey. Ref: TVFFSB: "outlaw with the powers of the devil." "Fantastic TV." Maltin/TVM. with Gene Barry, James Drury, Janice Rule, Slim Pickens, Charles McGraw.

DEVIL AND THE DEAD, The see LISA AND THE DEVIL

*DEVIL BAT 1941 Story: George Bricker. Ref: screen. TV. Lee.
DEVIL BAT, like most beloved camp classics, is not *unalloyed* joy. Approximately half its hour-plus running time is squandered on unfruitful intricacies of plot: if Bela Lugosi as the mad chemist Carruthers seems part *inspiration* and part *desperation*, the movie, as a whole, is more obviously a product of simple desperation. Fortunately, the "shock" scenes--in which flimsy *papier-mache* bats knock down full-grown actors--are as dumb as they are desperate. Lugosi's scenes themselves are (to put it mildly) uneven. One moment he approaches comic genius; the next he's embarrassing. He can seem to give a simple word like "*for-mu-la*" more stresses than it has syllables, and is wonderful trying to express the inexpressible--e.g., unholy delight in his brand-new devil bat. ("Splendid! You will be even greater than your unfortunate predecessor!") His performance is an involved mixture of the good, the bad, the pathetic, and the admirable--it might be his career in miniature.

DEVIL BEAR see CLAWS

DEVIL CAT see NIGHT CREATURE

The DEVIL COMMANDS 1941 (*WHEN THE DEVIL COMMANDS) Mus D: M.W. Stoloff. SdFX: Phil Faulkner. Ref: TV. LC.
The DEVIL COMMANDS is, in effect, a very strange "romantic comedy"--a comedy of frustrated love--capped by a little-short-of-terrific, three-installment horror payoff. Dr. Blair (Boris Karloff) and his dead wife (Shirley Warde)--with whom he is trying to communicate via thought-wave "aerials" (i.e., bodies, living or dead)--are continually being interrupted in "mid-kiss." If it's not his daughter (Amanda Duff) breaking into the lab, it's "folks talking," or the sheriff or housekeeper prying, or fellow scientists labeling the doctor's pursuits blasphemy. The script fritters away most of its 65 minutes--but not, it turns out, *all* of them: the three "brainstorms," with Blair attempting to contact his wife in the next world, are probably the weirdest "seances" on film--all brain rays, roaring winds, hunching corpses--the power of *amour fou*

unleashed, as it were. They're abundantly worth the wait--surreally horrific surprises perversely secreted in an old, forgotten, otherwise arid "B" horror.

DEVIL DOG: THE HOUND OF HELL L-R-Z(TV) 1978 color 93m. D: Curtis Harrington. SP: Stephen & Elinor Karpf. Ph: G.P. Finnerman. Mus: Artie Kane. AD: William Cruse. SpFxPh: Sam DiMaggio, Allen Blaisdell. Ref: TV. TVG. with Richard Crenna, Yvette Mimieux, Kim Richards, Ike Eisenman, Lou Frizzel, Martine Beswick, R.G. Armstrong, Victor Jory(shaman).

Aw! the cute little puppy couldn't be the devil dog, the hound of hell--though his eyes do light up funny, and he seems to make people around him burn up or drown (when noone else is looking)--and its master's children act strange and secretive (uh oh), and his wife seems to do its bidding (I think they better get rid of this dog), and she too acts strange, and socially unscrupulous ("Isn't this the American way?" she asks her husband, who should be catching on to the dog by now)--and, my God! it really is a gigantic horrible demon dog!--an Ecuadorian goblin-dog, to be specific, which the hero sends back to hell, finally--but (uh oh, a postscript) there were eight other puppies in the litter! (Somebody's gotta stop those postscripts!)

The DEVIL FROM THE BOTTOM OF THE SEA (H.K.) 197-? SpFX: Koichi Takano. Ref: JFFJ 13:32: "horde of monsters."

The DEVIL IN HER (H.K.) 1975 (cf. NIGHT OF THE DEVIL BRIDE) D: Chang Sen. Ref: IFG'76:215: "remake" of The EXORCIST.

The DEVIL MADE ME DO IT Univ-TV 1973 color 76m. Ref: TVFFSB: orig. episode of "The Snoop Sisters"; witch; satanist coven. with Helen Hayes, Mildred Natwick, Lou Antonio, Bert Convy, George Maharis, Alice Cooper, Cyril Ritchard.

DEVIL TIMES FIVE Cinemation 1974(1979) color 90m. (The HORRIBLE HOUSE ON THE HILL-'74 Barrister t. PEOPLETOYS-orig t?) D: Sean MacGregor. SP: John Durren. Story: Dylan Jones. Mus: William Loose. Ref: Baer/TFBC. Cinef IV:3:38. Bill Warren. LAT 2/2/79. Joe Dante. with Gene Evans, Sorrell Booke, Leif Garrett, Carolyn Stellar.

Crazy children commit brutal murders.

The DEVIL WITHIN HER (B) AI/Unicapital 1975('76-U.S.) color 94m. (I DON'T WANT TO BE BORN-B) D: Peter Sasdy. SP: Stanley Price. Story: Nato de Angeles. Ph: Kenneth Talbot. Mus: Ron Grainer. AD: Roy Stannard. SpFX: Bert Luxford. Mkp: Eddie Knight. Ref: MFB'75:155. Willis/SW. V 2/18/76. with Joan Collins, Eileen Atkins, Donald Pleasence, Ralph Bates, Caroline Munro, John Steiner.

Dwarf curses woman, who gives birth to monster-baby.

DEVIL WITHIN HER,The see BEYOND THE DOOR

DEVIL WOMAN (Fili) Lea 1970 SP,D: J.F. Sibal. Story: G.I. de Dios, from the comic strip. Ph: Steve Perez. Mus: D'Amarillo. Ref: Lee(Borst): woman with "snake-like things" on body. Meyers: sfa BRUKA,QUEEN OF EVIL('75-U.S.)?--bat men, "lady of snakes," "men of stone," "savage midgets." with D. Valencia.

DEVIL WOMAN JMG 1976 color D: Albert Yu, Felix Villars. Ref: Willis/SW. Meyers: the supernatural. V 11/24/76:11. with Rosemarie Gil, Alex T. Lec, Romy Diax, Robert Chen.

DEVILDAY(by A.Hall) see MADHOUSE

DEVILISH DOLLS (Braz) Nogueira 1975 color 90m. (BONECAS DIABOLICAS) SP,D: Flavio Nogueira. Ph: Henrique Borges. Mus: D.C. Sanches. Ref: Brasil Cinema'75. with Nogueira, Sonia Garcia, Maria do Rocio, Valter Prado.

Professor Sidrome's "living" dolls are made of steel and plastic.

DEVIL'S BALL, The see MASCOT, The

The DEVIL'S BARGAIN (B) C&M 1908 9m. D: A.E.Coleby. Ref:BFC.

Artist sells his soul for money.

DEVIL'S BED,The see SHE-WOLF OF DEVIL'S MOOR

The DEVIL'S DAUGHTER Para-TV 1972 color 74m. D: Jeannot Szwarc. Ref: TVFFSB. Scheuer/MOTV. with Shelley Winters, Belinda Montgomery, Joseph Cotten, R. Foxworth, J. Frid.

Mother sells daughter's soul to the Devil.

DEVIL'S DAUGHTER,The see POCOMANIA

DEVIL'S DOLL,The see SINTHIA THE DEVIL'S DOLL

DEVIL'S DUE Arno/Bacchus 1973 color 90m. D: Ernest Danna. SP: Gerry Pound. Mus: Ennepitti. Ref: V 4/4/73. with Cindy West, Catherine Warren, Lisa Grant.

Devil cult in Manhattan.

*The DEVIL'S HAND 1942 AD: Andre Andrejeu. Ref: screen. Everson. V 4/2/47. Cinef Smr'73:26. and with Pierre Larquey.

Maurice Tourneur's film is studded with ingenious effects--e.g., numbers magically "rearranging" themselves on a sheet of paper, the devil's agent "turning" a clock ahead--and the hero's paintings of wraiths and demons are a haunting presence throughout. But the film's centerpiece is a stunningly-conceived montage of the long history of the devil's hand, told in vivid, strikingly stylized vignettes. The macabre wit of Palau's emissary from the Devil ("C'est mon metier") anticipates, perhaps, the wit of Niall MacGinnis' Karswell in son _Jacques_ Tourneur's CURSE OF THE DEMON.

DEVIL'S MEN,The see LAND OF THE MINOTAUR

*The DEVIL'S MESSENGER 1962 Ph: William Troiano. Mus: Alfred Gwynn. AD: Robert J. Herts. Opt: CFI. Ref: TV. AFI: revised from Swedish TV series. and with Ralph Brown.

Three stories. 1) Visions of Satanya (Karen Kadler) drive man to death by heart attack. 2) 50,000-year-old girl found frozen in glacial ice. 3) Dreams and crystal foretell man's death. Poorly-told anecdotes, but #2 is pretty eerie anyway. The ice-bound girl suddenly opens her eyes; later, we see (but don't hear) her scream as her (reincarnated?) lover hacks away at the ice trying to free her. She then just seems to dissolve away--50,000 years down the drain....

DEVIL'S MOUNTAIN Gold Key-TV/Burrud-Hinshaw 1976 color 93m. D,P,Ph: Milas Hinshaw. Underwater Ph: B. Burton, B. Bell. Mus Sup: Doug Lackey, G. Kauer. Narr: Bill Burrud. Ref: GKey. TV. TVG.

Bones taken from Bora Bora burial ground seem to bring Tom Hinshaw bad luck. Home-movie-travelogue re: Polynesia, with a laughably limp narrative "hook"--every 10 minutes Burrud (who has all the vocal charm of John Agar) simply interjects a variation on "Tom was worried--he *still* hadn't returned the bones," "The bones must go back," etc. To *hell* with the bones....

DEVIL'S NIGHTMARE (Belg-I) (AI-TV)/Hemisphere/Cetelci-Delfino 1971('74-U.S.) color 95m. (La PLUS LONGUE NUIT DU DIABLE. AU SERVICE DU DIABLE) SP,D: Jean Brismee. SP: also Andre Hunebelle et al. Ph: A. Goeffers. Mus: A. Alessandroni. AD: Jio Berg. Ref: MFB'72:239. Cinef W'73:39. Willis/SW. TVFFSB. V 5/22/74:11. Cinef Smr'73:37. with Erika Blanc, Jean Servais, Daniel Emilfork, Shirley Corrigan, Jacques Monseu.

Curse renders every eldest daughter of noble family "an agent of the devil." (MFB)

*The DEVIL'S OWN Hammer-7A 1966 Mkp: George Partleton. Ref: TV. AFI. Lee.

Fairish mystery-shocker, with an overlong buildup and a letdown of a payoff. Funny bit with an enthusiastic butcher, though, and some nice "village day" atmosphere.

DEVIL'S PEOPLE,The see LAND OF THE MINOTAUR

DEVIL'S PLAYTHING see VEIL OF BLOOD

The DEVIL'S PROFESSION (B) Arrow 1915 55m. SP,D: F.C.S. Tudor. From G.S.W. James's novel. Ref: BFC. with Alesia Leon.

"Doctor is paid to inject rich people with madness simulant."

The DEVIL'S RAIN (U.S.-Mex) Bryanston/Howard 1975 color/scope 86m. D: Robert Fuest. SP: Gabe Essoe, J. Ashton, G. Hopman. Ph: Alex Phillips Jr. Mus: Al De Lory. PD: Nikita Knatz. Adv: Anton La Vey. SpPhFX: Film FX, Linwood Dunn, D.W. Weed. SpFX: Cliff & Carol Wenger, Thomas Fisher, F. Farfan. Mkp: The Burmans. SdFX: Gene Eliot. Ref: MFB'76:122. V 6/25/75.

TV. with Ernest Borgnine, Eddie Albert, Ida Lupino, William Shatner, Keenan Wynn, Tom Skerritt, John Travolta, Claudio Brook, Lisa Todd(Lilith), George Sawaya, Joan Prather.

Satan's minister (Borgnine) seeks disciples' book; disciples' souls--trapped in Devil's Rain in helmet--melt when latter smashed; woman with ESP. Incredibly cursory, slapdash devil-cult thriller, with lots of gratuitous oozing. The dialogue _means_ to be functional--"And eyeless faces, _hunhh_?--how about _that_ one?"--"literate" is an alternate universe.

The DEVIL'S TRIANGLE UFO/Libert/WNEW-TV(NY) 1973 color 52m. SP,D,P: Richard Winer. Mus: King Crimson. Narr: Vincent Price. Ref: Willis/SW. V 5/11/77:205(ad). 9/18/74:7(rated). 3/21/73:52: spacemen.

The mystery of the Bermuda triangle.

The DEVIL'S WEB (B) ABC-TV?/ITC-TV 1974 color 75m. (NURSE WILL MAKE IT BETTER-orig t?) D: Shaun O'Riordan. SP: Brian Clemens. Ph: M. Whitcutt, T. Mander. Mus: Laurie Johnson. Title Seq: Visualscope. Ref: TV. TVG. TVFFSB. with Diana Dors, Andrea Marcovicci, Linda Liles, Cec Linder, Ed Bishop.

The Devil--in the guise of a nurse (Dors)--both cures and converts his/her charges. Above-average ITC-TV horror show. It's good-against-evil again, but the battle is not taken over-seriously. Clemens' script has some pleasingly perverse glints of humor, and doesn't seem quite the usual hand-me-down from 100 other horror movies. Dors and Marcovicci are good.

The DEVIL'S WEDDING NIGHT (I) Dimension 1973('75-U.S.) color 85m. (COUNTESS DRACULA-orig U.S. t. Il PLENILUNIO DELLE VERGINI) D: Paolo Solvay. SP,P: M. Pupillo(aka Ralph Zucker). SP: also Alan Harris. Ref: TVFFSB. Murphy. Meyers. Glut/TDB. V 4/4/73:4(rated). 10/4/72:32. B.Warren. with Mark Damon, Sara Bay, Miriam Barrios, Stan Papps, Frances Davis, A.Getty.

Archaeologist with the Nibelungen ring (once owned by Dracula); Castle Karnstein; Castle Dracula; "the zombie," entranced girl; man possessed by Dracula's spirit.

DEVIL'S WIDOW,The or DEVIL'S WOMAN,The see TAM LIN

The DEVIL'S WOMAN (I) 1978 D: Enzo G. Castellari. Ref: V 10/18/78:176: "the terror of ancient magic!" with Leonora Fani, Patricia Adriani, Vincent Gardenia.

DEVUDE GELICHADU (India-Telugu) SVK 1976 color 145m. SP,D: Vijayanirmala. Story: M. Shanmugam. Mus: R. Naidu. Ref: Dharap: spirit haunts couple. with Krishna, Jaggaiah.

Le DIABLE EN BOUTEILLE (F) ACE-UFA 1935 95m. French version of *LOVE, DEATH AND THE DEVIL (with same D,SP,Mus credits). Adap: Serge Veber. Ph: Fritz Arno Wagner. AD: Otto Hunte, Willy Schiller. Ref: Chirat. with K. von Nagy, Pierre Blanchar, Gina Manes, Paul Azais, Gabriel Gabrio, Roger Karl.

Wish-granting demon in bottle--the last possessor of which

is damned. From Stevenson's story "The Imp in the Bottle."

Les DIABLESSES (F) Nordia-ABC-General 1974 Ref: V 5/8/74: 140: "horror pic."

DIABLO SE LLEVA LOS MUERTOS,El see LISA AND THE DEVIL

*The DIABOLICAL MEETINGS Lacy Int'l.-Prodimex 1971 color/scope 88m. (Les AMANTES DEL DIABLO. I DIABOLICI CONVEGNI) SP: Miguel Madrid, J.L. Navarro, Santoni, Elorrieta. Ph: E. di Cola. Mus: Carlo Savina. Ref: Bianco Index'72. Lee(V 10/27/71): mad doctor with satanic powers.

DIALOGHI CON LEUCO(by C.Pavese) see FROM THE CLOUD TO THE RESISTANCE

The DIAMOND SHIP (G) Images/Decla-Bioscop 1919 tinted 83m. (Das BRILLANTENSCHIFF. Das SKLAVENSCHIFF) Part II of series, The Spider (Die Spinnen); projected parts III,IV never made. SP,D: Fritz Lang. Ph: Karl Freund. AD: Otto Hunte, K.L. Kirmse, Hermann Warm. Ref: screen. Lee. FQ W'79:3. PFA notes 2/3/79. MFB'81:14-15. with Carl de Vogt, Ressel Orla.

Super-criminal "Spiders" out to rule Asia; subterranean city beneath San Francisco's Chinatown; Indian yogi in hypnotic trance who sees lost "Buddha-head diamond" and its possessors, past and present; heroine kept under villain's hypnotic spell; crater which emits poisonous fumes at night. Quaint, rather primitive Lang is now strictly a curiosity.

DIAMONDS ARE FOREVER (B) UA/Eon-Danjaq 1971 color/scope 119m. D: Guy Hamilton. SP: Richard Maibaum, Tom Mankiewicz, from Ian Fleming's book. Ph: Ted Moore. Mus: John Barry. PD: Ken Adam. SpFX: Leslie Hillman, W. McMahon. SpPhFX: Albert Whitlock, Wally Veevers. Ref: screen. MFB'72:29-30. Lee(V 12/15/71). B.Hill. with Sean Connery(James Bond), Jill St. John, Charles Gray, Lana Wood, Jimmy Dean, Bruce Cabot, Bruce Glover, Bernard Lee, Laurence Naismith, Lois Maxwell.

Giant, orbiting laser which detonates missile bases; "ape-woman" exhibit at carnival. Overplotty Bond, with flurries of excitement (e.g., Lana Wood). One knockout car stunt, a few funny gags, and lots of leaden ones.

DIARY OF A SPACE VIRGIN see GIRL FROM STARSHIP VENUS

DIAVOLO E I MORTI,Il see LISA AND THE DEVIL

DIDDLED! (B) C&M 1912 8m. D: C. Calvert? Ref: BFC.

"Man poses as mummy to fool professor...."

DIGBY--THE BIGGEST DOG IN THE WORLD (B) (AI-TV)/Cinerama/Shenson 1973('74-U.S.) color 88m. D: Joseph McGrath. SP: Michael Pertwee. Story: Charles Isaacs. From Ted Key's book. Ph: Harry Waxman. Mus: Edwin Astley. AD: Maurice Fowler. SpPhFX: Tom Howard. Ref: screen. MFB'73:246-7. TVFFSB.

Willis/SW. V 6/19/74. with Jim Dale, Spike Milligan, Angela Douglas, John Bluthal, Milo O'Shea, Victor Spinetti, Kenneth J. Warren, Victor Maddern, Edward Underdown.

Chemical turns sheepdog into giant; giant chimp at end. Simple boy-and-his-big-dog comedy. Spinetti's fractured German and eccentric movements are amusing.

DIKAYA OKHOTA KOROLYA STAKHA see KING STAKH'S WILD GAME CHASE

DINNER FOR ADELE (Cz) Dimension/CFP/Barrandov 1978 color 100m. (ADELA JESTE NEVECERELA. NICK CARTER IN PRAGUE-orig U.S.t. ADELE HASN'T HAD HER SUPPER YET-alt t) D: Oldrich Lipsky. SP: Jiri Brdecka. Ph: Jaroslav Kucera. Mus: Lubos Fiser. Sets: V. Labsky, M. Nejedly. SpFX: Jan Svankmaier. Ref: V 6/21/78: parody of Nick Carter stories, Fantomas. Cinef X:1:12. PFA notes: man-eating plant. with Michal Docolomansky, Rudolf Hrusinsky, Milos Kopecky, Nada Konvalinkova.

DINOSAUR 1980? clay anim short D: Will Vinton. Ref: PFA notes 1/24/81. V 7/1/81:30: "prehistoric life."

DIRECTION (Yug) Neoplanta 1974 anim short D: Zoran Jovanovic. Ref: IFG'75:476: "man pursued by great, white giants."

The DISAPPEARANCE OF FLIGHT 412 NBC-TV/Cinemobile 1974 color 72m. D: Jud Taylor. SP: George Simpson, Neal Burger. Ref: TVFFSB: jet chasing UFO disappears. Scheuer/MOTV: sf. TVG. TV Season. with Glenn Ford, Bradford Dillman, Guy Stockwell, David Soul, Kent Smith, Jack Ging, Greg Mullavey, R.F. Lyons.

The DISAPPEARANCES NBC-TV/Solow-Taft 1977 color 74m. D: Charles Dubin. From "The Man from Atlantis" TV series. Ref: TVFFSB: mad scientist. with Patrick Duffy, Belinda J. Montgomery, Alan Fudge, Darlene Carr.

DISCIPLE OF DEATH (B) Heritage/Chromage 1972 color 84m. SP, D,P: Tom Parkinson. SP,P: also Churton Fairman. Ph: William Brayne. AD: Dennis Pavitt. Mkp: Frank Turner. Ref: TVFFSB. MFB'72:230. V 8/23/72:7(rated). with Mike Raven, Marguerite Hardiman, Ronnie Lacey, Virginia Wetherell, Stephen Bradley.

18th Century. "Demon dwarf"; "occult weapons"; stranger from hell and his female zombies. (MFB)

DISCIPLES OF DEATH see ENTER THE DEVIL

Les DISPARUS DE SAINT-AGIL (F) Cinelde-Sigma/Dimeco 1938 99m. (MYSTERY AT ST.AGIL-cr t. BOYS' SCHOOL-U.S.?) D: Christian-Jaque. SP: Jean-Henri Blanchon, from Pierre Very's novel. Dial: Jacques Prevert. Ph: M. Lucien, A. Germain. Mus: Henri Verdun. AD: Pierre Schild. Ref: screen. Chirat. PFA notes 3/29/79. with Erich von Stroheim, Armand Bernard, Michel Simon, Robert Le Vigan("the invisible man"), Aime Clariond.

"Invisible man" who "disappears through walls" haunts French boys' school; hints of "occultism," "vampires"; abortive attempt by professor (Simon) to dictate Wells' "The Invisible Man" to students. (He punishes them by returning to "La Vie de Shakespeare.") By turns amusing and slack, this basically routine mystery-comedy is sparked by Prevert's dialogue. ("Le surnaturel...en le chambre de sciences naturelles!?") And von Stroheim and Simon have some winning moments.

DISTANT EARLY WARNING ABC-TV/Lenjen-Lefferts 1975 color 74m. D: Wes Kenney. Ref: TVFFSB. with Michael Parks, Herb Edelman, Mary Frann, Tony Geary.
"Visitation by long dead family members to...military station in the Arctic."

DISTRUGGETO KONG, LA TERRA E IN PERICOLO see GAPPA

DOC SAVAGE--THE MAN OF BRONZE WB/Pal 1975 color 100m. D: Michael Anderson. SP,P: George Pal. SP: also Joe Morhaim. From the book by Kenneth Robeson. Ph: Fred Koenekamp. Mus: Sousa. AD: Fred Harpman. SpFX: S. Bedig, R. MacDonald. Ref: MFB'75:153. V 5/7/75. with Ron Ely, Paul Gleason, Paul Wexler, Robyn Hilton, Pamela Hensley, Carlos Rivas.
Telepathy; "Green Death" ("fatally poisonous snakes"). (MFB)

DR. BLACK MR. HYDE Dimension 1976 color 83m. (The WATTS MONSTER '79 [illegible]) D: William Crain. SP: Larry Le Bron. Ph: Tak Fujimoto. Mus: Johnny Pate. Ref: V 10/24/79. 1/21/76. Boxo 7/2/79:22. AMPAS. FM 161:8. 165:11. Willis/SW. with Bernie Casey(Dr.Pride/Hyde), Rosalind Cash, Stu Gilliam.
Potion turns black doctor into "odd white" beast.

DR. DEATH: SEEKER OF SOULS Cinerama/Freedom Arts 1973 color 89m. D,P: Eddie Saeta. SP: Sal Ponti. Ph: Kent Wakefield, Emil Oster. Mus: Richard LaSalle. AD: Ed Graves. Mkp: Siegfried Geike. Ref: MFB'74:249. Willis/SW. V 11/14/73. with John Considine, Barry Coe, Cheryl Miller, Stewart Moss, Jo Morrow, Florence Marly, Sivi Aberg, Moe Howard, Larry Vincent.
Dr. Death has lived 1,000 years, his soul passing into the bodies of those he murders.

DR. DEVIL AND MR. HARE WB 1964 anim color 7m. (Bugs Bunny) D: Robert McKimson. Ref: Maltin/OMAM. LC. Glut/TFL.
Tasmanian Devil vs. the Frankenstein monster.

DOCTOR FRANKEN NBC-TV/Titus-Janus 1980 color 95m. D: Marvin J. Chomsky, Jeff Lieberman. SP: Lee Thomas, inspired by Mary Shelley's novel "Frankenstein." Ref: V 1/23/80:72. with Robert Vaughn, Robert Perault, David Selby, Teri Garr.
Transplant specialist keeps body alive with vital organs.

DR. FRANKENSTEIN see FRANKENSTEIN: THE TRUE STORY

DR. HECKYL AND MR. HYPE Cannon/Golan-Globus 1980 color 99m. SP,D: Charles B. Griffith, "with apologies to RLS." Ph: Robert Carras. Mus: Richard Band. PD: Maxwell Mendes. Ref: V

7/2/80. with Oliver Reed(Heckyl/Hype), Sunny Johnson, Maia Danziger, Mel Welles, Jackie Coogan, Corinne Calvet.
Potion turns deformed podiatrist into handsome (and literal) lady killer.

DOCTOR IN THE NUDE see SHOCK TREATMENT

DOCTOR JECKILL Y EL HOMBRE LOBO see DOCTOR JEKYLL AND THE WOLFMAN

DR. JEKYLL AND MR. BLOOD see MAN WITH TWO HEADS

DR. JEKYLL AND MR. HYDE Starlight 1914 Ref: Lee(MPN 11/28/14): comedy. no LC. no AF-Index.

*DR. JEKYLL AND MR. HYDE Para 1920 80m. SP: C.S. Beranger. Based also on T.R. Sullivan's play and on Oscar Wilde's "The Picture of Dorian Gray." AD: Robert Haas, C.O. Sessel. Ref: screen. MFB'75:208. Glut/CMM.
Dr. Jekyll--attempting to separate the good from the bad in man--turns himself into the purely evil Mr. Hyde; seq. with Hyde as huge spider-creature. Surprisingly perhaps, John Barrymore's interpretation of Hyde still retains much of its power. If the transformation scenes are unintentionally hilarious, Barrymore's later passages as Jekyll-succumbing-to-Hyde, and as the grotesquely comic Hyde, are at once creepy and funny, and even occasionally moving. Prime moment: Jekyll pleading with his love, Millicent, to leave him; then Hyde grinning lewdly and turning to the door to let her in.

*DR. JEKYLL AND MR. HYDE 1932 See also: BETTY BOOP,M.D. THREE'S A CROWD. Mkp: Wally Westmore. Ref: screen. Lee. Glut/CMM.
Fredric March's Hyde--a true grotesque, with obscenely fidgety, uncontrollable lips and fingers--isn't the whole show here, but this distinctly better-than-average version of the story divides pretty much, as usual, into two movies: MR. HYDE, a riveting spectacle re: the consequences of over-indulgence, and DR. JEKYLL, a stodgy tract on the perils of repression (not helped by the posturing of Rose Hobart, Holmes Herbert, and March as Jekyll).

*DR. JEKYLL AND MR. HYDE 1941 Mkp: Jack Dawn. EdFX: Peter Ballbusch. Ref: TV. and with Frederic Worlock, Lawrence Grant.
Long, generally uninspired version. The length of both the film and of individual sequences has several effects: 1) It tends to blur Stevenson's main point re: the inseparability of Jekyll-and-Hyde, made here finally by Jekyll's repeating "I am Dr. Henry Jekyll" at the end, as he again becomes Hyde; generally, Jekyll and Hyde seem to be simply two different characters belonging to two different worlds. 2) It allows Spencer Tracy (Hyde) and Ingrid Bergman (Ivy) to amplify and deepen their characterizations--his, however, becomes a bit too dependent on an insinuating rasp; hers is a touching (if slightly overstated) combination of vulnerability, sensuousness,

defensiveness, and spunk. 3) Hyde's cruelty to Ivy is so lovingly detailed that it virtually becomes the film's (partly of course because Bergman makes it felt)....Waxman's score is surprisingly conventional.

DR. JEKYLL AND MR. HYDE NBC-TV/Timex 1973 color 76m. D: David Winters. SP: Sherman Yellen. Mus: Lionel Bart, Mel Mandel, Norman Sachs. Ref: V 3/14/73:46. 1/24/73:26: shown theatrically outside U.S. with Kirk Douglas(Jekyll/Hyde), Susan George, Susan Hampshire, Stanley Holloway, Donald Pleasence, Michael Redgrave, Judi Bowker.
A (gasp!) musical Jekyll and Hyde.

DR. JEKYLL AND MRS. HYDE see ABBOTT AND COSTELLO MEET DR. JEKYLL AND MR. HYDE

DR. JEKYLL AND SISTER HYDE (B) AI/Hammer-EMI 1971 color 97m. D: Roy Ward Baker. SP: Brian Clemens, from "The Strange Case of Dr.Jekyll and Mr.Hyde" by RLS. Ph: Norman Warwick. Mus: David Whitaker. PD: Robert Jones. Mkp: John Wilcox. Ref: screen. MFB'71:218. Lee. V 10/27/71. with Ralph Bates(Jekyll), Martine Beswick(Hyde), Ivor Dean(Burke), Tony Calvin(Hare), Gerald Sim, Lewis Fiander, Virginia Wetherell, Bobby Parr.
Dr. Jekyll (here, aka Jack the Ripper) transforms himself into a woman. Fully clever script makes the best of a patently ludicrous situation, smoothly interweaving as it does its Jekyll-and-Hyde, Burke-and-Hare, and Jack the Ripper plot strands, though it reduces at times to a tired Jekyll-Hyde duel (or dual). Nice bits with a cigar, wine, a clock, and a dirty old undertaker.

DOCTOR JEKYLL AND THE WOLFMAN (Sp) Filmaco/Gonzalez 1971('74-U.S.) color 96m. (DOCTOR JECKILL Y EL HOMBRE LOBO. DOCTOR JEKYLL AND THE WEREWOLF-B) D: Leon Klimovsky. SP: Jacinto Molina. Sequel to MARK OF THE WOLFMAN. Ph: F. Fraile. Mus: A.G. Abril. AD: J. Alguero. SpFX: A. Molina. Mkp: Miguel Sese. Ref: MFB'76:97,222. V 12/12/73:28(rated). Glut/CMM. with Paul Naschy(aka J.Molina)(werewolf), Shirley Corrigan, Jack Taylor, Luis Induni.

DR. JEKYLL ET LES FEMMES (F; Eng.-lang.) Whodunit-Allegro 1981 color (The STRANGE CASE OF DR. JECKYLL AND MISS OSBOURN-orig t) SP?,D: Walerian Borowczyk. Ref: V 5/13/81:305: from RLS. 5/20/81:54. 8/12/81:34. with Udo Kier, Patrick Magee, Marina Pierro.

DR. JEKYLL JR. (I) Koral-Medusa 1978 (Il DOTTORE JEKILL JR. JEKYLL JR.) D: Steno. Ref: V 10/18/78:164. 5/9/79:288. 9/20/78:10(ad). 5/11/77:226: MR.JEKYLL JR. with Paolo Villaggio, Edwige Fenech.

DR. JEKYLL'S DUNGEON OF DEATH Rochelle 1979 color 91m. Ref: Boxo 7/2/79:23. 12/31/79:30. V 3/21/79:34(rated). with James Mathers.

DR. MABUSE (Sp-W.G.) Copercines/Telecines 1972 color (El DR. MABUSE. Der DOKTOR MABUSE) SP,D: Jesus Franco. SP: also A. Bernd. Based on David Kuhne's novel and on the Harbou-Lang character. Ph: Manuel Merino. Mus: Daniel White. AD: Karl Mayerberg. Ref: V 5/3/72:175. Lee. with Fred Williams, Ewa Stromberg, Roberto Camardiel.

DOCTOR MANIAC (S.Afr.) Worldwide/Associated 1973('76-U.S.) color 87m. (HOUSE OF THE LIVING DEAD-orig t. SKADUWEES OOR BRUGPLAAS) D: Ray Austin. SP: Marc De V Marais. Story: John Brason. Ph: Lionel Friedberg. Mus: Peter Elliot. PD: Anita Friedberg. SpFX: Protea Holdings. Mkp: Irene Haselau. Ref: MFB'76:97-8. Meyers. V 11/17/76:12. 5/8/74:244. 2/7/73:27. Willis/SW. with Mark Burns, Shirley Anne Field, David Oxley.

"Gothic smorgasbord": curse on family; old witch; theory that the soul "can be extracted from the body"; cloaked murderer; black magic. (MFB)

DR. PHIBES RISES AGAIN (U.S.-B) AI 1972 color 88m. SP,D: Robert Fuest. SP: also Robert Blees. Sequel to The ABOMINABLE DR. PHIBES. Ph: Alex Thomson. Mus: John Gale. PD: Brian Eatwell. Mkp: Trevor Crole-Rees. Ref: screen. Lee. V 7/19/72. MFB'72:230. with Vincent Price, Robert Quarry, Valli Kemp, Hugh Griffith, Fiona Lewis, Peter Cushing, Beryl Reid, Gerald Sim, Terry-Thomas, Milton Reid.

Dr. Phibes (Price) astrologically revived; elixir of life. Stray bits of wit; tired lines and gags are rifer. Fairly satisfying climactic encounter between Price and Quarry.

*DR. RENAULT'S SECRET 1942 (BURIED ALIVE-orig t) Ref: TV. Lee. LC. V 10/21/42.

Poor mystery-horror movie. Crudely sentimental treatment of J. Carrol Naish's ape-man-monster. Dr. Renault (George Zucco): "So you've discovered my secret!" (See title.)

El DR. SATAN (Mex) Espada? 1967 D: Miguel Morayta. SP: J.M. F. Unsain. Ph: R.M. Solares. Mus: L.H. Breton. AD: J.R. Granada. Ref: Lee: sequel: DR.SATAN AND BLACK MAGIC. with Joaquin Cordero, Alma D. Fuentes, Jose Galvez, Carlos Agosti.

Voodoo, zombies, King Devil.

DR. SEXUAL AND MR. HYDE 1971 color 68m. SP,D,P: Anthony Brzezinski. Ref: Lee. with Cindy Hopkins.

Old doctor made young.

DR. SIN FANG (B) MGM-Victory 1937 60m. D: Tony Frenguelli. SP: N. Byass, F. Reynolds. Story: K. Mason. See also: CHINATOWN NIGHTS. Ref: BFC. with H. Agar Lyons, Anne Grey.

"Professor's formula for curing cancer."

DR. STRANGE CBS-TV/Univ-TV 1978 color 94m. SP,D,Exec P: Philip DeGuere. Based on the comic-book character. Ph: Enzo A. Martinelli. Mus: Paul Chihara. AD: W.S. Tuntke. VisFX Cons: Thomas J. Wright. SpFX: Van Der Veer. Ref: TV. TVG.

V 9/13/78:66. with Peter Hooten, Jessica Walter(Morgan le Fay, Queen of the Sorcerers), Eddie Benton, John Mills, David Hooks (The Nameless One), Clyde Kusatsu, Philip Sterling.

The Guardian of the Light vs. The Nameless One and the forces of evil; spirit possession; nightmare visions; invisible barriers; astral projection (a la the "Little Girl Lost" ep. of "Twilight Zone"); magic pool; psychic rays; Asmodeus; transmutation of power from Merlin/Lindmer the Magician (Mills) to Strange; ABBOTT AND COSTELLO MEET FRANKENSTEIN on TV. Far from the worst of the TV superhero movies. If the fantasy elements are fairly standard, they're also plentiful (see above), and The Nameless One makes a fairly imposing anti-superhero, even if he is more talk than action. (It's his delivery.) Dialogue is restricted to lines of the "We were speaking of evil this afternoon" variety.

DR. SYN(by R.Thorndike) see NIGHT CREATURES

DR. TARR'S TORTURE DUNGEON (Mex) Group 1/Prisma 1973('76-U.S.) color 88m. (La MANSION DE LA LOCURA. HOUSE OF MADNESS-B) SP,D: Juan Lopez Moctezuma. SP: also Carlos Illescas. From Poe's story "The System of Dr.Tarr and Professor Fether." Ph: Rafael Corkidi. Mus: Nacho Mendez. Ref: MFB'74:102. Willis/SW. V 1/26/77:12. 8/22/73. 3/17/76:27(rated). with Claudio Brook, Arthur Hansel, Ellen Sherman, David Silva. M. Lasalle.

Criminal incites patients to take over asylum; "forest haunted by weird apparitions." (MFB)

*DOCTOR X 1932 From the play by Comstock & Miller. Ph: R. Towers;(color version) R. Rennahan. Mus D: Leo F. Forbstein. AD: Anton Grot. MaskFX: Max Factor Co. Ref: TV. MFB'78:121.

"Cannibal" killings traced to mad doctor and his electrified, "living, manufactured" flesh, which provides him with synthetic hand and monster-face; phobia-detector which measures heartbeat reactions to reenactments of murders; doctors at Blackstone Shoals experimenting with keeping hearts alive, brain-grafting, moon rays; climax: madman set afire and flung over cliff; creepy butler; morgue scene. Not to mention some great shrieking-wind effects (alternating eerily between howling and whistling) and the lighting, which makes <u>everyone</u> look like the mad medico. No doubt about it, DOCTOR X is a <u>horror movie</u>, an A-for-effort, highly energetic, fun-bad movie. Director Michael Curtiz whips up set-piece excitement so "intense" that the movie verges on self-parody--his staging is so calculated and so melodramatically outrageous that it's campily ingratiating. Lionel Atwill ("Meddling <u>fools</u>!") dominates with his authoritative blustering, while Lee Tracy annoys with his wise-guy act.

DOCTOR X (India-Hindustani) Fine Art 1972 color 140m. D,P, Ph: B. Gupta. Dial: K. Sherif, D.R. Gupta. Mus: Sonik-Omi. Ref: Dharap. with Som Dutt, Farida Jalal, Helen, Sudhir.

Professor invents invisibility pill; his son uses it "to bring justice" to crooks who try to steal formula.

DOCTOR'S SECRET,The(by W.J.Makin) see RETURN OF DR. X

DOGS Riddell/Mar Vista-La Quinta 1976 color 90m. D: Burt Brinckerhoff. SP: O'Brian Tomalin. Ph: Bob Steadman. Mus: Alan Oldfield. Mkp: Alan Friedman. Opt: Consolidated. Ref: TV. MFB'79:94. FFacts. with David McCallum, George Wyner, Sandra McCabe, Lance Hool, Linda Gray, Russ Grieve, E. Server.
Calif. Domestic dogs band together, attack humans, for unexplained reasons. Puppy-level terror; doggedly unfunny humor. Lots of barks, no bite. The only tingly note: the nocturnal howling.

DOKTOR MABUSE, Der see DR. MABUSE(1972)

DOLCE COME MORIRE see PSYCHIC, The

*The DOLL UFA-PAGU 1919 60m. SP: Ernst Lubitsch, Hans Kraly, from the operetta by A.E. Wilner (from themes of E.T.A. Hoffmann). Ph: Theodor Sparkuhl. Sets: Kurt Richter. Ref: screen. Weinberg/TLT. and with Hermann Thimig, Jacob Tiedtke.
A doll-maker briefly brings a human-size, mechanical doll to life; "smiling" moon; scientist's hair darkening in seconds. Very inventive, high-spirited fantasy-comedy. Ossi Oswalda's odd predicament--she must impersonate a mechanical doll--proves a coup (visually and comically) for Lubitsch and Kraly. Her movements (as she switches tenses from human to doll and back) are alternately stylized and impromptu, which alternating current makes for some very funny transitions.

DOMINIQUE (B) (Showtime-TV)/Sword & Sorcery(Grand Prize) 1978 color 95m. D: Michael Anderson. SP: Edward & Valerie Abraham, from Harold Lawlor's story "What Beckoning Ghost." Ph: Ted Moore. Mus: David Whitaker. AD: David Minty. Mkp: Tom Smith. Ref: MFB'79:120. TV. with Cliff Robertson, Jean Simmons, Jenny Agutter, Simon Ward, Ron Moody, Judy Geeson, Flora Robson, David Tomlinson, Jack Warner, Michael Jayston.
Man who drove wife to suicide with "ghosts" and "voices" is himself haunted by "ghost" (actually woman in lifelike mask of his wife). Thin-to-nonexistent fake-ghost story. The "haunted" Robertson never confronts the "apparitions"; he always, conveniently, turns or walks away, allowing them to "de-materialize." Otherwise, no story, right? Actually, no story anyway.

DON'T ANSWER THE PHONE! Crown Int'l/Scorpion-Manson Int'l 1980 color 95m. (The HOLLYWOOD STRANGLER-orig t) SP,D,P: Robert Hammer. SP,P: also Michael Castle. From Michael Curtis' novel "Nightline." Ph: James Carter. Mus: Byron Allred. AD: Kathy Cahill. SpFX: Dick Albain. Mkp: Teresa Austin. Ref: MFB'80:190. ad. SFExam 4/12/80. SFC 4/17/80. V 4/16/80. with James Westmoreland, Flo Gerrish, Nicholas Worth, Ben Frank, Pamela Bryant.
Psychotic killer rapes, kills, and "performs unspeakable mutilations" on his victims. (SFE)

DON'T BE AFRAID OF THE DARK ABC-TV/Lorimar 1973 color 74m. D: John Newland. SP: Nigel McKeiad(sp?). Ph: Andrew Jackson. Mus: Billy Goldenberg. PhFX: Howard Anderson. Mkp: Mike Hancock. Ref: TV. TVFFSB. with Kim Darby, Jim Hutton, Barbara Anderson, William Demarest, Pedro Armendariz Jr., William Sylvester, Felix Silla(creature).

Young couple's inherited old house is inhabited by gnome-like creatures who want the wife to join them. They turn out to be busy little creatures, but not quite busy enough to take up <u>all</u> the slack of the plot. And they should have remained heard and not seen. Heard, they're eerie; seen, they're comedy.

DON'T GO IN THE HOUSE FVI/Turbine 1980 color 82m. SP,D: Joseph Ellison. SP,P: Ellen Hammill. SP: also J. Masefield. Ph: Oliver Wood. Mus: Richard Einhorn. AD: Sarah Wood. SpFX: (coord) Peter Kunz; Matt Vogel. SpFxMkp: Tom Brumberger. Ref: V 6/11/80. MFB'81:65. Bob Moore. with Dan Grimaldi, Robert Osth, Ruth Dardick.

Punished boy incinerates mother's body; becomes incinerator worker who lures women to their deaths; at end he imagines his victims come to life, kill him.

DON'T GO INTO THE WOODS AFM 1980 D,P: Jim Bryan. SP: Garth Eliasson. Ph: Henry Zinman. Mus: G. Klien. PD: S.K. James. Ref: V 10/15/80:13,145: "horror pic." with Buck Carradine, Mary Gail Artz, Ken Carter, James P. Hayden.

DON'T LOOK IN THE BASEMENT (Gold Key-TV)/Hallmark/Camera 2 1973 color 89m. D: S.F. Brownrigg. SP: Tim Pope. Ph: Robert Alcott. Mus: Robert Farrar. Ref: Aros. TVFFSB. Willis/SW. Bianco Index'74. Maltin/TVM. with Rosie Holotik, Ann McAdams.

Asylum inmates stage bloody revolt.

DON'T LOOK NOW (B-I) Para/Casey-Eldorado 1973 color/scope 110m. (A VENEZIA...UN DICEMBRE ROSSO SHOCKING) D: Nicolas Roeg. SP: Allan Scott, Chris Bryant, from Daphne du Maurier's story. Ph: Anthony Richmond. Mus: Pino Donaggio. AD: Giovanni Soccol. Mkp: C. del Brocco. Ref: MFB'73:205. screen. Bianco Index'73. pr. V 10/24/73. with Julie Christie, Donald Sutherland, Hilary Mason, Adelina Poerio(dwarf), Leopoldo Trieste, Clelia Matania, Massimo Serato.

"Grotesque, tiny old woman" proves to be the "Venetian Jack the Ripper" (MFB); psychic messages. A mystery-shocker in which the killer is revealed to be a hundred-year-old version of Little Red Riding Hood already has one strike against it. Strike two is the diffuse plot; strike three is Roeg's over-fancy direction. Audiences booed, and who could blame them?

DON'T OPEN THE DOOR see ORPHAN, The

DON'T OPEN THE WINDOW (Sp-I) Hallmark(AI)/Newport/Star-Flaminia 1974('76-U.S.) color 93m. (FIN DE SEMANA PARA LOS MUERTOS. The LIVING DEAD AT THE MANCHESTER MORGUE-B) D: Jorge Grau.

SP: S. Continenza, M. Coscia. Ph: F. Sempere. Mus: Giuliano Sorgini. PD: Carlo Leva. SpFX: Luciano Bird. SpPhFX: G. De Rossi. Ref: MFB'75:78. Murphy. Willis/SW. V 12/24/75:6(rated, as BREAKFAST AT THE MANCHESTER MORGUE). with Ray Lovelock, Christine Galbo, Arthur Kennedy, Aldo Massasso.

Crop-dusting machine causes insects to invade and revive the recently-deceased.

DON'T SAY DIE (B) Primrose/Hagan/X Productions 1950 90m. SP, D: Vivian Milroy. SP: also Dido Milroy. Ref: TVFFSB: ghost-infested Irish castle. BFC. with Constance Smith, Tony Quinn, Sandra Dorne, Kenneth Connor, Thomas Gallagher(gorilla).

DOOMSDAY CHRONICLES Gold Key-TV/Jerry Johnson 1979 color 94m. D: James Thornton. SP: Kenneth J. Morris, Xavier Reyes, John C. Purvis. Mus: Joel Goldsmith. Narr: William Schallert. Ref: TV. TVG.

Un-electrifying speculation on how and when (perhaps about 1999?) the world will end.

The DOOMSDAY MACHINE Bless Int'l/Cine-Fund 1973 color 80m. (ARMAGEDDON 1975-orig t. DOOMSDAY-int t) D: Lee Sholem, Harry Hope. SP: Stuart James Byrne. Ph: Stanley Cortez. AD: James E. Schwarm. SpVisFX: David L. Hewitt;(ph) William C. Davies; (lighting) Mike Nussman. Ref: TV. V 10/18/78. 7/31/74:24: at Trieste. 5/16/73:23(ad). 1/24/73:17(ad). Lee(p). with Bobby Van, Ruta Lee, Henry Wilcoxon, Mala Powers, James Craig, Mike Farrell, Grant Williams, Casey Kasem.

Red Chinese set off device which, through a nuclear chain reaction, destroys Earth; U.S., however, sends manned rocket off to Venus _just in time_! Budget-conscious sf.

DOOMWATCH (B) Avco Embassy/Tigon 1972('76-U.S.) color 92m. D: Peter Sasdy. SP: Clive Exton. From the TV show by Kit Pedler & Gerry Davis. Ph: Kenneth Talbot. Mus: John Scott. AD: Colin Grimes. Ref: Lee(MFB'72:70). TVFFSB. TVG. with Ian Bannen, Judy Geeson, John Paul, Simon Oates, George Sanders, Percy Herbert, George Woodbridge.

Radioactive waste creates "hormone in fish which causes acromegaly in humans." (Lee)

DOOR,The(by R.C.-Hayes) see FROM BEYOND THE GRAVE

DORAENON II (J) 1981 anim feature Ref: V 7/29/81:40: robot cat. 5/13/81:258: sfa or sequel to DORAEMON-NOBITA'S DINOSAUR (Toho, 1980)?

DOTTORE JEKILL JR. see DR. JEKYLL JR.

*DOUBLE DOOR 1934 From the play by E. McFadden; suggested by Hermine _Klepac_. Ref: TV. LC.

Woman locked inside soundproof room. Slow, heavy-handed shock-drama. Near the end of the movie, everyone talks more loudly, as if excitement were building or being built. (It isn't.) Only the climactic scene and a flashback (involving a corpse) approximate the spirit of fun-ghoulish Grand Guignol.

DOUBLE POSSESSION see GANJA AND HESS

DOUZE TRAVAUX D'ASTERIX,Les see TWELVE TASKS OF ASTERIX,The

*DRACULA 1931 Sequel: DRACULA'S DAUGHTER. See also: FADE TO BLACK. Ref: screen.

The first Bela Lugosi film vampire, though not the best. The silent scenes of mist and gliding vampires are today the best part of DRACULA. Lugosi's pop-eyed idea of "supernaturalness" is actually the worst of it. His slow-motion speaking and movement are too self-consciously "menacing," although a few of his later scenes with Edward Van Sloan (played at a more normal speed) fare rather well. Dwight Frye gives the best performance, as Renfield--his "mad," "guilty," and "supercilious" acts are all quite enjoyable. As for the others: Van Sloan's overripe readings become monotonous, and David Manners is hopeless; but Helen Chandler is good.

DRACULA (B-U.S.) CBS-TV/Latglen-Curtis 1974(1973) color 98m. (BRAM STOKER'S DRACULA-cr t) D,P: Dan Curtis. SP: Richard Matheson, from Stoker's novel. Ph: Oswald Morris. Mus: Robert Cobert. PD: Trevor Williams. SpFX: Kit West. Ref: TV. MFB'74:148. FM 161:81. Glut/TDB. with Jack Palance(Dracula), Simon Ward, Nigel Davenport(Van Helsing), Pamela Brown, Fiona Lewis, Penelope Horner, Virginia Wetherell, John Challis.

An English solicitor finds himself a prisoner in Dracula's castle in Hungary. A rival for COUNT DRACULA(1971) as the blandest film Dracula, this version trots out all the old scenes again--the nicked finger (here, a throat), the picture in the locket, the attack of the vampire women. Full of effectless zooms and "disembodied" dialogue (i.e., loosely synched words over long-shots of actors--it may as well be the trees talking).

DRACULA Universal/Mirisch 1979 color/scope 112m. D: John Badham. SP: W.D. Richter, from the play by Hamilton Deane & John Balderston & the book by Bram Stoker. Ph: Gilbert Taylor. Mus: John Williams. PD: Peter Murton. SpFX: Roy Arbogast. SpVisFX: Albert Whitlock. Mkp: Peter Robb-King. Models: Brian Smithies. Ref: screen. MFB'79:195. V 7/4/79. with Frank Langella, Laurence Olivier, Kate Nelligan, Donald Pleasence, Trevor Eve, Jan Francis.

Count Dracula moves into Carfax Abbey on England's Yorkshire coast. Two critical casting mistakes hobble this splashy new DRACULA: a) casting the callow Langella (he's a holdover from the stage version) as Dracula is like casting David Manners as the Count, and, b) Laurence Olivier's Van Helsing proves to be as mechanical as Edward Van Sloan's (in the Lugosi version) and Lionel Barrymore's Van Helsing-like Zelen in MARK OF THE VAMPIRE. (The great tradition...!) One wonders what the _young_ Olivier would have done with the role of _Dracula_. Langella is merely flip, one of the least impressive screen vampires since Jermon Robles. And much of the film is simply a reshuffling of old lines and plot elements, or bendings or breakings of standard film-vampire rules re: crosses, daylight, transformations. There are, however, some magnificent shots of castles and Cornwall, enough stunts for a _series_ of vampire movies, plus a rousing Williams score and a pleasingly outrageous climactic sequence. The latter attempts to top every destroying-the-vampire sequence that came before it, and probably succeeds--it's a dandy.

DRACULA(novel by Bram Stoker) see also the following titles, and ALUCARDA. ANDY WARHOL'S DRACULA. ATTACK OF THE PHANTOMS. BARRY McKENZIE HOLDS HIS OWN. BLACULA. BLOOD('74). CAV.COSTANTE NICOSIA DEMONIACO OVVERO DRACULA IN BRIANZA. CEMETERY GIRLS. CHARLOTS CHEZ DRACULA JUNIOR,Les. COUNT DRACULA(P). COUNT DRACULA AND HIS VAMPIRE BRIDE. DAUGHTER OF DRACULA. DEAFULA. DEVIL'S WEDDING NIGHT,The. DRAGON VS.DRACULA. EVERY HOME SHOULD HAVE ONE. EVIL OF DRACULA. EYE OF COUNT FLICKENSTEIN. FADE TO BLACK. FANG-DANGO,El. GO FOR A TAKE. HALLOWEEN WITH THE ADDAMS FAMILY. HERZOG FILMS NOSFERATU(P). HOLLYWOOD ON PARADE NO. 8. IN SEARCH OF DRACULA. INFERNAL TRIO. INVASION DE LOS MUERTOS. JAILBREAK,The. JEUX DE LA COMTESSE DOLINGEN. JOVENCITO DRACULA. KATHAVAI THATTEEYA MOHNI PAYE. LADY DRACULA. LAST RITES. LISZTOMANIA. LOVE AT FIRST BITE. MAD BAKER,The. MAD LOVE LIFE OF A HOT VAMPIRE. MAMMA DRACULA. MEN OF ACTION MEET WOMEN OF DRACULA. MUNSTERS' REVENGE,The. MYSTERY IN DRACULA'S CASTLE,The. NAKED WORLD OF HARRISON MARKS. NOSFERAT,Le(P). NOSFERATU. OLD DRACULA. PASSION OF DRACULA(P). PEPITO Y CHABELO.... POBRECITO DRACULA. REINCARNATION OF ISABEL,The. SANTO Y BLUE DEMON CONTRA DRACULA Y EL HOMBRE LOBO. SATURDAY SUPERSTAR MOVIE(P). SATURDAY THE 14TH. SCREAM BLACULA SCREAM. 7 BROTHERS MEET DRACULA,The. SNOOP SISTERS,The(P). SON OF DRACULA. SPERMULA. TENDER DRACULA. TIEMPOS DUROS PARA DRACULA. TRAIN RIDE TO HOLLYWOOD. TWINS OF EVIL. VAMPIRE DRACULA COMES TO KOBE. VAMPYRES. VLAD TEPES. WEB OF THE SPIDER. WINTER WITH DRACULA (P). WORST CRIME OF ALL,The!

DRACULA A.D. 1972 (U.S.-B) WB/Hammer 1972 color 95m. (DRACULA TODAY-orig t. DRACULA '72. DRACULA CHELSEA '72. DRACULA CHASES THE MINI GIRLS-all int ts) D: Alan Gibson. SP: Don Houghton. Ph: Dick Bush. Mus: Michael Vickers;(songs) Stoneground. PD: Don Mingaye. SpFX: Les Bowie. Mkp: Jill Carpenter. Ref: MFB'72:230-31. V 10/25/72. TV. Glut/TDB. with Christopher Lee(Dracula), Peter Cushing, Stephanie Beacham, Marsha Hunt, Caroline Munro, Christopher Neame(Johnny Alucard).

Dracula conjured up (through black magic) in the 20th Century; potential victim kept in trance; one vampire dispatched with sunlight and shower water; Dracula, with hastily-blessed water and wooden spade. More Hammer how-to tips on reviving and destroying vampires. Here, hip London begins sporting fangs. The new Van Helsing (the same old Cushing) characterizes the vampire as a phoenix, dying and forever being re-born.

But the script doesn't make much of its novel link between Van Helsing and Dracula--to wit, the former's daughter, Jessica (Beacham), ticketed as the latter's bride. And the flip, hip kids are all-too-easily blown away by the no-nonsense supernatural.

DRACULA AND SON (F) Quartet/Gaumont-2000 1976('79-U.S.) color 105m.(88m.) (DRACULA, PERE ET FILS. PERE ET FILS) SP,D: Eduard Molinaro. SP: also Jean-Marie Poire, Alain Godard. From the novel "Paris-Vampire" by Claude Klotz. Ph: Alain Levent. Mus: Vladimir Cosma. AD: Jacques Bufnoir. Ref: Boxo 7/2/79:23. V 5/30/79. 5/11/77:335,291. 10/27/76:48. 9/29/76. Bianco #1/78:152. with Christopher Lee(pere), Bernard Menez (fils), Marie-Helene Breillat, Raymond Bussieres, Anna Gael.
Ousted from Communist Transylvania, Count Dracula "becomes the Dracula of the movies" in England. (V)

DRACULA AND THE 7 GOLDEN VAMPIRES see 7 BROTHERS MEET DRACULA

DRACULA AND TOK (Thai) 1979 Ref: V 1/10/79: filming begun. with Krung Srivilai(Dracula), Lo Tok.

DRACULA CERCA SANGUE DI VERGINE see ANDY WARHOL'S DRACULA

DRACULA CHASES THE MINI GIRLS see DRACULA A.D. 1972

DRACULA CHELSEA '72 see DRACULA A.D. 1972

DRACULA CONTRA DEL DR. FRANKENSTEIN see DRACULA VS. DR. FRANKENSTEIN

DRACULA EXOTICA Entertainment Ventures 1981 color Ref: V 7/1/81:4(rated). High Society 5/81: "lesbian vampire twins." with Jamie Gillis(Dracula), Vanessa Del Rio(vampire), Samantha Fox, Eric Edwards.

DRACULA IM SCHLOSS DES SCHRECKENS see WEB OF THE SPIDER

DRACULA IN THE PROVINCES see CAV.COSTANTE NICOSIA...

DRACULA IS DEAD AND WELL AND LIVING IN LONDON see COUNT DRACULA AND HIS VAMPIRE BRIDE

DRACULA, PERE ET FILS see DRACULA AND SON

DRACULA PRISONNIER DU DOCTEUR FRANKENSTEIN see DRACULA VS. DR. FRANKENSTEIN

DRACULA SAGA (Sp) Brandon/Profilmes 1972 color 91m. (La SAGA DE LOS DRACULAS. The SAGA OF DRACULA-alt t) D: Leon Klimovsky. SP: Erika Zsell. Ph: Francisco Sanchez. Ref: Brandon. Lee. V 5/9/73:144. CineFan 2:25. with Tina Sainz, Tony Isbert, Narcisco Ibanez Menta(Dracula), Helga Line.
Dracula's granddaughter bears blood-sucking infant.

DRACULA '72 see DRACULA A.D. 1972

DRACULA SUCKS MR/First Int'l/Kodiak 1979 color 98m. D: Philip Marshak. SP: David J. Kern, Darryl Marshak; William Margold. Ph: Hanania Baer. Mus: Lionel Thomas. Sets & SpFX: Richard King. Ref: Boxo 11/12/79:14. 12/31/79:21. V 2/6/80:37. MFB '80:90. with Jamie Gillis(Dracula), Annette Haven, John Holmes, Serena, Kay Parker, Reggie Nalder, John Leslie, Seka.
Dracula amok in Dr. Seward's sanitarium/castle.

DRACULA TODAY see DRACULA A.D. 1972

DRACULA VS. DR. FRANKENSTEIN (Sp-F) Fenix/CFdF 1972 color 84m. (DRACULA CONTRA EL DR. FRANKENSTEIN. DRACULA PRISONNIER DU DOCTEUR FRANKENSTEIN. La MALDICION DE FRANKENSTEIN) SP,D: Jesus Franco. Ph: Jose Climent. Mus: Daniel White, Bruno Nicolai. Mkp: M. Adelaide, E. Villanueva. Ref: Lee. Glut/TDB. V 5/3/72:175. Daisne. V 5/9/73:137. 10/25/72: "seedy werewolf," vampire women. with Dennis Price(Dr.Frankenstein), Alberto Dalbes, Howard Vernon(Dracula), Fernando Bilbao(the monster), Britt Nichols, Jossiane Gibert(aka Anne Libert), Mary Francis.

DRACULA VUOLE VIVERE see ANDY WARHOL'S DRACULA

DRACULA Y LAS MELLIZAS see TWINS OF EVIL

DRACULA'S BRIDE Backstreet 1980 color/scope (The ORGIES OF DRACULA-orig t. The COMING OF DRACULA'S BRIDE-ad t) D: Bart Storm. SP: William Margold. Ref: V 10/15/80:182(ad). poster. Leonard Wolf. with Annette Haven, Serena, Seka, John Holmes, Jamie Gillis(Dracula), John Leslie, Margold.

*DRACULA'S DAUGHTER 1936 Adap: John L. Balderston. Sequel to DRACULA(1931). Mkp: Jack Pierce. Ref: TV. Lee. MPH 12/28/35: 105: orig.to star Lugosi & Jane Wyatt. NYT 3/1/36.
Campily compelling when Gloria Holden as Marya Zaleska and Irving Pichel as Sandor are on. As Dracula's daughter she longs for "normality"; wet-blanket Sandor, though, is the voice of reality--for Dracula's daughter at least. He insists that she's doomed to "something ghastly" (i.e., him?).

DRACULA'S DOG Crown Int'l/Vic 1977 color 88m. (ZOLTAN... HOUND OF DRACULA-B. ZOLTAN-orig t) D: Albert Band. SP: Frank Ray Perilli. Ph: Bruce Logan. Mus: Andrew Belling. Mkp: Stan Winston, Zoltan Elek. Ref: MFB'77:133. V 6/21/78. 12/15/76:27(ad). Nancy Goldman. with Michael Pataki(Dracula), Jan Shutan, Libbie Chase, Reggie Nalder, Jose Ferrer.
Resurrected "half-vampire" servant of Dracula attempts to make the last of the clan his new master; vampire-dog pack.

DRACULA'S GREAT LOVE see CEMETERY GIRLS

DRACULA'S LAST RITES see LAST RITES

DRACULA'S TRANSYLVANIA see IN SEARCH OF DRACULA

DRACULA'S VIRGIN LOVERS see CEMETERY GIRLS

DRACULA'S WEDDING DAY Film-makers' Coop 1967 silent tinted 5m. D: Mike Jacobson. Ref: Lee. no LC. F-mC cat.
Dracula and his bride.

*The DRAGON MURDER CASE 1934 Ref: screen. LC.
The Stamm family curse holds that the dragon of their "dragon pool" (or "the place of the water monster," as the Indians called it) carries its victims off to "a place older than history, when the world was made" (i.e., glacier-created pot holes); 3-toed-claw marks (made by clawed diver's-glove) leading up to pool's edge; "dragon's shadow" seen over pool; theory that Rudolph Stamm may be "breeding a new type of beast." Okay mystery, okay comedy, and nice stabs at horror. The killer's identity is, unfortunately, rather obvious.

DRAGON VS. DRACULA (H.K.?) L&T(Ark)/Great China Film Co 197-? ('80-U.S.) color/scope 90m. D,P: Ting Chung. SP: Wai Shing. Ref: screen. poster. with Chen Kwn Chwn, Lung Chun Ern.
Not a Dracula movie--there's not even one fleeting reference to Dracula within the film (the villain is "Golden Mask"), although many people are found mysteriously murdered, with blood on their cheeks. However, there *are* other fantasy elements: a giant "ghost" in a nightmare sequence; flying-fireball weapons; flying-leaping kung fu; flying "buzz-saw" discs. There's also the line "This man is known as Big Pang, and *she* is the Foxy Lady." Unsophisticated, and dull to boot.

DRAGONSLAYER (U.S.-B) Para-Buena Vista 1981 color/scope 108m. SP,D: Matthew Robbins. SP,P: Hal Barwood. Ph: Derek VanIint. Mus: Alex North. PD: Elliot Scott. SpMechFX: Brian Johnson. Anim Sup: Samuel Comstock. Min & OptFX: Dennis Muren. SpFX Tech: David Watkins et al. PhFX: Industrial Light & Magic. Dragon:(des) David Bunnett;(fx) Phil Tippett, Ken Ralston. Model Sup: Lorne Peterson. Magic Adv: Harold Taylor. Mkp: Graham Freeborn. SdFX: Andy Aaron. Ref: screen. V 6/24/81. with Peter MacNicol(Galen), Caitlin Clarke, Ralph Richardson (Ulrich), John Hallam, Albert Salmi, Peter Eyre.
Kingdom terrorized by dragon and its whelp; sorcerer Ulrich and his apprentice Galen; magic amulet; visions; sorcerer conjured up from his scattered ashes. Rather timid mythmongering, at least until the excitingly-orchestrated climactic confrontation between sorcerers and dragons. The main dragon seems, graphically, kin to bats and gargoyles, and the wee ones are disgustingly voracious. The mother has the most touching moment in the movie, inquisitively nudging her offspring's dead little carcass.

DRAKULITA (Fili) RJF 1969 D: Consuelo P. Osorio. Ref: Glut/TDB: "vampire comedy set in a haunted house." with Rossana Ortiz(vampire), Lito Legaspi.

DRAWS see AMERICAN TICKLER

DREAM WORLD OF HARRISON MARKS,The see NAKED WORLD OF HARRISON MARKS,The

DRESSED TO KILL Filmways/Arkoff-Cinema 77 1980 color/scope? 105m. SP,D: Brian De Palma. Ph: Ralf Bode. Mus: Pino Donaggio. PD: Gary Weist. SpMkp: Robert Laden. SdFX: Hastings. Opt: Opt.House. Ref: screen. V 7/23/80. MFB'80:213. with Michael Caine, Angie Dickinson, Nancy Allen, Keith Gordon.

Brutal murder with razor; nightmares and daydreams of violence. Slight mystery-shocker, with for-the-most-part juvenile characterizations, and punctuated by a superfluous coda, a CARRIE-over. Okay for a stretch as a mystery, until a giveaway line (something about the doctor's "last patient"). De Palma's narrative tricks (e.g., using schizophrenia as a red herring at one point to "eliminate" the killer as a suspect) seem an end in themselves, and his film simply a vehicle for such piddling cleverness.

The DRILLER KILLER Rochelle/Navaron 1979 color 90m. D: Abel Ferrara. SP: Nicholas St. John. Ph: Ken Kelsch. Mus: Joseph Delia. Ref: Boxo 8/6/79:20. V 7/4/79. with Jimmy Laine, Baybi Day, Carolyn Marz, Tony Coca-Cola & the Roosters.

Artist cracks under pressure, "takes a carpentry drill to his friends and...winos." (Boxo)

DRIPPING DEEP RED see DEEP RED

DRUMS OF THE JUNGLE or DRUMS OF THE NIGHT see OUANGA

The DUALITY OF MAN (B) Wrench 1910 10m. From Stevenson's "The Strange Case of Dr.Jekyll and Mr.Hyde." Ref: BFC.

"Horror. Doctor's potion makes him steal banknotes and kill fiancee's father."

DUCK DODGERS OF THE 24½ CENTURY WB 1953 anim color 7m. Ref: Lee(LC). Maltin/OMAM. TVG 11/20/80. TV. V 11/26/80:106.

TV sequel: "Duck Dodgers and the Return of the 24½ Century," 1980 (on NBC-TV's "Daffy Duck's Thanks-for-Giving Special").

DUEL ABC-TV/Univ-TV 1971 color 75m. D: Steven Spielberg. SP: Richard Matheson, from his short story. Ph: Jack A. Marta. Mus: Billy Goldenberg. AD: Robert S. Smith. Ref: screen. V 9/12/73:32. MFB'72:231. '73:41. with Dennis Weaver, Eddie Firestone, Jacqueline Scott, Lou Frizzell, Dale Van Sickel.

A salesman traveling home by car on a quiet highway finds himself besieged by a homicidal driver in a mechanical-monster of a truck. The early sequences of DUEL set up unsettling counterpoints between the folksy car-radio chatter on the sound track and the looming figure of the monster-truck; between the hum of the car's motor and the nasty grating of the truck's. Later, however, a conventional "pounding" musical score replaces the low-key talk and music of the radio, as

Spielberg, on his part, amplifies the visual "noise." He tries so hard that he turns what begins as a truly unnerving anecdote into a conventional audience "grabber"--it's not just the car that gets overheated. In a sense, Spielberg is almost too adept visually. He has so many good sub-ideas--about where to shoot from, when to cut from the car to the truck, when to use slow motion (e.g., for the "death" of the truck)--that he obscures Matheson's main idea. What is happening to Weaver is crazy, but Spielberg doesn't just let the craziness happen--he's as aggressive and unrelenting as the truck. A high-gear, but relatively-superficial psychological intensity informs the movie's later scenes. Its most notable feature may, finally, be the winning human punctuation--the comic irrelevancies of the bystanders, and Weaver's hopping-and-whooping type of hysterical relief whenever he thinks he has outfoxed the truck.

DUFFY MASCOT see MASCOT, The

DUNE ROLLERS(by J.Ditky) see CREMATORS, The

DUVIDHA see TWO FACES, The

...E TU VIVRAI NEL TERRORE! L'ALDILA' (I) Fulvia 1981 color 89m. (The BEYOND-ad t?) SP,D: Lucio Fulci. SP: also G. Mariuzzo, D. Sacchetti. Ph: Sergio Salvati. Mus: Fabio Frizzi. Sets: Massimo Lentini. Ref: V 7/1/81. 7/29/81:30 & 5/13/81:154: sfa HOUSE OUTSIDE THE CEMETERY, aka QUELLA VILLA ACCANTO AL CIMITERO? with Katherine MacColl, David Warbeck, Sarah Keller(ghost).

"Haunted hotel...built on 1 of the 7 gates of hell."

E VENNE L'ALBA...MA TINTA DIROSSO see WEB OF THE SPIDER

EARTH II ABC-TV/MGM-TV 1971 color 95m. D: Tom Gries. SP: W.R. Woodfield, Allan Balter. Ph: M. Hugo. Mus: Lalo Schifrin. AD: G.W. Davis, E. Carfagno. SpFX: J.M. Johnson, R. Ryder, A. Cruickshank, Howard Anderson Jr. Ref: Lee(LAT 11/29/71). MFB'73:75. with Gary Lockwood, Tony Franciosa, Mariette Hartley, Gary Merrill, Hari Rhodes, Lew Ayres.

Space station becomes independent country.

*EARTH VS.THE FLYING SAUCERS 1956 (INVASION OF THE FLYING SAUCERS-orig t) Mus D: M. Bakaleinikoff. AD: Paul Palmentola. SpFX: also Russ Kelley. Ref: screen. Lee.

The movie's pacing, effects, and music stir up excitement; the "B"-sounding leads and supporting players quell it--a familiar sf-movie pattern, and not without the charm of the familiar. "Natch" dept.: (military officer) "When a powerful and threatening force lands on our nation's doorstep, we don't meet it with tea and cookies!"

EARTHBOUND Taft Int'l. 1981 color 94m. D,P: James L. Conway. SP: Michael Fisher. Ref: V 2/4/81. with Burl Ives; Chris Connelly, Meredith MacRae, Marc Gilpin(aliens); Joseph Campanella, John Schuck.
Alien family on Earth; invisibility; "space window."

EARTHQUAKE Univ 1974 color/scope/Sensurround 123m. (EARTHQUAKE 1980-orig t) D,P: Mark Robson. SP: George Fox, Mario Puzo. Ph: Philip Lathrop. Mus: John Williams. PD: Alexander Golitzen. SpPhFX: Albert Whitlock. SpFX: Frank Brendel, Jack McMasters. SpPh: Clifford Stine. Ref: MFB'75:7. V 11/13/74. with Charlton Heston, Ava Gardner, George Kennedy, Lorne Greene, Genevieve Bujold, Richard Roundtree, Marjoe Gortner, Lloyd Nolan, Barry Sullivan, Walter Matthau, Gabriel Dell.
Los Angeles razed.

EARTHQUAKE 7.9 (J) Toho 1980 (JISSHIN RETTO) SP: Kaneto Shindo. Mus: T. Tsubushima. SpFX: T. Nakano. Ref: JFFJ 13: 34. V 5/13/81:258,260(ad). with Yumi Takigawa.
Tokyo levelled.

EATEN ALIVE see DEATH TRAP

The ECHO (India-Hindi) Sangam 1974 color 136m. (GOONJ) SP, D: S.U. Sayed. Ph: V. Keshav. Mus: R.D. Burman. Ref: Dharap. with M. Sandhu, Reena Roy.
Mystery; fake ghost.

ECHO OF TERROR see FIEND WITH THE ELECTRONIC BRAIN

ECOLOGY OF A CRIME see TWITCH OF THE DEATH NERVE

ECOUTE VOIR... (F) Prospectacle 1978 color 125m. SP,D: Hugo Santiago. SP: also Claude Ollier. Ph: R. Aronovich. Ref: V 10/25/78. with Catherine Deneuve, Sami Frey, Florence Delay.
"Radiobeam" invention reduces people to automatons, influences their subconscious.

EDGAR ALLAN POE SPECIAL,The see EVENING OF EDGAR ALLAN POE,An

EDGAR ALLAN POE'S THE CONQUEROR WORM see CONQUEROR WORM,The

EDGAR POE CHEZ LES MORTS-VIVANTS see WEB OF THE SPIDER

EDICT see Z.P.G.

The EERIE MIDNIGHT HORROR SHOW (I) 21st Century/Tiberia 1974 ('78-U.S.) color 87m. (L'OSSESSA. The OBSESSED-ad t? The SEXORCIST-B) Story,D: Mario Gariazzo. SP: Ambrogio Molteni. Ph: Carlo Carlini. Mus: Marcello Giombini. AD: Ovidio Taito. SpFX: Paolo Ricci. Ref: MFB'77:49. V 7/17/74:26. Bianco Index'74: 1973? Boxo 2/4/80:23. Willis/SW: '78 release as The TORMENTED. with Stella Carnacina, Chris Avram, Lucretia Love,

Luigi Pistilli, Gabriele Tinti.
"Barabbas/Satan incubus"; statue that comes to life; possessed girl. (MFB)

EFFECTS Int'l.Harmony/The Image Works 1979 color 87m. SP,D: Dusty Nelson. From a novel by W.H. Mooney. Ph: C. Augenstein. AD: Ellen Hopkins. SpFX: Tom Savini. Ref: V 10/19/79: "gory, salacious." Cinef X:1:12. with John Harrison, Susan Chapek.
Cast and crew of low-budget horror movie discover that their director is really making "a film-about-a-film in which the deaths are for real...." (V)

*EGGHEAD'S ROBOT 1971 Sequel: The TROUBLESOME DOUBLE. AD: Peter Mullins. Ref: Lee.

ELECTRIC ESKIMO (B) CFF/Monument 1979 color 57m. D,Co-Sp,P: Frank Godwin. Ph: Ray Orton. Mus: Harry Robinson. AD: Mike Pickwoad. Ref: MFB'79:95. with Derek Francis, Diana King.
North Pole's electro-magnetic force electrifies Eskimo boy, gives him super-powers.

ELECTRIC TRANSFORMATIONS (B) Clarendon 1909 7m. D: Percy Stow. Ref: BFC: "professor's invention melts metal and people's faces."

ELEMENTAL,The(by R.C.-Hayes) see FROM BEYOND THE GRAVE

The ELEPHANT MAN (U.S.-B) Para/Brooksfilms 1980 scope 125m. SP,D: David Lynch. SP: also Christopher DeVore, Eric Bergren, from the books "The Elephant Man and Other Reminiscences" by Sir Frederick Treves and "The Elephant Man: A Study in Human Dignity" by Ashley Montagu. Ph: Freddie Francis. Mus: John Morris. PD: Stuart Craig. SpMkp:(des) Christopher Tucker; (exec) Wally Schneiderman. SpFX: Graham Longhurst. SpSdFX: Alan Splet, Lynch. Ref: screen. MFB'80:192: U.S.-made. V 10/1/80: British. with John Hurt(John Merrick, the Elephant Man), Anthony Hopkins, Anne Bancroft, John Gielgud, Wendy Hiller, Freddie Jones, Michael Elphick, Kenny Baker.
London, 1884. Treves, a surgeon, takes responsibility for transferring the horribly deformed John Merrick from a freak show to the London Hospital. As drama, The ELEPHANT MAN is surprisingly conventional--it provides lullingly regular doses of shock and pathos, and the script effects an over-neat "role reversal" between Merrick and his tormentors. (Treves even at one point accuses one of the chief exploiters-of-deformity: "<u>You're</u> the monster!") And the ambiguousness of Treves' position (as protector-<u>and</u>-exploiter) is in one scene reduced to his fretting, "Am I <u>a</u> good man or a bad man?" But if the film is fairly elementary as drama, the makeup and performance of Hurt as Merrick make his scenes discomfortingly effective as spectacle: the tensions between the viewer and Merrick's presence are not as readily classifiable as the tensions between Merrick and the other characters. Like Jean Marais' pre-transformation beast in BEAUTY AND THE BEAST(1946),

Merrick is both monster and man and does not dissolve away into simply one or the other. He puts the viewer's mind and eyes at war with each other. He's a unique, disturbing creation, or re-creation, though he also clearly belongs to the tradition of the "sympathetic monster"--that of Karloff's Frankenstein monster, Chaney's and Laughton's hunchbacks, Marais' beast.

Die ELIXIERE DES TEUFELS (W.G.) LW/Roxy-Divina 1977 color 113m. SP,D: Manfred Purzer. From the book by E.T.A. Hoffmann. Ph: C. Steinberger. Mus: Hans-Martin Majewski. Sets: Peter Rothe. Ref: V 7/27/77. with Dieter Laser, Sylvia Manas.
Magic elixir, Doppelganger, flagellations, murders.

ELLE CAUSE PLUS ELLE FLINGUE (F) La Boetie 1972 color 90m. SP,D: Michel Audiard. SP: also Jean-Marie Poire. Ph: Pierre Petit. Mus: Eddy Vartan. Ref: V 9/20/72. with Annie Girardot, Bernard Blier, Jean Carmet, Darry Cowl, Michel Galabru.
"Weird machine" that reduces people to "bone relics"; man with "occult powers."

EMANUELLE E FRANCOISE LE SORELLINE (I) Matra 1976 color 96m. (FRANCOISE AND EMMANUELLE-THE LITTLE SISTERS-ad t) SP,D,Ph: Aristide Massaccesi(aka Joe D'Amato). SP: also B. Mattei. TechFX: Camera Film Service. Ref: MFB'77:232. V 5/12/76:208. Bianco Index'76:24. with Luigi Mirafiore(aka George Eastman), Rose Mary Lindt, Patricia Gori, Karole A. Edel.
Hallucinations; torture; murder with meat axe; man "incarcerated forever behind a soundproof wall." (MFB)

EMBRYO Cine Artists/Plura(Howard) 1976 color 108m. D: Ralph Nelson. SP: Anita Doohan, Jack W. Thomas. Ph: Fred Koenekamp. Mus: Gil Melle. AD: Joe Alves Jr. SpFX: Roy Arbogast. Sp Mkp: Dan Striepeke, John Chambers et al. SdFX: Neiman-Tillar. Ref: TV. V 5/26/76. with Rock Hudson, Diane Ladd, Barbara Carrera(Victoria), Roddy McDowall, Ann Schedeen, Jack Colvin, Dr. Joyce Brothers, George Sawaya.
In 10 days, a scientist "grows" a woman from a fetus taken from the womb of a suicide and injected with a growth hormone called placental lactogen; ultimately, she must resort to murder to obtain the antidote to her accelerated aging. Or, Frankenstein meets Countess Dracula, as Hudson "plays God" and Carrera desperately fights advancing age. She lacks social or moral inhibitions and is exclusively book-and-tape taught. (Hence the one amusing sequence in which she, a neophyte player, humiliates chess-master McDowall.) A whiz kid--Charly II--she's a lesson that "there are some things you can't get out of books." You won't get them out of this cut-and-paste movie either, which is at best a vehicle for Carrera and (briefly) McDowall.

EMOTION (J) Brandon 197-? 40m. D: Nobuhiko Ohbayashi. Ref: Brandon
"Dracula-like lover....The vampirism dominating the final portion...refers to Vadim's...BLOOD AND ROSES."

EMPIRE OF PASSION (F-J) BCR/Argos-Oshima 1978 color 105m. (L'EMPIRE DE LA PASSION. AI NO BOREI. PHANTOM LOVE-ad t) SP,D: Nagisa Oshima. From N. Itoko's biography of N. Takashi. Ph: Yoshio Miyajima. Mus: Toru Takemitsu. AD: Jusho Toda. Ref: screen. MFB'79:23. HKFFest. V 5/9/79:381. 5/24/78. with Kazuko Yoshiyuki, Tatsuya Fuji, Takahiro Tamura.

Two lovers are haunted by the ghost of the woman's husband, whom they murdered. Some tingly "ghostly manifestations," but the script seems uncertain as to whether it wants to be a ghost story of retribution, a tale of *amour fou*, or "The Postman Always Rings Twice." The film has persuasive moments in all three modes, but seems to repeat rather than develop its thematic points.

EMPIRE OF THE ANTS AI/Cinema 77 1977 color 89m. Story,D,P, SpVisFX: Bert I. Gordon. SP: Jack Turley, from H.G. Wells' story. Ph: Reginald Morris. Mus: Dana Kaproff. PD: Charles Rosen. MinDes: Erik von Buelow. SpFX: Roy Downey. SpMkp: Ellis Burman. SdFX: Angel. VisFxAsst: Burt Harris Jr. Narr: Marvin Miller. Ref: MFB'78:64-5. TV. V(d) 7/1/77. with Joan Collins, Robert Lansing, John David Carson, Albert Salmi, Tom Fadden, Jacqueline Scott.

Radioactive waste proves responsible for giant ants attacking, attempting to control humans. Another B.I.G. movie with big animals ("Dozens of giant ants!") and even a Big Wheel (which *sounds* like a giant ant). Gordon was nurtured on THEM! and its ilk, and more recently seems to have been exposed to slow motion and INVASION OF THE BODY SNATCHERS. The giants still don't seem--visually or dramatically--to "belong," except for the queen ant, who is staffing an office in a sugar refinery and dispensing whiffs of her hypnotic gas to humans, who become her slaves. (Surrealists, please note.) The other ants just mill around, like effects "grafts" (from perhaps a documentary on ant farms) that, cinematically, don't "take."

The EMPIRE STRIKES BACK Fox/Lucasfilm 1980 color/scope 124m. D: Irvin Kershner. SP: Leigh Brackett, Lawrence Kasdan. Story & Exec P: George Lucas. Sequel to STAR WARS. Ph: Peter Suschitzky. Mus: John Williams. PD: Norman Reynolds. SpMkp: (des) Stuart Freeborn;(Yoda) Wendy Midener;(art) Graham Freeborn. SpVisFX: Brian Johnson, Richard Edlund. Stopmo Anim: Jon Berg, Phil Tippett. Anim & Roto: Peter Kuran. FxPh: Dennis Muren. Mattes: Harrison Ellenshaw. OptFX: Van Der Veer, Ray Mercer et al. MechFxSup: Nick Allder. SdDes: Ben Burtt. SpProjects: Gary Platek. ConcepArt: Ralph McQuarrie. Chief Model Maker: Lorne Peterson. Ref: screen. V 5/14/80. MFB'80: 129-30. with Mark Hamill, Harrison Ford, Billy Dee Williams, Carrie Fisher, David Prowse(Darth Vader; voice: James Earl Jones), Anthony Daniels(C-3PO), Peter Mayhew(Chewbacca), Kenny Baker(R2-D2), Frank Oz(Yoda master), Alec Guinness, Clive Revill, Julian Glover, Des Webb(snow creature).

STAR WARS, episode V. Luke Skywalker (Hamill) confronts his father, Darth Vader, an exponent of the dark side of the Force; ice planet Hoth; Empire probe-droids; imperial Walkers, machine-weapons; gigantic dinosaur-like monster; bog monster; asteroid field; laser swords; suspended animation. Outside, the kids line up again ("I've seen it so many times I don't know _how_ many times I've seen it"); inside, onscreen, the menagerie grows: this time there are monsters and machines that look like kangaroos, ostriches, airborne jellyfish, camels (the Walkers), and even koalas (Yoda). And this time Yoda, not Darth Vader, is the most unintelligible speaker (not counting of course R2-D2). (Yoda seems better seen than heard anyway.) Luke is again a mythic cipher--the themes of the Force and the education of heroes are not so much incarnated in him as floated _by_ him--while Han (Ford) and C-3PO emerge as the most engaging characters. (Was it Brackett who gave the former all the good (non-android) lines?) The first half of the movie contains most of the monsters and is livelier than the Luke-learns-more-and-more (more even than he cares to) second half, in which he begins to seem like, simply, a space in the screen which was reserved for some never-finished special effects.

EMPTY SEA (Norw.) Arctandria-Norsk 1979 (START HAV) SP,D: David Wingate. SP: also Nils Utsi, Magnar Mikkelsen, from the latter's novel. Ph: Agneta Ekman. Ref: IFG'80:249. with Utsi, Roald Kristiansen, Anne Gullestad.

"Northern Norway in the near future, when a multinational company has drained the sea...."

EN UN BATURRO TRES BURROS(by A.A. Gandolin) see FANTASMA DE MEDIANOCHE

The ENCHANTED CUP (B) Paul 1902 5m. D: W.R. Booth. Ref: BFC.

"Peasant uses magic cup and gorgon's head to save sweetheart from being burned by dwarfs."

ENCOUNTER OF THE SPOOKY KIND (H.K.) Golden Harvest/Bo Ho 1981 color 100m. SP,D: Samo Hung. SP: also Huang Ying. Ph: Ng Chowah, Lee Yau-tong. Mus: Chan Fun-kay. Ref: V 2/25/81. with Hung, Chung Fa, Chan Lung.

"Voodoo, black magic...death curse....kung fu theme with a funny horror twist."

ENCOUNTER WITH THE UNKNOWN (Gold Key-TV)/Libert/Centronics Int'l 1972 color 87m. D: Harry Thomason. Narr: Rod Serling. Ref: TVFFSB. Willis/SW. TVG. V 12/13/72:14. with Rosie Holotick, Gene Ross, Annabelle Weenick.

Three tales: 1) "death prophecy," 2) "mysterious 'deep hole'," 3) "chillingly beautiful ghost."

END OF THE WORLD Manson Int'l/Yablans/Band 1977 color 86m. D & Ed: John Hayes. SP: Frank Ray Perilli. Ph: John Huneck. Mus: Andrew Belling. PD: Serge Krizman. SpVideoFX: Sunrise Canyon. SpFX: Harry Woolman. Ref: MFB'79:24. V 10/19/77:12 (ad). with Christopher Lee(alien), Sue Lyon, Kirk Scott, Dean Jagger, L. Ayres, Macdonald Carey.

"Invaders from a utopian planet" plot to destroy a polluted Earth; "time-warp machine." (MFB)

ENDLESS NIGHT (B) NFTC-British Lion-EMI 1971 color 99m. (aka AGATHA CHRISTIE'S ENDLESS NIGHT) SP,D: Sidney Gilliat. From Christie's novel. Ph: Harry Waxman; R. Maasz. Mus: Bernard Herrmann. PD: Wilfrid Shingleton. Ref: Maltin/TVM. MFB'72:209. with Hayley Mills, Hywel Bennett, Britt Ekland, George Sanders, Per Oscarsson, Lois Maxwell, Leo Genn.
Deranged killer; woman (Patience Collier) paid to "haunt" rich young woman to death.

ENSAYO DE UN CRIMEN see CRIMINAL LIFE OF ARCHIBALDO DE LA CRUZ

ENTER THE DEVIL (Gold Key-TV)/Artists Int'l/Chisos 1971 color 86m. (DISCIPLES OF DEATH-orig t) SP,D: F.Q. Dobbs, David Cass. Ph: M.F. Cusack. Mus: Sam Douglas. SpFX: Jack Bennett. Ref: TV. TVFFSB. Lee(p). Willis/SW. V 5/8/74:256(ad). with Irene Kelly, Josh Bryant, Cass, Carle Benson, Linda Rascoe.
Anthropologist (Kelly) investigating "weird cults" in Texas desert comes across one; snake pit; human sacrifice. Not especially bad, but pretty dull. Most of the cast turn out to be members of the Disciples of Death. Desert setting the main plus; schlocky score the main minus.

EOLOMEA (E.G.) Defa 1973 color 90m. SP,D: Hermann Zschoche. Ph: Gunther Jaeuthe. Mus: Gunter Fischer. Ref: V 8/1/73: at Trieste; future space exploration. IFG. with W.W. Sanajew, Cox Habbens.

ERASERHEAD Libra/AFI 1977 90m. SP,D,P,PD,SpFX,SdFX & Ed: David Lynch. Ph & SpFxPh: Frederick Elmes. Ph: also Herbert Cardwell. SdFX: also Alan R. Splet. Ref: screen. MFB'79:44. V(d) 3/15/77. with Jack Nance, Charlotte Stewart, Jeanne Bates, Laurel Near.
Mutant baby (who looks like a skinned-alive fish-creature) gets on father's nerves; infanticide; nightmares re: mini-mutants; stopmo squiggle; man-made chickens which, baked, ooze. A monster-movie, or at least a monster, in the tradition of FIEND WITHOUT A FACE and ALIEN. Only the context is different--here, the horror is domestic and helpless, but still truly grotesque (and alarmingly lifelike). And it expires even more disgustingly than do the FIEND critters. On a (slightly) more serious level, the film seems to be about an ugly, imperfect life in search of a beautiful afterlife--if it's intermittently quite droll, it's also too diffuse for its own good. It's a monster-show with aspirations, but winds up simply a monster-show--ALIEN with laughs.

ERDGEIST(by F.Wedekind) see LULU

EROD,Az see FORTRESS,The

EROTIC ADVENTURES OF SIEGFRIED see LONG,SWIFT SWORD OF SIEGFRIED

EROTIC DR. JECKYL A.B.Ent./Webster 1976 color (The AMAZING DR.JEKYLL-alt t) D: T. McCoy. Ref: V 5/11/77:185(ad). Glut/ CMM: aka The INCREDIBLE DR.JEKYLL. Willis/SW. with Harry Reems, C.J. Laing, Bobby Astyr, Terri Hall, Susan Sparkle, Zebedy Colt.

EROTIC WITCHCRAFT see GOULVE, La

ERSCHEINUNGEN(by E.von Daniken) see MYSTERIES OF THE GODS

ESCALOFRIO DIABOLICO (Sp) 1971 color 90m. SP,D,P: George Martin. SP: also D. Ceballos. Ph: A. Nieva. Mus: Jose Espeitia. Ref: Lee(V 10/27/71). with Martin, Patty Shepard, Vidal Molina, Silvana Sandovel.

Devil worship, castle.

ESCAPE FROM BROADMOOR (B) IMP 1948 37m. SP,D: John Gilling. Ref: BFC. with John Stuart, Victoria Hopper, John le Mesurier.

"Murdered girl's ghost seeks vengeance on madman."

ESCAPE FROM NEW YORK Avco Embassy/City Film 1981 color/scope 99m. SP,D,Mus: John Carpenter. SP: also Nick Castle. Ph: Dean Cundey. Mus: also Alan Howarth; Debussy. PD: Joe Alves. SpFX:(sup) Roy Arbogast; (asst) Gary Zink. SpVisFX: New World/ Venice. Roto: Steve Elliott. MkpSup: Ken Chase. Opt: Pacific. GraphDes: Arthur Gelb. Ref: screen. V 6/17/81. with Kurt Russell, Lee Van Cleef, Ernest Borgnine, Donald Pleasence, Isaac Hayes, Season Hubley, Harry Dean Stanton, Adrienne Barbeau, Charles Cyphers.

New York City, 1997. Manhattan is a no-way-out maximum-security prison for the U.S.; literal human-time-bomb; President kidnapped; character ref. to BRIDE OF FRANKENSTEIN. A future vision of Manhattan as a nightmarish battleground-junkyard. Visually, that is, this qualifies as a vision; dramatically, it's vacant, yet another hollow suspense-vehicle. (The main motif is a wristwatch ticking away both the world's and the hero's fates.) In sum: great sets; no characters, only juvenile ideas of toughness and heroism. Comically and existentially a shell. (DARK STAR, it appears now, was the whole nut.) Only Stanton provides more than atmosphere.

ESCAPE TO WITCH MOUNTAIN BV 1975 color 97m. D: John Hough. SP: Robert M. Young, from Alexander Key's book. Ph: Frank Phillips. Mus: Johnny Mandel. AD: Mansbridge, Al Roelofs. SpFX: Cruickshank, Lee. Ref: MFB'75:105. TV. V 3/19/75. with Eddie Albert, Ray Milland, Donald Pleasence, Kim Richards, Ike Eisenmann, Denver Pyle, Dan Seymour(psychic), George Chandler.

Kids with psycho-kinetic powers prove to be from dying planet in another solar system; psychic "flashbacks." Bland story, periodically enlivened by the clever uses to which the kids put their powers, in order to baffle enemies (e.g., attack dogs psychically flummoxed, sicked on their pursuers). Sequel: RETURN FROM WITCH MOUNTAIN. See also: PEOPLE,The.

Un ESCARGOT DANS LA TETE (F) Link 1980 color 90m. SP,D: Jean-Etienne Siry. Ph: Francois About. AD: K. Doan, P. Mercier.

Ref: V 11/19/80. with Florence Giorgetti, Renaud Verley. Unbalanced artist assailed mentally, then physically, by snails.

ESCARLATA (Fili) 1969 D: Fely Crisostomo. SP: J.F. Sibal. Story: R.B. Omagap. Mus: Danny Holmsen. Ref: Lee. with A. Fuentes, Max Alvarado, Bella Flores.
Servant possessed by spirit of woman in portrait.

ESORCICCIO,L' see EXORCIST:ITALIAN STYLE,The

ESORCISTA NO.2,L' see NAKED EXORCISM

ESPANTO SURGE DE LA TUMBA,La see HORROR RISES FROM THE TOMB

ESPECTRO (Sp) Minguet 1977 D: Manuel Esteba(or Estevaz). Ref: V 5/17/78:389. 10/26/77:28: at Sitges. 6/15/77:44: "sci-fi." with Eduardo Fajardo, Daniel Martin, Julian Ugarte, Inka Maria.

El ESPECTRO DEL TERROR (Sp) Film Int'l. 1972 D: J.M. Elorrieta. Ref: V 5/9/73:137. 9/20/72:6: at Sitges. with Aramis Baglivi, Sancho Garcia.

ESPIRITU DE LA COLMENA see SPIRIT OF THE BEEHIVE

ESPY (J) Toho Eizo 1974 color 94m. D: Jun Fukuda. SP: H. Ogawa. Story: S. Komatsu. Ph: S. Ueda. Mus: Masaaki Hirao. AD: Shinobu Muraki. SpFX: Akinori Nakano. Ref: Bianco Index '76:25. V 10/22/75:115. 2/5/75. with Hiroshi Fujioka, Kaoru Yumi, Masao Kusakari, Yuzo Kayama.
Top-secret organization of ESP-blessed people.

ETRUSCAN KILLS AGAIN,The or ETRUSCO UCCIDI ANCORA,L' see DEAD ARE ALIVE,The

An EVENING OF EDGAR ALLAN POE AI-TV & Brandon 1971 color 52m. (The EDGAR ALLAN POE SPECIAL-alt t) D: Ken Johnson. Based on Poe's stories "The Tell-Tale Heart," "The Cask of Amontillado," "The Sphinx," and "The Pit and the Pendulum." Ref: TVFFSB. Brandon. with Vincent Price.

EVERY HOME SHOULD HAVE ONE (B) Example 1970 color 94m. (MARTY FELDMAN, VAMPIRE!-alt t?) D: Jim Clark. SP: Marty Feldman, B. Took, D. Norden. Ph: Ken Hodges. Mus: John Cameron. Ref: Lee(MFB'70:72-3). BFC. Murphy. with Feldman, Shelley Berman, Julie Ege, Judy Huxtable, Judy Cornwell.
Frankenstein movie on TV--hero imagines himself as Dracula battling the Monster.

EVERY SPARROW MUST FALL DCA/Jay Gee 1964 color 82m. D: Ronald R. Budsan. Mus: J.A. Kroculick. Ref: AFI. LC. with Robert Shea, Frank Salmonese.
Engineer invents "machine to eliminate humanity." (AFI)

EVERYBODY AND A CHICKEN Brandon 1979? anim 5m. D: Frank Gardner. Ref: Brandon: robot.

EVERYTHING HAPPENS TO ME (I) Leone 1980 Ref: V 5/13/81:160: sequel to The SHERIFF AND THE SATELLITE KID. with Bud Spencer, Cary Guffey.

EVERYTHING YOU ALWAYS WANTED TO KNOW ABOUT SEX (BUT WERE AFRAID TO ASK) UA/Rollins-Joffe 1972 color 87m. SP,D: Woody Allen. From the book by David Reuben. Ph: D.M. Walsh. Mus: Mundell Lowe. PD: Dale Hennesy. Ref: Lee. MFB'73:8-9. V 8/9/72. with Allen, John Carradine, Louise Lasser, Gene Wilder, Tony Randall, Burt Reynolds, Lynn Redgrave et al.

Two of seven sequences: monster-breast ravages countryside; parody of FANTASTIC VOYAGE.

The EVICTORS AI/Pierce 1979 color/scope 92m. SP,D,P: Charles B. Pierce. SP: also G. Rusoff, P. Fisk. Ph: Chuck Bryant. Mus: Jaime Mendoza-Nava. AD: John Ball. SpFX: Jack Bennett. Mkp: Tom Dickey. Opt: Jack Rabin. Ref: V 4/18/79. AMPAS. MFB'80:91. with Michael Parks, Jessica Harper, Vic Morrow, Sue Ann Langdon, Bill Thurman, Dennis Fimple.

"Centerpiece is an old house with a horrid history....Weak title won't help attract even the limited axe-murder fans the pic might appeal to." (V)

The EVIL New World/Rangoon 1978 color 89m. (CRY DEMON-orig t) D: Gus Trikonis. SP: Donald G. Thompson. Ph: Mario Di Leo. Mus: Johnny Harris. AD: Peter Jamison. SpFX: Hollywood Mobile Systems. ProsthMkp: Jack Young. Opt: Jack Rabin. Ref: TV. V 3/29/78. with Richard Crenna, Joanna Pettet, Andrew Prine, Victor Buono, Galen Thompson(ghost), Milton Selzer.

Old mansion in the "Valley of the Devils" haunted by ghost and by Satan (whom the former has trapped in the sulphur pits below the cellar); demonically-possessed dog, corpse; spirit possession; invisible force field. The Devil is a too-familiar (and thus reassuring) face (Buono); the eeriest presence is actually that of the helpful, non-threatening ghost. Thin skepticism-vs.-belief narrative frame. Silly albeit lively, with the standard ghost-story dialogue.

The EVIL EYE (Belg., with Flemish dial., F.titles) 1937 75m. (Het KWADE OOG. Le MAUVAIS OEIL) D: Charles Dekeukeleire. SP: Herman Teirlinck. Ph: Francois Rents. Mus: Marcel Poot. Ref: screen. PFA notes 5/14/80.

Man first glimpsed in burning windmill on the Flemish countryside believed to be "the evil eye"--a wizard, demon, or ghost. At the end he tells a villager that he and his beloved (a local girl) committed double suicide; that they became vampires (close shot here of sharp teeth and gushing blood). Intoxicating shots of clouds, buildings, trees, fields; absurd "narrative." The climactic, semi-experimental montage is a tour de force of something, but of what exactly is hard to say--*amour fou* perhaps, or *nature fou*. Nice time-lapse photography.

EVIL EYE see SUPERBEAST

The EVIL OF DRACULA (J) Toho 1975 Sequel to *DRACULA'S LUST FOR BLOOD? Ref: Murphy. V 4/2/75:44. JFFJ 13:30: sfa BLOODTHIRSTY ROSES?

EVIL STALKS THIS HOUSE see TALES OF THE HAUNTED

EVILSPEAK LIC-Coronet 1981? color D & Co-P: Eric Weston. SP: Joseph Garofalo. Ph: Irv Goodnoff. Ref: FM 176. V 10/15/80: 99-102. with Clint Howard, Charles Tyner, R.G. Armstrong.
Military school's computer used to conjure up pack of demonic wild pigs.

EVOLUTION (Can.) NFB 1971 anim color 5m. D: Michael Mills. Ref: screen. IFG'72:381. Lee.
A sometimes hilarious version of evolution, featuring a Martian.

EXCESS BAGGAGE (B) Real Art 1933 59m. D: Redd Davis. SP: H. Fowler Mear, from H.M. Raleigh's novel. Ref: BFC. with Rene Ray, Claude Allister, Gerald Rawlinson, Finlay Currie.
"Col. thinks he has killed superior while hunting ghost."

EXCITE ME (I) Lea 1972 color 96m. (IL TUO VIZIO E UNA STANZA CHIUSA E SOLO LO NE HO LA CHIAVE) D: Sergio Martino. SP: E. Gastaldi, A. Bolzoni, S. Scavolini, from Edgar Allan Poe's short story "The Black Cat." Ph: G. Ferrando. Mus: Bruno Nicolai. AD: G. Bertolini. Ref: MFB'73:156. Bianco Index'72. with Edwige Fenech, Anita Strindberg, Luigi Pistilli, Angela La Vorgna.
Old mansion; cat named Satan; corpse walled up in cellar.

EXOMAN NBC-TV/Univ-TV 1977 color 94m. D: Richard Irving. SP: Martin Caidin, Howard Rodman. Story: Henri Simoun, Caidin. Ph: Enzo A. Martinelli. Mus: Dana Kaproff. AD: J.W. Corso. SdFxEd: Kyle Wright. Ref: TV. TVFFSB. TV Season. with David Ackroyd, Harry Morgan, Jose Ferrer, Kevin McCarthy, Ann(e) Schedeen, A Martinez.
Exo-suit makes paralyzed professor mobile again, and also virtually invulnerable. Routine super-heroics.

EXORCISMO (Sp) Profilmes 1974 color/scope 92m. SP,D: Juan Bosch Palau. SP: also Jacinto Molina. Ph: Francisco Sanchez. Mus: Alberto Argudo. AD: Alfonso de Lucas. Ref: Bianco #5-6/77:234. V 5/7/75:243: EXORCIST-spawned. with Paul Naschy(aka J.Molina), Maria Perschy, Maria Kosti, Grace Mills, R.Leveder.

EXORCISM'S DAUGHTER (Sp) Mahler/Dauro 1971('74-U.S.) color 110m. (Las MELANCOLICAS) SP,D: Rafael M. Alba. Ph: Mario Pacheco. Mus: Jaime Perez. AD: R.C. Baleztena. Mkp: Miguel Sese. Ref: MFB'74:131-32. Willis/SW. V 2/13/74:14(ad). 5/24/72. with Analia Gade, Francisco Rabal, E.Santoni,H.Line.
Girl witnesses exorcism of mother's possessed body.

The EXORCIST WB/Hoya 1973 color 122m. D: William Friedkin. SP,P: William Peter Blatty, from his novel. Ph: Owen Roizman, Billy Williams. Mus: Jack Nitzche; Penderecki, Henze et al. PD: Bill Malley. SpFX: Marcel Vercoutere. Art: Eddie Garzero. Opt: Marv Ystrom. SpMkp: Dick Smith. SpSdFX: Ron Nagle et al. Sequel: EXORCIST II: THE HERETIC. See also: DEVIL IN HER, The. Ref: MFB'74:71: "no more nor less than a blood-and-thunder horror movie, foundering heavily on the rocks of pretension." V 12/26/73. screen. with Linda Blair, Max Von Sydow, Ellen Burstyn, Jason Miller, Lee J. Cobb, Mercedes McCambridge (demon's voice), Jack MacGowran, Kitty Winn, William O'Malley.

Jesuit archaeologist summoned to exorcise demon from 12-year-old girl. Some truly startling special-effects scenes admittedly make The EXORCIST an above-average blood-and-thunder horror movie. But director Friedkin apparently believes that (in non-effects sequences) the camera moves and that's a scene. Like ALIEN, The EXORCIST "delivers"--it has its nice shock "payoffs"--and in a sense that's all it needs, since most horror movies don't deliver even that much. But the only artists involved in these shock blockbusters are the effects and design men. Directors like Friedkin and Scott serve them.

The EXORCIST: ITALIAN STYLE (I) Ingra 1975 color 95m. (L'ESORCICCIO) Story,D: Ciccio Ingrassia. SP: Marino Onorati. Ph: G. Mancori. Mus: Franco Godi. AD: Giorgio Postiglione. Ref: CineFan 2:25. V 5/7/75:203(ad): "laugh at the devil." Bianco Index'75. with Ingrassia, Lino Banfi, Didi Perego.

EXORCIST II: THE HERETIC WB/Lederer 1977 color 117m. D & Co-P: John Boorman. SP: William Goodhart. Sequel to The EXORCIST. Ph: William A. Fraker. Mus: Ennio Morricone. PD: Richard Macdonald. SpVisFX: Albert Whitlock, Van Der Veer. SpFX: Chuck Gaspar et al. SpMkp: Dick Smith. SpPh: Oxford Scientific. Ref: V(d) 6/17/77. MFB'77:210-11. with Linda Blair, Richard Burton, Louise Fletcher, Max Von Sydow, Kitty Winn, Paul Henreid, James Earl Jones, Ned Beatty.

Thought-machine; ESP; demon.

The EXOTIC ONES Ormond 1968 60m. D,P: Ron Ormond. Ref: AFI: monster.

EXPERIMENT ALCATRAZ RKO/Crystal 1950 58m. D,P: Edward L.Cahn. SP: Orville Hampton. Story: George W.George, George F.Slavin. Ph: J.J. Rose. Mus: Irving Gertz. AD: Boris Leven. Ref: V 11/22/50. TV. TVG. LC. with John Howard, Joan Dixon, Walter Kingsford, Harry Lauter, Robert Shayne, Byron Foulger.

A doctor's experiments in using atomic radiation to fight blood diseases ultimately prove successful (he discovers a "secret ray," or new isotope, and gets a Newsweek cover), though the treatments apparently make one subject go berserk and stab another to death. Awkwardly plotted semi-sf-melodrama makes one grateful for small felicities (e.g., Shayne's "I'm a nice guy"), and there are few even of them. Here it's one brutal thug vs. the progress of science. (Script is on latter's side.)

EXPERIMENT PERILOUS RKO 1944 90m. D: Jacques Tourneur. SP,P: Warren Duff, from Margaret Carpenter's novel. Ph: Tony Gaudio. Mus: Roy Webb. AD: Albert S. D'Agostino, Jack Okey. SpFX: Vernon L. Walker. Ref: TV. LC. V 12/13/44: "strange and weird drama." with Hedy Lamarr, George Brent, Paul Lukas, Albert Dekker, Carl Esmond, Olive Blakeney, Julia Dean, M. Wycherley.
Woman "frightened to death" by madman-brother (Lukas), who with strength of will dominates wife (Lamarr) and son; latter has "nighttime terrors" induced by father's stories of "ugly witches." Hero Brent insists that there's a "simple and logical explanation" for the strange goings-on at the Bedereaux'--the fact that there isn't makes the movie fairly interesting. Lamarr at first appears to be under Lukas' hypnotic control; but fear, not hypnosis, is apparently the key. It's all psychological, and more involved than involving. Good, florid Webb score.

L'EXPLOITS EROTIQUES DE MACISTE DANS L'ATLANTIDE (F) CFFP 1974 D: Clifford Brown. Ref: V 5/8/74:139.

EXPLORING THE UNKNOWN 1977 color Narr: Burt Lancaster. Ref: TVG. TV: ESP, hypnotic regression explored.

EYE, The see EYEBALL

The EYE OF COUNT FLICKENSTEIN 1966 short D: Tony Conrad. Ref: Lee: Dracula-parody bit.

EYEBALL (I-Sp) Brenner/Pioneer-Estela 1974('78-U.S.) color/scope 91m. (GATTI ROSSI IN UN LABIRINTO DI VETRO. L'OCCHIO SBARRATO NEL BUIO-orig t. The EYE-ad t?) SP,D: Umberto Lenzi. SP: also Felix Tusell. Ph: A. Millan. Mus: Bruno Nicolai. AD: Jose Massague. Ref: V 11/1/78. 7/17/74:26. Bianco Index '75. with John Richardson, Martine Brochard, Silvia Solar, Jorge Rigaud, Marta May.
Murderer who extracts eyeballs of victims.

EYES see MANSION OF THE DOOMED

The EYES BEHIND THE STARS (I) (Gold Key-TV)/Novelli-Midia 1978 color 90m. (OCCHI DALLE STELLO) SP,D: Mario Gariazzo(aka Roy Garrett). Ph: E. Menczer. Mus: Marcello Giombini. AD: F. Cuppini. Ref: TV. TVG. V 5/17/78:250,242. 10/19/77:143. Bianco #3/78:163. GKey. with Nathalie Delon, Robert Hoffmann, Martin Balsam, Carlo Hinterman, Giorgio Ardisson, Sherry Buchanan.
Flying saucer; aliens who can make themselves invisible; telepathic woman who "sees" inside spacecraft; world-wide conspiracy to cover-up UFO data. Once again earthlings are menaced by a heavy-breathing, subjective camera (a type of creature which thrives in low-budget sf). Would that this (interminable) movie had been covered-up, deep-sixed, and otherwise withheld from us.

EYES OF A STRANGER WB/Georgetown 1981 color 85m. D: Ken Wiederhorn. SP: Mark Jackson, E.L. Bloom. Ph: Mini Rojas.

Mus: Richard Einhorn. AD: Jessica Sack. SpFX: Tom Savini. Ref: V 4/1/81. Boxo 6/9/80:7(ad). with Lauren Tewes, John Di Santi(killer), Jennifer J. Leigh, Peter DuPre.
"Women as bloodied prey of a sexual pervert....ugly." (V)

The EYES OF CHARLES SAND WB-TV 1972 color 75m. D: Reza Badiyi. SP: Henry Farrell, Stanford Whitmore. Ref: TV. TVFFSB: man with "second sight...led into a bizarre mystery." with Peter Haskell, Hugh Benson, Joan Bennett, Barbara Rush, Sharon Farrell, Bradford Dillman, Adam West, Ivor Francis.
The same old story (i.e., GASLIGHT, LOVE FROM A STRANGER), with a new set of actors. The script positively revels in familiar twists and situations.

EYES OF DR. CHANEY see MANSION OF THE DOOMED

EYES OF LAURA MARS Col/Jack Harris 1978 color 103m. D: Irvin Kershner. SP: John Carpenter, David Z. Goodman. Story: Jon Peters, Carpenter. Ph: Victor J. Kemper. Mus: Artie Kane. PD: Gene Callahan. SpPhFX: James Liles. Photographs: Rebecca Blake. SpFX: Edward Drohan. Ref: MFB'78:219. FC 3/80:12. TV. V 8/2/78. with Faye Dunaway, Tommy Lee Jones, Brad Dourif, Rene Auberjonois, Raul Julia, Darlanne Fluegel, Lisa Taylor.
Photographer who has visions of murders from murderer's viewpoint, schizophrenic "whose psychopathic 'half' hates" Laura for exploiting death in her pictures. (MFB) On just about any terms--sociological,psychological, romantic-dramatic, or thriller--EYES OF LAURA MARS seems _deja vu_. Laura's visions are a variation on the killer's-eye gimmick from the 1946 SPIRAL STAIRCASE; their only function in the story seems to be to make a nervous wreck of her. The climactic scene would _like_ to be romantic tragedy, but the movie by then has wasted too much time on Laura's kinky-psychic visions for it to be felt as such.

*The EYES OF THE MUMMY MA PAG-Union 1918 42m. Ref: screen. Weinberg/TLT.
Quasi-hypnotism: Emil Jannings' stare holds and turns Pola Negri; she can sense his presence. The kind of romantic schlock that the director, Ernst Lubitsch, later burlesqued in SO THIS IS PARIS(1926).

EZUSTMAJOM see OPERATION "SILVER MONKEY"

FABULOUS JOURNEY TO THE CENTER OF THE EARTH see WHERE TIME BEGAN

*The FACE BEHIND THE MASK 1941 From O'Connell's radio play "Interim." Ref: TV. Lee.
Another reason to wonder--why a Robert Florey cult? There's an occasional, evocative high-angle shot, but the hopelessly sappy plot pits kindness against unkindness and is peopled with saccharine caricatures of cops, gangsters, immigrants, etc.

Even Peter Lorre is a little-too-calculatedly lovable, though his bravura worm-turns revenge sequence, at the end, is highly enjoyable, one of those always-warmly-remembered Great Moments of "B"'s.

FACE IN THE NIGHT(by E.Wallace) see MALPAS MYSTERY, The

The FACE OF DARKNESS (B) Cromdale 1976 color 58m. SP,D,P: Ian F.H. Lloyd. Ph: P. Harvey. Mus: Martin Jacklin. AD: M. Audsley. Ref: MFB'77:6-7. with Lennard Pearce, John Bennett, David Allister(The Undead), Gwyneth Powell.
Politician resurrects man buried alive during the Inquisition.

FACE OF EVIL see NAME FOR EVIL, A

FADE TO BLACK American Cinema 1980 color 100m. SP,D: Vernon Zimmerman. Ph: Alex Phillips Jr. Mus: Craig Safan. Sets: L.L. Brookbank. SpFX: James Wayne. Ref: V 10/15/80:66,154. with Dennis Christopher, Linda Kerridge, Tim Thomerson.
Young man identifies with, masquerades as Lugosi-as-Dracula, Karloff-as-the-mummy, etc., revenges himself on "enemies."

The FAIRY'S SWORD (B) Hepworth 1908 10m. D: Lewin Fitzhamon. Ref: BFC: ogre, magic sword.

A FAITHLESS FRIEND (B) Hepworth 1908 8m. D: Lewin Fitzhamon. Ref: BFC: skeleton-to-life in dream.

*The FAKIR'S SPELL (B) 1914 Ref: BFC.
"Horror. Girl's British lover, changed into gorilla by her father, is captured by circus."

The FALCON AND THE CO-EDS RKO 1943 68m. D: William Clemens. SP: Ardel Wray, Gerald Geraghty, based on the Michael Arlen character. Ph: Roy Hunt. Mus D: Bakaleinikoff. AD: Albert D'Agostino? SpFX: Vernon L. Walker. Ref: TV. Maltin/TVM. LC. MPH 11/6/43. V 11/10/43. with Tom Conway, Jean Brooks, Rita Corday, Amelita Ward, Isabel Jewell, Cliff Clark, George Givot, Ian Wolfe, Dorothy Malone, Ed Gargan, Barbara Brown.
A psychic girl (Corday) foresees two deaths and fears that she, like her father, is insane; the wind ("Follow") and sea ("Your father--insane--only one answer--the sea") "speak" to her, and another woman attempts to drive her over the brink; "insane, disconnected murders"; music and shots of ocean from I WALKED WITH A ZOMBIE; cliff-overhang set from KING KONG. Decidedly the most offbeat of the Falcon films. Jean Brooks, Isabel Jewell, Ardel Wray, and Roy Webb's ZOMBIE music make it look and sound at times like a forgotten Val Lewton film, as it alternates between blanc (Falcon)and noir (Lewton). And if the Lewtons could have used more of Tom Conway's wryness, this Falcon profits by its occasional Lewtonesque somberness. Jean Brooks' tartness and melancholy here, in

fact, make her Vicky a cousin of her Jacqueline in The SEVENTH VICTIM.

*The FALL OF THE HOUSE OF USHER (F) 1928 Ref: screen. Wide Angle III:1:38-44. with M. and A. Gance.
Some pleasing visual effects--e.g., candles superimposed over trees; the camera barreling across a floor as leaves scatter. But the film is slow and confusing--you only wonder what Poe could possibly have had in mind. He paints her portrait; she dies; the house falls....

The FALL OF THE HOUSE OF USHER Sunn 1979 color D: James L. Conway. SP: Stephen Lord, from Poe's story. Ref: V 10/17/79: 116d(ad). 7/25/79(rated). with Martin Landau, Charlene Tilton, Ray Walston.

FAMILY OF A WURDALAK(by A.Tolstoy) see NIGHT OF THE DEVILS

El FANG-DANGO (Showtime-TV) 197-? 14m. SP,D,P: Tony deNonno. Ph: Nico. Mus: Donald Sosin. Mkp: S. Shendelman. Ref: TV. with Tony Travis(Dracula), Chris Jones, Susan Rockower.
Comedy, silent-movie style. Dracula has a fang-ache. Fangs but no fangs.

FANNY HILL MEETS DR. EROTICO Chancellor 1967 color 78m. D,P: Barry Mahon. Ref: AFI. with Sue Evans.
Mad doctor's monster brought to life.

FANTASMA D'AMORE (I-F-W.G.) IDF/AMLF/Roxy 1981 color 93m. SP,D: Dino Risi. SP: also Bernardino Zapponi, from M. Milani's novel. Ph: Tonino Delli Colli. Mus: Riz Ortolani. Sets: G. Mangano. Ref: V 5/13/81. with Marcello Mastroianni, Romy Schneider.
"Eerie atmosphere of the restless dead come back...to kill and destroy"; alchemist; hommage to NOSFERATU.

El FANTASMA DE MEDIANOCHE (Mex) Rex 1939 72m. (El MISTERIO SE VISTE DE FRAC-orig t) D: Raphael J. Sevilla. SP: G.S. de Sicilia, I. de Martino, from "En Un Baturro Tres Burros" by A.A. Gandolin. Ph: Fred Mandel. Mus: Raul Lavista. AD: Manuel Fontanals. Ref: "Historia Documental del Cine Mexicano," I:240-41: seance, strange house; ghost? with Sergio de Karlo, Victoria Blanco, Carlos L. Moctezuma, C. Orellana.

FANTASTIC PLANET (F-Cz) New World/Armorial-ORTF & Ceskosolvensky 1973 anim color 71m. (La PLANETE SAUVAGE. ***The SAVAGE PLANET) SP,D: Rene Laloux. SP,Des: Roland Topor. From the novel "Oms en Serie" by Stefan Wul. Mus: A. Goraguer. Ref: MFB'74:282. NYT 12/19/73. V 5/16/73. Voices: Barry Bostwick, Cynthia Alder, Olan Soule, Marvin Miller.
Androids and their pet Oms; telepathy; rockets; planet of "vast figures." (MFB)

FAREWELL TO THE PLANET OF THE APES see NEW PLANET OF THE APES

FARMER SPUDD AND HIS MISSUS TAKE A TRIP TO TOWN (B) Gaumont 1915 11m. D: J.L.V. Leigh. Ref: BFC.
"Country couple visit Madame Tussaud's exhibition and dream Chamber of Horrors comes to life."

El FARO DE CAYO SANGRE (Venez) Casnic 1975 40m. D: Antonio Castellet. SP: A. Mateo. Ref: IFG'76:368: "horror-fiction."

FASCINATION (F) ABC 1979 color D: Jean Rollin. Ref: V 5/7/80:474: "vampire thriller."

FATHER'S BABY BOY (B) Clarendon 1909 D: Percy Stow. Ref: BFC. "'Bovril' makes baby grow to enormous size."

FAUST (B) Hepworth 1911 sound D: Cecil M. Hepworth. From Gounod's opera. Ref: BFC. with Hay Plumb, Claire Pridelle.

FAUST (B) Master 1922 14m. (Tense Moments from Opera series) D: C. Sanderson. SP: Frank Miller, from Gounod's opera. Ref: BFC. with Dick Webb, Sylvia Caine, Lawford Davidson.

FAUST (B) Butcher 1923 22m. (Syncopated Picture Plays series) D: Bertram Phillips. SP: Frank Miller. Ref: BFC. with Queenie Thomas, Frank Stanmore.

FAUST (B) Song 1927 20m. (Cameo Operas series) D: H.B. Parkinson. From Gounod's opera. Ref: BFC. with Herbert Langley, A.B. Imeson, Margot Lees.
See also: BLUEBEARD(1944). PHANTOM OF THE PARADISE.

FEAR see NIGHT CREATURE

**The FEAR CHAMBER (U.S.-Mex) (Col-TV)/Azteca 1968 85m. SP, D: Jack Hill. Ref: TVFFSB. Lee. FM 54:6. with Boris Karloff, Yerye Beirut, Julissa, Carlos East.
Scientist requires chemicals produced by human body in a "state of extreme terror" to keep volcanic rocks "alive."

FEAR HAS 1,000 EYES (Swed) Swedish Film-production 1971 color 99m. (SKRACKEN HAR TUSEN OGON) SP,D: Torgny Wickman. Ph: L. Bjorne. Mus: Mats Olsson. AD: H. Garmland. Ref: MFB'72:101. with Solveig Anderssen, Anita Sanders, Hans Wahlgren.
Witch commits series of murders.

FEAR IN THE CITY OF THE LIVING DEAD (I) Nat'l.-Medusa-Dania 1980 color D: Lucio Fulci. Ref: V 5/13/81:160: "horror." with Christopher George, Catherine McCall, Janet Agren.

*FEAR IN THE NIGHT Pine-Thomas 1947 Mus: Rudy Schrager. AD: F. Paul Sylos. Ref: screen. V 2/19/47.
Hypnotized man kills in self-defense. Far-fetched premise, strained development, banal ending. However, the pre-credit shot of, simply, a ball of light flitting about the ink-black screen is a real attention-getter, and its "explanation" is

contained, tacitly, within the narrative. Six points.

FEAR IN THE NIGHT (B) Int'l Co-Prods/EMI/Hammer 1972('74-U.S.) color 85m. SP,D,P: Jimmy Sangster. SP: also Michael Syson. Ph: Arthur Grant. Mus: John McCabe. AD: Don Picton. Ref: MFB'72:160-61: "phantom prep school, with tape recordings echoing through the deserted buildings." TV. TVFFSB. Willis/SW. V 9/12/73:21(rated). with Judy Geeson, Joan Collins, Ralph Bates, Peter Cushing, James Cossins.

Sinister plots and counter-plots, all ingeniously diagramed for the viewer at the end--unfortunately, they _play_ ludicrously. The phantom-school idea actually seems rather extraneous, but does make for a nice credit sequence and a few frissons.

*FEAR NO EVIL 1969 Ph: _Andrew J. McIntyre_. AD: Howard E. Johnson. SpFxDes: Don Record. Mkp: Bud Westmore. Ref: TV.

Persian demon, Rakashi, in human form, attempts to lure woman into mirror world of the dead. Lax, diffuse black-magic thriller, with one or two shivery "Hungry Glass" ideas about mirrors (e.g., the woman's mirror image acting independently of her). Over-serious demon-cult nonsense.

FEAR NO EVIL Avco Embassy/C.LaLoggia 1981(1980) color 99m. (MARK OF THE BEAST-orig t) SP,D,Mus: Frank LaLoggia. Ph: Fred Goodich. Mus: also David Spear. Roto: Peter Kuran. Ref: V 1/7/81:18. 1/28/81: Lucifer summons zombies. 3/11/81:20. with Elizabeth Hoffmann, Dick Burt, R.J. Silverthorn(Lucifer).

Three archangels take human form to combat the Devil, who has been reborn in New York.

FEE FI FO FUM, I SMELL BLOOD see NIGHT STALKER, The

FELIX THE CAT IN BLUNDERLAND Educ/Sullivan 1926 anim 7m. Ref: screen. LC.

Felix follows Alice into Wonderland, encounters beaked "dinosaur," Jack and the Giant, etc.

See also: BOLD KING COLE.

FELLOWSHIP OF THE RING(by J.R.R.Tolkien) see LORD OF THE RINGS

FEMALE BUTCHER see LEGEND OF BLOOD CASTLE

FENG-SHEN PANG (H.K.?) 1967? Based on the folk novel "Feng-shen Yen-I." Ref: Eberhard.

Evil gods murder inhabitants of village, store their souls in gourd; girl "born from a banana."

FENG-SHEN YEN-I see FENG-SHEN PANG. NO-CH'A NAO TUNG-HAI

FENGRIFFEN(by D.Case) see --AND NOW THE SCREAMING STARTS!

FER-DE-LANCE CBS-TV/MGM-TV(Leslie Stevens) 1974 color 97m. (DEATH DIVE-B) D: Russell Mayberry. SP: Stevens. Ph: John M. Stephens. Mus & P: Dominic Frontiere. Mkp: Ted Coodley.

SpFX: Thomas L. Fisher. SdFX: Igo Kantor. Ref: MFB'76:50. TV. TV Season. with David Janssen, Hope Lange, Ivan Dixon, Jason Evers, Charles Knox Robinson, Ben Piazza.
Poisonous vipers loose on incapacitated sub. Fer-get it.

The FERTILITY GOD (India-Kannada) 1976? color SP,D,Ed: V.R.K. Prasad. Dial: G.V. Iyer. From Dr. Kambar's play. Ph: S. Ramachandra. Mus: B.V. Karanth. Ref: IFG'78:197.
A demon possesses a village chief--"every female he ravages dies"; oracle; ghost at bottom of well.

FETICHE see MASCOT, The

FETICHE CHEZ LES SIRENES (F) Starevitch 1935 See also: MASCOT, The. Ref: Ecran 73(Jan.,p24).

FETICHE EN VOYAGE DE NOCES (F) Starevitch 1935 Ref: Ecran 73.

FETICHE MASCOTTE see MASCOT, The

FETICHE NAVIGATEUR see NAVIGATOR, The

FETICHE PRESTIDIGITATEUR (F) Starevitch 1934 Ref: Ecran 73.

FETICHE SE MARIE (F) Starevitch 193[illegible] Ref: Ecran 73.

FIEND, The see BEWARE MY BRETHREN

The FIEND WITH THE ELECTRONIC BRAIN (AI-TV)/Hemisphere/Tal 1965 color/scope 90m. (PSYCHO A GO-GO-orig t. ECHO OF TERROR-int t? sfa BLOOD OF GHASTLY HORROR? The LOVE MANIAC?) Story,D,P: Al Adamson. SP: Chris Martino, Mark Eden. Ph: William Zsigmond. Mus: Don McGinnis;(lyrics) Billy Storm. Ref: AFI. ad. TVFFSB. FIR'79:464. with Roy Morton, Tacey Robbins, Kirk Duncan, John Carradine, The Vendells, Tanya Maree.
Mad doctor implants mind-control device in Vietnam veteran. (N.B.: at least in "revised" version of film.)

*FIEND WITHOUT A FACE MLC 1958 Sets: John Elphick. SpFX: Puppel & Nordhoff, Peter Neilson. Mkp: Jim Hides. Ref: TV. BFC.
Professor projects thoughts, creates "mental vampires"--fueled by electric and atomic energy--which suck out victims' brains and spinal cords. The ALIEN of its day. The human element is rudimentary here too--the "development" of the monsters is much more sophisticated than that of the characters. The brain-creatures are disgusting enough invisible--they make slurping and crunching sounds. Visible, and stopmo-animated, they're a <u>real</u> treat--brain-spines wriggling and writhing and (when shot) splattering ("pootpootpoot!") all over walls, rugs, and couches. The neatest trick, however: one wounded creeper <u>half</u>-blowing out the fuse that's about to send them all to oblivion. <u>Nice</u> touch--four extra points.

The FIENDISH PLOT OF DR. FU MANCHU WB/Orion-Playboy 1980 color 98m. (FU MANCHU-orig t) D: Piers Haggard. SP: Jim Moloney,

Rudy Dochtermann, based on Sax Rohmer's characters. Ph: Jean Tournier. Mus: Marc Wilkinson. PD: Alex Trauner. SpFX: Richard Parker. ElecFX: Serge Ponvianne. Mkp: Tom Smith. Ref: V 8/13/80. 6/30/76:28. MFB'80:192-3: cottage-into-flying-machine. TV. with Peter Sellers(Fu Manchu/Nayland Smith), Helen Mirren, David Tomlinson, Sid Caesar, Steve Franken, John Le Mesurier, Clement Harari, Burt Kwouk.

1933. Violent electric shocks keep evil genius Fu Manchu alive as he searches for ingredients for a youth serum; plant with sleep-inducing vapors; mechanical spiders. Aimless comedy-adventure. Sellers gives elocution lessons, while the elaborately silly plot unfolds, occasionally affording him a wry line (e.g., "Unroll the queen"). His deliberate, shell-shocked Smith might have been the basis for a _serio_-comic Fu Manchu movie, but his gravity seems misplaced here.

The FIFTH MAN Selig 1914 40m. SP,D: F.J. Grandon. From a story by James Oliver Curwood. Ref: Lee(MPW). LC. AF-Index. with Charles Clary, Lafe McKee, Roy Watson, Bessie Eyton.

Mad scientist adds man to his animal collection.

FIGHT FOR YOUR LIFE Mishkin 1977 color 89m. D: Robert A. Endelson. SP: Straw Weisman. Ph: L. Freidus. Mus: Jeff Slevin. Ref: V 12/21/77. with William Sanderson, Robert Judd, Catherine Peppers, Richard A. Rubin.

"Little more than a graphically violent and sadistic vengeance drama....a catalogue of atrocities."

FIGLIA DI FRANKENSTEIN see LADY FRANKENSTEIN

FILHAS DO FOGO see DAUGHTERS OF FIRE

FILLE A LA FOURRURE see NAKED LOVERS

FILLE DE DRACULA see DAUGHTER OF DRACULA

FILLES EXPERT EN JEUX CLANDESTINS see MAID FOR PLEASURE

FILMLAND MONSTERS Golden Eagle 1960 silent 3m. Ref: LC. Glut/CMM: Paul Blaisdell compilation film featuring "new footage of the She Creature" and "new and trailer footage from IT CONQUERED THE WORLD, DAY THE WORLD ENDED and INVASION OF THE SAUCERMEN."

FIN DE SEMANA PARA LOS MUERTOS see DON'T OPEN THE WINDOW

The FINAL CONFLICT (U.S.-B) Fox/Bernhard-Neufeld 1981 color/scope 103m. D: Graham Baker. SP & Assoc P: Andrew Birkin. Sequel to The OMEN. Ph: Robert Paynter, Phil Meheux. Mus: Jerry Goldsmith. PD: Herbert Westbrook. SpFxSup: Ian Wingrove.Mkp: Freddie Williamson. Opt: Rank, Camera FX. Exec P: Richard Donner. Ref: screen. V 3/25/81. with Sam Neill (Damien), Rossano Brazzi, Don Gordon, Lisa Harrow, H. Moxey.

Damien vs. the Nazarene, in Omen III (or Herod II), as the anti-Christ orders all male babies born on March 24th (the date foretold in the stars for the Second Coming) slaughtered. ("2,000 years has been long enough!") At the end, however, it looks like it's going to be another long haul for Satan. The Devil doesn't really get his due at all here. The script's conception of evil is trite: Damien's U.S. ambassador to England is your conventionally power-hungry, unscrupulous manipulator. And he (and the script) can't put over the good-is-evil-and-vice-versa conceit--his exhortation to his assembled followers ("Fail and you will be condemned to a numbing eternity in the flaccid bosom of Christ!") smacks a little too obviously of sour grapes.

The FINAL COUNTDOWN UA/Bryna 1980 color/scope 103m. D: Don Taylor. SP: David Ambrose, G. Davis, T. Hunter, P. Powell. Ph: Victor J. Kemper. Mus: John Scott. PD: Fernando Carrere. SpVisFX: Maurice Binder. Opt: Opt.House. SpFX: Pat Elmendorf et al. SpMkp: Bob Mills. SpSdFX: Alan S. Howarth. Ref: V 7/16/80. MFB'80:131-32. with Kirk Douglas, Martin Sheen, Katharine Ross, James Farentino, Ron O'Neal, Charles Durning.
Time-warp tale: nuclear-powered aircraft carrier U.S.S. Nimitz disappears on Dec. 7, 1980; reappears Dec. 7, 1941.

FINAL EXAM MPM 1981 color 90m. SP,D: Jimmy Huston. Ph: Darrell Cathcart. Mus: Gary Scott. Ref: V 6/17/81. with Joel S. Rice, Cecile Bagdadi, Timothy L. Raynor(killer).
"Beefy killer" stalks college campus.

FINAL PROGRAMME,The(by M.Moorcock) see LAST DAYS OF MAN ON EARTH

FINGERS AT THE WINDOW MGM 1942 90m. D: Charles Lederer. SP: Rose Caylor, Lawrence P. Bachmann. Ph: Harry Stradling, Charles Lawton. Mus: Bronislau Kaper. AD: William Ferrari, C. Gibbons. Ref: TV. LC. Lee(V 3/16/42). with Lew Ayres, Laraine Day, Basil Rathbone, Walter Kingsford, Miles Mander, Charles D. Brown, Cliff Clark, James Flavin, Russell Gleason.
Psychiatrist hypnotically compels lunatics to commit murders. Fairish thriller, with comedy.

FIOCCO NERO PER DEBORAH see DEBORAH

FIORE DELLE MILLE E UNA NOTTE see ARABIAN NIGHTS

FIRE BALLOONS,The(by R.Bradbury) see MARTIAN CHRONICLES,The

FIREBIRD 2015 A.D. see PHOENIX(1978)

The FIRST BAD MAN MGM 1955 anim color 7m. D: Tex Avery. SP: Heck Allen. Narr: Tex Ritter. Ref: screen. Adamson/TA.
Texas, one million B.C.; dinosaurs. Low-ebb Avery.

FIRST INNOCENT,The(by H.Golshiri) see TALL SHADOWS OF THE WIND

FIRST OF JANUARY,The see Z.P.G.

FIRST YANK INTO TOKYO RKO/Bren 1945 82m. D: Gordon Douglas. SP: J.R. Bren, Gladys Atwater. Ph: H.J. Wild. Mus: Leigh Harline. Ref: TV. LC. V 9/5/45: "mystery bomb of atomic proportions"; "special surgery job" that allows U.S. Army pilot to enter Japan as a spy. with Tom Neal, Barbara Hale, Marc Cramer, Richard Loo, Keye Luke, Benson Fong.

A drama of coincidence: everyone who turns up in the Japanese concentration camp already seems to know everyone else there. But only one lucky actor gets the movie's "plum" line: "America is a fat plum waiting to be shaken off the tree by the first great wind that blows across it."

The FISH AND THE RING (B) Natural Colour 1913 35m. D: F.M. Thornton, R.H. Callum. Ref: BFC. with H.Agar Lyons.

Fairies and animals save girl from "magical baron."

FISH MEN, The see SCREAMERS

FISHEYE (Yug) Zagreb 1979 anim color 10m. (RIBLJE OKO) D, Anim: J. Marusic. Ref: HKFFest.

Fish take revenge on fisherman.

FIVE DOLLS FOR AN AUGUST MOON (I) PAC 1970 color 85m. (CINQUE BAMBOLE PER LA LUNA D'AGOSTO) D & Ed: Mario Bava. SP: Mario Di Nardo. Ph: A. Rinaldi. Mus: Piero Umiliani. AD: Giuseppe Aldebaran. Ref: MFB'72:156-7. with Ira Furstenberg, Edwige Fenech, William Berger, Renato Rossini.

"Synthetic resin" formula; "truth drug"; stylish murders.

The FIVE DOOMED GENTLEMEN (G) Vandal-Delac 1931 (Die FUNF VERFLUCHTEN GENTLEMEN) D: Julien Duvivier. Ref: Chirat: G. version of UNDER THE MOON OF MOROCCO. Limbacher'79. with Anton Walbrook, Camilla Horn, Jack Trevor, Georges Peclet.

FLASH GORDON (U.S.-B?) Univ/De Laurentiis 1980 color/scope 105m. D: Mike Hodges. SP: Lorenzo Semple Jr. Adap: Michael Allin. Based on the Alex Raymond characters. Ph: Gil Taylor; Harry Waxman. Mus: Queen, Howard Blake. PD & Cost: Danilo Donati. SupAD: John Graysmark. SpPhFX:(sup) Frank Van Der Veer; Barry Nolan. Skies: Count Ul De Rico, Tom Adams. Elec SdFX: Theatre Three. SpFX:(models & skies) Richard Conway; (flying) Derek Botell;(sup) George Gibbs;(cons) Glen Robinson. Brain-drain Seq: Denis Postel. See also: FLESH GORDON. Ref: screen. V 12/3/80. MFB'80:235. with Sam J.Jones, Melody Anderson, Topol, Max Von Sydow(Ming), Ornella Muti(Aura), Brian Blessed(Vultan), Timothy Dalton, Peter Wyngarde, M. Melato.

Ming the Merciless of the planet Mongo plots to send the moon crashing into the Earth, after the latest of his periodic tests of our "life system" proves humans too dangerous to continue to exist; conditioning ray; thought amplifier; death-semblance injection; mesmerising ring; space-city's lightning field; "imagers"-creatures; octo-scorpion creature; giant lily-pad-spider creature; Hawkmen; energy globe; sea of fire; lantern ray; spaceships and rocket cycle; electrifying rays.

This is just about the best-looking other-universe since Kubrick's 2001, so good-looking that it's tempting to call it Donati's FLASH GORDON. There seems no end to eye-enthralling surprises of set, costume, and special effect. This is like a super-sf-con masquerade-ball-in-space--the many-hued swirls and whorls and splashes of Mongo's sky make the latter an engaging abstract film in itself, and the Arborian moon is like a giant, lost-floating-fragment-of-Disneyland treehouse. The parade of out-of-this-world costumes goes by so fast that the latter are in effect dazzling throwaways, with tantalizing hints of personality, culture, and art. The non-design elements in the film, from (roughly) most to least important: action/acting/plot/music/comedy/character/theme/dialogue. The category of ideas does not figure at all. (Good-vs.-evil is not an idea, simply an opposition.)

FLASH GORDON'S BATTLE IN SPACE (Turk.) Onuk-Lamek 1967 (BAYTEKIN FEZADA CARPISANLAR) SP,D: Sinasi Ozonuk. Based on Alex Raymond's comic strip. Ph: Fevzi Eryilmaz. Ref: WorldF '67. Limbacher'79. with Hasan Demirtas, Meltem Mete, S. San.
"The further adventures of Flash Gordon...." (WF)

FLEISCH see MEAT

The FLESH AND BLOOD SHOW (B) Entertainment Ventures/Heritage 1972('74-U.S.) color 96m. D,P: Pete Walker. SP: Alfred Shaughnessy. Ph: Peter Jessop. Mus: Cyril Ornadel. Ref: Willis/SW. V 3/28/73:4(rated). CineFan 2:27: Grand Guignol show within film. MFB'72:249. with Jenny Hanley, Ray Brooks, Luan Peters, Patrick Barr, Robin Askwith, Judy Matheson.
Madman lures actors to "dilapidated old theatre...to feed his obsessive hatred of actors...." (MFB)

FLESH FOR FRANKENSTEIN see ANDY WARHOL'S FRANKENSTEIN

FLESH GORDON Vanguard & Mammoth/Graffiti 1974(1972) color 65m. (78m.) SP,D: Michael Benveniste. Spoof of Raymond's "Flash Gordon." D: also Howard Ziehm. Ph: Ziehm. Mus: Ralph Ferraro. AD: Donald Harris. VisFX: David Allen, Jim Danforth. SpPhFX: Tom Scherman. SpProps: Rick Baker. Props: Tom Reamy. SpOptFX: Cinema Research, Ray Mercer. SpFX: Ziehm et al. Mkp: Bjo Trimble. Ref: MFB'75:55. screen. Willis/SW. V 7/31/74. 5/11/77:138(ad). with Jason Williams, Suzanne Fields, John Hoyt, Candy Samples, Mary Gavin, Joseph Hudgins.
Sex ray; phallic rocket; "penisauri and other gigantic creatures"; Destructo Beam; robots; "monstrous Idol of All Perversion"; "power pasties." (MFB) No funnier really than the Universal originals, though the stopmo-animated monsters are decidedly more impressive than Flash's rather motley bunch.

FLOODTIDE(by A.P.Herbert) see HOUSE BY THE RIVER

FLOWER LOVERS (Yug) Zagreb 1971 anim short D: B.Dovnikovic. Ref: IFG'72:397: exploding flowers wreck city.

FLY-BY-NIGHT Para/Siegel 1942 74m. D: Robert Siodmak. SP: F. Hugh Herbert, Jay Dratler. Story: Ben Roberts, Sidney Sheldon. Ph: John Seitz. AD: Hans Dreier, Haldane Douglas. Ref: W.K. Everson: "horror film." screen. P.LePage. LC. with Richard Carlson, Nancy Kelly, Albert Basserman, Walter Kingsford, Miles Mander, Marion Martin, Mary Gordon, Cy Kendall, Oscar O'Shea, Martin Kosleck, Ed Gargan, Clem Bevans, Arthur Loft.

G-32 invention (involving light, electricity, and gasses ignited in tubes) destroys human optic nerve; storm seq. in old dark insane asylum. Sprightly, engaging suspense-comedy, a "B" a la Hitchcock (specifically, 39 STEPS). Some genially outrageous stunts, some "A" lines, and a serviceable innocent-man-caught-between-cops-and-spies plot. A very early Richard Carlson sf-film.

*The FLYING SAUCER Colonial 1949 Ref: TV. V 1/11/50. LC. and with Garry Owens, Hantz Von Teuffen, Lester Sharpe.

Melo plot "A," plus Alaskan ice and a flying saucer. Scenery, and that's it--except for a startler of a scene in which the saucer roars right over an isolated shack.

The FLYING SORCERER (B) CFF/Anvil 1975 color 52m. SP,D: Harry Booth. SP: also Leo Maguire. Story: Hazel Swift. Ph: L. Dear. Mus: Harry Robinson. MechFX: Kenifex. Ref: MFB'75: 00. TVG. with Kim Burfield, Debbie Russ, Erik Chitty, John Bluthal, Tim Barrett(sorcerer).

Time machine takes inventor and nephew back to Middle Ages.

FLYING WITHOUT WINGS (Dutch) CFF/Castor 1977 color 93m. (VLIEGEN ZONDER VLEUGELS. PETER ENDE VLIEGENDE AUTOBUS) SP,D, Ed: Karst van der Meulen. Ph: C. Samson. Mus: T. Eyk. Ref: MFB'80:79. IFG'78:243. with M. van Kruyssen, L. Goudsmit.

Professor's zero-gravity rays make objects float in air.

FOES (Gold Key-TV)/BW/CAC 1977 color 90m. SP,D,SpFX: John Coats. Ph: Michael Sabo. Mus: Jeff Bruner. Anim: Lyn Gerry et al. SpFxPh: Scott Farrar, Christopher George. SpMkpFX: Susan Cabral. Ref: MFB'79:121. V 5/9/79:358(ad). 2/25/81:75 (ad). with MacDonald Carey, Jerry Hardin, Jane Wiley.

A flying saucer envelopes a section of the California coast in a mysterious force.

The FOG Avco Embassy/Entertainment Discoveries 1980 color/scope 91m. SP,D,Mus: John Carpenter. SP: also Debra Hill. Ph: Dean Cundey. PD: Tommy Wallace. SpFX: Richard Albain Jr., A&A Sp FX. SpPhFX: James F. Files. SpMkp: Rob Bottin. SpSdFX: Frank Serafine. Title Des: Burke Matisson. Ref: screen. MFB '80:214. V 1/16/80. Cinef X:1:41. with Adrienne Barbeau, Jamie Lee Curtis, Janet Leigh, Hal Holbrook, John Houseman(Mr. Machen), Charles Cyphers(Dan O'Bannon), D. Joston(Dr.Phibes).

Members of leper colony return to life after 100 years to wreak revenge on town responsible for their deaths (2000 MANIACS anyone?); refs. to Poe and Lovecraft. The FOG contains another John Carpenter *hommage* to The THING, but a talent further from that of Howard Hawks than Carpenter's--at least as demonstrated here--would be hard to imagine. The FOG is pathetically vacant in-between the shock sequences--the actors are simply filler material. The onslaught of the supernatural fog is amusing--it glows, frizzes power lines, and rolls photogenically across the bay and the town. But its explanation is labored, and the ghosts which it harbors are rather nondescript. (Like the other characters.)

*FOG ISLAND (Western-TV) 1945 From Bernadine Angus' play. Mus: Karl Hajos. Ref: TV. LC. V 4/11/45: "chiller."
Clairvoyant-astrologist; "psychic research lab"; clairvoyant session (with table rising up from floor); secret death-trap room; skeleton, skulls, and of course fog. The classic PRC dramatic structure: 1/3 exposition, 1/3 confrontations, 1/3 skulking. Notable only for the co-starring of horror-film veterans George Zucco and Lionel Atwill, who make the most of their three or four scenes together. (In his last scene, Zucco chews up Atwill and half the scenery, then chokes and dies, possibly of acute indigestion.)

FOLKS AT RED WOLF INN, The see TERROR HOUSE(1972)

The FOOD OF THE GODS AI 1976 color 88m. SP,D,P,SpVisFX: Bert I. Gordon. From H.G. Wells' novel. Ph: Reginald Morris. Mus: Elliot Kaplan. AD: Graeme Murray. Min: Erik von Buelow. SpFX: Tom Fisher et al. Ref: V 6/9/76. screen. MFB'76:213: "a truly appalling piece of s-f horror." with Marjoe Gortner, Pamela Franklin, Ralph Meeker, Ida Lupino, Chuck Courtney.
"Food of the gods" creates giant wasps, rats, etc. Noise, a busy camera, bad trick effects, and chicken suits. Gordon is still trading on the horror of sheer bigness. ("Those awful giant rats!") And his flip-the-ghastly-corpse-face-up shock effect dates back at least to The SPIDER(1958). Lots of blood gets spilled here, and the fact that those awful rats spill most of it doesn't make the carnage any less unpleasant.

FOOTSTEPS IN THE SAND see BLACK LIMELIGHT

FOR THE LOVE OF MARIASTELLA see MALACARNE

FORBIDDEN LOVE see FREAKS

The FORBIDDEN ROOM (F-I) Dear-Fox Europa 1977 color 102m. (ANIMA PERSA. LOST SOUL-ad t) SP,D: Dino Risi. SP: also B. Zapponi. From Giovanni Arpino's novel. Ph: Tonino Delli Colli. Mus: Francis Lai. Ref: V 1/26/77. 4/7/76:46. Bianco #1/77:128. with Vittorio Gassman, Catherine Deneuve.
"Mad brother"; "eerie, chilling atmosphere"; "uncanny" happenings in "crumbling mansion." (V)

FORBIDDEN ZONE Borack 1980 76m. SP,D,P: Richard Elfman. SP: also M. Bright, M.W. Nicholson, N. Jones. Ph: G. Sandor. Mus: Danny Elfman (Oingo-Boingo). PD: M.-P. Elfman. Ref: V

3/26/80. with Herve Villechaize, Susan Tyrell, Viva. Underground "Sixth Dimension" of "loony demons, ogres, cretins and assorted humans."

The FORCE BEYOND FVI 1978 color SP,D: William Sachs. SP,P: Donn Davison. Ref: V 2/8/78(rated). B.Warren. Boxo 12/5/77 (ad): new dimension? aliens? with Don Elkins, Peter Byrne, Renee Dahinden, Frances Farrelly.

The FORCE ON THUNDER MOUNTAIN (Gold Key-TV)/American Nat'l 1978 color 93m. D: Peter B. Good. Ph: K. Durden, G. Longsdale. Mus & with: Christopher Cain. Ref: TV. GKey. with Todd Dutson, Borge West, J.L. Strong.

"Mountain storms," "great ball of fire," falling trees, vanishing trail markers, and mysterious voice ("Go back!") traced to survivor of crash-landed spaceship from the planet Ariana, whose "thought translator" uses "the force" to translate thoughts into action. A Disney True-Life Adventure crossed with STAR WARS. "Rick--the force!" cries the old alien to the boy, as the bear attacks--a close call. (Almost plagiarism.) Scrappy, home-movie-level wilderness idyll.

FOREST OF FEAR see BLOODEATERS

FORGOTTEN CITY OF THE PLANET OF THE APES see NEW PLANET OF THE APES,The

The FORTRESS (Hung.) Hungarofilm/Mafilm 1979 color 119m. (Az EROD) SP,D: Miklos Szinetar. SP: also Gyula Hernadi. Ph: Miklos Biro. Ref: IFG'80:173. V 5/7/80:559: "social science fiction." 2/28/79. with Bella Tanai, S. Oszter, A. Rajhona.

"Enters the arenas of WESTWORLD and "Fantasy Island".... rich tourists paying to be humiliated by war games on a private estate." (IFG)

FORTUNE HUNTERS Fox 1946 anim color 7m. (GANDY GOOSE IN FORTUNE HUNTERS) D: Connie Rasinski. SP: John Foster. Ref: LC. Glut/TFL: Frankenstein-monster bit.

*The 4-D MAN 1959 Ref: TV.

The first half of The 4-D MAN is a loss: although Robert Lansing is effective (at least when not just moodily standing around), the other actors can hardly walk into a room, let alone through a wall. However, in the latter half, Lansing goes on a sometimes impressive, Invisible Man-like super-power trip, punctuated by choice stunts and bits of humor, as he sticks his arms through people, walls, and mailboxes (to varying effect--people age instantly and die). And if his climactic tirade is a bit actorish, it contains glints of real megalomania and desperation. And the final shot of his hand sticking out of the wall has a kind of perverse bravura to it.

FOUR FLIES ON GREY VELVET (I-F) Para/Seda & Universal 1971 color/scope 100m. (QUATTRO MOSCHE DI VELLUTO GRIGIO) Story,

SP,D: Dario Argento. Story: also Luigi Cozzi, M. Foglietti. Ph: Franco Di Giacomo. Mus: Ennio Morricone. AD: Enrico Sabbatini. Ref: Lee(LAT 8/4/72). MFB'73:56. V 1/19/72. Bianco Index'71. with Michael Brandon, Mimsy Farmer, Bud Spencer.

Laser-beam device that photographs the "last image on the retina" of murder victim's eye. (LAT)

FRACTURE (I) Triton 1978 anim color 18m. SP,D,Des: P.G. Brizzi. Ref: Zagreb 78 cat.: plants rule post-holocaust world.

FRANCIS THE FIRST (F) Meadow-Garner/Calamy 1937('47-U.S.) 85m. (FRANCOIS Ier. Les AMOURS DE LA BELLE FERRONNIERE) D: Christian-Jaque. SP: Paul Fekete. Ph: M. Lucien, A. Germain. Mus: Rene Sylviano. AD: Pierre Schild. Ref: V 4/23/47: "ghost sequence"; hypnotist. Chirat. Lee(p). DDC II:309. with Fernandel, Mona Goya, Alexandre Rignault, Sinoel(ghost), Mihalesco (Cagliostro), Alice Tissot.

FRANCOISE AND EMMANUELLE see EMANUELLE E FRANCOISE

*FRANKENSTEIN 1931 SP: F. Edwards Faragoh. Sequel: BRIDE OF FRANKENSTEIN. Mus: David Broekman. AD: Charles D. Hall. Sp FX: John P. Fulton. ElecFX: Kenneth Strickfaden. Ref: screen. TV. FM 169:41. Jim Shapiro. Lee.

Fifty years later, the creation sequences in FRANKENSTEIN still impress. Man and monster, however, are both eventually swallowed up in some creaking narrative machinery. (The merry/angry villagers are almost the stars of the second half of the film.) After carefully charting the monster's reactions to fire and sunlight, the script goes rather diffuse and sketchy, and loses its point until monster and maker meet again at the end. Boris Karloff's performance as the monster consists of suggestive fragments of disconnected scenes--a grunt, a snarl, a supplicating gesture, a tottering walk. And Colin Clive's intentness--which suggests both inspiration and madness--carries the first half. But it's primarily the sets and lighting which make this movie still watchable. You may forget John Boles, Mae Clarke, and Fred Kerr--who?--but you don't forget that cemetery, the watchtower, the lecture room shadows, the windmill.

FRANKENSTEIN (B) ABC-TV/Dan Curtis 1973 color 136m. Ref: TVFFSB. Glut/TFL: from Shelley's novel. Cinef F'73:37. with Robert Foxworth, Susan Strasberg, Bo Svenson(The Giant).

FRANKENSTEIN (novel by Mary Shelley) see also the following titles, and ANDY WARHOL'S FRANKENSTEIN. ATTACK OF THE PHANTOMS. BLACKENSTEIN. BLOOD PIE. DEATH RACE 2000. DR.DEVIL AND MR.HARE. DOCTOR FRANKEN. EVERY HOME SHOULD HAVE ONE. FORTUNE HUNTERS. FRANKENSTEIN('68)(P). FRANKENSTEIN CRIES OUT!(P). FUNHOUSE,The. GREAT PIGGY BANK ROBBERY. HAVE YOU GOT ANY CASTLES. HENDERSON MONSTER,The. HOLLYWOOD STEPS OUT. HORRIBLE SEXY VAMPIRE,The. INVASION DE LOS MUERTOS. INVENTORS,The. JAILBREAK,The. "KILLING" VS.FRANKENSTEIN. KING

TUT'S TOMB. LADY FRANKENSTEIN. LURK. MONSTER OF CEREMONIES. MUNSTERS' REVENGE,The. OUR HITLER(P). PEPITO Y CHABELO.... PORKY'S ROAD RACE. RETURN OF THE PINK PANTHER(P). SANTO Y BLUE DEMON VS.DR.FRANKENSTEIN. SATURDAY SUPERSTAR MOVIE(P). SNIFFLES AND THE BOOKWORM. SON OF DRACULA('74). SPIRIT OF THE BEEHIVE. TOYLAND PREMIERE. VICTOR FRANKENSTEIN. WHAT'S COOKIN',DOC? YOUNG FRANKENSTEIN.

FRANKENSTEIN AND THE MONSTER FROM HELL (B) Para/Hammer 1973 ('74-U.S.) color 99m. D: Terence Fisher. SP: Anthony Hinds (aka John Elder). Ph: Brian Probyn. Mus: James Bernard. AD: Scott MacGregor. Mkp: Eddie Knight. Ref: MFB'74:71-2. V 6/26/74. Willis/SW. with Peter Cushing, Shane Briant, Madeline Smith, John Stratton, Bernard Lee, Dave Prowse(the monster), Charles Lloyd Pack.

Baron Frankenstein, now running an asylum for the criminally insane (under the name of Dr. Victor), supervises the transplanting of the brain of a professor into his monster, "a brutish inmate." (MFB)

*FRANKENSTEIN CREATED WOMAN 1966 SP: Anthony Hinds(aka J.Elder). Ref: TV. Glut/TFL: AND FRANKENSTEIN CREATED WOMAN-orig t.

Baron Victor Frankenstein (Peter Cushing) attempts to prove that though the human body dies, the soul lives on--he scientifically transfers the soul of a dead man into the body of a woman. Intriguing premise wasted on labored (to put it charitably) revenge plot. Hammer at its most noxious, simplistic. A narrative vacuum.

FRANKENSTEIN EXPERIMENT, The see ANDY WARHOL'S FRANKENSTEIN

FRANKENSTEIN--ITALIAN STYLE (I) Euro Int'l/RPA 1976 color 97m. D: Armando Crispino. SP: M. Franciosa, M.L. Montagnana. Ph: G. Cipriani. Mus: Stelvio Cipriani. PD: Mario Molli. Ref: V 11/23/77: comedy a la YOUNG FRANKENSTEIN. 5/12/76:257 (ad),194. 10/22/75:58. with Aldo Maccione(the monster), Gianrico Tedeschi(Prof.Frankenstein), Ninetto Davoli(Igor), Jenny Tamburi.

FRANKENSTEIN JUNIOR see YOUNG FRANKENSTEIN

*FRANKENSTEIN MEETS THE WOLF MAN 1943 Sequel to both The WOLF MAN(1941) and GHOST OF FRANKENSTEIN. Sequel: HOUSE OF FRANKENSTEIN. Assoc AD: Martin Obzina. Ref: TV. V 2/24/43.

Arguably the nadir of Universal's Frankenstein series--hard to say if it's worse as a Frankenstein or as a Wolf Man movie. Here, Patric Knowles is Frank Mannering, a doctor very unconvincingly infused with the Frankenstein spirit--he gets a funny look on his face and suddenly simply has to restore the monster (Bela Lugosi and double Ed Parker) to its full strength. And this is Lon Chaney Jr.'s most annoying stint as Larry Talbot ("I'm not interested in <u>life</u>!" "I only want to <u>die</u>!" etc.)--where <u>are</u> Abbott and Costello? As in GHOST..., Lugosi and Lionel Atwill are wasted. Even the music and art direction are uneven. (But, in this context, stand out.) Wind machines, a moving camera, lighting, and music, however, combine to make the justly-renowned opening sequence satisfyingly atmospheric, though there is an embarrassing pause for poetry ("Even a man....") in a crypt.

FRANKENSTEIN 1980 (I) 1972 (MOSAIC-FRANKENSTEIN 1980. MOSAIQUE-FRANKENSTEIN 1980) D: Mario Mancini. Ref: Glut/TFL. Daisne. Limbacher'79. with John Richardson, Renato Romano, Xiro Papas, Gordon Mitchell.
Monster with self-destruct mechanism.

FRANKENSTEIN (PFALZ) (F) Richard 197-? color 14m. D: Jacques Richard. Ref: PFA notes 4/7/80.
"Accursed village"; man who vanishes.

FRANKENSTEIN: THE TRUE STORY (B) NBC-TV/Univ-TV(Stromberg) 1973 color 190m. (DR.FRANKENSTEIN-orig t) D: Jack Smight. SP: Christopher Isherwood, Don Bachardy. Ph: Arthur Ibbetson. Mus: Gil Melle. PD: Wilfrid Shingleton. SpFX: Roy Whybrow. Ref: MFB'74:250-51. TV. V 12/5/73:40. 6/29/73:26. with James Mason, Leonard Whiting, David McCallum, Jane Seymour, Michael Sarrazin(the monster), Michael Wilding, Agnes Moorehead, John Gielgud, Margaret Leighton, Ralph Richardson, Tom Baker.
Victor Frankenstein transplants a fellow doctor's brain into a creature composed of parts of dead bodies and brought to life with solar energy; another doctor blackmails Victor into constructing a female creature, dubbed Prima (Seymour). Themes of beauty and ugliness, on the level of The RAVEN(1935). The male monster beheads the female in public, and when asked why he did it replies, "Beautiful," which at least is succinct. Redeeming feature: Mason as the mastermind/bully Polidori.

FRANKENSTEIN'S CASTLE OF FREAKS (I) Aquarius/Classic Film Int'l (Straub) 1973 color 89m. (The MONSTERS OF DR.FRANKENSTEIN-orig t. The HOUSE OF FREAKS-alt t. TERROR CASTLE-ad t) D,P: Robert H. Oliver. Ref: TVFFSB. Lee. Willis/SW. V 10/3/73:5 (rated). 5/9/73:48,74(ad). 11/8/72:26. with Rossano Brazzi, Michael Dunn, Edmund Purdom, Gordon Michael, Christiane Royce.
With the aid of the Electric Accumulator, Dr. Frankenstein succeeds in discovering the secret of life; "Goliath the Giant," "Ook the Neanderthal Man," "Kreegin the Hunchback."

FRANKENSTEINS DAMON BEDROHT DIE WELT see GAMERA VS. JIGER

FRANKENSTEIN'S DRACULA see TENDER DRACULA

FRANKENSTEINS KAMPF GEGEN DIE TEUFELMONSTER see GODZILLA VS. THE SMOG MONSTER

The FREAK BARBER (B) Paul 1905 3m. D: J.Martin? Ref: BFC.
Barber cuts heads off customers, who in turn dismember him.

*FREAKS 1932 (FORBIDDEN LOVE-re-r t) Mus D: Gavin Barns. AD: Cedric Gibbons. Ref: screen. Cahiers de la Cin.#27:20. Lee.

It's still hard to know what to make of FREAKS. It seems as if it ought to be objectionable. It uses Siamese twins for perverse comedy, and a limbless man for bizarre spectacle. At its most banal it exploits stuttering. And (moving from the moral to the esthetic) it implicates both the normal and the abnormal in its broad melodramatics and contrived plotting. Yet the most melodramatic character--Cleo (Olga Baclanova)--is so despicable that she's amusing. Only she could possibly deserve what she gets. (Artificially-conferred freakism.) FREAKS seems suspended halfway between the enlightened and the benighted, compassion and exploitation. Its aims seem neither base nor noble, simply (and generally successfully) commercial.

FRENCH WITHOUT DRESSING (Can.) Sam Lake/IFA 1965 color 73m. D,P: Ted Leversuch. Ph: S. Lipinski. Mus: Jean Dore. Ref: AFI. with Laurie Darnell, Patricia Knight, Sharon Lynn.
Electronics company's new model TV set utilizes "fourth dimension" which gives viewer power over action on screen.

FRIDAY THE 13TH Para/Georgetown 1980 color 95m. D,P: Sean S. Cunningham. SP: Victor Miller. Sequel: FRIDAY THE 13TH PART 2. Ph: Barry Abrams. Mus: Harry Manfredini. AD: Virginia Field. SpMkpFX: Tom Savini; Taso Stavrakis. Atmospheric FX: Steve Kirshoff. SdFX: Ross Gaffney. Ref: FM 163:6-11. Boxo 1/7/80:5(ad). TV. SFC 5/14/80. MFB'80:132. V 5/14/80. with Adrienne King, Harry Crosby, Betsy Palmer, Mark Nelson.
Series of gory murders at Camp Crystal Lake--death by knife, arrow, hatchet, etc.; madwoman; nightmare coda. Little Lulu and Tubby at Summer Camp this isn't. Unfortunately. It's HALLOWEEN, with a touch of CARRIE and no class. The trailers told it all: 1,2,3,4....

FRIDAY THE 13TH PART 2 Para/Miner 1981 color 87m. D,P: Steve Miner. SP: Ron Kurz. Sequel to FRIDAY THE 13TH. Ph: Peter Stein. Mus: Harry Manfredini. PD: Virginia Field. SpFX: Steve Kirshoff. Titles: Modern. Ref: V 5/6/81. with Amy Steel, John Furey, Adrienne King, Warrington Gillette(Jason), Betsy Palmer.
More gore.

FRIDAY THE 13TH...THE ORPHAN see ORPHAN, The

FRIGHT (B) AA/British Lion/Fantale 1971 color 90m. D: Peter Collinson. SP: Tudor Gates. Ph: Ian Wilson. Mus: Harry Robinson. PD: Disley Jones. Ref: TV. TVG. MFB'71:219. V 10/27/71. VV 7/27/72. Cinef W'73:34. with Susan George, Ian Bannen, John Gregson, Honor Blackman, George Cole, C.L. Pack.
Homicidal maniac; babysitter alone in dark house; refs. to "ghosts" and horror movies; PLAGUE OF THE ZOMBIES on TV. Laughably transparent "maximum suspense" calculations.

FRIGHTMARE (B) Ellman/Heritage 1974('75-U.S.) color 86m. D: Pete Walker. SP: David McGillivray. Ph: Peter Jessop. Mus: Stanley Myers. AD: Chris Burke. Ref: MFB'75:8. Willis/

SW. with Rupert Davies, Sheila Keith, Deborah Fairfax, Paul Greenwood.
Married couple committed for murdering and devouring victims.

FRODO THE HOBBIT II see RETURN OF THE KING

FROG, The see PSYCHOMANIA(1972)

FROGS AI/Thomas-Edwards 1972 color 90m. D: George McCowan. SP: Robert Hutchison, Robert Blees. Ph: Mario Tosi. Mus: Les Baxter. Titles: Rabin. ElecFX: Joe Sidore. Ref: screen. MFB'72:138. Lee(V 3/29/72). VV 4/27/72. with Ray Milland, Sam Elliott, Joan Van Ark, Adam Roarke, Judy Pace, William Smith.
Ecological warfare, as frogs, snakes, lizards, spiders, and birds gang up on and kill humans. Some striking images--e.g., frogs hopping uncouthly across cakes, spiders spinning out long, feathery-elegant webs--and lots of croaking. (I can resist if you can.) But frogs and lizards just aren't very menacing, and most of the shocks are either telegraphed or otherwise muffed. Strained characterizations.

FROM BEYOND THE GRAVE (U.S.-B) WB/Amicus 1973('76-U.S., Mahler) color 98m. (The UNDEAD-orig t. TALES FROM BEYOND THE GRAVE-int t. TALES FROM THE BEYOND-ad t. The CREATURES-'80 re-r t) D: Kevin Connor. SP: Robin Clarke, Raymond Christodoulou. Based on R. Chetwynd-Hayes' stories "The Gate Crasher," "An Act of Kindness," "The Elemental," and "The Door." Ph: Alan Hume. Mus: Douglas Gamley. PD: Maurice Carter. SpFX: Alan Bryce. Mkp: Neville Smallwood. Ref: MFB'74:72. Lee. poster. Willis/SW. with Peter Cushing, David Warner, Donald and Angela Pleasence, Ian Bannen, Diana Dors, Margaret Leighton, Ian Ogilvy, Nyree Dawn Porter, Jack Watson, Lesley-Anne Down.
Four stories, involving spirit in magic mirror which demands victims, "witch-doll," invisible presence, magic room.

*FROM HELL IT CAME 1957 Story: Bernstein, J. Milner. AD: Rudi Feld. SpFX: James H. Donnelly. SpCostDes: Paul Blaisdell. Mkp: Harry Thomas. Ref: TV. Lee. and with Grace Mathews, Baynes Barron.
"It" is a "tabonga," a "wooden zombie" or "tree creature"--i.e., a two-legged tree. The scientists on its atoll talk about its "roots," but the fact that you can plainly see it walking about on two legs kind of ruins the "tree" effect. "Dialogue" means, primarily, exposition, and the script is charmingly ineffective at disguising that fact. (It often uses the ploy of having two characters just talking, that's all, just talking....)

FROM THE CLOUD TO THE RESISTANCE (I-F-W.G.-B) Straub-Huillet & RAI-TV/INA/JFuF/Artificial Eye 1979 color 103m. (DALLA NUBE ALLA RESISTENZA) SP,D,Ed: Jean-Marie Straub, Daniele Huillet. From Cesare Pavese's books "Dialoghi con Leuco" (Part 1) and "La Luna e I Falo" (Part 2). Ph: S. Diamanti, G. Canfarelli. Mus D: Gustav Leonhardt. Ref: MFB'80:45-6.

with Olimpia Carlisi, Guido Lombardi, Andrea Bacci, M. Monni.
Dialogue No.4 (of 6) in Part I: Two hunters, worried that the werewolf that they have just killed might still be part human, decide to bury it.

FROZEN FEAR(by R.Bloch) see ASYLUM

*The FROZEN GHOST 1945 Ref: TV. FM 169:40. V 6/13/45.
The works: missing persons kept in suspended animation as wax-museum exhibits; plot to drive hypnotist mad (latter thinks he "wished" man in trance dead); woman who uses telepathic hindsight to unravel mystery; mad plastic surgeon who fashions wax models. If Martin Kosleck as the madman makes acting look easy here, Lon Chaney Jr. (as the hypnotist) makes it look impossible, and he delivers the obligatory Chaney woe-is-me line: "Tragedy has determined to follow me wherever I go."

FROZEN SCREAM AFM/Renee Harmon 1980 D: Frank Roach. SP: Michael Soney, Celeste Hammond. Ph: Roberto Quazada. Ref: V 10/15/80:13,144: "horror pic....cryogenics." with R. Harmon, Thomas Gowan, Lee James, Sunny Bartholemew.

FU MANCHU see FIENDISH PLOT OF DR. FU MANCHU

FU MOON (J) Tezuka-TV 1980 anim 120m. Ref: JFFJ 13:30.
Alien visit to Earth in the future.

FUGITIVE FROM THE EMPIRE see ARCHER, The

FUKKATSU NO HI see VIRUS

FULL CIRCLE see HAUNTING OF JULIA, The

FUNF VERFLUCHTEN GENTLEMEN see FIVE DOOMED GENTLEMEN

The FUNHOUSE Univ/Neufeld-Power 1981 color/scope 96m. D: Tobe Hooper. SP: Larry Block. Ph: Andrew Laszlo. Mus: John Beal. PD: Morton Rabinowitz. SpFX: J.B. Jones. SpMkp:(des) Rick Baker;(exec) Craig Reardon. Ref: V 3/18/81: "carny Frankenstein." MFB'81:66: plot ref.to PSYCHO; clip from BRIDE OF FRANKENSTEIN. with Elizabeth Berridge, Cooper Huckabee, Miles Chapin, Sylvia Miles, William Finley, Wayne Doba(monster).
Teens trapped overnight with monster in carnival funhouse.

FURTHER MYSTERIES OF DR.FU MANCHU, The Stoll series D: Fred Paul. Ref: BFC. with H.Agar Lyons see CAFE L'EGYPTE,The. *COUGHING HORROR,The. *CRAGMIRE TOWER. *GOLDEN POMEGRANATES, The. GREEN MIST,The. GREYWATER PARK. KARAMANEH. MIDNIGHT SUMMONS,The.

FURTHER TALES FROM THE CRYPT see VAULT OF HORROR

The FURY Fox/Yablans 1978 color 118m. D: Brian De Palma. SP: John Farris, from his novel. Ph: Richard H. Kline. Mus: John

Williams. PD: Bill Malley. SpFX: A.D. Flowers. Mkp: William Tuttle. SpMkpFX: Rick Baker. Ref: MFB'78:200. TV. V 3/15/78. with Kirk Douglas, John Cassavetes, Carrie Snodgress, Charles Durning, Amy Irving, William Finley, Fiona Lewis, Carol Rossen.

Government research project develops individuals with psychic powers for use as potential weapons. But--as in The BOYS FROM BRAZIL--the sinister poli-sci-fi plot fails, again due to the uncontrollability of the subjects. (These masterminds just don't think ahead.) And the fact that the plotters here are our own officials--rather than a neo-Nazi network--doesn't really make the story more unnerving; it's just glib confirmation of popular cynicism. Hero Douglas is driven by various more-intense-and-simpler-than-life emotions (e.g., parental outrage, romantic guilt) that don't quite substitute for narrative drive. And while the psychic-emotional power of Irving and Andrew Stevens is showier than Douglas's theatrics, it's similarly unresonant. The "unifying" theme here seems to be revenge, that handy, all-purpose motivation. The film has its light moments, but needed a lot more of them.

FUTURE BOY CONAN (J) Toei/Nippon Anim-TV 1979 anim Ref: JFFJ 13:30: feature from TV-series footage.

FUTURE COP ABC-TV/Para-TV/Culzean-Tovern 1976 color 74m. D: Jud Taylor. SP,P: Anthony Wilson. See also: The COPS AND ROBIN. MAD BOMBER MYSTERY(P). Ref: TVFFSB: cybernetic rookie cop. TV Season. V 5/5/76:160. with Ernest Borgnine, Michael Shannon(android), John Larch, John Amos, Herbert Nelson.

FUTURE WOMEN (Gold Key-TV)/East West 1975?(1978?) color 90m. D: Jesus Franco. Ref: TVFFSB. V 2/25/81:75(ad). GKey: "supersonic electronic gadgetry." with Shirley Eaton, Richard Wyler, George Sanders.

Women of "Femina" plot to take over the world.

FUTUREWORLD AI 1976 color 107m. D: Richard T. Heffron. SP: Mayo Simon, George Schenck. Follow-up to WESTWORLD. Ph: H.Schwartz, G.Polito. Mus: Fred Karlin. AD: Trevor Williams. VisFxCoord: Brent Sellstrom. SpFX: Gene Grigg. Ref: MFB'76: 213-14. V 7/14/76. with Peter Fonda, Blythe Danner, Arthur Hill, Yul Brynner, John Ryan, Stuart Margolin, Allen Ludden, Robert Cornthwaite, Angela Greene, Judson Pratt.

Holiday center, Delos, reopens in 1985 with fail-safe robots.

GALAS DE LA PARAMOUNT see PARAMOUNT ON PARADE

GALAXIE (F) SGDP-Tanit-MRM 1972 D: Mathias Meregny. Ref: V 5/3/72:100: "cybernetic spies." Lee(p). with M.Green, H.Serre.

GALAXINA Crown Int'l/Marimar 1980 color 95m. SP,D: William Sachs. Ph: Dean Cundey. PD: Tom Turlley. SpPhFxSup: Chuck

Colwell. Ref: V 8/27/80: "ghoulish mutations." with Stephen Macht, Dorothy Stratten(robot), Avery Schreiber, H. Kaplowitz (alien), James D. Hinton.
3008 A.D. "Blue Star" force; space patrol.

GALAXY EXPRESS 999 (J) New World/Toei 1979 anim color (GINGA TETSUDO 999) D: Taro Rin. SP: Shiro Ishimori;(U.S.) Paul Grogan. Based on Leiji Matsumoto's TV series. Sequel: SAYONARA GINGA TETSUDO. Mus: Nozumi Aoki. Anim D: Kazuo Komatsubara. Ref: V 4/16/80(rated). 5/13/81:258. JFFJ 13: 8-9.
35th Century. Space train to the outer reaches of the universe.

GALAXY OF TERROR see PLANET OF HORRORS

GAME OF X, The see CONDORMAN

*GAMERA VS. GUIRON 1969 (KING KONG CONTRO GODZILLA-I) Ref: TV. Bianco #3/77:171.
Guest stars: "an outer-galaxy Gyaos," Guiron, and the cannibal girls of Tera, a twin planet to Earth on the far side of the sun. A film that defies you to suspend disbelief (just try), GAMERA VS. GUIRON (aka ATTACK OF THE MONSTERS on TV) is either impossibly naive or terribly knowing. Situation: two little boys fly away from Earth in a spaceship. Their earthbound playmate: "You get out of there or you'll get a scolding!" Situation: the cannibal girls catch the boys. Girl: "I'll check to see if the boys are poisonous. If not, they'll be our rations." Situation: same, later. Boy: "We're not good to eat!" Situation: Guiron's metal star smacks Gamera. Boy: "A go-go dancer! Gamera's doing a dance!" Situation: (see following). Doctor: "Gamera was seen headed this way, with a spaceship in his mouth." To be relished.

*GAMERA VS. JIGER 1970 (MONSTERS INVADE EXPO '70-SE Asia t. KING KONG L'IMPERO DEI DRAGHI-I. FRANKENSTEINS DAMON BEDROHT DIE WELT-G) Ref: Bianco Index'76:28. Lee. Glut/CMM.

*GAMERA VS. OUTER-SPACE MONSTER VIRUS 1968 scope (GAMERA TAI UCHU KAIJU BAIRUSU) D:(U.S.) Bret Morrison. Mus: Kenjiro Hirose. AD: Tomohisa Yano. SpFX(not Ph): Fujii, Kaneko. Ref: TV. WorldF'68. Lee.
Flying aliens in spaceship with "super-catch ray," laser ray, brain-control device, telepathic controls; 15-20m. of flashbacks to Barugon, the "quick-freeze monster," and Gyaos; friendly monster Gamera ("You can take his picture if you want")--his only weakness: "his overpowering kindness to children." Familiar cosmic melodramatics, relieved by some fun with the two scout-captives of the aliens, and by some strange story twists--e.g., the head alien divesting the others of their human bodies and absorbing them to become giant-size; Gamera using Virus as a surfboard. Tacky, idiotic, but sometimes damned hard to resist.

GAMERA VS. ZIGRA (J) Daiei 1971 color (GAMERA TAI SHINKAI KAIJU JIGURA) D: Noriaka Yuasa. Ref: Lee(Unijapan). with Ken Utsui, Yusuke Kawazu, Kayo Matsuo.
Gamera vs. giant ray-shooting fish.
See also: SUPER MONSTER GAMERA.

GANDAMU II (J) Shochiku 1981 anim feature Ref: V 8/19/81: 26: "sci-fier."

GANDY GOOSE IN FORTUNE HUNTERS see FORTUNE HUNTERS

GANJA AND HESS Heritage/Kelly-Jordan 1973 color 90m.(110m.) (VAMPIRES OF HARLEM-orig t. BLOOD COUPLE-alt t. DOUBLE POSSESSION-re-r t) SP,D: Bill Gunn. Ph: James E. Hinton. Mus: Sam Waymon. PD: Tom John. Ref: VV 3/14/74:75. Lee. Willis/SW. V 4/18/73. Cinef IX:3:39. TVFFSB. with Duane Jones, Marlene Clarke, Gunn, Waymon, Leonard Jackson.
Scientist "becomes afflicted with an ancient disease causing an insatiable addiction to blood." (TVFFSB)

*GAPPA--TRIPHIBIAN MONSTER AI-TV 1967 (aka MONSTER FROM AN UNKNOWN PLANET? DISTRUGGETO KONG,LA TERRA E IN PERICOLO-I) AD: K. Koike. SpFX:(& Story) Akira Watanabe;(ph) Isamu Kakita et al. Ref: TV. Bianco Index'76:44. WorldF'67.

GARDEN OF THE DEAD Entertainment Pyramid/Millenium 1972 color 59m. (TOMB OF THE UNDEAD-B) SP,D: John Hayes. Ph: Phil Kenneally. Mus: Jaime Mendoza-Nava. AD: Earl Marshall. SpFX: Richard Helmer. Ref: MFB'74:136. Willis/SW. Lee. V 9/20/72: 16(rated). with Duncan McLeod, John Dennis, Lee Frost, Susan Charney, Phil Hoover, Marland Proctor.
Formaldehyde revives dead convicts, turning them into "bloodthirsty zombies." (MFB)

GARDENER, The see SEEDS OF EVIL

GARGOYLES CBS-TV/Tomorrow Entertainment 1972 color 76m. D: B.W.L. Norton. SP: Stephen & Elinor Karpf. Ph: Earl Rath. Mus: Robert Prince. SpMkp: Ellis Burman, Stan Winston. SpFX: Milt Rice, George Peckham. Prologue: Michael S. Clark. Ref: TV. Lee. with Cornel Wilde, Jennifer Salt, Grayson Hall; Bernie Casey and Mickey Alzola(gargoyles); William Stevens.
After 500 years of incubation, hordes of gargoyle eggs begin to hatch deep within a system of caves in the American Southwest, fulfilling a prophecy that Satan's gargoyles would return to wage war on man. Fairly offbeat TV horror rates a merit award for venturesomeness at least. If the narrative framework is perfunctorily built, and the gargoyle mythology not very well developed, the half-human, half-reptile gargoyles themselves are hard not to watch. Except for Casey's banal "evil laugh," their scenes really _could_ be viewed fragments of life from another world.

GARRAS DE LORELEI, Las see WHEN THE SCREAMING STOPS

GASP! (Yug) Dan Tana/Avala 1977 color 91m. (KICMA) SP,D: Vlatko Gilic. Ph: Milic, Ivatovic. Mus: Walter Scharf. AD: V. Despotovic. Ref: Willis/SW. V(d) 9/23/77: "polluted Belgrade of the future." with D. Nikolic, S. Janjic.

GATE CRASHER,The(by R.C.-Hayes) see FROM BEYOND THE GRAVE

GATTI ROSSI IN UN LABIRINTO DI VETRO see EYEBALL

GATTO DI PARK LANE see BLACK CAT, The(1980?)

GAYATRI MAHIMA (India-Hindi) Bhatt Bros. 1977 color 124m. D: Harsukh Bhatt. SP: R. Priyadarshi. Mus: Chitragupta. Ref: Dharap. with Asis Kumar, Jaya Kaushalya, A. Bhatacharya.
"Sweets processed by black magic" drive man mad.

GAZ JAMEEN KE NEECHE see CRIME DOES NOT PAY

GEJAAGD DOOR DE WINST (Belg) Fugitive 1979 color D: Guido Henderickx, Robbe De Hert. Ref: V 5/9/79:500: "sci-fi trilogy."

GEMINI MAN NBC-TV/Univ-TV 1976 color 95m. (CODE NAME MINUS ONE-alt TV t. The NEW INVISIBLE MAN-orig t) D: Alan Levi. SP, P: Leslie Stevens, based on H.G. Wells' novel "The Invisible Man." Ph: Enzo Martinelli. Mus: Billy Goldenberg. AD: David Marshall. Ref: TV. TVFFSB: TV-series pilot. TVG. TV Season. V 5/19/76:98. Glut/CMM. with Ben Murphy, Katherine Crawford, Richard A. Dysart, Dana Elcar, Gregory Walcott, Austin Stoker, H.M. Wynant, Quinn Redeker, Paul Shenar, Cheryl Miller.
Injury gives special agent the power of invisibility.

GEMINI TWINS, The see TWINS OF EVIL

Le GENDARME ET LES EXTRA-TERRESTRES (F) SNC 1979 color 92m. D: Jean Giranet. SP: Jacques Vilfrid, based on Richard Balducci's characters; 5th in a series. Ph: M. Grignon, D.Tarot. Mus: Raymond Lefevre. Ref: V 4/4/79. 5/7/80:476: planned sequel "The Gendarme and the Revenge of the Aliens." with Louis de Funes, Michel Galabru, Maurice Risch, J.P. Rambal.
Metalloid space creatures that can assume human form land in St. Tropez to study human mores.

GENESIS II CBS-TV/Norway 1973 color 76m. D: John L. Moxey. SP,P: Gene Roddenberry. Ph: G.P. Finnerman. Mus: Harry Sukman. AD: Hilyard Brown. Mkp: Tom Burman? Ref: TV. Lee(V 3/28/73). with Alex Cord, Mariette Hartley, Ted Cassidy, Percy Rodrigues, Lynne Marta, Liam Dunn.
Man from 1979 awakens from suspended animation in 2133 A.D. (post-Great Conflict Earth). Transcontinental sub-shuttle; Pax, unisexual society preserving nature and art; Terranians, two-hearted mutants; fortress Phoenix, Ariz.; sonic pain/pleasure "stims." Low-grade "humanistic" sf uneasily yokes The TIME MACHINE, SPARTACUS, and LOST HORIZON. 1979 and 2133 both play like now-dated 1973. Hartley has a few interesting

scenes in an is-she-or-isn't-she? role.
See also: PLANET EARTH. STRANGE NEW WORLD.

GERTIE ON TOUR McCay 1917 anim 2m. D: Winsor McCay. Sequel to ***GERTIE THE DINOSAUR. Ref: Lee. PFA notes 12/15/76. no LC. screen: Gertie takes a streetcar.

GET SMART see NUDE BOMB, The

GETTING CLEAN (Cz) 1973? anim color 10m. See also: DEADLY ODOR,The. Ref: IFG'74:529.

GHASTLY ORGIES OF COUNT DRACULA see REINCARNATION OF ISABEL

***GHOSKS IS THE BUNK 1939 D: Dave Fleischer. Anim: W.Henning, A. Matthews. Ref: Maltin/OMAM: Popeye. LC.

*The GHOST AND MRS. MUIR 1947 AD: Richard Day, George Davis. SpFX: Fred Sersen. Ref: screen. V 5/21/47.
Mrs. Muir, as played by Gene Tierney, is vacuous, childish, pouty. Obviously, she hasn't a chance against George Sanders' comically self-conscious cad. It's cruel irony that this frail woman should fall into that man's clutches. A romantic dream world with ectoplasmic Captain Gregg (Rex Harrison) seems her only possible refuge from an unlovely real world. However, her patient anticipation of that world--in the film's latter scenes--is, oddly, treated as quiet triumph, and not as defeat. (Which tone might have tinged these scenes with something like bittersweet ambivalence.) One begins, in retrospect, to suspect that Tierney's poutiness was meant to be pluck, and her vacuousness was supposed to be some mysterious "inner reserve" of strength. Her ticket to dream-world is claimed, it seems, as a reward rather than as a cosmic consolation prize. Most of the irony of the Tierney-Sanders mismatch was, apparently, it transpires, an accident of casting. Mrs. Muir seems, after all, a conventional, conventionally-rewarded heroine (Mrs.Mere), rather than a tragically fragile woman, though Tierney's tenuousness as an actress succeeds in making the movie an interesting narrative conundrum. One can, to be sure, also be misled by Bernard Herrmann's score, which is less an enrichment of the film than its raison d'etre.

GHOST BUSTERS see SPOOK BUSTERS

GHOST EYES (H.K.) Shaw 197-? D: Kuei Chih-Hung. Ref: MFB '75:174: "horror movie."

A GHOST FOR SALE (B) Bushey 1952 31m. D: Victor M. Gover. SP: John Gilling. Ref: BFC: scenes from CURSE OF THE WRAYDONS. with Tod Slaughter, Patrick Barr, Tucker McGuire.
"Manor caretaker relates tale of mad squire, and vanishes."

GHOST GALLEON, The see HORROR OF THE ZOMBIES

The GHOST HUNTER (Braz) Circus 1975 color 80m. (O CACADOR DE FANTASMA) SP,D: Flavio Migliaccio, from Oscar Wilde's "The Canterville Ghost." Ph: J. Medeiros. Mus: Stefan Wohl. Ref: Brasil. with Migliaccio, Estelita Bell, Roberto Maia.
Inventor's machine takes him into parallel universe; "frightening house."

GHOST IN THE NIGHT see GHOSTS ON THE LOOSE

The GHOST LADY (Arg) San Miguel 1945 (La DAMA DUENDE) D: Luis Saslavsky. SP: Maria Teresa Leon, Rafael Alberto. Story: D.P.C. de la Barca. Ph: Jose M. Beltran. Ref: V 6/27/45. with Delia Garces, Enrique Diosdado, Ernesto Vilches.
Young widow poses as ghost in her castle.

The GHOST OF FLIGHT 401 NBC-TV/Para-TV & Lavery Jr. 1978 color 94m. D: Steven H. Stern. SP: Robert M. Young. From the book by John G. Fuller. Ph: Howard Schwartz. Mus: David Raksin. AD: Dan Lomino. Opt: Freeze Frame. Narr: Paul Frees. Ref: TV. TVG. TVFFSB. with Ernest Borgnine, Kim Basinger, Robert F. Lyons, Gary Lockwood, Eugene Roche, Carol Rossen, Tina Chen, Russell Johnson, Angela Clarke, Howard Hesseman.
Ghostly appearances of pilot (Borgnine) on ASA L-1011 flights are psychometrically linked with parts salvaged from crash in which he died; refs. to wolf's-bane, Karloff, etc. A serious ghost story based on incidents reported between 1972 and 1974. Like AUDREY ROSE it asks not just for suspended disbelief, but for belief, and relies a bit heavily on that old dramatic device, the skeptic (Lockwood). It's tasteful, occasionally touching, even convincing, but dramatically too conventional. The script brings back the dead, but it doesn't know what to do with them except startle the living. (The dead pilot's wife, who appreciates his continued presence, simply drops out of the picture.)

*The GHOST OF FRANKENSTEIN 1942 Sequel to SON OF FRANKENSTEIN. Sequel: FRANKENSTEIN MEETS THE WOLF MAN. Props: Ellis Burman. Ref: TV. FM 165:38. Glut/TFL: footage from FRANKENSTEIN(1931). with Cedric Hardwicke(Ludwig Frankenstein/ghost of his father).
This one has its novelties--at one point you get to hear Bela Lugosi's voice coming from Lon Chaney Jr.'s lips. (Ygor's brain has been placed in the Monster's head.) But the script employs the elements of the Thirties Frankensteins as only so many random building-blocks for the plot. GHOST has atmospheric music, lighting, and camerawork--it's watchable, but oh-so-empty. Even Lugosi, as Ygor--a high point of SON--is, like co-star Lionel Atwill, simply another, humorless "B"-ish villain here, and is given little time to relish his lines. In the Forties, he actually had (slightly) more interesting roles at PRC and Monogram than at Universal.

*GHOST PATROL Excelsior 1936 Ph: J. Greenhalgh. ElecFX: Kenneth Strickfaden. Ref: screen. Turner/Price.
Radium-tube invention "controls all electricity." An early

comic bit (in which some bad men joke about a death-ray-gunned plane) gives decidedly-false promise that there will be some kind of relief from the plot, and from Tim McCoy, who seems to have gotten a steely glint stuck in his eye.

**The GHOST SHIP RKO 1943 69m. P: Val Lewton. D: Mark Robson. SP: Donald H. Clarke. Story: Leo Mittler. Ph: Nicholas Musuraca. Mus: Roy Webb. AD: Albert S. D'Agostino, Walter E. Keller. SpFX: Vernon L. Walker. Ref: screen. V 12/29/43. Lee. Siegel/VL. Everson. with Richard Dix, Russell Wade, Edith Barrett, Ben Bard, Edmund Glover, Skelton Knaggs, Sir Lancelot, Lawrence Tierney, Alec Craig, Paul Marion, R. Bice.
The sailing ship Altair's captain proves to be a psychopathic killer. Dix is very good cast very much against type as the paranoid captain. ("Try! Try! Try!") But most of the other actors are at best bearable, and Edith Barrett has one long, dumbfounding speech which tops even the most embarrassing disquisitions in LEOPARD MAN. Typically, some of Lewton's best melancholic effects are immediately cancelled by false bits of optimism, and the film concludes limply with Knaggs' "men are basically good" speech. Some choice black-comedy bits help.

GHOST STORY NBC-TV/William Castle 1972 color 52m. D: John L. Moxey. SP: Richard Matheson. Ref: TV: pilot movie for series. V 9/20/72:30. Cinef III:2:19. with Barbara Parkins, Jeanette Nolan, Sam Jaffe, Sebastian Cabot.
Ghosts seem to possess baby, statue, radio. Some good plot twists; poor dialogue.

A GHOST STORY (India-Bengali) Mukul Roy 1973 141m. (KAYA HINER KAHINI) SP,D: Ajoy Kar. SP: also Salil Sen. Story: N. Ghosh. Ph: B. Chakraborty. Mus: M. Roy. Ref: Dharap. with Uttam Kumar, Aparna Sen, Bikash Roy, C. Devi.
"Suspense story": woman appears after her death to tell story of betrayal by lover.

GHOST STORY (B) Weeks 1974 color 89m. SP,D,P: Stephen Weeks. SP: also Rosemary Sutcliff. Ph: Peter Hurst. Mus: Ron Geesin. AD: Peter Young. Ref: MFB'75:154-55. V 2/12/75: 34: at Avoriaz. with Larry Dann, Murray Melvin, Vivian Mackerall, Marianne Faithfull, Barbara Shelley.
Ghost-seeker with scientific equipment; ghostly visions.

GHOST STORY 1981 D: John Irvin. Ref: V. New York. with Melvyn Douglas, Fred Astaire, John Houseman, D.Fairbanks Jr.

The GHOST WALKS (B) Central 1935 22m. D,P: Walter Tennyson. Ref: BFC. with George Bass, Barbara Gott.

A GHOSTLY AFFAIR (B) Hepworth 1914 D: H. Plumb? Ref: BFC.
"Burglar robs old castle where paintings come alive."

GHOSTS,The(by A.Barber) see AMAZING MR. BLUNDEN,The

The GHOSTS' HOLIDAY (B) Hepworth 1907 9m. D: Lewin Fitzhamon. Ref: BFC. with Gertie Potter.
"Ghosts rise from churchyard and hold ball in hotel."

The GHOSTS OF HANLEY HOUSE NTA-TV/Emerson 1974 80m. Ref: TVFFSB: "the ghosts...take over." with Elsie Baker, Barbara Chase, Wilkie De Martel, Cliff Scott.

*GHOSTS ON THE LOOSE 1943 (GHOST IN THE NIGHT-orig t) AD: David Milton. Ref: TV. V 7/7/43. 3/31/43:46.
Revolving portraits, trap doors, secret rooms, screams, and "spooky" music (Edward J.Kay's Charlie Chan themes played more slowly). The plot: "East Side Kids," cops, newlyweds, and Nazis wander around moving furniture back and forth from one old house to another. For all Bela Lugosi has to do he might as well _be_ a piece of the furniture--sample snappy line: "Idiots! Imbeciles! All of you!" Huntz Hall has two or three funny bits (out of 46).

GHOSTS THAT STILL WALK Gold Key-TV/Flocker 1978 color 96m. SP,D: James T. Flocker. Ph: Holger Kasper. Mus: Ronald Stein; Hod S(c)hudson et al. Sets: Timothy Doughten. SdFxEd: C.T. Welch. Ref: TV. GKey. with Matt Boston, Ann Nelson, Jerry Jensen, Caroline Howe, Phil Catalli.
Earthbound spirit of American Indian mummy possesses boy (while _his_ astral body is elsewhere), kills members of his family to keep its presence secret; rolling boulders terrorize couple travelling through desert in motor home. Or, the curse of the two-hour TV-time-slot, which causes every scene in syndicated made-for-TV movies to take at least 10 minutes, and featurettes-at-best to transform, before your eyes, into 95-minute features. This lethargic mixture of BACK FROM THE DEAD and The MUMMY(1932) at least has one inventive (if overlong) sequence--the desert rocks congregating, then practicing what looks like broad-jumping over the old folks' motor home. (The _Living_ Desert....)

*The GHOUL 1933 Ref: screen. Everson.
Sacred amulet, "The Eternal Light," supposedly confers immortality on its possessor. Boris Karloff's Egyptologist is _not_ a ghoul (of either the body-snatching or supernatural variety). He's simply a cataleptic who lopes about like a gangster-goon (and who _somehow_ acquired a shrivelled-up face and the ability to bend iron window-bars with his bare hands). The GHOUL is wonderfully rife with tree-shadow and other weird lighting effects, and there's a frantic, serial-like climax, in which the amulet changes hands more times than the earrings of Madame De. Unfortunately, this long-lost "classic" plays like a Forties PRC or Monogram which just happens to feature several renowned British actors: Cedric Hardwicke has a few bright lines and comes off least worst; Ernest Thesiger (as a Renfield-type) and Ralph Richardson (as a "parson") are both pretty much wasted; and Karloff is stuck in the most unfortunate role of all. Half the movie is just your basic

skulking. (It rivals NIGHT OF TERROR, of the same year, in that department.)

The GHOUL (B) Tyburn 1975 color 87m. (The THING IN THE ATTIC-U.S.,'78?) D: Freddie Francis. SP: Anthony Hinds(aka J.Elder). Ph: John Wilcox. Mus: Harry Robinson. AD: Jack Shampan. Mkp: Roy Ashton. Ref: MFB'75:155. Meyers. CineFan 2:42,46. V 6/11/75. with Peter Cushing, John Hurt, Alexandra Bastedo, Veronica Carlson, Don Henderson(the ghoul).
"Dr. Lawrence keeps a ghoulish creature who feeds off human flesh." (MFB)

GIANT IRON MAN ONE-SEVEN--The AERIAL BATTLESHIP (J) Toei-TV 1977 scope 20m. (DAITETSUJIN WANSEBUN--KUCHU SENKAN) D: Kan Wakabayashi. Ref: JFFJ 13:34.
Episode of TV series shown theatrically; "renegade robot."

The GIANT SPIDER INVASION Crest/Group 1/Transcentury(Cinema Group 75) 1975 color 76m. D,P: Bill Rebane. Sp,Story,P: Richard L. Huff. SP: also Robert Easton. Ph: Jack Willoughby. AD: Ito Rebane. SpFX: Richard Albain, Robert Millay. Ref: MFB'77:43. Meyers. ad. King/DM. LAT 2/27/76. TV. with Steve Brodie, Barbara Hale, Leslie Parrish, Alan Hale, Bill Williams.
Queen-monster spider and hordes of smaller spiders go on a rampage following a mysterious gamma ray shower, get into dresser drawers, blenders, etc.

GIFT FROM A RED PLANET see ALPHA INCIDENT, The

GINGA TETSUDO 999 see GALAXY EXPRESS 999

GINGERBREAD HOUSE see WHO SLEW AUNTIE ROO?

The GIRL FROM S.I.N. CIP/Bobmoral 1966 67m. (aka The GIRL FROM THE SECRET INNER NETWORK?) SP,D: C. Davis Smith. Ref: AFI. no LC. with Joyana, Sal Rogge, Barbie Kemp.
Scientist concocts invisibility pills.

The GIRL FROM STARSHIP VENUS (B) Intercontinental/Meadway 1975 ('78-U.S.) color 85m. (DIARY OF A SPACE VIRGIN-B. The SEX-PLORER-orig B.t) SP,D: Derek Ford. Ph: Roy Pointer. Mus: John Shakespeare. AD: E. Konkel. Ref: MFB'75:160-61. '76:66. AMPAS. with Monika Ringwald, Andrew Grant, Mark Jones.
Alien visits Earth in guise of young woman.

GIRLSAPOPPIN Preferred 1964 60m. Ref: AFI. no LC.
Chimpanzee scientist's banana-making machine explodes, propelling him through the time barrier.

*GLEN OR GLENDA Screen Classic 1953 75m. (GLENN OR GLENDA-'81 re-r t) Ph: William C. Thompson. Mus Cons: Sandford Dickinson. AD: Jack Miles. Mkp: Harry Thomas. Ref: screen. B. Hill: <u>not</u> sfa JAIL BAIT. with E. Wood(aka D. Davis).
Nightmare seq. with leering devil; Bela Lugosi shown

"creating life" in a beaker. Ed Wood employs all the resources of the cinema--split screen, voice-over, expressionistic lighting, montage, narrative ellipsis, dream imagery--and his industriousness is not unappreciated. GLEN OR GLENDA plays more like an experimental film than a narrative film. It is, however, a failed experiment, intermittently hilarious camp. Wood tries everything--nothing works. (Although there is something eerie about those split-screen shots of the "giant" Lugosi looking down upon the "ants" of the city....) Impossibly sincere exploitation film reduces to the inevitable howlers. ("Glen, is it another woman?" asks the closet-transvestite's girl friend at one point.)

The GLITTERBALL (B) CFF/Forstater 1977 color 56m. Story & D: Harley Cokliss. Story & SP: Howard Thompson. Ph: Alan Hall. Mus: Harry Robinson. SpFX: Charles Page. SpPhFX: Brian Johnson. Anim: Barry Leith. Ref: MFB'77:98-99,134. with Ben Buckton, Keith Jayne, Ron Pember, Marjorie Yates.
Spaceship discharges small metal spherical aliens.

GLUMP see PLEASE DON'T EAT MY MOTHER!

GO FOR A TAKE (B) Century 1972 color 90m. Story & D: Harry Booth. Story & SP: Alan Hackney. Ph: M. McDonald. Mus: Glen Mason. AD: Lionel Couch. SpFX: Les Bowie. Ref: Glut/TDB. MFB'73:9. with Dennis Price(Dracula), Reg Varney, Sue Lloyd, Julie Ege, Anouska Hempel.

GO TO THY DEATHBED(by S.Forbes) see REFLECTION OF FEAR

GOD TOLD ME TO see DEMON!

The GODSEND (U.S.-B) Cannon 1980 color 90m. D,P: Gabrielle Beaumont. SP: Olaf Pooley. From the novel by Bernard Taylor. Ph: Norman Warwick. Mus: Roger Webb. AD: Tony Curtis. Mkp: Di Biggs. Ref: ad. V 1/16/80. 5/7/80:503. TV. with Malcolm Stoddard, Cyd Hayman, Angela Pleasence, Patrick Barr; Wilhelmina Green & Joanne Boorman(Bonnie).
Occult albino child wreaks havoc with rivals. Push-button shocks-and-pathos, but the little girl who plays the killer-tyke is creepily angelic--she has a fixed, smug, unnerving half-smile, and white hair that positively shimmers. She always looks as if she's plotting unholy acts. (Whether she is or not.) Later (about three years on in the story), a bad little actress--given to narrowing her eyes effectlessly--takes over the role, and the film dies on the spot.

*GODZILLA, KING OF THE MONSTERS (Transworld-TV) 1954 (65m.-TV) (DAIKAIJU NO KAITEI NIMAN MARU-orig t) Story: Shigeru Kayama. AD: Satoshi Chuko, Takeo Kita;(sp fx) Akira Watanabe. SpCostDes: Ryosaku Takasugi. Ref: TV. Glut/CMM. JFFJ 13:16-21. Lee. and with Haru Nakajima(Godzilla).
H-bomb testing unleashes 100-million-year-old prehistoric monster. First but far-from-best of the series, GODZILLA (at

least in the hour-plus U.S. version) is mostly rote havoc. And, strangely, the movie's most distinctive feature now is the dolorous voice of Raymond Burr relating the story of the destruction of Tokyo. There are also some fairly eerie early scenes on a Pacific island, but Godzilla's more ingratiating performances came later.

See also the following films, and GAMERA VS. GUIRON. STAR GODZILLA(P). TERROR OF MECHAGODZILLA.

GODZILLA ON MONSTER ISLAND (J) Cinema Shares Int'l(Downtown)/ Toho Eizo 1972('78-U.S.) color/scope 89m. (GOJIRA TAI GAIGAN. GODZILLA VS.GIGAN-alt t. WAR OF THE MONSTERS-B) D: Jun Fukuda. SP: Shinichi Sekizawa. Ph: K. Hasegawa. Mus: Akira Ifukube. AD: Y. Honda. SpFX: Shokei Nakano. Ref: screen. MFB'77:99. with Hiroshi Ishikawa, Yuriko Hishimi, Haru Nakajima(Godzilla), Y. Omiya(Angurus), Kanta Ina(Ghidrah), K. Nakayama(Gigan), Tomoko Umeda.

The monsters from GIGANTIS vs. Ghidrah and Gigan (or Gilligan), the latter two controlled by tape by cockroaches from outer space. Highlights: the tapes arousing the two monsters; Godzilla and Angurus chatting; the climactic melee. These stray delights, unfortunately,merely punctuate a plot the fantasticalness of which never quite "takes," and which generally features slight variations on old monster-tricks. The cartoonist-hero saves the best monsters for his strip: Shukra, or Homework Monster, and Momagon, the Monster of Too-Strict Mothers.

GODZILLA VS. MECHAGODZILLA see GODZILLA VS.THE COSMIC MONSTER

GODZILLA VS. MEGALON (J) Cinema Shares Int'l/Toho-Eizo 1973 ('76-U.S.) color/scope 82m. (GOJIRA TAI MEGARO. KING-KONG, DA MONEN AUS DEM WELTALL-G) SP,D: Jun Fukuda. Story: Shinichi Sekizawa. Ph: Yuzuru Aizawa. Ref: Glut/CMM. TV. Lee. V 7/21/76:7. 6/16/76: "Borodan, a big, black chicken."

Three-million-year-old Seatopia, kingdom beneath the sea, unleashes Megalon on atom-happy Earth. Also: Godzilla; flying robot that becomes giant; bit with Rodan and Angurus on Monster Island; theme song for robot. Megalon's broad-jump-type hops when out of control are amusing, but most of the movie is just miscellaneous destruction, marking time until the long, nuttily-choreographed monster battle at the end. Hero to Jet Jaguar, the flying robot: "Get Godzilla--he's on Monster Island!"

GODZILLA VS. THE COSMIC MONSTER (J) Cinema Shares Int'l(Downtown)/Toho Eizo 1974('77-U.S.) color/scope 80m. (GOJIRA TAI MEKAGOJIRA. GODZILLA VS.THE BIONIC MONSTER-alt t. GODZILLA VS.MECHAGODZILLA-int t. KING KONG GEGEN GODZILLA-G) SP,D: Jun Fukuda. SP: also H. Yamaura. Story: S. Sekizawa, M. Fukushima. Sequel: TERROR OF MECHAGODZILLA. Ph: Yuzuru Aizawa. Mus: Masaru Sato. AD: Kazuo Satsuya. SpPhFX: Akiyoshi Nakano. Ref: MFB'77:122,179. Glut/CMM. TV. with Masaaki Daimon, Kazuya Aoyama, Akihiko Hirata, Hiroshi Koizumi.

And Godzilla, Angurus, Mechagodzilla (cyborg made of space titanium and controlled by aliens from the third planet of the Black Hole), and legendary monster King Seeser, who, revived by song, helps Godzilla defeat Mechagodzilla; wounded and dying aliens revert to beast-form; G. turns self into magnetic pole; M. first in G.'s image, then as flying, armored robot. Not one of the better Godzillas, but lively enough. Seeser looks and moves like a giant, demonic rodent-quarterback.

GODZILLA VS. THE SMOG MONSTER (J) AI/Toho 1971('72-U.S.) color/scope 85m. (GOJIRA TAI HEDORA. FRANKENSTEINS KAMPF GEGEN DIE TEUFELMONSTER-G) SP,D: Yoshimitsu Banno. SP: also Kaoru Mabuchi. Ph: Yoichi Manoda. Mus: Riichiro Manabe. AD: Inoue. SpFX: Shokei Nakano. Eng.-lang.vers: Lee Kresel. Ref: TV. MFB'75:82. Willis/SW. Glut/CMM. with Akira Yamauchi, Toshie Kimura, Hiroyuki Kawase.

The hideous Smog Monster fries people, corrodes metal--and even dares to propel sludge at Godzilla. It looks like a giant, horribly-tarred-and-feathered owl. Movie, like monster, demands a mixed response: awe, helpless laughter, dismay. If it's overlong and badly acted, it's also chock-full of cartoons, songs, and bizarre fantasies. One pair of shots matches men shuffling scrabble squares with Godzilla swinging the Smog Monster--to ask "Why?" is to ask the unanswerable.

GODZILLA'S REVENGE (J) UPA/Toho 1971(1969) color/scope 92m. (ORU KAIJU DAISHINGEKI. TERROR OF GODZILLA-int t?) D: Inoshiro Honda. SP: Shinichi Sekizawa. Ph: M. Tomioka. Mus: Kunio Miyauchi. AD: Takeo Kita. SpFX: Eiji Tsuburaya. Ref: screen. Lee. Glut/CMM: stock shots from FRANKENSTEIN CONQUERS THE WORLD, GODZILLA VS.THE SEA MONSTER, SON OF GODZILLA, KING KONG ESCAPES. with Kenji Sahara, T. Yazaki, Machiko Naka.

Boy dreams he meets monsters Baragon, Ebirah, Minyah (Godzilla's son), Spiega, etc., on Monster Island; Minyah shrinks himself to chat with him, then resumes monster-size to fight and defeat bully-monster Gabara. (A pat on the head here from Dad.) The boy's story might have been condensed a bit, but the boy-and-the-pint-size-Minyah scenes are crazily endearing. (Minyah to bad monster: "Nyah, nyah, nyah, nyah!") Priceless: Minyah flapping his arms to indicate intense pleasure. A small charmer (i.e., Minyah <u>and</u> film--relative to Godzilla, at least, Minyah is small).

GOJIRA TAI GAIGAN see GODZILLA ON MONSTER ISLAND

GOJIRA TAI HEDORA see GODZILLA VS.THE SMOG MONSTER

GOJIRA TAI MEGARO see GODZILLA VS.MEGALON

GOJIRA TAI MEKAGOJIRA see GODZILLA VS.THE COSMIC MONSTER

GOLD KEY "ZODIAC" SERIES Ref: TVFFSB. B.Warren. J.Dante: filmed? released under different ts.?

See: AGE OF PISCES. AQUARIAN,The. ARIES COMPUTER,The.

LEFT HAND OF GEMINI. LEO CHRONICLES,The. LOST WORLD OF LIBRA. PRELUDE TO TAURUS. SAGITTARIUS MINE,The. SCORPIO SCARAB,The. UNDER THE SIGN OF CAPRICORN. VENGEANCE OF VIRGO.

The GOLDEN HAIRPIN (H.K.-Cant.) H.K. Film Co. 1963 4-part serial (BIXIE JINCHAI) D: Chen Liepin. SP: Yin Haiqing. Story: Jin Tong. Ph: Liang Hong. Mus: Pan Chao. AD: Dong Peixin. Ref: HKFFest. with Zheng Yingcai, Yu Suqiu.
"Underground labyrinth which induces hallucinations"; "palm power"; super-human hero.

The GOLDEN SEA (G) Decla-Bioscop 1919 tinted 53m. (Der GOLDENE SEE) Part I of series, The Spiders (Die Spinnen). SP,D: Fritz Lang. Ph: Emil Schunemann. AD: O. Hunte et al. SpProps: Heinrich Umlauff. Ref: FQ W'79:3. Ott/FOFL. Lee. screen. MFB'81:14-15. with Carl de Vogt, Lil Dagover, R.Orla.
"Spiders," master criminals led by Lio-Sha, who leave stuffed spiders with victims; descendants of Incas who guard gold in caverns under lake; oval mirror which becomes viewing screen. Slow, naive early Lang, with some evocative gold and blue tinting.

The GOLDEN VOYAGE OF SINBAD (U.S.-B) Col/Morningside 1974 color/Dynarama 105m. (SINBAD'S GOLDEN VOYAGE-orig t) D: Gordon Hessler. Story & SP: Brian Clemens. Story,SpVisFX & Assoc P: Ray Harryhausen. Ph: Ted Moore. Mus: Miklos Rozsa. PD: John Stoll. Masks: Colin Arthur. Ref: screen. MFB'74:8. Lee. V 1/16/74. with John Philip Law, Caroline Munro, Tom Baker, Gregoire Aslan, Douglas Wilmer, Aldo Sambrell.
Lost land of Lemuria, magician, oracle, invisibility, demon, Griffin, living statue of Kali, cyclops. A "plus" for the Homunculi (which out-act the humans) and for the ship's figurehead (squeaking as it moves), and for portions of the other effects scenes. A "minus" for the acting, dialogue, story, and "humor."

Das GOLDENE DING (W.G.) Reitz 1971 color 118m. SP,D,P: Edgar Reitz et al. Mus: Nikos Mamangates. Ref: V 2/2/72. Lee. with Christian Reitz, Oliver Jovine, Colombe Smith.
Jason and the Golden Fleece; sea monsters, superhumans, clashing rocks of Bosporas.

GOLEM (Pol) Film Polski/PFU 1980 color & sepia 92m. SP,D: Piotr Szulkin. SP: also Tadeusz Sobolewski, from Gustav Meyrink's novel. Ph: Zygmunt Samosiuk. Sets: Z. Warpechowski, J. Wlasow. Ref: V 10/1/80. FM 169:7. with Marek Walczewski, Krystyna Janda, Joanna Zolkowska.
In a future society, scientifically-developed "monsters" are the norm.

GOLEM'S DAUGHTER see GOULVE, La

GOOD AGAINST EVIL ABC-TV/Fox-TV & Bolen-Frankel 1977 color 74m. D: Paul Wendkos. SP: Jimmy Sangster. Mus: Lalo Schifrin.

AD: Richard Y. Haman. Ref: TV Season. TVFFSB: Devil, witches, exorcism. with Dack Rambo, Elyssa Davalos, Richard Lynch, Dan O'Herlihy, Lelia Goldoni.

GOODBYE,SPACESHIP YAMATO see SPACE CRUISER YAMATO PART II

GOOFY GROCERIES WB 1941 anim 7m. D: Bob Clampett. SP: M. Millar. Ref: LC. Glut/CMM: "giant gorilla." Maltin/OMAM.

GOONJ see ECHO, The

GOONLAND see POPEYE IN GOONLAND

GOOPY GYNE BAGHA BYNE see ADVENTURES OF GOOPY AND BAGHA

The GORE GORE GIRLS Lewis 1972 color 90m. D,P,Mus: Herschell Gordon Lewis. SP: Alan J. Dachman. Ph: Alex Ameripoor. Ref: Lee. V 8/7/74:21. Medved/TGTA: aka BLOOD ORGY. with Frank Kress, Amy Farrell, Ray Sager, Henny Youngman, Hedda Lubin.

Series of brutal murders; gore, gore.

*The GORILLA 1939 Ref: screen: robot??

A man hires three detectives to protect him when "the gorilla" threatens to murder him at midnight in his old, dark mansion. Familiar horror and comedy--the Ritz Brothers followed by a gorilla, the Ritz Brothers followed by a dummy, etc. Some of the "takes" just go on and on. Bela Lugosi simply opening a peep-hole in one bit, however, is somehow very amusing.

The GORILLA MYSTERY Disney 1930 anim 7m. Ref: LC.

La GOULVE (F) Welp 1971 color 87m. (EROTIC WITCHCRAFT-B. GOLEM'S DAUGHTER. HOMO VAMPIRE-alt ts?) SP,D: M. Mercier. D,P: Bepi Fontana. Ph: Paul Soulignac. Mus: Guy Boulanger. Ref: MFB'73:97. with Herve Hendricks, Cesar Torres, Maika Simon(La Goulve), Anne Varese.

Spirit of snake goddess in portrait possesses humans.

GRADUATION, The see PROWLER, The

GRADUATION DAY IFI/Scope III 1981 color 85m. SP,D: Herb Freed. SP: also Anne Marisse. Ph: D. Yarussi. Ref: V 5/20/81. with Christopher George, E.J. Peaker, E.D. Murphy.

Murderer stalks small-town high school; death by sword, spear, etc.

GRAN AMOR DEL CONDE DRACULA see CEMETERY GIRLS

GRANDE TROUILLE, La see TENDER DRACULA

GRAVE OF THE VAMPIRE Entertainment Pyramid/Clover(Millenium) 1972(1975) color 95m. D & Adap: John Patrick Hayes. SP: David Chase, from his novel "The Still Life." Ph: Paul Hipp.

Mus: Jaime Mendoza-Nava. AD: Lee Fisher. Mkp: Tino Zacchia. Ref: MFB'74:175-6. Willis/SW. Lee. V 8/30/72:5(rated). with William Smith, Michael Pataki(vampire), Lyn Peters, Inga Neilsen, Diane Holden, Jay Adler.

Woman raped by vampire gives birth to boy who becomes vampire; seance, spirit possession.

GRAVEYARD OF HORROR see NECROPHAGUS

GRAVITY (Showtime-TV) 1976? live & anim 7m. SP,D,Ph,Ed: Michael Nankin, David Wechter. Mus: D. & Julius Wechter. Ref: TV.

Jiminy Gravity tells us what to do now that "the Earth is running out of gravity"; Carl La Fong Foundation for Gravitational Research. Amusing satire of educational shorts.

The GREAT LONDON MYSTERY (B) T&P 1920 serial (12 episodes) SP,D: Charles Raymond. SP: also Hope Loring. Ref: BFC: ch.1. The Sacred Snake Worshippers; ch.8. The Fraudulent Spiritualistic Seance; ch.9. The Living Dead. with David Devant(The Master Magician), Lady Doris Stapleton, Lester Gard(The Man Monkey), Lola de Liane(Froggie the Vampire).

The GREAT PIGGY BANK ROBBERY WB 1946 anim color 7m. (Daffy Duck) D: Bob Clampett. SP: Warren Foster. Ref: Glut/CMM/TFL. LC. Maltin/OMAM.

Character, Wolfman, with head of wolf; Frankenstein-monster-like character.

The GREEN MIST (B) 1924 22m. See also: Further Mysteries of Dr. Fu Manchu series. Ref: BFC.

The GREEN SLIME Ram 1968? scope (*BATTLE BEYOND THE STARS) SP: also Takeo Kaneko. Mus: Toshiaki Tsushima. SpFX: also Yukio Manoda & the Special Effects Co. Ref: WorldF'68. TV.

Space expedition discovers life form which thrives on energy and spawns new creatures from its own blood cells. ("My God!--it can heal itself!") The stout, one-eyed slime creatures are a cross between pugnacious mutant kids and tentacled, moss-covered fire hydrants. They may look silly, but they beep and flail about so much that they can't be ignored. Their battles with the humans are a riot of movement. The heroics of Robert Horton and Richard Jaeckel are just as silly and easier to ignore.

GREY CART, The see PHANTOM CHARIOT,The(1919)

GREYWATER PARK (B) 1924 30m. See also: Further Mysteries of Dr. Fu Manchu series. Ref: BFC.

El GRIPOTERIO (Sp) Procinsa 1971 anim color 12m. D: J.R. Sanchez. Ref: Lee(SpCinema).

Prehistoric animal that eats and grows.

See also: PET, The.

GRIZZLY FVI 1976 color/scope 91m. (KILLER GRIZZLY-TV) D: William Girdler. SP,P: Harvey Flaxman, David Sheldon. Ph: W. Asman. Mus: R.O. Ragland. SpFX: Phil Corey. Opt: CFI, Howard Anderson. Ref: TV. MFB'77:24. V 5/26/76. with Christopher George, Andrew Prine, Richard Jaeckel, Joan McCall.
Marauding, man-eating mammoth grizzly terrorizes national park. A grisly bore--elementary suspense, elementary characterization, and a mean bear.

The GROOVE ROOM Constellation/Unicorn 1974('77-U.S.)color/3-D 83m. (WHAT THE SWEDISH BUTLER SAW-B) SP,D: Vernon P. Becker. SP: also B.E. Downes, from the anon. novel "A Man with a Maid." Ph: T. Forsberg. Mus: H.C. Lundbye. PD: Ralph Larson. Ref: MFB'80:54,101. Willis/SW. with Sue Longhurst, Diana Dors, Martin Ljung(Jack the Ripper).

GROVE, The see NAME FOR EVIL, A

GUERRA DEI ROBOTS, La see WAR OF THE ROBOTS

GUSZTAV KIGOJA (Hung.) Pannonia 1977 anim color 5m. D: M. Jankovics, B. Ternovszky. Ref: Zagreb 78 cat.
Man finds himself transforming into snake.

H.G.WELLS' THE SHAPE OF THINGS TO COME (Can.) FVI/CFI 1979 color 98m. (The SHAPE OF THINGS TO COME-alt t) D: George McCowan. SP: Martin Lager. Based on Wells' screenplay THINGS TO COME. Ph: Reginald Morris. Mus: Paul Hoffert. AD: Gerry Holmes. VisFX: Wally Gentleman. Robots: Ralph Tillack. SpFX: Bill Wood. Ref: V 12/19/79. MFB'79:123. with Jack Palance, Carol Lynley, Barry Morse, John Ireland, Mark Parr.
A colony on the moon is established following nuclear destruction of the Earth.

HA KHEL SAVALYANCHA (India-Marathi) Madhu 1976 color 142m. D: Vasant Joglekar. SP: M. Kalelkar. Mus: H. Mangeshkar. Ref: Dharap. with K. Ghanekar, A. Kale, L. Sarang.
Woman fears servant's ghost haunts bungalow.

HACHA PARA LA LUNA DE MIEL see HATCHET FOR THE HONEYMOON

HAIR RAISING HARE WB 1945 anim color 7m. D: Chuck Jones. SP: T. Pierce. Ref: Glut/TFL: Peter Lorre-like monster. LC. TV. Maltin/OMAM.

HALLOWEEN Compass Int'l./Falcon Int'l. 1978 color/scope 91m. SP,D,Mus: John Carpenter. Ph: Dean Cundey. PD: Tommy Wallace. Mkp: Erica Ulland. Ref: screen: The THING & FORBIDDEN PLANET on TV. MFB'79:27. Cinef Smr'80:6: The BABYSITTER MURDERS-orig t. with Donald Pleasence, Jamie Lee Curtis, Nancy Loomis, P. J. Soles, Charles Cyphers, Nick Castle(The Shape).

A deranged boy who murders his sister and--15 years later--escapes from a sanitarium proves to be "the incarnation of evil." The last 20 or so minutes of HALLOWEEN--in which "the shape" just keeps coming back and begins to seem indomitable--are fun-scary. And the credit sequence (in which a jack-o'-lantern slowly and menacingly grows and ultimately fills the left side of the screen) is exquisitely conceived. But for all Carpenter's hommages to Hawks and Hitchcock, his movie is more indebted to William Castle, schlock-horror-specialist supreme. The little world of HALLOWEEN is the world of Bill Castle--sudden shocks, false alarms, wafer-thin (or thinner) characterizations. If Carpenter's camera here frames a girl tightly (as she walks, say, along the sidewalk) it's inevitably to set the audience up to jump when she bumps into someone. The director's "style" allows us to share his characters' every alarm--false or real--but nothing else of them.

HALLOWEEN WITH THE ADDAMS FAMILY NBC-TV/Fries 1977 color 75m. D: Dennis Steinmetz. SP: George Tibbles, based on the TV series "The Addams Family" and on Charles Addams' cartoons. Ref: SFC 10/31/80: TV-movie. TV Season: first telecast as special, "Halloween with the New Addams Family." with John Astin, Vito Scotti, Patrick Campbell, Parley Baer, Carolyn Jones, Jackie Coogan, Ted Cassidy(Lurch), Felix Silla(Cousin Itt), Lisa Loring, Suzanne Krazna(Countess Dracula).

HAMM (Hung.) Pannonia 1977 anim color 6m. SP,D,Des: I. Banyai. Ref: Zagreb 78 cat.

Man who swallows the Earth, the galaxy, the universe....

The HAND WB/Orion/Pressman-Ixtlan 1981 color 104m. SP,D: Oliver Stone. From Marc Brandel's book "The Lizard's Tail." Ph: King Baggot; George Koblasa. Mus: James Horner. PD: John Michael Riva. SpVisFX: Carlo Rambaldi. Hand FX:(coord) Gabriella Young. SpMkpFxCons: Stan Winston, Tom Burman. Sp SdFX: Stephen Katz. Illus: Barry Windsor-Smith. Ref: screen. V 4/29/81. with Michael Caine, Andrea Marcovicci, Annie McEnroe, Bruce McGill, Viveca Lindfors, Mara Hobel.

Comic-strip artist imagines that his lost, severed hand acts on his homicidal impulses; periodic monster's-eye-view shots suggest that his hand is actually alive...and that it has developed eyes....What the world needs now--another crawling-hand thriller. Is it fantasy or psychology? Does it matter?--it's the same old story either way. Caine is quite good, but his efforts are sacrificed on the altar of "suspense," a rather overworked celluloid god just now.

HAND OF POWER (W.G.) (AA-TV)/Indep.-Int'l./Rialto 1968('71-U.S.?) color 91m. (**IM BANNE DES UNHEIMLICHEN) D: Alfred Vohrer. SP: Ladislas Fodor, from Edgar Wallace's novel. Ph: Karl Loeb. Mus: Peter Thomas. AD: W. Vorweg, W. Kutz. Ref: WorldF'68. TVFFSB: fake zombie. Lee(p). Film 7/68. with Joachim Fuchsberger, Siv Mattson, Pinkas Braun, H.V. Meyerinck.

Murderer of 8 people wears Death's-head mask.

*HANDS OF THE RIPPER Univ 1971('72-U.S.) Mus: Christopher Gunning. AD: Roy Stannard. SpFX: Cliff Culley. Ref: TV. Lee. VV 8/10/72. Willis/SW. and with Katya Wyeth.

Sight of jewels' iridescence, or flickering light, hypnotically returns young woman to her childhood, in which state a kiss or embrace will spur her to relive the moment when her father (Jack the Ripper) stabbed her mother to death, and she too then kills. (Involved, isn't it?) Also: fake and real spiritualists. In added TV footage, the "author" of the story narrates and explicates (a la SECRET CEREMONY) the easily explicable; using everything but a pointer, he underlines the obvious in the narrative. Thus a routinely bad Hammer shocker becomes a studied exercise in redundancy (and arguably a more interesting artifact, if an admittedly even worse movie). Schizophrenia here is merely a pretext for violence and blood, though the climactic (slow motion) "suicide" of Anna (Angharad Rees) is at once silly, spectacular, and oddly touching.

HANGAR 18 Sunn 1980 color 93m. Story,D: James L. Conway. SP: Steven Thornley. Story: also Tom Chapman. Ph: Paul Hipp. Mus: John Cacavas. PD: Paul Staheli. SpFX: Harry Woolman. OptFxSup: John Forrest or J.F. Niss. Scenic Art: Doug Vandergrift. Models: Coast. Ref: V 7/30/80. SFC(ad). MFB'80:235-6. with Darren McGavin, Robert Vaughn, Gary Collins, James Hampton, Philip Abbott, Joseph Campanella, Pamela Bellwood, Tom Hallick, Cliff Osmond, William Schallert, H.M. Wynant.

U.S. government covers-up crash of NASA satellite and UFO.

HANGMAN AND THE WITCH, The see POISON AFFAIR, The

*HANGOVER SQUARE 1945 AD: Lyle Wheeler, Maurice Ransford. Ref: screen. V 1/17/45. Lee. and with Leyland Hodgson, Ann Codee.

Pianist whose depressions are "aggravated by excessive concentration" has mental lapses during which he commits murders. Sumptuously scored, carefully designed and lit, and strikingly photographed, HANGOVER SQUARE, frustratingly, merely toys with themes like the destructiveness of emotion and artistic-compulsion-as-self-destruction. It never quite settles on what Laird Cregar's lapses metaphorize until its very last shot, a bravura track back and up from Cregar at piano as he's engulfed by flames. Generally, the script fumbles all attempts to splice its fire/violence/music motifs together--it only succeeds during the climactic concerto, in the "flashback" orchestration of Cregar's mental images. It also scores a minor coup with a curtain cord: with it, the script neatly "ties" Cregar's murderous fits to his passion for Linda Darnell.

HANNAH--QUEEN OF THE VAMPIRES see CRYPT OF THE LIVING DEAD

HANSEL AND GRETEL see WHO SLEW AUNTIE ROO?

HANT, The see DARK AUGUST

HAPPINESS CAGE,The(by D.Reardon) see MIND SNATCHERS,The

HAPPY BIRTHDAY TO ME Col 1981 color 108m. D: J.Lee Thompson. SP: John Saxton, Peter Jobin, Timothy Bond. Ph: Miklos Lente. Mus: Bo Harwood, Lance Rubin. PD: Earl Preston. SpMkp: The Burmans. Ref: V 5/20/81. Cinef XI:3. with Melissa Sue Anderson, Glenn Ford, Tracy Bregman, Jack Blum, Sharon Acker.
Comedy. Murder by iron poker, motorcycle, barbells, shish kebab.

HAPPY EVER AFTER see TONIGHT'S THE NIGHT

HAPPY HOOLIGAN IN DR. JEKYL AND MR. ZIP IFS 1920 anim 6m. D: Bill Nolan. Ref: Lee(LC).

HAPPY MOTHER'S DAY...LOVE,GEORGE see RUN,STRANGER,RUN

HARDWARE WARS Pyramid/Kino Int'l 1978 12m. SP,D,Anim: Ernie Fosselius. Ref: J.Willis. screen. Boxo 7/28/80:2(ad).
Amusing parody of STAR WARS--toasters and waffle irons patrol outer space.

HARI DARSHAN (India-Hindi) Joy 1972 color 167m. D,P: Chandrakant. SP: N. Shyam. Story: R. Thakur. Ph: V.K. Joshi. Mus: K.-Anandji. Ref: Dharap. with Randhava, Asit Sen.
Lord Vishu assumes "shape of half animal and half man" to kill demon.

The HARLEM GLOBETROTTERS ON GILLIGAN'S ISLAND NBC-TV/Univ-TV & Redwood 1981 color 94m. D: Peter Baldwin. SP: Sherwood & Al Schwartz et al, based on the TV series. Ph: K.C. Smith. Mus: Gerald Fried. AD: Robert Crawley. Ref: TV. with Bob Denver, The Harlem Globetrotters, Martin Landau, Scatman Crothers, Alan Hale, Jim Backus, Barbara Bain, Russell Johnson, Dawn Wells, Natalie Schaefer.
The Globetrotters vs. a robot basketball team; very deadly tarantula; George the Robot. A laugh-track movie. (No audience needed.)

HARLEQUIN (Austral.) FGFP 1980 color/scope 93m. D: Simon Wincer. SP: Everett De Roche. Dial: Jon George, Neill Hicks. Ph: Gary Hansen. Mus: Brian May. PD: Bernard Hides. SpFX: Conrad C. Rothmann. Ref: MFB'80:176. with Robert Powell (Wolfe), David Hemmings, Carmen Duncan, Broderick Crawford.
"Enigmatic" man with "weird powers" returns from the dead, dies again, seems to possess man.

HARPYA (Belg) 197-? anim short D: Raoul Servais. Ref: SFC 7/4/80: "half-woman, half-predatory bird who devours everything."

HARVEST HOME(by T.Tryon) see DARK SECRET OF HARVEST HOME

HATCHET FOR THE HONEYMOON (Sp-I) GGP/Pan Latina & Mercury 1971 ('74-U.S.) color 93m. (**Una HACHA PARA LA LUNA DE MIEL. Il ROSSO SEGNO DELLA FOLLIA. BLOOD BRIDES-B) SP,D,Ph: Mario

Bava. SP: also S. Moncada. Ph: also A. Rinaldi. Mus: Sante Romitelli. AD: J.M. Herrero. Ref: MFB'73:29. FC 3/80:76: BLACK SABBATH on TV. Willis/SW. SpCinema. with Stephen Forsyth, Dagmar Lassander, Laura Betti, Gerard Tichy, Femi Benussi.
Man who murders brides of others haunted by ghost of his wife.

HATCHET MURDERS, The see DEEP RED

HAUNT OF FEAR see VAULT OF HORROR

HAUNTED GOLD (J) Toho 1979 Ref: JFFJ 13:33. with S. Katsu.
Female "ghost" haunts swamp.

The HAUNTED HOUSE (H.K.) Shaw 1977? (HSIUNG CHAI) SP,D: Li Han-hsiang. Ref: IFG'78:181,185: "horror film."

The HAUNTED MOUSE MGM 1965 anim color 9m. Ref: Meyers: Tom & Jerry & a haunted house. LC.

*The HAUNTED PALACE 1963 Mkp: Ted Coodley. Titles: Armand Acosta. Ref: screen. AFI. Lee.
The spirit of Charles Dexter Ward's great-grandfather Joseph Curwen seems to reach out of portrait to possess him; Curwen/Ward magically revives his long-dead mistress; town of Arkham cursed with mutants, the results apparently of Curwen's attempts to mate its women with creature ("elder god"?) kept in tank. Lip service to Lovecraft and Poe; more indebted to Stevenson and "Dr. Jekyll and Mr. Hyde," as the spirits of Ward and Curwen vie for tenancy of Ward's body. And the script pads its Jekyll-Hyde theme out with a revenge theme, a love-beyond-the-grave theme, and a 110-years-later-the-same-angry-villagers theme. Price provides a few moments of wit and relief from all the thunder, lightning, fog, and formula shock effects. And the travelling/scope shots lend every actor's every movement a bit of kinesthetic authority.

The HAUNTED SCENE PAINTER (B) Paul 1904 3m. Ref: BFC.
Theatre props (inc. dragon, ghost) come to life.

*HAUNTED SPOOKS 1920 20m. D: also Alf Goulding; Harold Lloyd? Titles: H.M. Walker. Ref: screen. Lee. LC. with Lloyd, Mildred Davis.
Top-notch Lloyd short. Hilarious first half was the model for the suicide gags in NEVER WEAKEN. Second half is a good "haunted" house free-for-all, a warmup for a similar sequence in HOT WATER.

The HAUNTING OF JULIA (B-Can.) Discovery/Fetter-Classic 1976 ('81-U.S.) color 97m. (FULL CIRCLE-orig t) D: Richard Loncraine. SP: H.B. Davenport; Dave Humphries, from Peter Straub's novel "Julia." Ph: Peter Hannan. Mus: Colin Towns. AD: Brian Morris. SpFX: Thomas Clark. Ref: MFB'78:89. V 9/28/77. 2/18/81:6(rated). with Mia Farrow, Keir Dullea, Tom Conti,

Jill Bennett, Cathleen Nesbitt, Peter Sallis, Mary Morris. Series of brutal murders; seance; mad woman (MFB); "gloomy house"; "ghostly child." (V)

The HAUNTING OF M. Nu-Image/Triangle 1979(1981) color 98m. SP,D,P: Anna Thomas. Ph: Gregory Nava. Mus: Chopin, Mahler, Janacek. Ref: screen. V 11/28/79. Boxo 4/81:54. with Sheelagh Gilbey, Nini Pitt, William Bryan(ghost), Evie Garratt.
Scotland, c.1900. A young woman is haunted by the ghost of an ancestor's lover. Spare, hesitantly-acted ghost story features a sensitive handling of the fantasy element, and of Mahler and Chopin. This ghost is not a menace; he's just there, and it's his mere presence that's threatening. His ultimate "defeat" is told--in the last shot of him--simply in his eyes. Fine photography.

The HAUNTING OF PENTHOUSE D ABC-TV/Clovis 1974 color 74m. D: Henry Kaplan. Ref: TVFFSB: "nightmare." with David Birney, Farley Granger, Tyne Daly.

The HAUNTING OF ROSALIND ABC-TV/Titus 1973 color 73m. Ref: TVFFSB: "eerie"; woman frightened by ghost. with Pamela Payton-Wright, Susan Sarandon, Beatrice Straight, Frank Converse.

The HAUNTING OF SILAS P. GOULD (B) Hepworth 1915 10m. D: Elwin Neame. Ref: BFC. Lee(p). with Ivy Close.
"Heiress sells home to American millionaire and poses as ghost to frighten him away." (BFC)

HAUNTS Intercontinental 1977 color 98m. (The VEIL-orig t) SP,D: Herb Freed. SP: also Anne Marisse. Ph: Larry Secrist. Ref: V(d) 7/15/77: "mad scissorer." with May Britt, Aldo Ray, Cameron Mitchell, E.J. Andre, William Gray Espy.

HAUSU see HOUSE

HAVE YOU GOT ANY CASTLES WB 1938 anim color 7m. D: Frank Tashlin. SP: Jack Miller. Ref: Glut/CMM. Maltin/OMAM. LC.
Frankenstein monster, Mr. Hyde, Phantom of the Opera, Dr. Fu Manchu.

HAY MUERTOS QUE NO HACEN RUIDO see THERE ARE DEAD THAT ARE SILENT

HE KNOWS YOU'RE ALONE UA/MGM/Ellanby 1980 color 92m. (BLOOD WEDDING-orig t) D: Armand Mastroianni. SP: Scott Parker. Ph: Gerald Feil. Mus: Alexander & Mark Peskanov. AD: Susan Kaufman. SpFX: Taso Stavrakis. Opt: Videart, MGM. Ref: V 8/27/80. 6/18/80. 5/7/80:308(ad). TV. MFB'80:214-15. with Don Scardino, Caitlin O'Heaney, Tom Rolfing(killer), P. Pease.
A 7-girls-stalked horror item that pretends at times to be about such horror items, featuring as it does a horror-movie-within-a-horror-movie, a dialogue ref. to PSYCHO, a plot ref. to PSYCHO (a pre-murder shower scene), a fairground horror

house, the (not exactly new) thought that by watching horror movies "you can face death without really dying," and a probably accidental plot ref. to The CORPSE VANISHES (the murderer favors brides). Easier to take than most of its ilk, but all the reflexive sophistication is rather wasted on a type of movie not really worth reflecting on. A few fun shocks and verbal felicities.

HE LIVED TO KILL see NIGHT OF TERROR

The HEADLESS EYES JER 1973 Ref: V 6/6/73:6(rated). Lee.

The HEADLESS GHOST (Thai) Sri Syarm 1980 color 100m. (Pi HUA KAD or Pee HUA KARAT) D: Vichit Usahajitr. SP: Songpet Senibodin. Story: T. Wisanukorn. Ph: S. Jaenphanit. Mus: S. Klongvesa. Ref: V 4/9/80: fantasy-horror-comedy. 1/10/79: 68. with Sorapong Chatri, Vasana Sittivej, Lor Tok.

Beheaded man's head and body return from the dead to seek revenge.

*The HEADLESS HORSEMAN, or The LEGEND OF SLEEPY HOLLOW 1922 70m. SP: C.S. Clancy. Ph: Ned Van Buren. Sets: Tec-Art. Ref: screen. AFI. Lee. no LC. and with Lois Meredith.

Title-clogged adaptation of the Irving story, with no suspense or atmosphere. The climactic "midnight" chase is actually shot in broad, undisguised daylight.

The HEARSE Crown Int'l/Marimark 1980 color 95m. D: George Bowers. SP: Bill Bleich. Idea: Mark Tenser. Ph: Mori Kawa. Mus: Webster Lewis. AD: Keith Michl. Opt: MGM. Ref: screen. V 9/24/80. FM 169:14-16. with Trish Van Devere, Joseph Cotten, David Gautreaux, Donald Hotton.

House and hearse haunted by man who made pact with the Devil for eternal life and wants heroine to join him. This fantastic-romantic premise is not unintriguing--but the script is a weak-tea concoction which includes a brazenly direct lift from REPULSION (the phantom-in-the-opened-mirror) and lots of tiresome false alarms. All the characters and props act as if they're in a horror movie.

HEARTBEAT Post/General-TV 1950 20m. D: William Cameron Menzies. From Edgar Allan Poe's story "The Tell-Tale Heart." Ref: Lee. LC. with Richard Hart.

HEARTBEEPS Univ 1981 color D: Allan Arkush. SP & Assoc P: John Hill. Mus: John Williams. SpMkpFX: Stan Winston. Sp VisFX: Albert Whitlock. SpDes: Jamie Shourt, Robbie Blalack. Ref: V 9/2/81:19(ad): robot comedy. with Andy Kaufman, Bernadette Peters, Randy Quaid, Melanie Mayron.

HEAVY METAL (Can.) Col/Guardian Trust(Reitman-Mogel) 1981 anim color 88m. D: Gerald Potterton. SP: Dan Goldberg, Len Blum. From stories by Richard Corben, Dan O'Bannon, Berni Wrightson et al. Mus: Elmer Bernstein;(songs) Stevie Nicks,

Devo, Black Sabbath et al. PD: Michael Gross. SpFX:(d) John Bruno;(anim) Lee Dyer; Camera FX, G. Coulthart, Barry & Lee Atkinson, Rex Neville et al. Stopmo Anim: Precision. Seq D: J.T. Murikami et al. Narr: John Huston? Ref: screen. V 8/5/81. Voices: John Vernon, Don Francks et al.

Sphere of all evil, the Loc-Nar; Valkyrie; futuristic New York; man-into-giant; robot; monster; ape & frog-creatures; flying insect-creatures; flying bat-dragons; ghoul-haunted bombers; alien worlds. Dramatically conventional, graphically (and musically) pleasing, but generally just innocuous. "Den" is the most amusing of the 7 tales; "Captain Sternn," the most morally pointed and interesting. In the latter, "honesty" is represented by an authoritatively-intimidating hulk, whose alter ego--a nerdish little "corruption"--ironically wins out. The other stories serve, at best, as simple vehicles for the animators.

*HEBA THE SNAKE WOMAN (B) 1915 16m. Ref: BFC.

"Horror. Aztec Princess changes into snake and kills doctor."

HECKLE AND JECKLE,THE TALKING MAGPIES,IN KING TUT'S TOMB see KING TUT'S TOMB

HEKSENE FRA DEN FORSTENEDE SKOG see WITCHES(1977)

HELL HOUSE(by R.Matheson) see LEGEND OF HELL HOUSE

HELL NIGHT Compass Int'l/BLT 1981 color 101m. D: Tom De Simone. SP: Randolph Feldman. Ph: Mac Ahlberg; Randy Wolen. Mus: Dan Wyman. AD: Steven Legler. SpFxMkp: Ken Horn, Tom Schwartz. SpFX: Court Wizard Prods. Ref: screen. V 9/2/81. with Linda Blair, Vincent Van Patten, Peter Barton, Kevin Brophy, Jenny Neumann.

Two huge, deformed killers haunt tunnels under old house; "ghost"; bloody murders. The contents must have settled--there's nothing _in_ this HALLOWEEN package. Oh, a _couple_ nice scares near the end, and a nifty monster-from-under-the-rug effect. But the characters seem to walk through the old dark house in slow motion--you keep expecting the next scene, and they're still walking through the last one.

HELP ME...I'M POSSESSED Riviera 1974(1976) color D: Charles Nizet. SP: William Greer. Ref: Willis/SW. V 7/10/74:5(rated). 5/8/74:53. with Greer, Deedy Peters, J.P. Agostin.

HELTER SKELTER (B) Gainsborough 1949 84m. D: Ralph Thomas. SP: Patrick Campbell, Jan Read, G. Bryant. Ref: BFC: clips from WOULD YOU BELIEVE IT? Lee: haunted castle. with Carol Marsh, David Tomlinson, Mervyn Johns, Terry-Thomas, Glynis Johns, V. Dyall, Wilfrid Hyde White(Dr.B.Jekyll/Mr.Hyde), H. Kendall, Z. Marshall, Harry Secombe, D. Price.

*HENCRAKE WITCH see HERNCRAKE WITCH, The

Rosher Jr. Mus: Charles Bernstein. SpMechFX: Milt Rice. AD: Gary Weist, Frank Sylos. Ref: MFB'75:57. V 9/19/73. with Tina Herazo, Keith Carradine, Gary Busey, Robert Walker Jr., Dan Haggerty, John Carradine.

Girl inherits supernatural powers from Indian father, casts spells on motorcycle gang.

HEXEN: GESCHANDET UND ZU TODE GEQUALT see MARK OF THE DEVIL, PART 2

HIDDEN CORPSE,The see STRANGERS OF THE EVENING

HI NO TORI see PHOENIX 2772

The HIDDEN FACE (JED-TV)/Howco 1954 72m. P: Edward D. Wood, Jr. Ref: TVFFSB: "horror." no LC. with Steve Reeves, Lyle Talbot, Dolores Fuller, Theodora Thurman.

Plastic surgeon forced to operate on man's face.

*The HIDDEN HAND 1942 SP: R. Schrock. Ref: TV. V 9/23/42.

Lorinda Channing (Cecil Cunningham) fakes death-by-heart-attack in order to watch her greedy family fight for the hidden fourth of her estate; death-semblance-serum counter-active; "ghost" (her brother, in cloak); thunderstorm; poisoned cherry which kills pet raven, Mr. Poe. A slightly different old-house-and-the-will plot, but it yields the usual "thrills." And it's disgracefully reliant on "comedy" with Willie Best's nervous butler, Eustace, though Milton Parsons as the madman, John Channing, is fun. Busy score.

HIFAZAT see SECURITY

HIGH PRIESTESS OF SEXUAL WITCHCRAFT Anonymous Releasing Triumvirate 1973 color 90m. (SEXUAL WITCHCRAFT-ad t) SP,D: Beau Buchanan. Ref: Aros. Willis/SW. V 6/20/73. 5/7/75:121 (ad). with Georgina Spelvin, Jean Palmer, Marc Stevens.

Greenwich Village. Devil worshippers; the occult.

HIJA DE DRACULA see DAUGHTER OF DRACULA

The HILLS HAVE EYES Vanguard/Blood Relations 1977 color 90m. SP,D: Wes Craven. Ph: Eric Saarinen. Mus: Don Peake. AD: Robert Burns. SpFX: John Frazier, Greg Auer. SpMkp: Ken Horn, Dave Ayres. Ref: screen. MFB'78:240-41. V 10/18/78:111. 12/20/78. with John Steadman, Janus Blythe, Arthur King, Russ Grieve, Virginia Vincent, Susan Lanier.

Cannibalistic hill family (modelled on Sawney Bean's 17th-century clan) flourishes, in its way, in the American Southwest. Hard to believe, but the rather notorious The HILLS HAVE EYES is actually kind of fun. The violent action is not so much graphic as hyperbolic and not I believe to be taken seriously. The main supporting data for a "light" interpretation: a cuddly little baby is threatened with death and worse throughout the movie, yet is hardly even touched. And a dog is the hero. The HILLS HAVE EYES is closer to Rin-Tin-Tin Meets the Cleggs than it is to The TEXAS CHAIN SAW MASSACRE. The antics of the mutant clan here are played for laughs and thrills, not gut-wrenching. What these mutants and humans do, or plan to do, to each other is just too horrible to be true. And if the bad guys are wittier, the good guys are more ingenious--the audience is encouraged to root for both sides. This AAC (alternating audience current) is, however, generated a bit too mechanically to be morally felt; audience identification with both human and mutant is strictly superficial, in this amusing world of cartoon characters and violence.

HINOTORI see PHOENIX(1978). PHOENIX 2772.

HIPOTEZA (Bulg) 1977 anim color 8m. D: A. Kulev. Ref: Zagreb 78 cat.: man destroyed by his technology.

HIRAK RAJA DESHE see KINGDOM OF DIAMONDS

HISTOIRE D'UNE PETITE FILLE QUI VOULAIT ETRE PRINCESSE see MAGIC CLOCK, The

*HISTOIRES EXTRAORDINAIRES Roto-Film 1932 89m. (UNHEIMLICHE GESCHICTEN) SP: also Heinz Goldberg, Eugen Szatmari. Ph: H. Gartner. Mus: Rolf Marbot, Bert Reisfeld. Ref: MFB'74:188. and with Harald Paulsen, Roma Balm, John Gottowt.

An "exhilarating battle of wits" between the hero and the villain, "conducted in three remarkable settings (waxworks museum, insane asylum, the Suicide Club), each more astonishing than the last."

La HISTORIA Y LA VIDA EXTRATERRESTRE (Sp) Etnos 1976 D: Juan G. Atienza. Ref: V 5/11/77:420: "sci-fi documentary."

HISTORY OF THE WORLD--PART I Fox/Brooksfilms 1981 color/scope 92m. SP,D,P: Mel Brooks. Ph: Woody Omens. Mus: John Morris. PD: Harold Michelson. SpVisFX: Albert Whitlock. Narr: Orson Welles. Ref: V 6/10/81. with Brooks, Dom De Luise, Madeline Kahn, Harvey Korman, Cloris Leachman, Sid Caesar et al.

Stone Age parody of 2001's "Dawn of Man"; "Jews in Space" number.

A HITCH IN TIME (B) CFF/Eyeline 1978 color 57m. D: Jan Darnley-Smith. SP: T.E.B. Clarke. Ph: T. Fletcher. Mus: Harry Robinson. AD: M. Pickwoad. Ref: MFB'79:123-4. with Michael McVey, Pheona McLellan, Jo M. Muller(witch), J.Rawle.

Professor's time machine sends students back in time, to 1953, 1816, 1645, and "a dangerous stop in the Stone Age."

The HOBBIT NBC-TV/Rankin-Bass & Xerox 1977 anim color 75m. D,P: Arthur Rankin Jr., Jules Bass. SP: Romeo Muller, from the book by J.R.R. Tolkien. See also: RETURN OF THE KING. LORD OF THE RINGS. Mus: Maury Laws. Ref: V 11/30/77:36.

11/23/77:101(ad): dragon. TV Season. Voices: Orson Bean, Hans Conreid, John Huston, Paul Frees, Theodore(Gollum) et al.

HOBITTO NO BOKEN see RETURN OF THE KING

*HOLD THAT GHOST 1941 Ref: screen. and with Ted Lewis.
Forrester's Club, deserted tavern "haunted" by "fiend with fangs" (owl), "ghost with fangs" (man in sheet), glowing-eyed ghost (never explained), levitating candles; Joan Davis as "screamer" for radio shows. The Hollywood-style ghost-comedy plot squeezes out Abbott and Costello's vaudeville-style patter. Davis's "fangs!" and keeping-eyes-open-and-on-candle pantomimes are, however, amusing, and H.J. Salter's music furnishes some atmosphere. Sort of a dry run for ABBOTT AND COSTELLO MEET FRANKENSTEIN. "Oh, Chuck!"

*The HOLE IN THE WALL 1929 Dial D: Irving Rapper. Ref: screen. and with Louise Closser Hale, Alan Brooks.
In climactic sequence, just-drowned man (Donald Meek) speaks through medium (Claudette Colbert) and alerts listeners to little girl's perilous situation; "Dogface," wild man/brute; TV screen (one-way mirror?); spiritualist's creepy props (e.g., "spectres" on wall, witch and monster masks, "buddha" with eyes alight). An impossible combination crook melodrama/fantasy/heart-tugger, in which all the crooks prove to have hearts of gold. Edward G. Robinson and Colbert are helpless with the talk in this early talkie, although _he_ has one good, mean line--"The tide is _rising_!" The charmingly un-actorish little girl and "Dogface" come off best, partly because they have so little dialogue.

HOLIDAYS WITH PAY (B) Manchester 1948 115m. D,P: John E. Blakeley. SP: Harry Jackson, F. Randle. Story: A. Toner. Ref: BFC: "haunted castle." with Tessie O'Shea, Sally Barnes.

The HOLLYWOOD MEATCLEAVER MASSACRE Group 1/Forest 1977 color 87m. (The MEATCLEAVER MASSACRE-alt t. REVENGE OF THE DEAD-B) D: Evan Lee. SP: Keith Burns, Ray Atherton; M. Gyulai, S. Singer. Ph: Guerdon Trueblood. Mus: Joe Azarello et al. SpMkp: Don Ling. Titles: Bob Greenberg. Ref: MFB'78:246. Willis/SW. Meyers. V 10/19/77:53(ad). with Christopher Lee, Larry Justin, J. Arthur Craig, Ed Wood, James Habif.
Professor summons up demon, Merak, to avenge deaths of his wife and children.

HOLLYWOOD ON PARADE NO.8 Para/Lewyn 1933 10m. Host: Eddie Borden. Ref: Barbara Hill. Classic Film Collector. LC.
Wax models of Bela Lugosi ("in his Dracula cape") and Gayne Whitman as Chandu come to life.

HOLLYWOOD STEPS OUT WB 1941 anim color 7m. Ref: screen. LC.
Frankenstein-monster bit; Peter Lorre caricature. Fairly amusing Tex Avery cartoon.

HOLLYWOOD STRANGLER, The see DON'T ANSWER THE PHONE!

HOLOCAUST 2000 see CHOSEN, The

HOLY TERROR see ALICE SWEET ALICE

HOME SWEET HOME (F) Unite Trois 1972 color 83m. SP,D: Liliane De Kermadec. SP: also Julien Guiomar. Ph: C. Creton. Mus: Roland Vincent. Ref: Lee. V 3/29/72. PFA. with Coline Deble, Jacques Monory, Guiomar.
"Old house...haunted" by past inhabitants. (V)

HOMEBODIES Avco Embassy/Cinema Entertainment 1974 color 96m. SP,D: Larry Yust. SP: also Howard Kaminsky, Bennett Sims. Ph: Isidore Mankofsky. Mus: Bernardo Segall;(song) Jeremy Kronsberg. AD: John Retsek. SpFX: Donald Courtney. Ref: MFB'77:71-2. Willis/SW. TV. V 9/4/74. with Paula Trueman (Mattie), Peter Brocco, Frances Fuller, William Hansen, Linda Marsh, Ian Wolfe, Douglas Fowley, Kenneth Tobey, Wesley Lau.
In order to delay their relocation, the elderly residents of a condemned tenement commit a series of bizarre murders; at the end, one victim--their ex-ringleader Mattie--seems to return from the dead. Low-key, dry, occasionally-very-funny black comedy. It never gets too cute or moralistic--but also, unfortunately, threatens never to end. The dramatically unfocussed script rambles from comedy to pathos to sociology and finally (apparently) to fantasy. At its sharpest--in the queasily comic murder-and-aftermath sequences--it makes wry use of the derisory plop of fresh cement, and of a furtively-pocketed half-foot-in-half-shoe.

O HOMEM LOBO (Braz) Pinheiro 1971 color (The WOLF MAN-tr t) SP,D,Ed: Raffaello Rossi. Ph: A.B. Thome. Mus: Gabriel Migliori. Ref: Lee(Higuchi). with Claudia Cerine, Lino Braga.
Scientist accidentally turns son into werewolf.

HOMER'S ODYSSEY, or The ADVENTURES OF ULYSSES (I) MOMA/Monopol/Milano 1911 30m. (L'ODISSEA) Ref: MOMA: "enormous Cyclops." Lee: from Homer's epic "The Odyssey." LC.

HOMME AU CERVEAU GREFFE see MAN WITH THE BRAIN GRAFT

L'HOMME QUI REVIENT DE LOIN (F) Gerin 1950 90m. D: Jacques Castanier. SP: Louis Chavance, from Gaston Leroux' novel. Ph: Georges Million. Mus: Yves Beaudrier. Ref: V 8/2/50: "eerie happenings." Lee(p). with Annabella, Maria Casares, Paul Bernard, Delmont, Jacques Serviere.
Mystery about a "series of strange visitations" and "spirit messages" from a man supposedly dead. (V)

HOMME SANS VISAGE, L' see SHADOWMAN

HOMO AUGENS (Yug.) Zagreb 1972? anim short D: Ante Zaninovic. Ref: IFG'73:492: "horror cartoon."

Recluse regresses to ape, begins to eat people, dies; people eat him.

HOMO VAMPIRE see GOULVE, La

HONTE DE LA JUNGLE see SHAME OF THE JUNGLE

HORLOGE MAGIQUE, L' see MAGIC CLOCK, The

HORRIBLE HOUSE ON THE HILL see DEVIL TIMES FIVE

HORRIBLE ORGIES OF COUNT DRACULA see REINCARNATION OF ISABEL

*The HORRIBLE SEXY VAMPIRE (Sp) Peppercorn-Wormser/Paragon/Cinefilms 1970('76-U.S.) color/scope 91m. (El VAMPIRE DE LA AUTOPISTA. Der VAMPIR VON SCHLOSS FRANKENSTEIN) D: Jose Luis Madrid. Ph: F. Madurga. Mus: Angel Arteaga. Ref: MFB '76:109-110. Lee(V). V 2/18/76:40(rated). with Waldemar Wohlfahrt, Patricia Loran, Luis Induni, Barta Barry.
"Ghostly manifestations" in "haunted castle"; vampire.

HORRIPILANTE BESTIA HUMANA, La see HORROR AND SEX

*HORROR AND SEX Jerand/Unistar 1969('72-U.S.) 82m. (NIGHT OF THE BLOODY APES-U.S. La HORRIPILANTE BESTIA HUMANA) AD: Carlos Arjona. SpFX: J.T. Torija. Mkp: Ma. Del Castillo. Ref: MFB'74:276. with C.L. Moctezuma, A.M. Solares.

The HORROR AT 37,000 FEET CBS-TV 1973 color 75m. (STONES-orig t) D: David Lowell Rich. SP: Ron Austin, Jim Buchanan. Story: V.X. Appleton. Ph: Earl Rath. Mus: Morton Stevens. AD: James Hulsey. Ref: TV. Lee(Warren). with William Shatner, Roy Thinnes, Chuck Connors, Lyn Loring, Buddy Ebsen, Tammy Grimes, Paul Winfield, Will Hutchins, France Nuyen, Russell Johnson, Darleen Carr, H.M. Wynant.
Still-potent Druid sacrificial stone unleashes cyclonic, freezing winds on airliner. Another ten-people-with-glossy-occupations-meet-disaster thriller. 1/10 scary; 9/10 silly. Vaguely Lovecraftian basis. (Ref. to "The Old Ones.")

HORROR CREATURES OF THE PREHISTORIC PLANET see HORROR OF THE BLOOD MONSTERS

HORROR EXPRESS (Sp-B) Scotia Int'l/Granada & Benmar 1972 color/scope 90m. (PANICO EN EL TRANSIBERIANO) Story & D: Eugenio Martin. SP: Arnaud d'Usseau, Julian Halevy. Ph: A. Ulloa. Mus: John Cavacas. AD: R.G. Guadiana. SpFX: Pablo Perez. Ref: screen. FC 3/80:76. MFB'74:79. V 10/25/72. with Peter Cushing, Christopher Lee, Telly Savalas, Silvia Tortosa, Alberto de Mendoza, Angel del Pozo, Helga Line, Peter Beckman.
Monstrous "missing link" absorbs and possesses minds of victims. Fairly tingly shocker, with an amusing cameo appearance by Savalas.

HORROR HIGH see TWISTED BRAIN

HORROR HOSPITAL (B) (Teleworld-TV)/Hallmark(AI)/Noteworthy (Richard Gordon) 1973('75-U.S.) color 88m. (COMPUTER KILLERS-alt U.S. t) SP,D: Antony Balch. SP: also Alan Watson. Ph: David McDonald. Mus: De Wolfe. AD: David Bill. Mkp: Colin Arthur. Ref: TV. TVFFSB. CineFan 2:26. V 1/16/74:26 (rated). MFB'73:126. with Michael Gough(Dr.Storm), Robin Askwith, Dennis Price, Vanessa Shaw, Skip Martin(Frederick).

Surgically-created, computer-controlled zombies; horribly-disfigured mad doctor with Michael Gough-like mask. The madman's mansion has a comically-ghastly facade--a self-consciously-menacing dwarf-servant, bloody bedsheets, a lurking "monster" (i.e., the doc sans mask). But behind that facade lies the same old horror story. One waits in vain for the parodic point, but one must content oneself with, simply, Michael Gough periodically cracking his knuckles.

HORROR! HOUSE OF THE GIANT SPIDERS (J) Tsuburaya-TV 1978 (KAIKI! KYODAIGUMO) D: Sei Okamura. Ref: JFFJ 13:30: movie.

*HORROR OF DRACULA Hammer-Cadogan 1958 SpFX: Sydney Pearson. Mkp: also Roy Ashton. Ref: TV. BFC. Borst. and with Charles Lloyd Pack, George Woodbridge, Olga Dickie, George Merritt.

This is perhaps, properly speaking, less Hammer's most exciting horror movie than it is James Bernard's most exciting score. The latter seems, roughly, half the film. It's clearly that wildly surging music that makes Christopher Lee's presence as Dracula as imposing as it is: _because_ Bernard's score is so overwhelming, all Lee need do is appear, or open his eyes, and it's a stunning moment. You won't find wolves, bats, or mist transforming into vampires here--but Lee's Dracula _will_ burst upon the scene as if he were a sudden materialization of the _music_. (Aural mist, as it were.) Jimmy Sangster's script features at least half-a-dozen memorable entrances for Dracula, not to mention a notable exit. Bernard and Lee make this repetition, or reiteration, seem like development--Dracula's presence seems, each time, a _fresh_ shock. He comes to seem omnipotent and omnipresent, an unshakeable nightmare. The film's female vampires like to smile and bare their fangs, and seem merely cutely perverse. But Dracula himself means business.

*The HORROR OF FRANKENSTEIN Levitt-Pickman 1970 (The CURSE OF FRANKENSTEIN-orig t) AD: Scott MacGregor. Ref: TV. Lee. V (d) 10/15/70. and with Dave Prowse(monster), James Hayters.

A slightly-amended version of writer-director Jimmy Sangster's earlier script for CURSE OF FRANKENSTEIN. Again we have the naughty maid, the aghast aide, Elizabeth, the dumped brain, the body-snatching, the monster-of-many-parts, and Victor (Ralph Bates) as a scheming cad. The one amendment: this time around Victor's callousness is at least _supposed_ to be amusing. It isn't really--Victor's "wit" is indistinguishable from mere smugness--but at least Sangster seems to have realized that he botched Victor One. Try, try again....

*HORROR OF THE BLOOD MONSTERS (U.S.-Fili) (AA-TV)/TAL-Tamaraw 1970 (VAMPIRE MEN OF THE LOST PLANET-TV. HORROR CREATURES OF THE PREHISTORIC PLANET-int t. sfa SPACE MISSION TO THE LOST PLANET?) Ph: William Zsigmond, W.G. Troiano. SpFX: David L. Hewitt. Mkp: Jean Hewitt. Ref: AFI. Cinef Spr'72:31. TVFFSB. Lee. V 5/17/78:210(ad). and with Jennifer Bishop, Joey Benson.
Snake men, vampire tribe, lobster men, bat men on lost planet.

HORROR OF THE ZOMBIES (Sp) Indep.-Int'l./Ancla Century 1974 ('76-U.S.) color 85m. (El BUQUE MALDITO. The GHOST GALLEON-ad t) SP?,D: Amando De Ossorio. Sequel to TOMBS OF THE BLIND DEAD. Ph: Raul Artigot. Mus: A.G. Abril. Sets: E.T. de la Fuente. Ref: V 5/8/74:207. 3/31/76:7(rated). Meyers. FM 165: 11. Willis/SW. V 9/25/74. 9/18/74:21(ad). with Maria Perschy, Jack Taylor, Carl Lemos(aka Leonard), Barbara Rey, Blanca Estrada, Manuel de Blas.
Cannibal-ghouls slaughter three models who board ghost ship.

HORROR ON SNAPE ISLAND (U.S.-B) Fanfare/EMI-Grenadier 1972 color 89m. (TOWER OF EVIL-TV & B t) SP,D: Jim O'Connolly. Story: George Baxt. Ph: Desmond Dickinson. Mus: Kenneth V. Jones. AD: Disley Jones. Ref: MFB'72:260-61. V 4/26/72. with Bryant Haliday, Jill Haworth, Anna Palk, Jack Watson, George Coulouris, Dennis Price, Robin Askwith, William Lucas, Candace Glendenning, John Hamill.
Madman, Phoenician superstition, murder on deserted island.

HORROR RISES FROM THE TOMB (Sp) Avco Embassy/Profilmes 1973 ('76-U.S.) color? 90m. (El ESPANTO SURGE DE LA TUMBA) SP, D,P: Carlos Aured Alonso. Ref: TVG. TVFFSB. V 5/9/73:144. CineFan 2:24. Willis/SW. with Paul Naschy, Emma Cohen, Vic Winner, Helga Line, Cristina Suriana, Luis Ciges.
Descendants of decapitated French knight and his mistress seem cursed to re-enact their crimes; head and body of knight return to life.

HORROR STORY (Sp) Cire 1973 D: Manuel E. Gallego. Ref: Lee. V 5/9/73:137. with M.G. Lozano, Silvia Solar, Marta May.

HOT DREAMS (I) Aquila 1974 color 86m. (AMORE LIBERO--FREE LOVE) SP,D: Pier L. Pavoni. SP,Story: Guido Leoni et al. Ph: Fausto Rossi. Mus: F. Frizzi. Ref: MFB'76:163. with Enzo Bottesini, Laura Gemser, Olga Bisera.
"Voodoo exponent" with "magical violins."

HOT PANTS HOLIDAY Avco Embassy/Moore-Weinbach 1971 color 81m. SP,D: Edward Mann. Story: Robin Moore. Ph: Michael Murphy. Ref: MFB'74:127. with Tudi Wiggins, Odette, Sabra Welles.
Charm obtained at "voodoo session" proves fatal.

*HOT WATER Kit Parker 1924 Ph:(asst) H.N. Kohler. AD: Liell K. Vedder. Ref: screen. LC. AFI.
The climactic "ghost" scenes in HOT WATER put hero Harold

Lloyd through the wringer--at first he fears that he has chloroformed his mother-in-law to death; then (after spotting a pamphlet titled "Do the Dead Return?")he's sure she has come back to haunt him. If he and his writers employ some of of the now-more-familiar comic-scare subjects--the mouse-in-the-glove (is this the first "crawling hand" movie?), the zombie-like sleepwalker, the yowling dog--they do so with a superior sense of invention and development. It's a joy just seeing all the narrative elements in the movie fall into their structural place in the last sequence, which manages to get <u>every</u> character and prop (including a turkey) into the act.

The HOTEL (Russ) 1980 D: Grigori Kromanov. Ref: V 7/23/80:5: at Trieste.

Mountain-hotel's boarders "turn out not to be human."

The HOUND OF THE BASKERVILLES ABC-TV/Univ-TV 1972 color 75m. D: Barry Crane. SP: Robert E. Thompson, based on Arthur Conan Doyle's book. Ph: Harry Wolf. Mus D: Hal Mooney. AD: H.E. Johnson. Ref: TV. Lee(V 2/16/72:43. Borst). with Stewart Granger(Sherlock Holmes), Bernard Fox, William Shatner, Sally Ann Howes, John Williams, A. Zerbe, J. Merrow.

Each new version of "The Hound..." seems a little worse than the last--perhaps the material is just too familiar.... The actors here sound like they're simply reading passages from the book--and their readings are far from inspired.

The HOUND OF THE BASKERVILLES (B) Michael White 1977 color 85m. SP,D: Paul Morrissey. SP: also Peter Cook & Dudley Moore. Ph: Dick Bush, John Wilcox. Mus: Moore. PD: Roy Smith. SpFxSup: Ian Wingrove. Ref: MFB'78:115-116.

with Cook, Moore, Denholm Elliott, Joan Greenwood, Terry-Thomas, Kenneth Williams, Hugh Griffith, Roy Kinnear, Irene Handl, Spike Milligan, Jessie Matthews.

Axe-murderer; seance; "infernal hound."

HOUSE (J) Toho 1977 color 87m. (HAUSU. IE-orig t) D,P,Sp FX: Nobuhiko Obayashi. SP: Chiho Katsura. Ph: Y. Sakamoto. Mus: Asei Kobayashi, Miki Yoshino. AD: Kazuo Satsuya. Ref: V 9/21/77: "Ten Little Indians" variation. JFFJ 13:32. with Kimiko Ikegami, Kumiko Oba, Ai Matsubara.

House's piano, clock, mirror devour people.

The HOUSE AND THE BRAIN ABC-TV/Titus 1973 color 73m. D: Gloria Monty. From the Bulwer-Lytton story? Ref: TVFFSB. with Keith Charles, Hurd Hatfield, Gretchen Corbett.

"Satanic guardian"; the occult; "18th century mansion."

The HOUSE BY THE LAKE (Can.) AI/Quadrant 1977 color 89m. (DEATH WEEKEND-B) SP,D: William Fruet. Ph: R. Saad. Mus & P: Ivan Reitman. AD: R.F. Smith. SpFX: Tony Parmalee. Ref: MFB'76:249-50: "ghoulish frissons." V(d) 3/15/77. with Brenda Vaccaro, Don Stroud, Chuck Shamata, Richard Ayres, D. Mattson.

Isolated country house; drownings; slashed throats.

HOUSE BY THE RIVER Republic/Fidelity 1950 88m. D: Fritz Lang. SP: Mel Dinelli, from the novel "Floodtide" by Alan P. Herbert. Ph: Edward Cronjager. Mus: George Antheil. AD: Boris Leven. SpFX: Howard & Theodore Lydecker. Ref: PFA notes 8/20/76. Everson. screen. V 3/29/50. Ott/FOFL. FQ W'79:8: "one of Lang's very worst." with Louis Hayward, Lee Bowman, Jane Wyatt, Dorothy Patrick, Ann Shoemaker, Kathleen Freeman, Sarah Padden, Will Wright.

Deranged killer haunted by "visions" of his victims; eerie night-scenes of the river.

The HOUSE IN NIGHTMARE PARK (B) Assoc.London-Extonation 1973 color 95m. (NIGHTMARE PARK-orig t) D: Peter Sykes. SP,P: Clive Exton, Terry Nation. Ph: Ian Wilson. Mus: Harry Robinson. AD: Maurice Carter. Ref: Lee(HR 12/8/72). MFB'73:98. with Frankie Howerd, Ray Milland, Kenneth Griffith, Hugh Burden, Rosalie Crutchley.

Horror-comedy re: family of maniacs in creepy mansion.

HOUSE IN THE BROKEN REEDS see UGETSU

HOUSE OF BLOOD see MANSION OF THE DOOMED

HOUSE OF CRAZIES see ASYLUM

*HOUSE OF DRACULA 1945 (The WOLF MAN'S CURE-8mm t) Sequel to HOUSE OF FRANKENSTEIN. Ref: TV. Glut/TDB/CMM. V 12/5/45.

The monsters are back again, but Dracula (John Carradine) and the Wolf Man (Lon Chaney Jr.) don't even kill anybody, and the Monster's (Glenn Strange) part is just a lumber-on. The highlight (relative to the rest): a busy nightmare sequence in which Dr. Edelmann (Onslow Stevens) sees good and bad versions of himself and footage from BRIDE OF FRANKENSTEIN. And where's Kharis?

HOUSE OF EVIL ABC-TV/Univ-TV 1974 color 74m. D: Bill Glenn. SP: Robert Van Scoyk. Ref: TVFFSB. Cinef IX:3:37. with Jamie Smith Jackson, Sarah Cunningham, Andy Robinson, Dabney Coleman, Salome Jens, Lou Frizzel.

Devil worshippers in New England.

HOUSE OF EXORCISM see LISA AND THE DEVIL

*The HOUSE OF FEAR 1939 (BACKSTAGE PHANTOM-orig t) Mus D: Charles Previn. AD: Jack Otterson, John Ewing. Ref: TV. MPH 4/1/39:85. 6/10/39.

Workmanlike but tepid--not a patch on the '29 version (The LAST WARNING), though Robert Coote is amusing as the producer's brother, and there's a fairly exciting spotlighted-killer-in-the-rafters chase. Not accounted for: "ghost" voice heard over dead phone. Accounted for: "ghost" faces in theatre (by a mask, a la PHANTOM OF CRESTWOOD).

*HOUSE OF FRANKENSTEIN 1944 Mus: also P. Dessau. Mkp: Jack Pierce. Sequel to FRANKENSTEIN MEETS THE WOLF MAN. Sequel: HOUSE OF DRACULA. Ref: TV. Jim Shapiro. V 12/20/44.

Some kinesthetic tracking shots, a rousing Salter-Dessau score, and a plot that's just one damn monster after another all work to foster the illusion that something is going on in the HOUSE OF FRANKENSTEIN. The movie is pure forward movement--a little too pure perhaps. There are some good actors in it, but little time for them. Two or three minutes, for instance, for George Zucco, while Boris Karloff provides little more than vocal plot-punctuation. And in terms of ideas, the movie is a vacuum, a mere repository for all the cliches of pathos, horror, and revenge. Each monster enters, dragging his own piece of exposition behind him--hilariously in the case of Lon Chaney Jr. as the Wolf Man/Larry Talbot. He's hardly revived from death before he begins begging to return to it. ("I can't go on killing and waiting and killing!") In the case of J. Carrol Naish's love-smitten hunchback Daniel, the cliches cancel each other out. He is introduced murdering two people, almost casually; later, we're asked to sympathize with him and his unrequited love for a gypsy girl (Elena Verdugo). It's a lot to ask.

HOUSE OF FREAKS see FRANKENSTEIN'S CASTLE OF FREAKS

*HOUSE OF FRIGHT (Col-TV) 1960 Ref: TV. TVFFSB. and with Joy Webster, Oliver Reed.

Hammer's first serious Jekyll-Hyde film is a not-wholly-unworthy addition to the ranks. It's fairly inventive at devising ways to confront Jekyll with Hyde and vice versa--e.g., Jekyll seeing himself as Hyde in a mirror; Hyde alarmed at signs of the encroaching Jekyll; Jekyll awaking to find one of Hyde's victims beneath him; Jekyll's voice conducting a duologue with Hyde's (with Jekyll as "host"). Unfortunately, the dramatic ball is bounced back and forth between them so often and so regularly that this begins to seem like a game: Dr. Ping and Mr. Pong. The movie threatens to become a comedy in spite of itself--one can picture it inspiring Jerry Lewis to make The _NUTTY_ PROFESSOR. And Paul Massie is one-dimensional as either Jekyll _or_ Hyde.

*HOUSE OF HORRORS 1946 Mkp: Jack Pierce. Ref: TV. FM 165:14-16. Les Otis.

Basically unrewarding "classic Universal" tail-ender; but each actor was apparently allotted one good line (e.g., Virginia Grey's "You don't get around much, do you?", directed at stuffy art critic Alan Napier). Rondo Hatton's Creeper (a character introduced in PEARL OF DEATH), like Harpo Marx, starts instinctively after every passing woman, but with somewhat different ideas in mind.

HOUSE OF MADNESS see DR. TARR'S TORTURE DUNGEON

HOUSE OF MORTAL SIN see CONFESSIONAL, The

*The HOUSE OF MYSTERY 1934 Ph: Archie Stout. Mus D: Abe Meyer. AD: E.R. Hickson. Ref: Turner/Price. FQ Smr'80:54. and with George Hayes, George Cleveland, Irving Bacon, Brandon Hurst.
The curse of Kali, in the form of a "ghostly ape," pursues a man who killed the sacred ape of a Hindu temple.

*HOUSE OF MYSTERY 1961 Based on the play "L'Angoisse" by P. Mills, C. Vylars. AD: Jack Shampan. Ref: BFC: ghost, medium.

The HOUSE OF PERIL (B) Astra 1922 62m. SP,D: Kenelm Foss, from the novel "Chink in the Armour" by Mrs. Belloc Lowndes & the play by H.A. Vachell. Ref: BFC. with Fay Compton, Roy Travers, Flora le Breton, A.B. Imeson.
Women lured to "haunted house" and killed for their jewels.

*HOUSE OF THE BLACK DEATH Taurus 1965 (sfa **NIGHT OF THE BEAST-int t) D: Harold Daniels. SP: Richard Mahoney, from the novel "The Widderburn Horror" (also film's orig. t) by Lora Crozetti. Ph: Murray De Atley. Mkp: N. Christie. Ref: TV. Lee. no AFI. FM 37:49. and with Dolores Faith, Sabrina, Jerome Thor, Kathrin Victor.
Werewolf (Tom Drake); warlocks; curse that destroys one warlock, Belial (Lon Chaney Jr.); invocation that sends another (John Carradine) to hell. Totally inept, stilted horror fantasy is candidate for worst-ever honors. So bad it isn't funny.

HOUSE OF THE LIVING DEAD see DOCTOR MANIAC

HOUSE OF THE LUTE (H.K.-Cant.) Hung Way 1979 color 95m. (YU-HUO FEN CH'IN) SP,D: Lau Shing-hon. Ph: J. Koo. Lute Mus: John Thompson. AD: D. Chan. Ref: V 8/8/79. IFG'81:166. with Yum Tat-Wah, Kwan Hoi-Shan, Chan Lap-Pun, Lok Bec-Kay.
"Well-made conventional ghost story"; "mysterious villa"; "unexpected horror." (V)

The HOUSE OF THE SEVEN CORPSES (Official-TV)/Emerson/Yordan 1973('74 Int'l. Amusements rel.) SP,D,P: Paul Harrison. Ph: Don Jones. AD: Ron Garcia. Ref: TVFFSB. Lee. Willis/SW. TV. TVG. V 11/13/74:12(ad). 8/15/73:17(rated). with Faith Domergue, John Ireland, John Carradine, Carol(e) Wells.
"Strange happenings" when movie company films in house with history of "witchcraft and black magic." (TVFFSB) Formula.

The HOUSE OF TOMORROW MGM 1949 anim color 7m. D: Tex Avery. SP: J. Cosgriff, R. Hogan. Ref: LC. Adamson/TA.
"Home improvements we can expect by 1975."

HOUSE OF WHIPCORD (B) AI/Heritage 1974 color 101m.(94m.) Story,D,P: Pete Walker. SP: David McGillivray. Ph: Peter Jessop. Mus: Stanley Myers. AD: Mike Pickwoad. Ref: MFB'74: 99-100: "psychological horror." Willis/SW. V 7/31/74:28(rated). with Barbara Markham, Patrick Barr, Ray Brooks, Anne Michelle.
Former magistrate and prison governor mete out punishment

to female "offenders" in their own private prison.

The HOUSE ON SKULL MOUNTAIN Fox/Hartsfield-Pinto-Film Fund 1974 color 89m. D: Ron Honthaner. SP: Mildred Pares. Ph: Monroe Askins. Mus: Jerrold Immel. AD: James Newport. Ref: Willis/SW. V 10/19/77:52(ad): sfa The HOUSE ON SKULL ISLAND (Group 1)? 10/22/75:8(ad). 10/16/74:18,20: "Ten Little Indians" formula; "voodoo ritual scenes." with Victor French, Ella Woods, Janee Michelle, Jean Durant, Lloyd Nelson, Mike Evans.

HOUSE OUTSIDE THE CEMETERY see QUELLA VILLA ACCANTO AL CIMITERO

The HOUSE THAT VANISHED (B) Hallmark(AI)/Blackwater 1973('74-U.S.) color 99m. (SCREAM...AND DIE!-B. PSYCHO SEX FIEND-alt B t) D: Joseph Larraz. SP: Derek Ford. Ph: Trevor Wrenn. Mus: Terry Warr. AD: John Hoesli. Ref: MFB'77:54. '74:14. V 6/26/74:6(rated). 9/21/77:6: at Sitges. Willis/SW. with Andrea Allan, Karl Lanchbury, Maggie Walker, Judy Matheson.
"Faceless menace in black coat and black leather gloves." (MFB)

HOW TO MAKE A DOLL Unusual/Argent 1968 color 81m. SP,D,P, SpSdFX: Herschell G. Lewis. SP: also Bert Ray. Ph: Roy Collodi. Mus: Larry Wellington. Sets: S. Horiatis. Ref: AFI. Lee. with Robert Wood, Jim Vance, Bobbi West, Elizabeth Davis.
Robot-women; man's mind part of computer.

HOW TO MAKE TIME FLY (B) Paul 1906 5m. Ref: BFC.
"Girl reverses clock's hands and life speeds up."

HOW TO SEDUCE A VIRGIN (F) CFdFP 1974 color 80m. (PLAISIR A TROIS) SP,D: Jesus Franco. Dial: Alain Petit. Ph: Gerard Brissaud. Mus: D. Janin, R. Hermel. Ref: MFB'75:159. with Alice Arno, Robert Woods, Howard Vernon, Tania Busselier.
Madwoman keeps "museum" of "bodies of beautiful girls, frozen in postures of terror on the point of death by a paralysing drug."

The HOWLING Avco Embassy/IFI-Wescom(Blatt) 1981 color 91m. D: Joe Dante. SP: John Sayles, T.H. Winkless, from the novel by Gary Brandner. Ph: John Hora. Mus: Pino Donaggio. AD: Robert A. Burns. SpFX: Roger George; Doug Beswick. SpMkpFX: Rob Bottin;(cons) Rick Baker; Greg Cannom. SdFX: The Provision Co. Anim: Peter Kuran;(stopmo) Dave Allen. Opt: Jack Rabin. Ref: screen. FM 174:22-24. Bill Warren. MFB'81:114-15. V 1/28/81. with Dee Wallace, Patrick Macnee, Dennis Dugan, Christopher Stone(R.William Neill), Belinda Balaski (Terry Fisher), Kevin McCarthy(Fred W.Francis), John Carradine(Erle Kenton), Slim Pickens(Sam Newfield), Kenneth Tobey, Dick Miller, Noble Willingham(Charlie Barton), Roger Corman, Forrest J Ackerman, Beverly Warren; Paul Bartel, Jonathan Kaplan?
Psychoanalyst George Waggner's (Macnee) California retreat, The Colony, proves to be a haven for a pack of werewolves;

clips from the 1941 WOLF MAN; refs. to "old Stu Walker," "Lew Landers," "Jerry Warren," "John Brahm (with the weather)." The HOWLING is a sort of celluloid Who's Who of Werewolfilms. All of the above-mentioned character names are hommages to directors of one or more werewolf movies. (Yes, even "Jerry Warren"--FACE OF THE SCREAMING WEREWOLF.) And FJA turns up carrying the WEREWOLF OF LONDON issue (no.24) of Famous Monsters. Which issue (this starts to get a bit tricky) contains a rebuttal (p.4) to an article(way back in FM no.18)by future-director Joe Dante, entitled "Dante's Inferno," being a roundup of the 50 worst horror movies. (By the bye, and not to confuse matters any further, but no.18 is also the first FM in which your author's name appeared--see p.2--a doubly historic issue.) Now, dud no.31 on Dante's list is MAD MONSTER (qq.v.), "the first horror film I ever saw," he admits--and also (hardly incidentally) a movie about a madman bent on creating an army of wolf-men; it was directed by Sam Newfield. (See above.) The HOWLING is obviously a very personal film for Dante. It is also (I guarantee) bound to be dear to anyone who collects credits for horror-movie checklists. Not that I intend to abdicate my higher, analytical responsibility--the movie has some extra-filmographic charms which merit mention. John Hora comes up with many atmospheric ferns-firs-and-fog compositions. John Carradine has one of his more amusing roles in recent years. And except for the bubbling-pudding effects, the werewolves are pretty formidable monsters. As a whole, however...well, there really is no whole, simply parts of a movie, most of them engaging enough. (The HOWLING is in no danger of being condemned to the Inferno.) But the script has little sense of purpose, except to suggest, wryly, that werewolves will be werewolves. Thematically, the film is as confused as--if brighter than--its fore-(uh)-bear, The WOLF MAN. The animal-liberation idea gets lost in thickets of effects and hommages....And did I somehow miss Henry Levin's name??

HSI-YU CHI see SUN-WU-K'UNG TA-CHAN CH'UN YAO. T'IEH-SHAN KUNG-CHU SHEN-HUO P'O T'IEN-MEN.

HSIAO-TZU NAO T'IEN-KUNG (H.K.?) 1960? Ref: Eberhard.
Fairy-gods vs. evil wolf-spirit.

HSIUNG CHAI see HAUNTED HOUSE,The(1977?)

HSUEH-NIANG see LADY SNOW

HU-MAN (F) Romantique-ORTF-Pauthe-Mascaro 1975 color 105m. SP,D: Jerome Laperrousaz. SP: also G. Laperrousaz et al. Ph: J. Glasberg. Mus: David Horowitz et al. Ref: V 10/22/75. 7/28/76:32. with Terence Stamp, Jeanne Moreau, A. Stevenin.
Organization that collects "mass emotion," uses it to send actor into the future.

HUA KAD or HUA KARAT see HEADLESS GHOST(1980)

HUA-KUANG CHIU-MU (H.K.-Chin.) 1970 color/scope From the "Nan-yu Chi." Ref: Eberhard. M.Luk: HUA-KUANG HELPING MOTHER-tr t.
Spirit of stone turns sinful man into stone; snake enters body of woman sent to hell; she eats child and is thought to be vampire; princess and others caught in the "net of the king of hell."

La HUELLA MACABRA (Mex) Clasa-Azteca 1963 D: Alfredo B. Crevenna. Ref: Lee: vampire children? with Guillermo Murray, Rosa Carmina, Elsa Cardenas, Jaime Fernandez, Carmen Molina.

HUGO THE HIPPO (U.S.-Hung.) (Worldvision-TV)/Fox/Brut 1975 anim color 78m. Story,D: William Feigenbaum. SP: Thomas Baum. Des: Graham Percy. Narr: Burl Ives. Ref: MFB'75:262. TVFFSB. AMPAS. V 7/14/76. Voices: Robert Morley, Paul Lynde.
Sultan's magician creates "an enormous iron man...garden full of monstrous fruit and vegetables....sharks." (MFB)

HUMAN EXPERIMENTS Pyramid/Brown-Goodell 1980 color 82m. D, Story: J. Gregory Goodell. SP: Richard Rothstein. Ph: Joao Fernandes. Mus: Marc Bucci. PD: Linda Spheeris. SpFX: James Dannaldson et al. Mkp: Alan Friedman. Ref: V 2/13/80. 10/18/78:127. MFB'80:91. with Linda Haynes, Geoffrey Lewis, Ellen Travolta, Aldo Ray, Jackie Coogan, Lurene Tuttle.
Deranged prison psychologist drives subjects mad, erases their memories, programs them with new identities.

*The HUMAN MONSTER 1939 Mus: Guy Jones. AD: Duncan Sutherland. Ref: TV. Lee. Lennig/TC: 1940-U.S.
Gruesome-toothed, monster-like blind murderer, Jake (Wilfred Walter), kills madman/boss Orloff; sound machine drives man deaf. The clues are tantalizing--a braille tape, an ad in code, tap water found in the stomach of a drowned man--but the scenes are formula, the comedy wan, and even Bela Lugosi as Dr. Orloff is dull. And he's dubbed as his alter ego Dearborn--in fact he's dubbed as Orloff at one point. In his one real "Lugosi" scene, he cackles crazily as he drags away a body and dumps it in the Thames.

The HUMANOID (I) Col/Merope 1979 color 100m. (L'UMANOIDE) SP,D: Aldo Lado(aka G.B.Lewis). SP: also A. Bolzoni. Ph: S. Ippoliti. Mus: Ennio Morricone. PD: Enzo Bulgarelli. SpFX Sup: Antonio Margheriti. SpFX: Armando Valcauda. Models: Emilio Ruiz. Ref: MFB'79:155-56. Cinef IX:1:43. with Richard Kiel, Corinne Clery, Barbara Bach, Arthur Kennedy, M. Serrato.
In the future: Metropolis(i.e., Earth); invention which turns space captain into humanoid; "obligatory cute robot"; 200-year-old woman kept alive artificially. (MFB)

HUMANOIDS FROM THE DEEP New World(Roger Corman) 1980 color 80m. (MONSTER-B. MONSTERS-W.G.) D: Barbara Peeters. SP: Frederick James. Story: Martin B. Cohen, Frank Arnold. Ph: Daniele Lacambre. Mus: James Horner. AD: Michael Erler.

SpMkpDes: Rob Bottin;(asst) Ken Myers, Shawn McEnroe, Steve Johnson. Ref: screen. V 4/23/80. 7/30/80:4. MFB'80:240. with Doug McClure, Ann Turkel, Vic Morrow, Cindy Weintraub, Lisa Glaser.

Coelacanth-like prehistoric fish devour DNA-5-stimulated salmon; go through four evolutionary stages in a single lifetime; become amphibious monsters which invade carnival, tear up the place and people; mate with women in order to advance their evolution yet further. Gorgeous girls and loathsome monsters--what more could one ask for? "Unsophisticated" as applied to _this_ movie and its determinedly-gory shock-scenes is less a criticism than a categorization. The movie doesn't _try_ for sophistication, except in the orchestration of the climactic carnival carnage. The postscript is a blatant lift from ALIEN (which in turn lifted the shock-effect from THEY CAME FROM WITHIN).

HUMANOMENON (I) Corona 1973 anim short Ref: IFG'74:534: "mechanical giant."

*The HUNCHBACK OF NOTRE DAME 1939 Ref: screen.

Terrifically ambitious RKO production at least constitutes an impressive display of energy. Characters and ideas busily bustle about and jostle each other--there are huge crowds, the church, the king, the press, Maureen O'Hara. But meaning fails to peep through. Charles Laughton, however, is emotion incarnate as the hunchback. His energy is as concentrated as the film's is diffused.

The HUNCHBACK OF NOTRE DAME (U.S.-B) NBC-TV/BBC-TV 1976 color 94m. D: Alan Cooke. SP: Robert Muller. From Victor Hugo's novel. Mus: Wilfred Josephs. Des: Don Taylor. Mkp: Maureen Winslade. Ref: TVFFSB. V 7/27/77:46. TV Season. with Warren Clarke(Quasimodo), Kenneth Haigh, Michelle Newell, Christopher Gable, David Rintoul.

See also: MUNSTERS' REVENGE,The. STORY OF THE DRAGON AND THE LION HUNCHBACK.

The HUNCHBACK OF THE MORGUE (Sp) Janus/Eva 1972('75-U.S.) color 90m. (El JOROBADO DE LA MORGUE) SP,D: Javier Aguirre. SP: also Jacinto Molina, Alberto Insua. Ph: R.P. Cubero. Mus: Carmelo Bernaola. SpFX: Pablo Perez. Ref: Willis/SW. Ecran 73(July,p.24). Lee. V 5/16/73. 9/12/73:21(rated). 5/9/73:137. with Paul Naschy(aka J.Molina), Rossana Yanni, Vic Winner, Maria Perschy, Alberto Dalbes.

Doctor feeds hunchback-supplied bodies to globular monster.

HUNGRY PETS see PLEASE DON'T EAT MY MOTHER!

HUNGRY WIVES see JACK'S WIFE

HUNTER, The see SCREAM OF THE WOLF

HURRICANE EXPRESS Mascot 1932 12-chapter serial/80m. feature D: Armand Schaefer, J.P. McGowan. SP: W. Gittens et al. Ph:

E. Miller, C. Wester. Mus: Lee Zahler. Ref: TV. Turner/Price. with John Wayne, Shirley Grey, Tully Marshall, Conway Tearle, J.Farrell MacDonald, Glenn Strange, Ed Parker, Lloyd Whitlock.
The mysterious "Wrecker" impersonates others with perfectly lifelike masks. Recurrent line: "So you're the wrecker!" Badly acted by all, including Wayne; but the game of the mask adds a quasi-surreal dimension to the movie. Everyone is the villain, at one time or another, if only for a moment or two. An idea is lurking about here....

HYAKUMANNEN CHIKIYU NO TABI--BANDABUKKU (J) Tezuka-TV 1978 anim D: O. Tezuka. Ref: JFFJ 13:30: TV-movie.
Pastiche of "space opera, time travel, weird-horror."

HYDE AND HARE WB 1955 anim color 7m. (Bugs Bunny) D: Friz Freleng. Ref: LC. Maltin/OMAM. Glut/CMM: Dr.Jekyll & Mr.Hyde.

HYOCHO NO BIJO (J) Shochiku-TV 1977 D: Umeji Inoue. From R. Edogawa's story "Kyuketsuki" or "Vampire." Ref: JFFJ 13:32.
TV-movie mystery, one of 8 Edogawa adaptations.

HYPNOS (I-Sp) Record 1971 color/scope (MASSACRE MANIA-alt t) SP,D: Paolo Bianchini. SP: also Max Corot. Mus: Carlo Savina. Ref: Lee. with Ken Wood(aka G.Cianfriglia), Robert Woods, Fernando Sancho, Rada Rassimov.
Subliminal TV messages turn people into murderers.

HYPNOTIST,The(by T.Browning) see MARK OF THE VAMPIRE(1935)

I AM THE DEVIL Brandon/Brodax 1975 anim color 31m.
History of the Devil; "spaced-out spookiness." (Brandon)

*I BELIEVE see MAN WITHOUT A SOUL

I DISMEMBER MAMA Europix Int'l/Romal 1972(1974) color (POOR ALBERT AND LITTLE ANNIE-orig t) D: Paul Leder. SP: William Norton. Ph: W. Swenning. Mus: H.B. Gilbert. Ref: Medved/TGTA. Willis/SW. Lee. V 1/3/73:45(ad). with Zooey Hall, Geri Reisch(1), Greg Mullavey, Joanna M. Jordan, Marlene Tracy.
Psychotic killer carves up victims.

I DON'T WANT TO BE BORN see DEVIL WITHIN HER, The

I HATE MY BODY (Sp-Swiss) Galaxia 1974 color 99m. (ODIO A MI CUERPO) D: Leon Klimovsky. SP: Soly. Ph: Paco Sanchez. Sets: Jose Alguero. Ref: V 6/5/74. 5/15/74:43. with Narciso Ibanez Menta, Alexandra Bastedo, Byron Mabe, Blanca Estrada.
Man's brain transplanted into woman.

I HATE YOU CAT!(by R.B.Hutton & R.Wootten) see TERROR OF SHEBA

I HAVE NO MOUTH BUT I MUST SCREAM see --AND NOW THE SCREAMING STARTS!

I LIKE MOUNTAIN MUSIC WB 1933 anim 6m. D: Bob Clampett. Ref: LC. Glut/CMM: "giant ape Ping Pong." TV: MAGAZINE RACK.

I, MONSTER (B) Cannon/Amicus-British Lion 1971('73-U.S.) color 3-D/2-D 75m. D: Stephen Weeks. SP: Milton Subotsky, from Robert Louis Stevenson's story "The Strange Case of Dr. Jekyll and Mr. Hyde." Ph: Moray Grant. Mus: Carl Davis. AD: Tony Curtis. Mkp: Harry & Peter Frampton. Ref: TV. Lee(MFB'71: 241). with Christopher Lee(Dr.Marlowe/Mr.Blake), Peter Cushing, Mike Raven, George Merritt, Susan Jameson, K.J. Warren.

A scientist separates the good from the evil in himself. (Or as he puts it, the ego and the superego from the id.) Lazy, unimaginative version of "Jekyll and Hyde" really introduces only one new twist to the story, and that's from "The Picture of Dorian Gray": as Mr. Blake's "pleasures increase," his face gets uglier. (He's his own portrait of corruption.) At first the only difference between the doctor and Blake is a smirk--the one transformation comes at the end, when the dying, ugly Blake becomes Marlowe again. Dr. Marlowe in fact hardly figures in the story. It's all Blake's (and Lee's as Blake), which fact rather defuses the Stevenson premise of interdependence between the two.

I SPIT ON YOUR GRAVE Cinemagic 1978 color 101m. (DAY OF THE WOMAN-orig t) SP,D,Ed: Meir Zarchi. Ph: Yuri Haviv. Ref: V 11/22/78:26. poster. with Camille Keaton, Eron Tabor, Richard Pace, Anthony Nichols.

Revenge-for-rape murders--e.g., castration with butcher knife; murder with rope, ax, outboard motor.

*I WALKED WITH A ZOMBIE 1943 Mus: Roy Webb. AD: Albert S. D'Agostino, Walter E. Keller. Ref: screen. TV. Siegel/VL. FC Smr'72:69-70. V 3/17/43.

The most frustratingly divided of the Lewton thrillers. On the one hand: atmospheric, unsettling sequences--e.g., the zombie Jessica "sleepwalking" at the gate, the walk itself, the sobbing in the shadowy courtyard. On the other: humorless ciphers of characters, and harried, cut-and-dried verbal presentation of the script's ideas on uncontrollable cruelty and guilt. The atmosphere of the film is moodily suggestive, of somber human and non-human affairs; it tells a sad, alluringly sensuous story. The story itself, however, is resolutely unmoving. There's no drama, simply dialogue-related facts re: the lives (past and present) of the characters. Even in the climactic scenes, exposition is still, rather tardily, being delivered. The story's lack of resonance is typical of mystery movies, in which relationships are generally established only at the end. By the time they've sorted out who did what to whom, it's over. J.Roy Hunt's photography and Roy Webb's music convey intimations of melancholy and evil; the dialogue conveys thoughts like "This is a sad place."

IDAHO TRANSFER Cinemation/Pando 1973(1975) color 87m. D: Peter Fonda. SP: Thomas Matthiesen. Ph: Bruce Logan. Mus: Bruce Langehorne. Ref: V 3/26/75. 6/20/73:7(rated). Willis/ SW. with Kelley Bohanan, Kevin Hearst, Keith Carradine.
Youths teleported into Idaho of the future to start new civilization.

IDLE ROOMERS Col 1944 17m. SP,D: Del Lord. SP: also E. Ullman. Ref: LC. Glut/CMM. Lee: werewolf-like monster. with The Three Stooges, Vernon Dent, Duke York(Lupe the Wolf Man).

IE see HOUSE

IF- (B) London 1916 80m. D: Stuart Kinder. Ref: BFC. with Iris Delaney, Ernest Leicester.
Plot to "divert defences with fake airships while hidden guns destroy London."

ILE MYSTERIEUSE, L' see MYSTERIOUS ISLAND,The(1972)

ILLUSTRATED MAN,The(by R.Bradbury) see MARTIAN CHRONICLES,The

ILLUSTRIOUS CORPSE,The(by T.Thayer) see STRANGERS OF THE EVENING

ILSA, HAREM KEEPER OF THE OIL SHEIKS Cambist 1976 color 93m. D: Don Edmonds. SP: Langton Stafford. Ph: Glenn Roland, Dean Cundey. AD: Mike Riva. SpMkpFX: Joe Blasco;(asst) David Ditmar. Ref: V 2/18/76: follow-up to ILSA, SHE WOLF OF THE SS. 1/21/76:57(ad). screen. with Dyanne Thorne, Michael Thayer, Wolfgang Roehm, Sharon Kelly, Su Ling, Marilyn Joy, Uschi Digart, Joyce Gibson.
Dismemberment and torture by rack, ants, tarantulas, rats, plastic vaginal explosive; death-semblance serum; hideous hunchback. As "exotic" as Pasadena, as "perverse" as Monty Rock III, ILSA II is essentially tame and unimaginative. It has plenty of awkwardly-done, sadistic stunts, but no spirit--of surrealism, general outrageousness, or whatever--informing them. It does, however, have some stunning actress-models, and one line: "More ants!" And it's admittedly not as dull as ILSA I.

ILSA, SHE WOLF OF THE SS Cambist 1974 color 72m. D: Don Edmonds. SP: Jonah Royston. Ph: G. Roland. SpMkp: Joe Blasco. Follow-up: ILSA,HAREM KEEPER OF THE OIL SHEIKS. Ref: screen. Bianco Index'76:32. with Dyanne Thorne(Ilsa), Gregory Knoph, Maria Marx, Uschi Digart, Jo Jo Deville; Donna Young?
World War II, Nazi Medical Camp #9. Commandant Ilsa is aka "The Black Widow," who castrates her lovers (afterwards); disease experiments with inmates ("The wound is now being infected with gangrene pus"); torture. Flairless pseudo-camp. Where is Fu Manchu when you need him?

IM BANNE DES UNHEIMLICHEN see HAND OF POWER

IM-HO-TEP see MUMMY,The(1932)

I'M NOT FEELING MYSELF TONIGHT (B) New Realm & Antler 1975 color 84m. D: Joseph McGrath. SP: David McGillivray. Idea: Laurence Barnett. Ph: Ken Higgins. Mus: Cy Payne. AD: Tony Curtis. Ref: MFB'76:30. with Barry Andrews, Sally Faulkner.
Odd-job man at sex-research institute invents "electronic aphrodisiac called Agnes."

IMAGES (Irish-U.S.) Col/Hemdale-Lionsgate 1972 color/scope 101m. SP,D: Robert Altman. Add'l Material & with: Susannah York. Ph: Vilmos Zsigmond. Mus: John Williams. PD: Leon Erickson. Ref: MFB'72:235. Lee. V 5/10/72. with Marcel Bozzufi, Rene Auberjonois, Hugh Millais, John Morley.
Hallucinations of a woman going insane: phantom dog, brutal murders, dead lover, evil alter ego.

IMMEDIATE POSSESSION (B) Starcraft 1931 42m. D: A. Varney-Serrao. SP: Brock Williams. Ref: BFC. with Herbert Mundin, Dorothy Bartlam, Leslie Perrins, Merle Tottenham.
Agent tries to sell "haunted" house.

IMMORAL TALES (F) Argos 1974 color 103m. (CONTES IMMORAUX) SP,D,AD,Ed: Walerian Borowczyk. Mus: Maurice Le Roux. Ref: MFB'77:120-21: "Erzsebet Bathory," 1 of 4 tales. V 8/21/74. with Paloma Picasso, Pascale Christophe.
Countess Bathory takes "rejuvenating baths" in blood of village maids.

The IMP IN THE BOTTLE Pyramid 1950 20m. Ref: Lee(LC): based on the Robert Louis Stevenson story.
See also: DIABLE EN BOUTEILLE, Le.

IMPATIENT PATIENT WB 1942 anim 7m. (Daffy Duck) D: Norman McCabe. SP: Don Christensen. Ref: LC. Maltin/OMAM. Glut/CMM: Dr. Jerkyl becomes "brute."

The "IMP"ROBABLE MR. WEE GEE Amer.Film Dist. 1966 color 75m. SP,D,P: Sherman Price. Ref: AFI: house haunted by voluptuous ghost. with Dick Richards, Hella Grondahl.

IN PREHISTORIC DAYS see BRUTE FORCE

IN SEARCH OF ANCIENT ASTRONAUTS Gold Key-TV/Landsburg 1975 color 52m. Narr: Rod Serling. Ref: TVFFSB. TVG: 1973?
Speculation re: alien visits to Earth.

IN SEARCH OF ANCIENT MYSTERIES Gold Key-TV/NBC-TV/Landsburg 1974 color 52m. SP,D,P: Fred Warshofsky. Narr: Rod Serling. Ref: TVG. TVFFSB: did aliens colonize Earth? V 2/13/74:57.

IN SEARCH OF DRACULA (Swed) Indep.-Int'l./Aspekt-SFP Int'l. 1972('76-U.S.) color 50m.(80m.) (PA JAKT EFTER DRACULA. DRACULA-orig t. DRACULA'S TRANSYLVANIA-int t. The LEGEND OF

The HENDERSON MONSTER CBS-TV/Titus 1980 color 94m. D: Waris Hussein. SP: Ernest Kinoy. Ph: E.R. Brown. Mus: Dick Hyman. AD: Marsha L. Eck. Ref: TV. V 6/11/80:61. with Jason Miller, Christine Lahti, Stephen Collins, David Spielberg, Nehemiah Persoff, Larry Gates, David Kilgore.

An updating of the "Frankenstein" story, with the doctor here a molecular geneticist experimenting with recombinant DNA, and potentially responsible for unleashing a "new life form" or "super-bacterium" on the world. The script all-too-neatly lays out the major social, scientific, and political issues of the day, in dialogue which alternates between pseudo-sophisticated banter and flat-footed earnestness. The film at times seems to take the side of the angry, torch-bearing "villagers," at others to suggest that the "monster" may be benign. Yet it still doesn't quite seem even-handed. Even at its most impartial it appears to offer sustenance to anti-intellectualism, if only, ultimately, half a loaf.

HEPHAESTUS PLAGUE,The(by T.Page) see BUG

**HERCULES AND THE PRINCESS OF TROY (U.S.-I?) Avco Embassy-TV 1966 color 52m. (HERCULES. HERCULES VS. THE SEA MONSTER-TV-movie ts.) D,P: Albert Band. SP: Larry Forrester, Ugo Liberatore. Ph: Enzo Barboni. Mus: Fred Stein(er). Narr: Everett Sloane. Ref: TV: series pilot? TVFFSB. FM 38:66. with Gordon Scott, Diana Hyland, Paul Stevens, Mart Hulswit, Steve Garrett, Gordon Mitchell, Roger Browne.

Maidens sacrificed to sea monster to appease gods. Tacky TV Hercules.

*HERCULES, PRISONER OF EVIL Royale Sodifilm 1967(1964?) scope (sfa *TERROR OF THE KIRGHIZ) Ref: RVB. Lee. and with Furio Meniconi.

Witch turns victims into werewolves.

HERCULES VS. THE SEA MONSTER see HERCULES AND THE PRINCESS OF TROY

HERE COMES THE BLOB see SON OF BLOB

HERE COMES THE BRIDE Unisphere/Golden Gate 1973 color 85m. (The BRIDE-orig t) SP,D: Jean-Marie Pelissie. SP,P: John Grissmer. Ph: Geoffrey Stephenson. Mus: Peter Bernstein. Ref: V 8/8/73. 4/7/76:15(ad). with Robin Strasser, John Beal, Arthur Roberts, Iva Jean Saraceni.

"Horror film....gory denouement....weird house."

HERETIC, The see EXORCIST II

The HERNCRAKE WITCH (B) Heron 1912 (*HENCRAKE WITCH-t.error) SP,D: Mark Melford. Ref: BFC. with Jakidawdra, Melford.

HEX Fox/Raab 1973 color 93m. SP,D: Leo Garen. SP: also Steve Katz. Story: D.W. Cannon, V. Zimmerman. Ph: Charles

DRACULA-alt t?) D,P,Mus: Calvin Floyd. SP: Yvonne Floyd, based on the book by Raymond McNally & Radu Florescu. Ph: Tony Forsberg et al. Ref: screen. MFB'75:166. V 2/18/76:40 (rated). 5/21/75. 5/3/72:164. Willis/SW. Boxo 9/24/79:29. Lee. Murphy. Daisne. with Christopher Lee.
Bland docu-drama re: the historical Dracula, featuring scenes from Dracula films and speculation on the abominable snowman, the Devil, and the Bermuda Triangle.

IN SEARCH OF BIGFOOT Atlantic/Bostonia 1976 color 75m. (cf. BIG FOOT--MAN OR BEAST?) D,P: Lawrence P. Crowley, William F. Miller. SP: Miller. Ph: Crowley. Narr: Phil Tonkin. Ref: Willis/SW. with Robert W. Morgan.

IN THE LAND OF KING HIRAK see KINGDOM OF DIAMONDS

IN THE SPIDER'S GRIP (F) Educ/PCC 1924('25-U.S.) object anim color 22m.(10m.) (DANS LES GRIFFES DE L'ARAIGNEE) SP,D,P, AD: Ladislas Starevitch. U.S.version: Morris Ryskind. Ref: Sadoul/Morris. Filmlexicon. Lee(MPN 31:1515,1664).

INCREDIBLE DR. JEKYLL see EROTIC DR. JECKYL

The INCREDIBLE HULK CBS-TV/Univ-TV 1977 color 93m. D: Kenneth Johnson, Sigmund Neufeld Jr. SP: Richard C. Matheson, K. Johnson, T.E. Szollosi. Based on Stan Lee's Marvel Comics character. Ph: H. Schwartz, J. McPherson. Mus: Joseph Harnell. See also: RETURN OF THE INCREDIBLE HULK. Ref: TVFFSB. MFB'79:252: 2 episodes from TV series. V 3/22/78:98. 11/9/77: 43. with Bill Bixby, Susan Sullivan, Lou Ferrigno(the hulk), Jack Colvin, Brandon Cruz, Sondra Currie.
After exposure to gamma rays, a scientist (Bixby) finds that anger transforms him into a 7-foot-tall man-beast.

**The INCREDIBLE INVASION (U.S.-Mex) Col/Azteca 1968 color (INVASION SINITESTRA) D: Juan Ibanez, Jack Hill. SP,P: Luis E. Vergara. SP: also Karl Schanzer. Ph: R. Dominguez, Austin McKinney. Mus: Enrico Cabiati. SpFX: James Tannenbaum. Ref: Lee(pb). with Boris Karloff, Enrique Guzman, Christa Linder, Maura Monti, Yerye Beirute.
Death ray; "energy aliens"; "man-into-monster."

The INCREDIBLE MELTING MAN AI/Quartet 1977 color 84m. SP,D: William Sachs. SP: also Rebecca Ross. Ph: Willy Curtis. Mus: Arlon Ober. AD: Michel Levesque. SpFxMkp: Rick Baker. SpFX: Harry Woolman. Ref: MFB'78:48. V 1/11/78. with Alex Rebar, Burr DeBenning, Myron Healey, Rainbeaux Smith, Michael Aldredge, Jonathan Demme, Mickey Lolich.
Saturn-flight survivor finds himself melting and craving human flesh.

The INCREDIBLE SHRINKING WOMAN Univ/Lija 1981 color 88m. D: Joel Schumacher. SP & Exec P: Jane Wagner. Suggested by Richard Matheson's novel "The Shrinking Man." Ph & SpFxSup:

Bruce Logan. Mus: Suzanne Ciani. PD: Raymond A. Brandt. Sp MkpDes: Rick Baker. SpFX: Roy Arbogast, Guy Faria, David Kelsey. Graphics: Michael Hamilton. Ref: screen. MFB'81:69. V 1/28/81. with Lily Tomlin, Charles Grodin, Ned Beatty, Henry Gibson, Maria Smith, John Glover, Mike Douglas, Terry McGovern.

Housewife (Tomlin), OD'd on product chemicals, finds herself shrinking, alienated from husband and children; finally restored to normal size, she finds herself growing; THIS ISLAND EARTH on TV; ape-and-shrunken-heroine team (a la Kong and Fay Wray). Movie (like heroine) has ID crisis. It's part black comedy, part effects stunts, part too-cute pr-parody, part Capra populism, and (most interestingly) part melancholic ode to mother-and-wife-hood. The main miscalculation (in a movie filled with them): the setting, Tasty Meadows, an incredible community-of-living-commercials--fantastic shrinking (or amazing colossal) women need more common, disbelief-suspending soil in which to thrive. The tone of the movie fluctuates grotesquely, though there are occasional inspired moments (e.g., the tiny Tomlin's drunken giggles during her wine-drenching; the "Volga boatman" bit with the giant slabs of bacon; the on-the-lam-from-the-giant-pursuing-dog throwaway).

INCREDIBLE TORTURE SHOW see BLOODSUCKING FREAKS

O INCRIVEL MONSTRO TRAPALHAO (Braz) Aragao 1981 Ref: V 2/25/81:23(ad): monster; Superman-type. with Renato Aragao, Dede Santana, Zacarias, Mussum.

INDIAN SPIRIT GUIDE,The(by R. Bloch) see JOURNEY TO MIDNIGHT

INFERNAL IDOL(by H. Seymour) see CRAZE

The INFERNAL TRIO (F-I-W.G.) Levitt-Pickman/Lira-Belstar & Oceania & T.I.T. 1974 color 100m. (Le TRIO INFERNAL) SP,D: Francis Girod. SP: also Jacques Rouffio. From a novel by Solange Fasquelle. Ph: Andreas Winding. Mus: Ennio Morricone. AD: J.-J. Caziot. SpFX: Pierre Roudeix. Ref: MFB '75:162. Willis/SW. V 5/15/74. with Michel Piccoli, Romy Schneider, Andrea Ferreol, Mascha Gomska.

"PSYCHO realms....acid bath murder....Philomene as Count Dracula....macabre humour...." (MFB)

The INFERNO (J) Toei 1979 132m. D: Tatsumi Kumashiro. Mus: Riichiro Manabe. SpFX: Nobuo Yajima. Ref: JFFJ 13:35: "supernatural/effects epic."

INFERNO (I) Fox/Intersound 1980 color 107m. SP,D: Dario Argento. Ph: Romano Albani. Mus: Keith Emerson. AD: Giuseppe Bassan. SpFX: Germano Natali, Mario Bava, Pino Leoni. Ref: V 4/2/80. MFB'80:196. with Irene Miracle, Leigh McCloskey, Eleonora Giorgi, Alida Valli, Daria Nicolodi, S. Pitoeff, Feodor Chaliapin.

"Lavish, no holds barred witch story"; curse; haunted palace; "apocalyptic holocaust" (V); suspended animation. (MFB)

INFRAMAN (H.K.) Brenner/Shaw 1975('77-U.S.) color/scope 92m. (ZHONGGUO CHAOREN. The SUPER INFRAMAN-alt t) D: Hua Shan. SP: Yi Kuang. Ph: Ho Lan-shan. Mus D: Chen Yung-yu. AD: Johnson-Tsao. SpFX: Yuan Hsiang-jen. Mkp: Wu Hsu-ching. Ref: screen. CineFan 2:26. PFA notes 9/27/80. V 3/31/76. Bianco #4/77:150. HKFFest V:211. with Li Hsiu-hsien, Wang Hsieh, Terry Liu, Y. Man-tzu.

Scientist transforms man into nuclear-powered Inframan, provides him with "thunderball fists" to fight legendary Princess Dragon Mom and her monster minions (inc. skeleton creatures, She-demon with ray-projecting eyes (in palms of hands!), fire-breathing monster, tentacled monster, spring-headed-and-handed monsters); brainwashing machine; deep-freeze; bottomless pit; freezing gas; rays of all colors; sequence in which Inframan and monster become giants and fight. (When it, foolishly, shrinks back to normal size, he squishes it.) Lots of fun with a seemingly endless parade of colorful monsters (see above), and their seemingly endless array of powers and funny growls and grunts. The monsters always seem to be shouting or muttering and bouncing about, and are so eager to help their mistress destroy civilization. Inframan's acrobatics are amusing too, but the monsters star, and there are lulls when they're not onscreen. (Very few when they are.)

*INGAGI RKO 1931(1930) D: Grace McKee? Story: N.H. Spitzer. Ph: Harold Williams et al. Mus: Edward Gage. Narr: Louis Nizor. Ref: FM 66:20. Turner/Price: footage from HEART OF AFRICA(1914). Lee. with Charles Gemora(gorilla), D. Swayne.

Poisonous prehistoric reptile.

See also: *SON OF INGAGI. A LAD AN' A LAMP(P).

The INITIATION OF SARAH ABC-TV/Fries-Stonehenge 1978 color 94m. D: Robert Day. SP: Don Ingalls, Kenette Gfeller, Carol Saraceno. Ph: Ric Waite. Mus: Johnny Harris. AD: Herman Zimmerman. SpFX: Cliff Wenger. Ref: TV. TVG. with Kay Lenz, Tony Bill, Kathryn Crosby, Shelley Winters, Tisa Farrow.

Psychic co-ed's anger can shatter mirrors, knock down mashers and snippy sorority sisters, frazzle ropes; housemother attempts to focus that power for evil purposes, almost turns sorority initiation into Black Mass. Too, too sweet, sincere fantasy-drama, though the acting is above average. And now, let's see, did CARRIE come first?

INNER SANCTUM series see CALLING DR.DEATH. DEAD MAN'S EYES. FROZEN GHOST,The. PILLOW OF DEATH. *STRANGE CONFESSION. *WEIRD WOMAN.

El INQUISIDOR (Peruv.-Arg.) Film Trust/Dusa & Arias 1975 D, P: Bernardo Arias. SP: Gustavo Ghirardi. Ph: P. Marcialetti. Ref: V 4/6/77:73(ad). 2/2/77:32. 9/17/75:3. IFG'75:76. '76. with Duilio Marzio, Olga Zubarry, Elena Sedova, M.A. Bisutti.

"Psycho gang" torturing family as witches comes up against real, "beautiful but powerful" witches. (V)

INSEMINOID (B) Shaw-Jupiter 1981 color 92m. D: Norman J. Warren. SP: Nick & Gloria Maley. Ph: John Metcalfe. Mus: John Scott. PD: Hayden Pearce. SpFX: Oxford, Camera FX. SpMkp: N. Maley, Makeup FX. SpOptFX: Axtell Assoc. Ref: V 10/15/80:175(ad). 11/19/80:33. MFB'81:93. with Robin Clarke, Jennifer Ashley, Stephanie Beacham, Judy Geeson(Sandy).
Woman possessed by alien on distant planet turns cannibalistic, gives birth to monster-twins.

INSUL DER SELIGEN see ISLANDS OF BLISS

INTERIM(by T.E.O'Connell) see FACE BEHIND THE MASK

***INTERPLANETARY REVOLUTION SFT 1924 6m. (MEZHPLANETNAYA REVOLUTSIYA) AD: E. Komissarenko et al. Ref: screen. Lee.
Capitalist and National Socialist "ghouls" vampirize woman, drink her blood through straws. Bizarre, offhand-psychedelic animated comedy.

INTERRUPTED JOURNEY(by J.G.Fuller) see UFO INCIDENT,The

The INTRUDER Texture/YFFFC 1973 clay anim short D: Scott Morris. Ref: IFG'78:380: "hilarious monster film." '74:536: prehistoric animals.

The INTRUDER WITHIN ABC-TV/Furia-Oringer 1981 color 95m. (The LUCIFER RIG-orig t) D: Peter Carter. SP: Ed Waters. Ph: James Pergola. Mus: Gil Melle. AD: G. Holmes. SpMkpDes: James Cummins; Henry Golas;(devel) Shafton Inc. Opt: Howard A. Anderson. Ref: TV. TVG. FM 176. with Chad Everett, Jennifer Warren, Joseph Bottoms, Joe Finnegan(final creature).
Prehistoric eggs from the ocean floor hatch monsters which more or less recapitulate ALIEN. Confusing continuity; derivative thrills and monster-design. PANIC OFFSHORE-int t.

The INUGAMIS (J) Toei & Toho 1977 (INUGAMIKE NO ICHIZOKU) D: Kon Ichikawa. From Seishi Yokomizo's novel. Mus: Yuji Ohno. Ref: V 5/11/77:148(ad): "haunted mansion"; the Devil? 5/4/77:54. with Koji Ishizaka, Yoko Shimada, Mieko Takamine.

*INVADERS FROM MARS 1953 Ref: screen. MFB'81:122.
Great moments in sf: the cut in the flashback montage from (a) father Arthur Franz slapping son Jimmy Hunt, to (b) the detonation of the explosives. Or, the objective correlative with a vengeance. Also: the "sand symphony"'s heavenly chorus seeming, perversely, to promise a glorious (zombie-like) future for all. But, oh! that stock footage and those *terrible* moments.

La INVASION DE LOS MUERTOS (Mex) Azteca 1972 color D: Rene Cardona. Ref: Lee(M/TVM). with Blue Demon, Crista Linder, Jorge Mistral, Cesar Silva(Dracula), Tarzan Moreno(Frankenstein monster).

INVASION FROM INNER EARTH (Gold Key-TV)/United Int'l/North Star (Bill Rebane) 1977 color 95m. D: Ito Rebane. Ph: Jack Willoughby. Opt: CFI. Ref: TVFFSB. V 2/14/79:71(ad). 12/22/76:26. TV. TVG. with Paul Bentzen, Debbi Pick, Nick Holt, Karl Wallace.
"Red ray" wreaks havoc on Earth. Plodding sf.

The INVASION OF CAROL ENDERS ABC-TV/Dan Curtis 1974 color 68m. Ref: TVFFSB. with Meredith Baxter, Chris Connelly, C. Aidman.
Personality transfer between a living and a dead woman.

*INVASION OF THE ANIMAL PEOPLE (Medallion-TV)/Unger-Fortuna 1958 73m.(55m.) (RYMDINVASION I LAPPLAND) SP: also Arthur C. Pierce. Ph: Hilding Bladh. Mus: Allan Johannson. AD: Nils Nilsson. Ref: TV. AFI. Lee. and with Ake Gronberg.
Monster escaped from spaceship terrorizes countryside. Endearingly inept sf-mystery, with so few elements to its mystery-plot that the script has to dispense them very carefully. The "star" is a big, rather-too-adorable-looking monster which runs around starting avalanches and wrecking houses. It also likes to lumber around carrying a young woman (for unstated reasons). The narration (by John Carradine) is gobbledygook. ("And without the future, there would be no present," etc.)

INVASION OF THE BEE GIRLS Centaur/Sequoia 1973 color 85m. D: Denis Sanders. SP: Nicholas Meyer. Ph: Gary Graver. Mus: Charles Bernstein. Ref: screen. Lee. PFA notes 11/24/78. CineFan 2:29. V 6/30/73:7(rated). with William Smith, Anitra Ford, Victoria Vetri, Rene Bond, Cliff Osmond, Anna Aries.
Scientist alters cellular structure of female subjects, turns them into deadly "queen bees" with voracious sexual appetites. Not quite consistent enough to be parody; too suspiciously intentional to be honest camp; not artful enough to bring off a sex-as-death metaphor, BEE GIRLS is still intermittently tackily charming. The notion of "plot" is treated quite cavalierly. It hinges (such as it is) on the hero's recalling "something the captain said: 'They're dropping like flies'," which recollection somehow leads him to bees, which subject quickly leads him to the "bee girls." (Who are also, in most cases, "D" (cup) girls.) Highlight: the making-of-a-queen-bee sequence, a cockeyed *tour de force* of willed-camp, eroticism, and horror (and a favorite of Roger Ebert).

INVASION OF THE BLOOD FARMERS NMD 1972 color 80m. SP,D,P: Ed Adlum. SP: also Ed Kelleher. Ref: Lee. Boxo 7/28/80:9. LAT. Willis/SW. with Norman Kell(e)y, Cynthia Fleming (Onhorrid), Tanna Hunter, Bruce Detrick.

INVASION OF THE BODY SNATCHERS UA/Solofilm 1978 color 115m. D: Phil Kaufman. SP: W.D. Richter, from Jack Finney's novel "The Body Snatcher." Ph: Michael Chapman. Mus: Denny Zeitlin. PD: Charles Rosen. SpFX: Dell Rheaume, Russ Hessey.

Space Seqs: Ron Dexter, Howard Preston. MkpFX: Tom Burman, Edouard Henriques. SpSdFX: Ben Burtt. Opt: Pacific Title. Ref: screen. MFB'79:47. V 12/20/78. Arthur McMillan. with Donald Sutherland, Brooke Adams, Leonard Nimoy, Veronica Cartwright, Jeff Goldblum, Art Hindle, Lelia Goldoni, Kevin McCarthy, Don Siegel, Tom Luddy, Albert Johnson, Robert Duvall.

Spores from a dying world drift through space, fall over San Francisco, transform into seed pods capable of duplicating and replacing humans. The movie itself is a remake and (as long as the original 1956 version isn't destroyed, like a pod-copied human) rather superfluous. There are admittedly enough changes rung on the original, and there are even some improvements. (The '78 garden of budding bodies is more horrific than the '56 greenhouse equivalent.) But the first half of the new version seems to be searching, mistakenly, for "relevance." It suggests that the finger-pointing aliens are emotionally atrophied San Franciscans--i.e., it's indulging in some finger-pointing of its own. And the fact that the aliens are emotional blanks finally counts for less than the fact that they are annoyingly messianic: the movie is (in effect if not intention) about people with a cause, not people without a soul, and, yes, these people _are_ everywhere, and they _want to get you_. (Only in the movie, however, do they have pods at their disposal.) Somewhere within this story lies dormant a very funny satire on proselytism....The second half of the film dwindles into a mere retelling of the original, with embellishments (e.g., the aliens appropriate ships as well as trucks).

INVASION OF THE FLYING SAUCERS see EARTH VS.THE FLYING SAUCERS

INVASION OF THE LOVE DRONES Drones 1977 color 72m. D?,SP, Ph,Ed: Jerome Hamlin. Ref: Meyers. V 12/7/77. Willis/SW. with Viveca Ash, Jamie Gillis, Eric Edwards, Bree Anthony.

Doctor who creates race of love drones; spaceship from another universe which runs on sexual energy.

INVASION SINITESTRA see INCREDIBLE INVASION, The

INVENTING TROUBLE (B) Cricks 1915 10m. D: W.P. Kellino. SP: Reuben Gillmer. Ref: BFC.

"Inventor demonstrates labour-saving devices, until prehistoric monster eats him."

The INVENTORS Educ/Christie 1934 22m. SP: W. Watson, S. Herzig. Ref: LC. Lee. with "Col.Stoopnagle" and "Budd."

Frankenstein-monster-like robot made of car parts goes berserk.

L'INVENZIONE DI MOREL (I) Mount Street-Alga 1974 color 110m. SP,D: Emidio Greco. SP: also Andrea Barbata. From the novel by Adolf Bioy Casares. Ph: Silvano Ippoliti. Mus: Nicola Piovani. AD: Amedeo Fago. Ref: V 9/25/74. Bianco Index'74: 1973? with Giulio Brogi, Anna Karina, John Steiner, Ezio

Marano.
Time travel?; "sci-fi twist." (V)

INVISIBLE ADVERSARIES (Austrian) Export 1978 color 112m. (UNSICHTBARE GEGNER) D,P: Valie Export. SP: Peter Weibel. Ph: Wolfgang Simon. Mus: Hartl-Kalchauser. Ref: V 5/10/78. VV 1/14/81. with Susann Widl, P. Weibel.
Mysterious force called Hyksos invades people of Earth.

*INVISIBLE AGENT 1942 SpFX: John P. Fulton. Ref: TV. Glut/CMM: not really sequel to '33 INVISIBLE MAN. and with Keye Luke.
Hokey plot, dialogue, invisibility stunts, relieved occasionally by humor from Peter Lorre. (Listen for his "Naturally" in the fishhook sequence.) Fulton's effects are generally familiar, occasionally impressive, and there _is_ one offbeat effect: Ilona Massey's lips flattening as the invisible Jon Hall kisses her. _That_ one you don't expect.

*INVISIBLE GHOST 1941 AD: David Milton. Ref: TV. Lennig/TC.
Monogram at low ebb. (That's _low._) The purpose of the ungainly script seems to be to make Bela Lugosi look ridiculous--he spends half his screen time just carrying around his coat. And who wants to hear _Bela Lugosi_ deliver lines like "Apple pie--that will _be_ a _treat!_" Could _this_ be Monogram's worst? Is the search finally over...?

*The INVISIBLE MAN 1933 AD: Charles D. Hall. Sequel: The INVISIBLE MAN RETURNS. Ref: TV. Glut/CMM: _not_ based on the Wylie book, even in part. Lee.
A classic horror-fantasy which works best as, simply, a Claude Rains "reading" of his role as Griffin, the invisible man. If this is the first and best of its kind it's primarily thanks to the voice of Rains. The movie is also satisfying as effects stunts-and-comedy. (The "gathering nuts in May" bit is perfection.) But it's rather filmsy as narrative: Henry Travers' exposition-clogged scenes are like afterthought inserts intended solely to explain Rains' plight. And in about an hour the plot travels from William Harrigan's "He meddled in things men should leave alone" to Rains' "I meddled in things that man must leave alone," which is not a hell of a long way.

The INVISIBLE MAN NBC-TV/Univ-TV & Silverton 1975 color 72m. D: Robert M. Lewis. SP,P: Steven Bochco. From the H.G.Wells novel. Ref: TVG. V 5/14/75:138. with David McCallum(the invisible man), Melinda Fee, Jackie Cooper, Arch Johnson.

INVISIBLE MAN,The(novel by H.G.Wells), and scientific invisibility
See also: ASA-NISSE I AGENTFORM. DISPARUS DE SAINT-AGIL. DOCTOR X(1972). GEMINI MAN. GIRL FROM S.I.N. INVISIBLE REVENGE. LUSTY TRANSPARENT MAN. MAYA MANUSHYA. MORE WILD WILD WEST. NOW YOU SEE HIM,NOW YOU DON'T. OSCAR,KINA Y EL LASER. PARCHIS VS.EL INVENTOR INVISIBLE,Los. PER,JOM,PHEN. PHANTOM OF THE MOULIN ROUGE. PINK LADIES' MOTION PICTURE. WHERE'S JOHNNY?

*The INVISIBLE MAN RETURNS 1940 Ref: TV. Glut/CMM.
Flat sequel to the Whale-Rains INVISIBLE MAN. The one evocative scene: this new invisible man (Vincent Price) appropriating a scarecrow's clothes. For the most part, though, this is pulp tragedy, with actors Price, Cedric Hardwicke, and John Sutton all striking the same sinned-against attitude at one time or another.

*The INVISIBLE MAN'S REVENGE 1944 Mus: H.J. Salter. Ref: TV. V 6/7/44. Glut/CMM: not really sequel to '33 INVISIBLE MAN.
There's no ambivalence about Jon Hall's invisible man (as there was about Rains')--he's simply unpleasant, a murderer and a madman who evokes no awe or sympathy. And the writing is forced. But John P. Fulton's invisibility effects are amazing: e.g., the hand-in-the-aquarium, the flour-on-the-face, the darts-sailing-right-into-the-bull's-eye, the dog-harness, the parrot-perch.

*The INVISIBLE RAY 1936 Story: H. Higgin. Mus: Franz Waxman. AD: Albert D'Agostino. ElecFX: Kenneth Strickfaden. Ref: TV. Turner/Price. Lee. and with Paul Weigel.
Ray from the Andromeda nebula trapped, its record of time and space projected; "journey" by it to Andromeda at the speed of "electric magnification"; "flashback," via ray, to meteorite from A. crashing to Earth a "few thousand million years" ago; Radium "X" from meteorite, unfiltered, makes Dr. Janos Rukh's (Boris Karloff) touch deadly; filtered, is a cure-all; counteractive keeps Rukh from incinerating; ultraviolet camera captures image of murderer in victim's eyes. The science here is fascinating, the drama not, and the latter consumes much more running time. Music, effects, and art direction star, by default. Karloff and Bela Lugosi both have dry, humorless roles, although Lugosi's matter-of-fact delivery of the line "They die" produces a little tingle, and heroine Frances Drake has some of the direct emotional appeal of Margaret Sullavan.

The INVISIBLE REVENGE Kit Parker/Fox 1925 anim 10m. D: Raoul Barre. From Bud Fisher's "Mutt & Jeff" comic strip. Ref: KParker. no LC. Lee: solution-produced invisibility.

*The INVISIBLE WOMAN 1940 SpFX: John P. Fulton. Ref: TV. Lee.
John Barrymore's doddering scientist here is an amusing creation--but he's only in effect an oasis in a desert of painfully prankish actors and tired gags re: invisibility. His best line: "Hereditary!"

INVOCATION OF MY DEMON BROTHER Film-makers' Coop 1969 12m. (ZAP-alt t?) SP,D,Ph,P,AD: Kenneth Anger. Mus: Mick Jagger. Ref: Lee: Black Mass. MFB'73:179-80: "comic-book demon." with Speed Hacker, Bobby Beausoleil(Lucifer), Anton LaVey.

IO see OUTLAND

IO E CATERINA (I-F) RAI-TV & Ital.Int'l/Carthago 1981 color SP,D: Alberto Sordi. SP: also R. Sonego. Ph: S. D'Offizi. Mus: Piero Piccioni. Sets: L. Baraldi. Ref: V 2/4/81: "women & robots." with Sordi, Edwige Fenech, Catherine Spaak, Rossano Brazzi, Valeria Valeri.

ISLA MISTERIOSA see MYSTERIOUS ISLAND(1972)

The ISLAND Univ/Zanuck-Brown 1980 color/scope 114m. D: Michael Ritchie. SP: Peter Benchley, from his novel. Ph: Henri Decae;(sea) Neil Roach;(matte) Bill Taylor. Mus: Ennio Morricone; R. Strauss. PD: Dale Hennesy. SpVisFX: Albert Whitlock. SpFX: Cliff Wenger. Mkp: J.A. Sanchez, Bob Westmoreland. Ref: V 6/4/80: modern-day pirates in the Bermuda triangle. MFB'80:177. D.Dworkin. TV. with Michael Caine, David Warner, Angela McGregor, Frank Middlemass, Colin Jeavons.

Science-pirate-fiction, as fifth-or-sixth-generation pirates take on the U.S. Coast Guard (and win). High adventure, and a dark vision of man and violence, are meant to comment upon each other, but more often just confuse each other, as the Caine character's son becomes a moral football. (Both sides--civilized and uncivilized--seem occasionally to have possession of him at the same time. This is either ambiguity or an infraction.) Caine's dryness plays very well off the outrageousness and general unbelievability of the situation, but can't dispel same.

ISLAND OF DEATH see WOULD YOU KILL A CHILD?

The ISLAND OF DR. MOREAU AI/Cinema 77 1977 color 98m. D: Don Taylor. SP: John H. Shaner, Al Ramrus, from H.G. Wells' novel. Ph: Gerry Fisher. Mus: Laurence Rosenthal. PD: Philip Jefferies. SpMkp: John Chambers, Dan Striepeke, Tom Burman. SpFX: Cliff Wenger. Ref: TV. V(d) 7/12/77. with Burt Lancaster(Moreau), Michael York, Nigel Davenport, Barbara Carrera(Maria), Richard Basehart(Sayer of the Law), Nick Cravat(M'Ling), Fumio Demura.

A doctor conducting eugenic experiments on animals and humans on a Pacific island discovers the cell particle which controls evolution. ("He was perfect, but he's still an animal!") Rubbery makeup makes the "manimal" scenes look like carnival time in Costa Rica. Superfluous variations on Cocteau's BEAUTY AND THE BEAST, the Laughton ISLAND OF LOST SOULS, and the Lugosi APEMAN.

*ISLAND OF LOST SOULS 1932 Ref: screen. FM 66:20. 28:30-39. 169:42-3. and with Charles Gemora.

Charles Laughton as the brilliant, mad Dr. Moreau makes every furrow of his brow, twitch of his lips, and crook of his finger count. He's showily subdued--he gets his bizarre effects effortlessly, it appears, while most of the other actors here struggle with the simplest lines. (Paul Hurst and Arthur Hohl, however, are also good.) The Moreau thoroughly deflated, after his guinea pig (or panther) Lota's (Kathleen Burke's) reversion to panther-hood, is at once a pitiable and contemptible figure, both tragic and petty--it's not, after all, just his defeat. Bela Lugosi as another of Moreau's experiments looks like a bit character in a W.C. Fields comedy--Mr. Muckle with hair.

ISLAND OF MUTATIONS see SCREAMERS

ISLAND OF THE DAMNED see WOULD YOU KILL A CHILD?

ISLAND OF THE LIVING DEAD see ZOMBIE

ISLAND OF THE TWILIGHT PEOPLE see TWILIGHT PEOPLE

ISLAND OF THE ZOMBIES (I) Kristal 1980 color D: Joe D'Amato. Ref: V 5/7/80:412. with Laura Gemser.

The ISLANDS OF BLISS (G) Brandon 1913 50m. (Die INSUL DER SELIGEN) D: Arthur Kahane. Ph: F. Weimann. AD & P: Max Reinhardt. Ref: Brandon. Lee. with W. Diegelmann, W. Prager.

Circe--on an island of Roman gods--turns two adventurers into pigs.

*ISLE OF THE DEAD 1945 Inspired by the Arnold Boecklin painting, "The Isle of the Dead." Sd: Jean L. Speak, James G. Stewart. Ref: TV. V 9/12/45. MFB'81:122-23. Siegel/VL.

Greece, 1912, during the First Balkan War. General Pherides, "the watchdog," tries to confine an outbreak of septicemic plague within a group of nine people taking refuge at an island inn built upon a cemetery. ISLE OF THE DEAD is nothing if not downbeat; in fact it perhaps tries too hard to be grim. One of Val Lewton's most humorless films, it suffers some from its over-seriousness. Only occasional accidentally-risible lines break the morbid spell the film casts. Some may find this monotone merely monotonous. I find it for the most part absorbing. The script proceeds as single-mindedly as its protagonist, the general (Boris Karloff), a man who puts his faith in what he can "see and feel and know about." He rejects the words of the dying doctor (Ernst Dorian): "Fight death all your days and die knowing you know nothing," the words of a man who can accept the irrational (i.e., a truly rational man). Pherides' eventual conversion from the doctor's science to Kyra's (Helene Thimig) and Albrecht's (Jason Robards) superstition is only superficially a conversion: he is only exchanging weapons in his fight against the unknown. The last shot of the general--his eyes open even in death--is a testament to unyielding character. It survives even Albrecht's eulogy, which is spoken over it, and which, not incidentally, illustrates a weakness of even the better Lewton films. The general is portrayed as a rigidly authoritarian, even cruel man--Albrecht's "He wanted to protect us" sounds as if it's meant simply to excuse him and his actions. The more blatant cruelties of the Karloff characters in The

BODY SNATCHER and BEDLAM are also excused with similar, last-minute apologies. These absolutions obscure Lewton's main point--that the morality of his characters is finally subordinate to the fact of their mortality. In ISLE OF THE DEAD, Thea (Ellen Drew) may be "good," yet all her efforts can't save her mistress, Mrs. St.Aubyn (Katherine Emery), from the disease that is slowly killing her; good or bad, the general can't save himself from the plague. (The film even, at one point, identifies the general with a statue of Cerberus, the guardian of the dead.) Mrs. St.Aubyn's attributions to Thea of goodness, and Kyra's of evil, seem intended to check and balance each other--the woman's illness and her eventual death have nothing to do with Thea's character. The performances of Karloff, Dorian, and Drew; Leigh Harline's autumnally-toned score, and the atmospheric sound and visual effects all work, I think, against the apologetic tenor of some of the dialogue, and towards a philosophic stance that seems at once half-dread, half-acceptance of death, and that affirms the latter's independence of will or character.

ISN'T IT SHOCKING ABC-TV/ABC Circle 1973 color 72m. D: John Badham. SP: Lane Slate. Ph: Jack Woolf. Mus: David Shire. AD: Joseph Alves Jr. SpFX: Cliff Wenger. Mkp: E.T. Case. Opt: Consolidated. Ref: TV. Cinef IV:3:37: "horror thriller"; "murder machine" which induces death by heart attack. with Edmond O'Brien, Alan Alda, Louise Lasser, Ruth Gordon, Will Geer, Dorothy Tristan, Lloyd Nolan, Liam Dunn, Pat Quinn.
A superlative cast in a routine mystery-with-a-touch-of-sf. Generally pleasant, but formula. Nice moments with Lasser and Alda.

ISOLA DEGLI UOMINI PESCE see SCREAMERS

ISOLA MISTERIOSA... see MYSTERIOUS ISLAND(1972)

IT see IT! THE TERROR FROM BEYOND SPACE

*IT CAME FROM BENEATH THE SEA 1955 SpFX: Jack Erickson. Ref: TV.
Eerie ascending-tentacle shots punctuate a very cheap-looking sf-er. A more typical shot: three actors standing around a desk marking time between Ray Harryhausen's effects. At one point an actor (demonstrating how fast an octopus can travel) inflates and lets fly a balloon--they couldn't even afford a filmstrip! In sum: nice tentacle, lousy arm.

IT CAME...WITHOUT WARNING Filmways/Heritage 1980 color 89m. (The WARNING-orig t. WITHOUT WARNING-alt t) D,P: Greydon Clark. SP: Lyn Freeman, D. Grodnik, et al. Ph: Dean Cundey. Mus: Dan Wyman. PD: Jack DeWolf. SpFX: P.J. Quinlivan III; (asst) Dana Rheaume. SpMkp: Greg Cannom. SpCost: Elois Jenssen;(asst) Vera Mordaunt. Opt: Modern. Ref: TV. V 9/24/80. 8/6/80:26. with Jack Palance, Martin Landau, Tarah Nutter, C.S. Nelson, Cameron Mitchell, Neville Brand, Sue Ane Langdon, Larry Storch, Ralph Meeker, Kevin Hall(alien).

Alien being sends out discus-shaped, flying sucker-creatures; icky corpses stored in shed. Another showcase for a few determinedly-disgusting effects. Not as effective-of-kind as FIEND WITHOUT A FACE or ALIEN.

IT FELL FROM THE SKY see ALIEN DEAD, The

IT HAPPENED AT LAKEWOOD MANOR ABC-TV/Landsburg 1977 color 93m. (PANIC AT LAKEWOOD MANOR-alt t. ANTS-orig t) D: Robert Scheerer. SP: Guerdon Trueblood. Ph: Bernie Abramson. Mus: Ken Richmond. AD: Ray Beal. SpFX: Roy Downey. Opt: Westheimer. Ref: TV. TVFFSB. V 5/17/78:185(ad). TV Season. with Suzanne Somers, Robert Foxworth, Myrna Loy, Lynda Day George, Bernie Casey, Anita Gillette, Steve Franken, Stacey Keach Sr.
Hordes of poisonous ants (products of a "toxic world") terrorize a summer resort-hotel. ("Ants are ants." "Not these!") Complete with Fifties-style filmstrip on ants, and lots of ants. (Cast of millions!) It's certainly no Picnic at Lakewood Manor. Signed, Sick-of-Ants.

*IT HAPPENED HERE Rath-Long Distance 1966 Mus: Jack Beaver. AD: A. Mollo, Jim Nicolson. Ref: screen. AFI. Lee.
A sometimes bitingly witty depiction of the German occupation of England, mid-World War II. Of course it didn't happen there, and this film plays on your knowledge of that fact. It's like watching a double-movie--from one angle it's a documentary, from another, science fiction: this could be France; this is England. The "schizophrenic" high point of this sf-documentary: the National Socialist newsreel, which rewrites history in order to fashion a vision of a warm, enduring German-British brotherhood. The more straightforward, dramatic sections of the movie are less certainly written, more didactic than ironic, and not far from well-meaning but muddled anti-Nazi dramas like The MAN I MARRIED(1940), in which the "true nature" of fascism slowly dawns on the protagonist. (Somehow these dawns always seem false, imposed.) The straightforwardness of the Kevin Brownlow-Andrew Mollo script does, however, allow for acts of violence by both Nazis and partisans.

IT LIVES AGAIN WB/Larco 1978 color 91m. SP,D: Larry Cohen. Sequel to IT'S ALIVE(1973). Ph: Fenton Hamilton. Mus: Bernard Herrmann; Laurie Johnson. SpMkp: Rick Baker. Ref: MFB '78:242. Meyers. V 5/10/78. with Frederic Forrest, Kathleen Lloyd, John P. Ryan, John Marley, Eddie Constantine, A.Duggan.
Mobile-clinic doctor responsible for delivering mutant killer-babies.

IT LIVES BY NIGHT see BAT PEOPLE, The

*IT! THE TERROR FROM BEYOND SPACE 1958 (IT-orig t) SpMkp: Paul Blaisdell. Ref: TV. Lee.
The plot, in the characters' own words: "If nothing else works--maybe gas?" "Bullets, grenades--nothing stops it!"

"Grenades, gas, and bullets have failed to stop the beast--but perhaps it can be electrocuted." Silly/tense sf-suspense, depending on which moment you happen to be watching. If the script's suspense ploys are elementary, the monster's bulk and snarls are intimidating. "TV Key" (2nd ed.) was right: "Laughable at times but fun for the kiddies."

ITIM see RITES OF MAY

IT'S A BIRD, IT'S A PLANE, IT'S SUPERMAN ABC-TV/Twain 1975 color 93m. D: Jack Regas. SP: Romeo Muller(sp?). Based on the Strouse-Newman play & the "Superman" characters created by Siegel & Shuster. Ref: TVFFSB. Cinef IV:3:37. with David Wilson, Lesley Warren, David Wayne, Kenneth Mars, Loretta Swit, Allen Ludden.

Superman vs. a mad scientist.

IT'S ALIVE WB/Larco 1973 color 91m. (BABY KILLER-I) SP,D,P: Larry Cohen. Ph: Fenton Hamilton. Mus: Bernard Herrmann. SpMkp: Rick Baker. Titles: Imagic. Sequel: IT LIVES AGAIN. Ref: V 10/16/74. screen. MFB'75:137. Bianco Index'75. with John Ryan, Sharon Farrell, Andrew Duggan, Guy Stockwell, Michael Ansara, Robert Emhardt, William Wellman Jr., J. Dixon.

Santa Monica, Calif. An infant killer-mutant is born to a perplexed couple. Real horror and fake pathos, sensationalistically blended. This monster both snarls and sobs, confounding human responses (at least its parents'). The comic-dramatic conflict: it _is_ a baby, but it'll rip up anyone (except kin) in leaping range. Key discombobulating image: the milkman's _milk_ and the milkman's _blood_ combining and pouring out the back of his truck and down the street. If nothing else, the script effectively illustrates its own wisdom: "People without children these days don't realize how lucky they are." Unfortunately, the movie leans more toward the dramatic than the comic. It takes itself too sociologically seriously--the script invokes "Frankenstein," finding figurative monsters in scientists, doctors, pr men, and cops, and even Herrmann's music can't help bring off _that_ analogy. One thing is certain: you will see scenes in Larry Cohen's films which you'll never see in anyone else's--which certainty is perhaps more fortunate than unfortunate.

IT'S ALIVE see BAT PEOPLE, The

IT'S NOT THE SIZE THAT COUNTS see PERCY'S PROGRESS

IZBAVITELJ see REDEEMER,The(1977)

J.D.'S REVENGE AI 1976 color 95m. D,P: Arthur Marks. SP: Jaison Starkes. Ph: Harry May. Mus: Robert Prince. Ref: V 6/30/76. Willis/SW. with Glynn Turman, Lou Gossett, Joan

Pringle, David McKnight(J.D.), Carl Crudup.
"Law student possessed by spirit of dead hoodlum."

J-MEN FOREVER see DAY THE EARTH GOT STONED

JAANI DUSHMAN (India-Hindi) Kohli 1979 Ref: V 5/30/79:42: "India's first multistar horror movie." FM 161:12.

JABBERWOCKY (B) Cinema 5/Umbrella 1977 color 101m. SP,D: Terry Gilliam. SP: also Charles Alverson. Title from the poem by Lewis Carroll. Ph: Terry Bedford. Mus: DeWolfe. PD: Roy Smith. SpDes: Valerie Charlton, Clinton Cavers, Jen Effects. Ref: MFB'77:72-3. V(d) 4/11/77. Jim Shapiro. with Michael Palin, Max Wall, Deborah Fallender, John Le Mesurier, Harry H. Corbett, Bernard Bresslaw, Peter Salmon(Monster Man).
"Jabberwock, a hideous monster...a proper special-effects monster with horns, beak, wings, claw and scaly tail." (MFB)

JACK AND THE BEANSTALK (J) Col/Commodore & Film-Rite 1976 anim color 90m. SP,D: (Eng.vers.) Peter J. Solmo. Ref: Willis/SW. V 11/12/75:28. TV: monstrous, fanged ogre. NYT 4/16/76.

JACK THE RIPPER (U.S.-B?) Medallion-TV/Pathe-Alpha(Hal Roach) 1958 98m. D: David MacDonald. SP: Michael Plant. Ph: Stephen Dade. Mus: Edwin Astley. Ref: TV. TVFFSB. with Boris Karloff(host/Dr.Mason/Mr.Atterbury/Capt.Elwood), Niall MacGinnis, Nora Swinburne, Clifford Evans, Thomas B. Henry, Robert Griffin, Morris Ankrum.
Four episodes from the unsold TV series "The Veil," involving precognition, ghostly visitation, ghostly revenge, Jack the Ripper. Cut-and-dried anecdotes, with perhaps a pinch or two of narrative interest. MacGinnis, however, is fine in the fourth story; he's a clairvoyant tormented by visions of the Whitechapel murders. This fleetingly-glimpsed Ripper is a mad surgeon who begins by torturing animals. ("Then there were the bats.") Karloff has incidental roles in the first two stories, and an uncertainly-written lead role in the third keeps forcing him to switch gears abruptly.

*JACK THE RIPPER (Sp-I) Cinefilms & Apollon 1971 color/scope 98m. (JACK,EL DESTRIPADOR DE LONDRES. SETTE CADAVERI PER SCOTLAND YARD) SP: J.L. Madrid, Jacinto Molina, S. Continenza, T. Carpi. Ph: D. Ubeda. Mus: Piero Piccioni. AD: J.A. Soler. SpFX: Antonio Molina. Ref: Bianco Index'73. Lee(SpCinema). with Paul Naschy(aka J.Molina), Patricia Loran, Andres Resino, Renzo Marignano.

JACK THE RIPPER (W.G.-Swiss) (Showtime-TV)/Cineshowcase/Export 1978 color 86m. D: Jesus Franco. Ref: Boxo 7/30/79:21. V 5/17/78:369. 1/25/78:94. with Klaus Kinski, Josephine Chaplin, Herbert Fux, Lina Romay.
Straightforward, unremarkable version of the story.
See also: BIZARRE-BIZARRE(P). BLACK THE RIPPER. DR.JEKYLL

AND SISTER HYDE. GROOVE ROOM,The. LULU. MURDER BY DECREE. PHANTOM OF THE OPERA(1962). TERROR IN THE WAX MUSEUM. TIME AFTER TIME.

JACK THE RIPPER GOES WEST see KNIFE FOR THE LADIES, A

JACK'S WIFE Jack Harris/Latent Image 1973 color 89m. (HUNGRY WIVES-alt t) SP,D,Ph,Ed: George A. Romero. Mus: Steve Gorn. Ref: Lee. V 4/18/73. 1/10/73:4(rated). FC 3/80:32. with Jan White, Ray Laine, Anne Muffly, Bill Thunhurst.
Housewife becomes witch, joins coven.

*The JADE MASK 1945 66m. (CHARLIE CHAN IN THE JADE MASK-alt t) Mus D: Edward J.Kay. Ref: TV. V 1/24/45. and with Cyril Delevanti.
Killer who manipulates dead scientist (or "zombie"), puppet-like, on lines from hall landing to living room below, to make it appear as if his victim is still alive (honest!); mechanism in ventriloquist's dummy which shoots poison darts; door which only scientist's voice can open. Sluggish, kookily-plotted Charlie Chan mystery.

JADU TONA (India-Hindi) Guru 1977 color 134m. SP,D: Raveekant Nagaich. Story: Rani Nagaich. Dial: Aziz Quasi. Mus: H. Bhosle. Ref: V 3/19/80:34. Dharap. with Ashok Kumar, Feroz Khan, Prem Chopra, Prem Nath.
Spirit possesses rich man's daughter.

JAGAN MOHINI (India-Telugu) Vittal 1978 color 164m. SP,D: B.V. Acharya. Mus: V. Krishnamurthy. Ref: Dharap. with Narasimharaju, Prabha, Jayamalini.
Spirit of girl deceived in former life by king returns to possess him.

Los JAGUARES CONTRA EL INVASOR MISTERIOSO (Colombian?) Victor Films 197-? color D: Juan M. Herrera. Dial?: Elias Campos. Mus: Albert Levy. Ref: TVG. TV: aliens with furry-faced "master"? with Julio Cesar Luna, Fedra, Gilberto Fuentes.

The JAILBREAK Fox 1946 anim color 7m. (MIGHTY MOUSE IN THE JAIL BREAK-alt t) D: Eddie Donnelly. SP: J. Foster. Ref: LC. Glut/TFL: bit with Frankenstein monster and Dracula.

JAKKA DENGEKITAI (J) Toei-TV & Asahi Comm. 1977 scope 20m. D: Minoru Yamada. Ref: JFFJ 13:34: episode of TV series rel. theat.; "superhero cyborgs."

JAKKA DENGEKITAI VS. GORENJA (J) Toei-TV 1978 24m. D: K. Taguchi. Ref: JFFJ 13:34: sequel to JAKKA DENGEKITAI.

JAMES BOND (character created by Ian Fleming) see DIAMONDS ARE FOREVER. FOR YOUR EYES ONLY(P). LIVE AND LET DIE. MAN WITH THE GOLDEN GUN. MOONRAKER. NAKED WORLD OF HARRISON MARKS. SPY WHO LOVED ME,The.

JANGAL MEIN MANGAL (India-Hindi) Kiron 1972 color 152m. D, P: R. Bhatia. SP: S. Khalil. Story: Kottarakara. Ph: K.K. Hapadia. Mus: S.-Jaikishan. Ref: Dharap: "ghost" murders. with Pran, Kiran Kumar, Reena Roy.

JASEI NO IN see UGETSU

JAWAI VIKAT GHENE AAHE see WANTED: SON-IN-LAW SALE

JAWS Univ/Zanuck-Brown 1975 color/scope 125m. D: Steven Spielberg. SP: Peter Benchley, Carl Gottlieb, from Benchley's novel. Ph: Bill Butler;(underwater) Rexford Metz;(shark) Ron & Valerie Taylor. Mus: John Williams. PD: Joseph Alves Jr. SpFX: Robert A. Mattey. Sequel: JAWS 2. Ref: MFB'75:263. V 6/18/75. TV. with Roy Scheider, Robert Shaw, Richard Dreyfuss, Lorraine Gary, Murray Hamilton.

A Great White Shark terrorizes the Long Island resort community of Amity. Funny, engaging adventure/monster movie, the kind of film it seems only Steven Spielberg knows how to make nowadays. The dramatic tensions may be elementary--mayor vs. police chief, shark hunter (Shaw) vs. shark expert (Dreyfuss), man vs. shark--but the script is good-naturedly self-conscious about it. If we've been here before (in films and books), Spielberg & co. trade on that familiarity and make us glad to be back. JAWS is good, non-serious filmmaking, and better than a lot of serious filmmaking. (Good examples of either kind are uncommon enough.) John Williams' score makes <u>water</u> exciting.

JAWS OF THE JUNGLE Jay Dee Kay 1936 60m. (JUNGLE VIRGIN-alt t) D,P: J.D. Kendis. SP: Eddy Graneman. Narr: C. Howell. Ref: Turner/Price. LC. with Teeto, "Walla"(orangutang).

"Horde of giant vampire bats" attacks village in Ceylon.

JAWS 2 Univ/Zanuck-Brown 1978 color/scope 116m. D: Jeannot Szwarc. SP: Carl Gottlieb, Howard Sackler, Dorothy Tristan. Sequel to JAWS. Ph: Michael Butler;(shark) Ron & Valerie Taylor. Mus: John Williams. PD: Joe Alves. SpMechFX: Robert Mattey, Roy Arbogast. Ref: MFB'78:243. V 6/7/78. TV. with Roy Scheider, Lorraine Gary, Murray Hamilton, Barry Coe, Joseph Mascolo, Ann Dusenberry, John Dukakis.

A second monster-shark terrorizes the same Long Island resort community. Dreyfuss and Shaw are gone; Spielberg too; and maybe we (and John Williams, who's back) aren't really <u>that</u> interested in sharks after all. The sights and sounds of Amity are about all that's left. And since it's about 80 minutes before people <u>begin</u> to realize that there's another shark at large, we have plenty of time to take them in. Meanwhile, police chief Scheider is sacked, the shark is fed, and, well, that's about it....

JEFF GORDON STRIKES AGAIN (F) FIDA 1964 (DES FRISSONS PARTOUT) D: Raoul Andre. SP: Michel Lebrun. Ref: TVFFSB. FIR'68:443. Cahiers 5/64:61. with Eddie Constantine, Perrette Pradier,

Clement Harari, Daniel Emilfork.
"Bizarre keepers" in private asylum (FIR); FBI agent "threatened with brain surgery that will leave him insane." (TVFFSB)

The JEKYLL AND HYDE PORTFOLIO HMS/Xerxes 1972 color 85m. Story,D,P: Eric J. Haims. SP: Don Greer. Story: also Shelley Haims. Ph: Arch Archambault. Mus: Randy Scott. Ref: Lee(HR 1/24/72): schizophrenic killer. V 6/6/73:6(rated). with Gray Daniels, Mady Maguire, Rene Bond, Sebastian Brook, Bonnie Jean.

JEKYLL JR. see DR.JEKYLL JR.

JEN KUI HU see MAN,GHOST,FOX

JENNIFER AI/Krantz 1978 color 90m. D: Brice Mack. SP: Kay C. Johnson. Story: Steve Krantz. Ph: Irv Goodnoff. Mus Sup: Jerry Styne. Ref: V 5/24/78: "for the young in head." with Lisa Pelikan(Jennifer), Bert Convy, Nina Foch, Amy Johnston, John Gavin, Jeff Corey, Florida Friebus.
Psychic schoolgirl conjures up snakes to wreak revenge on enemies.

JERUSALEM'S LOT see SALEM'S LOT

***La JETEE Argos 1963 still photos (The PIER) SP,D: Chris Marker. Ph: Jean Chiabaud. Mus: Trevor Duncan. SpFX: C.S. Olaf. Ref: screen. Sadoul/Morris. Lee. with Helene Chatelain, Davos Hanich, Jacques Ledoux.
Slight, memory-themed sf-fantasy, with pretentious score and narration. A few nice photos.

JEU DE MASSACRE see KILLING GAME, The

Les JEUX DE LA COMTESSE DOLINGEN DE GRATZ(STYRIE) (F) Nautile-Prospectacle-Perec-Zajdermann 1981 color 115m. SP,D: Catherine Binet. From Unica Zurn's book & a chapter of Bram Stoker's novel "Dracula." Ph: William Lubtchansky et al. Ref: V 6/3/81. with Michel Lonsdale, Carol Kane, Katia Wastchenko, Robert Stephens, Marina Vlady, Marilu Marini.
"Family friend who may be a vampire."

JEWEL OF SEVEN STARS,The(by B.Stoker) see AWAKENING,The. CURSE OF THE MUMMY.

JIBAN RAHASYA see MYSTERY OF LIFE(1973)

JIGAZO NO KAI--OTTO NO BOREI NI OBIERU ONNA (J) Toho Eizo-TV 1979 D: Kazuyoshi Yoshikawa. Ref: JFFJ 13:30.
Woman haunted by husband's ghost.

JISSHIN RETTO see EARTHQUAKE 7.9

*JITTERBUGS 1943 Mus: Charles Newman. AD: Chester Gore. Ref: TV. V 5/26/43. Lee.

You know a comedy is in trouble when the straight lines are as funny as the punch lines, and the highlight is a song with the lyrics "The stars danced a little polka last night/The moon kissed the Mississippi last night." The plot goes further out of its way for that song than it does for Laurel-and-Hardy comedy.

**The JOHNSTOWN MONSTER (B) CFF/Sebastian 1971 color 54m. SP,D: Olaf Pooley. Mus: Harry Robinson. AD: Arnold Chapkis. Ref: M/TVM. Lee(MFB'71:222). with Connor Brennan, Simon Tully, Michael Goodliffe.

Fake and real lake-monsters.

JOROBADO DE LA MORGUE see HUNCHBACK OF THE MORGUE

JOUISSEUSES, Les see UNFAITHFUL WIVES, The

JOURNEY BACK TO OZ (WB-TV)/Filmation 1971 anim color 88m. (RETURN TO THE LAND OF OZ-orig t) D: Hal Sutherland. SP: Fred Ladd et al. Sequel to The WIZARD OF OZ. Ph: S.A. Alcazar. Mus: Sammy Cahn, James Van Heusen. AD: Don Christensen. Anim: Amby Paliwoda. SdFX: Horta-Mahana. Ref: TV. MFB'73:10-11. V 5/22/74:32. Lee. Voices: Liza Minnelli (Dorothy), Milton Berle, Mel Blanc, Margaret Hamilton, Paul Lynde, Ethel Merman, Mickey Rooney, Danny Thomas, Jack E. Leonard.

Mombi (Merman), sister of the Wicked Witch of the West, and her magic, green elephants; spooky forest; monster-chair; tree-monsters; goblins; montage of witches (inc. one who turns into bat); potion for shrinking. Signally uninspired, bland cartoon-invocation of Oz. Lots of meant-to-be-uplifting speeches and song lyrics. Dorothy's return to Oz turns out to be a non-event.

JOURNEY INTO DARKNESS (U.S.-B) ABC-TV/Fox-TV & Anthony Hinds 1968 color 95m. D: 1) James Hill; 2) Peter Sasdy. SP: 1) Oscar Millard; 2) Millard, John Gould. Story: 1) L.P. Davies; 2) Charles Beaumont. Episodes from the "Journey to the Unknown" TV series. Mus: J.P. Scott. AD: William Kellner. Host: Patrick McGoohan. Ref: TV. TVG. TVFFSB. with Robert Reed, Jennifer Hilary, Michael Tolan, Nanette Newman, Patrick Allen, Michael Ripper, Milo O'Shea.

1) "Paper Dolls": genetically-produced boy ("the whelp") with sixth sense psychically directs his three brothers to wreak havoc with the minds of their "enemies." OK premise; but VILLAGE OF THE DAMNED and SCANNERS do it better. 2) "The New People": wealthy, bored man "collects" people, conducts Black Mass, murders for kicks. Unintriguing intrigue.

JOURNEY INTO MIDNIGHT see JOURNEY TO MIDNIGHT

A JOURNEY INTO THE BEYOND (W.G.) Burbank Int'l/Telecontact 1975('77-U.S.) color 95m.(113m.) (REISE INS JENSEITS--DIE WELT DES UBERNATURLICHEN) D: Rolf Olsen. SP: Paul Ross.

Ph: Frank X. Lederle. Mus: Sonoton;(U.S.) Don Great. Narr: John Carradine. Ref: MFB'77:105-6. V 12/22/76:7(rated). Willis/SW.
   Parapsychology, exorcism, spiritualism, gore.

JOURNEY TO MIDNIGHT (U.S.-B) ABC-TV/Fox-TV & Hinds 1968 color 100m. (JOURNEY INTO MIDNIGHT-ad t) D: 1) Alan Gibson; 2) Richard Baker. SP: 1) Jeremy Paul; 2) Robert Bloch. Story: 1) William Abney; 2) Bloch. Episodes from the "Journey to the Unknown" TV series. Mus: David Dabney? AD: William Kellner. Host: Sebastian Cabot. Ref: TV. TVG. TVFFSB. with Chad Everett, Julie Harris, Edward Fox, Tom Adams, Tracy Reed, Bernard Lee, Catherine Lacey, Marne Maitland.
   1) "Poor Butterfly": a costume party at an English country house proves to be a "masquerade of dead souls," ghosts who died in a fire 40 years before. Thin, predictable ghost story. 2) "The Indian Spirit Guide": an opportunist fleecing a wealthy widow loses his life at a seance, the victim of arrows belonging to an Indian dead 80 years. Slight.

JOURNEY TO THE CENTER OF THE EARTH(by J.Verne) see WHERE TIME BEGAN

JOURNEY TO THE UNKNOWN (U.S.-B) ABC-TV/Fox-TV & Hinds 1969 color 106m. Episodes from the TV series. See also: JOURNEY INTO DARKNESS. JOURNEY TO MIDNIGHT. Hostess: Joan Crawford. Ref: TVFFSB. TVG. with Vera Miles, Patty Duke.
   1) Young woman "pledged to the Devil." 2) Girl "terrorized by psycho landlady." (TVFFSB)

El JOVENCITO DRACULA (Sp) Films del Mediterraneo 1976 D: Carlos B. Parra, Jorge Gigo. Ref: V 5/11/77:420. with Parra, Victor Israel.

The JOVIAL FLUID (B) EcKo 1913 7m. Ref: BFC. with Sam T. Poluski.
   Professor invents "laughter liquid."

JUBILEE (B) Libra/Megalovision 1978 color 104m. SP,D: Derek Jarman. SP: also James Whaley. Ph: Peter Middleton. Mus: Brian Eno et al. AD: Christopher Hobbs. Ref: MFB'78:66. V 2/1/78: "vicious killings...black humor." AMPAS. Willis/SW: Cinegate. with Jenny Runacre, Little Nell Campbell, Toyah Willcox, Richard O'Brien, Adam Ant.
   Court astrologer's angel Ariel transports Queen Elizabeth I to an England of the future "where law and order has been abolished." (MFB)

JUDGE DEE: THE MONASTERY MURDERS ABC-TV/ABC Circle 1974 color 95m. D: Jeremy Kagan. SP: Nicholas Meyer, from Robert Van Gulick's novel "Judge Dee at the Haunted Monastery." Ph: Gene Polito. Mus: Leonard Rosenman. PD: Jan Scott. SpFX: John J. De Bron. MkpDes: Stan Winston. Opt: CFI. Ref: TV. TVFFSB. TV Season. V 1/1/75:28. with Khigh Dhiegh, Mako, Soon-Taik

Oh, Miiko Taka, Irene Tsu, Keye Luke.
690 A.D. Visions of 100-year-old "ghosts" in Chinese monastery; gallery of horrors (with one living exhibit); secret room; killer-bear. Mild monastery mystery-intrigue, with nice atmosphere and all sorts of masquerades and plot twists.

JUEGO,El(by J.J.Plans) see WOULD YOU KILL A CHILD?

JUEGOS DE SOCIEDAD (Sp) Promofilm 1974 D: J.L. Merino. Ref: V 5/8/74:207,208(ad): "macabre witches' Sabbath." IFG'75:317. with Manuel Summers, Eva Czemerys.

Le JUIF POLONAIS (F) Jacques Haik 1931('37-U.S.) 95m. D: Jean Kemm. Dial: Pierre Maudru. From the novel by Erckmann-Chatrian. Ph: Paul Cotteret, R. Le Febvre. Mus: Andre Sablon. AD: Jean d'Eaubonne. Ref: Chirat. Lee. Limbacher'79. with Harry Baur, Georges la Cressonniere, Mady Berry, S. Mareuil.
Murderer dreams he's discovered; wakes up, falls dead.
See also: BELLS,The(1914 & 1931).

JULES VERNE'S MYSTERY ON MONSTER ISLAND see MONSTER ISLAND

JULES VERNE'S THE MYSTERIOUS ISLAND see MYSTERIOUS ISLAND(1972)

JULIA(by P.Straub) see HAUNTING OF JULIA, The

JUNGLE BURGER see SHAME OF THE JUNGLE

*The JUNGLE CAPTIVE 1945 Ref: TV. FM 165:14,15. V 6/13/45. and with Charles Wagenheim, Eddy Chandler.
The not-so-fine art of a JUNGLE CAPTIVE is the art of stitching random plot-scraps together. At its most tortuous/ingenious, the script (step 1) has ape-woman Vicky Lane escape from madman Otto Kruger's country house; its objective: get the hero (Phil Brown) out there too. So: (step 2) Otto's assistant (Rondo Hatton) goes into town to alert Otto--Rondo (step 2a) just happens to be wearing the pin that Phil gave his girl (Amelita Ward, Otto's non-jungle-captive-in-the-country). Phil (step 3) spots pin, puts two and two together, and....(There must have been an easier way.) Very Poor Taste Dept.: when Otto catches deformed aide Rondo eyeing Amelita, he tells him (indicating the ape-woman), "This is more in your line." Crude.

JUNGLE GENTS AA 1954 64m. SP,D: Edward Bernds. SP: also Elwood Ullman. Ph: H. Neumann. Mus: Marlin Skiles. AD: David Milton. SpFX: Augie Lohman. Ref: TV. LC. Lee. TVG. with Leo Gorcey, Huntz Hall, Bennie Bartlett, Laurette Luez, Bernard Gorcey, David Condon, Rudolph Anders; Woody Strode?
Wonder drug makes Bowery Boy (Hall) sensitive to the smell of diamonds; Tarzan-and-Jane-like couple; horror sequence in African caves haunted by giant, faceless "ghost." By 1954, practically only Gorcey (Mr. Malaprop) and Hall (apoplexy-as-

comic-style) are left of the original Bowery Octogenarians, and just barely. In this one they at least get into the "jungle" and out of that damn soda fountain. Laurette Luez (from PREHISTORIC WOMEN) is the only reason to open your eyes.

JUNGLE JIM(character created by Alex Raymond) see MARK OF THE GORILLA. PYGMY ISLAND.

JUNGLE VIRGIN see JAWS OF THE JUNGLE

*JUNGLE WOMAN 1944 Mus D: Paul Sawtell. Ref: TV. V 5/24/44.
Rote Lewtonisms, stock footage, and flashbacks to CAPTIVE WILD WOMAN. Notable principally for asylum inmate Willie's (Edward M.Hyans Jr.) reaction to the jungle woman (Acquanetta): "Oh boy oh boy oh boy! This place is getting better all the time!" Worst in the series, if distinctions are possible at this level. Film actually contains stock footage (from The BIG CAGE) within stock footage (from CAPTIVE WILD WOMAN)! Acquanetta was probably the most beautiful actress to work for Universal--and the worst. Her face, voice, and role here recall Simone Simon in CAT PEOPLE; but there's rather a gap in talent between the two.

**JUNIOR G-MEN Univ 1940 serial 12 chapters D: F. Beebe, J. Rawlins. SP: G.H. Plympton, B. Dickey. Ph: Jerome Ash. AD: Ralph DeLacy. Ref: TV. Lee: Little Tough Guys movie. LC. Showmen's 8/3/40. with Billy Halop, Huntz Hall, Gabriel Dell, Bernard Punsley, Phillip Terry, Russell Hicks.
Remote-control device detonates explosives up to 100 miles away; tested, it blows up shack. Slapdash serial.

*JUNKET 89 1971 Sequel: The TROUBLE WITH 2B.

*JUST IMAGINE 1930 (The WORLD IN 1981-orig t) AD: Stephen Goosson, Ralph Hammeras. Chor: Seymour Felix. Ref: screen.
Pretty silly sf-comedy-musical, though one gag in 50 still clicks, and there's a drinking-song sequence that comes to resemble the near-apocalyptic war-sequence in DUCK SOUP. But most of it is simply actors at odds with dialogue.

JWALA MOHINI (India-Kannada) Premier 1973 133m. D: S.N. Singh. Story: D.S. Singh. Ph: Murthy. Mus: Satyam. Ref: Dharap. with Ranga, Sampath.
Spirit of woman spurned by member of family casts curse on it.

K-9000: A SPACE ODDITY Haboush 1968? anim color 10m. D: Robert Mitchell, Robert Swarthe. Ref: Lee: spoof of 2001.

KAALI RAAT (India-Hindi) Bohra Bros. 1977 color 120m. D: S. Bohra. SP: H.M. Singh. Mus: L. Pyarelal. Ref: Dharap. with

Vinod Mehra, Jogeeta Bali, L. Pawar, Ramkumar.
Ghosts of murdered family return to kill killers.

KADARU MASAM (India-Malayalam) Blessed 1976 125m. D: P. Balakrishnan. SP: S. Alway. Story: Moorthy. Mus: B.A. Chidambaranathan. Ref: Dharap. with Vincent, Dwarkesh.
Doctor's serum turns victims into criminals.

KADOYNG (B) (JED-TV)/CFF/Shand 1972 color 60m. D: Ian Shand. SP: Leo Maguire. Ph: Mark McDonald. Mus: Edwin Astley. Ref: MFB'72:215. TVFFSB. with Teresa Codling, Adrian Hall, L. Maguire(alien), Bill Owen, Gerald Sim, David Williams.
Friendly humanoid alien comes to Earth in egg-shaped ship.

KAETTEKITA ULTRA MAN (J) Toho 1971 color 44m. D: Yoshiharu Tomita. Ref: UFQ 56: Ultraman vs. Sea Gorath.

KAIKI! KYODAIGUMO see HORROR! HOUSE OF THE GIANT SPIDERS

The KAISER'S SHADOW, Or THE TRIPLE CROSS Ince 1918 55m. D: R. William Neill. SP: O.R. Cohen, J.H. Giesy. Ref: LC. Lee (FIR'66:285): ray-gun rifle. with Dorothy Dalton, T. Hall.

KAMPON NI SATANAS (Fili) Tamaraw 1970 color SP,D: Mar B. Isidro. Mus: Manuel Franco. Ref: Lee(Borst). with Jimmy Morato, Eva Montes, Gil De Leon, Marion Douglas.
Girl's deal with Devil brings mother back to life.

KAN PI see KUN PI

KANE see BROTHER JOHN

KARAMANEH (B) 1924 30m. See also: Further Mysteries of Dr. Fu-Manchu series. Ref: BFC.

KASTURI (India-Hindi) Dutt 1978 color 131m. SP,D,P: Bimal Dutt. Ph: Mahajan. Mus: Utam Singh. Ref: IFG'80:186. Dharap: "mix-up of science and superstition" leaves man dead. with Nutan, P. Sahni, Dr. S. Lagoo, Agha.
Professor accidentally breaks egg of rare bird--"events then take a weird turn." (IFG)

KATHAVAI THATTEEYA MOHNI PAYE (India-Tamil) Anuradha Int'l. 1975 117m. SP,D: M.A. Rajaraman. Mus: C.N. Pandurangan. Ref: Dharap. with C.R. Patiban, Sanjivirajan, Desikan, Liza.
"A film, inspired by the "Dracula" series of films, tells of the curse of a vampire prince and how his hoary and macabre reign of terror is ended by a daring private-eye."

KAYA HINER KAHINI see GHOST STORY(1973)

The KEEPER (Can.) Lions Gate 1976 color 88m. SP,D: Tom Drake. Story,P: Donald Wilson. Story: also D. Curnick. Ph: Doug McKay. Mus: Eric Hoyt. AD: Keith Pepper. Ref: V

5/26/76: "a spoof of the horror genre." with Christopher Lee (The Keeper), Tell Schrieber, Sally Gray, Ross Vezarian.
Asylum administrator plots to take over the world, using hypnosis, murder.

KHORDA see DEATHMASTER

KICMA see GASP!

KILL AND KILL AGAIN FVI 1981 color 100m. D: Ivan Hall. SP: John Crowther. Ph: Tai Krige. Mus Sup: Igo Kantor. Ref: V 5/13/81. with James Ryan, Anneline Kriel, Ken Gampu.
Mind-controlling drug (by-product of energy formula).

KILL THE BEAST see BEAST MUST DIE, The

KILL TO LOVE (H.K.) DDI-FPC 1981 color 90m. D: Tam Kav Ming. SP: Joyce Chan. Ph: Brian Lai. Mus: Tam Kar Ming. Ref: V 9/2/81. with Ching Hsia, Chung Cheung Lin.
Madman kills students "in various horrifying ways...."

KILLDOZER Univ-TV 1974 color 74m. D: Jerry London. SP: Theodore Sturgeon, Ed MacKillap. Adap & P: Herbert Solow. Based on Sturgeon's novella. Ph: Terry K. Meade. Mus: Gil Melle. AD: J. Bachman. SpFX: Albert Whitlock. Ref: TVFFSB. TV. with Clint Walker, James Wainwright, Carl Betz, Neville Brand, Robert Urich, James A. Watson Jr.
An island off Africa. A strange "blue light" from a meteorite possesses an earth-mover; latter commences destruction of a construction crew. This imitation of DUEL is a comedy and doesn't know it. The idea of a rogue bulldozer remains more risible than horrible, despite a flashy show of lights and levers and metal. "Do you _believe_ that thing?" one character asks. Silly question.

KILLER BEES Worldvision-TV/ABC-TV/RSO 1974 color 74m. D: Curtis Harrington. SP: Joyce & John William Corrington. Ph: Jack Woolf. Mus: David Shire. PD: Joel Schumacher. SpFX: Henry Millar. SpVisFX: Van Der Veer. Mkp: Paul Stanhope. Ref: TV. TV Season. TVFFSB. with Gloria Swanson, Edward Albert, Kate Jackson, Roger Davis, Craig Stevens, Liam Dunn.
Matriarch (Swanson) of Van Bohlen family, winegrowers, controls African bees which seem to have a single mind and kill for her. ("Grandmother's bees aren't ordinary.") Nice Hermannesque score is most notable feature of routine TV-movie, in which animated flecks stand in for swarming bees. (_Not_ frightening.) Heroine Jackson's assumption of the role of keeper-of-the-flecks (at the end) may be a plot necessity, but it's a character non sequitur, just another fizzled "macabre" touch.

KILLER FISH (B-Braz-F?) AFD/ITC/Filmar do Brasil-Victoria 1979 color 101m. (TREASURE OF THE PIRANHA-orig t) D: Antonio Margheriti. SP: Kenneth Ross. Story: Simonelli,

Princi. Ph: A. Spagnoli. Mus: G.& M.De Angelis. AD: Bronze. SpFX: A. Possanza, W. Reis;(ph) R. Pallottini. SpSeqs: Herbert V. Theiss. Mkp: G. Morosi. SdFX: Cine Audio. Ref: TV: B-I-U.S.(Grade & Ponti & Fawcett-Majors)? V 10/24/79: Braz-I? MFB'79:147. Boxo 12/3/79. with Lee Majors, Karen Black, James Franciscus, Margaux Hemingway, Marisa Berenson, Dan Pastorini, Anthony Steffen, Gary Collins.

Criminal mastermind stocks reservoir with man-eating piranha to protect jewel cache. The beautiful people and the piranha. Only Karen Black does more than look beautiful. Drearily vacant production.

KILLER GRIZZLY see GRIZZLY

KILLER SPORES NBC-TV/Solow-Taft 1977 color 95m. D: Reza Badiyi. From the "Man from Atlantis" TV series. Ref: TVFFSB. with Patrick Duffy, Belinda Montgomery, Alan Fudge, K. Tigar.

Space probe returns carrying "ectoplasmic matter" which renders humans catatonic.

KILLER WHALE, The see ORCA

KILLER WITH TWO FACES (B) ABC-TV/ITC-TV 1974 color 74m. D: John Scholz-Conway. SP: Brian Clemens. Mus: Laurie Johnson. Title Seq: Visualscope. Ref: TV. TVG. TVFFSB. with Donna Mills, Ian Hendry, David Lodge, Roddy McMillan.

Woman in peril, unsure which twin is mad strangler. Laughably contrived "suspense." Good thing they weren't triplets.

KILLER'S MOON (B) Rothernorth 1978 color 90m. SP,D: Alan Birkinshaw. Ph: A. Lavis. Mus: John Shakespeare, D. Warne. AD: Carolyn Scott. Ref: MFB'78:243-44. with Anthony Forrest, Tom Marshall, Georgina Kean, Nigel Gregory, David Jackson.

"Four homicidal maniacs under the influence of remedial lysergic acid escape from a lunatic asylum" and go on a killing spree.

The KILLING AT OUTPOST ZETA Gold Key-TV 1980 color 92m. Ref: GKey. with Gordon DeVol, Jackie Ray, James A. Watson Jr.

"Mysterious disappearances" at U.S. space outpost.

The KILLING GAME (F) (MCA-TV)/Regional/A.J.-Francinor-LFM 1967 color 94m. (JEU DE MASSACRE. COMIC STRIP HERO. ALL WEEKEND LOVERS-both alt ts?) SP,D: Alain Jessua. Ph: Jacques Robin. Mus: Jacques Loussier. AD: Claire Forestier. Illustrator: Guy Peelaert. Ref: AFI. TV. SFC. with Jean-Pierre Cassel, Claudine Auger, Michel Duchaussoy, E. Hirt, Anna Gaylor.

Young couple produce comic strips based on real-life adventures of odd young playboy; characters in theatre see bit of vampire movie (original footage?); line: "He liked her because she looked like the daughter of Dracula." Offbeat, intriguing comedy-drama.

"KILLING" VS. FRANKENSTEIN (Turk) Omur 1967 (KILLING FRANKESTAYNA KARSI) SP,D,P: Nuri Akinci. Ph: C. Ar. Ref:

WorldF'67. Limbacher'79. with Oktay Gursel, Oya Peri.
Master-criminal "Killing" vs. the Frankenstein monster.

The KING AND THE MOCKINGBIRD (F) Grimault-Gibe-Antenne 2 1952/1979 anim color 87m. (Le ROI ET L'OISEAU) SP,D,AD,Ed: Paul Grimault. SP: also Jacques Prevert. From Andersen's fairy tale "The Shepherdess and the Chimney Sweep." Ph: Gerard Soirant. Mus: Wojciech Kilar. Songs: Prevert, Kosma. Collab: Pierre Prevert. SdFX: Henri Gruel. Ref: V 4/23/80. Lee. Voices: Jean Martin, Raymond Bussieres, Roger Blin.
Revised version of the 1952 La BERGERE ET LE RAMONEUR aka CURIOUS ADVENTURES OF MR.WONDERBIRD. The King of Takicardie's secret weapon proves to be a huge robot.

*KING KONG 1933 (The BEAST-orig t. KING APE. KONG-int ts) Ph: also Vernon L. Walker, J.O. Taylor. Tech Asst: Marcel Delgado. Ref: Glut/CMM. Lee.
The Fay-in-nightmare-land sequences on Skull Island make KONG our best, most durable horror/monster movie from the Thirties--while the 1976 remake has already almost been forgotten....
See also the following titles, and APE(1976). *HOLE IN THE MOON. I LIKE MOUNTAIN MUSIC. *MONSTER GORILLA. PARADE OF THE WOODEN SOLDIERS. PET STORE,The. ROBOT,The(1978). SON OF KONG. SYNTHETISCHER FILM. TARZAN AND KING KONG.

KING KONG ABC-TV/Videocraft Int'l.-TV 1966 anim color 50m. Ref: Glut/CMM: TV-movie; character Dr. Who also in *KING KONG ESCAPES. no LC.

KING KONG Para/De Laurentiis 1976 color/scope 134m.(190m.-'80 TV version) (KING KONG: THE LEGEND REBORN-orig t) D: John Guillermin. SP: Lorenzo Semple Jr. Remake of KING KONG (1933). Ph: Richard H. Kline. Mus: John Barry. PD: Mario Chiari, Dale Hennesy. SpDes: Carlo Rambaldi;(sculptor) Don Chandler. PhFX: Van Der Veer, Barry Nolan, H.E. Wellman. Sp FX: Glen Robinson, Joe Day. Ref: V(d) 12/10/76. MFB'77:25. TV. Glut/CMM. with Jeff Bridges, Charles Grodin, Jessica Lange, John Randolph, Rene Auberjonois, Dennis Fimple, John Agar, Ed Lauter, Rick Baker(Kong).
Giant ape found on fog-enshrouded island is transported to New York for exhibition. The new Kong just doesn't seem very formidable--lighting, sets, camera, music, and sound effects all fail him. Apparently in compensation, the director devotes an unconscionable amount of time simply to showing actors looking up and gaping at him. (As if he's so huge.) Never mind the original KONG--give me SON OF KONG...MIGHTY JOE YOUNG...KING KONG VS.GODZILLA even. Comparison to KONGA seems more in order here.
See also: AMERICAN TICKLER. GAPPA. INCREDIBLE SHRINKING WOMAN,The. KINO. KING OF KONG ISLAND. MIGHTY PEKING MAN. QUEEN KONG.

KING KONG CONTRO GODZILLA see GAMERA VS.GUIRON

KING-KONG,DA MONEN AUS DEM WETTALL see GODZILLA VS. MEGALON

KING KONG GEGEN GODZILLA see GODZILLA VS. THE COSMIC MONSTER

KING KONG L'IMPERO DEI DRAGHI see GAMERA VS. JIGER

KING MONSTER see MYSTERY OF THE GOLDEN EYE

KING OF KONG ISLAND (Gold Key-TV)/Monarch 1968('77-U.S.) 92m. (*EVE THE WILD WOMAN) Mus: Roberto Pregadio. Ref: TVG. Boxo 7/23/79:21. V 5/11/77:282(ad). GKey.
"The mighty ape King, descendant of the original Kong," vs. an army of remote-controlled apes. (GK)

KING OF THE DEAD see MUMMY,The(1932)

*KING OF THE ZOMBIES 1941 Sets: David Milton. Ref: TV. FM 169:36.
Enemy agent attempts, through voodoo, to "transmigrate" admiral's knowledge into woman's brain. Very sluggish horror-comedy. One funny scene in which Mantan Moreland thinks he has been turned into a zombie. Hardly Monogram's best horror movie.

KING OF THE "Z"S NYU 1979? 20m. D: Karl Tiedemann. SP: Stephen Winer. Ref: screen. V 9/26/79:34. W.K.Everson.
"Interview" with William K. Everson re: Vespucci Pictures and their films ("really dreadful"), with clips from "The Dog That Got Real Big"(1955) and "Block and Tackle Meet Scary People"(1952). Amusing fabricated-film-history.

KING STAKH'S WILD GAME CHASE (Russ) Sovexport/Belarusfilm 1980 color 124m. (DIKAYA OKHOTA KOROLYA STAKHA) SP,D: Valeri Rubinchik. SP: also V. Korotkevich. Ph: T. Loginova. Mus: Y. Glebov. AD: A. Chertovich. Ref: Soviet Film 80/5. V 8/27/80. with Boris Plotnikov, Valentina Shendrikova.
"Curse" on nobleman's family--marshes "haunted" by 13 "ghostly horsemen." (SF)

KING TUT'S TOMB Fox 1950 anim color 9m. (HECKLE AND JECKLE, THE TALKING MAGPIES,IN KING TUT'S TOMB-alt t) Ref: LC. Lee. Glut/TFL.
Egyptian dancer who transforms into Frankenstein's monster; ghosts; mummies.

The KINGDOM OF DIAMONDS (India-Bengali) MOMA/GOVWB 1980 color 118m. (HIRAK RAJA DESHE. IN THE LAND OF KING HIRAK-tr t) SP,D,Mus,Des: Satyajit Ray. Sequel to The ADVENTURES OF GOOPY AND BAGHA. Ph: Soumendu Roy. AD: Ashoke Bose. Ref: screen. IFG'80:187. V 12/17/80. FC 3/81:3. PFA notes 10/3/81. with Robi Ghose, Tapen Chatterjee, Utpal Dutt, Soumitra Chatterjee.
King's subjects brainwashed in professor's machine in "the Mumbo-Jumbo Room"; magic. An uncustomarily simplistic Ray film. Broad comedy and broad politics, as comic characters Goopy and Bagha--Abbott and Costello on an off-day--learn the

ABC's of authoritarianism.

KINGDOM OF THE SPIDERS Dimension/Arachnid 1977 color 95m. D: John "Bud" Cardos. SP: Richard Robinson, Alan Caillou. Story: J.M. Sneller, Stephen Lodge. Ph: John Morrill. Mus: Igo Kantor. SpFX: Greg Auer. Mattes: Cy Didjurgis. Mkp: Ve Neill, Kathy Agron. Ref: MFB'78:92. V 11/16/77. TV. with William Shatner, Tiffany Bolling, Woody Strode, Altovise Davis, Joe Ross, Hoke Howell, Marcy Lafferty.

Arizona. Tarantulas with venom five times more toxic than normal band together into an "aggressive army," attack cows, dogs, then humans, wrapping their victims in cocoons for future use as food. Far from sophisticated--but who needs sophistication when you've got what looks like about 5,000 live spiders scudding about? You may have seen this before, but not with 40,000 hairy legs. How could the film _not_ be harrowing? It is, finally, in spite of the laughably "serious" characterization and strained dialogue and plot development. From above (plop!), from below (pitter-patter, scurry), from behind (surprise!) they come. Amusingly disgusting, with a good, logical "kicker" at the end.

KINO (Cz) Slovenska 1977 anim color 6m. SP,D,Des: V.Kubal. Ref: Zagreb 78 cat.

KING KONG, JAWS, etc. fail to excite, give way to "new tricks" at movie theatre.

KIRLIAN EFFECT,The or KIRLIAN FORCE,The see PSYCHIC KILLER

The KIRLIAN WITNESS Sarno 1978 color/scope 91m. SP,D,P: Jonathan Sarno. SP: also Lamar Sanders. Ph: Joao Fernandes. Mus: Harry Manfredini. Ref: V 11/22/78: DAY OF THE TRIFFIDS on TV. Cinef IX:1:44. with Nancy Snyder, Ted Laplat, Lawrence Tierney, Joel Colodner.

Household plant's "picture" of murder communicated to next intended victim of murderer.

KISERTET LUBLON see PHANTOM ON HORSEBACK

The KISS (B) ICF/Oppidan 1977 color 18m. D: Kevin Pither. Ref: MFB'77:203. with Digby Rumsey(Death).

KISS IN ATTACK OF THE PHANTOMS or KISS MEETS THE PHANTOM OF THE PARK see ATTACK OF THE PHANTOMS

KISS OF THE TARANTULA (Gold Key-TV)/Omni/Cinema-Vu 1976 color 85m. (SHUDDER-B) D: Chris Munger. SP: Warren Hamilton Jr. Story: Daniel B. Cady. Ph: Henning Schellerup. Mus: Phillan Bishop. PD: John Burrows. Ref: TVFFSB. AMPAS. MFB'77:80. with Eric Mason, Suzanne Ling, Herman Wallner, Patricia Landon.

Young girl uses pet tarantulas as weapons.

KITTY IN DREAMLAND (B) Klein/Urban 1911 9m. Ref: BFC: dream of witches and ogre. Lee: French?

KLABAUTERMANDEN see WE ARE ALL DEMONS!

A KNIFE FOR THE LADIES Bryanston 1973 color 85m. (JACK THE RIPPER GOES WEST-orig t) D: Larry G. Spangler. SP: G.A. Bloom. Ref: V 5/9/73:163. 7/4/73:23(ad): 19th-century Jack the Ripper in U.S. Willis/SW. Cinef IX:3:39. with Jack Elam, Ruth Roman, Jeff Cooper, Gene Evans, John Kellogg, Joe Santos.

A KNIGHT ERRANT (B) Paul 1907 8m. D: J.H. Martin. SP & with: Langford Reed. Ref: BFC.
Ogre, witch, dwarf, fairy.

The KNOCKING ON THE DOOR (B) 1923 20m. See also: Mystery of Dr. Fu-Manchu series. Ref: Lee.

KOKO SEES SPOOKS Para?/Fleischer 1925 anim 6m. (Out of the Inkwell series) Ref: Maltin/OMAM. no LC.

KOKO'S EARTH CONTROL Para/Fleischer 1928 anim 8m. Ref: LC. Meyers: Earth destroyed.

KOLCHAK PAPERS,The or KOLCHA(C)K TAPES,The see NIGHT STALKER

KONG see KING KONG(1933)

KOSHOKU TOMEI NINGEN see LUSTY TRANSPARENT HUMAN

KOU-HUN CHIANG T'OU see BLACK MAGIC 2

KOUMANI see CONTACT

*KRAKATIT Brandon/CFC 1947('51-U.S.) 97m.(110m.) SP: J. & O. Vavra. Ph: Vaclav Hanus. Mus: Jiri Srnka. Ref: Brandon. V 5/2/51. Lee. and with Karel Hoger, Frantisek Smolik.
See also: BLACK SUN.

KRAZY SPOOKS Col/Mintz 1933 anim 7m. (Krazy Kat) SP: R. Zamora, H. Love. Ref: Maltin/OMAM. LC.

*KRONOS 1957 (KRONOS,DESTROYER OF THE UNIVERSE-'79 re-r t) Ref: TV. Boxo 8/6/79:27.
Mechanical energy "accumulator" from flying saucer absorbs Earth's electrical and atomic energy; man possessed by alien blob of light aids monster. MAGNETIC MONSTER without the latter's panache. Ludicrously sketchy continuity--there's no plot-character-dialogue flesh on the bare-bones premise. Exclamations such as "Great Caesar's ghost!" are about as inventive as the dialogue gets.

KRONOS see CAPTAIN KRONOS--VAMPIRE HUNTER

KRVAVA PANI (Cz) CFP-Koliba 1981 anim color 80m. SP,D,Des: Viktor Kubal. Ph: Otto Geyer. Mus: Juraj Lexmann. Ref: V 3/18/81: cartoon version of the Lady Bathory legend.

KU-WU I-YUN (H.K.-Chinese) 196-? (The MYSTERIOUS OLD HOUSE-tr t) Ref: Eberhard. M.Luk.
A brother and sister find out that their home is a haunted house.

KUN PI (Thai-Chinese) Five Stars & Shaw 1975 color 110m. (KAN PI. PREGNANT BY A GHOST-tr t) SP,D: Rom Bunnag. Story: Sumon Sirima. Ph: Wang Yonglong. Mus: Sahat Tuchinda. Ref: V 5/7/75:128. 4/30/75. 9/10/75:28. 12/4/74:30. with Lo Lieh, Krung Sriwilai, Fang Ye, R. Sripatimakul.
"Evil ghost" possesses man's body, making woman pregnant through him.

KWADE OOG see EVIL EYE(1937)

KYAPUTEN FUYUCHO see CAPTAIN FUTURE

KYUKETSUKI(by R.Edogawa) see HYOCHO NO BIJO

KYUKETSUKI DORAKYURA KOBE NI ARAWARU see VAMPIRE DRACULA COMES TO KOBE

Het LAASTE OORDEEL (Belg) 1972 short Ref: Cinef W'73:39. Lee.
Deadly gas forces population underground.

LABIRINT (Russ) 1971 anim Ref: Reveaux: by A.S.-Blotskaya; Theseus vs. the minotaur.

LABORATORY Gold Key-TV 1980 color 93m. Ref: GKey. with Camille Mitchell, Corinne Michaels, Garnett Smith.
Alien scientists on Earth study humans in special lab.

LABYRINTH see REFLECTION OF FEAR

Le LAC DES MORTS VIVANTS (F) Eurocine 1980? Ref: V 5/13/81: 283: horror.

*The LADY AND THE MONSTER 1944 (The MONSTER-orig t. The MONSTER'S CASTLE-int t. The MONSTER AND THE LADY-int t?) SpFX: Theodore Lydecker. Ref: TV. MPH 12/25/43:1687. V 3/22/44. 11/3/43. Lee.
The hypnotic/telepathic powers of a dead man's brain dominate a living man. Walter Scharf's score and the light-and-shadow play are small plusses here, but the changes rung on the possession theme are slight. Actors and director just try too hard, and with no dramatic meat, Erich von Stroheim just chews. At one point, Vera Hruba Ralston screams "You...*monster*!" at him--from a casual insult a title grew. (See above.)

LADY DRACULA (W.G.) TV 13 1977 D: F.J. Gottlieb. Ref: V 5/11/77:396. 12/8/76:40: vampire send-up. with Evelyn Kraft.

LADY DRACULA see LEMORA

LADY FRANKENSTEIN (I) New World/Condor Int'l. 1971 color 99m. (La FIGLIA DI FRANKENSTEIN. MADAME FRANKENSTEIN-orig U.S.t) D,P: Ernst von Theumer(aka Mel Welles). SP: Edward Di Lorenzo. Story: Dick Randall;(uncred.) Bill Warren? Ph: R. Pallotini. Mus: Alessandro Alessandroni. AD: Francis Mellon. SpFX: Cipa. Ref: MFB'72:94-5. Bianco Index'72. Lee. Glut/TFL. with Joseph Cotten, Sara Bay, Mickey Hargitay, Herbert Fux, Paul Muller.
The doctor's monster vs. his daughter's monster.

LADY JAMES BOND (India-Hindi) Anand Lakshmi 1972 143m. SP,D: K.S.R. Doss. Story: K. Mohan. Ph: P. Devraj. Mus: Sathyam. Ref: Dharap. with Vijayalalitha, Ramkrishna.
"Science-thriller...in the style of old movie Frankenstein and recent Bond films...."

The LADY OF SHALLOT (B) Hepworth(Ivy Close) 1912 SP,D: Elwin Neame. From Tennyson's poem. Ref: BFC. with I. Close.
"Lady looks in cursed mirror to see knight, and dies."

LADY SNOW (H.K.?) 1970? (HSUEH-NIANG) Based on a story in the "Liao-chai Chih-i." Ref: Eberhard.
Female ghost murders man; his wife eats mad-monk's cake and vomits it up into dead husband's open heart; he revives; the monk turns the ghost into smoke and imprisons her in a gourd.

LAGARTIJA CON PIEL DE MUJER see LIZARD IN A WOMAN'S SKIN

LAMYATA (Bulg) BC 1976 anim color 7m. D: D. Donev. Ref: Zagreb 78 cat.: five-headed dragon.

LAND OF CELTIC GHOSTS Gold Key-TV/Johnson 1980? color 97m. D,P,Ph,Ed: Jerry Johnson. SP: Maureen Curtis. Mus Sup: Don Great. Narr: Richard Basehart. Ref: TV: filmed in Ireland. GKey. with P.F. Byrne.
Ghosts of Irish history: tales of spectral laughter, ghostly screams, lake monsters, murder holes, poltergeists; haunted cottages, castles, halls, and billiard rooms; spirits of the famine, and the ghost of W.B. Yeats. Pleasant, leisurely combination travelogue/ghost-story-compilation features a better variety of interviews/stories and settings than the "Bigfoot"-type semi-documentaries, and a stronger sense of history.

The LAND OF THE MINOTAUR (B-Greek) (Gold Key-TV)/Crown Int'l./ Getty & Poseidon 1976 color 94m. (The DEVIL'S PEOPLE-orig t? The DEVIL'S MEN-B) D: Costas Carayiannis. SP: Arthur Rowe. Ph: Aris Stavrou. Mus: Brian Eno. AD: Petros Copourallis. Ref: Meyers. MFB'76:211-12. V 5/12/76:335(ad). 12/10/75:37. 2/25/81:75(ad). with Donald Pleasence, Peter Cushing, Luan Peters, Nikos Verlakis, Vanna Revilli, Costas Skouras.
"Bizarre sacrificial ritual"; the Devil "in the guise of a stone, fire-breathing minotaur." (MFB)

The LAND THAT TIME FORGOT (B) AI/Amicus/Land 1975 color 91m. D: Kevin Connor. SP: James Cawthorne, Michael Moorcock, from Edgar Rice Burroughs' novel. Ph: Alan Hume;(process) Charles Staffel. Mus: Douglas Gamley. PD: Maurice Carter. SpFX: Derek Meddings;(dinos.seqs.) Roger Dicken. Mkp: Tom Smith. Ref: MFB'75:34. TV. V 4/9/75. with Doug McClure, John McEnery, Susan Penhaligon, Anthony Ainley, Bobby Parr(prehistoric man).

1916. The lost island of Caprona proves to be a prehistoric world in which each inhabitant recapitulates all evolutionary stages and each epoch is represented. Dinosaurs represented: the diplodocus, allosaurus, styracosaurus, pterodactyl, stegosaurus, triceratops, tyrannosaurus. Filmographically, the script recapitulates The LOST WORLD(1925), KING KONG(1933), ONE MILLION B.C.(1940), UNKNOWN ISLAND(1948), etc. Okay as a prehistoric travelogue. But the time-lapse-world idea doesn't make for much drama. Lots of dinosaurs at least.

See also: AT THE EARTH'S CORE. PEOPLE THAT TIME FORGOT.

LAOKOON (Cz) Kratky 1970 anim short SP,D,AD: Vaclav Mergl. Ref: IFG'72:383. Lee.

Eggs hatch tentacled monsters.

LASERBLAST Manson Int'l/Yablans/Band 1978 color 80m. D: Michael Rae. SP: Franne Schacht, Frank Ray Perilli. Ph: Terry Bowen. Mus: Joel Goldsmith, Richard Band. AD: Pat McFadden. AnimFX: Dave Allen. SpFX: Harry Woolman. LaserFX: Paul Gentry. SpFxMkp: Steve Neill. Ref: MFB'79:48. AMPAS. V 3/8/78. 10/19/77:13(ad). with Kim Milford, Cheryl Smith, Gianni Russo, Ron Masak, Keenan Wynn, Roddy McDowall.

"Prehistoric-style creatures"; pendant left by dead alien which turns boy into alien; laser gun. (MFB)

The LAST BRIDE OF SALEM ABC-TV/Fox-TV 1974 color 74m. D: Tom Donovan. SP: Rita Lakin. Ref: TVFFSB. TV Season. with Bradford Dillman, Lois Nettleton, Joni Bick, Paul Harding.

"Demonic forces" threaten a young mother's family. (TVFFSB)

LAST CANNIBAL WORLD, The see LAST SURVIVOR, The

The LAST CHASE Crown Int'l 1981 color 101m. SP,D,P: Martyn Burke. SP: also C.R. O'Christopher, Taylor Sutherland. Ph: Paul Van Der Linden. AD: Roy Forge Smith. SpFX: Tom Fisher, Michael Lennick. Ref: V 5/6/81. with Lee Majors, Burgess Meredith, Chris Makepeace, Alexandra Stewart.

Oil-less and car-less 1980s U.S.; strange epidemic.

The LAST DAYS OF MAN ON EARTH (B) New World/Goodtimes-Gladiole 1973 color 78m.(89m.) (The FINAL PROGRAMME-B) SP,D,PD: Robert Fuest. Based on Michael Moorcock's novel "The Final Programme." Ph: Norman Warwick. Mus: Paul Beaver, Bernard Krause;(sax) Gerry Mulligan. Opt: Camera FX. Mkp: Ann Brodie, Alan Boyle. Ref: MFB'73:206. Willis/SW. V 10/29/75. screen. with Jon Finch, Jenny Runacre, Sterling Hayden, Harry Andrews, Hugh Griffith, Julie Ege, Patrick Magee, George Coulouris.

The near-future. Solar incubator and super-computer in Lapland lab combine man and woman to produce immortal "New Messiah," a hermaphroditic, self-regenerating human being--who is revealed to be an ape-man monster. Fussily futuristic details, flip dialogue, hip pessimism re: science and man. At once too light and too heavy--the script all-too-easily undercuts its own tired pretensions. Trimmed for U.S. release, thank goodness.

The LAST DAYS OF PLANET EARTH (J) UPA/Toho(T.Tanaka) 1981 (1978?) color/scope 90m.? D: Toshio Masuda. SP: Toshio Yasumi. Story: T. Goto. SpFX: T. Nakano. Ref: TV. with Tetsuro Tanba.

Prophecies of Nostradamus and Revelations fulfilled: eugenic mutations in people (yielding supernormal children) and plants (yielding super-weeds); SST explosions (resulting in destruction of ozone layer); mass traffic jams and destruction on freeways; youth movement towards suicide; mirror-like sky reflecting Earth back upon itself; hallucinations; vision of mutant-populated, nuclear-devastated Earth. The works. Chaos and pathos, in what plays like a sloppy collage of disaster movie epics. Three or four of the hundred-plus narrative fragments are briefly provocative.

The LAST DINOSAUR (U.S.-J) ABC TV/Rankin-Bass 1977 color 91m. D: Alex Grasshof(f), Tom Kotani. SP: William Overgard. Ph: Shosi Ueda;(sp fx) Sadao Sato. Mus: Maury Laws. AD: K. Fujiwara;(sp fx) Tetsuzo Ohsaw. SpFX: Kazuo Sagawa, Tsuburaya Prods. SpOptFX: M. Nakano, M. Miyashige. Ref: MFB'78:48. TV. JFFJ 13:30. TVFFSB. TV Season. with Richard Boone, Joan van Ark, Steven Keats, William Ross, Carl Hansen.

"Polar-borer" drills into polar ice-cap, surfaces in volcanic lake in land of savages--and Tyrannosaurus Rex. Cribs from UNKNOWN WORLD (and its earth-borer), BEAST OF HOLLOW MOUNTAIN (and the dinosaur-trapping-actor-in-cave bit), BEAST WITH FIVE FINGERS ("Rex" rising out of the smoke, refusing to die, like the hand crawling out of the fireplace). The dinosaurs look like balloons, and the actors might as well _be_ balloons. One monster's-eye-view shot suggests that the monster has a zoom lens.

The LAST HORROR FILM 1981? D: David Winters. Ref: V 9/16/81:5: at Paris sf-fest. Starburst: with Caroline Munro.

LAST HOUSE ON THE LEFT Hallmark(AI)/Cunningham 1972 color 85m. SP,D,Ed: Wes Craven. Ph: Victor Hurwitz. Mus: David Alex Hess. Ref: Willis/SW. Bianco Index'73. V 11/8/72:25(ad). F Facts. Cinef F'73:35. with Hess, Lucy Grantham, Sandra Cassell, Marc Sheffler, Fred Lincoln.

Sadistic cons rape and murder two girls; father of one of the two murders _them_.

See also: NEW HOUSE ON THE LEFT.

LAST RITES Cannon/New Empire 1980 color 88m. (DRACULA'S LAST RITES-ad t) SP,D,Ph: Domonic Paris. SP: also Ben

Donnelly. Mus: Paul Jost, George Small. Ref: V 3/26/80. 5/7/80:32-3(ad). with Patricia Lee Hammond, Gerald Fielding, Victor Jorge, Mimi Weddell.
Village of vampires headed by mortician "Lucard."

The LAST SURVIVOR (I) AI/Erre(F.D.) 1976('78-U.S.) color/ scope 92m. (ULTIMO MONDO CANNIBALE. CANNIBAL HOLOCAUST-ad t. The LAST CANNIBAL WORLD-ad t. CANNIBAL-B) D: Ruggero Deodato. SP: T. Carpi, G. Clerici, R. Genta, A. Tellini. Ph: M. Masciocchi. Mus: Ubaldo Continiello. PD: W. Patriarca. SpFX: Paolo Ricci. Ref: V 5/7/80:368. 6/14/80: "not so grand bouffe." 12/28/77:26. MFB'79:103-4: "the gory details of cannibalism." with Massimo Foschi, Me Me Lay, Ivan Rassimov, Suleiman.
Tribe of cannibals in the Philippine jungle.

The LAST WAVE (Austral.) World Northal/Ayer/M&M-Power-SAFC-AFC-UA 1977 color 104m. SP,D: Peter Weir. SP: also Tony Morphett, Petru Popescu. Ph: Russell Boyd. Mus: Charles Wain. PD: Goran Warff. SpFX: Monty Fieguth, Bob Hilditch. OptFX: Optical & Graphic. Ref: MFB'78:66-7. IFG'80. V 11/16/77. screen. AMPAS. with Richard Chamberlain, Olivia Hamnett, Gulpilil, Frederick Parslow(e), Nandjiwarra Amagula.
A Sydney lawyer discovers that changes in weather patterns in Australia herald the end of the world, or (more precisely) the end of a cycle in its history. An intriguing cultural-mystical exercise, The LAST WAVE is like an aboriginal Revelations told as a Lovecraft-like mystery. (Substitute "Old Gods' time" for "dream time.") If the script doesn't really play that dramatically--what could the hero possibly do with his terrible knowledge?--the meteorological details (or clues) tantalize: the rain and hailstones from the cloudless sky; the rain of mud; the altered Sydney skyline; the leaky radio. The characters are less characters than simply pieces of the puzzle.

The LATE GREAT PLANET EARTH Pacific Int'l/Amram-RCR 1978 color 86m. SP,D: Robert Amram. SP: also Rolf Forsberg. From the book by Hal Lindsey & C.C. Carlson. Ph: M. Werk. Mus: Dana Kaproff. Anim: Jim Veillieux. SpFX: R.W. Peterson. Narr: Orson Welles, Lindsey. Ref: MFB'80:24. V 2/14/79: "not so great." 5/3/78:47(ad). with Beaumont Bruestle, Del Russell.
Armageddon, in the near future, as foretold by Revelations.

The LATHE OF HEAVEN PBS-TV 1980 color 95m. D,P: David Loxton, Fred Barzyk. SP: Roger E. Swaybill, Diane English, from Ursula K. LeGuin's book. Ph: Robbie Greenberg. Mus: Michael Small. PD: John W. Stevens. SpFX: Jack Bennett. VisCons: Ed Emshwiller. Ref: TV. CineFan 2:62. with Bruce Davison, Kevin Conway, Margaret Avery, Niki Flacks, Peyton Park.
Portland, Ore., the near future. A young man whose "effective" dreams alter reality falls into the clutches of a psychiatrist who attempts to make him dream a better world--with disastrous results. This flimsy teleplay funnels the LeGuin book's humor and invention into a more conventional dramatic mold, and irons out all the narrative "surprises"--each "new

reality" is "announced" and immediately explained, and is introduced in the same manner as the last one. The script is lamely dramatized and dialogued and retains only the book's plot fundamentals. And it reduces LeGuin's bravura climactic de-creations of the world to limp abstract images.

*LEAVES FROM SATAN'S BOOK Brandon 1919 (BLADE AF SATANS BOG) Adap: Dreyer, from M. Corelli's novel "Satans Sorger." Ref: screen. Brandon. MOMA.

Four-episode film is simply the same Judas-Satan-Christ story told four times, with each telling a bit more wearying than the last. The influence may be Griffith, but the spirit is Tod Slaughter--the acting is all the noble looks and ignoble leers of melodrama at its melo-est.

The LEFT HAND OF GEMINI Gold Key-TV("Zodiac" series) 1972 color 92m. Ref: TVFFSB. with Ian McShane, Ursula Theiss, R. Egan.

"Emperor of all worlds"; "key to all human power."

The LEGACY (B) Univ/Pethurst(Turman-Foster) 1978 color 102m. D: Richard Marquand. SP: Jimmy Sangster, Patrick Tilley, Paul Wheeler. Ph: Dick Bush, Alan Hume. Mus: Michael J. Lewis; (song) Kiki Dee. PD: Disley Jones. SpFX: Ian Wingrove. Sp FxMkp: Robin Grantham. Ref: TV. MFB'78:221. V 10/3/79. FM 101.28-34. with Katharine Ross, Sam Elliott, John Standing, Ian Hogg, Margaret Tyzack(Adams), Charles Gray, Roger Daltrey.

The satanic power of "the six" devolves on one of them, Maggie (Ross), the apparent reincarnation of the first holder of the power; the other five receive delayed punishments for past crimes; death-by-drowning-in-frozen-over-pool, chicken-bone-in-throat, shattering-mirror-slivers; were-cat-like nurse-familiar Adams; scalding shower (a la PSYCHIC KILLER); dog-pack attack (a la The OMEN, DOGS, The PACK). And of course the time-gap-punishment plot is courtesy of AND THEN THERE WERE NONE. The only new, amusing effect is the all-roads-lead-to-the-estate one, a bit of topographical necromancy "capped" by the great, unwitting straight line, "What brought you here?" (Any self-respecting ROCKY HORROR audience would cry as one, "A car!") (The LEGACY OF MAGGIE WALSH-TV)

LEGACY 197-? clay anim D: Will Vinton. Ref: SFC 7/4/80: dinosaurs.

LEGACY OF BLOOD Heritage/Studio West 1971 color 89m. (BLOOD LEGACY-alt t) D,P: Carl Monson. SP: Eric Norden. Ph: Ben Rombouts, Jack Beckett. Mus: Jaime Mendoza-Nava. AD: Mike McCloskey. Mkp: Rick Sagliani. Ref: TV. MFB'75:58. TVFFSB. V 3/21/73:24(rated): sfa LEGACY OF BLOOD(Fanfare)? with Faith Domergue, John Russell, Merry Anders, Jeff Morrow, Rodolfo Acosta, Dick Davalos, John Carradine, Buck Kartalian.

Rich man who plays dead; murder-among-heirs; severed head in 'frig; human lampshade; body in fish tank; electrocution-by-lamp; death-by-bee-sting; masochistic servant, Igor. An excuse for some venerable and not-so-venerable actors to get together and over-act. Undistinguished in the extreme.

LEGACY OF BLOOD Ken Lane/Take One 1978 color 82m. SP,D,P,Ph, Ed: Andy Milligan. Ref: V 3/8/78. with Elaine Boies, Chris Broderick, Marilee Troncone, Jeannie Cusick.

"Three sisters and their mates progressively murdered and disemboweled" at inn as they wait for the reading of their father's will.

LEGACY OF SATAN Film Productions/Damiano 1973 SP,D,P: Gerard Damiano. Ref: Lee(Boxo 7/30/73). Murphy. V 1/31/73:6(rated). with Lisa Christian.

Black magic; blood-drinking satanists.

The LEGEND OF BIGFOOT Palladium 1975 color 76m. SP,D: Harry S. Winer. SP: also Paula Labrot. Mus: Don Peake. Ref: V 5/12/76:42(ad). 10/22/75:3(rated). Willis/SW.

LEGEND OF BLOOD CASTLE (Sp-I) FVI/X-Luis 1972('74-U.S.) color 85m. (CEREMONIA SANGRIENTA. BLOOD CEREMONY-orig U.S.t. FEMALE BUTCHER-re-r t?) D: Jorge Grau. SP: Juan Tebar, S.Continenza. Ref: Murphy: the Bathory story. B.Warren. Willis/SW. V 5/15/74: 43(ad). 2/27/74:7(rated). 10/17/73:18. with Ewa Aulin, Lucia Bose, Espartaco Santoni.

**The LEGEND OF BLOOD MOUNTAIN Craddock 1965 color 61m. D, SP: Massey Cramer. SP: also Don Hadley, Bob Corley. Ref: AFI. Miami Herald 4/5/68. with George Ellis, Zenas Sears, Erin Fleming.

Small-town reporter discovers a monster.

The LEGEND OF BOGGY CREEK (Cinema Shares-TV)/Halco/Pierce-Ledwell 1972 color/scope? 90m. D,P,Ph: Charles B. Pierce. SP & Assoc P: Earl E. Smith. Mus: Jaime Mendoza-Nava. Narr: Vern Stearman. Ref: TV. TVFFSB. Lee. Willis/SW. V 12/6/72. with Willie E. Smith, John P. Hixon, Travis Crabtree, J.W. Oates.

Ape-like monster terrorizes small Arkansas town, perhaps because (as the narration and the song lyrics suggest) he's lonely. Pathos and suspense, if you can manage an enormous suspension of disbelief, and endure the wistful songs, the "interviews" with the folk of Fouke, and the "dramatic reconstructions" of incidents.

See also: RETURN TO BOGGY CREEK.

LEGEND OF DOOM HOUSE see MALPERTIUS

LEGEND OF DRACULA see IN SEARCH OF DRACULA

The LEGEND OF HELL HOUSE (U.S.-B) Fox/Academy(Nicholson) 1973 color 94m. D: John Hough. SP: Richard Matheson, from his novel "Hell House." Ph: Alan Hume. Elec Mus: Brian Hodgson, Delia Derbyshire. AD: Robert Jones. SpPhFX: Tom Howard. Sp FX: Roy Whybrow. Mkp: Linda Devetta. Ref: MFB'73:193. screen. Lee. V 5/30/73. with Pamela Franklin, Roddy McDowall, Clive Revill, Gayle Hunnicutt, Roland Culver, Michael Gough.

"Psychic energy" of mansion's dead owner generates ghostly manifestations; "reversor" counteracts electro-magnetic energy;

mental and physical mediums. An amusing series of effects--embracing "shadows," bottled ectoplasm, exploding fireplaces, possessed cats--alternating with hasty, semi-hysterical theorizing by the characters. Not much atmosphere, but fun anyway. Nice electronic-music "emanations."

The LEGEND OF HILLBILLY JOHN Harris/Two's Co. 1972(1975) color 89m. D: John Newland. SP: Melvin Levy, from the book "Who Fears the Devil?" by Manly Wade Wellman. Ph: F. Olsen. Mus: Roger Kellaway. SpFX: Gene Warren. Ref: Willis/SW. Lee. V 9/12/73:38. 11/1/72. with Hedge(s) Capers, Severn Darden, Susan Strasberg, R.G. Armstrong, Denver Pyle, Harris Yulin, Alfred Ryder, Val Avery, Percy Rodriguez.
Hillbilly vs. the Devil; demon bird; black magic.

LEGEND OF HORROR Ellman/General 1972 80m. D: Bill Davies. From Edgar Allan Poe's story "The Tell-Tale Heart." Ref: Lee. Ecran 12/77:30. with Karin Field.

The LEGEND OF LOCH NESS Gold Key-TV/Martin 1976 color 92m. D,P: Richard Martin. SP: Christian Davis. Ph: Jack Monahan. Narr: Arthur Franz. Ref: TV. TVFFSB.
"The search for the world's most famous monster...." (TVFFSB) Scrappy semi-documentary.

The LEGEND OF LODZ (Pol) 1975? anim short D: A. Piliczewski. Ref: IFG'76:456.
Factory plagued by "smoke devil."

The LEGEND OF SLEEPY HOLLOW Bosustow 1972 anim color short Mus: Larry Woolf. Narr: John Carradine. Ref: Lee.

The LEGEND OF SLEEPY HOLLOW (NBC-TV)/Sunn/Taft 1979(1980-TV r) color 90m. D: Henning Schellerup. SP: Malvin Wald, Jack Jacobs, Tom Chapman, from Washington Irving's story. Ph: Paul Hipp. Mus: Bob Summers. PD: Paul Staheli. SpFX: Harry Woolman. SdFX: Jim Bryan. Ref: TV. TVG. V 7/4/79(rated). 10/17/79:116d(ad). with Jeff Goldblum, Paul Sand, Dick Butkus, Meg Foster, Laura Campbell, James Griffith, John S. White.
Feeble re-telling of the Irving story, featuring both fake and (apparently) real Headless Horsemen. Determinedly flavorless production. Foster and Campbell, however, improve the scenery considerably.

The LEGEND OF SPIDER FOREST (B) New Line/Cupid-Action Plus 1971 ('74-US) color/scope 91m. (VENOM-B) D: Peter Sykes. SP: Donald & Derek Ford. Story: Stephen Collins. Dial: Christopher Wicking. Ph: Peter Jessop. Mus: J.S. Harrison. AD: Hayden Pearce. SpFX: Roy Whybrow. Ref: MFB'74:136-7. Bianco #1/77:136. Willis/SW. V 11/13/74:17. 5/10/72:32(rated). with Simon Brent, Neda Arneric, Derek Newark, Sheila Allen.
"Spider goddess" supposedly brings death to anyone she loves--this legend a front for Nazi war criminal's work on spider-venom nerve drug.

LEGEND OF THE MOUNTAIN (H.K.-Mand.) Prosperity 1979 color/ scope 186m. (SHAN-CHUNG CH'UAN-CH'I) D,AD,Ed: King Hu. SP: Chung Ling, based on the 11th-century tale "A Cave Full of Ghosts in the West Mountain." Ph: Ch'en Chun-chieh. Mus: Wu Ta-chiang. Ref: IFG'80:16m,170-71. V 4/25/79. with Hsu Feng, Chang Ai-Chia, Shih Chun.

"Story of a young scholar's attraction to two wandering female spirits," one of whom is deadly. (IFG)

LEGEND OF THE 7 GOLDEN VAMPIRES see 7 BROTHERS MEET DRACULA

LEGEND OF THE WEREWOLF (B) Tyburn 1974 color 90m. D: Freddie Francis. SP: John Elder. Ph: John Wilcox. Mus: Harry Robinson. AD: Jack Shampan. SpPhFX: Charles Staffel. Mkp: Jimmy Evans, Graham Freeborn; Roy Ashton? Ref: MFB'75:265. Glut/CMM: WOLF BOY. PLAGUE OF THE WEREWOLVES-project ts. with Peter Cushing, Ron Moody, Hugh Griffith, Roy Castle, David Rintoul(Etoile,the werewolf), Renee Houston, Michael Ripper.

Travelling showman discovers strange boy with "werewolf instincts." (MFB)

The LEGEND OF THE WOLF WOMAN (I) Dimension/Cinestampa/Amanda (Dialchi) 1976 color/scope 100m. (La LUPA MANNARA. The WOLF WOMAN-alt t. WEREWOLF WOMAN-B. DAUGHTER OF A WEREWOLF-orig t) SP,D: Rino Di Silvestro. SP: also Renato Rossini (aka Howard Ross). Ph: Mario Capriotti. Mus: Coriolano Gori. AD: Arrigo Peri. Ref: Bianco Index'76. MFB'80:216. Willis/SW. Cont.Film Rev.'80. V 4/6/77:34. 5/12/76:212. 5/9/73:48,75(ad). Meyers. with Annik Borel("licantropa"), Frederick Stafford, Rossini, Dagmar Lassander, Osvaldo Ruggieri.

Woman's dream of wolf-woman ancestor prefigures her own transformation into a werewolf.

LEGENDARY CURSE OF LEMORA see LEMORA

The LEMON GROVE KIDS MEET THE GREEN GRASSHOPPER AND THE VAMPIRE LADY FROM OUTER SPACE Steckler 196-? color 30m. D: Ted Rotter. SP: E.M. Kevke. Story: Ray Dennis Steckler. Ref: Lee(Warren). no LC. with Carolyn Brandt(vampire), Coleman Francis, Steckler.

Alien insect-man and vampire-woman on Earth.

LEMORA--A CHILD'S TALE OF THE SUPERNATURAL Heritage/Media Cinema (Blackfern) 1975 color 90m. (LADY DRACULA. The LEGENDARY CURSE OF LEMORA-alt ts. LEMORA,THE LADY DRACULA-ad t) SP,D: Richard Blackburn. SP,P: Robert Fern. Ph: Robert Caramico. Mus: Daniel Neufeld. AD: Sterling Franck. SpMkp & VisFX: Byrd Holland. Opt: Consolidated. Ref: TV. Willis/SW. TVG. TVFFSB. J.Shapiro. Murphy. with Lesley Gilb, Cheryl Smith, William Whitton, Maxine Ballantyne, Hy Pyke.

A comic allegory of innocence and experience, as a nice Baptist girl loses her way in a world peopled with vampires and hideous monsters. A very strange horror movie. Evil is comically rampant--every man wants sweet, blond Lila (Smith).

(Or, as the film's ballad runs, "She was holy and divine, and I wish that she were mine.") The vampiric Lemora seems to offer Lila a compromise, best-of-both-worlds existence--sensual fulfillment short of indulgence. (The indulgent state is represented by the foul forest-monsters, who apparently got there by being _really_ decadent.) The vampire here is _la creature moyenne sensuelle_, as it were. However, it's not really that easy to pin things down in this sly, oddly adventurous, stylized comedy. Other narrative elements include some kids, a diary, and a strange disease--God only knows if it all adds up. Film's main drawback: Gilb's awkwardness as Lemora.

LENG-YUEH LI-HUN (Cantonese) 1968? (MOON OF THE GHOST-tr t) Ref: Eberhard. M.Luk.
"Ghosts" and "dead people" abound in house of recently remarried man.

The LEO CHRONICLES Gold Key-TV("Zodiac" series) 1972 color 94m. Ref: TVFFSB. with George Montgomery, Maria Perschy.
Spaceship in danger of crash-landing on Jupiter.

LEONOR (Sp-F-I) New Line/Goya-Uranus-Arcadie & Films 66 & Transeuropa 1975('77-U.S.) color 100m. SP,D: Juan Bunuel. SP: also J.-C. Carriere, C.B. Wood, B. Zapponi et al. Story: Ludwig Tieck. Ph: Luciano Tovoli. Mus: Ennio Morricone. Ref: screen. AMPAS. Willis/SW. PFA notes 6/28/77. V 9/10/75. 5/7/75:242. 3/5/75:28: "a touch of vampirism." with Liv Ullmann, Michel Piccoli, Ornella Muti, Angel Del Pozo.
A mysterious figure (the Devil?) appears and seems to resurrect the wife of a 14th-century nobleman; she proceeds to sap the life of the children of the countryside. Some striking images, and Ullmann is at times provocatively alluring/menacing. But the narrative details are unintriguing, and the performances generally bland. If Juan Bunuel has father Luis' subject here--the climactic images of _amour fou_ are plundered from ABISMOS DE PASION--he has Jesus Franco's sensibility.

*The LEOPARD MAN 1943 Ref: screen. Siegel/VL. V 5/5/43. and with Brandon Hurst, Russell Wade, Jacqueline DeWitt,J.Dilson.
Flimsiest and least interesting of the nine Lewton thrillers. Everyone in LEOPARD MAN is a philosopher, or talks as if he were one. Dennis O'Keefe is the most "philosophical"--a ping-pong ball in a fountain is his chief source of existential inspiration. ("Galbraith said we're like that ball....") James Bell has good dramatic bits, and the scare sequence in the arroyo is good, but _so_ contrived.

LET'S LOVE AND LAUGH (B) Wardour/British Int'l 1931 84m. (aka BRIDEGROOM FOR TWO) D,P: Richard Eichberg. SP: Frederick Jackson, Walter Mycroft, from the play "The Bridegroom's Widow" or "A Welcome Wife" by Fred Thompson, Ernest Paulton. Ref: BFC. no LC. MPH 5/30/31: "two 'victims' reappear" at seance. with Muriel Angelus, Denis Wyndham, Gene Gerrard.

*LET'S SCARE JESSICA TO DEATH Jessica 1971 SP: N. Jonas. Mkp: Irvin Carlton. Ref: TV. and with Gretchen Corbett, Mariclare Costello.

Unbalanced, jealous woman is beset (or is she imagining it all?) by female vampire and her victims. Take away that parenthetical question, and there's no movie--there's hardly one as is. Dead-end ambiguity.

LEVRES DE SANG (F) ABC? 1976 color? D: Jean Rollin. Ph: J. F. Robin. Mus: D.W. Lepauw. Ref: Murphy: vampires? with J.L. Phillipe, Annie Briand, Nathalie Perrey, Paul Bisciglia.

LEWDNESS OF THE FEMALE VIPER see UGETSU

LIANG SHA TA-NAO T'AI-K'UNG (H.K.?) 196-? (TWO GOOFS IN OUTER SPACE-tr t) Ref: Eberhard. Margaret Luk.

Rocket-factory workers find Mars is run by robots; death rays.

LIAO-CHAI CHIH-I see LADY SNOW. LIEN SO. MAN,GHOST,FOX. SHEN-KU CH'I-T'AN.

LICENSED TO LOVE AND KILL (B) Shonteff(Palm Springs) 1979 color/scope 94m. (An ORCHID FOR NO.1-orig t) D & Assoc P: Lindsay Shonteff. SP: Jeremy Lee Francis. Ph: Bill Paterson. Mus: Simon Bell. SpFX: Christopher Verner. Ref: MFB'79:196-7. V 9/28/77:27(ad). with Gareth Hunt, Nick Tate, Fiona Curzon, Gary Hope, Geoffrey Keene, John Arnatt.

"Mad professor" creates duplicates of British secret agent and American Vice President. (MFB)

LIEN SO (H.K.) 196-? color Based on a chapter of the "Liao-Chai Chih-I." Ref: Eberhard: Ming period.

Ghost, hell, magic, wizard, exorcism.

LIFE AFTER DEATH see DEATH: THE ULTIMATE MYSTERY

LIFE FOR A LIFE see NECROMANCY(1972)

LIFE,LIBERTY AND PURSUIT ON THE PLANET OF THE APES see NEW PLANET OF THE APES

LIFE POD Gold Key-TV 1980 color 94m. Ref: GKey. with Joe Penny, Jordan Michaels, Kristine DeBell.

"Half-computer, half-human" brain terminal of space cruiser goes berserk.

LIFESPAN (U.S.-B-Dutch) Whitepal 1975 color 85m. SP,D: Alexander Whitelaw. SP: also Judith Roscoe, Alva Ruben. Ph: Eddy van der E(n)den. Mus: Terry Riley. AD: Dick Schillemans. Ref: MFB '79:176. V 9/24/75. with Hiram Keller, Tina Aumont, Klaus Kinski, Fons Rademakers, Eric Schneider.

"Longevity serum"; ghost (MFB); "grave desecration." (V)

The LIGHTNING WARRIOR Mascot 1931 serial 12 chapters D: Armand Schaefer, B. Kline. SP: Ford Beebe et al. Ph: E. Miller et al. Mus: Lee Zahler. Ref: Turner/Price. with Frankie Darro, Hayden Stevenson, George Brent, Pat O'Malley, Georgia Hale, Lafe McKee, Yakima Canutt, Kermit Maynard.
"Cloaked madman, the Wolf Man" and his "eerie wail."

LIGHTNING WOMAN (Fili) Lea 1964 (BABAING KIDLAT) D: Tony Cayado. Ref: Lee. with Liza Moreno, Dolphy.
Girl whose parents were killed by lightning at her birth is able to fly and kill.

LIKENESS OF JULIE,The(by R.Matheson) see TRILOGY OF TERROR(1975)

LIPS OF BLOOD (F-Sp) Films de L'Epee & Orbita 1972 color 85m. (Les CHEMINS DE LA VIOLENCE. Le SANG DES AUTRES. PERVERSIONS SEXUELLES. El SECRETO DE LA MOMIA) D: Ken Ruder; A.M. Gelabert? SP: Vincent Didier, from a story by David S. Cooper. Ph: Raymond Heil. Ref: MFB'73:95. Lee: mummy. V 5/9/73:106, 137. with Michel Flynn, Richard Vitz, Georges Rigaud, Manon Treviere, Catherine Frank, Teresa Gimpera.
Revived body of cataleptic Egyptian requires blood to survive; its severed hand strangles man.

LISA AND THE DEVIL (I-Sp-W.G.) (AA-TV)/Euro-America & Leone Int'l./Tecisa/Roxy 1972 color 93m. (Il DIAVOLO E I MORTI. El DIABLO SE LLEVA LOS MUERTOS. La CASA DELL'EXORCISMO. The DEVIL AND THE DEAD-ad t) D: Mario Bava. SP: A. Cittini, A. Leone. Ph: Cecilio Paniagua. Mus: Carlo Savina. AD: Nedo Azzini. SpFX: Franco Tocci. Mkp: Franco Freda. Ref: TVFFSB. V 5/9/73:144. 12/6/72:28. FC 3/80. TV. Lee. MFB'77:120. '78: 230: shot as LISA E IL DIAVOLO; re-edited as HOUSE OF EXORCISM (1975) with Robert Alda. with Elke Sommer, Telly Savalas, Sylva Koscina, Alida Valli, G. Tinti, E. Santoni, E. Fajardo.
Double of dead woman forced to join in macabre ritual; skeletons, coffins, "shrine of death." Slow-moving mixture of shock, melodrama, and romantic drama. Sommer screams every five minutes or so. Savalas is dubbed, but he and this other voice have some incidental fun with wax dummies and lollipops. Amusing if confusing five-or-six-zoom climactic shock scene.

LISZTOMANIA (B) WB/VPS-Goodtimes 1975 color/scope 104m. (LISZT-orig t) SP,D: Ken Russell. Ph: Peter Suschitzky. Mus: Rick Wakeman; Liszt, Wagner. AD: Philip Harrison. SpFX: Colin Chilvers, Roy Spencer. Mkp: Wally Schneiderman. Ref: MFB'75:240-41. V 10/15/75. 2/5/75:6. with Roger Daltrey, Sara Kestelman, Paul Nicholas, Fiona Lewis, John Justin, Wakeman (Thor/Siegfried), Ringo Starr, Oliver Reed, Georgina Hale.
Mechanical "superman" created by Wagner in the image of Siegfried; Wagner rising from the grave as Hitler; spaceship; "Whale/Hammer/Corman horror-movie references"; refs. to Dracula, Harker. (MFB)

LITAN, Or THE FACE-SNATCHERS (F & Eng-lang versions) M.Films-Films A2 1981 SP,D: Jean-Pierre Mocky. SP: also Jean-Claude

Romer;(Eng.vers.) Scott Baker. Ref: V 5/13/81:286: "sci-fi adventure." 9/9/81:50. with Mocky, Marie-Jose Nat.

A LITTLE BIT LIKE MURDER ABC-TV/Univ-TV 1973 color 73m. Ref: TVFFSB. with Elizabeth Hartman, Roger Davis, Sharon Farrell, Nina Foch.

"Ancient family curse" may be behind woman's mental illness.

LITTLE DEVIL (Indonesian) P.T.Sinar Tekun 1979 color (TUYUL) D: Bay Isbahi. Ref: V 5/9/79:405(ad): "shocker." with Darto Helm(Tuyul), Muny Cader, Debby Dewi, W.D. Mochtar.

Midget menace? cannibalism?

The LITTLE PRINCE Para/Donen 1974 color 89m. D,P: Stanley Donen. SP: Alan Jay Lerner, from the book "Le Petit Prince" by Antoine De St.-Exupery. Ph: Christopher Challis. Mus, Songs: Lerner & Loewe. PD: John Barry. SpFX: John Richardson. SpPhFX: Thomas Howard. Mkp: Ernie Gasser. Ref: MFB'75:177. screen. V 11/6/74. with Richard Kiley, Steven Warner(prince), Bob Fosse(snake), Gene Wilder, Clive Revill, Victor Spinetti.

Prince from asteroid B-612 arrives on Earth; tour of other planets and asteroids. Fosse's bravura number is highlight of generally disappointing adaptation of famous story.

LITTLE RED RIDING HOOD see ONCE UPON A RHYME

*The LITTLE SHOP OF HORRORS 1960 Mus: Fred Katz. Mkp: Harry Thomas. Ref: screen. Lee. MFB'73:78.

Talking, carnivorous plant (a cross between a butterwort and a Venus' fly-trap) hypnotizes stooge into going out and bringing back food for it. Funny (if one-note) characters, in a very strange situation comedy. Alternately awful and inspired. Each actor has his or her shining moments, but only the plant seems to have <u>all</u> shining moments. (It's its delivery.)

LIVE AGAIN, DIE AGAIN Univ-TV/Victor 1974 color 74m. D: Richard A. Colla. Ref: TVFFSB. with Walter Pidgeon, Donna Mills, Cliff Potts, Geraldine Page, Vera Miles, Mike Farrell.

Woman placed in suspended animation 34 years.

LIVE AND LET DIE (B) UA/Eon 1973 color 121m. D: Guy Hamilton;(shark seqs) William Grefe. SP: Tom Mankiewicz, from Ian Fleming's novel. Ph: Ted Moore. Mus: George Martin;(songs) Paul & Linda McCartney. AD: Syd Cain. SpFX: Derek Meddings. SpPhFX: Charles Staffel. Titles: Maurice Binder. Ref: MFB'73: 171-72. Lee. V 6/27/73. NYT 6/28/73. B.Warren. with Roger Moore(James Bond), Yaphet Kotto, Jane Seymour, Clifton James, David Hedison, Bernard Lee, Lois Maxwell.

"Voodoo snake ceremony"; fortune teller (MFB); "killer sharks" (V); Geoffrey Holder as supernatural being. (BW)

The LIVE MUMMY (B) Pathe 1915 15m. Ref: BFC.

"Man poses as Egyptian mummy to fool scientist."

A LIVELY SKELETON (B) LCC 1910 24m. Ref: BFC.
"Girl's suitor uses skeleton to scare away father's patients."

*The LIVING DEAD 1934 Ref: screen. BFC. TVG.
Catalepsy is discovered to be a germ. There's one "mystery" touch (i.e., a flashlight probing a coffin-filled cellar) but no mystery here--the viewer knows that Masters is the mastermind, and the script scores feeble points on our inside knowledge (e.g., the question "Who's behind all this?" cueing a cut to Masters). George Curzon's insolence as Masters, however, is winning. He's his own best audience. ("Ingenious, isn't it?")

LIVING DEAD,The see PSYCHOMANIA

LIVING DEAD AT THE MANCHESTER MORGUE see DON'T OPEN THE WINDOW

*The LIVING GHOST (UA-TV) 1942 Ref: TV. TVFFSB. V(d) 10/22/42. HR 10/22/42. and with Jan Wiley, Laurence Grant, Howard Banks.
An anesthetic paralyzes the cortical cells of a man's brain, leaving the "de-corticated" man a "zombie." Plus!--an old dark house, a woman (Minerva Urecal) with a mystical bent, and an illustrated lecture on the properties of the brain. (The latter a sort of flash-forward to the educational filmstrips of Fifties monster movies.) The comic opening sequence is amusing, but most of the (abundant) humor here is forced, and James Dunn overplays. The script fails to explain why the "zombie" stalks around trying to kill people.

LIZA (India-Malayalam) Dhanya 1978 color 146m. SP,D: Baby. Dial & Songs: Vijayan. Mus: K.J. Joy. Ref: Dharap. with Prem Nazeer, Ravi Kumar, Jayan, V. Radha, Vidhu.
Suicide possesses girl, scares to death those who drove her to suicide, and is finally exorcised.

**A LIZARD IN A WOMAN'S SKIN (I-F-Sp) AI/Int'l Apollo & Corona & Atlantida 1971 color 105m. (SCHIZOID-alt t. Una LUCERTOLA CON LA PELLE DI DONNA. Una LAGARTIJA CON PIEL DE MUJER) D & Co-SP: Lucio Fulci. Ph: L. Kuveiller. Mus: Ennio Morricone. PD: R. Calatayud. Ref: MFB'73:150. Lee. with Florinda Bolkan, Jean Sorel, Stanley Baker, Leo Genn, Anita Strindberg.
"Prophetic" dream of murder; "bat attack." (MFB)

LIZARD'S TAIL,The(by M.Brandel) see HAND,The

LOCATAIRE,Le or LOCATAIRE CHIMERIQUE,Le see TENANT, The

*The LODGER--A STORY OF THE LONDON FOG 1926 84m. (The CASE OF JONATHAN DREW-U.S.) Ph: also Hal Young. Titles: I. Montagu. Ref: screen. BFC. MFB'76:156.
"The Avenger" leaves the sign of the triangle on his "fair-haired" victims. One of Alfred Hitchcock's best comedies, unfortunately unintended as such. "The lodger" is just too, too

"tormented" to be taken seriously. A few cute bits (e.g., the hero breaking the cookie-heart in two), but, visually, generally undistinguished.

*The LODGER 1944 SpFX: Fred Sersen. Ref: screen. Lee.
Laird Cregar triumphs, at odd moments, over a pedestrian script punctuated by dull-eared "philosophical" exchanges. But his Jack the Ripper here is basically a conventional, love-as-hate, women-the-root-of-all-evil psychopath.

LOGAN'S RUN UA/MGM 1976 color/scope 118m. D: Michael Anderson. SP: David Z. Goodman, from the novel by William F. Nolan and George Clayton Johnson. Ph: Ernest Laszlo. Mus: Jerry Goldsmith. AD: Dale Hennesy. SpFX: Glen Robinson;(ph) L.B. Abbott; Van Der Veer. Holograms: Multiplex. Mattes: Matthew Yuricich. Ref: TV. MFB'76:215-16. V 6/16/76. with Michael York, Richard Jordan, Jenny Agutter, Roscoe Lee Browne(Box), Peter Ustinov, Farrah Fawcett-Majors, Michael Anderson Jr.
The "breeder"-born people of the year 2274 are sealed inside a huge, domed city and live for pleasure to the age of 30, when they enter the "Carousel" for "renewal" (read: extermination); "Sandmen" liquidate "Runners" (read: fugitives); "New You" super-plastic-surgery; flying (robot?) people-disposers; super-man-machine Box, who deep-freezes humans; flame-ray guns. Sort out the disorienting terms and gizmos here, and you'll find the usual future-shocked society. Nostalgia for the simple things in life prevails: aging, mothers, fathers. Lots of action, but it's a <u>long</u> run, and Ustinov's belated appearance as the old mutterer is like manna. ("It's just a place--<u>you</u> <u>know</u>.") Apparently, characterization (like old-age) survives <u>only</u> <u>outside</u> the dome. The final scene--in which the past (Ustinov) is on exhibit for the people of the future--is silly, sentimental, and yet (despite all) somehow quite touching.

LONG HARD NIGHT, The see PACK, The

LONG LIVE GHOSTS! (Cz) CFP/Barrandov 1979 color 92m. (AT ZIJI DUCHOVE!) D: Oldrich Lipsky. SP: Zdenek Sverak. Story: Jiri Melisek. Ph: Jan Nemecek. Mus: Jaroslav Uhlir. Sets: Vladimir Labsky. Ref: V 2/28/79. with Jiri Sovak(ghost), Dana Vavarova, Jiri Prochazka, Tomas Holly.
Knight's ghost haunts castle; his daughter ("another ghost") "enters the world of humans."

The LONG,SWIFT SWORD OF SIEGFRIED (W.G.-U.S.) Atlas/Entertainment Ventures 1971 color 89m. (SIEGFRIED UND DAS SAGENHAFTE LIEBESLEBEN DER NIBELUNGEN. The EROTIC ADVENTURES OF SIEGFRIED-B) D: Adrian Hoven;(U.S.vers.) David Friedman. SP: Al de Ger. Ph: H. Staudinger. Mus: D. Patucchi; Wagner. Ref: MFB'72:146. Lee. with Raymond Harmstorf, Sybill Danning, Heidi Bohlen.
Dragon, invisibility, magic cap.

LONG WEEKEND (Austral.) Dugong 1978 color/scope 97m. D,P: Colin Eggleston. SP: Everett de Roche. Ph: Vincent Monton. Mus: Michael Carlos. PD: Larry Eastwood. SpFX: Ivan Durrant. Ref: MFB'80:137. IFG'80:61. V 5/10/78. with John Hargreaves, Briony Behets, Mike McEwen, Michael Aitkins.
"Ecological apocalypse" in Australia. (MFB)

LOOK WHAT'S HAPPENED TO ROSEMARY'S BABY ABC-TV/Para-TV & Culzean 1976 color 95m. (ROSEMARY'S BABY II-orig t) D: Sam O'Steen. SP,P: Anthony Wilson. Sequel to ROSEMARY'S BABY. Ph: John Alonzo. Mus: Charles Bernstein. AD: Lester D. Gobruegge. SpFX: Joe Mercurio. Mkp: Jack Petty. Opt: Howard Anderson. Ref: TV. TVFFSB. TV Season. V 11/10/76:42. with Ruth Gordon, George Maharis, Ray Milland, Patty Duke Astin, Stephen McHattie (Adrian), Broderick Crawford, Tina Louise, Donna Mills.
The demon-child grows up, reforms, and gives way to another potential anti-Christ. Adrian is Dr. Jekyll, Mr. Hyde, and a rebel without a cause all rolled into one, as the script awkwardly attempts to account for evil in today's world. Lots of chanting, a few hokily-spectacular images, and welcome deflating punctuation from Gordon. The coven now even owns its own bus. (No driver needed.)

LOOSE IN LONDON Mono(AA) 1953 65m. SP,D: Edward Bernds. SP: also Elwood Ullman. Ph: Harry Neumann. Mus: Marlin Skiles. AD: C. Steensen(sp?). SpFX: Ray Mercer. Ref: TV. LC. with Leo Gorcey, Huntz Hall, Bennie Bartlett, Bernard Gorcey, Norma Varden, Angela Greene, David Condon, W. Kingsford, Clyde Cook.
English manor house "haunted" by hooded hangman dead 400 years; tolling tower bell which heralds murder; torture chamber. ("Looks like a day nursery for monsters.") The Bowery Boys' London is just like New York--no laughs there either. The script writes itself, following the easiest joke routes.

LORD ARTHUR SAVILE'S CRIME (Russ) 1916 D: S. Viessielovski. From Oscar Wilde's story. Ref: Daisne. with Nikolai Rimski.
See also: WORLD OF HORROR.

The LORD OF THE RINGS UA/Fantasy Films 1978 anim & live color 133m. D: Ralph Bakshi. SP: Chris Conkling, Peter S. Beagle, based on "The Fellowship of the Ring" & "The Two Towers," novels by J.R.R. Tolkien. Ph: Timothy Galfas;(anim) Nick Vasu Inc. et al. Mus: Leonard Rosenman. SdFX: Sam Shaw. Ref: MFB'79:148. V 11/8/78. ad. Voices: Christopher Guard, William Squire, John Hurt, Dominic Guard, Norman Bird, Andre Morell, Peter Woodthorpe(Gollum). with Billy Barty, Angelo Rossitto.
Mythical Middle-Earth, inhabited by Hobbits, wizards, "vile, cave-dwelling creature known as "Gollum"," living tree, "grisly Ring Wraiths and hordes of Orcs." (MFB)
See also: HOBBIT,The. RETURN OF THE KING.

*LOST ATLANTIS (Eng.-lang.vers.) Janus/SIC 1932 75m. SP: also Alexandre Arnoux. Dial: Jacques Deval. Ph: also Joseph Barth. Ref: screen. Chirat. TVFFSB.

Flavorless version of the Benoit novel isn't a patch on SIREN OF ATLANTIS. The script's disjointedness makes the main characters seem simply romantically whimsical, their relationship just another variation on the eternal triangle. Gibb McLaughlin is inconsequentially eccentric in the Henry Daniell role of greeter-to-Atlantis. Here the last shots are of the legionnaires as they lose St.-Avit's track, and of the great stone image of Antinea. (The latter, the only good use of the prop in the movie.)

*The LOST CITY (Classic Int'l-TV) 1935 74m. & 108m. feature versions (CITY OF LOST MEN-feature t) SP: P.P. Sheehan et al. Story: G.M. Merrick et al. Ph: Roland Price, Ed Linden. Mus: Lee Zahler. AD: Ralph Berger. SpFX: Norman Dawn. Elec FX: Kenneth Strickfaden. Ref: TV. TVFFSB. Turner/Price. V 2/27/35. and with George Hayes, B. Bletcher, Henry Hall.

"Ultra-short-wave transmitter" broadcasts to entire world; "cosmic condenser" unleashes electricity into Earth's atmosphere; "destroying ray"; no-transmitter TV sees and hears all within 1,000-mile radius; combo metal-plate-and-"enlarging machine" makes men into giant zombies; "light key" unlocks door with ray; "freezing gun" freezes rays, electricity, life, etc. ("That's quite a contraption"); "magnetic detector" detects source of electrical disturbances. See Strickfaden's effects carry whole scenes! See the hero nearly choked to death by a zombie-giant, who is dispatched (and none too soon) by electricity! (Cut to the heroine standing nearby, wringing her hands and crying "I'm so glad!") Hear the hero's comic sidekick Jerry (Eddie Featherstone) unfailingly make the most inane observations! (Hero: "What are those drums?" Heroine: "They're the drums of death!" Jerry: "The drums of death!") See Gabby Hayes as the "human interest"; William Boyd as the inhuman interest, the evil Zolok! See The LOST CITY! (Epochally awful it may be, but it is not dull.)

The LOST CITY OF ATLANTIS Gold Key-TV/Globe Cinema Arts 1978 color 93m. D,P: Richard Martin. SP: Sara Nickerson. Ph: Steve Shuttack. Mus: Aminadav Aloni. Ed: H.L. Strock. Ref: TV. V 3/1/78:100(ad). TVG. GKey.

Speculation re: Atlantis, involving ghosts, reincarnation, aliens, Mars. Familiar mythic musing. ("Did Earth almost collide with Mars?" "Are the Basques ex-Atlanteans?" "Did the ancient Egyptians colonize southern Idaho?")

LOST SOUL see FORBIDDEN ROOM(1977)

The LOST WORLD OF LIBRA Gold Key-TV("Zodiac" series) 1972? color 92m. Ref: TVFFSB. with J.Darren,T.Savalas,S.Whitman.

Death and destruction befall students of the occult studying papyrus scrolls for the "secret of the ages."

LOVE AT FIRST BITE AI/Simon 1979 color 96m. D: Stan Dragoti. SP,Story: Robert Kaufman. Story: also Mark Gindes. Ph: Edward Rosson. Mus: Charles Bernstein. PD: Serge Krizman. SpFX:

Allen Hall. Mkp: William Tuttle. Opt: Modern. SdFX: Popsicle. Ref: MFB'79:177-8. V 4/11/79. TV. with George Hamilton(Dracula), Susan Saint James, Richard Benjamin, Dick Shawn, Arte Johnson(Renfield), Barry Gordon, Ronnie Schell, Michael Pataki, John Dennis.

Dracula and the New York night life. Here he spews vapors, melts knives, and makes cars do tricks. He even gets a few laughs, but this is no YOUNG FRANKENSTEIN or even a FEARLESS VAMPIRE KILLERS. (Okay--it beats out SPOOKS RUN WILD.) The basic idea--pitting the romantic, European, Lugosi-styled Dracula vs. a hip New York--isn't bad, but it's diluted by ethnic jokes, Renfield jokes, bat (very bat) jokes, sight gags, etc. Hamilton's performance is, essentially, a 90-minute Lugosi impression.

*LOVE FROM A STRANGER 1947 Ref: TV.

Rote suspense/period drama. So contrived that--trucks and cars being unavailable--a horse-and-carriage runs down murderer John Hodiak at the end. One effective contrivance: Hodiak forcing wife Sylvia Sidney to read him his catalogued exploits, as he prepares to kill her.

LOVE MACHINE(S),The see PLEASURE MACHINES,The

LOVE MANIAC,The see FIEND WITH THE ELECTRONIC BRAIN

LOVE ME SPACE (Swed) 1974 anim D: L.-A. Hult. Ref: IFG'75: 472: "visitors from another planet."

LOVE OF THE WHITE SNAKE (H.K.) First Films/Wong 1978 color 98m. SP,D: Szu-Ma Ke. Ph: C.C. Chu. SpFX: Tadashi Nishimoto. Ref: V 8/23/78. 5/17/78:425(ad). with L.C. Hsia, C.Chi, L.Kun.

Man discovers woman he married is a snake goddess.

LOVE TRAP see CURSE OF THE BLACK WIDOW

LOVE: VAMPIRE STYLE see BITE ME, DARLING

*The LOVE WANGA 1941 See: OUANGA. POCOMANIA.

LUCERTOLA CON LA PELLE DI DONNA see LIZARD IN A WOMAN'S SKIN

The LUCIFER COMPLEX Gold Key-TV/Vista 1978 color 90m.? SP,D: David L. Hewitt. Ph: David E. Jackson. Mus: William Loose. SpFX: Ray Mercer? Ref: TV. TVG. GKey. with Robert Vaughn, Keenan Wynn, Aldo Ray, Merrie E. Ross, Lynn Cartwright.

Nazi plot to conquer the world in the Seventies, employing clones of Hitler, the hero, world leaders; laser-ray weapon; computerized history of the 20th Century. Crude sf-actioner. The "history" is just an excuse for stock-footage padding.

LUCIFER PROJECT, The see BARRACUDA

LUCIFER RIG, The see INTRUDER WITHIN

LUCIFER'S WOMEN Constellation 1975? color D: Paul Aratow. Ref: Meyers: devil cult. V 5/11/77:177(ad). Willis/SW'79. with Larry Hankin, Jane Brunel-Cohen, Emily Smith.

LUCY COMES TO STAY(by R.Bloch) see ASYLUM

LULU (Austrian) Vienna 1962 100m. (NO ORCHIDS FOR LULU-B) D: Rolf Thiele. SP: Herbert Reinecker, from the plays "Erdgeist" & "Der Buchse der Pandora" by F. Wedekind. Ph: Michel Kelber. Mus: Carl de Groof. Ref: Lee(FIR). no AFI. with Nadja Tiller, Hildegarde Kneff, O.E. Hasse, Mario Adorf, Charles Regnier(Jack the Ripper).

LULU Chase 1978 color 94m. D,P,Ph,Ed: Ronald Chase. From Wedekind's plays. Mus: Alban Berg. AD: V. Martin, D. Eastman. Ref: V 5/24/78: "visual shocks." 7/9/80:5. with Paul Shenar, Elisa Leonelli, Thomas Roberdean(Jack the Ripper).

LULU (F-W.G.-I) Elephant & Whodunit/TV 13/Medusa 1980 color 95m. SP,D,Des: Walerian Borowczyk. From Wedekind's plays. Ph: Michael Steinke. Ref: V 7/23/80: "vacuous." with Ann Bennent, Udo Kier(Jack the Ripper), Jean-Jacques Delbo.

LUNA E I FALO(by C.Pavese) see FROM THE CLOUD TO THE RESISTANCE

LUNCH ON THE GRASS see PICNIC ON THE GRASS

LUPA MANNARA,La see LEGEND OF THE WOLF WOMAN

LURE OF THE DEVIL'S TRIANGLE 1977 D: Philip Ronald. Ref: Willis/SW. with M. Cone.

LURK Film-makers' Coop 1965 38m. D: Rudy Burckhardt. SP & Narr: Edwin Denby. Ref: Lee. Glut/TFL: satire of FRANKENSTEIN (1931). with Red Grooms(monster), Mimi Grooms.

*LUST FOR A VAMPIRE (Teleworld-TV)/Levitt-Pickman 1971 From Le Fanu's story "Carmilla." Sequel to The VAMPIRE LOVERS. Ref: TV. Glut/TDB. Lee. TVFFSB. and with Michael Johnson, Mike Raven(Count Karnstein).

Horror-story writer Richard Lestrange (Johnson) falls in love with Mircalla (i.e., the vampire Carmilla Karnstein restored to life by black rites). Low-ebb Hammer which fails even to make much of the irony that its hero writes stories like this one. ("Life" imitates "art," so, loosely, to speak.) Film periodically threatens to turn into a comedy, but the threats may not have been intentional.

LUSTY TRANSPARENT HUMAN (J) Nikkatsu 1979 (KOSHOKU TOMEI NINGEN) D: Shinya Yamamoto. Sequel to LUSTY TRANSPARENT MAN? Ref: V 10/17/79:248.

LUSTY TRANSPARENT MAN (J) Nikkatsu 1978 (TOMEI NINGEN--OKASE) D: Isao Hayashi. Ref: V 5/9/79:371. JFFJ 13:33: "womanizing invisible man."

LYNN HART,THE STRANGE LOVE EXORCIST see STRANGE EXORCISM OF LYNN HART,The

M3: THE GEMINI STRAIN (Can.) Group 1/Harmony Ridge 1979 color 88m. (MUTATION-orig t. PLAGUE-int t) SP,D,P: Ed Hunt. SP,P: also Barry Pearson. Mus: Eric Robertson. Ref: Boxo 2/4/80. V 10/18/78:102(ad). 5/17/78:400. SFC 5/5/79(ad). with Daniel Pilon, Kate Reid, Celine Lomez, Michael J. Reynolds.
"Deadly bacterial mutation" kills scientist, spreads through city.

MACABRA see DEMONOID

O MACABRO DR. SCIVANO (Braz) Natus 1971 72m. SP,D,Ph: Raul Calhado. D: also Rosalvo Cacador. Ph: also W. Silva. AD: N. Resende. SpFX: Josef Reindl. Ref: Lee: vampire; voodoo. with Calhado, Luiz Leme, Oswaldo de Souza.

MACBETH(by W.Shakespeare) see BOOKWORM,The. REAL THING AT LAST,The.

MACCHIE SOLARI see AUTOPSY

The MACHINE TO KILL BAD PEOPLE (I) Brandon/Universalia-Tevere 1948 80m. (La MACCHINA AMMAZZACATTIVI. The CAMERA THAT KILLS BAD GUYS-cr t) SP,D: Roberto Rossellini. SP: also Franco Brusati et al. Ph: Tino Santoni, E.B. Berutto. Mus: Renzo Rossellini. SpFX: Eugenio Bava. Ref: screen. Brandon. MFB '81:37-8. Guarner/RR. with Gennaro Pisano, Giovanni Amato, Aldo Nanni, Marilyn Bufferd.
113,000-year-old minor devil gives photographer magic camera which kills and petrifies anyone whose picture it photographs. Cheerful little social satire. Those designated as "evil" (everyone, himself included, as it transpires), and dispatched by the hero, instantly assume the poses in the old photos that he photographs, and "freeze." They rush frantically, in effect, to pose for their own deaths.

MACUNAIMA (Braz) New Line/Serro-Grupo-Condor 1969('72-U.S.) color 108m. SP,D,P: J.P. de Andrade. From the novel by M. de Andrade. Ph: G. Cosulich, A. Beato. Mus: M. de Andrade et al. AD & Cost: Anisio Medeiros. Ref: MFB'74:130-31: "a mess." Willis/SW. with Grande Otelo, Paolo Jose, Dina Sfat.
Magic spring which turns Brazilian native white; sorceress; magic stone; cannibal family; man-eating water sprite.

The MAD BAKER Regency/Crunch Bird 1972 anim color 10m. Ref: Lee. PFA notes 12/23/80. Glut/TDB.
"Dracula-like" mad baker creates monster-cake (Lee); spoof of "old Universal horror films." (Glut)

The MAD BUTCHER Ellman/Universal Entertainment 1972(1974) color (The VIENNA STRANGLER-orig t. MEAT IS MEAT-TV) D: Guido Zurli. SP: Charles Ross. Ref: Willis/SW. Lee. V 5/10/72:18(ad). 11/15/72:3(rated): sfa 3 ON A MEATHOOK(Studio I)? TVFFSB. with Victor Buono, Karin Field, Brad Harris, John Ireland.
Butcher turns victims into sausages.

The MAD DOCTOR Disney 1933 anim 7m. D: David Hand. Ref: LC. Jim Shapiro. Maltin/OMAM/TDF.
"All the stops pulled out to create a miniature horror movie." (TDF)

*The MAD GHOUL 1943 (MYSTERY OF THE GHOUL-orig t) Mkp: Jack Pierce. Ref: TV. V 11/3/43. 3/31/43:46. Lee.
Dr. Morris (George Zucco), a chemist, has discovered vapors which produce in animals a temporary-but-recurrent, hypnotic state of "death-in-life" which, unchecked, leads to death itself. The only antidote: an herbal distillation, mixed with an extract from the hearts of fresh corpses. When Isabel (Evelyn Ankers), the fiancee of his surgeon-assistant Ted (David Bruce), confides to Dr. Morris that she wants out of their engagement, he subjects Ted to the gas, and plants the suggestion in his subconscious that Isabel no longer loves him. (Adding, a bit prematurely as it transpires, "She loves _me_.") Later, learning that it's the singer's accompanist, Eric (Turhan Bey), whom she loves, Morris sends the zombie-like Ted out to kill, first, Eric, then himself....Better movies have been written off for lesser crimes than those committed (in the name of acting and dialogue) in The MAD GHOUL. But the Hans Kraly material has a bite and tartness unusual for a Universal horror movie (at least from the Forties), and it features an intriguing "anti-heroine" role for Evelyn Ankers. In the film's more-surely-written second half, the doctor's quasi-hypnotic power over Ted comes (most surprisingly) to resonate as an objectification of _both_ men's alienation from Isabel--and "death-in-life" comes to seem an unexpectedly sound, insinuating metaphor for the dead-end corrosiveness of obsessive love. (Or as the doctor puts it: "The world in a test tube.") The script suggests that Dr. Morris--in attempting (in the climactic sequence) to revenge himself on Isabel--is, in effect, killing himself (literally as well as emotionally), his fate echoing that of Ted, who is _programmed_ to self-destruct. (The doctor is mortally dependent on the good-as-dead Ted's surgical expertise after exposure to his own hypnotic fumes.) _L'amour fou...la mort folle_. The script quirkily intertwines the literal and the figurative: Isabel's impassivity, it implies, sends her rejected lovers to the hearts of corpses (rather grisly surrogates)--the last shot: Dr. Morris futilely digging at the dirt over a grave, then dying. (Spurned again.) But if the script, tactfully, does not quite show the blood drying on the fingernails of Isabel (as an accessory before the fact), neither does it leave her hands spotless--_vide_, the pleasant irony of the line, "Only _she_ was

tearing their hearts out with music," and of her song lyrics: "Our love will live through the years" and "The lovely things of life are made all for love....We were meant for this and this...."--the latter words sung as Ted is about to murder Eric in front of her, on stage. Universal's funny valentine....

The MAD LOVE LIFE OF A HOT VAMPIRE 1971 Ref: Lee. Glut/TDB: hunchback. with Jim Parker(Dracula), Jane Bond, Kim Kim.

MAD MAX (Austral.) AI/Mad Max 1979 color/scope 100m. Story, SP,D: George Miller. SP: also James McCausland. Story: also Byron Kennedy. Ph: David Eggby. Mus: Brian May. AD: Jon Dowding. SpFX: Chris Murray. SdFX: Ned Dawson. Ref: IFG'80: 55. V 5/16/79. MFB'79:228: "luridly bottom-of-the-barrel." with Mel Gibson, Joanne Samuel, Steve Bisley, Roger Ward.
Future cops vs. highway marauders.

*The MAD MONSTER 1942 AD: Fred Preble. SpFX: Gene Stone. Mkp: Harry Ross. Ref: TV. with Anne Nagel, John Elliott--
and the doctor's-revenge-via-monster plot of the previous year's PRC, DEVIL BAT. George Zucco and a wolf-man (Glenn Strange) replace Bela Lugosi and his bats. The script, in a quasi-ingenious stroke, crams a raft of exposition into one, short flashback sequence near the beginning of the movie--the better to get on with its terribly tortuous (yet, oddly, sort of suspenseful) revenge story. Though the dialogue is wordy and ungainly, Zucco brings his part an odd sort of conviction. Lots of shadows, moss, fog, bottles, and other determinedly-atmospheric trappings.
See also: The HOWLING.

MADAME FRANKENSTEIN see LADY FRANKENSTEIN

MADAME SIN (U.S.-B) ABC-TV/ITC-TV 1972 color 90m. SP,D: David Greene. SP: also Barry Oringer. Story: Lou Morheim, Barry Shear. Mus: Michael Gibbs. PD: Brian Eatwell. Ref: MFB'72:117-18: "dull script." Lee. with Bette Davis, Robert Wagner, Denholm Elliott, Roy Kinnear, Charles Lloyd Pack.
Machine for erasing memories.

MADAME ZENOBIA Screencom/Cemano 1973 color 80m. D,Ph,P: Eduardo Cemano. Ref: V 12/12/73: "black occult leader...a kind of voodoo Dr. Joyce Brothers." with Tina Russell, Rick Livermore, Elizabeth Donovan(voodoo woman), Derald Delancey.

MADHOUSE (U.S.-B) AI/Amicus 1974 color 92m. (The REVENGE OF DR.DEATH-orig t. DEATHDAY-int t. sfa The MADHOUSE OF DR. FEAR-TV?) D: Jim Clark. SP: Greg Morrison, from the novel "Devilday" by Angus Hall. Adap: Ken Levison. Ph: Ray Parslow. Mus: Douglas Gamley. AD: Tony Curtis. SpFX: Kerss & Spencer. Mkp: George Blackler. Ref: MFB'74:278. Glut/TDB. V 3/27/74. 8/15/73:16. Lee. Cinef Smr'73:46. with Vincent Price, Natasha Pyne, Adrienne Corri, Peter Cushing, Robert Quarry.

Series of murders parallels scenes from actor Paul Toombes' "Doctor Death" movies; costume-party Dracula (Cushing) and Count Yorga (Quarry).

The MADMAN'S BRIDE (B) Hepworth 1907 7m. Ref: BFC.
"Mad lord buys girl from father, kills her during night...."

MAENAK AMERICA see POT, The

MAGDELENA--VOM TEUFEL BESESSEN see BEYOND THE DARKNESS

The MAGGOTS Studio 1979 D: Bill Rebane? Ref: Boxo 9/17/79:34. with Otis Young, John Goff, Katherine Hopkins.

MAGIA (Hung.) Corvin 1917 D: Alexander Korda. SP: K. Sztrokay, F. Karinthy. Ref: Lee. with Mihaly Varkonyi.
Baron Merlin, an ancient magician, drinks the blood of a young man "every thousandth moon" to sustain his life.

MAGIC Fox/Levine 1978 color 107m. D: Richard Attenborough. SP: William Goldman, from his novel. Ph: Victor J. Kemper. Mus: Jerry Goldsmith. PD: Terence Marsh. SpFX: Robert MacDonald Jr. SpCons: Dennis Alwood. Ref: MFB'79:8-9. TV. V 11/1/78. with Anthony Hopkins, Ann-Margret, Burgess Meredith, Lillian Randolph, Ed Lauter, E.J. Andre, David Ogden Stiers.
A schizophrenic ventriloquist dominated by his dummy resorts to murder in order to protect himself. The ending is touching, and Hopkins as the tormented Corky has some strong scenes. But they're more or less the regulation tormented-ventriloquist scenes found in every boy-and-his-dummy movie or TV show. The film is in effect a lovingly observed and scored cliche. It pretends to be a thriller, a psychological study, and a love story--all at once--but it doesn't become very romantically imaginative or psychologically telling until it's just about over.

The MAGIC BLADE (H.K.-Chinese) Shaw 1976 color 101m. D: Chu Yuan. SP: Yi Kuang, Szu Tu An. Ph: H. Chieh. Ref: V 8/4/76. with Ti Lung, Lo Lieh, Ching Li.
"Magical secret weapon"; "Devil Grandma"; "an eerie and sinister mood."

The MAGIC CLOCK (F & G versions) MOMA/Star 1926 object anim & live tinted 40m. (L'HORLOGE MAGIQUE. Die WUNDERUHR. The STORY OF A LITTLE GIRL WHO WANTED TO BECOME A PRINCESS-alt t. L'HISTOIRE D'UNE PETITE FILLE QUI VOULAIT ETRE PRINCESSE) SP,D,Ph,AD & Anim: Ladislas Starevitch. Ref: screen. Sadoul/DOFM. Lee. PFA notes 6/23/77. MOMA: 1917? Filmlexicon: 1928? with Nina Star(aka Nina Starevitch).
Dragon that flips victims up and into its mouth; Black Knight who proves to be Death; huge serpent guarding "immoral" apple; grotesque living trees; giant of the forest. An extraordinarily deft and witty blending of animation and live action, this comic fairy tale is a series of seemingly unending

visual delights. Among the many imaginative details and touches: the Sylph painting butterflies, the flower catching the (shrunken) girl, the giant clutching her, etc. If The MAGIC CLOCK hasn't quite the emotional undertow of Starevitch's other classic, The MASCOT, it's funnier and more free-ranging. The story of the clockmaker gives way to the story of the clock and clock figures, which in turn gives way to an intermingling of the two stories, which finally gives way to a depiction of a dream fairy-land. The narrative culmination--the union of the clockmaker's daughter and the prince of the clock--also seals the union of real, fantasy, and dream worlds.

MAGIC CURSE (H.K.) 197-? color 94m. SP,D: Tommy Loo-Chun, To Man Po. Ph: S. Wong. Mus: Wong Chu Yen. Ref: MFB'78:93. with Jason Pia Piau, Pinky De Leon, Peter Chen Lau, T.C. Bee.
Borneo. High priestess of Snake Tribe curses man--any woman he kisses will die violently.

The MAGIC GARDEN (B) Paul 1908 Ref: BFC.
"Drunken gardener sees giant frog, snake, etc."

MAGIC SKIN, The see DESIRE

The MAGIC SNOWFLAKE SWORD (H.K.-Cant.) H.K. Film Co. 1964 Ref: HKFFest: villainess uses hypnotic drug on victims.

*The MAGICIAN 1926 Ref: screen. Everson.
It's only 1926 and already, in The MAGICIAN, many of the standard horror-movie elements are apparent: the mad doctor (it's certified--he spent time in an asylum); the slim-to-none premise (he needs a "maiden's heart-blood" for a life-creation formula); the lab (in an "ancient sorcerer's tower"); the funny dwarf-assistant; the fiery finish; the dumb lines/intertitles (e.g., "Sometimes I think I shall go mad with the horror of it all"). The Rex Ingram script includes elements of SVENGALI (hypnotist, artists), The HUNCHBACK OF NOTRE DAME (Paris, gargoyles), DRACULA (hypnotism, sanitarium, heroes racing to the villain's domain), and CURSE OF THE DEMON (ancient formula, magician, library setting). And though The MAGICIAN is inferior to most of its filmic pre-and-post-1926 cross references, it does have its modest virtues--a bit of comedy; Paul Wegener's infernal vision of Alice Terry, himself, and a satyr; the dwarf-in-the-closet, and Wegener's self-consciously melodramatic acting style.

MAGIE MODERNE (F) Para(France) 1931 color seqs. 65m. (TELEVISION-alt t) D: Dimitri Buchowetzki. SP: Michel Duran, from H.I. Young's play. Ref: Chirat: TV invention; also Eng., G., Dutch, Pol., Rum., Swiss, Cz., & Ital. versions. with Lucien Galas, Gaston Jacquet, Madeleine Guitty.

*The MAGNETIC MONSTER A-men 1953 SpFX: Harry Redmond Jr. Sp PhFX: Jack Glass, Leo Britt? Ref: TV. V 2/11/53. Lee. and with Strother Martin.

Unipolar, magnetic isotope, created by bombarding "Serenium" with alpha particles, destroyed in Deltatron in Nova Scotia. Sf film is fairly intriguing as a mystery; risible as drama or horror. The "monster" hardly seems as "monstrous" or scary as everyone in the movie is pretending. At the end, hero Richard Carlson's "multiplication" theory--i.e., hate or fear begets monsters; love, babies--very neatly ties together the script's scientific and personal co-plots. (Ho ho ho!)

MAGNIFICENT MAGICAL MAGNET OF SANTA MESA NBC-TV/Col-TV & Gerber 1977 color 74m. D: Hy Averback. SP: Gerald Gardner. Ref: TVFFSB. TV Season. with Michael Burns, Susan Blanchard, Harry Morgan, Tom Poston, Conrad Janis.
Scientist's disk invention could solve world's energy problem.

MAGNIFICENT MS. TTR/Orangewood 1979 color 84m. (STAR WOMAN-orig t. SUPERWOMAN-int t) SP?,D,P: Damon Christian. Ph: R. McCallum. AD: Bill Wolf. SpFX: Opt.Systems. Ref: Cinema-X 3/80. Boxo 7/30/79:22. V 7/18/79:25. SFC 7/4/79(ad). with Desiree Cousteau(Superwoman), Jennifer Welles, Jesie St.James.
Spaceships; flying heroine.

MAID FOR PLEASURE (F) Europrodis 1974 color 91m. (FILLES EXPERTES EN JEUX CLANDESTINS) D,P: Guy Maria. SP: Serge Mareuil. Ph: J. Ledoux. Mus: B. Gerard, O. Toussaint. Ref: MFB'75:8. with Marcel Charvey, O. Mathot, V. Boisgel.
Hypnotism; visions; black-hooded witch of the 15th Century.

MAIDSTONE Supreme Mix 1971 color 110m. SP,D: Norman Mailer. Ph: R. Leacock et al. Mus: Isaac Hayes. Ref: Lee(FFacts). with Mailer, Rip Torn,Joy Bang, Ultra Violet, Harris Yulin.
Docu-drama re: the making of a movie set in the near future when all political leaders have been assassinated.

MAISON QUI PLEURE, La see CRYING HOUSE, The

MAKAI TENSHO (J) Toei/Kadokawa 1981 Ref: V 7/1/81:39: "spooky"; "other worldly evil." 7/22/81:24. with K. Sawada.

MAKE ROOM! MAKE ROOM!(by H.Harrison) see SOYLENT GREEN

MAL OCCHIO (Mex) Orofilms 1976 Ref: V 3/31/76:67(ad): "Mas alla del exorcismo."

MALACARNE (I) Sicilian Films 1948 103m. (FOR THE LOVE OF MARIASTELLA-alt t?) D: Natale Di Cristina. SP: Ovidio Imara. Story: Zucca Mercanti. Ph: Giuseppe La Torre. Ref: no LC. V 11/17/48. with Mariella Lotti, Otello Tosi, Amedeo Nazzari, Giovanni Grasso, Umberto Spadaro(Fifi the Hunchback).
A "sea monster" drives tuna away from a small Sicilian fishing port.

MALATESTA'S CARNIVAL OF BLOOD Int'l Co-Prods/Windmill 1973 (MALATESTA'S CARNIVAL-orig t) SP,D: Christopher Speeth.

Story: Werner Liepholt. Sets: Alan Johnson et al. SdFX: S. Speeth. SpFX: Richard Grosser. Ref: Lee(pb). Ecran 73(July, p29). V 10/31/73:6: at Sitges. 8/15/73:17(rated). with Janine Carazo, Jerome Dempsey, Herve Villechaize, William Preston.
Ghouls, gore, mutilation, etc.

MALDICION DE FRANKENSTEIN see DRACULA VS.DR.FRANKENSTEIN

MALDICION DE LA BESTIA see NIGHT OF THE HOWLING BEAST

MALEVIL (F-W.G.) Films A2 & Gibe Telecip/Stella & NEF-Diffusion 1981 color/scope 119m. SP,D: Christian de Chalonge. SP: also Pierre Dumayet. From Robert Merle's novel. Ph: Jean Penzer. Mus: Gabriel Lared. AD: Max Douy. Ref: V 2/4/81:51: post-nuclear-holocaust. 5/13/81:286. 6/17/81. with Michel Serrault, Jacques Dutronc, Robert Dhery, Jean-Louis Trintignant.

The MALPAS MYSTERY (B) (Bloom-TV)/Schoenfeld/Independent Artists 1960 60m. D: Sidney Hayers. SP: Paul Tabori, Gordon Wellesley, from Edgar Wallace's novel "Face in the Night." Ph: Michael Reed. Mus: Elizabeth Lutyens. AD: Eric Saw. Ref: AFI. TV. TVG. BFC. TVFFSB. with Maureen Swanson, Allan Cuthbertson, Geoffrey Keene, Sandra Dorne, Ronald Howard.
Man in house with automatic doors and lights wears weird, featureless mask, apparently to give the impression that it conceals a horrible face, or no face. (Malpas: "No--she'd never marry something that looks like a nightmare!") Blandly plotted and acted mystery, sprinkled with suggestively sinister lines like "And dead men don't walk!"

MALPERTIUS (F-Belg-W.G.) SdEdS & LPAA/Sofidoc/Artemis 1972 color 124m. (MALPERTIUS:HISTOIRE D'UNE MAISON MAUDITE. The LEGEND OF DOOM HOUSE-B) D: Harry Kumel. SP: Jean Ferry, from Jean Ray's novel. Ph: Gerry Fisher. Mus: Georges Delerue. AD: Pierre Cadiou. SpPhFX: M. Bernard. Mkp: John O'Gorman. Ref: MFB'77:262. '79:138. Lee. V 5/17/72. with Orson Welles, Susan Hampshire(gorgon), Michel Bouquet, Jean-Pierre Cassel, Mathieu Carriere, Walter Rilla, Sylvia Vartan.
House haunted by dying Greek gods.

MAMMA DRACULA (F-Belg;Eng.-lang.) SND & RTBF/Valisa 1980 color 90m. SP,D,P: Boris Szulzinger. SP: also P. Sterckx, M.H. Wajnberg. Dial: Tony Hendra. Ph: Willy Kurant. Mus: Roy Budd. Mkp: Pascale Kellen. Ref: V 3/5/80:49. 5/28/80. 12/3/80. 5/13/81:305,348. with Louise Fletcher(Mamma), Maria Schneider, Jimmy Shuman, M.H. & Alexander Wajnberg.
Vampire woman remains young by bathing in the blood of virgins; scientist working on formula for artificial blood.

*MAN ALIVE 1945 Ref: TV. V 9/26/45. and with Carl Switzer.
"Dead" man's (Pat O'Brien) presence scares fake medium, Prof. Zoroda (Fortunio Bonanova), away from seance; oracular "apparition" during thunderstorm; Adolphe Menjou as Lucifer in stage show. Determinedly "whacky" farce. Ellen Drew should

not have been informed that she was playing comedy, though the other actors whoop it up a bit too. Good Leigh Harline score (except when it does some whooping-up of its own).

The MAN AND THE SNAKE (B) Jocelyn 1972 color 26m. SP,D: Sture Rydman. SP: also Brian Scobie. From Ambrose Bierce's story. Ph: Gerry Fisher. Mus: Marc Wilkinson. PD: Bryan Graves. Ref: MFB'72:264. with John Fraser, Andre Morell.

Man frightened to death by king cobra.

The MAN FROM ATLANTIS NBC-TV/Solow-Taft 1977 color 100m. D: Lee H. Katzin. SP: Mayo Simon. Mus: Fred Karlin. SpFX: Tom Fisher. Ref: TVFFSB. V 3/9/77:46. TV Season. with Patrick Duffy, Belinda Montgomery, Victor Buono, Art Lund, Steve Franken, Larry Pressman, Virginia Gregg.

Man with gill-like tissue instead of lungs.

See also: DEATH SCOUTS. DISAPPEARANCES,The. KILLER SPORES

*The MAN FROM <u>1997</u> <u>1957</u> Ref: TVFFSB.

The MAN FROM NOWHERE (B) CFF/Barker 1976 color 59m. D: James Hill. SP: John Tully. Ph: Desmond Dickinson. Mus: John Cameron. AD: Hazel Peiser. Ref: MFB'76:57. with Sarah Hollis-Andrews, Ronald Adam, Shane Franklin.

"Period-thriller-cum-ghost story": "dark-coated man" pops up and down around "old dark house."

MAN, GHOST, FOX (Mandarin) 1969 color (JEN,KUI,HU) Based on the "Liao-chai Chih-I." Ref: Eberhard.

Student in love with ghost; fox spirit; "18th hell"; "1000 years in the ice palace."

The MAN IN MOTLEY (B) London 1916 80m. D: Ralph Dewsbury. From Tom Gallon's novel. Ref: BFC. with H. Willis, H. Hobbs.

"Man poses as ghost to force killer to confess."

*MAN MADE MONSTER 1941 SP: G. Waggner(aka J.West). AD: Jack Otterson. SpFX: John P. Fulton. Mkp: Jack Pierce. Ref: TV. Les Otis. Lee. FM 169:40.

Tepid, straightforward Universal horror-show is worth a look for Lionel Atwill's Dr. Rigas, whose hilarious disdain for all "these nonentities" is quite amusing. ("The forces of creation--bah!") His lively acidity occasionally counteracts Lon Chaney Jr.'s mopey, Larry Talbot-like Dan (Anne Nagel: "There's something tragic about this") and the plot, which is merely a pretext for a wan "payoff"--the electrocution scene, in which Dan lights up and lights out. Alternately sweet and stirring H.J. Salter score.

MAN ON A SWING Para/Jaffilms 1974 color 109m. D: Frank Perry. SP: David Z. Goodman. Ph: Adam Holender. Mus: Lalo Schifrin. PD: Joel Schiller. Ref: TV. V 2/27/74. with Cliff Robertson, Joel Grey, Dorothy Tristan, Elizabeth Wilson, Gil Gerard.

Is Franklin (Grey), an apparent clairvoyant, <u>leading</u> his audience during his trances, or is he himself led by occult forces? Is the film a psychological or parapsychological study? Or both? As embodied in Grey's performance, the ambiguity is tantalizing. His dervish act has elements of both the psychic and the charlatan--if it's just an act it's a good one. Generally, however, the film's ambiguity is frustrating, limiting. The only points of interest are the above questions, and though they sustain interest, they don't deepen it. We're left, simply, with a lot of arrows pointing in different directions.

*The MAN THEY COULD NOT HANG 1939 72m. Ref: TV. FM 169:41.

Nicely paced and smartly plotted, The MAN THEY COULD NOT HANG is one of Boris Karloff's better "B" vehicles of the Thirties. The highlight, and a real coup: the sound of his ominous, oracular voice (as Dr. Savaard) piped in by speaker from the top of a living-room wall. His measured, sepulchral tones make his "gracious" welcoming of his "guests"--the judge and jury who sentenced him to hang--as menacing as dire threats. Such god-like aural richness is, however, a bit overpowering for the more mundane, non-ironic moments between scientist-father and daughter, and the script wastes some time at the beginning trying to work up sympathy for Savaard. ("Here's a man who spent his whole life trying to do nothing but good.")

The MAN WHO FELL TO EARTH (B) Cinema 5/British Lion 1976 color/scope 138m. D: Nicolas Roeg. SP: Paul Mayersberg, from the novel by Walter Tevis. Ideas: Donald Cammell. Ph: Anthony Richmond. Mus D: John Phillips. AD: Brian Eatwell. SpPhFX: P.S. Ellenshaw, Camera FX. Mkp: Linda De Vetta. SpOceanographicFX: Desmond Briscoe(sp?), Woods Hole Ocean.Inst. Ref: screen. MFB'76:86. V 3/24/76. with David Bowie(alien), Rip Torn, Candy Clark, Buck Henry, Bernie Casey, James Lovell.

Alien being from dying planet lands in New Mexico; in human guise founds business empire; becomes distracted by TV images and by Earth lady; seems about to embark on return flight to his planet when thugs wreck his work and blow up his space base; doctors experiment on him; he escapes or is let go and winds up drinking alone at a cafe table. (Diffuse, isn't it?) Roeg, Mayersberg, and co. apparently put a lot into this film--would that they had found some way for us to get something out of it. There are lyrical moments (e.g., the psychically-sensitive alien picking up bits of his and our past); but also thoughts like "I know all things begin and end in eternity." The import of the script is dissipated in displays of both human and alien pathos and kinkiness. (The point evidently being that people are and aren't alike all over.)

MAN WITH A MAID, A see GROOVE ROOM, The

*The MAN WITH NINE LIVES 1940 AD: Lionel Banks. Ref: TV. Lee.

Repeat dose of chemical formula--intended to restore frozen bodies to life--instead kills. The plot of The MAN WITH NINE

LIVES--none too believable at the beginning--becomes progressively more incredible. And Boris Karloff as a Mr. Nice Guy is just too sanctimoniously self-righteous to be believed. Unintentional high point: Kraaval (Karloff) shooting a man in the back, then grumbling, "You call everything murder, Doc." Roger Pryor has a "B" voice.

The MAN WITH THE BRAIN GRAFT (F-I-W.G.) Parc-UPF-UPG/Verona/Bavaria Atelier 1972 color 90m. (L'HOMME AU CERVEAU GREFFE) SP,D: Jacques Doniol-Valcroze. From novel by V. Viacs & A. Franck. Ph: Etienne Becker. AD: Claude Pignot. Ref: Lee. V 4/19/72. 10/4/72:29: sfa TRANSPLANTE A LA ITALIANA? IFG'73: 185. with Mathieu Carriere, Jean-Pierre Aumont, Michel Duchaussoy, Nicoletta Machiavelli.
Doctor's brain transplanted into patient.

The MAN WITH THE GOLDEN GUN (B) UA/Eon 1974 color 125m. D: Guy Hamilton. SP: Richard Maibaum, Tom Mankiewicz, from Ian Fleming's novel. Ph: Ted Moore, Oswald Morris. Mus: John Barry. PD: Peter Murton. SpFX: John Stears. Min: Derek Meddings. Titles: M. Binder. Gun: Colibri Lighters. Computers: Calspan. Ref: MFB'75:11. V 12/11/74. with Roger Moore(James Bond), Christopher Lee, Britt Ekland, Maud Adams, Herve Villechaize, Clifton James, Soon Taik Oh, Richard Loo, Marc Lawrence, Bernard Lee, Lois Maxwell, Marne Maitland.
Device for harnessing solar energy; flying car.

The MAN WITH THE LIMP (B) 1923 20m. See also: Mystery of Dr. Fu-Manchu series. Ref: BFC. Lee.

The MAN WITH THE POWER NBC-TV/Univ-TV 1977 color 95m. D: Nicholas Sgarro. SP,P: Allan Balter. Ph: J.J. Jones. Mus: Patrick Williams. AD: Frank Greico Jr. Ref: TV. TVFFSB. TV Season. with Bob Neill, Vic Morrow, Roger Perry, Persis Khambatta, Austin Stoker, Tim O'Connor.
Young man inherits psycho-kinetic powers from father, an alien being; mystic figure. Typical super-hero stuff.

MAN WITH THE SYNTHETIC BRAIN see BLOOD OF GHASTLY HORROR

The MAN WITH TWO HEADS (U.S.-B) Mishkin 1972 color 80m. (DR. JEKYLL AND MR. BLOOD-orig t) SP,D,Ph: Andy Milligan. From "The Strange Case of Dr.Jekyll and Mr.Hyde" by RLS. AD: Elaine. Mkp: Lois Marsh. Ref: FFacts. Aros. Lee. with Denis DeMarne, Julia Stratton, Berwick Kaler, Jacqueline Lawrence.
London, 1835. Dr. Jekyll's secret potion brings out his evil nature, in the person of Mr. Blood.

MAN WITH TWO HEADS see THING WITH TWO HEADS

*The MAN WITHOUT A SOUL 1916 (sfa *I BELIEVE) SP: Kenelm Foss. Ref: BFC.
"Church student loses soul after scientist revives his body."

MANDRAKE NBC-TV/Univ-TV 1979 color 95m. D: Harry Falk. SP: Rick Husky, from the comic strip "Mandrake the Magician" by Falk & Davis. Ph: V.A. Martinelli. Mus: Morton Stevens. AD: J.P. Bruce. Ref: TV. V 1/31/79:59. with Anthony Herrera, Simone Griffeth, Ji-Tu Cumbuka, Gretchen Corbett, Robert Reed.

Magician with ability to conjure up invulnerable tigers, spiders, brick walls, subjects' memories; hypnotically-programmed saboteurs (a la TELEFON); death-semblance serum; drug-induced hypnosis. Insipid, "hip" banter and "Kung Fu"-type mystical mumbo-jumbo don't mix. Only the "telepathic projection" tricks break up the monotony.

MANIAC Analysis/Magnum(Maniac) 1981(1980) color 91m. D: William Lustig. SP: C.A. Rosenberg, Joe Spinell. Ph: Robert Lindsay. Mus: Jay Chattaway;(elec) Peter Levin. SpMkpFX: Tom Savini. SdFX: Sandy Rackow. Opt: Cinopticals. Ref: screen. V 10/15/80:53(ad). 2/4/81. with Spinell(Frank), Caroline Munro, Gail Lawrence, Savini.

Schizophrenic who misses his mother murders and scalps women to get wigs for his mannequin-surrogates; hallucinations (mother's hand from grave; victims returning, undoing his head). Better-than-competent-of-kind, MANIAC begins as an almost Bunuelian examination of madness, but takes a few too many William Castle turns to achieve feature length. (At that, it's still better-than-average Castle.) The script makes its own cross reference to TAXI DRIVER and sticks equally closely to its warped protagonist--too closely for conventional-shocker comfort. At its best the film has a disturbing, documentary directness; at its worst it has dialogue sequences which are decidedly less convincing than the madman's voice-over growls and interior duologues.

The MANITOU Avco Embassy/Enterprise 1978 color/scope 105m. SP,D,P: William Girdler. SP: also Jon Cedar, Thomas Pope. From Graham Masterton's novel. Ph: Michael Hugo. Mus: Lalo Schifrin. PD: Walter S. Herndon. ConcepDes: Nikita Knatz. SpFX: Gene Grigg, Tim Smythe;(asst) Sam Price, Dale Newkist. SpFxMkp: Tom Burman. MkpSup: Joe McKinney. SdFX: Fred Brown. SpPhFX: CFI, Van Der Veer. Ref: MFB'78:177-78. V 3/1/78. TV. with Tony Curtis, Michael Ansara, Susan Strasberg, Cedar, Stella Stevens, Ann Sothern, Burgess Meredith, Paul Mantee, Jeanette Nolan; Felix Silla & Joe Gieb(Misquamacus).

Greatest Indian medicine man of all reincarnated for fifth time by hatching from lump on woman's neck; Misquamacus summons up lizard demon, spirit of the North Wind, Great Old One (Satan) and is vanquished by computer/machine manitous directed at it by woman. Engaging, imaginative supernatural thriller. The continuity is functional, but each new, mind-boggling effect is calculated to top (and does top) the last one, as one medicine man (Ansara) takes on what seems to be the whole <u>universe</u> of the supernatural. Your average fantasy-thriller is usually content with (attempting) one or two "payoffs," but The MANITOU is payoff after payoff--e.g., the hospital-tenth-floor-as-ice-palace (that North Wind), the room-with-the-view (NSEW, up, and down) but no roof, floor, or walls. The effects are simultaneously enthralling and absurd--suspension of disbelief is not possible--but also not necessary. You're not asked to believe, only to be amazed.

MANOOT COMPUTER see COMPUTER SUPERMAN

MANNIKINS OF HORROR(by R.Bloch) see ASYLUM

*MAN'S GENESIS Biog 1912 17m. (PRIMITIVE MAN-orig t) SP,D: D.W. Griffith. SP: also Frank Woods. Sequel: BRUTE FORCE (1914). Ph: Billy Bitzer. Ref: AF-Index. Henderson/DWG. with Mae Marsh, Wilfred Lucas, R. Harron, C.H. Mailes.
See also: PRIMITIVE MAN,The(1913).

MANSION DE LA LOCURA see DR.TARR'S TORTURE DUNGEON

MANSION DE LA NIEBLA see MURDER MANSION

MANSION OF THE DOOMED Group 1/Charles Band 1976 color 89m. (EYES-orig t. EYES OF DR.CHANEY-int t. HOUSE OF BLOOD-int t. The TERROR OF DR.CHANEY-B) D: Michael Pataki. SP: Frank Ray Perilli. Ph: Andrew Davis. Mus: Robert O. Ragland. AD: Roger Pancake. Mkp: M. Bacarella, T. Hoeber. Ref: MFB'78:98, 256. Willis/SW. V 3/30/77:5. 5/26/76:4(rated). SFC 12/10/76. Ind.Film Jnl. 11/12/75:11. with Richard Basehart(Dr.Leonard Chaney), Trish Stewart, Gloria Grahame, Lance Henriksen, Vic Tayback, Arthur Space, Marilyn Joi.
Surgeon attempts eye transplant for his blind daughter.

MARCIA NUZIALE see WEDDING MARCH(1966)

MARIANNE Toluca/Cinema Systems 1975 D: Noel Black. SP: Sidney Stebel. Story: Black, Stebel. Ph: Michael Murphy. Ref: V 9/8/76:34: "voodoo pic." 4/30/75:27. 6/12/74:6. 6/5/74:3. with Kitty Winn, Peter Donat, Mary-Robin Redd, William Burns.

MARINE EXPRESS (J) Tezuka-TV 1979 anim Ref: JFFJ 13:30: TV-movie; "sf mystery."

*The MARK OF DEATH 1962 See also: CREATURE OF THE WALKING DEAD. Ref: TV: the latter's dandy musical motif originates here.

MARK OF THE BEAST see FEAR NO EVIL(1981)

*MARK OF THE DEVIL Hallmark(AI)/HFS 70-Hoven 1970('72-U.S.) 95m. (AUSTRIA 1700. SATAN-ad ts) SP: Sergio Cassner. Sequel: MARK OF THE DEVIL,PART 2. Ph: E.W. Kalinke. Sets: Max Melin. Ref: screen. Lee. Willis/SW. and with Reggie Nalder, Udo Kier, Olivera Vuco.
The torture scenes sold MARK OF THE DEVIL to the public, but the film's subject seems, oddly enough, to be the passing of the era of your local witchfinder, and the script occasionally seems to be getting at something. But the broader

narrative strokes are all predictable ironies, and one must settle, finally, for bits of humor and stray aural and visual felicities.

MARK OF THE DEVIL, PART 2 (W.G.-F) Hallmark(AI)/TV 13 & Monaco-SND 1972('74-U.S.) color 90m. (HEXEN: GESCHANDET UND ZU TODE GEQUALT) D: Adrian Hoven. SP: Max Hunter, Fred Dagar. Sequel to MARK OF THE DEVIL. Ph: E.W. Kalinke. Mkp: Josef Cosfeld. Ref: Willis/SW. Lee: witches tortured. V 1/30/74: 5(rated). Bianco Index'74. with Erica Blanc, Anton Diffring, Reggie Nalder, Percy Hoven, Jean Pierre Zola.

MARK OF THE GORILLA Col/Katzman 1950 68m. D: William Berke. SP: Carroll Young, from Alex Raymond's "Jungle Jim" comic strip. Ph: Ira Morgan. Mus D: Bakaleinikoff. AD: Paul Palmentola. Ref: V 2/22/50. TV. "Great Movie Series." with Johnny Weissmuller, Trudy Marshall, Suzanne Dalbert, Onslow Stevens, Selmer Jackson, Robert Purcell.

Phony zoologist's henchmen masquerade as gorillas to scare natives away from cache of Nazi gold; shots of "gorilla" and its huge shadow as it skulks about at night (Jim: "He's pretty smart for a gorilla"); huge snake; vulture. A veritable stock-footage museum, with choice stock-dialogue exhibits: "This isn't gorilla territory." "It looked like a gorilla, but that yell sounded almost human." "Jungle Jim is loose!" "That jungle guy is hard to kill."

*MARK OF THE VAMPIRE 1935 61m. Add'l Dial: H.S. Kraft, Samuel Ornitz, John L. Balderston. From Tod Browning's story "The Hypnotist." Mkp: Jack Dawn; Bill Tuttle? Ref: screen. MFB '79:59: "the film goes from strength to strength as Wong Howe's photography caressingly illuminates the horrendously beautiful images...." (Tom Milne) MPH 4/16/35: orig. 80m. and with Henry Stephenson(vampire actor).

In the fantasy sequences of MARK OF THE VAMPIRE, the vampires are less monsters/menaces than, simply, other-worldly beings that seem to float on mist and that have their own form of society, with its own set of laws. Except for Carroll Borland's hiss, they communicate noiselessly, and seem as elemental as the dog, bats, beetles, rats, and spiders which also inhabit this strange realm. The mystery-plot, narrative framework of MARK OF THE VAMPIRE is the showcase for this supernatural world, which, as Milne notes, is not really dispelled by the climactic revelations. (The "vampires" are actually actors in a plot to expose a murderer.) The two worlds of the film exist independently of each other. The unearthly sounds of the night world seem to be a cross between the sound of wind and the howling of unidentifiable animals. This is Bela Lugosi's (and Browning's, and Hollywood's) premier vampire movie.

MARK OF THE WITCH Favorite Films/Presidio 1970 color 84m. D: Tom Moore. SP: Mary Davis, Martha Peters. Ph: Robert E. Bethard. Mus: Whitey Thomas. Sets: Jim Carver. Mkp: Lynn

Brooks. Ref: AFI. Lee(Boxo) with Robert Elston, Anitra Walsh, Darryl Wells, Marie Santell(witch), Barbara Brownell.
300-year-old witch possesses co-ed, terrorizes college.

*The MARK OF THE WOLFMAN Indep.-Int'l. 1968('71-U.S.) (The WOLFMAN OF COUNT DRACULA-SE Asia. VAMPIRE OF DR.DRACULA-alt t) U.S. version: Anim: Bob Le Bar. Art: Gray Morrow. Ref: Lee. Glut/CMM: Dr. Frankenstein as a werewolf. TVG.
Sequels: La NOCHE DEL HOMBRE LOBO. *DRACULA VS. FRANKENSTEIN(1969). *The FURY OF THE WOLFMAN. The WEREWOLF VS. THE VAMPIRE WOMAN. DR.JEKYLL AND THE WOLFMAN. CURSE OF THE DEVIL. NIGHT OF THE HOWLING BEAST. RETORNO DEL HOMBRE LOBO.

MARKHEIM(by R.L.Stevenson) see MIRROR AND MARKHEIM, The

MARRIED BEFORE BREAKFAST MGM/Zimbalist 1937 70m. D: Edwin L. Marin. SP: George Oppenheimer, Everett Freeman. Story: Harry Ruskin. Mus: David Snell. Ref: TVFFSB: "crazy inventions." LC. NYT 7/23/37. B.Warren. V 7/28/37. with Robert Young, Florence Rice, June Clayworth, Warren Hymer, Hugh Marlowe.
"Shaving cream which calls for no razor." (V)

The MARTIAN CHRONICLES NBC-TV/Fries-Stonehenge 1980 color 300m. D: Michael Anderson. SP: Richard Matheson, based on the book by Ray Bradbury (& on the story "The Fire Balloons" in his "The Illustrated Man"). Ph: Ted Moore;(models) Bob Kindred. Mus: Stanley Myers;(elec) Richard Harvey. AD: Assheton Gorton. SpFxD: John Stears. Mkp: George Frost. Ref: V 10/18/78:108(ad). Bill Warren: 3-part miniseries with foreign theatrical version. Cinef X:1:19-23. with Rock Hudson, Fritz Weaver, Darren McGavin, Roddy McDowall, Maria Schell, Barry Morse, Bernie Casey, Gayle Hunnicutt, Robert Beatty, Chris Connelly, Bernadette Peters, Michael Anderson Jr., Jon Finch, Terence Longdon, Richard Masur.
Stories of men, Martians, robots, ghosts on Mars.

MARTIN Libra/Laurel(Braddock) 1976 color 95m. SP,D: George A. Romero. Ph: Michael Gornick. Mus: Donald Rubinstein. Mkp & SpFX: Tom Savini. Ref: screen. MFB'78:9-10. V 1/10/79. 10/1/75:47(ad): aka BLOOD? AMPAS: 1977? with John Amplas (Martin), Lincoln Maazel, Christine Forrest, Sarah Venable.
MARTIN is CAT PEOPLE in reverse: in the latter film, the psychiatrist tries to convince the heroine that she isn't a cat person. (She is.) In MARTIN, Martin's uncle tries to convince him that he is a vampire. (He isn't.) In both films, superstition (debunked or not) is the agent of suppression and death. At least this is the idea that seems to be struggling to the surface in each film, and that finds its subtlest expression in Simone Simon's affecting performance in CAT PEOPLE. Both Irena and Martin achieve sexual consummation only through violence. (She with fangs; he with hypo and razor.) But the films see two different worlds: Lewton's portrays Irena's plight as sad because she's cut off from a "normal" world. (Never mind that the Kent Smith and Jane

Randolph characters could set standards of normality only for mannequins.) Romero sees Martin's plight as sad too, perhaps, but not because he's cut off from some "normal" world--that world is shown to be as sad and screwed-up as Martin is. Romero's cynical view, however, seems as one-dimensional and one-sided as Lewton's more sentimental one. In MARTIN hope is extinguished before it even begins to burn.

MARTY FELDMAN,VAMPIRE! see EVERY HOME SHOULD HAVE ONE

MARY, MARY, BLOODY MARY (U.S.-Mex) (Four Star-TV)/Black Lion/ Translor-Proa-CM 1975 color 101m. D: Juan Lopez Moctezuma. SP: Malcolm Marmorstein. Story: Don Rico, Don Henderson. Ph: Miguel Garzon. Mus: Tom Bahler. Ref: V 5/21/75. Willis/SW. TVFFSB. with Christina Ferrare(vampire), David Young, Helena Rojo, John Carradine(vampire).

Fashion-model vampire mercifully put to death by vampire-father.

MAS ALLA DE LA AVENTURA (Arg) Guimef SRL 1980 color 95m. D: O.B. Finn. SP: Vicente Caputo. Dial: Oscar Viale. Ph: Paz, Marizialetti. Mus: L.M. Serra. Sets: Iglesias, Ferrari. Ref: V 1/7/81. IFG'81:53. with Andy Pruna, Catherine Alric, Marcos Zucker.

Alien beings; "extinction of several animal species"; nature in revolt. (IFG)

MAS ALLA DEL TERROR see BEYOND TERROR

The MASCOT (F) Film Images/Gelma-Film 1933 object anim & live action 26m. (FETICHE. FETICHE MASCOTTE. The DEVIL'S BALL. DUFFY MASCOT. The CHARM-alt ts. PUPPET LOVE-15m. vers.) SP,D,Ph,AD,Anim: Ladislas Starevitch. See also: titles under FETICHE. NAVIGATOR, The. Ref: screen. Ecran 73(Jan.,p24). Kit Parker. PFA notes 6/23/77. Filmlexicon.

A stuffed dog, animated by a doll-maker's teardrops and searching for an orange for the woman's daughter, loses its way in an eerie midnight world inhabited by the Devil, creatures made of paper, straw, and refuse, vegetable beings, balloon-creatures, and living bird-skeletons and dolls. The little dog is utterly winning; the nightmare creatures are eerily entranced. The MASCOT opposes sweet, determined "selflessness" with a grotesque "selfishness," crazy purposefulness with an enticing, cold purposelessness. Starevitch conjures up a haunted, haywire world which is, at once, seemingly moral and amoral, and which contrasts fullness of spirit with emptiness of spirit. He sketches spiritual or psychic states--warm, alive; cold, dead--with uncanny exactness. The nature of the film's mysterious emotional undercurrent is suggested by the odd, oddly affecting connection between the mother's tears and the tears (in the latter part of the night-world sequence) of a ballerina-doll. (The latter weeps when serenaded by a clown-doll, whose severed head has been replaced by a potato or an onion.) If the dream characters vanish with the daylight, their effect as fantastical correlatives lingers. It doesn't really matter if the ballerina is crying over the beauty of the music, the memory of the apache-doll she seems to have lost, or the sordidness of her (literal) gutter life. What matters is, simply, that this dream-doll (which the mother created) also cries, then disappears. Real tears here summon up a fantasy world; a doll's dream-tears, conversely, evoke an emotional reality, or surreality, which, curiously, is intensified rather than dispelled by the fact that the (animated) ballerina and clown promptly fade away into the (real) shrubbery: suggestion reinforced by discretion, the poetic enriched by the prosaic.

*The MASK OF FU MANCHU 1932 AD: Cedric Gibbons. Ref: screen.
Boris Karloff at his most amusingly perverse and vicious, as that "hideous yellow monster" (heroine Karen Morley's partisan, inflammatory words) Fu Manchu. Flamboyant hokum, interrupted every other scene by delusions of "continuity." Myrna Loy as Fu Manchu's daughter is a lump, but Karloff and Morley are very much in the spirit of the thing. More horrific fun from the inexhaustible early Thirties--terribly irresponsible and all, but that seems to be the general idea here.

MASSACRE MANIA see HYPNOS

*MASTER MINDS 1949 Mkp: Jack Pierce. Ref: TV. V 1/11/50. Lee. and with Chester Clute.
Mad scientist planning "new race of supermen" uses serum from human lymphatic glands to turn ape into man; switches ape-man's brain for a better(?) one, Satch's (Huntz Hall); "Legend of Forsythe House says that it's haunted"; "haunted knight" (actually Bernard Gorcey). Miles above most Bowery Boys comedies, thanks mainly to Glenn Strange's impression (as Atlas, the monster) of Huntz Hall. He plays him as a dippy, effeminate clod, and Hall's mannerisms are amusing coming from Strange, as they rarely are from Hall himself. Thanks also, partly, to Hall's impression of Strange as a big dumb brute. Some of Leo Gorcey's malapropisms are so far-fetched that the original word is quite lost. ("Omar Khayyam's ruby" is, unhappily, retrievable.) "Miles above most Bowery Boys comedies" does not of course mean, and is not intended to mean, a whole hell of a lot.

MASTER OF LOVE (I) Chiara 1973 color 109m. (RACCONTI PROIBITI DI NULLA VESTITI) D,Co-Sp: Brunello Rondi. Ph: L. Trasatti. Mus: Stelvio Cipriani. AD: G. Ramacci. Ref: MFB'74: 183. with Rossano Brazzi, Magali Noel, Arrigo Masi, Barbara Bouchet, Tina Aumont(witch), Monica Strebel(Lady Death).

MASTER OF THE HOUNDS(by A.Budrys) see TO KILL A CLOWN

The MASTER RACE RKO/Golden 1944 96m. SP,D: Herbert J. Biberman. SP: also Anne Froelick, Rowland Leigh. Ref: Bill Warren. NYT 11/2/44. Maltin/TVM. with George Coulouris, Stanley

Ridges, Osa Massen, Carl Esmond, Nancy Gates, Morris Carnovsky, Lloyd Bridges, Gavin Muir, Paul Guilfoyle, Jason Robards.
Post-World-War-II Nazi sabotage.

The MATHEMATICIAN (B) BFI 1976 computer anim color 3m. D, P: Stan Hayward. Ref: MFB'78:35.
Mathematician discovers equation which destroys Earth.

MAUVAIS OEIL, Le see EVIL EYE,The(1937)

MAXWELL SMART AND THE NUDE BOMB see NUDE BOMB,The

MAYA MANUSHYA (India-Kannada) Sudarshan 1976 151m. SP,D: K. V.S. Kutumba Rao. Story: Susheela. Dial: Priya. Mus: Vijaya Bhaskar. Ref: Dharap. with Rajesh, Vadiraj, Sudhir, B. Radha.
Doctor's invisibility drug enables youth to take on smugglers.

MAYHEM see SCREAM,BABY,SCREAM

MAZINGER Z VS. DEVILMAN (J) Toei 1973 anim short Ref: JFFJ 13:35: giant robot.

MEAT (W.G.) Pentagramma 1979 color 108m. (FLEISCH) SP,D,P: Rainer Erler. Ph: W. Grasshof. Mus: Eugen Thomass. AD: Paul Winslow. Ref: V 12/5/79. 10/17/79:328(ad). with Jutta Speidel, Wolf Roth, Herbert Herrmann, Charlotte Kerr.
Multi-national corporation abducts young people, sells their organs to transplant organ banks.

MEAT IS MEAT see MAD BUTCHER, The

MEATCLEAVER MASSACRE,The see HOLLYWOOD MEATCLEAVER MASSACRE,The

*The MEDIUM Film Tests 1934 38m. SP: V. Sewell, from the play "L'Angoisse" by P. Mills & C. de Vylars. Remakes: The LATIN QUARTER(1945). HOUSE OF MYSTERY(1961). Ref: BFC. with Nancy O'Neil, Shayle Gardner, Barbara Gott, Ben Welden.
"Psychic model reveals that mad sculptor hid dead wife in statue."

The MEDUSA TOUCH (B-F) WB/Bulldog & Citeca/Coatesfilm 1978 color 109m. D: Jack Gold. SP: John Briley, from the novel by Peter van Greenaway. Ph: Arthur Ibbetson. Mus: Michael J. Lewis. AD: Peter Mullins. SpFX: Brian Johnson. OptFX: Doug Ferris. Mkp: Eric Allwright. Ref: MFB'78:138-9. V 2/8/78. TV. AMPAS. with Richard Burton, Lino Ventura, Lee Remick, Harry Andrews, Alan Badel, Marie-Christine Barrault, Jeremy Brett, Michael Hordern(fortune teller), Derek Jacobi, Gordon Jackson, Robert Flemyng, Jennifer Jayne, Norman Bird.
Novelist (Burton) can kill and destroy with telekinetic power; his brain-waves shake Westminster Cathedral (cf. The CREEPING UNKNOWN). Big, bland co-production. The script attempts to link accidents and natural disasters to personal

volition. Charles Bennett has done the man-with-the-power theme better (esp. in CURSE OF THE DEMON), and the script also taps, weakly, DONOVAN'S BRAIN and The OMEN (family-as-obstacle to "special" child). The climactic sequence, however, quirkily and suspensefully ties falling plaster to EEG squiggles, as the brain of Burton imitates the brawn of Samson.

MEINE WELT IN BILDERN(by E.von Daniken) see MYSTERIES OF THE GODS

MEKAGOJIRA NO GYAKUSHU see TERROR OF MECHAGODZILLA

MELANCOLICAS, Las see EXORCISM'S DAUGHTER

MEN OF ACTION MEET WOMEN OF DRACULA (Fili) Villanueva 1969 D: Artemio Marquez. Mus: Britz. SpFX: T. Torrente. Ref: Lee. with Dante Varona, Eddie Torrente, Norman Henson.
Dracula, vampire women.

*MESA OF LOST WOMEN (AA-TV) 1952 Dial D: Orville Hampton. Narr: Lyle Talbot. Ref: TV. TVFFSB. LC. and with Fred Kelsey, Chris-Pin Martin, Tandra Quinn(Tarantella).
Delectably awful sf-horror. So bad it <u>can't</u> have been an accident, or so you tell yourself as the narrator intones, "I admit I felt a little uneasy when my driver turned into the Muerto Desert." Or, later, as he exclaims (of Jackie Coogan's mad scientist), "Dr. Aranya!" and the hero clarifies: "That's Spanish for spider!" At one point, the hero actually <u>says</u> "I want a girl who's <u>sincere</u>, real. Someone who'll stick by me when the chips are down." At another point, the heroine actually <u>says</u> "I looked up and saw some women and <u>little men</u>. It was unreal." <u>That's</u> the word. Unfortunately unforgettable guitar-and-piano score.

MESSAGE FROM SPACE (J) UA/Toei-Tohokushinsha 1978 color 105m. (UCHU KARA NO MESSEEJI) Story,D: Kinji Fukasaku. Story,SP: H. Matsuda. Ph: T. Nakajima. Mus: K. Morioka. AD: Tetsuzo Osawa. SpFxD: Nobuo Yajim. SpPhFX: Minoru Nakano. Ref: V 5/9/79:381. 11/1/78. AMPAS. with Vic Morrow, Sonny Chiba, Philip Casnoff, Peggy Lee Brennan, Tetsuro Tamba.
Robot, spaceships, "bizarre creatures." (V)

MESSAGE FROM SPACE: GALACTIC BATTLE (J) Toei 1978 21m. (UCHUKARA NO MESSEEJI--GINGA TAISEN) D: M. Yamada. Ref: JFFJ 13:34: based on TV series (adapted from MESSAGE FROM SPACE).

MESSE NERE DELLA CONTESSA DRACULA see WEREWOLF VS.THE VAMPIRE WOMAN

MESSIAH OF EVIL Int'l.Cinefilm/VM 1975(1972?) color/scope 90m. (The SECOND COMING-orig t. REVENGE OF THE SCREAMING DEAD. RETURN OF THE LIVING DEAD-re-r ts. DEAD PEOPLE-'81 Bedford Ent. re-r t) SP,D,P: Willard Huyck, Gloria Katz. Ph: Stephen

Katz. Mus: Phillan Bishop. AD: Jack Fiske, Joan Mocine. Ref: V 10/11/78. 4/30/75: "cannibalistic zombies." 9/23/81:26. Willis/SW. with Michael Greer, Marianna Hill, Joy Bang, Anitra Ford, Royal Dano, Elisha Cook Jr.

METAMORFOSIS (Sp) Filmscontacto 1971 color 90m. SP,D: Jacinto Esteva. SP: also J.M. Nunes. Mus: Carlos Maleras. Ref: Lee(SpCinema).
Scientists turn imperfect being into perfect one.

METAMORPHOSES(by Ovid) see WINDS OF CHANGE

METEOR AI/Arkoff 1979 color/scope 103m. D: Ronald Neame. SP: Stanley Mann, Edmund H. North. Ph: Paul Lohmann. Mus: Laurence Rosenthal. PD: Edward Carfagno. VisFX:(sup) Margo Anderson; William Cruse;(ed) Martin Jay Sadoff. SpFX:(sup) Robert Staples, Glen Robinson; Jim Doyle et al. ElecFX: Craig Hundley. Ref: TV. MFB'80:9. V 10/17/79. with Sean Connery, Natalie Wood, Karl Malden, Brian Keith, Martin Landau, Trevor Howard, Richard Dysart, Henry Fonda, Joseph Campanella, Clyde Kusatsu, Sybil Danning, Stu Nahan, Clete Roberts, James Bacon, G. Gay.
A comet strikes the Asteroid Belt, setting a large meteor, Orpheus,and fragments of it on a collision course with Earth. The U.S. and U.S.S.R. re-direct their orbiting nuclear weapons in an attempt to intercept and destroy Orpheus in space. Laughably thin effects-vehicle. The writers lose the war <u>and</u> the battles; they interest one in neither the fate of the whole planet <u>nor</u> individual earthlings. The movie is in effect a misguided "A" hommage to sf-disaster "B"'s of the Fifties like EARTH VS.THE FLYING SAUCERS--the line "Do you want to go out there and meet it with <u>sling shots</u> and <u>BB guns</u>?" in particular has a very familiar ring to it.

MEZHPLANETNAYA REVOLUTSIYA see INTERPLANETARY REVOLUTION

MICKEY THE GORILLA TAMER see PET STORE, The

MICROWAVE MASSACRE Reel Life 1979 D: Wayne Berwick. SP: Thomas Singer. Ref: V 11/22/78:28. Bill Warren. with Jackie Vernon, Loren Schein, Al Troupe, Claire Ginsberg, Sarah Alt.

MIDARE KARAKURI (J) Toho 1979 D: Susumu Kodama. Ref: JFFJ 13:33. with Yasuku Masuda, Hirako Shiro.
"Cursed doll" may be killer.

MIDDLE TOE OF THE RIGHT FOOT(by A.Bierce) see RETURN, The

MIDNIGHT Indep.-Int'l. 1980? SP,D: John Russo, from his novel. Ref: Boxo 4/7/80:11(ad). V 11/19/80:31: "horror pic."

A MIDNIGHT EPISODE (F) Star 1899 1m. (Un BON LIT) D: Georges Melies. Ref: Lee: giant bugs.

*MIDNIGHT MENACE (Eros-TV) 1937('39-U.S.) (BOMBS OVER LONDON-U.S.) SP: also D.B.Wyndham Lewis. Ref: FDY.and with L.Hanray.

MIDNIGHT OFFERINGS ABC-TV/Stephen J.Cannell 1981 color 95m. D: Rod Holcomb. SP: Juanita Bartlett. Ph: Hector Figueroa. Mus: Walter Scharf. AD: A.D. Jefferies Sr. SpFX: John Coles. Mkp: Jack Obringer. SdFX: Jack May. Ref: TV. TVG. with Melissa Sue Anderson(bad witch), Mary McDonough(good witch), Cathryn Damon, Patrick Cassidy, Gordon Jump, Marion Ross.
Two students--both 7th-daughters-of-7th-daughters majoring in witchcraft (heavy course-load of rituals)--conduct an occult duel. A few cute tricks, a few dumb lines ("Good and evil--that's the classic struggle." "What did we learn from John Wayne?--good guys have limits."), and you've got another 7th-daughter-of-the-7th-daughter-of-The EXORCIST.

The MIDNIGHT PARASITES (J) 1973? anim D: Yoji Kuri. Ref: IFG'74:534: "Bosch's monsters."

The MIDNIGHT SUMMONS (B) 1924 22m. See also: Further Mysteries of Dr. Fu-Manchu series. Ref: BFC.

MIGHTY MOUSE IN THE JAIL BREAK see JAILBREAK, The

The MIGHTY PEKING MAN (H.K.-Cant.) Shaw 1977 color 100m. D: Ho Meng-hua. Ph: Tsao Hui-chi, Wu Cho-hua. Ref: IFG'78:178 (ad). V 8/31/77: "high camp." 2/2/77:32: sfa The RETURN OF KING KONG? with Evelyne Kraft, Li Hsiu-hsien, H. Yao, K. Feng.
Gigantic apeman of the Himalayas taken to Hong Kong.

MIJN NACHTEN MET SUSAN OLGA ALBERT JULIE PIET & SANDRA (Dutch) Scorpio 1975 color/scope 100m. SP,D: Pim de la Parra. SP: also Harry Kumel et al. Ph: M. Felperlaan. Mus: E. Lutyens. Ref: MFB'77:263: "sex-cum-horror." V 5/21/75. with Willeke Van Ammelrooy, Nelly Frijda.
"Secret dark room"; "mad man"; "crazy woman lurking." (V)

MILAP (India-Hindi) Nitin 1972 color 124m. Story,D: B.R. Ishara. Ref: Dharap.
Spell; curse; man who takes the form of a snake.

MILITARY SECRET (Russ) Artkino/Soyuzdet 1945 73m. D: Vladimir Legoshin. SP: Leonid & Peter Tur, Leo Sheynin. Ph: Sergei Uruseysky. Mus: Konstantin Korchmarev. Ref: V 8/8/45: inventor; "secret weapon." with Sergei Lukianov, Ivan Malishevsky.

The MILPITAS MONSTER Ayer 1976 color 78m. Story,D,P,Ed: Robert L. Burrill. SP:David Boston. Story: also David Kottas. Ph: Marilyn Odello et al. Mus: Robert R. Berry Jr. AD & Sp FX: Duane D. Walz. Anim: Stephen C. Wathen. Narr: Tennessee Ernie Ford. Ref: CineFan 2:10-14. with Doug Hagdohl, Walz, Joseph House, Priscilla House, Bob Wilkins.
Monster spawned by pollution preys on garbage.

The MIND SNATCHERS (AI-TV)/Cinerama/IFV 1972 color 94m. D: Bernard Girard. SP: Ron Whyte, from Dennis Reardon's play "The Happiness Cage." Ph: Manny Wynn. Mus: Phil Ramone. AD: William Molyneux. SdFX: Ross-Gaffney. Ref: V 7/12/72. Lee.

VV 8/10/72. with Christopher Walken, Joss Ackland, Ralph Meeker, Ronny Cox.

Army scientists install electrodes in people, stimulate their pleasure centers.

MINDSWEEPERS, The see CLONES, The

MINDWARP see PLANET OF HORRORS

MIRACLES OF THE GODS see MYSTERIES OF THE GODS

MIRAI SHONEN KONAN (J) Nippon Anim 1977 anim color 29m. D, Des,Mus: H. Miyazaki. Ref: Zagreb 78 cat.: World War III.

The MIRROR AND MARKHEIM (B) Motley 1954 28m. SP,D: John Lamont, from Robert Louis Stevenson's story, "Markheim." Narr: Marius Goring. Ref: BFC. with Philip Saville, Arthur Lowe, Christopher Lee(visitant), Lloyd Lamble.

"Mirror figure shows man what would happen if he stabbed antique dealer."

MISS GOLEM (Cz) 197-? Ref: V 7/31/74:24. with Jana Bolotava.

"Satire-tinged tale of a female Frankenstein."

MISS LESLIE'S DOLLS World-Wide 1972 color 88m. SP,D: Joseph G. Prieto. SP: also R.J. Remy. Ph: G. Sandor. Mus: Imer Leaf. AD: Jerry Remy. Ref: MFB'73:128. V 5/17/72:26(rated). with Salvador Ugarte, Terry Juston, Kitty Lewis, C.W. Pitts.

Transvestite's spirit enters unconscious woman's body; his "dolls" are embalmed corpses.

MISS MORRISON'S GHOSTS (B) ITV/Anglia-TV 1981 100m. D: John Bruce. SP: Ian Curteis. Ref: V 9/9/81:72. with Wendy Hiller, Hannah Gordon, Bosco Hogan, Vivian Pickles.

"'Ghost story' values"; Oxford faculty women report seeing ghost of Marie Antoinette.

*MISS PINKERTON (UA-TV) 1932 (67m.) Mus D: Leo F. Forbstein. AD: Jack Okey. Ref: screen. TVFFSB. and with Lyle Talbot?

Sinister crookbacked butler; screams; skulking; odd-angle shots; opening shot: huge shadow falling across facade of old house; dial. ref. to Frankenstein. This thunderstorm mystery is much slower than the remake, The NURSE'S SECRET. The actors seem bored, there's no musical or editing elan, and Lee Patrick is snappier (as a Joan Blondell-type) in the remake than Blondell is in the original. Limp doses of "atmosphere," comedy, human interest.

*The MISSING GUEST 1938 Mus D: Charles Previn. AD: Jack Otterson. Ref: TV. Lee.

Masquerade party in "haunted" house; pianos and organs "played" by the wind. Bad but pleasant. Lighter than the first version of the story (SECRET OF THE BLUE ROOM); less mechanical than the third (MURDER IN THE BLUE ROOM). And substantially rewritten from the first, if not really much improved. Some passable puns in the dialogue, and a nice subjective-camera trick with a "ghost" crashing the party.

The MISSING JUROR Col 1944 63m. D: Budd Boetticher. SP: Charles O'Neal. Story: L. Abrams, R.H. Wilkinson. Ph: L.W. O'Connell. Mus D: Bakaleinikoff. Ref: LC. V 12/20/44. with Jim Bannon, Janis Carter, George Macready, Joseph Crehan, Mike Mazurki, Carole Mathews, Cliff Clark, Edmund Cobb.
"A phantom killer...has murdered six members of a jury that once wrongly convicted a man of murder." (V)

The MISSING LINK (F-Belg) Pils & SND 1980 anim color 95m. D,Des,Story: Picha. SP: Tony Hendra. Story: also P. Bartier, J. Collette. Mus D: Roy Budd. Ref: V 5/14/80.
Prehistory. "Missing link," brontosaurus, pterodactyl, dragon, Amazons; parodies of JAWS, STAR WARS, 2001, etc.

MISSION GALACTICA see BATTLESTAR GALACTICA: THE LIVING LEGEND

MR. JEKYLL JR. see DR. JEKYLL JR.

MR. MACKINLEY'S FLIGHT (Russ) Mosfilm 1977 color 100m. D: Mikhail Schveitzer. SP: Leonid Leonov. Mus: I. Schvartz. Ref: PFA(Trieste pr). with Donatas Banionis, G. Bolotova.
Man preserved by new gas awakens in year 2225.

**MR. MOTO TAKES A VACATION see MUMMY'S HAND,The(note)

MR. TVARDOVSKI (Russ) 1916 (PAN TVARDOVSKIJ) D,Ph: Ladislas Starevitch. From I.J. Kraszevski's story. Ref: Lee. Filmlexicon. with N. Saltikoff, S. Tchapelski.
Deal with the Devil.

*MR. WONG, DETECTIVE (UA-TV) 1938 Ph: Harry Neuman(n). AD: E.R. Hickson. Ref: TV. TVFFSB. V 11/23/38.
Solution to murder (i.e., the how): police-car sirens shattered poison-gas-filled glass balls. Boris Karloff as Mr. Wong is flavorless at best, embarrassing at worst, as he tries to match "comic" wits with Grant Withers' ever-exasperated Captain Street. Try Mr. Moto instead.

MISTERIO SE VISTE DE FRAC see FANTASMA DE MEDIANOCHE

MISTRESS OF THE APES Cineworld 1979 color 84m. SP,D: Larry Buchanan. Ph: Nicholas Josef von Sternberg. Mus: The Missing Link. Mkp: Greg Cannom;(asst) Rob Bottin. Ref: MFB'80:9. V 5/17/78:184(ad). with Jenny Neumann, Garth Pillsbury, Paula Sills, Barbara Leigh, Walt Robin.
Safari discovers tribe of ape-men (missing links?) in the Congo.

*The MODERN BLUEBEARD 1946 100m. Ref: TV.
This Mexican comedy is far from good, but it does feature

haunting traces of Buster Keaton's comic genius. In fact the first half is, in effect, a Keaton silent--his "sketches" alternate with plot-and-dialogue sequences. (In the latter half he himself becomes embroiled in the plot.) In one bit, he pantomimes "Charge!" as he mounts a horse, upon which command it proceeds to saunter off. (A deadpan horse?!) No miracle, but certainly preferable to something like GOD'S COUNTRY (of the same year), in which Keaton does a putting-up-the-tent routine while another actor watches him, and the camera is on the other actor!

MODERN INVENTIONS Disney 1937 anim color 9m. D: Jack King. Ref: screen. Lee. LC. Maltin/OMAM.
Donald Duck cartoon featuring robot-butler and automated barber-chair and baby-tender. Prime vintage Disney.

MOINE, Le see MONK, The

MOLCHANIYE DOKTORA IVENSA (Russ) Mosfilm 1974 (SILENCE OF DR. IVENS-tr t) SP,D: Budimir Metalnikov. Ph: Sokol, Bondarev. Ref: IFG'74:352. with Sergei Bondarchuk, Z. Bolotova(alien).
Three aliens land on Earth.

MOLECULA EN ORBITA (Sp) Cruz Delgado 1970 anim color 8m. Ref: Lee: aliens, monsters.

Las MOMIAS DE GUANAJUATO (Mex) 1972 Ref: Glut/CMM: mummies return to life. with "Santo," "Blue Demon," "M. Mascaras."
Sequels: El CASTILLO DE LAS MOMIAS DE GUANAJATO. El ROBO DE LAS MOMIAS DE GUANAJATO.

MONACHE DI SANT'ARCHANGELO see SISTERS OF SATAN

MONDO KEY or MONDO KEYHOLE see WORST CRIME OF ALL,The!

MONIHARA see THREE DAUGHTERS

MONISMANIEN 1995 (Swed) Fant/SR-2 1975 color 93m. SP,D,P: Kenne Fant. Ph: Sven Nykvist. Mus: Berlioz. Ref: V 8/20/75: "futuristic nightmare." with Erland Josephson, Ingrid Thulin.

The MONK (F-I-W.G.) Maya-Comacico-IP-Peri/Tritone/Studio 1973 color 92m. (Le MOINE) D: Ado Kyrou. SP: Luis Bunuel, Jean-Claude Carriere, from "Monk" Lewis's novel. Ph: Sacha Vierny. Mus: Piero Piccione; Ennio Morricone? AD: Max Douy. Ref: MFB'74:132. V 7/11/73. Lee. with Franco Nero, Nathalie Delon, Nicol Williamson, Nadja Tiller, Maria Machado.
Pact with the Devil; hallucinations; violence.

*The MONSTER (Gold Key-TV) 1925 Ref: screen. MFB'81:81. TVFFSB.
Mad doctor (Lon Chaney) and trance-bound assistant attempt to transfer man's soul into woman. A few fine, but too-brief high-comic scenes, with Chaney parodying all horror-movie doctors ("You dare call me mad!?") who came before and after:

he goes through several alarming facial contortions, catches himself, then suffers a few residual tics. Most of the movie, however, is limp "comedy" with the hero (Johnny Arthur), punctuated by a few "thrills."

MONSTER see HUMANOIDS FROM THE DEEP. MONSTROID

MONSTER,The or MONSTER AND THE LADY,The see LADY AND THE MONSTER

The MONSTER CLUB (B) ITC/Sword & Sorcery(Chips) 1981 color 97m. D: Roy Ward Baker. SP: Edward & Valerie Abraham, from the story collection by Ronald Chetwynd-Hayes. Ph: Peter Jessop. Mus: Douglas Gamley, John Giorgiadis;(elec) Alan Hawkshaw. AD: Tony Curtis. Mkp: Roy Ashton, E. Gasser. Ref: V 5/27/81. MFB'81:94. with Vincent Price & Donald Pleasence (vampires), John Carradine(Hayes), Stuart Whitman, Richard Johnson, Britt Ekland, Simon Ward, Patrick Magee, Anthony Steel.

Three stories, involving "the shadmock, a species endowed with a lethal whistle," vampires, and "the hungoo (the off-spring of a human and a ghoul)." (MFB)

MONSTER DOG, The see PET, The

MONSTER FROM AN UNKNOWN PLANET see GAPPA

MONSTER ISLAND (Sp-U.S.) Almena & Fort 1980 color/Dinavision 100m. (JULES VERNE'S MYSTERY ON MONSTER ISLAND-ad t. aka MYSTERY ON MONSTER ISLAND?) SP,D,P: J. Piquer Simon. SP: also J. Grau, R. Gantman. Ph: Andres Berenguer. Mus: A. Agullo(sp?). AD: G. Andres. VisFX: Emilio Ruiz. Ref: V 10/15/80:291(ad). 12/3/80:36. 5/13/81:108. 4/22/81. with Peter Cushing, Terence Stamp, Blanca Estrada, Frank Brana, Paul Naschy, Ian Serra, Gerard Tichy.

Volcanic island of (fake) monsters.

*The MONSTER MAKER 1944 Mkp: Maurice Siederman. Ref: TV. Jim Shapiro. V 5/17/44.

PRC (not necessarily to be congratulated) latched on to a truly disgusting idea here: acromegaly-as-a-weapon. (The scene in which the girl discovers her deformed father is a gem of its kind.) The scientist's acromegalic wife and the heroine's father are the "monsters," but the witless script leaves this in-family irony undeveloped. For your "snappy comebacks" file: J. Carrol Naish (responding to the line, "The dead have no place among the living"): "I'll be the judge of that." The odd, plaintive musical score was Albert Glasser's first.

MONSTER OF CEREMONIES Univ/Lantz 1966 anim 7m. D: Paul J. Smith. Ref: Maltin/OMAM. no LC. Glut/TFL.

Mad doctor turns Woody Woodpecker into Frankenstein-like monster.

MONSTER OF THE MARSHES see BRIDE OF THE MONSTER

*The MONSTER STRIKES 1959 Ref: V 8/25/76:24: sfa ZARKOFF--HALF MAN, HALF BEAST(D:CHS;Dimension;Wells story)?

*The MONSTER THAT CHALLENGED THE WORLD 1957 SpFX: August Lohman;(des) E.S. Haworth;(ph) Robert Crandall. Mkp: Abe Haberman. Ref: TV. and with Barbara Darrow.

Giant prehistoric snails drain victims of blood and water. Undistinguished monsters and movie. Clogged with mawkish "human interest." The voracious snails in the filmstrip-within-the-film are more fearsome than the actual monsters, which look rather innocuous (even if they do drool).

MONSTER (THE LEGEND THAT BECAME A TERROR) see MONSTROID

*The MONSTER WALKS 1932 Mus D: Lee Zahler. AD: Ben Dore. Sets: Ralph Black. Ref: screen. Turner/Price.

A long series of awkward dialogue-sequences, enlivened only by the "killer" chimp Yogi's periodic screeches, and by the climax, in which Mischa Auer, strangled by Yogi, dies cross-eyed. Deadly ape; deadly film.

MONSTERS see HUMANOIDS FROM THE DEEP

MONSTER'S CASTLE, The see LADY AND THE MONSTER, The

MONSTERS FROM AN UNKNOWN PLANET see TERROR OF MECHAGODZILLA

MONSTERS INVADE EXPO '70 see GAMERA VS. JIGER

MONSTERS OF DR.FRANKENSTEIN see FRANKENSTEIN'S CASTLE OF FREAKS

MONSTROID M&M/AID 1980(1976) color (MONSTER (THE LEGEND THAT BECAME A TERROR)-orig t) SP,D: Herbert L. Strock. SP: also W.R. Schmidt, G. Scott. Story,P: Ken Hartford. From the novel by Peter Crowcroft. Ph: J.W. Mincey. SpFX: David Hewitt. Ref: V 10/17/79:6. 5/9/79:219(ad). 10/11/78:47(ad). 10/22/75:45(ad): gigantic, clawed monster? 5/30/79:42: sfa Die BESTIEN? 8/27/80:24(rated). F.O.Ray. with Jim Mitchum, John Carradine, Keenan Wynn, Diane McBain, Anthony Eisley, Aldo Sanbrell.

El MONSTRUO (Sp) Castillo 1971 anim color 9m. D: Amaro Carretero. Ref: Lee: monster-lizard.

MONTAGNA DEL DIO CANNIBALE see PRISONER OF THE CANNIBAL GOD

MONTE DE LAS BRUJAS see WITCHES MOUNTAIN

MONTY PYTHON AND THE HOLY GRAIL (B) Cinema 5/EMI-Python-White 1975 color 86m. SP,D & with: Terry Gilliam, Terry Jones. SP & with: also Graham Chapman, John Cleese, Eric Idle, Michael Palin. Ph: Terry Bedford. Mus: Neil Innes, De Wolfe. PD: Roy Smith. SpFX: John Horton. SpPhFX: Julian Doyle. Anim: Gilliam. Ref: TV. V 3/19/75. MFB'75:84. Meyers. and with John Young, Innes, Bee Duffell.

Black Beast of Aaaargh ("cartoon peril"); vicious, springing rabbit ("That rabbit's dynamite!"); fireball-flinging sorcerer; gore; monster-claw turning pages of Story of the Film. Spectacle! Adventure! Romance! (All deftly deflated.) Episodic, but more-consistently-funny than the TV Pythons. It isn't far at all here from the sublime (chivalry, knights, Arthur) to the ridiculous (e.g., a discussion of the migratory patterns of coconuts). Often, the mere turn of a phrase is all it takes: e.g., the won't-admit-defeat Black Knight, plopped upright on the ground like an urn, after King Arthur has hacked off his limbs: "Let's call it a draw." Or: Arthur's right-hand man, confronted with a note attached to an arrow sticking out of his own chest: "Message for you, Sir." The phrase "British understatement" comes to mind, but doesn't quite do justice to the sense of disproportion here between action and diction, which seems both very British and a bit surreal.

The MOON MASK RIDER (J) Nippon Herald 1981 SP,D: Yukihiro Sawada. SP,Mus,Exec P: Kohan Kawauchi, from his novel. Ref: V 5/13/81:103(ad). JFFJ 13:30: based on Toei's Gekko Kamen, alien super-hero.

MOON OF THE GHOST see LENG-YUEH LI-HUN

MOON OF THE WOLF ABC-TV/Filmways-TV 1972 color 75m. D: Daniel Petrie. SP: Alvin Sapinsley, from the novel by Leslie H. Whitten. Ph: Richard C. Glouner. Mus: Bernardo Segall. AD: James Hulsey. Mkp: Tom & William Tuttle. Opt: Cinefx. Ref: TV. Janet Willis. Lee. with David Janssen, Barbara Rush, Bradford Dillman(werewolf), John Beradino, Royal Dano, John Chandler, Geoffrey Lewis, George Sawaya.

A strange old man possesses the secret of the "loukerouk" that's at large in the Louisiana bayous; it proves to be Andrew Rodanthe, a victim of Lycanthropy veritam, a strain of lycanthropy only-temporarily-controllable by drugs. Routine TV horror simplifies what seems to be a rather more intricate work on contemporary werewolves. Lycanthropy here is a sort of ultimate decadence. (See also TWINS OF EVIL and its hedonistic vampirism.) Some nice down-South atmosphere, broken up by lines like "Andrew Rodanthe is out there and he's turnin' into a wolf!"

MOONCHILD (Bloom-TV)/Filmakers Ltd/American Films 1972(1974) color 90m. SP,D: Alan Gadney. Ph: E. Alston. Mus: Pat Williams, Bill Byers. AD: R. Tamburino. Mkp: Jane Alexander. Ref: Lee. TVFFSB. CineFan 2:30. Cinef Spr'72:6-7. Willis/SW. V 2/27/74:7(rated). with Victor Buono, John Carradine, Janet Landgard, Pat Renella, Mark Travis, William Challee.

Deformed reincarnate repeats life cycle every 25 years.

MOONRAKER (B-F) UA/Eon-LPAA 1979 color/scope 126m. D: Lewis Gilbert. SP: Christopher Wood, from Ian Fleming's novel. Ph:

Jean Tournier. Mus: John Barry. PD: Ken Adam;(space) Harry Lange. VisFxSup: Derek Meddings;(ph) Paul Wilson. SpFX: John Evans, John Richardson et al. Ref: MFB'79:179-180. screen. V 6/27/79. with Roger Moore(James Bond), Lois Chiles, Michael Lonsdale, Richard Kiel("Jaws"), Corinne Clery, Geoffrey Keene, Lois Maxwell, Bernard Lee, Alfie Bass, Brian Keith.

Billionaire Hugo Drax plots to destroy life on Earth with "space bombs"; starts his own "colony" in space. Fun last-half-hour of outer-space thrills. And parts of the set-pieces and stunts (e.g., the parachute sequence, the cable-car tussle, the space battle) are amusing. But most of the jokes (verbal and visual) fizzle, and the movie seems mainly to be James Bond wandering about from one city to another, in a never-ending search for new backdrops to old gags.

MORE THAN SISTERS 1980 color 84m. SP: "Lars Tobin." Ref: J. Shapiro: telepathy; nightmare seqs.,; Herrmann music from PSYCHO, VERTIGO, SISTERS. with Jamie Gillis.

MORE WILD WILD WEST CBS-TV/Jacks 1980 color 94m. D: Burt Kennedy. SP: William Bowers, Tony Kayden. Based on "The Wild Wild West" TV series. Ph: C. Arnold. Mus: Jeff Alexander. AD: Albert Heschong. Ref: TV. TVG. with Robert Conrad, Ross Martin, Jonathan Winters, Avery Schreiber, Joyce Brothers.

Madman's plot to rule the world; several invisible men.

MORT EN DIRECT see DEATHWATCH

MORTE IN VACANZA(by A.Casella) see DEATH TAKES A HOLIDAY

MORTE NEGLI OCCHI DEL GATTO see SEVEN DEAD IN THE CAT'S EYES

MOSAIC-FRANKENSTEIN 1980 or MOSAIQUE-FRANKENSTEIN 1980 see FRANKENSTEIN 1980

MOSCOW CASSIOPEA see CASSIOPEA

MOSQUITO DER SCHANDER see BLOODLUST(1976)

MOST DANGEROUS GAME,The(by R.Connell) see SEVEN WOMEN FOR SATAN

MOSTRO E IN TAVOLA see ANDY WARHOL'S FRANKENSTEIN

MOTEL HELL UA/Camp Hill 1980 color 106m. D: Kevin Connor. SP,P: Robert & Steven-Charles Jaffe. Ph: T. Del Ruth. Mus: Lance Rubin. AD: J.M. Altadonna. SpFX: Adams R. Calvert. SpSdFX: Craig Hundley. Mkp: Marie Carter. Ref: V 10/22/80: chainsaw duel. TV. MFB'81:74. with Rory Calhoun, Paul Linke, Nancy Parsons, Nina Axelrod, Wolfman Jack, Dick Curtis.

Combination motel-meat-packing-plant (a la Sweeney Todd); clips from MONSTER THAT CHALLENGED THE WORLD. Scrappy, occasionally amusing light-hearted Grand Guignol, along the lines of The HILLS HAVE EYES. Farmer Vincent's (Calhoun) operation is (as he puts it) "creative"--he detours cars with herds of cardboard cows, and plants his "stock" in a well-tended garden. The mixture of the hokey and the macabre is sometimes taking; but neither the humor nor the horror of the story is escalating.

MOTHER'S DAY UFDC 1980 color 98m. SP,D: Charles Kaufman. SP: also Warren D. Leight. Ph: Joe Mangine. Mus: Phil Gallo, Clem Vicari. Ref: V 9/24/80. with Nancy Hendrickson, Deborah Luce, Tiana Pierce, Holden McGuire.
Retarded brothers play gory "games" with trio of ex-coeds.

MOTOR MANIA RKO/Disney 1950 anim color 9m. D: Jack Kinney. Ref: TV. J.Shapiro. LC. Maltin/OMAM.
Goofy as Mr. Walker (mild-mannered pedestrian) and alter ego Mr. Wheeler (maniacal motorist), a la "Dr. Jekyll and Mr. Hyde." (And he makes a convincing Jekyll _and_ Hyde.)

The MOUNTAIN BRINGS FORTH (F) SGdP 1973? anim short? D: J. Colombat. Ref: IFG'74:532.
Female astronauts land on a planet of "voracious creatures."

MOVINI'S VENOM see NIGHT OF THE COBRA WOMAN

MRIG TRISHNA (India-Hindi) Naheta 1975 color 134m. SP,D: R. Shukla. SP: also T. Faruquie. Mus: S. Sen. Ref: Dharap. with Yogita Bali, Rakesh, Jalal Agha.
"Weird illusions"; "strange adventure"; evil spirits.

MS. 45 Rochelle/Navaron 1981 color 84m. D: Abel Ferrara. SP: Nicholas St. John. Ph: James Momel. Mus: Joe Delia. Ref: V 5/6/81. with Zoe Tamerlis, Steve Singer, Jack Thibeau.
Revenge-for-rape story with "'gross' elements."

MUCH ADO ABOUT MURDER see THEATER OF BLOOD

Los MUCHACHOS DE ANTES NO USABAN ARSENICO (Arg) 1974 D: Jose M. Suarez. Ref: V 9/10/75:32: "horror comedy." with Narciso Ibanez Menta, Barbara Mujica, Marie Soffici, Mecha Ortiz.

MUJER MURCIELAGO see BATWOMAN

Las MUJERES PANTERAS (Mex) Azteca/Calderon 1967? D: Rene Cardona. SP: Alfredo Salazar. Ref: Lee. with Ariadne Welter, Elizabeth Campbell, Eric del Castillo, "Loco" Valdes.
Goddess of evil gives women power and features of panthers to battle the wrestling women.

MULHER DO DESEJO see WOMAN OF DESIRE

MUMIA KOZBESZOL,A see MUMMY INTERFERES,The

MUMMIES, and Egyptology see the following titles, and ATTACK OF THE PHANTOMS. AWAKENING,The. BETTY BOOP'S MUSEUM. BORN OF THE WIND. CAT CREATURE,The. CRUISE INTO TERROR. CURSE OF BIGFOOT. CURSE OF KING TUT'S TOMB. CURSE OF THE MUMMY. DAWN

OF THE MUMMY. DEATH:THE ULTIMATE MYSTERY. DEMONOID. DIDDLED! GHOSTS THAT STILL WALK. KID MILLIONS(P). KING TUT'S TOMB. LIPS OF BLOOD. LIVE MUMMY,The. titles under MOMIAS DE GUANAJATO. MUNSTERS' REVENGE,The. PEPITO Y CHABELO.... PERILS OF PORK PIE. PHARAOH'S CURSE. SANTO EN LA VENGANZA DE LA MOMIA. SATURDAY THE 14TH. SON OF DRACULA(1974). STORY OF TUTANKHAMUN. TANGO THROUGH GERMANY. TUT-TUT AND HIS TERRIBLE TOMB. YSANI THE PRIESTESS.

The MUMMY (B) Pathe-Britannia 1912 9m. D: A.E. Coleby? Ref: BFC.

"Man poses as revived mummy to fool sweetheart's father."

*The MUMMY 1932 (CAGLIOSTRO-orig t. IM-HO-TEP. The KING OF THE DEAD-int ts) AD: Willy Pogany. SpFX: John P. Fulton. Ref: TV. Lee. Glut/CMM.

Best scenes: the synecdochic Imhotep-to-life sequence (shots of the mummy's hand, the trailing bandages), and the flashback to ancient Egypt, where the love of Imhotep (Boris Karloff)--"the name of a man unspoken since before the siege of Troy"--and Ankhesenamon (Zita Johann) began. Admirable in its single-minded, hyper-romantic way, the original MUMMY is finally just too serious for its own good. It veers in tone from the genuinely romantic (the flashback, the crane shot up over the magic pool which introduces it) to the gooey (the Johann-David Manners scenes). There's no comic edge to Karloff's Imhotep/Ardath Bey (as there is, say, to his Fu Manchu of the same year), though such forbidding solemnity soon enough becomes (unintentionally) comical. (Karloff's eyes even, at one point, literally light up for Johann.) And the characters are given to sudden, dire-sounding exclamations--Manners' "The white cat--Bast!--the goddess of evil sendings!" is my personal favorite.

See also: The MUMMY(1959). FADE TO BLACK.

*The MUMMY 1959 88m. Ref: BFC: based on the screenplays for The MUMMY(1932) & The MUMMY'S TOMB(1942). TV. Lee. and with George Pastell, Michael Ripper, Harold Goodwin.

A hash of scenes from old Universal mummy movies (the above-named included), "updated" with more graphic violence. Static cloud formations and flora and poor sound recording and lighting make outdoor scenes seem indoor.

**The MUMMY INTERFERES (Hung.) Mafilm 1967 90m. (A MUMIA KOZBESZOL) SP,D: Gabor Olah. Ph: I. Lakatos. AD: T. Vayer. Ref: WorldF'67. with Janos Koltai(mummy), Laszlo Mensaros (dead prince), Tamas Major(Pharaoh), Eva Ruttkai, I. Avar.

*The MUMMY'S CURSE 1944 Mus & Lyrics: Oliver Drake, Frank Orth. Mkp: Jack Pierce. SpFxPh: John P. Fulton. Ref: TV. Lee. V 12/20/44. and with Dennis Moore.

One of the more interesting entries in one of Universal's less interesting series. Some of the scenes with the solar-rejuvenated mummy Ananka (Virginia Christine) have an almost surreal tinge--they evoke her yearning for life far more flavorfully than comparable scenes in DRACULA'S DAUGHTER evoke Countess Zaleska's life-wish. (For one thing they depend not on dialogue, but simply on the image of the sun.) Eerie I WALKED WITH A ZOMBIE-like shot: Ananka's white-draped figure as she runs through the woods at night. And the mummy's murders are always shown as shadow play--art or tic? (Sunlight and life vs. darkness and death?) The rest of the news, however, is bad. The Louisiana characters and settings are aggressively "colorful"; most of the actors are "B"-minus, and the dialogue runs to inanities like "Always she walk like she's asleep--swamp plenty bad for people like that." My favorite here, however: "Goobie"'s artfully varied,hyperbolic: "The Devil's on the loose and he's dancing with the mummy" and, later, "The mummy's on the loose and he's dancing with the Devil."

*The MUMMY'S GHOST 1944 (The MUMMY'S RETURN-orig t) Ref: TV. Glut/CMM. V 7/5/44. 3/31/43:46.

Like The MUMMY'S CURSE, his GHOST features a couple of surprising sequences--the mummified Princess Ananka's wrappings crumbling at the touch of Kharis (Lon Chaney Jr.), who then tears up the museum. (Her soul has vacated and entered Amina Mansori (Ramsay Ames).) Later: Amina withering away as Kharis carries her into the swamp. (Shots here of her aging arm/feet/face.) Ramsay Ames, however, is a less interesting actress than Virginia Christine--Ms. Ames' expressed pain hardly seems mystical. And Robert Lowery is a surly lump as the hero. (Hallowe'en-party-game question: is the latter's last glimpse of Amina's hag-face a stroke of cruel or kind fate?) Chaney gets what he (at best) deserves: sixth billing in the credits....What you're likely to remember from GHOST are stray images: Kharis busting through the log fence; Amina's hair streaking white; the mill and the length of tracks leading up to it.

*The MUMMY'S HAND 1940 Mus D: H.J. Salter. AD: Jack Otterson, Ralph M. DeLacy. Mkp: Jack Pierce. Ref: Lee. TV. Glut/CMM.

Generally vapid, with perfunctory comedy (from Wallace Ford) and awkward dramatic moments (from all). As with the 1932 original (The MUMMY) the highlight is the mummy's revival. The here-he-comes-again shock-scenes that follow are rote Universal....Note: in "The Detective in Film," William K. Everson seems to confuse a scene in MR.MOTO TAKES A VACATION (in which Lionel Atwill steps on a camera) with a scene in The MUMMY'S HAND,in which George Zucco (as Andoheb) purposely drops Dick Foran's vase. (The two scenes do have a certain interchangeability.)

MUMMY'S RETURN, The see MUMMY'S GHOST, The

The MUMMY'S REVENGE (Sp) (Avco Embassy-TV)/Lotus-Sara 1973 color/scope (La VENGANZA DE LA MOMIA. The VENGEANCE OF THE MUMMY-alt t) D: Carlos A. Aured. SP: Jacinto Molina. Ph:

Francisco Sanchez. AD: G. Andres. SpFX: Julio Sanchez-Caballero. Mkp: Miguel Sese. Ref: Lee. TVFFSB. V 5/8/74:207. 5/9/73:143(ad). with Paul Naschy(mummy), Rina Otolina, Jack Taylor, Helga Line, Luis Davila.

Revived mummy seeks body for wife's soul.

*The MUMMY'S TOMB 1942 Stock footage from FRANKENSTEIN(1931). See also The MUMMY(1959). Ref: TV. V 10/14/42. Glut/CMM: Eddie Parker as Kharis in long shots.

If you must see The MUMMY'S HAND, watch the first 10 minutes of The MUMMY'S TOMB--it consists of neatly-compressed, flashback highlights from The MUMMY'S HAND. If you have to see The MUMMY'S TOMB, there is, unfortunately, only one way. The latter is one of Universal's most cursory horror movies. The actors from HAND--George Zucco, Dick Foran, Wallace Ford--continue their roles here, briefly: Zucco for about a minute, Ford a few minutes--just time enough to exclaim "Greyish marks!"--and Foran not much longer. So slapdash that heroine Elyse Knox's last line is dubbed in over her closed mouth.

The MUNSTERS' REVENGE NBC-TV/Univ-TV 1981 color 95m. D: Don Weis. SP: Arthur Alsberg, Don Nelson, based on "The Munsters" TV series. Ph: H.L. Wolf. Mus: Vic Mizzy. AD: J.M. Bachman. SdFX: Glen Hoskinson. Ref: TV. TVG. V 3/11/81:110. with Fred Gwynne, Al Lewis, Sid Caesar, Yvonne De Carlo, Robert Hastings (cousin Phantom of the Opera), Jo McDonnell, Gary Vinson.

Wax museum's models are actually remote-controlled robot versions of the Munsters (inc. Frankenstein-monster-like Herman and Dracula-like Grandpa), the hunchback of Notre Dame, the creature from the Black Lagoon, werewolf, Tor Johnson-masked monster; youth-and-life-restoring formula; Herman-as-mummy (in place of restored-to-life baby-mummy); Bride of Frankenstein relative. Lots of laughs--90% of them on the laugh-track, though Gwynne and Caesar are good for a few too. (Wot!--no scream-track?!)

The MUPPET MOVIE (U.S.-B) AFD/ITC & Henson 1979 live & puppets color 97m. D: James Frawley. SP: Jerry Juhl, Jack Burns. Based on "The Muppet Show" TV series. Ph: I. Mankofsky. Mus: Paul Williams, Kenny Ascher. PD: Joel Schiller. SpFX: Robbie Knott. Ref: MFB'79:149-50. V 5/30/79. TV. AMPAS. with Mel Brooks, Dom DeLuise, Bob Hope, Madeline Kahn, Steve Martin, Orson Welles, Milton Berle, Edgar Bergen, et al.

Professor Krassman (Brooks) attempts to liquefy Kermit's brain with an "electronic cerebrectomy"; Dr. Bunsen's growing pills enlarge prune and Animal; Jack and other strange creatures; song ref. to King Kong. Rather sloppy and amorphous, but charmingly punctuated by Kermit's asides. The sloppiness--they would call it "informality"--is of course part of the Muppet modus operandi, but 97 minutes is a lot of informality. (What the hey, 30 minutes is a lot....) Martin and Brooks have the best guest bits. 2:1 resistibility-to-irresistibility ratio.

MURDER BY DEATH Col/Rastar 1976 color/scope 95m. D: Robert Moore. SP: Neil Simon. Ph: D.M. Walsh. Mus: Dave Grusin. PD: Stephen Grimes. SpFX: Augie Lohman. Art: Charles Addams. SdFxEd: Frank Warner. Ref: MFB'76:216. V 6/23/76. TV. with Eileen Brennan, Truman Capote, James Coco, Peter Falk, Alec Guinness, Elsa Lanchester, David Niven, Peter Sellers, Nancy Walker, Maggie Smith, Estelle Winwood.

Killer at large in Gothic mansion equipped with electronically-produced "weather," "screaming" doorbell, fake cobwebs, falling gargoyles, African death-masks; hostess/host with lifelike rubber masks. Caricatures of detectives Sam Spade, Miss Marple, Charlie Chan, Hercule Poirot, Nick and Nora Charles. (Wot!--no Moto?) In this murder-mystery parody, comedy is the victim, and Neil Simon did it. Our favorite sleuths are reduced to quips, and neither sleuths nor quips mix well, though Falk as Sam Diamond is in a slightly-different key and plays off well against the rest. Oh, there are _moments_....

MURDER BY DECREE (Can.-B) Avco Embassy/Ambassador 1979 color 112m. (SHERLOCK HOLMES AND SAUCY JACK-orig t. SHERLOCK HOLMES: MURDER BY DECREE-int t) D: Bob Clark. SP: John Hopkins. Based on the book "The Ripper File" by John Lloyd & Elwyn Jones, and on the Arthur Conan Doyle characters. See also: A STUDY IN TERROR. Ph: Reginald Morris. Mus: Carl Zittrer, Paul Zaza. PD: Harry Pottle. SpFX: Michael Albrechtson. Ref: screen. MFB'80:50. V 5/9/79:334. 1/24/79. 2/2/77:43(ad). 1/12/77:3. with Christopher Plummer, James Mason, Anthony Quayle, Donald Sutherland(psychic), John Gielgud, Susan Clark, Genevieve Bujold, Michael Hemmings, F. Finlay, C. Kessler.

"Jack the Ripper" is discovered to be the product of a conspiracy by the British government. Plummer and Mason head a ridiculously distinguished cast for a Sherlock Holmes mystery. The former is satisfactory as Holmes; Mason has inspired moments in his not-particularly-well-written role of Watson. Handsome-bland production is short on substance--the revelations of conspiracy and cover-up seem anti-climactic. One brief, startling, "caught-in-the-act" scene of murder and violence.

MURDER BY MAIL see SCHIZOID

MURDER BY ROPE (B) B&D Para 1936 64m. D: G. Pearson. SP: R. Neale. Ref: BFC. with Wilfrid Hyde-White, D.A. Clarke-Smith.

Hanged man "returns to kill judge and hangman."

*MURDER BY TELEVISION 1935 SP: Joseph O'Donnell. Story: C. Hennecke, C. Coolidge. Ph: James Brown Jr., A. Reed. Song: Oliver Wallace. AD: Louis Rachmil. TV Tech: M.M. Stern. Ref: screen. TV. TVG. and with Hattie McDaniel, Henry Hall.

TV-tube invention used as death ray. Occasionally endearingly clumsy mystery. The actors take all day to accomplish the simplest of scenes--they seem to be going _very slowly_ in order to get them right--and the dialogue sometimes reaches giddy heights of unnaturalness. More often, though, just dull, with a motley collection of actors, all (it seems) in grey suits and grey dialogue. Positive note: Bela Lugosi delivering one long, impossible line with great flair.

*MURDER BY THE CLOCK 1931 Also based on the play by Charles Beahan. Ph: Karl Struss. Ref: TV. and with Martha Mattox.

A drug restores a murderer to life, but the sound of a tomb siren (signaling the revival of his victim) proves too much for his heart, and he dies again. The villainess then employs a death mask of the woman whom she had her husband (the aforementioned victim) murder, in order to frighten him back to death too. Death is weirdly uncertain in MURDER BY THE CLOCK ....The actors move like mechanical dolls, each one carrying, robot-like, his or her own little share of exposition. One admirably silly/macabre scene in which the villainess experiences the thrill of murder vicariously. Offbeat but awful.

MURDER, HE SAYS Para/Leshin 1945 91m. D: George Marshall. SP: Lou Breslow. Story: Jack Moffitt. Ph: T. Sparkuhl. Mus: Robert Emmett Dolan. SpFX: Gordon Jennings, Paul Lerpae. Ref: screen. NYT 6/25/45. LC. V 4/11/45. with Fred MacMurray, Helen Walker, Marjorie Main, Porter Hall, Jean Heather, Peter Whitney, Barbara Pepper, Mabel Paige.

Poison which turns victims phosphorescent; glowing dog that heralds death; ref. to GHOST BREAKERS(1940); fake-ghost bit. Some sly moments--e.g., MacMurray reading by the late-Grandma's light; whips and sofa springs cracking and creaking (respectively) outrageously. But plot and players are, generally, not especially inspired, and there's just no relief from the relentlessly-mad Fleagle family.

*MURDER IN THE BLUE ROOM 1944 Ph: George Robinson. Mus D: Sam Freed Jr. AD: John B. Goodman, H.H. MacArthur. Ref: TV. V 11/1/44. Lee.

Universal (apparently desperate for material) made three versions of Erich Philippi's "Secret of the Blue Room" between 1933 and 1944. MURDER, the third and no charm, turns the story into a mystery-horror-musical about the reopening of a haunted mansion. It adds a female songs-and-jokes trio--an incredible combination of the Andrews Sisters and Abbott and Costello--a weird cabbie, and a frolicsome ghost, to no avail.

**MURDER IN THE MUSEUM Progressive(Willis Kent) 1934 55m. D: Melville Shyer. SP: E.B. Crosswhite. Ph: James Diamond. Ref: FD 6/27/34. Turner/Price. with Henry B. Walthall, John Harron, Phyllis Barrington, Joseph Girard, Donald Kerr.

"Diabolical invention...whereby a .45-caliber gun can be transformed to fire a .38-caliber bullet"; "The Human Ape."(T/P)

MURDER IN THE PRIVATE CAR MGM 1934 58m. D: Harry Beaumont. SP: Edgar Allan Woolf, Al Boasberg, Ralph Spence. Adap: Harvey Thew. From the play "The Rear Car" by E.E. Rose. Ph: James Van Trees, Leonard Smith. AD: Cedric Gibbons. Ref:

screen. Limbacher'79. B.Warren. TVFFSB. LC. with Una Merkel, Charlie Ruggles, Mary Carlisle, Russell Hardie, Porter Hall, Berton Churchill, Snowflake, Sterling Holloway, W. Robertson.

Mysterious voice that warns passengers in train's private car that they have only five hours to live; "strange sounds and voices"; huge paw-print on wall (left by circus gorilla); man stabbed to death through eye; secret compartment with controls for car's lights and openings. Ruggles' comedy fizzles, and there's a plot to be gotten through; but the runaway-private-car climax is both pretty funny and exciting. MGM lion in-joke (but no batteries) included.

MURDER MANSION (Sp-I) (Avco Embassy-TV)/Mundial & Tritone 1972 color 90m. (La MANSION DE LA NIEBLA. QUANDO MARTA URLO DALLA TOMBA) D: F. Lara Polop. Ref: V 5/9/73. Bianco Index. TVFFSB. with Analia Gade, Evelyn Stewart, Andres Resino.

"Old mansion with an eerie legend." (TVFFSB)

*MURDERS IN THE RUE MORGUE 1932 Mkp: Jack Pierce. Ref: TV. FM 66:20. Lee. and with Charles Gemora(gorilla).

It seems that with many of Bela Lugosi's performances you can't quite be sure that the actor was in on the joke--that he knew, for instance, how funny-endearing his Dr. Vollin (The RAVEN) was, or that he knew how fondly silly his dead-serious Vitus Werdegast (The BLACK CAT) appeared. But with SON OF FRANKENSTEIN; with parts also of DEVIL BAT, MYSTERIOUS MR. WONG, and The CORPSE VANISHES; and with MURDERS IN THE RUE MORGUE, you know he knew--you know he's in control. His Dr. Mirakle here seems delighted to outrage others, and to delight in his own outrageousness. He is only too glad to confront others with the grotesque--his ape, his theories, himself. Mirakle seems to relish his adversary relationship with humanity. (He even invites his audience, at one point, to burn him as a heretic.) To him, the refusal of his interlocutors to accept his theories ("I will prove your kinship with the ape!")--to accept the obvious--is pathetically amusing. (They're not in on the joke.) He positively swills in their squeamishness....The film as a whole, however, is pretty slipshod. The other actors speak their lines as if stilted English might sound like French (this is, supposedly, Paris, 1835), while Lugosi speaks a language of his own invention, in perhaps the Lugosi performance.

*MURDERS IN THE RUE MORGUE 1971 SpMkp: Jack Young. Ref: TV.

Secret of "shallow breathing" allows man (Herbert Lom) to return from the grave, commit acid-murders, assume guise of ape, Erik, in Grand Guignol production; heroine (Christine Kaufmann) suffers from nightmares stemming from the shock of seeing her mother killed; hypnotic trance enables her to relive her mother's death; nightmare-prophecy. Nightmares and murders alternate here with numbing regularity, the film all the while building (as it were) to the (rather expected) revelations. The plot-to-padding ratio is about 1:1. (Conservative estimate.)

MUSCLE BEACH PARTY AI/Alta Vista 1964 color/scope 94m. Story, D: William Asher. Story,SP: Robert Dillon. Ph: H. Wellman. Mus: Les Baxter. AD: L. Croxton. Mkp: Ted Coodley. PhSpFX: Butler-Glouner, Pat Dinga. Ref: TV. AFI: entry in BEACH PARTY series. with Frankie Avalon, Annette Funicello, Luciana Paluzzi, Peter Lorre et al.
Scenes with super-strong Mr. Strangdour (Lorre); bit with his apeman-monster assistant, Igor. Silly, slapsticky comedy.

MUSEUM PIECE NO. 13(by R.King) see SECRET BEYOND THE DOOR...

MUTATION see M3: THE GEMINI STRAIN

The MUTATIONS (B) Col/Cyclone(Getty) 1973 color 92m. (The MUTATION-orig t) D: Jack Cardiff. SP: R.D. Weinbach, Edward Mann. Ph: Paul Beeson. Mus: Basil Kirchin. AD: Herbert Smith. SpFX: Mike Hope. SpPhFX: Ken Middleham. SpMkp: Charles Parker. Ref: MFB'75:12. Willis/SW. V 5/29/74. 12/6/72:7. with Donald Pleasence, Tom Baker, Julie Ege, Michael Dunn, Jill Haworth.
Bio-chemist attempts to synthesize plant and animal forms through scientifically-induced mutation.

MUTILATED see SHRIEK OF THE MUTILATED

MUTT AND JEFF(by B.Fisher) see INVISIBLE REVENGE

MY BLOODY VALENTINE (Can.) Para/Secret-CFDC 1981 color 91m. D: George Mihalka. SP: John Beaird. Idea: Stephen Miller. Ph: Rodney Gibbons. Mus: Paul Zaza. AD: Penny Hadfield. SpMkpFX: Tom Burman et al. SpMechFX: Cosmi-Kinetics. SdFX: Jeff Bushelman. Ref: V 2/18/81. MFB'81:117-18. with Paul Kelman, Lori Hallier, Neil Affleck, Don Francks, Cynthia Dale.
"The deadly pick ax of the crazed coal miner." (V)

MYSTERIES FROM BEYOND EARTH (Gold Key-TV)/CineVue/American Nat'l 1975 color 95m. D,P: George Gale. SP: Ralph & Judy Blum, Don Scioli. Mus: Jaime Mendoza-Nava. Ref: TV. TVFFSB. TVG. Willis/SW. with Charles Hickson, Dr.Thelma Moss, Maj.Donald Keyhoe, Carl Anderson, James McDivitt.
UFO's (inc. clip from INVADERS FROM MARS); witchcraft; the Bermuda Triangle; Black Holes; ESP; Atlantis; Kirlian photography and the "phantom leaf phenomenon"; haunted houses; cloning. Psychic flotsam and jetsam, though Dr. Moss's presentation on Kirlian photography intrigues. Host: Lawrence Dobkin.

MYSTERIES FROM BEYOND THE TRIANGLE Gold Key-TV 1977 color 94m. D: William Miller?; L. Crawle. SP: Daphne Deane. Ph: Adam Crow; E. Joyce. Mus: J. Gilman, R. Mounsey. Models: Robert Randall. Ref: TV. GKey. TVG. with Chet Curtis, Ann Swain.
Scientists and psychics exploring the Bermuda Triangle; "magnetic deviations"; unexplained forces. ("Are these strange formations the work of aliens?") Lackluster sea saga/speculation.

MYSTERIES OF THE GODS (W.G.) Hemisphere/Hirschberg-Kalmowicz 1976 color 97m. (BOTSCHAFT DER GOTTER. MIRACLES OF THE GODS-ad t. PHAENOMENE--DIE WELT ERREGEN-orig t) D:Harald Reinl. SP & Exec P: Manfred Barthel. From the books "Aussaat und Kosmos," "Meine Welt in Bildern," & "Erscheinungen" by Erich von Daniken. Mus: Peter Thomas. Ref: MFB'76:230. '77:54. V 11/17/76:27(rated). 5/26/76. 5/12/76:375(ad). 5/14/75:56(ad).

Proposes that "extra-terrestrial astronauts" implant "programmes" in specially-selected humans.

*The MYSTERIOUS DR. FU MANCHU 1929 Ref: screen.

A "gigantic melodrama" about a "diabolical genius of a madman"; hypnotized woman who kills. Atmospheric locales: China, 1900; Limehouse; Redmoat Grange, a castle overlooking the sea. Fu Manchu: "When the moonbeam touches the dragon I shall return." Heroine (Jean Arthur), throughout: "Oh, no!" She's sweet and sexy; the film is, well....

Sequels: *DAUGHTER OF THE DRAGON.*RETURN OF DR.FU MANCHU.

*MYSTERIOUS ISLAND 1929 Ref: screen.

Sea midgets turn into "vampires" ("blood!"), swarm over humans, in fascinating undersea scenes. Otherwise, it's substandard adventure and romance, in what sounds like <u>the</u> microphone-bound early talkie. This structural/stylistic predecessor of ATTACK OF THE MAYAN MUMMY alternates between interminable dialogue-sequences and pure-action scenes. Highlight of former: an hilarious 10-minute marathon in which Lionel Barrymore stands and reads his lines from (offscreen) cards, over another actor's shoulder, and tries (most unsuccessfully) to distract our attention by waving one hand about.

The MYSTERIOUS ISLAND (I-F-Sp-Cameroon) Cinerama/Cinematografica-Cite-Copercines-Cameroons 1972('74-U.S.) color 96m. (L'ISOLA MISTERIOSA E IL CAPITANO NEMO. L'ILE MYSTERIEUSE. El CAPITAN NEMO. La ISLA MISTERIOSA. The MYSTERIOUS ISLAND OF CAPTAIN NEMO-alt t. JULES VERNE'S THE MYSTERIOUS ISLAND OF DR. NEMO-ad t) D: J.A. Bardem, Henri Colpi. SP: Bardem, Jacques Champreux, from Verne's novel. Ph: E. Serafin, G. Delecluze. Mus: Gianni Ferrio. AD: J.L. Galicia, J.P. Cubero. Ref: Bianco Index'73. Daisne. Lee. Willis/SW. Meyers. V 11/28/73. 5/9/73:137. with Omar Sharif, Philippe Nicaud, Jess Hahn, Gerard Tichy, Gabriele Tinti, R. Bataglia.

Nemo and the Nautilus; radiation beams?

*The MYSTERIOUS MR. WONG (UA-TV/Manbeck) 1935 Adap: L. <u>Levenson</u>. Add'l Dial: James Herbuveaux. Mus D: Abe Meyer. <u>AD: E. R.</u> Hickson. Ref: screen. TVFFSB. Turner/Price.

Bela Lugosi, irresistibly hammy as the cruel, flamboyant Wong ("A few hours with the <u>rats</u> will make him <u>speak</u> the <u>truth!</u>"), alternates here between menace and mock-menace, melodrama and send-up, as he slinks and skulks about. ("Time (pause) came (pause) before (pause) Man (double pause)--there'splentyofit!") Wong occasionally masquerades as a funny old shopkeeper, and it proves a lark for Lugosi, but this charade gets a bit tiring for the audience, and the film keeps cutting back to Wallace Ford (and his failed comedy), so Lugosi is only able to perk up scenes here and there. Still, way above average for Monogram.

The MYSTERIOUS MONSTERS Sunn/Wolper 1975 color 93m. (BIGFOOT--THE MYSTERIOUS MONSTER-alt t) SP,D: Robert Guenette. Ph: David Myers et al. Mus: Rudy Raksin. Narr: Peter Graves. Ref: TVFFSB. Willis/SW. V 8/4/76. 10/29/75:7(rated). with Peter Hurkos.

Speculation re: the Abominable Snowman, the Loch Ness Monster, Bigfoot; "hokey dramaturgy...involving actors dressed up as monsters." (V)

MYSTERIOUS OLD HOUSE, The see KU-WU I-YUN

MYSTERY AT ST.AGIL see DISPARUS DE SAINT-AGIL

The MYSTERY IN DRACULA'S CASTLE NBC-TV/Buena Vista 1972 color 95m. D: Robert Totten. Ref: TVFFSB. Glut/TDB: first shown on TV's "World of Disney." with Johnny Whitaker, Scott Kolden, Clu Gulager, Mariette Hartley.

Dracula-film fan and his brother decide to use an old lighthouse as a horror-movie location.

MYSTERY OF DR. FU-MANCHU, The Stoll series D: A.E. Colby. Ref: BFC. with H. Agar Lyons, Fred Paul. see AARON'S ROD. CALL OF SIVA,The. CLUE OF THE PIGTAIL. *CRY OF THE NIGHT-HAWK. *FIERY HAND,The. *FUNGI CELLARS,The. KNOCKING ON THE DOOR,The. MAN WITH THE LIMP. *MIRACLE,The. *QUEEN OF HEARTS. *SACRED ORDER,The. SCENTED ENVELOPES,The. *SHRINE OF THE SEVEN LAMPS. *SILVER BUDDHA,The. WEST CASE,The.

The MYSTERY OF LIFE (India-Bengali) Jagrata 1973 (JIBAN RAHASYA) Story,D: Salil Roy. SP: Tapesh Ghosh. Ph: Biman Sinha. Mus: A. Banerjee. Ref: Dharap. with Pran, Dilip Roy.

Woman possessed by spirit of murdered lover.

MYSTERY OF THE GHOUL see MAD GHOUL, The

MYSTERY OF THE GOLDEN EYE Gold Key-TV/WEC/Jack Harris 1977 color 78m. (KING MONSTER-orig t) D: Richard Martin. Ref: TVFFSB: horror. TVG. GKey. with Robert White, Basil Bradbury, K.K. Mohajan.

U.S. senator's son disappears while exploring Komodo Island.

MYSTERY OF THE MARIE CELESTE see PHANTOM SHIP(1935)

MYSTERY ON MONSTER ISLAND see MONSTER ISLAND

NAA NINNA BIDENU (India-Kannada) Magnet 1978 121m. D?,SP: K. Nagabhusan. Story: M.A. Rajaram. Mus: G.K. Venkatesh. Ref: Dharap. with Ramakanth, Purandar, Nanjundappa.
Spirits of boy and girl--killed by firm's directors--return to kill them.

NAAG CHAMPA (India-Hindi) Chitra Kunj 1976 color 139m. D & Mus: S.N. Tripathi. SP: R. Priyadarshi. Ref: Dharap. with Kanan Kaushal, Shahi Kapoor, B.M. Vyas.
Magician, death-curse.

NACHT DER VAMPIRE see WEREWOLF VS. THE VAMPIRE WOMAN, The

NAGAM EN DEIVAM see DEVATHALARA DEEVINCHANDI

NAGIN (India-Hindi) Shankar 1976 color 145m. D: Rajkumar Kohli. SP: J.R. Paul, C. Shokh. Story: R. Singh. Mus: L. Pyarelal. Ref: Dharap. with Sunil Dutt, Feroz Khan, Sanjay.
A female cobra "takes the form of women" to revenge herself on the five men responsible for the death of her lover.
See also: DEVATHALARA DEEVINCHANDI.

NAKED EXORCISM (I) Colosseum-Manila 1975 color 88m. (Un URLO DALLE TENEBRE. L'ESORCISTA NO.2-orig t) SP,D: Angelo Pannaccio. SP: also Aldo Crudo, F. Brocani. Story: Guido Albonico. Ph: Villa, Centini. Mus: M. Sorgini. Ref: MFB'77: 199-200. Bianco Index'76:71. V 1/8/75:76. with Richard Conte, Francoise Prevost, Jean-Claude Verne, Mimma Monticelli.
A nun fears her brother is possessed by the Devil.

NAKED LOVERS (F) Pierson 1977 color 85m. D,P: Claude Pierson. SP: Elisabeth Leclair. Ph: Claude Masson. Mkp: Roland Warnod. Ref: MFB'79:44-5,219. with Ursula White, Alban Ceray, Didier Aubriot, Barbara Moose.
Aliens from the planet Eros reanimate and inhabit the dead of Earth.

**The NAKED WITCH Alexander(Mishkin) 1964(1961) color 60m. (The NAKED TEMPTRESS-alt t) D & Ph: Andy Milligan. SP: Clay Guss. Ref: Boxo 3/6/67. AFI: '67 re-r with 20m. added. with Beth Porter(vampire-witch), Robert Burgos, Lee Forbes.
Student removes stake from heart of executed witch, who then revives; hunchback(Forbes).

The NAKED WORLD OF HARRISON MARKS Manson/Token 1967 color 84m. (The DREAM WORLD OF HARRISON MARKS-alt t) D,P,Co-Sp: Marks. Ph: Len Harris. Mus: John Hawksworth. Narr: Valentine Dyall. Ref: AFI. with Marks, Pamela Green, June Palmer.
Photographer daydreams he's Count Dracula, James Bond, etc.

NAMAKUBI JOCHI JIKEN (J) Okura Eiga 1967 D: Kinya Lgawa. Ref: WorldF'67. with H. Tsuruoka, K. Hinotori.
Woman's ghost returns to haunt her killers.

A NAME FOR EVIL Cinerama/Penthouse 1972 color (The GROVE-orig t. THERE IS A NAME FOR EVIL. The FACE OF EVIL-int ts) SP,D: Bernard Girard. From novel by Andrew Lytle. Mus: Dominic Frontiere. Ref: Lee. V 5/3/72:196. with Robert Culp, Samantha Eggar, Mike Lane.
Murderous ghost haunts Southern mansion.

NAME IS BLACULA, The see SCREAM, BLACULA, SCREAM

NAN-YU CHI see HUA-KUANG CHIU-MU

The NAVIGATOR (F) Film Images/Starevitch 1934 12m. (FETICHE NAVIGATEUR) Ref: FI'74 cat.: sequel to The MASCOT.

NAZARENO CRUZ Y EL LOBO (Arg) Choila 1974 color 92m. D,P: Leonardo Favio. SP: Zuhair Jury, from a radio play by J.C. Chiappe. Ph: J.J. Stagnaro. Mus: J.G. Caffi. AD: M.A. Lumaldo. Ref: V 9/10/75:32. 6/18/75. with Alfredo Alcon(the Devil), Juan Jose Camero(Cruz), Nora Cullen(witch), M. Magali.
Family's 7th son cursed by ancient legend to turn into wolf during night of the full moon; old woman who can turn into "any kind of animal."

NECROMANCY Cinerama/Zenith Int'l 1972 color 82m. (The TOY FACTORY-orig t. A LIFE FOR A LIFE-ad t) SP,D,P: Bert I. Gordon. Ph: Winton Hoch. Mus: Fred Karger. AD: Frank Sylos. SpFX: William Vanderbyl. Ref: V 10/11/72. Lee. TV. with Orson Welles, Pamela Franklin, Lee Purcell, Michael Ontkean.
Occultist attempts to restore dead son to life. Dawdling Gordon thriller.

**NECROPHAGUS (Sp) (AI-TV)/FISA 1971 color/scope 86m. (El DESCUARTIZADOR DE BINBROOK. GRAVEYARD OF HORROR-TV) SP,D: Miguel Madrid(aka Michael Skaife). Ph: A. Nieva. Mus: A. Santisteben. AD: B. Hyde. SpFX: Antonio Molina. Ref: TV. TVFFSB. Lee(SpCinema). V 5/3/72:175. with William Curran, Catharine Ellison, Beatriz Lacy, Frank Brana, Yocasta Grey.
Man turned into animal-mineral-vegetable monster which lives on fresh corpses. Dubbed and unwatchable.

NEDOKONCENY WEEKEND see UNFINISHED WEEKEND, The

NEITHER THE SAND NOR THE SEA (B) Int'l Amusements/Tigon 1972 ('74-U.S.) color 94m. D: Fred Burnley. SP: Gordon Honeycombe, from his novel. Add'l Dial: Rosemary Davies. Ph: D. Muri. Mus: Nahum Heiman. AD: Michael Bastow. Ref: MFB'72: 255. V 1/30/74. Willis/SW. with Susan Hampshire, Michael Petrovitch, Frank Finlay, Jack Lambert, Michael Craze.
Woman continues to care for her lover's living corpse after he dies of a heart attack.

NELLA STRETTA MORSA DEL RAGNO see WEB OF THE SPIDER

The NEPTUNE FACTOR--AN UNDERSEA ODYSSEY (Can.) Fox/Quadrant & Bellevue-Pathe 1973 color/scope 98m. (The NEPTUNE DISASTER-

TV. CONQUEST OF THE DEEPS-orig t) D: Daniel Petrie. SP: Jack DeWitt. Ph: Harry Makin. Mus: Lalo Schifrin, W. McCauley. PD: D.L. Clark, J. McAdam. SpFX: Film Opticals, Lee Howard. Ref: TV. V 5/23/73. MFB'73:172-3. Lee. with Ben Gazzara, Yvette Mimieux, Walter Pidgeon, Ernest Borgnine, Chris Wiggins.
Sub finds giant eel and other giant fish in lost grotto. Dreary sf-adventure.

NERO VENEZIANO see VENETIAN BLACK

The NESTING FFD/Sam Lake 1981(1980) color 104m. (PHOBIA-orig t) SP,D,P: Armand Weston. SP: also Daria Price. Ph: Joao Fernandez. Mus: Jack Malken, Kim Scholes. SpFX: Matt Vogel. Ref: V 10/15/80:152(ad). 3/18/81:232(ad). 4/29/81. with Robin Groves, Christopher Loomis, John Carradine, Gloria Grahame, David Tabor.
Ghosts haunting Victorian mansion use heroine in plot to revenge their murder.

NEVER COMPLAIN TO YOUR LAUNDRESS (B) Hepworth 1907 D: Lewin Fitzhamon. Ref: BFC.
Customer who complains is "scrubbed, mangled and parcelled."

NEVER TOO YOUNG TO ROCK (B) GTO 1975 color 99m. SP,D: Dennis Abey. SP: also Ron Inkpen. Ph: H. Harrison. AD: Denis Gordon-Orr. Ref: MFB'75:142-43. with Peter Denyer, Freddie Jones, Sheila Steafel, John Clive, Peter Noone.
The near future. "Group Detector Van" seeks out rock groups, finds one in a haunted house.

The NEW ADVENTURES OF TARZAN Rep/Burroughs-Tarzan 1936 serial 12 chapters & 75m. feature (TARZAN IN GUATEMALA-orig t. TARZAN AND THE LOST GODDESS-int t. TARZAN'S NEW ADVENTURE-alt feat.t. TARZAN AND THE GREEN GODDESS-'38 feat. with added scenes) D,Co-Ph: Edward Kull. SP: Charles F. Royal, Edwin F. Blum. Story: Edgar Rice Burroughs, based on his books. Mus D: Abe Meyer. AD: Charles Clague. SpFX: Ray Mercer, Howard Anderson. Ref: TV. Turner/Price. Lee. TVG. with Herman Brix (aka Bruce Bennett), Ula Holt, Earl Dwire;('38) Jack Mower.
"Monsters--black-robed emissaries of the Princess Maya"; crystal ball; idol containing formula for explosive "powerful enough to blow cities sky high." Stilted, crude action-adventure movie. The credits at least warn you: "Sound recording variable--filmed under difficult conditions, and your kind indulgence is craved in this direction." Guatemala and some nice shots of clouds star, by default.

NEW HOUSE ON THE LEFT Central Park 1978 color D,P: Evans Isle. Ref: Willis/SW. with Kay Beal, Patty Edwards, Norma Knight.
See also: LAST HOUSE ON THE LEFT. cf.LAST STOP...(P)

NEW INVISIBLE MAN see GEMINI MAN

NEW KING KONG, The see APE(1976)

The NEW, ORIGINAL WONDER WOMAN ABC-TV/WB-TV 1975 color 74m. D: Leonard Horn. SP: Stanley Ralph Ross, based on the Charles Moulton characters. Ph: Dennis Dalzell. Mus: Charles Fox. SpAnim: Phill Norman. Ref: TV Season. TVFFSB. TV. V 11/12/75: 45. with Lynda Carter, Lyle Waggoner, Cloris Leachman, Red Buttons, Stella Stevens, Kenneth Mars, Henry Gibson.

From a tribe of Amazons (ex-slaves from Rome and Greece) on Paradise Island in the Bermuda Triangle, Wonder Woman comes to aid the Allies in World War II; invisible plane; magic lasso; bullet-deflecting bracelets. Tepid adventure-fantasy.

NEW PEOPLE,The(by C.Beaumont) see JOURNEY INTO DARKNESS

The NEW PLANET OF THE APES: BACK TO THE PLANET OF THE APES CBS-TV/Fox-TV 1974('80 feature version) color 74m. D: Don Weis, Arnold Laven. SP: Arthur Wallace, Edward J. Lakso. From the "Planet of the Apes" TV series. Ph: G.P. Finnerman. Mus: Lalo Schifrin, Richard LaSalle. AD: Arch Bacon. Mkp: Dan Striepeke. Ref: TV. TVG. V 9/18/74:42. with Roddy McDowall(Galen), Ron Harper, James Naughton(regulars); Royal Dano, Biff Elliot, Cindy Eilbacher, Norm Alden, Mark Lenard.

A radioactive disturbance sends human astronauts into the ape-ruled Earth of 3085 a.d. ("What kind of planet _is_ _this_?!") More re-cycled ape-masks. But, by God, Roddy McDowall _is_ _still_ winning. (If his hard questions as Galen--e.g., "Why should _truth_ be against the law?"--aren't hard enough.)

The NEW PLANET OF THE APES: FAREWELL TO THE PLANET OF THE APES 1974(1980) D: Don McDougall, J.M. Lucas. SP: R. Lenski et al. Mus: Earle Hagen. Ref: TV. and with Roscoe Lee Browne, Joanna Barnes, Frank Aletter.

The NEW PLANET OF THE APES: FORGOTTEN CITY OF THE PLANET OF THE APES 1974(1980) Ref: TVG.

The NEW PLANET OF THE APES: LIFE,LIBERTY AND PURSUIT ON THE PLANET OF THE APES 1974(1980) D: Arnold Laven, Alf Kjellin. SP: Barry Oringer, Richard Collins. Ref: TV. TVG. and with Beverly Garland, Jamie Smith Jackson, Mark Lenard.

The NEW PLANET OF THE APES: TREACHERY AND GREED ON THE PLANET OF THE APES 1974(1980) D: Don McDougall, Bernard McEveety. SP: Arthur Wallace, Robert Hammer. Mus: Earle Hagen, Lalo Schifrin. Ref: TV. and with William Smith, John Hoyt, Zina Bethune, Victor Kilian.

NEW YEAR'S EVIL Cannon(Golan-Globus) 1980 color 85m. SP,D: Emmett Alston. SP: also Leonard Neubauer. Ph: Edward Thomas. Mus: W.M. Lewis, Laurin Rinder. AD: J.K. Towery. Mkp: Julie Purcell. SpCost: Let It Rock. Ref: screen. V 1/21/81. with Roz Kelly, Kip Niven(Evil), Grant Cramer(Evil Jr.),C.Wallace.

Psychopathic killer ("That's right--I'm evil") times his murders to coincide with across-the-U.S. TV coverage of New Year's Eve celebrations; drive-in previews of "Blood Feast" and "Blood Bath" (but not the BLOOD FEAST and BLOOD BATH). Another holiday assassinated. Programmed shocks and whimsy.

The NEWCOMER (Benin) Iris-Int'l Tropic 1979 color 87m. (Le NOUVEAU VENU) SP,D: Richard De Meideros. SP: also R. Ewagnion, B. Lawani. Ref: V 8/22/79. with Michel Djondo, Sikirou Ogoujobi, A. Capo-Cichi.

Tribal chief exorcises government official under hex.

NIBELUNGEN, The see WHEN THE SCREAMING STOPS

NICK CARTER IN PRAGUE see DINNER FOR ADELE

NIGHT ANDY CAME HOME, The see DEATHDREAM

NIGHT CREATURE (Time-Life-TV)/Dimension/Woolner 1979(1977) color 83m. (FEAR-orig t. OUT OF THE DARKNESS. DEVIL CAT. CAT-all int ts) Story,D,Exec P: Lee Madden. SP: Hubert Smith. Ph: Pemylot Cheydon. Mus: Jim Helms. Ref: V 10/3/79: "action-horror." 5/7/80:470. 5/17/78:143(ad). 7/30/80:68. 10/19/77:63 (ad). 5/11/77:167(ad). AMPAS. with Donald Pleasence, Nancy Kwan, Ross Hagen, Jennifer Rhodes, Lesly Fine.

Writer in Southeast Asia "becomes obsessed with man-eating black leopard." (V)

*NIGHT CREATURES Merlin 1962 SP: Anthony Hinds. From the novel "Dr. Syn" by Russell Thorndike. SpFX: Les Bowie. Mkp: Roy Ashton. Ref: BFC. AFI. TV. Lee. FM 165:29.

"Marsh phantoms" scare man to death. Fast and plotty Hammer, but otherwise quite empty, undistinguished. Lots of "shock cuts."

NIGHT CRIES ABC-TV/Stonehenge 1978 color 94m. D: Richard Lang. SP: Brian Taggert. Ph: C.G. Arnold. Mus: Paul Chihara. AD: Bill Ross. SpFX: Robby Knott. Ref: TV. TVFFSB. TVG. with Susan Saint James, Michael Parks, William Conrad, Jamie Smith Jackson, Cathleen Nesbitt, Lee Kessler, Ellen Geer.

Nightmares and psychic phenomena. Images from a woman's nightmares lead her to, a) a secret in her past, locked behind a closet door which terrifies her, and, b) her kidnapped baby. Perfunctory psychology, with a touch of fantasy--she and her psychiatrist are both right. Saint James gives a one-note (i.e., petulant) performance. Ludicrous climactic-revelations sequence.

The NIGHT EVELYN CAME OUT OF THE GRAVE (I) (Gold Key-TV)/Phase I/Phoenix 1971('72-U.S.) color/scope 103m. (La NOTTE CHE EVELYN USCI DALLA TOMBA. The NIGHT SHE AROSE FROM THE TOMB-B) SP,D: Emilio P. Miraglia. SP: also F. Pittor(r)u, M.Felisatti. Ph: G. Di Giovanni. Mus: Bruno Nicolai. AD: Lorenzo Baraldi. Ref: MFB'72:255-56. Lee. GKey. V 7/26/72. Bianco Index'71. with Antonio De Teffe, Erika Blanc, Marina Malfatti, Giacomo Rossi Stuart, Umberto Raho.

"Corpse" that appears to return to life; "apparition" at

seance; mad killer; murder-with-snake; corpse left in fox cage. Tepid plotting-and-counterplotting intrigue, with an inordinate amount of skulking.

NIGHT FRIGHT 196-? c80m. D: James A. Sullivan. SP: Russ Marker. Ph: Robert C. Jessup. Mus: Christopher Trussell. AD: Bill Mitchell. SpFX: Jack Bennett. Ref: TV. no AFI. with John Agar, Carol Gilley, Roger Ready, Bill Thurman.

"Fireball"/flying saucer crashes to Earth at Satan's Hollow; girl's body found later, nearby, "all chewed up," with "gator"-like tracks leading away from the scene. Truly tacky.

NIGHT GAMES Avco Embassy/Pan Pacific 1980 color 105m. D: Roger Vadim. SP: Anton Diether, Clarke Reynolds. Story: B.J. Sussman, Diether. Ph: Dennis Lewiston. Mus: John Barry. PD: Robert Laing. SpFX: Gene Grigg. Ref: V 1/30/80. VV 4/21/80: "zero." MFB'80:10: "inept psychodrama." with Cindy Pickett, Joanna Cassidy, Barry Primus, Mark Hanks("The Phantom").

Housewife "left alone in oversized manse...screaming her lungs out at the mere approach of another human being...." (V)

The NIGHT GOD SCREAMED Cinemation/Lasky-Carlin 1971 color 85m. (The NIGHT THAT GOD SCREAMED-orig t. NIGHTMARE HOUSE-int t. SCREAM-B) D: Lee Madden. SP: Gil Lasky. Ph: S. Larner. Mus: Donald Vincent. AD: Jim Newport. Ref: MFB'74:13-14. CineFan 2:27. Bianco Index'74. Lee(p). with Jeanne Crain, Alex Nicol, Daniel Spelling, Barbara Hancock.

"Hooded monk"; "macabre dummy"; "bloody corpses"; "mysterious telephone calls" threatening preacher's widow.

*NIGHT KEY 1937 Assoc Art D: Loren Patrick. Ref: TV.

New, improved alarm system; "night key" which matches the frequency of any alarm and which allows inventor to enter and exit buildings undetected; stick which emits web-like ray. Intricately-silly juvenilia, with Boris Karloff helpless in another sweet-old-scientist-type role. Gangster Alan Baxter's intimidating monotone, however, is kicky. The business-vs.-science revenge story is more enjoyable as DEVIL BAT. Prize line: (Warren Hull) "Petty Louie doesn't write on tables for the fun of it!"

*NIGHT MONSTER 1942 Ref: TV. V 10/21/42. and with Robert Homans, Eddy Waller.

Hindu mystic's (Nils Asther) occult theory--that all matter is "cosmic substance in vibration" (which will power can reduce to its basic elements and reassemble in another place)--allows legless man to materialize limbs and commit murders; "curse of death"; ref. to King Tut curse; horror-story writer (Don Porter). Outside, there's fog; inside, Bela Lugosi and Lionel Atwill. But the latter are wasted, and--despite its more outre supernatural elements--NIGHT MONSTER is a resolutely mundane mystery. Even the score is just recycled H.J. Salter. Only the light-and-shadow effects pass.

*The NIGHT MY NUMBER CAME UP 1955 Story: Sir Victor Goddard. AD: Jim Morahan. SpFX: Sydney Pearson. Art: W.S. Robinson. Ref: TV. Barr/ES. and with Hugh Moxey, Percy Herbert.

This is, in effect, a feature-length (looking backwards) DEAD OF NIGHT segment, or (looking forward) "Twilight Zone," and is about as thin as such a characterization might indicate. Okay, though, in the air, where details of navigation take over from one-dimensional characters. But generally too cold-sober and serious-minded re: premonitory dreams and fate. Only Malcolm Arnold's score approximates the chilly tenor of the better "Twilight Zone"'s. Script features a flash-forward (a visualized re-telling of the dream) within a flashback (the body of the film), and cultural notes on the Chinese "Night of the Returning Spirit."

The NIGHT OF SUBMISSION 1977? 60m. Ref: screen.

Restaurant-front for voodoo cult; wax voodoo-doll; photos of voodoo ceremony (and 200-page report on same) which turn out blank (like, in effect, the movie).

*NIGHT OF TERROR 1933 (**HE LIVED TO KILL-re-r t) SP: also Lester Nielson. Ph: J.A. Valentine. Tech D: W.L. Vogel. Ref: TV. Lee. Screen World'57. Lennig/TC: HE LIVED...-also orig t?

NIGHT OF TERROR is a genially lousy horror movie featuring a three-ring-circus of horror gimmicks: Bela Lugosi and his mediumistic wife; the lurking, fanged menace; the "suspended animation" stunts. It's filmmaking as shell game--just keep things moving fast enough and no one will know there is no pea. This might have been titled "Night of Skulking"; there are three professional skulkers--Lugosi, his wife, and the maniac--but some amateurs get into the act too. ("You don't know who might be listening.") The maniac himself (played by Edwin Maxwell) is actually rather likably seedy--he's always grinning, and at the end he warns the viewer not to reveal the ending or he'll tear you limb from limb. But it's all in fun. (There have been no known casualties from exposure to NIGHT OF TERROR.)

NIGHT OF THE BEAST see HOUSE OF THE BLACK DEATH

NIGHT OF THE BLIND DEAD see TOMBS OF THE BLIND DEAD

NIGHT OF THE BLOODY APES see HORROR AND SEX

NIGHT OF THE COBRA WOMAN (U.S.-Fili) New World 1972 color 85m. (MOVINI'S VENOM-ad t) SP,D: Andrew Meyer. SP,P: Kerry Magnus. Ph: Nonong Rasca. AD: Ben Otico. SpFX: Feling Hilario. Ref: screen. Lee. V 3/3/74. with Joy Bang, Marlene Clark, Roger Garrett, Vic Diaz, Slash Marks.

Snake-bitten woman turns into cobra, sucks the life out of men during intercourse. Slightly cuckoo, fuzzily-plotted horror-fantasy has some effects and turns of plot which are real jaw-droppers--e.g., the cobra woman packing the skin she has just shed into her handbag...one victim's teeth suddenly dropping out...pieces of chopped-up snake transforming into more snakes...!?! (I pass.)

The NIGHT OF THE DAMNED (I) Primax 1971 color 87m. (La NOTTE DEI DANNATI) D: F.M. Ratti. SP: Aldo Marcovecchio, Ted Rusoff. Ph: G. La Rosa. Mus: Carlo Savina. PD: Elio Balleti. SpFX: Rino Carboni. Ref: MFB'72:142. M/TVM. with Pierre Brice, Patrizia Viotti, Angela De Leo, Mario Carra.
Reincarnated witch hypnotizes woman.

NIGHT OF THE DARK FULL MOON see SILENT NIGHT, BLOODY NIGHT

NIGHT OF THE DEMON Aldan 1980 color 90m. D: Jim Wasson. SP: Paul Cassey. Ref: Boxo 12/31/79:19. with Mike Cutt, Joy Allen, Richard Fields.
Anthropology students find "creature and its half-human offspring" in Pacific Northwest.

NIGHT OF THE DEVIL BRIDE (H.K.?) Shaw 1974? (cf.DEVIL IN HER) Ref: V 5/14/75:86(ad). with Lo Lieh, Chen Ping.

NIGHT OF THE DEVILS (I-Sp) Hallmark(AI)/Filmes Cinematografica-Due Emme & Copercines 1972('73-U.S.) color 88m. (La NOTTE DEI DIAVOLI. La NOCHE DE LOS DIABLOS) D: Giorgio Ferroni. SP: R. Migliorini et al. From the story "The Wurdalak" or "Family of a Wurdalak" by A. Tolstoy. Ph: M. Berenguer. Mus: Giorgio Gaslini. AD: Liverani, Galicia. SpFX: Rambaldi. Ref: MFB'73:32-3: "putrefaction is the main visual motif...." Murphy. Ecran 73(July,p27). V 10/3/73:5(rated). Bianco Index'73. with Gianni Garko, Agostina Belli, Teresa Gimpera, Maria Monti.
Young man fears girl is one of a family of witches.

*NIGHT OF THE GHOULS (Crown Int'l-TV) 1958 60m. (REVENGE OF THE DEAD-TV) Ref: TVFFSB. Pitts/HFS: sequel to BRIDE OF THE MONSTER? and with Kenne Duncan, Jeanie Stevens.
A phony medium and his accomplice, on the run from cops, meet "dead men...deep in the tombs." (TVFFSB)

NIGHT OF THE HOWLING BEAST (Sp) Constellation/Profilmes 1975 ('77-U.S.) color (La MALDICION DE LA BESTIA. The WEREWOLF AND THE YETI-alt t) D: M.I. Bonns. Sequel to MARK OF THE WOLFMAN. Ref: CineFan 2:24. V 5/12/76:414(ad),406. 10/22/75: 52. 4/13/77:6(rated). Glut/CMM. Willis/SW. with Paul Naschy (Waldemar, werewolf), Gil Vidal, Silvia Solar, L.Induni,G.Mills.
Member of Tibetan expedition "attacked by strange creatures," turned into werewolf (that, at climax, fights Yeti.)

NIGHT OF THE LEPUS MGM/Lyles 1972 color 88m. (RABBITS-orig t) D: William F. Claxton. SP: Don Holliday, Gene R. Kearney, from Russell Braddon's novel "The Year of the Angry Rabbit." Ph: Ted Voigtlander. Mus: Jimmie Haskell. PD: Stan Jolley. SpPhFX: Howard Anderson Co. Ref: MFB'73:55: "Rabbits, too, are not exactly alive with menace...." V 7/5/72. with Stuart

Whitman, Janet Leigh, Rory Calhoun, DeForest Kelley, Paul Fix.
Pest-control serum turns rabbits into wolf-sized, man-eating monster-rabbits.

*NIGHT OF THE LIVING DEAD Image 10 1968 Sequel: DAWN OF THE DEAD. SpFX: Regis Survinski, Tony Pantanello. Ref: screen.
Note: I regret my rather strident remarks re: NIGHT in the '72 volume, yet still can't quite be objective about the film. It's disturbing, yes, but "disturbing" is not my idea of a good time. George Romero seems, fortunately, in his subsequent films, not to have realized what made the first one tick. (I won't tell him if you don't.)

NIGHT OF THE SEAGULLS (Sp) Better Global Films/Profilmes-Ancla Century 1975('77-U.S.) color SP,D: Amando De Ossorio. Sequel to TOMBS OF THE BLIND DEAD. Ph: F. Sanchez. Mus: A.G. Abril. Sets: G. Andres. Ref: CineFan 2:25. V 7/20/77:7 (rated). 5/12/76:414(ad),406. with Victor Petit, Maria Kosti, Sandra Mozarosky, Julie James.
Village cursed by blood-drinking, undead knights. Original title: La NOCHE DE LAS GAVIOTAS.

NIGHT OF THE SORCERERS (Sp) (Avco Embassy-TV)/Profilmes-Hesperia 1973 color 89m. (La NOCHE DE LOS BRUJOS) D: Amando De Ossorio. Ref: TV. TVFFSB. V 5/8/74:207. CineFan 2:24. with Jack Taylor, Simon Andreu, Kali Hansa, Maria Kosti, J.Thelman.
Members of African expedition variously sacrificed, turned into monsters; leopard woman/sorceress. Tacky horror-fantasy.

The NIGHT OF THE THOUSAND CATS (Mex) Ellman/Avant 1972('74-U.S.) color 85m. (La NOCHE DE LOS MIL GATOS) SP,D: Rene Cardona. SP: also M. Marzac. Ph: Alex Phillips. Mus: Raul Lavista. Ref: V 10/25/72: "gorilla-like butler." Lee. Willis/SW. Bianco #2/78:158. V 10/9/74:19(rated). with Anjanette Comer, Zulma Faiad, Hugo Stiglitz, Christa Linder.
Madman feeds his cat-hordes human flesh; jars of severed heads.

A NIGHT OF THRILLS Univ/Rex 1914 25m. D: Joseph De Grasse. Ref: Lee: haunted-house comedy. AF-Index. with Lon Chaney.

NIGHT SCHOOL see TERROR EYES

NIGHT SHE AROSE FROM THE TOMB see NIGHT EVELYN CAME OUT OF THE GRAVE

The NIGHT STALKER ABC-TV/Dan Curtis 1972 color 74m. (The KOLCHAK PAPERS or The KOLCHA(C)K TAPES-orig t) D: John L. Moxey. SP: Richard Matheson. Ph: M. Hugo. Mus: Robert Cobert. AD: Trevor Williams. Mkp: Jerry Cash. Sequel: The NIGHT STRANGLER. Ref: TV. Lee. Murphy: FEE FI FO FUM, I SMELL BLOOD-int t? with Darren McGavin, Carol Lynley, Simon Oakland, Ralph Meeker, Barry Atwater(vampire), Kent Smith, Claude Akins, Charles McGraw, Elisha Cook Jr., Stanley Adams.

Officials in Las Vegas cover-up the fact that a vampire is loose. Nothing much new here but the setting. Juvenile comedy from McGavin, familiar vampire lore from Matheson, and a vampire with superhuman strength from SCREAM AND SCREAM AGAIN.

The NIGHT STRANGLER Time-Life-TV/ABC-TV/Fox-TV 1973 color 72m. (The TIME KILLER-orig t) D,P: Dan Curtis. SP: Richard Matheson. Sequel to The NIGHT STALKER. Ph: R. Hauser. Mus: Robert Cobert. PD: T. Williams. SpFX: Ira Anderson. Mkp: William Tuttle. Ref: TV. Lee. with Darren McGavin, JoAnn Pflug, Simon Oakland, Scott Brady, Wally Cox, Margaret Hamilton, John Carradine, Richard Anderson(alchemist), Nina Wayne.

"Killer from time" requires human blood during 18-day cycle, every 21 years, to sustain life (beginning in Chicago in 1868); leaves "residue of rotted flesh" on victims' necks. More formula horror-and-fun from Curtis and Matheson. McGavin's conniptions as Kolchak may make you feel that the real menace isn't finished off at the end.

NIGHT THAT GOD SCREAMED see NIGHT GOD SCREAMED, The

The NIGHT THAT PANICKED AMERICA ABC-TV/Para-TV 1975 color 95m. D,P: Joseph Sargent. SP: Nicholas Meyer, Anthony Wilson; radio transcript of H.G. Wells' "The War of the Worlds" by Howard Koch. Ph: Jules Brenner. Consul: Paul Stewart. Ref: TV. TV Season. with Paul Shenar(Orson Welles), Vic Morrow, Cliff De Young, Michael Constantine, Eileen Brennan, Tom Bosley, Will Geer, Meredith Baxter, Liam Dunn, Casey Kasem.

Dramatization of events surrounding the famous broadcast. The re-creation of the Welles/Wells production itself is intriguing enough, but the "surrounding events" consist of singularly witless mini-dramas: father accepting son's desire to fight, couple deciding to stay together, etc.

NIGHT TRAIN see TRAIN RIDE TO HOLLYWOOD

NIGHT WALK, The see DEATHDREAM

NIGHT WATCH (B) (Worldvision-TV)/Avco Embassy/Brut 1973 color 98m. D: Brian G. Hutton. SP: Tony Williamson, from the play by Lucille Fletcher. Add'l Dial: Evan Jones. Ph: Billy Williams. Mus: John Cameron. AD: Peter Murton. Ref: MFB'73: 194. TVFFSB. V 8/8/73. with Elizabeth Taylor, Laurence Harvey, Billie Whitelaw, Tony Britton, Linda Hayden, Bill Dean.

Madwoman makes her "visions" come true by killing couple; "old-fashioned thriller....almost continuous thunderstorm.... extremely bloody murders." (MFB)

NIGHTLINE(by M.Curtis) see DON'T ANSWER THE PHONE

*NIGHTMARE ALLEY 1947 Ref: screen. V 10/15/47: "horror yarn."

Good "mentalist" acts, and snappy byplay with Tyrone Power, Coleen Gray, Helen Walker, Joan Blondell. Routine rise-and-fall story. The fade-in/action/fade-out progression of the film's sequences is lullingly "even."

NIGHTMARE HOTEL (Sp) (Gold Key-TV)/Verga-Mercofilms-Veza 1973 color 92m. (Una VELA PARA EL DIABLO. A CANDLE FOR THE DEVIL-B) SP,D: Eugenio Martin. SP: also Antonio Fos. Ph: J.F. Aguayo. Mus: A.P. Olea. AD: Adolfo Cofino. SpFX: Pablo Perez. Ref: MFB'75:18: "formulary horror film." GKey. TVFFSB. V 5/15/74:43(ad). with Judy Geeson, Aurora Bautista, Victor Alcazar, Esperanza Roy, Lone Fleming, Blanca Estrada.

Murder victims hidden in "huge wine jars accidentally used for cooking." (MFB)

NIGHTMARE HOUSE see NIGHT GOD SCREAMED, The

NIGHTMARE IN BLOOD PFE/Xeromega 1978(1974) color/scope 90m. SP,D,P: John Stanley. SP,P: also Kenn Davis. Ph: Charles Rudnick. Ref: V 7/26/78: "frequently quite amusing." 7/11/73: 3. AMPAS. Willis/SW. Maltin/TVM. with Kerwin Mathews(Prince Zaroff), Jerry Walter, Barrie Youngfellow, Hy Pyke, Kathleen Quinlan, Dan Caldwell.

Vampire-movie actor really is vampire; two assistants kept alive with blood transfusions. Rarely-shown horror-comedy by the man who dared to replace Bob Wilkins as host of KTVU-TV's "Creature Features."

*NIGHTMARE IN WAX (Gold Key-TV)/RKO/A&E 1969 (CRIMES IN THE WAX MUSEUM-ad t) Ph: Glenn Smith. Mus Sup: Igo Kantor. AD: James Freiberg. Mkp: Martin Varnaud. Ref: TV("Creature Features"). AFI. GKey. and with John "Bud" Cardos.

Mad makeup man boiled in vat of wax; suspense-movie director named Alfred Herman; refs. to Lon Chaney, movie "The Vampires"; all-a-nightmare ending. Verbose, plodding shocker trusts too much to the ghastliness of its wax-museum-zombies premise and to the perversity of the Cameron Mitchell character. (The latter is quite a meaty role for him--mostly bologna.)

NIGHTMARE PARK see HOUSE IN NIGHTMARE PARK

NIGHTMARES (Austral.) Roadshow/Bioscope 1980 D,P: John Lamond. SP,P: Colin Eggleston. Ph: Gary Wapshott. Ref: V 10/15/80: 164(ad): "screams of terror." IFG'81:65. with Jenny Neumann, Gary Sweet, Briony Behets, Maureen Edwards.

The NIGHTS OF YASSMIN (Egy) 1979? Ref: IFG'80:115: "adapted by Barakat from the American film, CARRIE...."

NIGHTWING Col/Ransohoff 1979 color 103m. D: Arthur Hiller. SP: Steve Shagan, Bud Shrake, Martin Cruz Smith, from Smith's novel. Ph: Charles Rosher. Mus: Henry Mancini. PD: James Vance. SpVisFX: Carlo Rambaldi. SpFX: Milt Rice. SdFX: Sam Shaw. Opt: Van Der Veer. Ref: V 7/4/79. MFB'80:50-51. with Nick Mancuso, David Warner, Strother Martin, Kathryn Harrold.

Plague-bearing vampire bats responsible for series of deaths; end-of-the-world prophecy.

The NINE LIVES OF FRITZ THE CAT AI/Two Gees 1974 anim color 76m. D & Co-Sp: Robert Taylor. Sequel to FRITZ THE CAT. SpPhDes: Gregg Heschong. SpPhFX: Modern. SpFX: Bernice Bissett et al. Ref: MFB'74:182. V 5/22/74.
Trip to Mars; space adventures; 1984; gay Devil.

NINOS, Los see WOULD YOU KILL A CHILD?

The NINTH HEART (Cz) Czeskoslovensky 1980 color 90m. SP,D: Juraj Herz. Ph: Jiri Machane. Mus: Petr Hapka. AD: Vladimir Labsky. Ref: V 10/22/80. with Ondrej Pavelka, Julie Juristova, Anna Malova, Juraj Kukura.
"Astrologer who steals hearts literally."

NIPPON CHINBOTSU see TIDAL WAVE

*The NITWITS 1935 Mus D: Roy Webb. AD: Van Nest Polglase. Ref: TV. LC.
Fog, screeching cat, spider's huge shadow on wall, mummy case, "dangerous maniac" "The Black Widow" (and about 10 other people) skulking about, man in skeleton-suit ("Death taking a holiday"), all in long, "spooky" midnight sequence. A few laughs and thrills, if you wait long enough (like about an hour). The balmy-songwriter character here is actually (slightly) funnier than Wheeler and Woolsey and he's not exactly a riot.

NO-CH'A NAO TUNG-HAI (H.K.?) 1968? color Based on the novel "Feng-Shen Yen-I." Ref: Eberhard.
"The Dragon King of the East China Sea" can turn himself into a snake.

NO ORCHIDS FOR LULU see LULU(1962)

NO SUCH THING AS A VAMPIRE(by R.Matheson) see DEAD OF NIGHT(1977)

NOAH'S ARK (F) Nayfack/PIC 1947('50-U.S.) 97m. (L'ARCHE DE NOE) D: Henry Jacques. SP: Jacques Prevert, P. Laroche, A. Paraz, from latter's novel "Bitru." Ph: Henry Tiquet. Mus: Joseph Kosma. Ref: V 2/26/47. Lee. Martin/"France." with Pierre Brasseur, Alerme, Georges Rollin, Jeanne Marken.
Auto-motor invention runs on water-as-fuel.

NOBODY'S GHOUL Fox/CBS-TV 1962 anim color 7m. (Deputy Dawg) D: Dave Tendlar. Ref: Maltin/OMAM. LC.

NOBODY'S HOUSE(by A.M. Burrage) see RETURN, The

NOCHE DE LAS GAVIOTAS see NIGHT OF THE SEAGULLS

NOCHE DE LAS ORGIAS DE LOS VAMPIROS see VAMPIRE'S ALL NIGHT ORGY

NOCHE DE LOS BRUJOS see NIGHT OF THE SORCERERS

NOCHE DE LOS DIABLOS see NIGHT OF THE DEVILS

NOCHE DE LOS MIL GATOS see NIGHT OF THE THOUSAND CATS

La NOCHE DE LOS MONSTRUOUS (Mex) America 1973 D: Fernando Cortes. Ref: V 5/8/74:238.

La NOCHE DE LOS VAMPIROS (Sp) Richard 1975 (cf.VAMPIRE'S ALL NIGHT ORGY) D: Leon Klimovsky. Ref: V 5/12/76:406. with Emma Cohen, Carlos Ballesteros.

NOCHE DE WALPURGIS see WEREWOLF VS.THE VAMPIRE WOMAN

La NOCHE DEL HOMBRE LOBO (Sp-F) Kin-Films 1968 color D: Rene Govar. SP: Jacinto Molina et al. Sequel to MARK OF THE WOLFMAN. Ref: Lee. Glut/CMM. with Paul Naschy(aka J.Molina) (Waldemar, werewolf), Monique Brainville, Helene Vatelle.
Mad doc uses werewolf to kill enemies.
See also: RETORNO DEL HOMBRE LOBO.

NOCHE DEL TERROR CIEGO see TOMBS OF THE BLIND DEAD

NOCTURNA (GRANDDAUGHTER OF DRACULA) Compass Int'l/Bonet 1979 color 83m. SP,D: Harry Tampa. Story & with: Nai Bonet. Ph: Mac Ahlberg. Mus: Reid Whitelaw, Norman Bergen. AD: Jack Krueger, Steve De Vita. Anim: Bob Le Bar. Ref: Boxo 7/2/79:22. Murphy. MFB'79:180. Willis/SW. V 10/18/78:94(ad). with John Carradine(Count Dracula), Yvonne De Carlo(Jugulia), Brother Theodore, Adam Keefe, John Blyth Barrymore.
Comedy. Dracula follows his granddaughter to New York.

*NON-STOP NEW YORK Janus 1937 71m. SP: also Kurt Siodmak, Derek Twist. Mus D: Louis Levy. Ref: BFC. screen. TVFFSB. Lee. with Frank Cellier, Peter Bull, William Dewhurst.
Plane with outside observation-deck makes non-stop (18-hour) trans-Atlantic flight; hero at one point climbs across plane's roof to reach cockpit (plane still in flight)....The deceptively dawdling first half of NON-STOP NEW YORK constitutes a rather laborious assembling of the principals for the big flight. Midway, however, the movie begins to transform into a NUMBER SEVENTEEN-like parody of itself, with just the right note of self-conscious absurdity--e.g., the steward announcing dinner with a bugle; a blackmailer shaking his finger disapprovingly at a gangster about to shove the heroine out of the plane. Hilarious sequence with Francis L. Sullivan imitating a Paraguayan general. ("Maybe he wanted to tell you a limerick.") Monty Python, where are you?

The NORLISS TAPES NBC-TV/Curtis-Metromedia 1973 color 75m. D,P: Dan Curtis. SP: William F. Nolan. Story: Fred Mustard Stewart. Ph: Ben Colman. Mus: Robert Cobert. AD: Trevor Williams. SpFX: Roger George. Mkp: Fred Phillips. Ref: TV. Lee. with Roy Thinnes, Don Porter, Angie Dickinson, Claude Akins, Michele Carey, Vonetta McGee, Hurd Hatfield, Stanley Adams, Nick Dimitri(monster), Bob Schott(demon).
Monterey, Calif. Living dead man fashions demon, Sargoth, made of clay and blood, in exchange for immortality; Egyptian

ring, the Osiris scarab, allows him to leave coffin at night; victims found drained of blood ("vampire" scare); "blood circle" (medieval alchemy) restrains demon. Flimsy continuity, formula shock-scenes, tepid score. The bright side: at least Darren McGavin isn't in it.

The NORMING OF JACK 243 ABC-TV/Sullivan 1975 color 74m. D: Robert Precht. Ref: TVFFSB. with David Selby, Leslie Charleson. Future society outlaws individuality.

*NOSFERATU 1922 tinted 88m. Mus: Hans Erdmann. Ref: screen. MFB'74:37-8. E.Patalas. Lee. TVFFSB.

If a Rene Clair fantasy-comedy can fairly be described as having an air of "delicate inevitability," F.W. Murnau's NOSFERATU might be characterized as having an air of _indelicate_ inevitability. Murnau makes every movement of character and object here seem fated, entranced--e.g., the vampire Orlok's reanimated-corpse-like movements and locomotion; the death-ship gliding in and out of frame; the cloaked, fast-motion scuttling of the stage-coach; Orlok standing rigidly in the rowboat--like Conrad Veidt in his introductory scene in Murnau's 1920 Der GANG IN DIE NACHT--as it drifts to shore; the waves washing the seashore. This spectral-seeming manner of movement is suggestive of other-than-human guidance--all the lesser, individual actions (of actor, object, and camera) in the film seem to be traceable to the workings of a single mainspring. While the real-estate agent, for instance, is fiddling with papers, Orlok's eyes are fixed on the locket-portrait of the agent's wife. Hutter's preoccupation here--like all the bustling-about and to-do in the film--seems incidental to Orlok's fixed look, seems simply an unwitting adjunct of it. While others are distracted by this and that, Orlok's stare is directed towards the end matter, and _his_ implacability is anything _but_ delicate. Even his body seems incidental to--and only a vehicle for--the forces behind that stare.

See also: NOSFERATU THE VAMPYRE.

NOSFERATU THE VAMPYRE (W.G.-F) Fox/Herzog-Gaumont 1979 color 107m. (NOSFERATU: PHANTOM DER NACHT) SP,D,P: Werner Herzog. Based on the film NOSFERATU(1922) and on Bram Stoker's novel "Dracula." Ph: Jorg Schmidt-Reitwein. Mus: Popol Vuh, Florian Fricke; Wagner, Gounod. PD: Henning von Gierke, Ulrich Bergfelder. SpFX: Cornelius Siegel. Mkp: Reiko Kruk, Dominique Collandant. Ref: screen. MFB'79:151. V 1/24/79. with Klaus Kinski(Dracula), Isabelle Adjani, Bruno Ganz, Roland Topor (Renfield), Walter Ladengast, Jacques Dufilho, Beverly Walker.

Werner Herzog's gift to horror-film fans is very welcome, and is also, incidentally, one answer to the question, Is there life (in the horror film) after Romero-Cronenberg-Hooper?--after, that is, the Savage Seventies? Horror movies--with their systematic brutalization of characters and viewers alike--may have gotten to be a bit too horrifying for their (and our) own good in the Seventies. Herzog, here, returns to the Twenties and borrows not only the old Murnau-Galeen script, but the Max Schreck vampire as well; and yet he makes something new of both, and a work sufficiently horrific, but unbrutal. Klaus Kinski's Dracula may look like Schreck's Orlok, but he doesn't play like him. Kinski's dead-white Dracula is discomfortingly "intimate"--here, in the dining room, in the bedroom, is this undead creature, this corpse, pretending to be simply another player in the drama...while the other players seem understandably uncertain as to how to take him and his funny-creepy, fidgety cadaverousness. And their registered uncertainty is very amusing. This Dracula's tactless, impatient lust--and his periodic groans--make it quite clear that he is simply not one of them....Herzog, moreover, attempts to make the plight of his vampire-as-outsider tragic (as well as comic). Unfortunately, the tragic aspects of the situation are rather muffled by some indifferent acting and dialogue, and by arbitrary alterations in the Dracula plot and characterizations. These narrative improvements seem superficial, whereas Herzog and Kinski wholly reconceive the role of Dracula. If, dramatically, NOSFERATU seems unsatisfying, it's visually quite out of the ordinary, and it's probably the funniest intentionally-funny vampire movie of all. See also: HERZOG FILMS NOSFERATU(P).

NOTHING BUT THE NIGHT (B) Cinema Systems/Charlemagne 1972('75-U.S.) color 90m. (The RESURRECTION SYNDICATE-'76 Intercontinental re-r) D: Peter Sasdy. SP: Brian Hayles, from John Blackburn's novel. Ph: Ken Talbot. Mus: Malcolm Williamson. AD: Colin Grimes. SpFX: Les Bowie. Ref: MFB'73:32: "flabby, laborious." Willis/SW. V 7/31/74:28(rated). 2/11/76:34. Bill Warren. with Christopher Lee, Peter Cushing, Diana Dors, Georgia Brown, Keith Barron, Duncan Lamont.

Orphans injected with life-essence of dead trustees of orphanage "in order to perpetuate their existence."

NOTRE DAME DE PARIS(by V.Hugo) see TENDERNESS OF THE DAMNED

NOTTE CHE EVELYN USCI DALLA TOMBA see NIGHT EVELYN CAME OUT OF THE GRAVE

NOTTE DEI DANNATI see NIGHT OF THE DAMNED

NOTTE DEI DIAVOLI see NIGHT OF THE DEVILS

NOUVEAU VENU, Le see NEWCOMER, The

NOVIA ENSANGRENTADA, La see BLOOD SPATTERED BRIDE, The

NOW YOU SEE HIM, NOW YOU DON'T Buena Vista 1972 color 88m. D: Robert Butler. SP: Joseph L. McEveety. Sequel to The COMPUTER WORE TENNIS SHOES. Story: R.L. King. Ph: F.Phillips. Mus: R.F. Brunner. SpPhFX: Lycett, Lee. Ref: MFB'72:142-43. V 7/5/72. with Kurt Russell(Dexter Riley), Cesar Romero, Joe Flynn, Jim Backus, William Windom, Edward Andrews, Dave Willock, Frank Aletter, Ed Begley Jr.

"Freak electrical storm" gives student's elixir "power to render objects invisible." (MFB)

The NUDE BOMB Univ & Time-Life 1980 color 94m. (MAXWELL SMART AND THE NUDE BOMB-orig t) D: Clive Donner. SP: Arne Sultan, Bill Dana, Leonard B. Stern, based on the "Get Smart" TV series. Ph: Harry L. Wolf. Mus: Lalo Schifrin. PD: W. Tuntke. Sp FX: W. Krumm, R. Lea. Ref: V 5/7/80. MFB'81:8: "hordes of clones." with Don Adams, Sylvia Kristel, Rhonda Fleming, Dana Elcar, Norman Lloyd, Vittorio Gassman, Pamela Hensley.
Plot to denude world's population with missile-launched bombs.

La NUIT DU CIMETIERE (F) ABC 1973 color 85m. (La ROSE DE FER-alt t) SP,D: Jean Rollin. SP: also Maurice Lemaitre. Ph: J.J. Renon. Mus: Pierre Raph. Ref: V 5/9/73:106. Cinef F'73:38. Ecran 73(July,p24). with Francoise Pascal, Hughes Quester, Mireille D'Argent, Pierre Dupont.
Couple locked overnight in cemetery.

NUITS ROUGES see SHADOWMAN

NURSE KEATE(by M.G.Eberhart) see WHILE THE PATIENT SLEPT

NUN AND THE DEVIL, The see SISTERS OF SATAN

NURSE SHERRI Indep.-Int'l./JER 1977 color 88m. Story,D: Al Adamson. SP: M. Bockman, G. Tittinger. Ph: R. Michaels. AD: Ann McDonald. SpVisFX: Bob Le Bar. Mkp: Tom Schwartz. Ref: MFB'80:218. Meyers. AMPAS. Willis/SW. V 5/11/77:177(ad). with Geoffrey Land, Jill Jacobson, Marilyn Joi.
Woman possessed by spirit of dead man.

NURSE WILL MAKE IT BETTER see DEVIL'S WEB, The

The NURSEMAID'S DREAM (B) Hepworth 1908 8m. D: Lewin Fitzhamon. Ref: BFC. with Gertie Potter.
Dream: giants after baby.

The NURSE'S SECRET WB-FN 1941 65m. D: Noel M. Smith. SP: Anthony Coldeway, from Mary Roberts Rinehart's story "Miss Pinkerton." Ph: James Van Trees. Ref: TV. B.Warren. TVFFSB. LC. with Lee Patrick, Regis Toomey, Faye Emerson, Virginia Brissac, Frank Reicher, Charles Trowbridge, Julie Bishop.
Arsenic-in-hypo murder; old house; screams; skulking, cloaked figure; howling dog; "A"-film chiller music (stock?); "ghost" scare. Generally humdrum blend of mystery, horror, and comedy, though the solution is agreeably twisty, and the movie is at least livelier than the original (MISS PINKERTON, 1932).

NUTCRACKER FANTASY (U.S.-J) Sanrio 1979 puppet anim color 82m. D: Takeo Nakamura;(key anim) F. Magari, T. Nakamura. SP: T. Joachim, E. Fournier. Story: S. Tsuji, from "The

Nutcracker and the Mouseking" by E.T.A. Hoffmann. Ph: F. Otani et al. Sets: Kaburagi, Yamashita. Ref: V 8/8/79. JFFJ 13:11,14. Voices: Christopher Lee, Roddy McDowall, et al.
Princess turned into sleeping mouse, her heart "stolen by an army of evil mice." (V)

*The NUTTY PROFESSOR Lewis Ent. 1963 AD: Hal Pereira, Walter Tyler. Mkp:(sup) Wally Westmore; Jack Stone. Ref: screen. Lee. and with Richard Kiel, Doodles Weaver.
Chemistry teacher Julius Kelp transforms himself into a horrible, hairy monster, then into hip Buddy Love, the idol of everyone (especially himself). Jerry Lewis accomplishes the double feat of making both his Dr. Jekyll and his Mr. Hyde interesting--his Julius Kelp may in fact be the most engaging screen Jekyll. Both Julius and Buddy are more likely closer to aggravations of the real Lewis--logical personal extremes--than they are (as they have on occasion been supposed to be) to portraits of Lewis and Dean Martin, resp. Both personae seem figures of self-deflation, or comic apology, rather than vindictiveness. And his Julius-Buddy vocal confusions--one voice segueing right into the other--suggest a composite (Lewis himself, perhaps). Unfortunately, the script offers only suggestions of a more complex character, and fails to develop either protagonist very far beyond amusing schtiks. The dual role seems, finally, a technical feat, the only interest of an otherwise patchily-written-and-charactered movie.

OBSESSED, The see EERIE MIDNIGHT HORROR SHOW, The

OBSZONITATEN see CONFESSIONS OF A MALE ESCORT

OCCHI DALLE STELLE see EYES BEHIND THE STARS

OCCHIO NEL LABIRINTO see BLOOD(1971)

OCCHIO SBARRATO NEL BUIO see EYEBALL

OCTA-MAN (Heritage-TV)/Filmers Guild 1971 color 83m. (OCTO-MAN-orig t) D: Harry Essex. Mkp: Rick Baker;(des) George Barr. Ref: TVFFSB. Lee. with Pier Angeli, Kerwin Mathews, Jeff Morrow, Harry Guardino.
Earth visited by part-man, part-octopus creature from space.

ODIO A MI CUERPO see I HATE MY BODY

ODISSEA,L' or ODYSSEY, The see HOMER'S ODYSSEY

OEUFORIQUES (F) Phar 3 1975 anim D,P: Henri Heidsieck. Ref: IFG'75:469: "three frightening robots."

*OF GODS AND THE DEAD New Yorker 1969('72-U.S.) (97m.) Sets & Cost: F. Imperio. Ref: screen. Willis/SW. Lee. NYT 6/19/72.

with Norma Bengell, Othon Bastos, Nelson Xavier.
A modernist endurance test from Brazil--one-hundred-minutes' worth of "tableaux." (Refuse to take it.)

OF THE DEAD see DES MORTS

OH THAT MOLAR! (B) Alpha 1906 3m. D: Arthur Cooper. Ref: BFC.
"Man with toothache dreams of demon teeth dancing in head."

OILY MANIAC (H.K.) Shaw 1976 color 90m. D: Ho Meng-hua. SP: Chua Lam. Ph: T. Hui-chi. AD: C. Ching-shen. Ref: V 10/20/76. with Li Hsiu-hsien, Chen Ping, Lily Li.
Incantation turns plantation manager into monster.

OISEAU DE NUIT (F) 1975? anim D: B. Palacios. Ref: IFG'76:455.
"Winged bird-woman...from another world."

Los OJOS SINIESTROS DEL DR. ORLOFF (Sp) Manacoa 1973 D: Jesus Franco. Sequel to The AWFUL DR.ORLOF. Ref: V 5/17/78:389. 5/7/75:243: "horror." 8/22/73:20. with Montserrat Prons, Loretta Tovar, Robert Woods.

*The OLD DARK HOUSE 1932 AD: Charles D. Hall. Mkp: Jack Pierce. Ref: screen. MFB'79:159. Lee.
Eva Moore, Boris Karloff, Ernest Thesiger, and Brember Wells are very entertaining as the peculiar members of the old dark household--Moore especially is amusing/alarming with her vitriolic Puritanism. Charles Laughton, Melvyn Douglas, Raymond Massey, Lilian Bond, and Gloria Stuart, however, are a rather tiresome lot as their guests--we're actually asked to take them *seriously*. While Moore's dialogue as Rebecca Femm works to create a genuine comic-monster character, Laughton's speeches as Porterhouse simply spell out *his*--in his case it's just words. The movie is half delightful and half pretty awful; the shrilly optimistic, laughably compressed whirlwind-romance between Bond and Douglas is the worst of it. The Femms may be bad examples for their guests, but they're at least good theatre.

OLD DRACULA (B) AI/WFS 1974('75-U.S.) color 88m. (VAMPIRA-B. VAMPIRELLA-orig t. VAMPIR. VAMPIRE-int ts) D: Clive Donner. SP: Jeremy Lloyd. Ph: Tony Richmond. Mus: David Whitaker; (Vampira theme) Anthony Newley. AD: Philip Harrison. Mkp: Phil Leakey. Ref: MFB'74:257. TV. Murphy. FM 163:23. Willis/SW. V 11/12/75. 8/13/75:4(rated). 8/1/73:22. with David Niven (Vladimir Dracula), Teresa Graves, Jennie Linden, Veronica Carlson, Nicky Henson, Linda Hayden, Bernard Bresslaw.
Dracula requires extremely-rare-type blood to restore wife (dead 50 years) to life; telepathy; body-switching; by end, both are black. Fast, loose, but only very occasionally funny. The point of too many of the gags is simply that Dracula and Vampira are vampires. (Niven: "*Night* is *my* time of day.") But so many parodic darts get tossed that a few were bound to hit *some* target, and Teresa Graves as Vampira has some of Paula Prentiss' brash, offhand goofiness and charm.

OMBRA NELL'OMBRA see RING OF DARKNESS

The OMEGANS (U.S.-Fili) (Para-TV)/Wilder 1967 color 85m. D, P: W. Lee Wilder. SP: Waldon Wheeland. Ph: Herbert V. Theis. Mus: Albert Elms. SpFX: Francis Rooker. Ref: TV. Les Otis. TVFFSB. Lee. with Keith Larsen, Ingrid Pitt, Bruno Punzalan.

Overdose of phosphorous in Malayan river's waters makes victims phosphorescent, ultimately "cremates" them. A slow bore, with none of the old W. Lee Wilder spark. Telling line: "And you won't chicken out at the last minute like you did with the snake?" (Or, how to admit guilt, in an overheard conversation.) The Ingrid Pitt character here just suffers and suffers.

The OMEN Fox 1976 color/scope 111m. (The ANTI-CHRIST-orig t) D: Richard Donner. SP: David Seltzer. Sequels: DAMIEN-OMEN II. The FINAL CONFLICT. Ph: Gilbert Taylor. Mus: Jerry Goldsmith. AD: Carmen Dillon. SpFX: John Richardson. Mkp: Stuart Freeborn. Ref: MFB'76:170. TV. V 8/4/76:6. 6/9/76. with Gregory Peck, Lee Remick, David Warner, Billie Whitelaw, Leo McKern, Harvey Stephens(Damien), Martin Benson, Sheila Raynor.

The baby Damien, the anti-Christ, is substituted for the murdered newborn of an American couple, and the Devil protects his own with nanny, dogs, storm, fire, truck, and (last but not least) paternal feeling. This combination of the Book of Revelations and "The Twilight Zone" is chock-full of diabolical revelations (e.g., the anti-Bethlehem star, the "devil's shafts" in the photos) which, in your average mystery, would be called "clues," and The OMEN in fact does pretty well as a mystery. Its "sleuths" (Peck and Warner) make the rounds of hospitals, monasteries, and cemeteries--but the "murderer" wins _this_ round in the trilogy. It should, perhaps, be noted that The OMEN does _less well_ as drama (there are more clues than characters), horror (the shocks seem manufactured), or metaphysics (Revelations is reduced to a code book).

OMS EN SERIE(by S.Wul) see FANTASTIC PLANET

ON PROBATION Peerless 1935 71m. D: Charles Hutchison. SP: Sherman L. Lowe. Story: Crane Wilbur. Ph: Henry Kruse. Sets: Jennett. Ref: Turner/Price. no LC. with Monte Blue, Lucile Browne, William Bakewell, Barbara Bedford, Henry Hall.

"Old hag fortune-teller's" curse of death-by-lion fulfilled.

ONCE UPON A RHYME (Harvey-TV)/Para 1950 anim color 8m. D: I. Sparber. SP: I. Klein. Ref: TV. LC. Maltin/OMAM.

Casper in Mother Goose Land, saving Little Red Riding Hood from the wolf; haunted house, ghosts. Bland.

ONCE UPON A SPY ABC-TV/Col-TV & David Gerber 1980 color 94m. D: Ivan Nagy. SP,Story: Jimmy Sangster. Story: also Lemuel Pitkin. Ph: Dennis Dalzell. Mus: John Cacavas. PD: Duane Alt. SpFX: John Unsinn. Ref: TV. TVG. with Ted Danson, Mary Louise Weller, Christopher Lee, Eleanor Parker, Leonard Stone.

Shrinking machine which employs cosmic rays; super-computer;

helicopter with super-magnet which lifts up car; "mass-reducer" rays, bounced off satellite, shrink aircraft carrier; human maze-game; madman's plot to take over U.S. foiled by "100% refraction" of rays (back to source). Slick, empty sf-spy TV-movie. Slight but inoffensive. Highlight: the cat-and-the-canary maze-game. Sangster and Lee together again!

ONCE UPON A VIRGIN see PHANTASMES

ONDATA DI PIACERE see WAVES OF LUST

ONE-ARMED BANDIT (Swed) Svenska 1974 anim D: Peter Kruse. Ref: IFG'75:472: gamblers "swallowed up by Frankenstein fruit-machines."

ONE DEADLY OWNER (B) ABC-TV/ITC-TV 1974 color 74m. D: Ian Fordyce. SP: Brian Clemens. Mus: Laurie Johnson. Anim: Dolphin. Ref: TV. TVFFSB. with Donna Mills, Jeremy Brett, Laurence Payne, Robert Morris.
Rolls Royce "has a mind of its own and a terrifying past."

ONE MAN'S SECRET(by R.Weiman) see POSSESSED(1947)

*ONE TOO-EXCITING NIGHT 1922 (Q-Riosities series) SP,D: Gaston Quiribet. Ref: BFC.

ONE WOMAN'S REVENGE see REVENGE!

ONI (J) 1973? puppet anim D,P: K. Kawamoto. Ref: IFG'74:534.
Mother turns into witch "who haunts her own sons."

ONLY A ROOM-ER (B) Cricks 1916 10m. D: Toby Cooper. SP: E. Dangerfield. Ref: BFC. with Jack Jarman.
Men play tricks on friend sleeping in "haunted" room.

OPERATION BORORO (Cz) Barrandov 1973 color 90m. (AKCE BORORO) SP,D: Otakar Fuka. Ph: Josef Hanus. Mus: Petr Hapka. Ref: V 7/25/73: at Trieste. with S. Matyas, B. Turzonova.
Woman from another planet; miracle drug.

OPERATION "SILVER MONKEY" (Hung.) 1971 anim color 10m. (EZUSTMAJOM) D: Otto Foky. SP: J. Nepp. Elec Mus: J. Toth. Ref: Hungarofilm bltn #3(1972). Cinef W'73:39.
Alien spy sent to Earth.

OPOWIESCI O PILOCIE PIRXIE see TEST PILOT PIRX

ORCA Para/De Laurentiis 1977 color/scope 92m. (The KILLER WHALE-orig t. ORCA, THE KILLER WHALE-alt t) D: Michael Anderson. SP,P: Luciano Vincenzoni. SP: also S. Donati. Ph: Ted Moore. Mus: Ennio Morricone. PD: M. Garbuglia. SpPhFX: Van Der Veer. SpFX: Alec C. Weldon. Ref: V 6/2/76:34.(d) 7/13/77. MFB'77:171: "pallid." with Richard Harris, Charlotte Rampling, Will Sampson, Bo Derek, Keenan Wynn, "Red" Barry, R. Carradine.
Killer whale seeks revenge for death of its mate.

ORCHID FOR NO.1,An see LICENSED TO LOVE AND KILL

ORGIA DE LOS MUERTOS see BRACULA

ORGIES OF DRACULA see DRACULA'S BRIDE

*ORLAK, THE HELL OF FRANKENSTEIN Col/Independiente 1961 90m. Ph: F. Colin. Mus: R. Fuentes; F.J. Perez? Ref: TV. Lee. and with David Reynoso, Antonio Raxel, Rosa de Castilla, A. Calvo, Joaquin Cordero, Andres Soler.

Remote-controlled monster, Orlak, used as super-strong, invulnerable murderer; "vampire" killings. Protracted horror-western-romance. Alarming climactic scene of the monster's now-haywire head smoking and melting.

The ORPHAN New World?/World Northal 1979 color 85m. (DON'T OPEN THE DOOR-final t? FRIDAY THE 13TH...THE ORPHAN-orig t) SP,D: John Ballard, from Saki's short story "Sredni Vashtar." Ph: Beda K. Batka. Mus: Ted Macero. AD: S.A. MacKenzie. Ref: Boxo 12/3/79: "for late horror shows." V 12/12/79. 2/25/80:35. 9/10/80:42. AMPAS. Willis/SW. with Mark Owens, Peggy Feury, Joanna Miles, Donn Whyte, Eleanor Stewart.

Disturbed boy subject to violent fantasies (e.g., toy ape attacking aunt).

ORRORI DEL CASTELLO DI NORIMBERGA see BARON BLOOD

ORU KAIJU DAISHINGEKI see GODZILLA'S REVENGE

OSCAR, KINA Y EL LASER (Sp) Signo 1978 color 92m. SP,D: Jose Maria Blanco. SP: also S. Porqueras. Story: Carmen Kurtz. Ph: J. Gelpi. Mus: Castro Dario. SpFX: Juan Palleja. Ref: V 3/14/79. 10/18/78:228(ad). with Jose M. Alonso, Manuel Alberto, C. Castellanos, Monica Garcia.

Talking, home-made laser-ray machine makes boy invisible.

OSSESSA, L' see EERIE MIDNIGHT HORROR SHOW, The

The OTHER Fox/Rex-Benchmark 1972 color 100m. D: Robert Mulligan. SP & Exec P: Thomas Tryon, from his novel. Ph: R.L. Surtees. Mus: Jerry Goldsmith. PD: Albert Brenner. Ref: screen. MFB'72:256. Lee(V 5/24/72). with Uta Hagen, Diana Muldaur, Chris & Martin Udvarnoky, Victor French, John Ritter.

1935. Schizophrenic boy blames series of deaths on twin brother, who's dead; (anachronistic) ref. to MURDER IN THE BLUE ROOM(1944). The script of The OTHER springs its one surprise (as if it were a coup) some 60 minutes into the movie. And a few minutes later the first "objective" shot finally occurs: Niles is shown talking, not to dead-brother Holland, but to...air. There are hints of this subjective trick--Holland is not seen with Niles whenever anyone else is present. But it's still a cheat, and one used before in films (in, for instance, PILLOW OF DEATH, 1945). The movie itself seems schizophrenic, successful neither as an evocation of a sick-child's fantasy-world, nor as a shocker. It's quietly but crassly exploitative, not of violence (which is ellipsed), but of schizophrenia, which is reduced to a narrative stunt.

The OTHER PERSON (B) Granger-Binger 1921 66m. D: B.E. Doxat-Pratt. SP: B. James, from Fergus Hume's novel. Ref: BFC. with Zoe Palmer, A. Migliar, Arthur Pusey,Ivo Dawson, N.Hayden.
"Seance proves ghost impelled spiritualist to kill father."

The OTHER SMILE (W.G.) BA-Van Ackeren 1978 color 115m. (Das ANDERE LAECHELN) SP,D: Robert Van Ackeren. SP: also Joy Markert, Peter Stripp. Ph: Janken Janssen. Ref: V 6/21/78. with Katja Rupe, Elisabeth Trissenaar, Heinz Ehrenfreund.
"Vampire theme": wife and girl friend slowly exchange personalities.

The OTHERS NBC-TV/McCleery 1957 color 54m. Based on Henry James's novella "The Turn of the Screw." Ref: TVFFSB. with Sarah Churchill, Tommy Kirk, Geoffrey Toone.
"Governess battles evil spirits for two children's souls."

OUANGA Hoffberg 1935 63m. (DRUMS OF THE NIGHT-orig t. CRIME OF VOODOO. DRUMS OF THE JUNGLE-alt ts. sfa *The LOVE WANGA?) SP,D,P: George Terwilliger. Remake: POCOMANIA. Ph: Carl Berger. Ref: Turner/Price. Lee. with Fredi Washington, Sheldon Leonard, Philip Brandon, Marie Paxton, Winifred Harris.
Voodoo priestess who plots to destroy plantation owner's fiancee through hypnosis and voodoo; voodoo tree; curse.

OUT OF THE DARKNESS see NIGHT CREATURE

The OUTER SPACE CONNECTION (Gold Key-TV)/Sunn/Landsburg 1975 color 92m. SP,D: Fred Warshofsky. From the book by Alan & Sally Landsburg. Ph: Jeri Sopanen et al. Mus: Roger Wagner. Narr: Rod Serling. Ref:MFB'78:94. TVFFSB. V 1/29/75:28(rated).
Alien-colonization-of-Earth theories, involving cloning, the Bermuda Triangle, reincarnation, Egypt's pyramids.

OUTER SPACE JITTERS Col 1957 16m. D,P: Jules White. SP: Jack White. Ref: Lee. LC. with The 3 Stooges, Gene Roth, Emil Sitka, Dan Blocker, Philip Van Zandt.
Aliens with electricity for blood; prehistoric man.

OUTER TOUCH (B) Three-Six-Two 1979 color 78m. D: Norman J. Warren. SP: Andrew Payne, from an idea by David Speechley. Ph: J. Metcalfe, P. Sinclair. AD: Hayden Pearce. Mkp: Robin Grantham. Ref: MFB'79:198. with Barry Stokes, Tony Maiden, Glory Annen, Michael Rowlatt, Ava Cadell.
"Three women from a parthenogenic civilization" seek out human specimens for a galactic zoo.

OUTLAND (U.S.-B) WB/Ladd Co.(Outland) 1981 color/scope 109m. (IO-orig t) SP,D: Peter Hyams. Ph: Stephen Goldblatt. Mus: Jerry Goldsmith. PD: Philip Harrison. SpFX: John Stears. SpOptFxSup: Roy Field. Wire FX: Bob Harman. Laser FX: Holoco.

Video: Richard Hewitt. SdFX: R.M. Thirlwell. Mkp: Peter Robb-King. Ref: screen. V 5/20/81. 6/3/81:36. with Sean Connery, Peter Boyle, Frances Sternhagen, James Sikking, Kika Markham.
Super-production of Con-Am mining operation on Io, a moon of Jupiter, is traced to company-supplied amphetamines which promote industriousness--and insanity. As a reworking of HIGH NOON, OUTLAND is less provocative and amusing than RIO BRAVO; as sf it's almost non-existent (the space setting merely provides an excuse for a few nice effects and stunts); as an actor vehicle (for Connery and Sternhagen) it passes--both have bright moments. The "suspense" is hardly killing.

OVERLORDS OF THE UFO Gold Key-TV 1977 color 92m. Ref: TVFFSB: "examination" of UFO's. TVG.

OVERSEXED Scotia American 1974 color 75m. SP,D: Joe Sarno, based on Stevenson's story "The Strange Case of Dr. Jekyll & Mr. Hyde." Ph: Bill Godsey. Ref: MFB'75:143. with Veronica Parrish(Shirley Jekyll/Sherry Hyde), Eric Edwards, S. Landham.
Dr. Shirley Jekyll experiments on herself with serum which increases her sexual appetite and bustline.

PA JAKT EFTER DRACULA see IN SEARCH OF DRACULA

The PACK WB 1977 color 99m. (The LONG HARD NIGHT-B) SP,D: Robert Clouse. From Dave Fisher's novel. Ph: Ralph Woolsey. Mus: Lee Holdridge. SpFX: Milton Rice. Ref: V(d) 8/24/77. MFB'77:237. '78:107,126. with Joe Don Baker, Hope Alexander-Willis, Richard B. Shull, R.G.Armstrong, Richard O'Brien.
"Unseen horror" as wild dogs menace residents of remote island. (V).

PAN TVARDOVSKIJ see MR. TVARDOVSKI

PANG HSIEN see CLAM FAIRY

PANIC AT LAKEWOOD MANOR see IT HAPPENED AT LAKEWOOD MANOR

PANIC IN THE WILDERNESS Gold Key-TV 1975 color 93m. Ref: GKey. TVG: Canadian Bigfoot-type.

PANICO EN EL TRANSIBERIANO see HORROR EXPRESS

PANIK (Hung.) Pannonia 1979 anim color 10m. D & Anim: Sandor Reisenbuchler. From Karel Capek's sf novel "War with the Newts." Ref: HKFFest.

PANNA A NETVOR see BEAUTY AND THE BEAST(1979)

PANTHER ISLAND see BOMBA ON PANTHER ISLAND

PAPER DOLLS(by L.P.Davies) see JOURNEY INTO DARKNESS

PARAMOUNT ON PARADE Para 1930 b&w & color 77m.(100m.) D: Rowland V. Lee, Edward Sutherland, et al. Ph: H. Fischbeck, V. Milner. Sets: John Wenger. Ref: Everson/TDIF. TVFFSB. AFI. NYT 4/21/30. Chirat: F. version with M. Moreno; GALAS DE LA PARAMOUNT-Sp. vers. with Barry Norton; Cz. vers. with J. Werich; also Dutch, Pol., I., Rum., Dan. versions.

Skit with Clive Brook(Sherlock Holmes), William Powell(Philo Vance), Warner Oland(Fu Manchu), Eugene Pallette(Sgt.Heath).

PARADE OF THE WOODEN SOLDIERS Para 1933 anim 8m. D: Dave Fleischer. Ref: LC. Lee: "features parody of KING KONG."

PARASITE MURDERS, The see THEY CAME FROM WITHIN

Los PARCHIS VS. EL INVENTOR INVISIBLE (Arg) PA & ATC 1981? SP,D: Mario Sabato. SP: also V. Proncet. Ref: V 5/13/81:377. with the Parchis, Julio de Grazia, Javier Portales.

PARIS-VAMPIRE(by C.Klotz) see DRACULA AND SON

PARTS THE CLONUS HORROR Group 1/Clonus 1979 color 90m. (The CLONUS HORROR. CLONUS-early ts) SP,D,P: Robert S. Fiveson. SP,P: Myrl A. Schreibman. SP:also R. Smith, B. Sullivan. Ph: Max Beaufort. Mus: Hod David Schudson. AD: Steve Nelson. SpFX: Steve Karkus. SpMkp: Joe Blasco. Ref: screen. AMPAS. V 10/18/78:86. 7/18/79:13. 11/14/79. with Timothy Donnelly, Paulette Breen, Keenan Wynn, Peter Graves, Lurene Tuttle.

Specially-bred clone escapes Clonus, organ-bank research center providing parts for selected Americans. Flat-footed, almost amateurish sf-horror--the "horror," "humor," "drama," "action," and "social significance" never leave their qualifying quotes. Cookie-cut from standard sf/adventure/drama patterns.

PAS DE VIOLENCE ENTRE NOUS see QUEM E BETA?

PASSIONE D'AMORE (I-F) Massfilm & Cocinor 1981 color 118m. SP,D: Ettore Scola. SP: also Ruggero Maccari, from a novel by Tarchetti. Ph: C. Ragona. Mus: Armando Trovajoli. Sets: F. Senese. Ref: V 5/20/81. S&S Smr'81:162: from TV serial. with Valeria D'Obici, Bernard Giraudeau, Laura Antonelli, Jean-Louis Trintignant, Massimo Girotti, Bernard Blier.

"Beauty and the Beast" tale; woman with "face like Nosferatu"; man "transformed into a grizzly bear." (V)

The PASSIONS OF CAROL Ambar 1975 color 76m. SP,D,Ed: Amanda Barton. From Dickens' "A Christmas Carol." AD: G. Esposito. Ref: Willis/SW. V 3/19/75: "eerie." with Mary Stuart, Marc Stevens(Marley), Jamie Gillis, Kim Pope; A. Millhouse, K. Andre, H. Richler(ghosts).

PASTEL DE SANGRE see BLOOD PIE

PATAYIN MO SA SINDAK SI BARBARA! (Fili) Rosas 1974 color 96m. Story,D: C.A. Castillo. SP: Mike Makiling. Ph: R. Remias.

Mus: Ernani Cuenco. Ref: V 9/25/74. 8/14/74:28. with Susan Roces, Dante Rivero, Rosanna Ortiz.
An EXORCIST-inspired "story of possession."

PATH TO SAVAGERY(by R.E.Alter) see RAVAGERS

PATRICK (Austral) Vanguard(Monarch)/AIFC 1978 color 90m.(110m.) D: Richard Franklin. SP: Everett de Roche. Ph: Don McAlpine. Mus: Brian May. AD: L. Binns. SpFxSup: C.C. Rothmann. Mkp: J.L. Perez. Ref: MFB'79:127. TV. V 7/26/78: Filmways? Willis/ SW. with Susan Penhaligon, Robert Helpmann, Rod Mullinar, Julia Blake, Robert Thompson(Patrick).
Comatose man's compensatory-plus, psycho-kinetic powers peak, lethally, when others threaten him. Cold, mechanical exercise in psycho-kinetic legerdemain. Typewriter tricks, elevator tricks, flower-pot tricks, etc., enliven an otherwise drab program of hospital-staff one-upmanship and impossible love (i.e., Patrick's for his nurse). Mediocre.

PAUK (Yugos) Zagreb 1969 anim 12m. D & Des: A. Marks, V. Jutrisa. Mus: Klobucar. Ref: Lee.
After killing man-sized spider, man turns into one too.

PAYSAGE (F) 1975? anim D: Jan Lenica. Ref: IFG'76:455.
"Land where bodiless skulls chase and bite one another."

*The PEARL OF DEATH 1944 Ref: TV. FM 165:14. V 8/30/44.
The "monster at large" in London proves to be the "Oxton horror," aka the Creeper (Rondo Hatton), who breaks the backs of his victims (and always at the third lumbar vertebra). He also smashes a lot of china. (Holmes: "But why bric-a-brac and nothing but bric-a-brac?") Enough "why?"'s to make a (barely) passable mystery. The "horror" (Hatton) here seems a last-minute graft to the mystery plot; the latter depends overly on limp masquerades by Sherlock Holmes (Basil Rathbone) and Giles Conover (Miles Mander). Nigel Bruce as Watson, however, is quietly delightful in this one. He's the ideal counterpoint to Rathbone's vigorousness and Dennis Hoey's Lestradian exasperation.
See also: BRUTE MAN,The. HOUSE OF HORRORS.

La PEAU DE CHAGRIN (Yugos) Zagreb 1960 anim color 10m. (SAGRENSKA KOZA) D & Des: Vladimir Kristl. D: also Ivo Vrbanic. From Balzac's story. Mus: Prohaska. Ref: TV. Lee.
Youth receives wish-fulfilling skin from the Devil.

La PEAU DE CHAGRIN (F) 1981 D: Michel Favart. Ref: V 8/12/81: 34: TV-movie.
See also: DESIRE. PIEL DE ZAPA, La.

PECADO NA SACRISTIA see SIN IN THE VESTRY

*PEEPING TOM Corinth-Libra 1959('79-re-r) 109m.(90m.-U.S., Astor, '62) AD: Arthur Lawson. Ref: screen. Lee. FQ Spr'80:

2-10. and with Miles Malleson, Jack Watson.

An offbeat black-comedy-drama, tart on the surface but a bit soft at the center. Bravura sick/shock ending, funny in-jokes ("You won't see that in Sight and Sound."), and a wry contribution from Malleson. But all the lines and details re: sight dovetail too neatly, and the story is, after all, about another poor guy who must kill what he, in his twisted way, loves/hates. (See also WEREWOLF OF LONDON, The WOLF MAN, The LODGER, POWER OF THE WHISTLER, Spike Jones, etc.)

Una PELEA CUBANA CONTRA LOS DEMONIOS (Cuban) ICAIC 1972 120m. SP,D: Tomas G. Alea. SP: also Jose Triana et al. From the book by F. Ortiz. Ph: Joya. Mus: Leo Brower. Ref: V 8/9/72. with J.A. Rodriguez, Raul Pomares, Olivia Belizaire.

17th-century Cuba. Demon possession, exorcism, pirates.

The PEOPLE ABC-TV/American Zoetrope(Coppola)-Fries 1972 color 74m. D: John Korty. SP: James M. Miller, from the book "Pilgrimage: The Book of the People" by Zenna Henderson. Ph: Edward Rosson. Mus: Carmen Coppola. AD: Jack Degovia. SpFX: Ken Phelps. Ref: TV. Lee. with Kim Darby, William Shatner, Dan O'Herlihy, Diane Varsi, Laurie Walters.

Miracle-working folk with ESP powers (inc. levitation) in secluded valley prove to be survivors of extinct planet. Too too sweet-and-simple tract on intolerance is well-meant but plays awkwardly.

See also: ESCAPE TO WITCH MOUNTAIN.

PEOPLE Damiano 1979 color 85m. D,P: Gerard Damiano. Ref: Cinema-X Review 1/80. SFC 9/22/79(ad). with Eric Edwards, Kasey Rodgers, Serena, Jamie Gillis, Susan McBain, Kelly Green.

Six stories. Third in hardcore version titled "Vampires."

The PEOPLE THAT TIME FORGOT (U.S.-B) AI/Amicus 1977 color 90m. D: Kevin Connor. SP: Patrick Tilley, from Edgar Rice Burroughs' novel. Ph: Alan Hume;(process) Charles Staffel. Mus: John Scott. PD: Maurice Carter. SpFX: John Richardson, Ian Wingrove. Mkp: Robin Grantham. Ref: V(d) 6/21/77. MFB '77:172. TV. with Patrick Wayne, Sarah Douglas, Dana Gillespie(cave woman), Thorley Walters, Doug McClure, Shane Rimmer, Tony Britton, Dave Prowse, Milton Reid(Sabbala), John Hallam.

Back to Caprona: flashbacks to LAND THAT TIME FORGOT; pterodactyl; stegosaurus; armadillo-like dinosaur; cave with monsters in holes-in-walls; skull-shaped mountain; big spider; couple allosaur-types. Juvenile, occasionally agreeably daft sf-adventure. The dinosaur effects aren't sophisticated but are kind of fun--e.g., the "armadillo"'s relentless plod-plod-plod through the forest, towards the three bound protagonists; the pterodactyl pecking inquisitively at the plane's wing. (The latter image belongs somewhere in the great Cinema Scrapbook.) Reid is the only actor worth mentioning--he looks as if time might have lost track of him.

Sequel to The LAND THAT TIME FORGOT. See also: AT THE EARTH'S CORE.

The PEOPLE WHO OWN THE DARK (Sp) Newcal(Cunningham)/Trefilms 1975('80-U.S.) color 86m. (PLANETA CIEGO) D: Leon Klimovsky. SP: Vicente Aranda, Harry Narunsky. SpFX: Jesus Pena. Ref: screen. ad. V 8/1/79(rated). 5/12/76:416. with Maria Perschy, Tony Kendall, Paul Naschy, A.de Mendoza, T. Gimpera.
A nuclear holocaust which blinds most people spares a group conducting a Sadean ceremony in the cellar of a chateau. The spared lash out at the blind, and vice versa. All the principals but two are killed; the two are "rescued" by a decontamination crew "from the south," then put to sleep and buried alive as (with terrible irony) Beethoven's Ninth blares forth from a radio. Ill-conceived mixture of horror, sf, and dollar-book cynicism.

PEOPLETOYS see DEVIL TIMES FIVE

PEPITO Y CHABELO VS. LOS MONSTRUOUS (Mex) Alameda 1973 (CHABELO Y PEPITO CONTRA LOS MONSTRUOUS-alt t) D: Jose Estrada. Ref: V 5/8/74:238. Glut/CMM.
Comedy featuring the Wolf Man, Dracula, the Frankenstein monster, Mr. Hyde, the mummy, and a gorilla.

PER, JOM, PHEN (Thai) Saha Mongkol 1980 color 125m. D: Sompong Tribupa. SP: Laem Bandit. Ph: Vudhichai. Mus: Buan Savatcho. AD: Permpohem. Ref: V 10/29/80. with Thep Thienchai, Long Kaomonkadee, B. Savatcho, Sitao.
Comedy dealing with the power of invisibility.

*PERCY MGM 1971 Sequel: PERCY'S PROGRESS. Mus: R.Davies.Ref:Lee.

PERCY'S PROGRESS (B) Brenner/Box-Thomas 1974('79-U.S.) color 101m. (IT'S NOT THE SIZE THAT COUNTS-U.S. PERCY'S PRIVATE PARTS-alt U.S.t) D: Ralph Thomas. SP: Sid Colin; Ian La Frenais. Ph: Tony Imi. Mus: Tony Macauley. AD: A. Witherick. Ref: MFB'74:204-5. V 4/4/79. 10/1/75:47(ad). with Leigh Lawson, Elke Sommer, Denholm Elliott, Judy Geeson, Harry H. Corbett, Vincent Price, Julie Ege, Milo O'Shea, George Coulouris.
Chemical dumped in world's water supplies makes all men impotent.

PERE ET FILS see DRACULA AND SON

The PERILS OF PORK PIE (B) Homeland 1916 50m. D: W.P. Kellino. SP: Reuben Gillmer. Ref: BFC. with Billy Merson.
Man dreams mummy in British Museum comes to life.

PERSECUTION see TERROR OF SHEBA

PERSEI (Russ) 1973 anim 10m. D: A. Snezhko-Blotskaya. Ref: Reveaux: Perseus vs. the Gorgon.

PERSEY see STORY OF PERSEUS, The

PERVERSIONS SEXUELLES see LIPS OF BLOOD

The PET McCay 1921? anim 7m. (The MONSTER DOG-alt t) D: Winsor McCay. "Dream of a Rarebit Fiend" series. Ref: PFA notes 12/7/76(Reveaux). screen. Lee: 1917. VV 1/26/76.

Woman's new pet--a stray dog/cat/calf which she calls Cutey--frisks about, licks faces, and does what comes naturally to it--principally eating. It eats (and grows) and eats, beginning with small objects, progressing to larger ones, including its new owners (its appetite increasing with its size); then to houses, planes, Chicago. ("Maybe Rough on Rats will kill it!"--No.) This monster-pet isn't mean or vindictive, just there and hungry and rather frighteningly inexorable. Finally, it simply bursts. (Gastronomical logic.) With The PET, the Monster Movie is born, and arguably has its finest (as well as first) moment.

See also: El GRIPOTERIO.

The PET STORE UA/Disney 1933 anim 7m. (MICKEY THE GORILLA TAMER-8mm t) D: Wilfred Jackson. Ref: Glut/CMM: Mickey Mouse spoof of KING KONG. LC. Maltin/OMAM.

PETER EN DE VLIEGENDE AUTOBUS see FLYING WITHOUT WINGS

PETEY WHEATSTRAW Tronsue 1978 color 93m. SP,D: Cliff Roquemore. Ph: Nickolas Von Sternberg. Ref: V 5/3/78. with Rudy Ray Moore, Jimmy Lynch, G.Tito Shaw(the Devil).

Lucifer restores murder victims to life; deal with Devil.

PETIT POUCET see TOM THUMB(1972)

PETIT PRINCE,Le(by A.De St.-Exupery) see LITTLE PRINCE,The

PHAENOMENE see MYSTERIES OF THE GODS

PHANTASM Avco Embassy/New Breed 1978 color 89m. SP,D,Ph: Don Coscarelli. Mus: Fred Myrow, Malcolm Seagrave. PD: S. Tyer. SpFX: Paul Pepperman. Models: Silver Sphere, Willard Green. Mkp: Shirley Mae. Ref: screen. MFB'79:182. FM 165:4, 8. V 3/7/79. with Angus Scrimm(The Tall Man), Michael Baldwin, Bill Thornbury, Reggie Bannister, Kathy Lester.

Dead bodies furnish raw material for homunculi (used as slaves in another dimension); spy-sphere which drills into victim's head; alien being's severed finger becomes vicious little, crazed-Muppet-like creature. Fun horror stunts and jack-in-the-box-like shocks make criticisms about character (there are none) and continuity (there is none) seem secondary here. The ends justify the wobbliness of means. PHANTASM practically invents a new movie-category or classification--comic-horror-science-fantasy. It's quirky and inventive; each new stunt or surprise seems the best yet: e.g., the "Muppet" terror, trapped in someone's coat, buzzing about angrily; headstones popping up out of the ground before the characters. The film has a sort of rabbits-out-of-the-hat, undisciplined charm to it. It's episodic, but cheery about it.

PHANTASMES (F) Impex-ABC 1975 color 88m. (ONCE UPON A VIRGIN-B) SP,D: Jean Rollin. Ph: Allinh. Mus: D.W. LePauw. Ref: MFB'78:179. V 5/12/76:271. with Mylene d'Antes, Jean-Louis Vattier, Rachel Mhas, C. Castel, Rollin.

Castle's owner "bound by diabolic forces to martyrise those he loves"; "ominous exhalations from the lake." (MFB)

The PHANTASTIC WORLD OF MATTHEW MADSON (W.G.) Cinegrafik-ZDF 1974 color 94m. SP,D & with: Helmut Herbst. SP: also K. Wyborny. Ph: Deppe, Perraudin. Mus: N. Busch, A. Moore. Sets: Uwe Pohlmann. Anim: Robert Darroll, Michael Ruediger. Ref: V 4/17/74: historical "review of special effects."

Astronauts land on unknown planet in search of "scientist from another era."

PHANTOM see PHANTOM OF THE PARADISE

*The PHANTOM BARON CDPDF 1943 Cost: Dior. Ref: screen. MFB '77:55. and with Jean Cocteau(Baron Carol).

A Gallic attempt at a fairy tale, this plays more like Hollywood romantic-comedy, with the love-pairs changing every other scene. Over-loaded with symbolism, and a bit dull, but there is one breathtaking image--involving a reflection seen in a stream--and there are some nice "ghostly" effects (e.g., the contents of the baron's room "vanishing").

*The PHANTOM CHARIOT 1919 (aka The GREY CART. The PHANTOM HORSE) Ref: screen. Lee.

The amusingly complicated fantasy-flashback structure of Victor Sjostrom's The PHANTOM CHARIOT redeems a rather conventional, black-and-white moral drama re: one's responsibility towards others. Simple yet evocative effects (e.g., the chariot "riding" on the water). Sjostrom (the actor) is evil and unrelenting; Hilda Borgstrom is good and unrelenting--the conflict is resolved by a contrived, trick "happy ending." Good but relatively minor Sjostrom.

*The PHANTOM CREEPS (Classic Int'l-TV) 1939 also 75m. feature Ph: also W. Sickner. Mus:(stock) Waxman, Skinner, et al. AD: Ralph DeLacy. Ref: TV. TVFFSB.

"Devisualizer belt" uses "light waves too intense for the human eye"; Z-ray machine destroys objects imbued with invisible gas; cute little mechanical spiders. Awkward Moments Dept.: (hero, to just-discovered stowaway on crash-diving plane): "Who are you? Never mind--bail out!"

PHANTOM HORSE, The see PHANTOM CHARIOT(1919)

PHANTOM LOVE see EMPIRE OF PASSION

*PHANTOM OF CRESTWOOD 1932 Mus: Max Steiner. AD: Colbert Clark. Assoc P: Merian C.Cooper. Ref: TV. MFB'79:259.

Don't be misled by the "names" behind the title (i.e.,

Selznick, Cooper, Steiner). PHANTOM is creaky, dull, theatrically-acted, simply another "I wanted to kill her but I didn't" mystery, complete with bats and secret passages. At its most determinedly "horrific" it has a man wear his son's death-mask in order to frighten a woman. And at one point, hostess Karen Morley's kid sister complains, "This is a fine graduation party!" A minute later sis is dead with a dart in her neck....It's a downright lousy graduation party.

The PHANTOM OF HOLLYWOOD CBS-TV 1974 color (The PHANTOM OF LOT 2-orig t) D: Gene Levitt. Mkp: William Tuttle. Ref: Glut/CMM. Scheuer/MOTV. with Jack Cassidy(Phantom), Skye Aubrey, Broderick Crawford, Jackie Coogan.
Scarred Phantom haunts backlots of Worldwide Studios.

PHANTOM OF THE FILLMORE see PHANTOM OF THE PARADISE

*The PHANTOM OF THE MOULIN ROUGE 1925 88m. Ref: screen. Everson. and with Sandra Milowanoff, M.S.Schutz, Paul Olivier.
Dr. Renault, a psychologist, hypnotically wills the unhappy Julien Boissel's spirit out of his body. This intriguing fantastique premise is, unfortunately, effected only after a near-hour's worth of limp, non-fantastique narrative. It's as if writer-director Rene Clair wanted to test his conventional-narrative skills before embarking on a non-conventional Clair comedy-drama-suspense-fantasy. In the real-Clair (final) third, Julien initially exults in his freshly-granted freedom from earthly worries and restraints--he flies, or floats, about Paris, in double-exposure. But he despairs when he begins to miss earthly attractions like love. This is the Clair version, clearly, of the fantasy sequences in Capra's IT'S A WONDERFUL LIFE(1946). Julien's non-born, double-exposure state or status cuts two ways--the fact that he can, physically, pass right through the bodies of others is deceptively "liberating." This is an invisible-man movie (or third of a movie) with bite, a strange mix of the farcical and the poignant.

*The PHANTOM OF THE OPERA 1925 SP: R. Schrock. D: also Edward Sedgwick, Lon Chaney. AD: A.H.(Charles D.? Dan?) Hall, E.E. Sheeley. Catacombs Des: Ben Carre. Titles: Tom Reed. Ref: S&S'80. AFI. and with Chester Conklin.

*PHANTOM OF THE OPERA 1943 Adap: John Jacoby. Stage D: William Wymetal. Mkp: Jack Pierce. Operatic Score: Ward & Waggner; Tchaikovsky, Chopin. Ref: TV. V 8/18/43. Glut/CMM.
The terribly-scarred Erique Claudin (Claude Rains), wanted for the murder of a music publisher, finds refuge in the catacombs below the Paris Opera House, which he haunts in the guise of the Phantom...."Phantom" is right--blink, and you'll miss him. He's lost in the background of this exasperatingly bland comic opera. Trivial comedy dominates, in the persons of Nelson Eddy and Edgar Barrier. The famous scenes--the cutting of the great chandelier (or, the Paris Hacksaw Massacre), the unmasking of the Phantom--seem almost incidental to the

incessant warbling, and are thus robbed of their imaginative power. This is a damn musical.

*The PHANTOM OF THE OPERA 1962 SP: Anthony Hinds(aka J.Elder). Stage D: Dennis Maunder. Ref: screen. TV. AFI. and with Liam Redmond, Ian Wilson(dwarf), Renee Houston.

The Phantom Professor Petrie (Herbert Lom) and his hunchbacked assistant haunt London opera house; Scotland Yard's Black Museum (Jack the Ripper exhibit). Fair version of Leroux's book proceeds neatly and plausibly until the catch-all climactic scenes, in which, a) the Phantom is unmasked (not by his protegee Heather Sears, but by his nemesis, publisher Michael Gough); b) his "St. Joan" opera and protegee are great hits, and, c) the chandelier--as it must--falls (on him!). Thus are all audience expectations (based on past "Phantoms") and plot requirements (of this "Phantom"'s script) screwily satisfied. (Credulity, however, is strained a bit.) But here, at least, it's Edward De Souza and Michael Gough--and not Nelson Eddy and Edgar Barrier--who bear most of the dramatic weight.

See also: HAVE YOU GOT ANY CASTLES. MUNSTERS' REVENGE, The. PINK PANTHER STRIKES AGAIN,The. SONG AT MIDNIGHT(P). PHANTOM OF THE PARADISE.

PHANTOM OF THE PARADISE Fox/Harbor 1974 color 91m. (PHANTOM. PHANTOM OF THE FILLMORE-early ts) SP,D: Brian De Palma, based on the "Faust" & "Phantom of the Opera" stories. Ph: Larry Pizer. Mus: Paul Williams; G.A. Tipton. PD: Jack Fisk. Sp FX: Greg Auer. Mkp: Rolf Miller. Sets: Sissy Spacek. Ref: MFB'75:112. screen. V 10/30/74. 9/18/74:7. Photon 26:15-18. with Williams, William Finley(Phantom), Jessica Harper, Gerrit Graham, Henry Calvert, George Memmoli, Keith Allison.

Disfigured songwriter who haunts rock-concert hall; "Faust" rock opera; man whose life/soul is contained in videotapes. Many striking images, and a few amusing musical numbers, with sets dressed-to-kill; but (apart from the numbers) indifferently-staged. Stylish, but not especially funny or dramatic. Most of the best moments of the patchwork story belong to Williams (as the ageless Swan). As PHANTOMS OF THE OPERA go, not bad.

The PHANTOM ON HORSEBACK (Hung.) Budapest Studio 1977 color 111m. (KISERTET LUBLON) SP,D: Robert Ban. SP: also P.M. Gal, from a novel by Kalman Mikszath. Ph: Tamas Somlo. Mus: Emil Petrovics. Ref: V 3/2/77. with Gyorgy Czerhalmi, Iren Bordan, Dezso Garas, Imre Raday.

Ghost of wine merchant haunts Hungarian village.

**The PHANTOM SHIP (B) Hammer 1935 80m. (The MYSTERY OF THE MARIE CELESTE-B) SP,D: Denison Clift. Adap: C. Larkworthy. Ph: Geoffrey Faithfull, Eric Cross. AD: J.Elder Wills. Ref: screen. BFC. Lee. FM 20:25. with Bela Lugosi, Shirley Grey, Ben Welden, Dennis Hoey, Gibson Gowland, Terence de Marney.

Mad sailor murders all on board sailing ship. Slow, tired

melodrama. A few half-eerie scenes of a maddened Lugosi alone on the derelict. His best line: "Whiskey!" (It's that delivery.)

The PHANTOM SIGNAL Edison 1913 33m. D: George Lessey. SP: H.J. Collins. Ref: Lee. AF-Index. with Charles Ogle.
Railway accidents heralded by skeleton's appearance; wrecker haunted by dreams of victims.

*PHARAOH'S CURSE 1957 (CURSE OF THE PHARAOH-orig t) AD: Bob Kinoshita. SpFX: Jack Rabin, Louis DeWitt. Mkp: Ted Coodley. Ref: TV. Lee.
Soul of 3,000-year-old mummy of high priest enters Egyptian's body, turns him in effect into vampire who drains blood of men (and horse) to keep from turning into dust; one severed arm does turn to dust; vampire's sister casts cat-like shadow. The characters here spend most of their time in a tomb, running around passageways and bumping into the monster, who looks like an old man in pajamas. (Not frightening.) Strained mystery, comedy, drama, horror.

PHASE IV (U.S.-B) Para/Alced 1974 color 84m. D: Saul Bass. SP: Mayo Simon. Ph: Dick Bush. Mus: Brian Gascoigne;(elec) D. Vorhaus. AD: John Barry. SpAntPh: Ken Middleham. SpFX: John Richardson. Ref: MFB'74:220. V 10/9/74. with Nigel Davenport, Lynne Frederick, Michael Murphy, Alan Gifford.
Ants unite, destroy enemies in the Arizona desert, battle humans holed up in scientist's "experimental dome," plan to make two of them part of their world.

PHOBIA (Can.) Para/Borough Park 1980 color 90m. D: John Huston. SP: Lew Lehman, Jimmy Sangster, P. Bellwood. Story: Gary Sherman, Ronald Shusett. Ph: Reginald Morris. Mus: Andre Gagnon. PD: Ben Edwards. SpFX: Martin Malivoire. Ref: MFB'81:77: "horror." Cinef X:1:38. with Paul Michael Glaser, John Colicos, Susan Hogan, Alexandra Stewart, Robert O'Ree.
Mad doc confronts phobic patients with what each fears most.

PHOBIA see NESTING, The

PHOENIX (J) Merritt-White/Toho 1978('81-U.S.?) (HINOTORI) D: Kon Ichikawa. Mus: Jun Fukamachi. Anim D: Osamu Tezuka, based on his comic series. SpFX: Teruyoshi Nakano. Ref: JFFJ 13:33: futuristic "sf/fantasy." V 3/18/81:4(rated): sfa FIREBIRD 2015 A.D.? 10/22/80: "people-animal carnage"; wasp pit.

The PHOENIX ABC-TV/Mark Carliner 1981 color 75m. D: Douglas Hickox. SP: Anthony & Nancy Lawrence. Ph: Birnkant. Mus: Arthur Rubinstein. SpFX: Apogee. Ref: TV. V 4/29/81:60. with Judson Scott(Bennu), Fernando Allende, Shelley Smith, E. G. Marshall.
Mind-reading, self-healing, thought-projecting Phoenix, a god ("practically a Superman") comes to Earth to aid humans ("a wellspring of hope for humanity"); amulet with energy shield

is symbol of "The Golden Light." Suffocatingly high-minded super-heroics, with stray amiable moments. "Love is something I don't know too much about," admits the disillusioned heroine. The hero has some gaps to close too, but all come out ahead. (She seems to turn into a rose.)

PHOENIX 2772 (J) Toho/Tezuka 1980 anim color 100m. (SPACE FIREBIRD-alt t. HI NO TORI-2772 AI NO KOSUMOSU ZONU) SP,D: Taku Sugiyama. SP: also Osamu Tezuka. Mus: Yasuo Higuchi. AD: K. Nakamura. Ref: PFA notes 3/24/80. FM 170:14. V 5/13/81: 258. 5/7/80:459(ad). JFFJ 13:33.
"Romantic space-fantasy set in an overpopulated future.... fearful Firebird's boundless powers." (PFA)

PHOTO SOUVENIR (F) FR3 Lyon 1978 color 90m. SP,D: Edmond Sechan. SP: also Jean-Claude Carriere. Ph: Guy Delattre. Mus: G. Delerue. Ref: V 2/1/78. with Vania Vilers, D. Ayme.
Photos from Polaroid predict deaths.

PICNIC AT HANGING ROCK (Austral.) Atlantic/Picnic-M&M-BEF-SAFC-AFC 1975 color 116m. D: Peter Weir. SP: Cliff Green, from Joan Lindsay's novel. Ph: Russell Boyd;(nature) David Sanderson. Mus: Bruce Smeaton; Beethoven. AD: David Copping. Ref: screen. MFB'76:196. IFG'80. V 11/5/75. Willis/SW. with Rachel Roberts, Dominic Guard, Helen Morse, Anne Lambert.
Haunted rock swallows four women, spits one back. (Apparently, it accepts only those sufficiently sensuous.) The mystery of the missing women is half-intriguing, half-ludicrous; the other, non-mystery narrative elements merely take up time. Sparsely-scattered clues--Roberts' "Nothing changed--ever," a painting, the nature photography, a reference to Botticelli--hint that the women have entered some sort of timeless, sensuous Utopia. 116 minutes of "hints"....

PICNIC ON THE GRASS (F) Contemporary/Renoir 1959 color 91m. (Le DEJEUNER SUR L'HERBE. LUNCH ON THE GRASS-B) SP,D: Jean Renoir. Ph: G. Leclerc. Mus: Joseph Kosma. Sets: M.-L. Dieulot. SpFX: LAX. Ref: screen. Lephoron/JR: "Alexis... future president of a United Europe." Durgnat/JR: "not so much science-fiction as future-history-fiction." Newsweek 10/24/60. S&S'77:238: "smugly anti-intellectual." with Paul Meurisse, Catherine Rouvel, Jacqueline Morane, Fernand Sardou, Jean-Pierre Granval, Charles Blavette, Paulette Dubost, M. Cassan.
A relatively minor, yet very pleasing idyll from Renoir. Definitely pro-nature, but not necessarily anti-intellectual: Meurisse's stuffy biologist is a subject not so much of ridicule as of affectionate kidding. PICNIC is engagingly playful, where Renoir's best films are serious and playful. Here, the scientist can finally and unreservedly profess, "Happiness is succumbing to nature's order." In the more ambiguous natural order described in The ELUSIVE CORPORAL or DAY IN THE COUNTRY, the expression of such a sentiment would have to be intended ironically (on Renoir's part at least). Uneven Kosma score which (like the film) gets too cute at times.

PICNIC ON THE ROAD(by the Strugatskys) see STALKER

The PICTURE OF DORIAN GRAY (Dan) Regia Art 1910 short Ref: Lee: from Oscar Wilde's book. with Valdemar Psilander.

The PICTURE OF DORIAN GRAY (U.S.-B?) ABC-TV/Dan Curtis 1973 color 136m. D: Glenn Jordan. SP: John Tomerlin. Based on Wilde's book. Mus: Robert Cobert. Sets: Reginald Allen. Ref: TVFFSB. Cinef F'73:46. with Shane Briant(Dorian), Nigel Davenport, Charles Aidman, Fionnula Flanagan, John Karlen.

The PICTURE OF DORIAN GRAY (F) Daunou 1977 D: Pierre Boutron. From Boutron's drama, based on Wilde's book. Ref: V 5/17/78.
See also: DR.JEKYLL AND MR.HYDE(Para,1920). TAKE OFF.

The PIED PIPER (B) Para/Sagittarius-Goodtimes 1971 color 90m. SP,D: Jacques Demy. SP: also Andrew Birkin, Mark Peploe. Ph: P. Suschitzky. Mus: Donovan. PD: Assheton Gordon. SpFX: John Stears. Ref: MFB'72:193. VV 7/6/72. V 5/10/72. with Donovan, Donald Pleasence, Jack Wild, Michael Hordern, John Hurt, Cathryn Harrison, Roy Kinnear, Diana Dors.
Vengeful minstrel spirits children away from Hamelin with his music. From Robert Browning's poem.

La PIEL DE ZAPA (Arg) EFA 1943 82m. D: Luis Bayon Herrera. SP: Leopoldo Torres Rios, Raimundo Roxal, based on Balzac's story "The Wild Ass's Skin" or "La Peau de Chagrin." Ph: Roque Funes. Mus: A.G. del Barrio. Ref: V 12/15/43. with Hugo del Carril, Florence Marly, Aida Luz, Santiago Gomez Cou.
Magic skin from curio shop grants owner's wishes--and shortens his life.

PIER, The see JETEE, La

PILGRIMAGE(by Z.Henderson) see PEOPLE, The

*PILLOW OF DEATH 1945 67m. SpFxPh: John P. Fulton. Ref: TV. V 12/12/45. Lee.
"Creepy old house" with "ghost in the attic"; "psychic investigator"; man (Lon Chaney Jr.) who "hears" his dead wife talking to him. The hero, Chaney, who seemingly only appears to be guilty, proves, actually, to be guilty of three murders. But the movie cheats, in order to make it seem as if someone's plotting against him: the first time the dead woman "speaks" (during a seance), others present hear her too, and there's no attempt, cinematically, to distinguish this earlier "objective" voice from the later "subjective," imagined one. (A sin of omission to go with the film's many sins of commission.)

The PINK LADIES' MOTION PICTURE (J) Toho 1978 (PINKU REDEI NO KATSUDOSHASHIN) D: Tom Kotani. Ref: JFFJ 13:33. with Mitsuyo Nemoto, Keiko Masuda.
Sf-movie parody (one of several movie-parodies) features giant dog, alien, power of invisibility.

The PINK PANTHER STRIKES AGAIN UA 1976 color/scope 103m. SP,D,P: Blake Edwards. SP: also Frank Waldman. Sequel to The PINK PANTHER. Ph: Harry Waxman. Mus: Henry Mancini. PD: Peter Mullins. Anim: Richard Williams Studio. Ref: J.Shapiro. V(d) 12/8/76. MFB'77:29. with Peter Sellers, Herbert Lom, Lesley-Anne Down, Marne Maitland, Colin Blakely, Burt Kwouk.
Scientist's Doomsday Machine destroys UN building, makes villain disappear; reprise of Lom at organ, a la PHANTOM OF THE OPERA('62); Sellers in "Quasimodo" disguise; animated credit bit with Kong on the Empire State Building; old castle.

PIRANHA New World-UA/Piranha 1978 color 94m. D: Joe Dante. Story,SP: John Sayles. Story: also Richard Robinson. Ph: Jamie Anderson. Mus: Pino Donaggio. AD: Bill & Kerry Mellin. SpFX: Jon Berg. SpDes&Anim: Phil Tippett. Anim: Adam Beckett. SpPhFX: Peter Kuran, Bill Hedge, Rick Taylor. Ref: MFB'78: 224. V 8/9/78. 11/30/77:4. TV. with Bradford Dillman, Heather Menzies, Kevin McCarthy, Keenan Wynn, Dick Miller, Barbara Steele, Bruce Gordon, Barry Brown, Paul Bartel, Richard Deacon.
Man-eating strain of piranha released into Texas waterways. Typical animals-on-the-rampage movie, featuring a fun-exciting water-skier-in-jeopardy sequence.

The PIT (Can.) Amulet 1980 color 99m. (TEDDY-orig t) D: Lew Lehman. SP: Ian A. Stuart. Ph: Fred Guthe. Mus: Victor Davies. Ref: V 10/15/80:63. 3/18/81:150(ad). IFG'81:96. with Sammy Snyders, Jeannie Elias.
Child's teddy bear wreaks havoc in small western town.

PIT AND THE PENDULUM,The(by E.A.Poe) see EVENING OF EDGAR ALLAN POE,An. UNCANNY,The.

A PLACE TO DIE (B) ABC-TV/ITC 1974 color 74m. D: Peter Jefferies. SP: T. Feeley. Story: B. Johnson. Mus: Laurie Johnson. AD: R. Lake. Anim: Dolphin. Ref: TV. TVFFSB. with Alexandra Hay, Bryan Marshall, Lila Kaye, Juan Moreno.
Devil-worshippers in English village await woman with "cloven hoof."

PLAGUE see M3: THE GEMINI STRAIN

PLAGUE OF THE WEREWOLVES see LEGEND OF THE WEREWOLF

PLAISIR A TROIS see HOW TO SEDUCE A VIRGIN

*PLAN 9 FROM OUTER SPACE (Gold Key-TV)/Reynolds 1958 SpFX: Charles Duncan. ElecFX: Jim Woods. Mkp: Tom Bartholomew. Ref: screen. TVFFSB. VV 4/14/80:46. Murphy: footage from "The Vampire's Tomb" (project). and with Dudley Manlove, Tom Keene, Conrad Brooks, Criswell, Vampira(Vampire Lady), Gloria Dea.
Ultimate explosive, solaranite(sp?). Near-legendary filmic atrocity is too-well-known-and-loved by now to need any further introduction. Suffice it to say that, with a little larger budget, PLAN 9 could have been another COSMIC MAN--and noone

would remember it now either. Noted-in-passing: the characters' gravitation towards the same patch of the tiny cemetery set gets to be almost surreally comic, accidentally eerie (like a recurrent nightmare-scene)--atmosphere on a dime.

PLANE DIPPY WB 1936 anim 7m. D: Tex Avery. Mus: Bernard Brown. Ref: LC. Adamson/TA: "robot plane."

PLANET EARTH ABC-TV/WB-TV & Norway 1974 color 74m. D: Marc Daniels. SP: Gene Roddenberry, Juanita Bartlett. Ph: Arch Dalzell. Mus: Harry Sukman. AD: R. Kinoshita. Ref: Maltin/TVM. TV. V 5/1/74:36. with John Saxon, Diana Muldaur, Janet Margolin, Ted Cassidy, Aron Kincaid, Majel Barrett, C. Cary.
Post-Great-Conflict, 22nd-century Earth: female-dominated society; suspended animation; mutant army; mind-and-body-controlling extracts, used to domesticate Dinks (male slaves). Embarrassingly coy "reverse world" sf-sitcom-drama. The strain to be "contemporary" shows. Wretched.

PLANET OF DINOSAURS Wells 1980(1978) color D,P: James K.Shea. SP: Ralph Lucas. Mus: Kelly Lammers, John O'Verlin. SpVisFX: Stephen Czerkas, James Aupperle, Doug Beswick. Ref: V 10/18/78: 148(ad). 7/25/79:5: "silly story line." 7/2/80:6(rated). with James Whitworth, Pamela Bottaro, Harvey Shain. (A)

PLANET OF HORRORS New World/Corman 1981 color (GALAXY OF TERROR-alt t. QUEST-orig t. MINDWARP: AN INFINITY OF TERROR-int t) SP,D: Bruce Clark. Sp,Co-P: Marc Siegler. Ph: J. Haitkin. Ref: V 7/8/81:5(rated). Cinef XI:4. with Edward Albert, Erin Moran, Ray Walston.
Planet of "mind-creatures." (A)

*PLANET OF THE APES 1968 From Pierre Boulle's novel "Le Planete des Singes." Mkp: also Ben Nye, Dan Striepeke. Ref: TVG. Lee.
Sequels: BATTLE FOR THE PLANET OF THE APES. CONQUEST OF THE PLANET OF THE APES.
See also NEW PLANET OF THE APES, The.

PLANETA CIEGO see PEOPLE WHO OWN THE DARK, The

PLANETE DES SINGES(by P.Boulle) see PLANET OF THE APES

PLANETE SAUVAGE see FANTASTIC PLANET

PLAYGIRL KILLER see DECOY FOR TERROR

PLEASE DON'T EAT MY MOTHER! Boxo Int'l 1972 color 98m. (GLUMP-orig t? PLEASE RELEASE MY MOTHER. PLEASE NOT MY MOTHER-ad ts? HUNGRY PETS-re-r t) D,P: Carl Monson. Ph: Jack Beckett. AD: Mike McClosky. Mkp: Harry Woolman. Ref: FFacts. Medved/TGTA. Lee(Boxo). Indep.Film Jnl. 4/27/72:24 (ad). Willis/SW. with Rene Bond, Buck Kartalian, F. Wisel, Alicia Friedland, Lyn Lundgren.
Talking, carnivorous female plant.

The PLEASURE MACHINES Pacific Int'l. 1969 70m. (aka The LOVE MACHINE(S)) D & Exec P: Ron Garcia. SP: R.G. Vicry. Ph & Exec P: Paul Hunt. Ref: AFI. no LC. with Barbara Lynn, Beverly Walker, Patricia Miller.
Inventor builds lifelike male and female robots.

PLENILUNIO DELLE VIRGINI see DEVIL'S WEDDING NIGHT

PLUK, MAROONED IN SPACE (F) Image 1974 anim D: Jean Image. Ref: V 5/7/75:206.

PLUS LONGUE NUIT DU DIABLE, La see DEVIL'S NIGHTMARE

PLUTOPIA RKO/Disney 1950 anim color 7m. D: Charles Nichols. Ref: LC. Maltin/OMAM: Mickey and Pluto; "surrealistic nightmare."

El POBRECITO DRACULA (Sp) Mezquiriz 1976 D: Juan Fortuny. Ref: V 5/11/77:429. M.Carbajal. with Joe Rigoli.

*POCOMANIA 1939 (aka The DEVIL'S DAUGHTER. sfa *LOVE WANGA?) Remake of OUANGA. Ph: Jay Rescher. Mus: John Killman. Ref: Turner/Price. Lee. MPH 12/9/39.

PODER DE LAS TINIEBLAS see DEMON WITCH CHILD

*The POISON AFFAIR Gaum 1955 (**The HANGMAN AND THE WITCH-TV) Ref: TVFFSB.

The POISON PEN World 1919 50m. Story,D: Edwin August. SP: J.C. Miller. Ref: Lee(MPN). LC. with June Elvidge, Earle Metcalfe, Joseph Smiley, George Bunny.
Hypnosis and "violet rays" cure patient with dual personality.

POODLE (Sp) Figaro 1979 color 90m. (CANICHE) SP,D: Bigas Luna. Ph: P. Aznar. AD: Carlos Riart. Ref: V 5/16/79. with Angel Jove, Consol Tura, Linda P. Gallardo, Sara Grey.
Brother and sister living in old country-house are "found dead, seemingly clawed and bitten to death....Presumably each has killed the other in canine ecstasy."

POOR ALBERT AND LITTLE ANNIE see I DISMEMBER MAMA

POOR BUTTERFLY(by W.Abney) see JOURNEY TO MIDNIGHT

POPEYE IN GOONLAND Para 1938 anim 9m. (GOONLAND-alt t) D: Dave Fleischer. Ref: Meyers. Lee. LC.
Popeye vs. monster-giants.

PORKY'S ROAD RACE WB 1937 anim color 7m. D: Frank Tashlin. Mus: C.W. Stalling. Voices: Mel Blanc. Ref: Lee. Glut/TFL. LC.
Bit with Frankenstein-monster-type named Borax Karoff.

POSSESS MY SOUL see ABBY

POSSESSED WB 1947 108m. D: Curtis Bernhardt. SP: Silvia Richards, Ranald MacDougall, from Rita Weiman's story "One Man's Secret!" Ph: Joseph Valentine. Mus: Franz Waxman. AD: Anton Grot. Ref: screen. Lee. V 6/4/47. NYT 5/30/47. LC. with Joan Crawford, Van Heflin, Raymond Massey, Geraldine Brooks, Stanley Ridges, Douglas Kennedy, Monte Blue, Erskine Sanford, Moroni Olsen; John Ridgely?

Woman with split personality; old dark house with "ghost"; fantasy of vanishing body; clutching-hand bit. Film displays some good camera sense, if little dramatic sense. It's just, in effect, a recital of events in a woman's life, though Crawford occasionally provides insights into the connections between the character's two selves. There's a tantalizing, opening teaser-sequence, and a stunning, offscreen-scream scene. But otherwise little suspense and lots of contrivance.

The POSSESSED NBC-TV/WB-TV 1977 color 75m. D & Exec P: Jerry Thorpe. SP: John S. Young. Ph: C.G. Arnold. Mus: Leonard Rosenman. AD: F. Hope. Ref: TV. TV Season. V 5/4/77:116. with James Farentino, Joan Hackett, Harrison Ford, Eugene Roche, Claudette Nevins, P.J. Soles.

Doubting minister given second chance at life to fight evil, finds same at girls' school in Salem, Oregon, in the form of mysterious fires and possessed schoolmistress who spits nails. Investigation-into-evil falls somewhat short of "The Minister's Black Veil," plays like a pilot for a super-minister series. Serious schlock. (The worst kind.) "There is no why." "I believe in evil, and that it can be taken on." Like that.

POSSESSION (B) ABC-TV/ITC-TV 1973 color 74m. D: John Cooper. Ph: Roy Simper. PD: Henry Graveney. Ref: TV. TVFFSB. with John Carson, Joanna Dunham, James Cossins, Athol Coats.

Newlyweds vs. evil presence in English country-house; ghost?; skeleton; strange whistling; rabbit; seance summoning up images from 1953.

POSSESSION (F-W.G.) Oliane-Soma-Marianne 1981 color 127m. SP,D: Andrzej Zulawski. Dial: Frederic Tuten. Ph: Bruno Nuytten. Mus: Andrzej Korzynski. Ref: V 5/27/81. with Isabelle Adjani, Sam Neill, Heinz Bennent, Margit Carstensen.

Woman creates loathsome monster "from herself."

The POSSESSION OF JOEL DELANEY Para/ITC-Haworth 1972 color 108m. D: Waris Hussein. SP: Matt Robinson, Grimes Grice. From Ramona Stewart's novel. Ph: A.J. Ornitz. Mus: Joe Raposo. PD: Peter Murton. Mkp: Saul Meth. Ref: MFB'72:216. V 5/17/72. TV. with Shirley MacLaine, Perry King, Michael Hordern, David Elliott, Lovelady Powell, Paulita Iglesias.

New York City. Spirit of Puerto Rican murderer takes possession of young man (King); murders again; attempted exorcism; hint that spirit passes from brother to sister (MacLaine) upon death of former. The atmosphere of racial tension (Norah Benson's ostentatious furs, juxtaposed with the insolent glances of the Spanish Harlem poor) may be different, but the story is the same. Why doesn't a nice, sweet spirit ever possess a louse?

The POT (Thai) Hollywood Film 1975 color 95m. (MAENAK AMERICA) D,Ed: Lek Kitipraporn. SP: Leo V. Gordon. Ph: Tom Lau. Ref: V 1/14/76. 5/7/75:128. with Lisa Farringer, Krung Srivilai, Sitao.

Woman returns from the dead; "ghost-and-horror effects."

POVESTEA DRAGOSTEI see STORY OF LOVE

POWDER TOWN (UA-TV)/RKO 1942 79m. D: Rowland V. Lee. SP: David Boehm. From an idea by Vicki Baum & a novel by Max Brand. Ph: Frank Redman. Mus: Roy Webb. AD: Albert D'Agostino. SpFX: Vernon L. Walker. Ref: TV. V. TVFFSB. LC. with Victor McLaglen, Edmond O'Brien, June Havoc, Eddie Foy Jr., Roy Gordon, Mary Gordon, Frances Neal, George Cleveland.

Chemist invents ray-like, remote-control explosive, based on the principle of "skip distance." McLaglen has a few winning scenes, but O'Brien as a Cary Grant-like bumbling scientist is (like the film) gruesomely miscalculated. Movie plays like a straight drama into which "comic" characters have been forcibly injected.

*The POWER OF THE WHISTLER 1945 Mus: Wilbur Hatch. Ref: Lee. screen. V 3/28/45.

Richard Dix's "George" (a temporary amnesiac) is "charming" and "good-looking." But he can't help throttling a kitten, a canary, a squirrel. Something is wrong, as these hilariously casual manglings suggest. The man that Jean (Janis Carter) has just met and already is considering marrying may be (goodness!) a madman. As in SECRET BEYOND THE DOOR..., the horror-beneath-the-hero's-charming-surface irony is cornily blatant. This is the camp version of "appearance vs. reality." The movie's every move--in dialogue, character, and incident--seems unerringly "wrong," and the invariable miscalculation makes it campily likeable. To top it all off, there's a climax involving thunder and lightning, a barn, a pitchfork, and a birthday cake laced with rat poison.

The POWER WITHIN ABC-TV/Spelling 1979 color 75m. D: John L. Moxey. SP: E.J. Lasko. Ref: V 5/23/79:68: "kid stuff." with Art Hindle, Edward Binns, Joe Rassulo, Eric Braeden, David Hedison, Susan Howard, John Dennis.

Man struck by lightning can project electric rays from hands.

PRAIRIE CHICKENS UA/Hal Roach 1943(1942) 46m. D: Hal Roach Jr. SP: A. Belgard, E. Snell. Story: D. Hough. Ph: Robert Pittack. Mus: Edward Ward. Ref: V 7/14/43: supposedly haunted ranch-house. LC. with Jimmy Rogers, Noah Beery Jr.

PREGNANT BY A GHOST see KUN PI

The PREHISTORIC MAN (Hung.) Star 1917 D: Alfred Desy. SP: Z. Somlyo, E. Gyori. Ref: Lee.
Rays give monkey intelligence of man.

PRELUDE (B) Knight 1927 8m. SP,D & with: Castleton Knight. From Edgar Allan Poe's story "The Premature Burial." Ref: BFC: "horror."
Man listening to Rachmaninoff's "Prelude" dreams he is victim of premature burial.

PRELUDE TO TAURUS Gold Key-TV("Zodiac" series) 1972? color 94m. Ref: TVFFSB. with Pamela Tiffin, Robert Walker Jr.
Survivors of 900,000-year-old civilization found frozen in Arctic ice.

PREMATURE BURIAL,The(by E.A.Poe) see PRELUDE

The PREMONITION Avco Embassy/Galaxy 1975(1972?) color 90m. SP,D,P: Robert Allen Schnitzer. SP: also A. Mahon, L. Pastore. Ph: V.C. Milt. Mus: Henry Mollicone;(elec) Pril Smiley. AD: John Lawless. Ref: V 11/26/75. 8/9/72:4(rated): Transview. TVFFSB. with Sharon Farrell, Richard Lynch, Jeff Corey.
Mother and carnival mime attempt to regain her daughter "through parapsychological means." (V)

The PRESIDENT VANISHES Para/Walter Wanger 1934 86m. D: William Wellman. SP: Carey Wilson, Cedric Worth, from a novel by Rex Stout. Adap: Lynn Starling. Ph: B. McGill. EdFX: Slavko Vorkapich, John Hoffman. Ref: screen. PFA notes 1/15/76. 11/11/80. New Rep. 12/26/34. NYT 12/8/34. LC. with Paul Kelly, Arthur Byron, Janet Beecher, Sidney Blackmer, Edward Arnold, Rosalind Russell, Andy Devine, Osgood Perkins, J.Carrol Naish, Charles Grapewin, Jason Robards, Edward Ellis, Clara Blandick, Walter Kingsford, Paul Harvey; Irving Bacon?
To counteract a fascistic plot--hatched by industrialists, bankers, and the secret Grey Shirt Army--to take over the U.S. and go to war, the President "vanishes"; the Secretary of War takes his place, declares a state of martial law, and unleashes the secret service. Right up until the last few minutes of this weirdly irresponsible poli-sci-fi-fantasy, the message comes through loud and clear: reject the wicked warmongers. Then: model-citizen Andy Devine (yes) humbly declares that he will fight for his beloved President (Byron) if he can be an officer. This bizarre turn of events would knock the movie into a cocked hat if the movie were not already there. The final message then, delivered by the gushing Devine: trust (not to say nuzzle) your President. This theme is couched in very "human," folksy terms--the President playfully tweaking the First Lady's nose; Andy's mom pampering him before acting president Arnold. And the script employs mystery, comedy, romance, and action-movie elements, the "better" to get its message across. An unintentional joy.

PRETHANGALUDE THAZVARA see VALLEY OF GHOSTS

PREY (B) Tymar 1977 color 85m. D: Norman J. Warren. SP: Max Cuff. Story: Quinn Donoghue. Ph: D.V. Browne. Mus: Ivor Slaney. AD: Hayden Pearce. Ref: MFB'78:119. V 6/8/77:34. with Glory Annen, Sally Faulkner, Barry Stokes(alien).
Alien from UFO possesses man's body, cannibalizes humans.

PREY(by R.Matheson) see TRILOGY OF TERROR(1975)

PRICKLY PROBLEMS see Q

*The PRIMITIVE MAN 1913 SP,D: D.W. Griffith. Ref: Lee: sfa BRUTE FORCE? AF-Index: includes MAN'S GENESIS (adding frame story). with Mae Marsh, Wilfred Lucas, Robert Harron, Edwin August, Alfred Paget, C.H. Mailes.

PRIMITIVE MEN see MAN'S GENESIS

PRISONER OF THE CANNIBAL GOD (I) Dania 1978 color/scope 99m. (La MONTAGNA DEL DIO CANNIBALE) SP,D: Sergio Martino. SP: also Cesare Frugoni. Ph: G. Ferrando. Mus: G.& M. De Angelis. PD: M.A. Geleng. Ref: MFB'79:253-54. with Ursula Andress, Stacy Keach, Claudio Cassinelli, Franco Fantasia, A. Marsina.
Expedition to "haunted" New Guinea island discovers tribe of masked cannibals.

PRISONNIER DE L'ARAIGNEE see WEB OF THE SPIDER

The PRIVATE EYES New World/Tri-Star 1980 color 91m. D: Lang Elliott. SP: Tim Conway, John Myhers. Ph: J. Haitkin. Mus: Peter Matz. AD: V. Peranio. Ref: V 11/26/80. with Tim Conway, Don Knotts, Trisha Noble, Bernard Fox, Grace Zabriskie.
"Monster called a Wookalar"; "semi-haunted house"; torture chamber; "time gun" invention; "Quasimodo character."

PRIVATE PARTS Premier(MGM)/Penelope/Gene Corman 1972 color 82m. D: Paul Bartel. SP: Phil Kearney, Les Rendelstein. Ph: A. Davis. Mus: Hugo Friedhofer. PD: John Retsek. Ref: MFB'73: 211: "languid direction." V 9/27/72. with Ayn Ruymen, Lucille Benson, John Ventantonio, Gene Simms, John Lupton.
"Apartment-house horror"; transvestite killer. (MFB)

PROBE see SEARCH

Le PROCUREUR HALLERS (F) Albatros 1930 D: Robert Wiene. SP: Johannes Brandt, from Paul Lindau's book "Der Andere." French version of The OTHER(1930). Ph: N. Farkas. Mus: F. Hollander. Ref: Chirat. with Jean Max, Colette Darfeuil, Suzanne Delmas.
D.A. with split personality.

PROFESSOR DIDLITTLE AND THE SECRET FORMULA (W.G.) Rhewes-Atlas Int'l 1972 color D: W.V. Chmielewski. Ref: Lee(M/TVM): superman formula. with Bill Ramsey, Boyd Bachmann.

*PROFESSOR HOSKINS' PATENT HUSTLER (B) Thanhouser-Martin 1913 D: D. Aylott? Ref: BFC.
"Invention makes things accelerate."

PROFESSOR POPPER'S PROBLEM(S) (B) (JED-TV)/CFF/Mersey 1974 color serial 6 episodes 91m. D: Gerry O'Hara. SP: Leo McGuire. Story: R. Loncraine. Ph: Ken Hodges. Mus: Kenneth V. Jones. AD: G. Provis. SpPhFX: Tommy Howard. Ref: MFB'75: 37. TVFFSB. with Adam Richens, Debra Collins, Milo O'Shea.
Prof and pupils take pills, shrink till they're two inches tall; "The Monster" (chapter three): "huge spider."

PROFONDO ROSSO see DEEP RED

PROHADKA O HONZIKOVI A MARENCE (Cz) CFP-Barrandov 1981 puppet & cartoon anim & live color 66m. SP,D: Karel Zeman. Ph: Zdenek Krupa. Mus: Karel Svoboda. Des: Eugen Spaleny et al. Ref: V 3/18/81.
"Evil spell that makes (the hero) half-monster, half-human."

PROM NIGHT Avco Embassy/Simcom(Guardian) 1980 color 91m. D: Paul Lynch. SP: William Gray. Story: Robert Guza Jr. Ph: Robert New. Mus: Carl Zittrer, Paul Zaza. AD: Reuben Freed. SpFX: Al Cotter. Opt: Film FX. Ref: V 7/23/80. SFC 9/2/80. TV. MFB'80:218-19. with Leslie Nielsen, Jamie Lee Curtis, Casey Stevens, Antoinette Bower, Michael Tough, Eddie Benton.
Children's-game-of-death; not just one but three or four "weird" characters; triple-revenge plot; nervous guilt; shattering glass; suspense "building"; then: some dissipating disco, and disclosure of an unforgivable red monster-herring; and only then (finally!--what relief!) the ax-murders, and a tip of the hat to pathos. CARRIE + HALLOWEEN = PROM NIGHT, or zero.

PROPHECY Para/Rosen 1979 color/scope 102m. D: John Frankenheimer. SP: David Seltzer. Ph:Harry Stradling,Jr. Mus: Leonard Rosenman. PD: W.C. Smith. SpMkp:(des) Tom Burman; (mfgd) T. & Ellis Burman, Edouard Henriques. SpFX: Robert Dawson. SdFxEd: W.R. Kowalchuk. Opt: Modern. Props: Ray Mercer Jr. Ref: TV. MFB'79:233. V 6/13/79. with Talia Shire, Robert Foxworth, Armand Assante, Richard Dysart, Graham Jarvis, Victoria Racimo, Evans Evans.
Mercury-poisoned Maine waters produce huge, mutant, Bigfoot-like bear-creature, fulfilling (or inspiring) the Indian legend of the Catayda(sp?), a "part of all things created." Public health department official Foxworth initially finds a big fish and funny bush-roots, sees a giant tadpole, hears about deformed babies, and is attacked by a mad raccoon. "There's definitely something wrong." The baby monsters are nasty, pint-sized, skinned-alive-looking creatures and make wailing sounds; papa-bear-monster makes crunch-snap-slurp sounds. But apart from these rather obscene sights and sounds, the movie is undistinguished, a series of wan chills, with an underpinning of topicality.

PROVIDENCE (F-Swiss; Eng.-lang.) Cinema 5/Action-SFdP-FR3 & Citel 1977 color 107m. D: Alain Resnais. SP: David Mercer. Ph: Ricardo Aronovitch. Mus: Miklos Rozsa. PD: Jacques Saulnier. Mkp: M.-H. Yatschenkoff et al. SdFX: Jean Schwarz. Ref: screen. V(d) 1/14/77. MFB'78:51-2. FQ Smr'77:21-4. with Dirk Bogarde, John Gielgud, David Warner, Elaine Stritch, Ellen Burstyn, Samson Fainsilber(werewolf), Peter Arne.

Aging author's notes and nightmares re: relatives and werewolves all run together. Amusing structural conceits--e.g., the god-like Clive (Gielgud) introducing words into the mouths of his characters/relatives, or injecting characters into (and ejecting same from) the scenes of the film--and "devastatingly" witty dialogue (by Clive--he intends it to be devastating). And the "real life"/"real scenery"/"real characters" post-script is in unforced and touching (if expected) contrast to Clive's mental ramblings. (Rozsa's music ensures that it's touching.) But the gaps so described--between imaginings and reality and between characters (especially father and sons)--don't seem that rich or fine an esthetic yield; they _are_ like, simply, a ps. to Clive's (too) fully-illustrated art/life. In his imaginings, Clive makes his sweetly-simple relatives superficially "complicated"--they share his way with words, drinks, and sex. He provides "juicy" but dimensionless roles for Bogarde, Warner, and of course Gielgud. (Though he badly miscasts Burstyn as his daughter-in-law-in-his-image. She is very ill-dreamt.) "It's the world seen through his eyes" is both the point and the problem. Clive is rather-willfully myopic, and so, necessarily, is much of the film. The fact that scriptwriter and director devote so much time to his dreaming implicates _them_ in Clive's fuzzy vision. The ps. doesn't quite let them off _his_ hook.

The PROWLER Sandhurst 1981 color (The GRADUATION-orig t) D: Joseph Zito. SpMkpFX: Tom Savini. Ref: Cinef XI:3: horror.

PRZEKLADANIEC see ROLY-POLY

PSI FACTOR Gold Key-TV 1980 color 91m. Ref: GKey. with Peter Mark Richman, Gretchen Corbett, Tom Martin.

"Mischievous aliens from another dimension."

PSYCHED OUT BY A 4D WITCH Emerson/New Art 1972 "4-D" Ref: V 10/18/72:4(rated). (d)11/72. Bill Warren.

Comedy re: witchcraft, demons, and the astral world.

The PSYCHIC (I) Group 1/Brandon Chase 1979 color 89m. (SETTE NOTE IN NERO. DOLCE COME MORIRE-orig t) D: Lucio Fulci. Ph: Sergio Salvati. Ref: TV. V 5/16/79. 5/11/77:243. 5/2/79 (rated). 10/27/76:50. AMPAS. with Jennifer O'Neill, Gabriele Ferzetti, Marc Porel, Gianni Garko, Evelyn Stewart.

Woman's vision of past murder turns out to be premonition of her own (near) death; "haunted" house. Hollow suspenser. The only interest lies in seeing the pieces of the puzzle of O'Neill's vision fall into place--e.g., the musical watch, the "old lady," the man with the limp--a rather mechanical pleasure, but better than nothing. The one real frisson: O'Neill suddenly realizing that her vision is premonition and not recollection.

PSYCHIC KILLER Avco Embassy/Syn-Frank(Lexington) 1975 color 89m. (The KIRLIAN EFFECT-orig t. The KIRLIAN FORCE-int t) SP,D: Raymond Danton. SP: also Greydon Clark, Mikel Angel. Ph: Herb Pearl. Mus: William Kraft. AD: Joel Leonard. Mkp: Tino Zacchia. Opt: F-Stop. Tech Adv: K.L. Johnson. Ref: MFB'79:31. TV. V 11/5/75. 5/15/74:7. Willis/SW. Meyers. with Paul Burke, Jim Hutton, Julie Adams, Nehemiah Persoff (parapsychologist), Neville Brand, Aldo Ray, Whit Bissell, Rod Cameron, John Dennis, Della Reese, Marland Proctor.

Medallion gives man's malevolent energy the power to operate independently of his body. This offbeat thriller is a jumble of tones and styles, but it has some wild, must-see sequences. It's alternately (and sometimes simultaneously) tawdry and inspired, a combination perfect-crime-yarn/fantasy-shocker. The climax is a pip of a variation on "The Monkey's Paw." But the best sequence: Joseph Della Sorte as a power-happy construction engineer exulting in his latest project, to the strains of "La Donna Mobile" ("Every stick, every brick--all all mine"), as, far and directly above him, a (psychically-operated) crane maneuvers into bombs-away position the building's cornerstone. This choice, black-comic sequence is so right, so, well, brilliant--how can so much of the rest be so <u>wrong</u>!? Hutton's role of "perfect criminal" is unevenly written, but its remote-control-murder wizardry generates excitement.

*PSYCHO 1960 Mkp: Jack Barron, Robert Dawn. Titles: Saul Bass. Ref: screen. Lee: Universal re-r.

Schizophrenic assumes dead-mother's personality, kills intruders into "their" lives. A witty, intelligent, beautifully-crafted psychological-horror-comedy, PSYCHO seems, finally, a little too ingenious for its own good; the wit ultimately seems less a means than an end in itself. Even the sharpest of the double entendres in the dialogue begin to sound redundant as the actors (excluding Perkins) come to seem more and more like props for, purely, an exercise in suspense. ("Mother" isn't the only mannikin.) Certain individual shots--the track past the tree to Perkins (as Norman) at the bog; the not-of-this-world look on his face as he attacks Vera Miles in the cellar--suggest frightening, <u>unplumbed</u> abysses, places from which Hitchcock's wit effectively and forever bars him (and places to which perhaps only Bunuel, among directors, has esthetic access). That said, it should also be acknowledged that Hitchcock's senses of when, where, and how to use close shots--for an intimate, claustrophobic effect (like Janet Leigh's anxiousness as she drives from Phoenix to the Bates Motel)--are unerring in PSYCHO, as is his use of the camera in general. One crane shot, up and over Perkins as he carries "mother" to the cellar, seems particularly evocative, in its

movement from the more familiar, actor-level position to an overhead view; in its suggestion of psychological as well as spatial dislocation. Of course this shot serves one strictly-narrative function; but here at least there seems to be more than pure ingenuity at work.
See also: DERANGED. TEXAS CHAIN SAW MASSACRE, The.

PSYCHO A GO-GO! see FIEND WITH THE ELECTRONIC BRAIN

PSYCHO SEX FIEND see HOUSE THAT VANISHED, The

PSYCHOMANIA (B) (Official-TV)/Benmar(Scotia-Barber) 1972 color 91m. (The LIVING DEAD-orig t. The FROG-int t) D: Don Sharp. SP: Arnaud D'Usseau, Julian Halevy. Ph: Ted Moore. Mus: John Cameron; David Whitaker. AD: Maurice Carter. SpFX: Patrick Moore. Mkp: Neville Smallwood. Ref: MFB'73:82. TV. TVFFSB. Lee. no V. with George Sanders, Beryl Reid, Nicky Henson(Tom), Mary Larkin, Robert Hardy, Roy Holder.
Spiritualist's pact with the Devil allows, first, her son, then other members of his anti-social, thrill-seeking motorcycle gang, "The Living Dead," to become exactly that--they die, only to return as invulnerable anti-social thrill-seekers. Or, biker anarchy compounded by immortality--The WILD ANGELS crossed with SON OF DRACULA. The result: the ultimate thrill for the bikers; the ultimate horror for those who cross their path. The deftly absurd script delights in indulging the unholy terrors in their toy of immortality--and takes it away from them only when playtime is over. (Mom turns into a frog; they, into stone.) This is a charmingly brazen "What if...?" story. There's no more than a beat between Tom's demonstration of his invulnerability--a harmless knife-in-the-back--and a girl gang-member's excited "What are we waiting for?"

The PSYCHOTRONIC MAN Int'l.Harmony/Spelson-Sell 1980 color 90m. SP,D,Ph: Jack M. Sell. SP & with: Peter Spelson. Mus: Tommy Irons. AD: Fred Becht. SpFX: Bob Vanni. Ref: V 5/7/80: "for the product hungry only." with Christopher Carbis, Curt Colbert, Robin Newton.
"Subconscious forces" compel potbellied barber to kill.

PUPPE, Die see DOLL, The

PUPPET LOVE see MASCOT, The

PYGMY ISLAND Col 1950 69m. D: William Berke. SP: Carroll Young, from Alex Raymond's "Jungle Jim" comic strip. Ph: Ira Morgan. Mus D: Bakaleinikoff. AD: P. Palmentola. Ref: V 11/22/50. "Great Movie Series." with Johnny Weissmuller, Ann Savage, David Bruce, Steven Geray, William Tannen, Billy Barty, Tris Coffin, Billy Curtis, Rusty Wescoatt.
"Mad gorilla"; "renegade whites" impersonating "witch devils"; "valuable fiber plant."

The PYX (Can.) Cinerama/Samuels-Roffman 1973 color 111m. D: Harvey Hart. SP: Robert Schlitt, from John Buell's novel.

Ph: Rene Verzier. Mus: Harry Freedman;(songs & with) Karen Black. Ref: screen. V 10/3/73. Lee. with Christopher Plummer, Donald Pilon, Jean-Louis Roux.
Black Mass; demon possession. Portentous, ambitious, elliptical, and probably empty fantasy-drama. The film may be about hypocrisy, or perhaps about guilt--only The Shadow knows. Poor post-dubbing makes this hard on the ears.

Q (I-F-B) Monti/SND-Contrechamp/Valise 1974 color 85m. (PRICKLY PROBLEMS-alt t) SP,D: Jean-Francois Davy. From Peter Knack's novel "Y a Plus Qu'a." Ph: Marc Fossard. Mus: Raymond Ruer. Ref: MFB'76:172. with Philippe Gaste, Corinne O'Brian, Malisa Longo, Rita Cadillac, Jean Roche.
France, the 1980s. Private cars are almost unknown, and women are "thoroughly liberated and expert in karate."

QUANDO ELAS QUEREM.... see WHEN WOMEN WANT....

QUANDO LE DONNE PERSERO LA CODA see WHEN WOMEN LOST THEIR TAILS

QUANDO MARTA URLO DALLA TOMBA see MURDER MANSION

QUASI AT THE QUACKADERO Pyramid/Sally Cruickshank 1976 anim color 10m. Ref: LC Films'76.
"Amusement park of the future"; robot; time travel.

The QUATERMASS CONCLUSION (B) Euston 1979 color 105m. D: Piers Haggard. SP: Nigel Kneale. Sequel to *The CREEPING UNKNOWN. Ph: Ian Wilson. Mus: Marc Wilkinson, Nic Rowley. Ref: V 2/13/80: TV-movie? with John Mills, Simon MacCorkindale, Margaret Tyzack, Barbara Kellerman, Ralph Arliss.
"Space beam" ionizes "world youth."

QUATTRO MOSCHE DI VELLUTO GRIGIO see FOUR FLIES ON GREY VELVET

QUEEN KONG (B-I) Dexter & Grafitti Italiana(La Boetie) 1976 color SP,D: Frank Agrama. SP: also Ron Dobrin. Ref: Glut/CMM. Meyers: parody of KING KONG. V 10/20/76:130. 5/19/76:59 (ad). 5/12/76:208. with Rula Lenska, Robin Askwith.
Giant female gorilla transplanted from dinosaur-infested African domain to London.

QUEEN OF EVIL see SEIZURE

*The QUEEN OF SPADES PFA 1916 53m. SP: F. Otsep. Also based on Tchaikovsky's opera. Ph: Y. Slavinsky. AD: V. Ballieuzek et al. Ref: screen. PFA notes 9/25/81.
Ghost of Countess whom man scared to death seems to tell him the secret of winning at cards; hallucinations of spider web, countess. Dramatically, flat-footed and dated. (The film belongs to the silent staring-as-acting school.) But

even here the climactic scenes have a "Twilight Zone"-like kick to them, and the man-going-mad effects at the end are fun.

*The QUEEN OF SPADES Stratford 1949 Mkp: Robert Clarke. Assoc P: Jack Clayton. Ref: screen. and with Valentine Dyall, Gibb McLaughlin, Hay Petrie, George Woodbridge, Aubrey Mallalieu.
Countess Ranevskaya (Edith Evans) learns the secret of the cards from the satanic Count de Saint Germain; seems to return from the dead to pass it on to young man (Anton Walbrook). Atmospheric, involving horror story, with notable performances by Walbrook, Evans, and Yvonne Mitchell, and a good score by Auric. Choice horror moments and comic bits, though the characterizations finally seem a bit cramped by the anecdotal nature of the material. And the script appears to begin in fantasy and end firmly in good-old-psychology. (As if realism were integrity and fantasy just frou-frou.)

**QUEEN OF THE JUNGLE Screen Attractions/Wohl 1935 serial (12 chapters) & feature (60m.) D: Robert Hill. SP: J. Griffin Jay. Ph: W. Hyer. Mus D: Hal Chasnoff. Tech D: Fred Preble. Ref: Turner/Price. Lee: stock from '22 serial JUNGLE GODDESS. with Reed Howes, Mary Kornman, Dickie Jones, Lafe McKee, George Chesebro, Eddie Foster.
Lost kingdom of Mu. Radium death-ray from idol's eyes; lion men; Leopard Woman; killer-ape; Tree Man; Fish Men.

•QUEENS OF EVIL (I-F) Flavia & Carlton-Labrador 1971 color 91m. (Il DELITTO DEL DIAVOLO. La REGINE) SP,D: Tonino Cervi. SP: also Benedetti, Troisio. Ph: S. D'Offizi. Mus: A.F. Lavagnino. PD: M. De Rossi. Ref: MFB'72:137. Cinef Smr'73: 37. with Haydee Politoff, Silvia Monti, Ida Galli(aka Evelyn Stewart), Guido Alberti.
Emissary of the Devil; three sisters who chop up man.

QUELLA VILLA ACCANTO AL CIMITERO (I) 1981 (HOUSE OUTSIDE THE CEMETERY-ad t. sfa...E TU VIVRAI NEL TERRORE!?) D: Lucio Fulci. Ref: V 9/16/81:5:at Paris sf-fest. 5/13/81:154. with Catherine McCall, Paolo Malco, Antoine St. John.

QUELQU'UN A TUE (F) Forrester-Parant 1933 90m. (Le CHATEAU DE LA TERREUR-orig t) D: Jack Forrester. Dial: J.-J. Frappa. French version of *CRIMINAL AT LARGE. Ph: Hubert. Mus: Carl Tucker. AD: Wakhevitch, Gys. Ref: Chirat: "sinister chateau." with Pierre Magnier, Marcelle Geniat, Raymond Cordy, G. Modot.

QUEM E BETA? (Braz-F) Regina & Dahlia 1973 color 80m. (PAS DE VIOLENCE ENTRE NOUS) SP,D: Nelson Pereira Dos Santos. SP: also G.L. Clerc. Ref: Lee. V 6/27/73: post-atomic-holocaust story. with Frederic De Pasquale, Noelle Adam, R. Rosembourg.

QUEST see PLANET OF HORRORS

QUEST FOR LOVE (B) (Viacom-TV)/Rogers 1971 color 91m. D: Ralph Thomas. SP: Bert Batt, from John Wyndham's short story

"Random Quest." Ph: Ernest Steward. Mus: Eric Rogers;(theme) Peter Rogers. AD: Robert Jones. Titles: GSE. Ref: TV. TVG. TVFFSB. Lee. MFB'71:202. with Joan Collins, Tom Bell, Simon Ward, Denholm Elliott, Laurence Naismith, Sam Kydd,N.McCallum.

During an experiment, a physicist is thrust into a parallel world of 1971 in which he replaces his double. Occasionally lightly charming, occasionally bittersweet, this science-fantasy-romance about "second chances" at life and love is finally rather severely diluted by too much shuttling back and forth between worlds and airports. Some quite lovely moments; some quite "romantic" moments (the latter invariably swelled by the ludicrously-swelling "Ottilie's Theme").

The QUESTOR TAPES NBC-TV/Univ-TV 1974 color 95m. D: Richard A. Colla. Sp & Exec P: Gene Roddenberry. SP: also Gene L. Coon. Ph: M. Margulies. Mus: Gil Melle. AD: Phil Barber. SpPhFX: Albert Whitlock. Ref: TV. Lee. V 1/30/74:34. TVG. with Robert Foxworth(android), Mike Farrell, John Vernon, Lew Ayres(android), James Shigeta, Robert Douglas, Dana Wynter, Majel Barrett, Walter Koenig, Alan Caillou.

Questor is the last of a line of god-like androids that has for 200 millennia assisted mankind towards its childhood's end. Philosophically ambitious sf-drama plays, alternately, like a lost book of the Bible and a pilot for a TV series, and waxes sentimental over human emotions in the worst way--Questor is hardly operational before he begins pining for feeling. (This, the basic android-cliche.) His gaucherie while at large in the strange, non-android world, however, does make the movie's midsection amusing.

QUIEN PUEDE MATAR A UN NINO? see WOULD YOU KILL A CHILD?

QUINTET Fox/Lion's Gate 1979 color 118m. SP,D: Robert Altman. SP: also P. Resnick, F. Barhydt, L. Chetwynd. Ph: J. Boffety. Mus: Tom Pierson. PD: Leon Ericksen. SpFX:(des) David Horton; Tom Fisher, John Thomas. Ref: MFB'79:152-3. V 2/7/79: "impenetrable." with Paul Newman, Vittorio Gassman, Fernando Rey, Bibi Andersson, Brigitte Fossey, Nina Van Pallandt.

In an Earth paralyzed by a new ice age, citizens of a snowbound city play a board game of life and death--Quintet.

R---! see WORST CRIME OF ALL,The!

RABBITS see NIGHT OF THE LEPUS

RABID (Can.) New World/Cinepix-Dibar 1977 color 91m. SP,D: David Cronenberg. Ph: Rene Verzier. Mus: Ivan Reitman. AD: Claude Marchand. SpMkp:(des) Joe Blasco;(exec) Byrd Holland. SpFX: Al Griswold. Ref: screen. MFB'77:240. V(d) 6/21/77. FC 3/80: 38. with Marilyn Chambers(Rose), Frank Moore, Joe Silver, Howard Ryshpan(Dr.Keloid), Patricia Gage.

Skin graft leaves woman's underarm with "puffy red infection with a telescopic syringe that sucks out a pint or two of blood from Chambers' victims, and infects them with (a new strain of) rabies." (V) They in turn bite others, go into a coma and die, while she lives on, an immune transmitter who lives on blood. Guaranteed "Yuchh!" material, what with everyone getting punctured by everything from scissors, hooks, and teeth to needles, pneumatic drills, and the phallus-in-the-vagina creature--Rose's thorn--in our heroine's armpit. A special bonus: the victims and their victims bleed red and froth grey-green at the mouth. The film is wholly functional. There's little or no attempt at characterization, no straining for meaning, no social comment, no comic relief. And it's debatable whether there are Freudian overtones or simply puncture wounds. Cronenberg's admitted purity of intent and effect is rather a mixed blessing considering the film's intent and effect.

RACCONTI PROIBITI DI NULLA VESTITI see MASTER OF LOVE

RACE WITH THE DEVIL Fox/Saber-Maslansky 1975 color 88m. D: Jack Starrett. SP: Lee Frost, Wes Bishop. Ph: Robert Jessup. Mus: Leonard Rosenman. SpFX: Richard Helmer. Ref: MFB'75: 203. V 6/11/75. TV. with Peter Fonda, Warren Oates, Loretta Swit, Lara Parker, R.G. Armstrong, Phil Hoover.

Texas. Witnesses of human sacrifice at witches' sabbath are pursued by members of the cult. Routine, occasionally exciting chase-suspense actioner. Stunt-work galore. It seems that everyone in the county belongs to the cult and has a car, truck, or bus--but nothing stops our protagonists' camper....

RACER,The(by I.Melchior) see DEATH RACE 2000

RADS 1001 (I) 1973? short Ref: V 7/25/73:18: post-"worldwide holocaust." with John Steiner.

RAGGEDY ANN AND ANDY Fox/ITT 1977 color/scope anim & live 85m. D: Richard Williams. SP: P. Thackray, Max Wilk. Based on Johnny Gruelle's stories. Mus: Joe Raposo. PD: C. Cole. Ref: MFB'78:204-5. V 3/16/77. Voices: Didi Conn, Arnold Stang, Joe Silver(Greedy), Paul Dooley(Gazooks).

Girl's dolls (which come to life) include Greedy (a sweet-eating monster) and Gazooks (a sea serpent).

RAIDERS OF THE LOST ARK Para/Lucasfilm 1981 color/scope 115m. D: Steven Spielberg. SP: Lawrence Kasdan. Story: George Lucas, Philip Kaufman. Ph: Douglas Slocombe. Mus: John Williams. PD: Norman Reynolds. VisFX:(sup) Richard Edlund; Industrial Light & Magic. SpFxSup: Kit West. SpMkp: Chris Walas. Clouds: Gary Platek. Art: M. Lloyd, Ron Cobb. SdFX: S.H. Flick. Opt: MGM, Modern. Ref: screen. V 6/10/81. with Harrison Ford, Karen Allen, Paul Freeman, Ronald Lacey, John Rhys-Davies, Denholm Elliott.

Long-lost Ark of the Covenant--when opened--unleashes spectral hordes; snake pit; mummy chamber. What Republic could have done if it had been able to invest 12 years in production on a single super-serial. Gargantuan adventure movie works best when wryly acknowledging its own peril-a-minute absurdity--when, for instance, John Williams' thunderous score or the hyperbolic sound effects (e.g., cracking whips, hissing snakes) take over. Williams makes every incident, every stunt not just dramatic, but epochal. The script occasionally kids itself; but the element of parody in the score is inherent. Like the action, the music is not merely "enough"; it's more-than-enough. But it doesn't strain--as the script and direction sometimes do--for its exciting effects. It's always hyping the action and casually kidding its own aural hype. The movie has to scramble to keep up with Williams, and when it does catch up (as it does in the snake-pit and truck-and-jeep sequences), it becomes both exhilarating and amusing. When it lags behind, its hollowness becomes rather too apparent.

RAJA NARTAKIYA RAHASYA (India-Kannada) Sree Padmalakshmi 1976 color 161m. D & Ed: B. Harinarayana. SP: G. Venkatarao. Story: G.V. Rao. Mus: B. Vasantha. Ref: Dharap. with Rajesh, Udayakumar, Ramgopal.

Girl poses as ghost in "haunted mansion."

The RAJAH'S TIARA (B) Big Ben-Union 1914 38m. D: H.Martinek. SP: L.C. MacBean. Ref: BFC. with James Carew, Ivy Montford.

"X-ray device to see through walls."

RAJDHANI EXPRESS (India-Hindi) 1972 131m. D: B.J. Patel. SP: Govind Raman. Ph: Arvind. Mus: L. Chakraborty. Ref: Dharap. with Jonibond, Renu, Rajoo.

"Science-fiction story" about professor's "device to cure all diseases."

RAMA SUPERMAN INDONESIA (Indon.) Serama 1975 color/scope Ref: IFG'76:229(ad): super-hero.

RANDOM QUEST(by J.Wyndham) see QUEST FOR LOVE

RANDY THE ELECTRIC LADY 1980? color 75m. (RANDY-cr t) D: Philip Schuman? SP:Terry Southern? Ref: FC 9/81:68. J. Shapiro. with Desiree Cousteau, Jesie St. James.

Feedback from "human" computer makes girl produce "orgasmee, the world's greatest aphrodisiac." (JS)

RAPTO EN LAS ESTRELLAS (Sp) Castilla 1971 anim color 7m. D: Amaro Carretero. Ref: Lee(SpCinema).

"Villainous Astros"; robot.

RATATAPLAN (I) Cineriz 1979 color 90m. SP,D: Maurizio Nichetti. Ph: Mario Battistoni. Mus: Detto Mariano. Ref: V 9/5/79: electronic double. with Edy Angelillo, Roland Topor.

The RATS ARE COMING! THE WEREWOLVES ARE HERE! Mishkin 1972 color 92m. SP,D,Ph: Andy Milligan. Sets: Elaine. Mkp: Lois Marsh. Ref: FFacts. Lee. Aros. with Hope Stansbury, Jacqueline Skarvellis, Berwick Kaler, Noel Collins.

Family of werewolves ("unique species"), including girl who raises man-eating rats.

RATTLERS Boxo Int'l 1976 color 82m. D,P: John McCauley. SP: Jerry Golding. Ph: Richard Gibb, Irv Goodnoff. SpFX: Harry Woolman. Mkp: John Landon. Ref: FFacts. Willis/SW. with Sam Chew, Elizabeth Chauvet, Dan Priest, Celia Kaye.

Effect of discarded nerve gas on rattlesnakes makes them attack humans.

RAVAGERS Col/Saul David 1979 color/scope 91m. D: Richard Compton. SP: Donald S. Sanford, from Robert E. Alter's novel "Path to Savagery." Ph: V. Saizis. Mus: Fred Karlin. PD: R.E. Hobbs. SpFX: Fred Cramer. Ref: HR 5/25/79. V 5/30/79. PFA. with Richard Harris, Ann Turkel, Art Carney, Ernest Borgnine, Woody Strode, Seymour Cassel, Alana Hamilton.

Devastated world of the future inhabited by tribes of ravagers.

*The RAVEN 1935 Mus Sup: Gilbert Kurland. AD: Albert S. D'Agostino. Ref: TV. B.Hill. and with Maidel Turner.

"Universal presents Karloff and Lugosi" read the credits--no further identification of the two stars is necessary. The movie itself is unique; The RAVEN would be a classic American comedy if it could be proven that comedy was intended. Bela Lugosi here is perhaps as engaging as he is in MURDERS IN THE RUE MORGUE(1932). However, in the latter film, his Dr. Mirakle seems both aware of--and amused by--his own outre malevolence and its effect on others. Dr. Vollin (in The RAVEN) is more amusing than amused. At base, Lugosi seems to take this odd character <u>seriously</u>, as a <u>serious</u> part--rather than (as he does with Mirakle) seriously, as a <u>comic</u> part. He overloads every line with portent and suggestiveness ("It's <u>more</u> than a <u>hobby</u>!"), while the folks about him seem oddly oblivious of his unseemliness, and play dumb, or tactful, stranding him and making him look pretty foolish. Boris Karloff, meanwhile, plays his (impossible) role of Bateman <u>straight</u>--of such stuff are camp classics made of.

The RAVEN Para/Fleischer 1940 anim color 22m. SP: C. Meyer, P. Colvig. Ref: Cabarga/TFS. LC. Maltin/OMAM: based on the poem by Edgar Allan Poe.

See also: BOOKWORM, The. HIDDEN HAND, The(1942).

RAW MEAT (B) AI/K-L 1972 color 87m. (DEATH LINE-B) Story, D: Gary Sherman. SP: Ceri Jones. Ph: Alex Thomson. Mus: Jeremy Rose, Wil Malone. AD: Denis Gordon-Orr. SpFX: John Horton. Mkp: Harry & Peter Frampton. Ref: MFB'73:6. Lee. VV 11/15/73. with Donald Pleasence, Norman Rossington, David Ladd, Christopher Lee, Sharon Gurney.

Descendants of people buried alive in cave-in under British Museum in 1892 live on humans who wander into their tunnels from above.

RAYS THAT ERASE (B) Martin 1916 9m. Ref: BFC.
"Rays from professor's lamp make objects disappear."

The REAL THING AT LAST (B) British Actors 1916 33m. SP,D: James M. Barrie. D: also L.C. MacBean. Ref: BFC. Lee. with Ernest Thesiger(witch), Gladys Cooper(American witch), Edmund Gwenn, Godfrey Tearle, Owen Nares, A.E. Matthews.
Shakespeare's "Macbeth" modernized--"gaudy and vulgar American version; more witches and goblin." (Lee)

REAR CAR,The(by E.E.Rose) see MURDER IN THE PRIVATE CAR

REBELION DE LAS MUERTAS see VENGEANCE OF THE ZOMBIES

RECORDED LIVE (Showtime-TV)/Blackhawk/USC 1975 color 8m. D, Anim: S.S. Wilson. Mus: George Winston. Ref: TV. Blackhawk. with John Goodwin.
Reels of video tape come to life, consume humans; magnet temporarily repels monster(s). Droll comedy, with amusing stopmo animation and sound effects. (The latter sound like tactical chatter by the tape-creature.)

RED (B) Marro 1976 color 24m. SP,D: Astrid Frank. Ph: Robert Krasker. Mus: Anthony Bowles. AD: Harry Evans. Ref: MFB'79:110. with Ferdy Mayne, Mark Wynter, Frank.
Mysterious, bewitching girl haunts country house.

The RED DRAGON Mono 1945 64m. D: Phil Rosen. SP: George Callahan, based on Earl Derr Biggers' characters. Ph: Vincent Farrar. Mus: Edward J. Kay. Ref: TV. V 1/2/46. LC. with Sidney Toler(Charlie Chan), Fortunio Bonanova, Benson Fong, Robert Emmett Keane, Willie Best, Carol Hughes, Don Costello.
Sf-mystery: 95th element could (if used in bomb) "wipe out a country"; thermostat device stuck into wall "sends out radio-electric impulse" which allows killer to fire bullets from mechanism by remote control. Near rock-bottom for the Chans, with ghastly "humor" from Fong and Best (who make one wistful for Sen Yung and Mantan Moreland) and the same old Kay music. Toler and Bonanova talk out the mystery so lethargically that their scenes verge on self-parody. Each time a gun goes off, the suspects, helpfully, converge, like a line of chorus girls, or tactful vultures.

The REDEEMER (Yugos) Jadran-Croatia 1977 color/scope 87m. (IZBAVITELJ) SP,D: Krsto Papic. SP: also Ivo Bresan. From Alexander Greene's story. Ph: I. Rajkovic. Mus: B. Zivkovic. AD: Drago Turina. Ref: V 3/9/77. IFG'78:342-3. with Ivica Vidovic, Mirjana Majurec, Relja Vasic.
Europe, 1931. A rat-people, led by a rat-savior, overwhelm the population "by impersonating their victims"; "eerie." (IFG)

The REDEEMER...SON OF SATAN! Dimension/MLTD 1978 color? 83m. D: Constantine S. Gochis. Mus: Philip Gallo, Clem Vicari. AD: John Allee. SpFX: Jack Thompson. Ref: MFB'78:119-120: 1976? Willis/SW. with Michael Hollingsworth, Damien Knight, Gyr Patterson, T.G. Finkbinder(Redeemer), Nikki Barthen.
Mysterious boy who rises from mountain lake responsible for deaths of group of "grave sinners." (MFB)

A REFLECTION OF FEAR Col/Jaffe 1973(1971) color 89m. (AUTUMN CHILD-orig t. LABYRINTH-int t) D: William A. Fraker. SP: Edward Hume, Lewis John Carlino, from the novel "Go To Thy Deathbed" by Stanton Forbes. Ph: Laszlo Kovacs. Mus: Fred Myrow. AD: Joel Schiller. Mkp: Emile Lavigne. Ref: MFB'73: 56-7. Scheuer/MOTV. Cinef III:2:27. V 3/14/73. Lee: "horror murders." TVFFSB. J.Shapiro. TVG: "old mansion." FFacts. with Robert Shaw, Sally Kellerman, Sondra Locke, Mary Ure, Signe Hasso, Mitchell Ryan, Gordon DeVol, Liam Dunn.
Schizophrenic's imaginary half commits murders.

REGINE, La see QUEENS OF EVIL

REINCARNATION OF ISABEL (I) GRP 1973 color/scope 100m. (The GHASTLY ORGIES OF COUNT DRACULA-ad t. RITI, MAGIE NERE E SEGRETE ORGE DEL TRECENTO. The HORRIBLE ORGIES OF COUNT DRACULA, OR BLACK MAGIC-RITES-REINCARNATIONS-ad t?) D: Ralph Brown. SP: Renato Polselli. Ph: Ugo Brunelli. Mus: Gianfranco Reverberi, Romolo Forlai. Ref: CineFan 2:25. V 5/7/75:198(ad). Bianco Index'76:56. Glut/TDB. with Mickey Hargitay, Rita Calderoni, Raoul, Moschera Consolata, Max Dorian.
Satanic priests attempt to revive 400-year-old witch with blood of virgin.

The REINCARNATION OF PETER PROUD AI/BCP(Bing Crosby) & F/I 1975 color 104m. D: J.Lee Thompson. SP: Max Ehrlich, from his novel. Ph: Victor J. Kemper. Mus: Jerry Goldsmith. AD: Jack Martin Smith. Mkp: Jack H. Young, Robert O'Bradovich, M. Maggi. Ref: MFB'75:223. V 4/2/75. TV. with Michael Sarrazin, Jennifer O'Neill, Margot Kidder, Debralee Scott, Steve Franken, Cornelia Sharpe, Paul Hecht.
Parapsychologist discovers man who had previous existence. Smooth but contrived, with a very unsatisfying ending. The latter makes a sort of ironic, <u>cyclical</u> sense--as a nasty squelch (the second-time-around's no charm <u>here</u>)--but it makes no <u>dramatic</u> sense. It's simply the same ending tacked onto two different stories (present-tense Peter's and past-tense Jeff's), for an ironic quick-kill.

REISE INS JENSEITS see JOURNEY INTO THE BEYOND

RENDEZVOUS EN FORET (F) Argos-Two World 1972 color 80m. SP, D: Alain Fleischer. Ph: Marcel Grignon. Ref: V 5/3/72:93. Lee. with Catherine Jourdan, Laurence Trimble.
"Adult fairy tale of beauty and the beast." (V)

RENDEZVOUS 24 Fox/Wurtzel 1946 70m. D: James Tinling. SP: Aubrey Wisberg. Ph: Ben Kline. Mus: Emil Newman. Ref: Bill Warren. LC. V 5/1/46. with William Gargan, Pat O'Moore, Kurt Katch, David Leonard, Maria Palmer, Herman Bing.
Nazi scientists "working on development of atomic explosions by remote radio control" almost destroy Paris. (V)

The RENEGADE SATELLITE Official-TV/Reed-Space Ranger 1954 78m. SP: Warren Wilson? From the "Rocky Jones, Space Ranger" TV series. Ph: Walter Strenge. Mus: Alexander Laszlo. AD: Maclure Capps. PhFX: Jack Glass. Ref: TVFFSB. script. Space War #2/78,p63. with Richard Crane, Jimmy Lydon, Sally Mansfield, Maurice Cass, Scotty Beckett, Ann Robinson.

RENTADICK (B) Paradine-Virgin 1972 color 94m. D: Jim Clark. SP: John Cleese, Graham Chapman. Ph: John Coquillon. Mus: Carl Davis. SpFX: Michael Albrechtsen. Ref: MFB'72:143-4. with James Booth, Julie Ege, Tsai Chin, Spike Milligan.
Chemist's nerve-gas paralyzes people from the waist down.

*REPULSION 1965 SP: also David Stone. Ref: screen. AFI.
This clinically absorbing study of a young woman (Catherine Deneuve) both obsessed with and repulsed by "maleness" may still be Roman Polanski's best film. The camera follows her--taking in objects and phenomena which happen to distract her--in her time, dawdling and lingering as she does. "Her time" is, at first, only slightly out-of-synch with "their time." It becomes increasingly out-of-synch, until, finally, it's a matter of "her world" and "their world." The latter half of the film (in, principally, "her world") is a good shock-show, and yet it's somewhat unsatisfying; it dwells on effects (in both psychological and cinematic senses)rather than probing causes. It's simply a more spectacular recapitulation of the first half. Polanski appears to choose to stay on the psychological surface of his subject, and his discretion is at least preferable to glib analysis, if it leaves his study tantalizingly incomplete, unfinished.

REQUIEM POUR UN VAMPIRE see CRAZED VAMPIRE

RESURRECTION SYNDICATE, The see NOTHING BUT THE NIGHT

El RETORNO DE LOS VAMPIROS (Sp) Uranzu 1972 D: Jose M. Zabalza. Ref: V 5/9/73:144. Lee. with Simon Andreu, M. Monterrey.

RETORNO DE WALPURGIS, El see CURSE OF THE DEVIL

El RETORNO DEL HOMBRE LOBO (Sp) 1980 (La NOCHE DEL HOMBRE LOBO-orig t) SP,D,P: Jacinto Molina. Sequel to MARK OF THE WOLFMAN? Ref: V 8/20/80:44: "werewolf yarn." 10/1/80:47,67. 4/15/81:26. with Paul Naschy(aka Molina), Julia Saly, Narciso Ibanez Menta.

The RETURN (B) Pyramid/Jocelyn 1973 color 30m. SP,D: Sture Rydman. SP: also B. Scobie. From the short stories "Nobody's

House" by A.M. Burrage & "The Middle Toe of the Right Foot" by Ambrose Bierce. Ph: Douglas Slocombe. Mus: Marc Wilkinson. PD: Bryan Graves. Ref: TV. MFB'73:257. with Peter Vaughan.
Ghost reputedly haunts isolated house. Anecdote begins mundanely, works to a satisfyingly chilly conclusion.

RETURN FROM WITCH MOUNTAIN BV 1978 color 93m. D: John Hough. SP: Malcolm Marmorstein. Sequel to ESCAPE TO WITCH MOUNTAIN. Ph: Frank Phillips. Mus: Lalo Schifrin. AD: Mansbridge, Senter. Stopmo Anim: Joe Hale. SpFX: Lycett, Cruickshank, Lee. Ref: MFB'79:51. V 3/15/78. TV. with Kim Richards, Ike Eisenmann, Bette Davis, Christopher Lee, Jack Soo, Denver Pyle, Ward Costello, Helene Winston, D. Bakalyan, Lloyd Nelson.
Scientist uses mind-control device to harness alien boy's telekinetic energy; with his aid sabotages plutonium plant's emergency cooling system. A Disney fantasy-comedy nadir. "Plot" is too strong a word for the sad little thread on which an unending series of embarrassingly cute telekinetic stunts is strung. "Character" is another dimension altogether.

RETURN OF BLACKENSTEIN see BLACKENSTEIN

RETURN OF CAPTAIN NEMO see AMAZING CAPTAIN NEMO

*The RETURN OF CHANDU (Classic Int'l-TV) 1934 Ph: John Hickson. Mus D: Abe Meyer. AD: Robert Ellis. Ref: TV: Universal?? TVFFSB. Turner/Price: cliff-hangers from first 4 chapters of 12-chapter serial re-filmed for "smoother" feature. and with Wilfred Lucas, Iron Eyes Cody(Cat Man), Edward Piel, H. Hall.
Yogi master ("Have faith, my son") on call through finger-ring; invisibility; mind control; Bubasti cult; princess who's drugged, placed in sarcophagus. Dull skullduggery, distinguished only by Bela Lugosi's presence.

*The RETURN OF DOCTOR X (UA-TV) 1939 From Makin's story "The Doctor's Secret." Mus: Bernard Kaun. Ref: TV. TVG. Lee.
Lines: "Synthetic blood!" "Interesting stuff, blood." "His interest in blood almost equals my own." Data: Humphrey Bogart as Dr. Maurice J. Xavier/Marshall Quesne (1897-1937; 1939) enters carrying a rabbit. The bad news: this is for the most part a typical Warners blend of "toughness" and comedy, with a cast of actors you'd least want to see in a horror movie--Dennis Morgan, Bogart, Wayne Morris, Rosemary Lane, Huntz Hall. The only eerie note: Lya Lys's "cold, graveyard look" as an actress whose body is found drained of that interesting stuff, blood.

RETURN OF KING KONG see MIGHTY PEKING MAN

*RETURN OF THE APE MAN (NTA-TV) 1944 Sets: David Milton. Ref: TV. TVFFSB. Lennig/TC. Lee. V 7/26/44. and with J. Farrell MacDonald, Ernie Adams.
A scientist "advances the brain" of a revived prehistoric ape man "20,000 years in a few hours," by implanting in it a part of a fellow-scientist's brain. So lifeless and

perfunctory that the actors sound as if they're reading the script for the first time, for some arcane, non-narrative experiment. John Carradine is a blank, and Bela Lugosi's line readings are as mechanical as Edward J. Kay's stock musical motifs. A shoo-in for Monogram's worst if it weren't for The INVISIBLE GHOST.

The RETURN OF THE EVIL DEAD (Sp) Ancla Century 1973 color 91m. (El ATAQUE DE LOS MUERTOS SIN OJOS) SP,D: Amando De Ossorio. Sequel to TOMBS OF THE BLIND DEAD. Ph: M.F. Mila. Mus: A.G. Abril. Ref: MFB'76:211. V 5/9/73:137. Bianco Index '74. with Tony Kendall, Fernando Sancho, L. Fleming, E. Roy.
"Satanist group of Templars" returns from the dead. (MFB)

The RETURN OF THE INCREDIBLE HULK Univ-TV 1977 color 94m. D: Alan Levi. Ref: TVFFSB. with Bill Bixby, Lou Ferrigno, Jack Colvin, Laurie Prange, Dorothy Tristan, William Daniels.
See also: The INCREDIBLE HULK.

The RETURN OF THE KING...A STORY OF THE HOBBITS (U.S.-J) ABC-TV/Rankin-Bass & Toei 1980 anim color 95m. (HOBITTO NO BOKEN. FRODO THE HOBBIT II-orig t) D: Akiyuki Kubo;(U.S.) Arthur Rankin Jr., Jules Bass. SP: Romeo Muller, based on the books "The Return of the King" and "The Hobbit" by J.R.R. Tolkien. Mus: Maury Laws. Anim: Toru Hara, T. Kubo. Ref: V 5/7/80:581(ad). 5/9/79:381. 12/6/78:12(ad). JFFJ 13:35. Panorama 5/80. PFA. Voices: Orson Bean, Theodore Bikel, William Conrad, John Huston, Roddy McDowall.
Cadaverous Lord of the Nazgul; Armies of Darkness; dragon.
See also: HOBBIT,The. LORD OF THE RINGS.

RETURN OF THE LIVING DEAD see MESSIAH OF EVIL

*The RETURN OF THE VAMPIRE 1944(1943) (VAMPIRES OVER LONDON-orig t?) SpFX: Aaron <u>Nibley</u>. Ref: TV. V 2/2/44. Lennig/TC. LC.
RETURN OF THE VAMPIRE is emblematic of the generally prosaic "B" horrors of the Forties. The film is over before it starts: in virtually the first shot, a werewolf steps into close shot and begins chatting with a vampire. (So much for suspension of disbelief!) And casting baby-faced Matt Willis as Bela Lugosi's lycanthropic aide Andreas is like casting Wayne Morris as a werewolf. Only Lugosi's delivery as Armand Tesla ("the depraved Rumanian scientist" who becomes a vampire) has any sense of other-worldliness to it. But it's not for no reason that you never hear fans quoting Lugosi lines from this film.

RETURN TO BOGGY CREEK 777/Gates(Bayou) 1978 color/scope 85m. Story,D: Tom Moore. SP: John David Woody. Ph: R.E. Bethard. Mus: Darrell Deck. Sets: Ken Kennedy. SpDes: Tery Moore, Jane Grubb. Opt: Pacific. Ref: TV. Willis/SW. with Dawn Wells, Dana Plato, Louis Belaire(monster), John Hofeus.
Hairy but friendly monster; hurricane; kids; ballad. Low-key, rambling, not-exactly-riveting.
See also: LEGEND OF BOGGY CREEK.

RETURN TO THE LAND OF OZ see JOURNEY BACK TO OZ

REVAMP Film-makers' Coop 196-? 6m. D: Peter Hudiburg. Ref: Lee. "Vampire film about vampire films."

REVENGE! ABC-TV/Carliner 1971 color 72m. (aka ONE WOMAN'S REVENGE. THERE ONCE WAS A WOMAN) D: Jud Taylor. SP: Joseph Stefano. Ph: John Alonzo. Mus: Dominic Frontiere. AD: Joseph Jennings. Ref: TV. Lee. TVFFSB. TVG: "Gothic horror." with Shelley Winters, Bradford Dillman, Carol Rossen, Stuart Whitman(psychic), Roger Perry, Gary Clarke.

Madwoman chains man (whom she holds responsible for her daughter's suicide) in cellar; his wife (who has ESP) and psychic search for him. Typically hollow TV-movie-slot plot provides a few piquant moments for Winters, precious little for viewer.

REVENGE OF BIGFOOT Splendora Int'l. 1979 Ref: V 7/25/79:32 (rated).

REVENGE OF DR. DEATH see MADHOUSE

*The REVENGE OF FRANKENSTEIN Hammer-Cadogan 1958 Add'l Dial: Hurford Jaynes. Sequel to CURSE OF FRANKENSTEIN. Mkp: Phil Leakey. Ref: TV. BFC. and with Michael Ripper, John Welsh.

Manufactured body ("Dr.Franck") contains brain of manufacturer, Dr. Stein, aka Baron Frankenstein (Peter Cushing); another body (Michael Gwynne's) with brain of dwarf (Oscar Quitak); chimp with brain of orang.; body snatcher (Lionel Jeffries). A cute ending, and a "monster" (Gwynne) who almost makes a go of it; but the essentially pointless script doesn't ring any resonant changes on the Frankenstein themes. Cushing's Baron is at least a bit wittier than he was in CURSE.

REVENGE OF MECHAGODZILLA see TERROR OF MECHAGODZILLA

REVENGE OF THE DEAD see HOLLYWOOD MEATCLEAVER MASSACRE, The

REVENGE OF THE MYSTERONS FROM MARS (B) Showtime-TV/ITC-TV 1981 puppets color 95m. D: Brian Burgess, Robert Lynn, Ken Turner. SP: Tony Barwick. Sequel to ***THUNDERBIRDS ARE GO? Mus: Barry Gray. SupAD: Bob Bell. VisFX:(sup) Derek Meddings; Shaun Whittaker-Cooke;(2nd unit d) Peter Wragg. Ref: TV. TVG. Voices: Paul Maxwell et al.

REVENGE OF THE SCREAMING DEAD see MESSIAH OF EVIL

REVENGE OF THE STEPFORD WIVES NBC-TV/Scherick 1980 color 92m. D: Robert Fuest. SP: David Wiltse. Re-working of The STEPFORD WIVES. Ph: Ric Waite. Mus: Laurence Rosenthal. AD: Tom H. John. Mkp: Christina Smith. Ref: TV. TVG. with Sharon Gless, Julie Kavner, Arthur Hill, Don Johnson.

Ten years later. The men of Stepford are now chemically re-programming (or "neutralizing") their women to be perfect wives; pills and sirens periodically reinforce their subservience. The method this time is closer to brainwashing than to duplication; the results are the same. REVENGE simply and limply re-cycles the basic terrible-paradise premise, without adding any ideas of its own. More suffocating irony; more glib anti-anti-feminism, capped by a silly, horror-movie-formula "revenge." Julie Kavner has a few good post-neutralization scenes (i.e., "coming out" and "haywire").

*REVENGE OF THE ZOMBIES (UA-TV) 1943 Ref: TV. V 9/1/43.
This oddball Monogram--like their KING OF THE ZOMBIES--features a casual, semi-comic treatment of zombies, and Mantan Moreland doing one-liners. There's also a risible "zombie call," one zombie dubbed Lazarus (James Baskett) ("Ah, yes!--in the Bible--he rose from the dead"), and the mad doctor's (John Carradine) fiercely independent, strong-willed wife (Veda Ann Borg), who "goes her own way, living or dead." The line here between zombie and non-zombie actors is sometimes thin--heroine Gale Storm and Bob Steele as a U.S. agent are particularly ambiguous.

RIBLJE OKO see FISHEYE

*The RIDER OF THE SKULLS Col 1966 D: Alfredo Salazar. Ref: Lee. Glut/CMM: vampires, headless horsemen.

RING OF DARKNESS (I) Tanit 1977 (Un OMBRA NELL'OMBRA) D: Pier Carpi. Ref: V 5/11/77:288: "satanic thriller." 10/20/76: 84. 9/2/81:6: at Sitges. with Anne Heywood, Valentina Cortese, John Philip Law, Marisa Mell, Irene Papas, Lara Wendell.

RIPPER FILE,The(by J.Lloyd & E.Jones) see MURDER BY DECREE

RISHYA SHRUNGA see FERTILITY GOD, The

RITES DES MORTS, Les see DES MORTS

The RITES OF MAY (Fili) LVN/de Leon 1976 color 116m. (ITIM) D,P: Mike de Leon. SP: Doy de Mundo, Gil Quito. Ph: Ely Cruz, R. Lacap. Mus: Max Jocson. Ref: V 3/21/79: spiritualism, seance. with Tommy Abuel, Charo Santos, Mona Lisa.

RITI, MAGIE NERE E SEGRETE ORGE DEL TRECENTO see REINCARNATION OF ISABEL

RITUALS (Can.) Aquarius/Day & Date Int'l 1978 color 94m. D: Peter Carter. SP: Ian Sutherland. Ph: Rene Verzier. AD: Karen Bromley. Ref: IFG'78:93. V 4/26/78: unseen madman. Willis/SW. with Hal Holbrook, Lawrence Dane, Robin Gammell.
Doctors menaced by "strange force." (IFG)

El ROBO DE LAS MOMIAS DE GUANAJUATO (Mex) Agrasanchez 1972 86m. D: Tito Novaro. SP: Miguel Morayta. Sequel to Las MOMIAS DE GUANAJATO. Ph: A. Ruiz. Mus: Rafael Carreon. Ref: Lee. Glut/CMM. with Mil Mascaras, Blue Angel, Tito Novaro.

Electronically-controlled, resurrected mummies play part in attempt to conquer the world.

The ROBOT MacMillan 1978 object anim color 18m. D: Frank & Joan Gardner. Ref: PFA notes 7/30/80. Brandon.
"Toy robot with delusions of being King Kong." (Brandon)

*ROBOT MONSTER (Medallion-TV) 1953 SpPhFX: Jack Rabin, David Commons. SpProp: N.A. Fisher. Mkp: Stan Campbell. Ref: screen. TVFFSB. Glut/CMM: footage from LOST CONTINENT. with Selena Royale, George Barrows(Ro-Man), John Brown(robot voice).
Ape-like alien's death ray destroys civilization. ROBOT MONSTER is one of our odder legacies from early-middle-Fifties sf. The dialogue goes on beyond pretentiousness into cosmic delirium. At one point the heroine cries (passionately if disjointedly) "Even if it means that man's millions of years of struggle up from the sea, the slime, the fight to breathe air, to stand erect, to think, to conquer nature--do you believe all this can be stopped by a doting father and a jealous suitor?" Lines like this don't just fall flat--they fall so far it's dizzying. Barrows' Ro-Man--torn between sex and duty--"makes" the movie. Makes it, that is, above-average camp. Andrew Sarris's comment about the poignancy of male lechery seems apposite here, in an inverse way.

ROBOT RUMPUS (J) Toei 1977 anim 25m. (WAKUSEI ROBO DANGADOO ACE) D: Teruo Ishii. SP: Yasuo Yoshino. Sequel: WAKUSEI ROBO DANGADO ESU--UCHU DAIKAISEN. Ref: V 5/17/78:420. JFFJ 13:34: "insect robot army."

ROBOTS see WAR OF THE ROBOTS

The ROCKY HORROR PICTURE SHOW (B) Fox/White-Adler 1975 color 101m. SP,D: Jim Sharman. SP: also Richard O'Brien, from his play "The Rocky Horror Show." Ph: Peter Suschitzky. Mus: O'Brien. AD: T.A. Snow. SpFX: Wally Veevers. Mkp: Peter Robb-King. Ref: MFB'75:181-82. screen. V 9/24/75. with Tim Curry(Frank N.Furter), Susan Sarandon, Barry Bostwick, Charles Gray, Peter Hinwood(Rocky), Meatloaf, O'Brien.
Aliens from the planet Transsexual in the Transylvania Galaxy; transvestite, bisexual leader's life-creating experiments; laser guns. It may have been a "Picture Show" once, but it's an event now, a landmark not so much in film history as in film-audience history. How good this do-it-yourself movie is depends pretty much on how witty the audience of the moment is--my audience saw to it that there were few lulls. (Some "interior dialogue" was especially sharp.) The pretext (i.e., the movie itself) seems marginally more amusing than young-couple-lost-in-old-house predecessors like HORROR OF IT ALL, but such observations are neither here nor there. The most popular character (with my group): Little Nell Campbell's Columbia. The theme (almost lost in the excitement): sexual expression vs. sexual repression.
See also: SHOCK TREATMENT(P).

ROCKY JONES, SPACE RANGER see RENEGADE SATELLITE, The

The ROGUES' TAVERN (JED-TV)/Puritan/Mercury 1936 67m. D: Bob Hill. SP: Al Martin. Ph: Bill Hyer. Mus D: Abe Meyer. Sets: Fred Preble. Ref: Turner/Price. TVFFSB. LC. with Wallace Ford, Barbara Pepper, Joan Woodbury, Clara Kimball Young, Jack Mulhall, John Elliott, Earl Dwire, A. Loft, Ed Cassidy.
Murder victims' throats torn open by "hand-operated device shaped like a dog's head and equipped with fangs"; "vengeful scientist"; "mysterious warning voice." (T/P)

ROI ET L'OISEAU, Le see KING AND THE MOCKINGBIRD, The

ROLLERBABIES Classic 1976 color 84m. D,P: Carter Stevens. Ref: Meyers. Willis/SW. with Alan Marlo, Suzanne McBain.
Overpopulated future in which sex is forbidden.

ROLLERBALL UA 1975 color 129m. D,P: Norman Jewison. SP: William Harrison, from his short story "Rollerball Murders." Ph: Douglas Slocombe. Mus: Andre Previn; Shostakovich, Bach, J. Strauss. PD: John Box. SpFX: Sass Bedig, John Richardson, Joe Fitt. Multivision: Brian Smedley-Aston. Ref: MFB'75:223-24. V 6/25/75. TV. with James Caan, John Houseman, Maud Adams, John Beck, Moses Gunn, Pamela Hensley, Ralph Richardson, Burt Kwouk, Shane Rimmer.
In the corporate world of 2018, poverty, sickness, and war have been eliminated, and an ultra-violent game known as Rollerball--instituted to discourage individual initiative--is the favorite spectator sport; flame guns; Zero, super-computer with memory pool. There is a perhaps-intriguing anecdote here re: collective-vs.-individual interests. But the script takes cinematic eons simply to establish its most basic premises, the better (apparently) to establish them. (And it seems rather incredible that the "stats freaks" of even so docile a future-society would let the Corporation's arbitrary re-writing of rollerball rules--and hence history--go unremarked.)

ROLY-POLY (Polish) 1968 color 35m. (PRZEKLADANIEC) D: Andrzej Wajda. Ref: Cinef W'73:39. Lee. screen.
Clever transplant-comedy.

ROMANTIC AGONY, The see VAARWEL

RONGRAM PI (Thai) Jirabanterng 1975 Ref: V 12/3/75:32. 11/19/75:28. 10/1/75:42: "horror film"; haunted inn.

ROSE DE FER see NUIT DU CIMETIERE

*ROSEMARY'S BABY 1968 Sequel: LOOK WHAT'S HAPPENED TO ROSEMARY'S BABY. PD: Richard Sylbert. Process Ph: F. Edouart. Mkp: Allan Snyder. Ref: AFI. and with Charles Grodin, Tony Curtis(voice), W. Castle, Wende Wagner, Almira Sessions.

ROSSO SEGNO DELLA FOLLIA see HATCHET FOR THE HONEYMOON

ROUGE DE CHINE see CHINESE RED

RUBY Dimension/Krantz 1977 color 84m. (BLOOD RUBY-orig t) D: Curtis Harrington. SP: George Edwards, Barry Schneider. Story: Steve Krantz. Ph: William Mendenhall. Mus: Don Ellis. AD: Tom Rasmussen. SpFX: Knott Ltd., Alfred Shelly. Ref: V (d) 5/19/77. MFB'77:214. V 2/2/77:32. 12/8/76:19. TV. with Piper Laurie, Stuart Whitman, Roger Davis, Fred Kohler, Len Lesser, Janit Baldwin, Crystin Sinclaire.

Parapsychologist attempts to exorcise murderous evil spirit; ATTACK OF THE FIFTY-FOOT WOMAN playing at drive-in.

RUN, STRANGER, RUN (Swiss-Can.?) Cinema 5/Taurean 1973 color 90m. (HAPPY MOTHER'S DAY...LOVE, GEORGE-orig t) D,P: Darren McGavin. SP: Robert Clouse. Ph: W. Lassally. Mus: Don Vincent. PD: Wuethrich. Mkp: Tony Lloyd. Ref: TV. Scheuer/ MOTV: "Gothic horror." Maltin/TVM. FFacts. with Patricia Neal, Cloris Leachman, Ron Howard, Bobby Darin, Simon Oakland, Tessa Dahl, Kathie Browne, Joe Mascolo, Thayer David.

Nova Scotia. Mad girl commits brutal murders; corpses everywhere.

RUNNING SILENT see SILENT RUNNING

RUSLAN I LJUDMILA (Russ) 1914 82m. D,Ph,AD: Ladislas Starevitch. Based on Pushkin's narrative poem. Ref: Filmlexicon: 1915. Lee. with Ivan Mosjoukine(Devil), S. Vassilieva.

RUSLAN I LUDMILA (Russ) Sovexportfilm/Mosfilm 1973 color 225m. SP,D: Alexandre Ptouchko. SP: also Bolotine, from Pushkin's poem. Ph: Guelein, Zakharov. Mus: Tikon Khrennikov. Ref: Filmex'74. screen: giant head. V 4/17/74. with Natalia Petrova, Valeri Kosinets, Vladimir Fiodorov.

"Sorcerers and witches"; "sinister dwarf" whose strength is in his beard. (V) Fine effects; ploddingly-told story, with awkwardly-rhymed "heroic" dialogue. Alternately amusing and wearying--and long enough to alternate many times.

RYMDINVASION I LAPPLAND see INVASION OF THE ANIMAL PEOPLE

RYU NO TARO (J) Toei-TV 1979 anim color 75m. SP,D: K. Urayama. Ref: JFFJ 13:35: feature from TV-series footage.

"Evil spirits"; dragon.

S.F. SAIYUKI see STARZINGER

S.O.S. (I) 1979? anim D: Guido Manuli. Ref: IFG'80:372: "sci-fi."

*SOS COAST GUARD 1937 Ref: TV. Lennig/TC. and with Lee Ford.

Radioactive disintegration gas which, vaporized in containers or bombs, could destroy whole cities; machine for detecting radioactivity; "half-mad giant" who's virtually impervious to bullets. Flat, colorless "featurized" serial. Bela Lugosi as the mad Boroff is only allowed to interject an occasional order. (Coast Guard officer: "Boroff and his kind must be annihilated regardless of cost!")

SABBAT OF THE BLACK CAT (Austral.) 1974 color 85m. D,P: Ralph Marsden. Ref: Lee: from Poe's "The Black Cat." V 5/5/76:98.

SABRE TOOTH TIGER, The see DEEP RED

Le SADIQUE AUX DENTS ROUGES (Belg) Cinevision 1971 color 80m. D: Jean-Louis Van Belle. Ph: J. Crevin. Mus: Raymond Legrand. Ref: Lee(Ecran). Cinef F'73:39. with Jane Clayton, Albert Simono, Daniel Moosman.
Scientist turns young man into vampire.

Le SADIQUE DE NOTRE DAME (F) Eurocine 1979 color D: Jesus Franco. Ref: V 5/7/80:475. 5/13/81:283: horror.

SAGA DE LOS DRACULAS see DRACULA SAGA

The SAGITTARIUS MINE Gold Key-TV("Zodiac" series) 1972? color 91m. Ref: TVFFSB. with Steve Forrest, Diane Baker, R.Danton.
Invisible menace threatens seekers of the Lost Dutchman gold mine; occult book.

SAGRENSKA KOZA see PEAU DE CHAGRIN(1960)

SAIBOOGU 009 see CYBORG 009

SAIEHAIEN BOLAN DE BAD see TALL SHADOWS OF THE WIND

SAIYUKI see STARZINGER

SALEM'S LOT CBS-TV/WB-TV 1979 color 190m. D: Tobe Hooper. SP: Paul Monash, from Stephen King's novel. Ph: Jules Brenner. Mus: Harry Sukman. PD: Mort Rabinowitz. SpFX: Frank Torro. SpMkp: Jack Young. Ref: TV. V 7/22/81:4(rated): WB feature version. 5/7/80:234: aka JERUSALEM'S LOT? Cinef. TVG. with David Soul, James Mason, Lance Kerwin, Bonnie Bedelia, Lew Ayres, Reggie Nalder(vampire), Fred Willard, Julie Cobb.
Vampire in Maine. Generally conventional vampire movie. The mist-and-bobbing-and-clawing-kid-at-the-window effect is very deceptive--it seems evocative of so much more (both psychologically and supernaturally) than the story goes on to deliver. The vampire-in-the-kitchen sequence is also fairly exciting. But most of the sequences take forever "building tension."

The SAME NIGHT, THE SAME VOICE (India-Hindi) Mayur 1973 color 136m. (WOHI RAAT WOHI AWAAZ) SP,D: Dev Kishen. Story: V. Desai. Ph: R. Layton. Mus: Sonik-Omi. Ref: Dharap.

with Radha Saluja, Sonia Sahni, Sameet Bhanja.
Murders in "haunted haveli" supposedly committed by spirit of raped girl.

SAMMY'S SUPER T-SHIRT (B) CFF/Monument 1978 color 58m. D: Jeremy Summers. SP: Frank Godwin. Story: H.L. Robertson. Mus: Harry Robinson. Ref: MFB'78:95-6. with Reggie Winch, David Young, Richard Vernon, Michael Ripper.
Chemical solution soaks into boy's T-shirt, makes wearer super-strong.

SANG DES AUTRES, Le see LIPS OF BLOOD

*SANTA CLAUS CONQUERS THE MARTIANS JaLor 1964 Story,P: Paul L. Jacobson. Mus: Milton DeLugg. SpPhFX: Haberstroh Studios. SpLighting FX: Duke Brady. SpProps: Fritz Hansen. Mkp: George Fiala. Ref: TV. AFI. and with Victor Stiles, Vincent Beck.
Robot, Tor; electronic mind-programmers; 800-year-old wise man of Mars; tickling and immobilizing rays; sleep spray; toy-producing machine; nuclear curtain; Martian rocket with magniscope, radar shield, and anti-gravity generator. Forced jollity, as Santa's laughter proves contagious with kids of all planets. Older viewers may find some jollity in the dialogue: (Martian, disgustedly) "Santa Claus! Toys! Games! Laughing children!"; (TV newscaster) "And Mrs. Claus has positively identified the kidnappers as Martians." Not one of the real high-water marks of children's fantasy.

SANTO CONTRA LA MAGIA NEGRA (Mex) Latino-americana & Flama 1972 color 100m. D: A.B. Crevenna. SP: R.G. Travesi. Story: F. Oses. Ph: A. Uribe. Mus: G.C. Carreon. Ref: Lee. with Santo, Elsa Cardenas, Sasha Montenegro, Carlos Suarez.
Voodoo; zombies; man-into-tiger.

SANTO EN LA VENGANZA DE LA MOMIA (Mex) Calderon 1971 color 88m. D: Rene Cardona. SP: Alfredo Salazar. Ref: TV. Lee. M/TVM 10/70. with Santo, Eric del Castillo, Mary Montiel, Cesar del Campo, Carlos Suarez.
Hideous mummy with bow-and-arrows menaces expedition. Lots of "la momia!"

SANTO EN LA VENGANZA DE LAS MUJERES VAMPIROS (Mex) Latino-americana & Flama 1969 color 90m. (La VENGANZA DE LAS MUJERES VAMPIROS-alt t) D: F. Curiel. SP: F. Oses, J.G. Besne. AD: A. Lopez. Mkp: F.L. de Guevara. Ref: Glut/TDB: 1974? Lee. with Santo, Norma Lazareno, Gina Romand(vampire).
Vampire horde; resurrected vampire countess; synthetic man.

SANTO VS. CAPULINA (Mex) Clasa-Mohme & Azteca 1972 color Ref: Lee. with Santo, Capulina, Liza Castro, Crox Alvarado.
Personality-transforming machine.

SANTO VS. INVASION DE LOS MARCIANOS (Mex) Azteca 1967? (cf. *MURDERERS FROM ANOTHER WORLD) Ref: Lee(FDY'68). with Santo.

SANTO Y BLUE DEMON CONTRA DRACULA Y EL HOMBRE LOBO (Mex) Azteca & Calderon 1972 color 90m. D: Miguel M. Delgado. SP: Alfredo Salazar. Ph: R. Solano. Mus: G.C. Carreon. AD: A. Lopez. Mkp: M. Ortega. Ref: Lee(Warren). with Santo, Blue Demon, Aldo Monti(Dracula), Carlos Suarez, Eugenia San Martin.
Dracula; wolf man; hunchback; zombies; misc. vampires.

SANTO Y BLUE DEMON VS. DR. FRANKENSTEIN (Mex) Calderon 1973 D: Miguel Delgado. Ref: V 5/8/74:238.

SANTO Y MANTEQUILLA NAPOLES EN LA VENGANZA DE LA LLORONA (Mex) Calderon 1975 D: Miguel M. Delgado. SP: Francisco Cavazos. Ref: V 11/5/75:41. with Santo, Mantequilla, Kiki Calles, Carlos Suarez, Ana Lilia Tovar, Sonia Cavazos, A. Castano.

SARABA UCHU SENKAN YAMATAO see SPACE CRUISER YAMATO PART II

SASQUATCH, THE LEGEND OF BIGFOOT (Gold Key-TV)/NAFP/Fabian 1976 color 101m. D: Ed Ragozzini. SP: Ed Hawkins. Story: R.D. Olson. Animal Ph: Dick Robinson. Mus: Al Capps. Ref: MFB '78:181-82. TVFFSB. Meyers. V 1/18/78. S Union 3/13/76. Lee (p): 1974? with George Lauris, Jim Bradford, William Emmons.
Ape-like creatures discovered in British Columbia.

SATAN see MARK OF THE DEVIL

The SATAN MURDERS (B) ABC-TV/Clovis 1974 color 74m. D: Lela Swift. SP: I.G. Neiman. Ref: TVFFSB: satanists. Lee. with Salome Jens, Larry Blyden, Susan Sarandon, Douglass Watson.

SATANAS DE TODOS LOS HORRORES (Mex) America 1972 color 93m. D: Julian Soler. SP: A. Ruanova. Ph: Ruvacalba. Mus: Ernesto Cortazar. Ref: Lee. Ecran 12/77:30. with Enrique Lizalde, Enrique Rocha, Carlos Lopez Moctezuma.
Human sacrifice; catalepsy.

SATANIC RITES OF DRACULA see COUNT DRACULA AND HIS VAMPIRE BRIDE

**The SATANIST Olympic Int'l. 1968 64m. (aka SUCCUBUS?) D: Spence Crilly. Ref: LAT. AFI. no LC.
"Devil's bride"; "student of the occult." (AFI)

SATAN'S BLACK WEDDING IRMI 1975 color 62m. D: Phillip Miller. Ref: V 3/26/75:5(rated). B.Warren. Cinef V:3.
"Coven of Satan worshippers." (Cinef)

SATAN'S BLOODY FREAKS see BLOOD OF FRANKENSTEIN

SATAN'S CHEERLEADERS WAC/Clark 1976 color SP,D: Greydon Clark. SP,P: Alvin L. Fast. Mus: Gerald Lee. Ref: Meyers. Willis/SW. with John Ireland, Yvonne De Carlo, Jack Kruschen, John Carradine, Sydney Chaplin, Kerry Sherman.
Satan mates with high-school cheerleader.

SATAN'S SCHOOL FOR GIRLS Spelling-Goldberg 1973 color 73m. D: David Lowell Rich. SP: A.A. Ross. Ph: Tim Southcott. Mus: Laurence Rosenthal. AD: Tracy Bousman. SpFX: Logan Frazee. Mkp: H. Smit. Ref: TV. with Roy Thinnes(Satan), Pamela Franklin, Jo Van Fleet, Lloyd Bochner, Kate Jackson, Jamie Smith Jackson, Cheryl Ladd, Bill Quinn, Terry Lumley.

Satan teaches (incognito) at a girls' school, "collects" the lonely and unwanted; school built on site of Salem witch trials; storm. Franklin and Jackson are oh-so-easy on the eyes; but the script is rather hard on the intelligence. "Suspense" here is, supposedly, Pamela and Kate snooping around old rooms in the dark--but don't count on it.

SATAN'S SLAVE (B) Crown Int'l/Monumental 1976('79-U.S.) color/scope 86m. D: Norman J. Warren. SP & with: David McGillivray. Ph: Les Young. Mus: John Scott. AD: Hayden Pearce. Ref: MFB'77:10: "archaic second feature." Willis/SW. with Michael Gough, Martin Potter, Candace Glendenning.

Father-and-son necromancers plan to resurrect 18th-century witch.

SATANS SORGER(by M.Corelli) see LEAVES FROM SATAN'S BOOK

SATAN'S TRIANGLE Worldvision-TV/ABC-TV/Danny Thomas 1975 color 75m. D: Sutton Roley. SP: William Read Woodfield. Ph: L.J. South. Mus: Johnny Pate. SpFX: Gene Grigg. SpPhFX: Howard Anderson. Ref: TV. TV Season. with Kim Novak, Doug McClure, Alejandro Rey, Ed Lauter, Jim Davis, Michael Conrad.

The Devil--in the guise of a priest--plies the waters of the Bermuda Triangle, angling for souls. Ludicrous double-twist plot is worthy of dear old Monogram, as "strange lightning" and bodies found floating in air are explained, first, scientifically, then supernaturally. Winner, BOWERY AT MIDNIGHT Memorial Award (for transcendently idiotic plotting), 1975.

SATURDAY THE 14TH New World/Julie Corman 1981 color 75m. SP, D: Howard R. Cohen. Story & Co-P: Jeff Begun. Ph: Daniel Lacambre. Mus: Parmer Fuller. AD: Arlene Alen. SpFX: Richard Lacey. PyrotechFX: Roger George. CreatureFX: Rick Stratton, Steve Neill. SpVisFX: E.D. Farino;(ph) Gary Wagner. Opt: Jack Rabin. Ref: screen. J.Willis. S Union 9/6/81. with Richard Benjamin, Paula Prentiss(temp.vampire), Severn Darden(Van Helsing), Stacy Keach Sr., Rosemary De Camp, Roberta Collins;Jeffrey Tambor & Nancy Lee Andrews(vampires).

Book of Evil which, opened, unleashes horde of monsters (inc.mummy); Dracula-like vampire; inferno barring exit; refs. to ROSEMARY'S BABY, JAWS, LITTLE SHOP OF HORRORS, The OMEN, "Twilight Zone." Horror-movie parody touches all bases--The EXORCIST & co., HALLOWEEN & co., DRACULA & co.--but in the wrong, or no, order. The gags fail thick and fast, though Benjamin and Prentiss play the comedy as straight as they can to the horror. But monsters and effects proliferate, suggesting a puzzling lack of confidence in the leads. (If you can't trust these two farceurs, who can you trust?) A smattering of laughs.

SATURN 3 (U.S.-B) AFD/ITC-Transcontinental 1980 color 88m. D,P: Stanley Donen. SP: Martin Amis. Story: John Barry. Ph: Billy Williams; Bob Paynter. Mus: Elmer Bernstein. PD: Stuart Craig. SpFX:(sup) Colin Chilvers;(asst) Roy Spencer, T. Schubert et al. SdFX:John Poyner, Tony Message;(elec) Roger Limb. Computer Graphics: System Simulations. OptFX: Roy Field, Wally Veevers, Peter Parks. Ref: V 2/20/80. TV. MFB'80:94. with Farrah Fawcett, Kirk Douglas, Harvey Keitel.
Lascivious robot, Hector, on space station is programmed by "direct input" from assembler's brain. A slight anecdote padded out with some pleasant sight-and-sound effects. Stronger on robot technology than on human psychology, though the drift is skeptical re: machines, and the script roughly recapitulates FRANKENSTEIN(1931). Here, however, the "bad brain" is the creator's/assembler's own. The new look in robots is "skeletal"--Hector's "veins," "muscles," "brain," etc. are all exposed. The movie passes only as a fashion show, for Hector and Farrah.

The SAVAGE BEES NBC-TV/Col-TV & Landsburg-Kirshner 1976 color 94m. D,P: Bruce Geller. SP: Guerdon Trueblood. Ph: Richard Glouner. Mus: Walter Murphy. SpBeeFX: Norman Gary, Kenneth Lorensen. Mkp: Maurice Stein. Opt: Westheimer. Ref: MFB'78: 69. TV. TV Season. with Ben Johnson, Michael Parks, Gretchen Corbett, Paul Hecht, Horst Bucholz, James Best.
"Suspense" in this TV-movie means a woman driving an African-killer-bee-covered Volkswagen through the deserted streets of New Orleans to the Super Dome (where the bees are to be frozen off), with the car engine slowly dying of bee-congestion. Well, "suspense" is one word....Old pros like Johnson and Best, however, make the less-strained first half of the movie easier to take than most bee-movies, and there's a good horror bit with a farmer in a stream (no refuge there even) and a good comic bit with a voodoo chicken.
Sequel: TERROR OUT OF THE SKY.

The SAVAGE CURSE (B) ABC-TV?/ITC-TV 1974 color 75m. D,P: John Sichel. SP: Terence Feely. Story: Brian Clemens. Ph: Phil Brown. Mus: Laurie Johnson. PD: Michael Eve. Mkp: Sheila Mann. Title Seq: Visualscope. Ref: TV. with George Chakiris, Jenny Agutter, Anton Diffring, Russell Hunter.
Variation on Edgar Allan Poe's "The Cask of Amontillado," as young men are walled up alive in cellar; ref. to "The Pit and the Pendulum" too.

SAVAGE PLANET see FANTASTIC PLANET

SAVAGE WEEKEND see UPSTATE MURDERS, The

SAYONARA GINGA TETSUDO 999 (J) Toei 1981 anim feature Ref: V 8/26/81:45: "sfer"; sequel to GALAXY EXPRESS 999.

SCANNERS (Can.) Avco Embassy/Filmplan Int'l.-CFDC 1981 color 102m. SP,D: David Cronenberg. Ph: Mark Irwin. Mus: Howard Shore. AD: Carol Spier. SpMkpFX:(cons) Dick Smith; Stephen Dupuis et al. SpFX: Gary Zeller; Henry Piercig;(asst) Don Berry, Louis Craig. Sculptures: Tom Coulter et al. Opt: Film Opts. Micro FX: Dennis Pike. Ref: screen. MFB'81:78. V 1/21/81. 1/28/81:6: TELEPATHY 2000-tx t. See also: STEREO. with Stephen Lack, Jennifer O'Neill, Patrick McGoohan, Lawrence Dane, Michael Ironside(Revok), Robert Silverman(Pierce).

Drug Ephemerol (for pregnant women) produces ability in offspring of telepathic scanning. SCANNERS is a generally exciting, imaginative thriller, one of the more inventive of the EXORCIST-sired effects shockers. It even threatens, at times, to become more than a thriller, as Cronenberg makes metaphoric links between scanning and madness and art. Eventually, however, he opts more for surface excitement. The movie is rather stronger on demonstrating the destructive than the constructive uses of scanning. In fact it's downright ingenious at showing the 101 uses of human-scanners-as-weapons--but it could have been a fuller, better film if it had had fewer demonstrations, more implications. Cronenberg describes the specialness of his characters--people with "people in their heads"--but not their commonness. They all turn out, it seems, to be related (literally) to one another, but not to anyone we know.

SCARED TO DEATH Lone Star-Malone 1980 color 96m. (The ABERDEEN EXPERIMENT-orig t) SP: William Malone. Ref: Boxo 7/7/80:3. 8/81:54. FM 169:11. V 11/5/80:6(rated). 1/21/81:50 & 5/13/81:152: sfa THERE WAS ONCE A CHILD(Creative)? with John Stinson, Diana Davidson.

"Genetic mutant monster" inhabits L.A. sewers.

*The SCARLET CLAW 1944 Ref: screen. V 5/24/44.

"Eerie glow" heralds attacks of phosphorescent "fiend" in Canadian village; refs. to werewolves, "The Hound of the Baskervilles," "The Sussex Vampire." A foggy-moors-and-strangely-tolling-bell montage makes a good, creepy opening for this Sherlock Holmes entry--but subsequent chills are distinctly mild. And the random murders of the plot are not quite (as Basil Rathbone's Holmes puts it) "beads on a string"--they're just beads, with no string of narrative interest. Nigel Bruce's more-extended baskings in the spotlight (as Watson) here are less amusing than his occasional sotto voce mutterings (which sound for all the world like his stomach rumbling).

*The SCARLET CLUE 1945 (CHARLIE CHAN IN THE SCARLET CLUE-ad t) Ref: TV. V 5/16/45.

Horror-movie and radio-show star Horace Carlos(sp?) wears mask as "The Mad Monster" that's a "combination of Dracula and a zombie"; electric-arc invention; climatic tunnel; gelatin capsule the contents of which are deadly when combined with nicotine. The plethora of sf and horror gimmicks, and Mantan

Moreland-and-friend's double-talk routine, make this a shade more tolerable than most of the later Chans.

*SCARS OF DRACULA Levitt-Pickman 1970 SP: Anthony Hinds(aka J.Elder). AD: Scott MacGregor. SpFX: Roger Dicken. Mkp: Wally Schneiderman. Ref: TV. AFI. Glut/TDB. and with Dennis Waterman, Michael Ripper, Anouska Hempel(vampire).

Vapid Hammer Dracula is strong on cleavage, weak on bats. Only the title is new, though the old James Bernard music is still stirring. The Count is an authority figure here, challenged first by his mistress and then by his servant. At least that's what you'll find if you're looking for more than fangs. A few, very-welcome lighter moments.

The SCENARIO WRITER'S DREAM Univ 1915 Ref: Menville/TTC. AF-Index: sfa The SCENARIO EDITOR'S DREAM(Powers,1914)?

New York City destroyed by death-ray-equipped aircraft.

The SCENTED ENVELOPES (B) 1923 30m. See also: Mystery of Dr. Fu-Manchu series. Ref: BFC. Lee.

SCHLANGENEI,Das see SERPENT'S EGG, The

SCHIZO (B) Heritage 1976 color 109m. D,P: Pete Walker. SP & with: David McGillivray. Ph: Peter Jessop. Mus: Stanley Myers. AD: Chris Burke. Ref: MFB'76:256. with Lynne Frederick, John Leyton, Stephanie Beacham, J. Fraser, J. Watson.

"Studiously nasty murders....beleaguered heroine and bloodthirsty killer are one and the same."

SCHIZOID Cannon 1980 color 91m. (MURDER BY MAIL-orig t) SP,D: David Paulsen. Ph: Norman Leigh. Mus: Craig Hundley. AD: Kathy C. Cahill. Ref: V 10/22/80: "shocker." 7/15/81:4. with Klaus Kinski, Mariana Hill, Craig Wasson, Donna Wilkes.

Series of scissor murders.

SCHIZOID see LIZARD IN A WOMAN'S SKIN

SCHLOCK Jack Harris/Gazotskie 1973(1971) color 81m. (The BANANA MONSTER-alt t) SP,D: John Landis. Ph: Bob Collins. Mus: David Gibson. SpFX & Props: Ivan Lepper. SpMkp: Rick Baker. Ref: screen. Lee. pr. V 1/10/73:4(rated). 3/28/73: KING KONG and FRANKENSTEIN(1931) refs. with Landis(apeman), Saul Kahan, Eliza Garrett, Forrest J Ackerman, Don Glut.

Defrosted prehistoric apeman commits series of murders. Generally amusing and charming, if rather slight monster-movie spoof. "Look, there's Forry!" "Look, 2001!"

SCIENCE FICTION (Pol) SMF 1971 anim D: M. Kijowicz. Ref: IFG'72:387: spaceman's adventures on another planet.

The SCORPIO SCARAB Gold Key-TV("Zodiac" series) 1972? color 93m. Ref: TVFFSB. with George Hamilton, Angie Dickinson.

"Strange beings" are duplicates of government officials.

SCREAM see NIGHT GOD SCREAMED, The

SCREAM...AND DIE! see HOUSE THAT VANISHED, The

SCREAM, BABY, SCREAM Westbury 1969 color 83m. (MAYHEM) D,P,Ed: Joseph Adler. SP: Laurence R. Cohen. Ph: Julio Chavez. Mus: The Charles Austin Group. Sets: David Trimble. SpMkp: Douglas Hobart. Ref: AFI. Lee. V 1/24/73:6(rated). with Ross Harris, Eugenie Wingate, Chris Martell, S. Stuart.
Mad artist gets grotesque subjects for his macabre paintings by surgically deforming models.

SCREAM BLACULA SCREAM AI/Naar 1973 color 95m. (BLACULA II-orig t. The NAME IS BLACULA. BLACULA LIVES AGAIN! BLACULA IS BEAUTIFUL--all int ts) D: Bob Kelljan. SP: Joan Torres, R. Koenig, M. Jules. Sequel to BLACULA. Ph: I. Mankofsky. Mus: Bill Marx. AD: Al Brocchicchio. SpFX: Jack De Bron. Mkp: Alan Snider. Ref: screen. pr. Glut/TDB. V 7/4/73. Lee. Murphy. MFB'75:114. with William Marshall(Blacula/Mamuwalde), Pam Grier, Don Mitchell, Richard Lawson(vampire), B. Rhoades.
The vampire Blacula, resurrected by voodoo, attempts to force a voodoo priestess to exorcise the vampire-demon within him. Unplayable scenes and unspeakable lines, relieved now and then by a bit of humor (e.g., a vain novice-vampire who misses his reflection).

SCREAM, EVELYN, SCREAM! Cougar 1977 color Ref: V 5/17/78: 188(ad): "horrifying." 5/11/77:205(ad). with Stafford Repp.

SCREAM OF THE WOLF ABC-TV/Metromedia-Curtis 1974 color 74m. (The HUNTER-alt t) D,P: Dan Curtis. SP: Richard Matheson. Story: David C(h)ase. Ph: P. Lohmann. Mus: R. Cobert. AD: Walter Simon. Ref: TV. TVFFSB. Lee. with Peter Graves, Clint Walker, Philip Carey, JoAnn Pflug, Don Megowan.
Brutal murders made to appear work of werewolf. Surprisingly undistinguished Matheson script. Walker's macho-mystical hunter is a ludicrous conception--his outre "motivations" are simply not to be believed.

SCREAM, PRETTY PEGGY Univ-TV/Morheim 1973 color 74m. D: Gordon Hessler. SP: Jimmy Sangster, Arthur Hoffe. Ph: L.J. South. Mus: Bob Prince. PD: J. Alves Jr. Ref: TV. TVFFSB. with Bette Davis, Ted Bessell, Sian Barbara Allen, Charles Drake, Allan Arbus.
Schizophrenic sculptor assumes personality of dead sister (whom he has killed), encases her body in statue depicting "the ultimate evil." PSYCHO revisited _again_, in spare, low-key, transparent mystery.

SCREAMERS (I) New World/Dania-Medusa 1979('81-U.S.) color/scope 82m.(99m.) (L'ISOLA DEGLI UOMINI PESCE. ISLAND OF MUTATIONS-B. The FISH MEN-ad t) SP,D: Sergio Martino;(U.S.) Miller Drake. SP: also Donati, Frugoni. Ph: Ferrando;(U.S.) Gary Graver. Mus: L. Michelini; Sandy Berman. PD & SpDes:

M.A. Geleng. SpFX: Paolo Ricci, Cataldo Galiano. SpMkpFX: (U.S.) Chris Walas. Ref: screen. MFB'79:175. FM 161:13. with Barbara Bach, Claudio Cassinelli, Richard Johnson, Beryl Cunningham, Joseph Cotten;(U.S.) Cameron Mitchell, Mel Ferrer.

Geneticist creates "fish-man" mutants from humans in attempt to solve world's food problem; voodoo scorpion, the "custodian of the souls of the (mummified) living dead" ("It's just a big bug and a bunch of rags!"); sunken land of Atlantis; living corpse in haunted Cave of the Dead (in added U.S. footage). Flaccid, contrived. The gory (added) prologue promises another HUMANOIDS FROM THE DEEP, but turns out to be the most--or, rather, only--hackle-raising sequence. It's just fog and monsters, but that's really all you need--and all you _get_ here.

The SCREAMING SKULL ABC-TV/Specter 1973 color 75m. D: Gloria Monty. SP: N. Borisoff, from a story by F. Marion Crawford. Sets: A. Kimmel. Ref: Lee. with David McCallum, Carrie Nye.

Murdered-woman's skull haunts husband and brother-in-law.

The SCREAMING WOMAN ABC-TV/Univ-TV 1972 color 75m. D: Jack Smight. SP: Merwin Gerard, from Ray Bradbury's short story. Ph: Sam Leavitt. Mus: John Williams. AD: J. Chilburg II. Ref: Lee. TVG. with Olivia de Havilland, Ed Nelson, Joseph Cotten, Walter Pidgeon, Charles Drake, Jan Arvan.

Mental patient finds woman buried alive on her estate.

SCREAMS OF A WINTER NIGHT Dimension/Full Moon 1979 color 92m. D: James L. Wilson. SP: R.H. Wadsack. Ph: R.E. Rogers. Mus: Don Zimmers. Sets,Cost: M.S. Wilson. SpFX: W.T. Cherry III. Ref: V 10/3/79: "no screams here." Willis/SW. Boxo 7/2/79:22. FM 165:11. AMPAS. with Gil Glasgow, Mary Cox, Robin Bradley, Matt Borel, Patrick Byers.

Kids at remote lake tell stories re: "Bigfoot type," "haunted apartment," psychopathic "child woman." (Boxo)

SEA CREATURES see BEYOND ATLANTIS

SEA GOD AND GHOSTS (H.K.) 197-? Ref: JFFJ 13:32: "period monster movie."

SEARCH NBC-TV/WB-TV 1972 color 94m. (aka PROBE) D: Russell Mayberry. SP,P: Leslie Stevens. Ph: J.M. Stephens. Mus: Dominic Frontiere. AD: Fred Harpman. SpFX: J.C. Strong. Ref: TV. Lee. K.Bunce. with Hugh O'Brian, Elke Sommer, John Gielgud, Burgess Meredith, Lilia Skala, Angel Tompkins, Kent Smith, Alfred Ryder, A. Martinez.

World Securities organization with super-computer; agent with neuro-implant, a miniature camera/shortwave/infrared/ultrasonic/sniperscope gadget linked with computer; man who wants to "revitalize the SS movement" and who alters his ID (down to his fingerprints). Standard imitation-"Mission: Impossible" TV-movie, with scads of computer pyrotechnics and Gielgud's and Meredith's good humor to see you through (or not). A TV-series pilot.

SEARCH FOR THE EVIL ONE Ambassador 1967 color/Technoscope 82m. D: Joseph Kane. SP: Don Fearheiley. Ph: G. Galbraith. SpFX: Ira Anderson. Ref: MFB'78:162-3: "outlandish." no AFI. with Lee Paterson, Lisa Pera, Henry Brandon(Bormann), Pitt Herbert(Hitler), Ivan Triesault, H.M. Wynant, Anna Lisa.
Adolf Hitler is alive and well in Argentina and still plotting with Martin Bormann to conquer the world.

SEARCH FOR THE GODS ABC-TV/WB-TV & Cramer 1975 color 94m. D: Jud Taylor. SP: Ken Pettus. Story: Herman Miller. Ph: Matt Leonetti. Ref: TVG. V 3/12/75:50: hypnosis. TV. with Kurt Russell, Stephen McHattie, Ralph Bellamy, Victoria Racimo, Raymond St.Jacques, Albert Paulsen.
"Quest for evidence of ancient visitors to Earth." (TVFFSB)

SECOND CHANCE(by J.Finney) see DEAD OF NIGHT(1977)

SECOND COMING, The see MESSIAH OF EVIL

The SECRET (H.K.) Unique 1979 color 100m. D: Ann Hui. SP: Joyce Chan. Ph: C.M. Chung. Mus: Violet Lam. Ref: V 11/7/79. with Sylvia Chiang, Chiu Ah Chi, Tsui Siu Keung.
"Achieves its objective of pleasurably scaring its viewers with...what looks like "ghosts"."

SECRET BEYOND THE DOOR... Univ/Diana 1947 98m. D,P: Fritz Lang. SP: Silvia Richards, from Rufus King's story "Museum Piece No.13." Ph: Stanley Cortez. Mus: Miklos Rozsa. PD: Max Parker. Ref: screen. V 12/31/47. Lee. FQ W'79/80:10. Eisner/FL. with Joan Bennett, Michael Redgrave, Anne Revere, Barbara O'Neil, James Seay, Paul Cavanagh.
Psychopath driven to murder those he loves; sinister house with "eerie" masks on walls, and rooms which are replicas of murder scenes; secret room reserved for bride's death; horror scenes in thunderstorm, fog....The works. Of the many woman-menaced-by-her-beloved thrillers of the Forties (see also SUSPICION, GASLIGHT, POWER OF THE WHISTLER, The TWO MRS. CARROLLS, LOVE FROM A STRANGER), SECRET... is probably the funniest. The message of this peculiar sub-genre: the outward sign or symptom of the homicidal maniac is _charm_. This message is probably not taken very seriously by very many people, and possibly was not so taken even by the makers of the movie. The theme must have _some_ kind of cautionary resonance for women, but it eludes these films (at least on any articulate level). Or perhaps pairing a woman with a closet madman is simply the most expedient narrative means to a horror movie's end of getting the heroine alone with the "monster." Here, at any rate, the overblown narration ("I heard his voice and then I didn't hear any more because the beating of my blood was louder"), dialogue, acting, and music succeed in making SECRET... a real camp-collector's find.

SECRET RITES (B) Meadway 1971 color 47m. SP,D: Derek Ford. Mus: B. Walton. AD: E. Konkel. Ref: Lee(MFB'72:58).
Documentary re: witchcraft, with horror-movie opening.

SECRETO DE LA MOMIA see LIPS OF BLOOD

**SECRETS OF CHINATOWN Syndicate/Northern-PLI 1935 63m. D: Fred Newmeyer. SP: Guy Morton, from his novel. Ph: William Beckway. Tech D: Li-Young. Ref: Turner/Price. FD 2/20/35. no LC. with Nick Stuart, Lucile Browne, Raymond Lawrence, James Flavin, Arthur Legge-Willis(yogi).
Hypnotized heroine; "weird ceremony" and "strange temple" of killer-cult, the Order of the Black Robe. (T/P)

The SECRETS OF HOUSE NO.5 (Russ) Pathe 1912 Ref: Lee.
"Mysticism" and ghosts; "vampires"?

SECRETS OF THE BERMUDA TRIANGLE WB 1978 SP,D,P: Donald Brittain. Story,P: Alan Landsburg. Mus: Laurin M. Rinder, W. Michael Lewis. Ref: V 2/1/78:25(ad).

SECURITY (India-Hindi) Balakrishna 1973 color 143m. (HIFAZAT) D: K.S.R. Das. Dial: Prem Kapur. Ph: V.S.R. Swamy. Mus: R.D. Burman. Ref: Dharap. with Vinod Mehra, Ashok Kumar.
Series of murders in "haunted house."

SEDUZIDAS PELO DEMONIO (Braz) ECDIC 1975 color 108m. SP,D, Ed: Raffaele Rossi. Ph: Nobile. Mus: S. Coelho. Ref: Brasil. with Roberto Cesar, Cassiano Ricardo, Shirley Screch.
Student possessed by demon freed of it when stabbed with crucifix.

SEEDS OF EVIL KKI/United Mktg. 1973(1981) color 81m. (The GARDENER-orig t) SP,D: Jim Kay. Ph: M. Zingale. Mus: Marc Fredericks. Ref: V 2/18/81. 4/11/73:5(rated). with Joe Dallesandro, Katharine Houghton, Rita Gam, James Congdon.
"Human tree";killer-flowers.

SEIS PASAJES AL INFIERNO (Arg) Mural SCA 1975 D: F. Siro. Ref: IFG'76:89: "for the horror market." with John Russell, Mala Powers.

SEIZURE (Can.) AI/Cinerama/Intercontinental-Queen of Evil 1974 color 94m. (QUEEN OF EVIL-orig t) SP,D: Oliver Stone. SP: also Edward Mann. Ph: R. Racine. Mus: Lee Gagnon. AD: N. Stone. Mkp & SpFX: Thomas Brumberger. Ref: MFB'76:219. V 11/20/74. screen. Ecran 6/74:25. Willis/SW. with Jonathan Frid, Martine Beswick(Queen), Joe Sirola, Herve Villechaize, Troy Donahue, Mary Woronov.
Characters (inc. dwarf, giant, ghost, Queen) from author's novel of the supernatural seem to come to life. Offbeat but unremarkable horror-fantasy.

SELF-PORTRAIT IN BRAINS Jackpot/Artboro 1980 SP,D,P: Brian Yuzna. SP: also Jimmy Dobbins. Ph: M. Muscal. Mus: James D. Lumsden. Ref: V 7/16/80:22(ad): "sci-fi murder mystery." 7/22/81:4(rated). with Gary Christopher, Kim Brattain, Lou Bello, Billy Arthur Jr.

SENGOKU JIEITAI see TIME SLIP

SENSUOUS VAMPIRES 1981? Ref: V 7/15/81:16: in Miami.

The SENTINEL Univ 1977 color 91m. SP,D,P: Michael Winner. SP,P: also Jeffrey Konvitz, from his novel. Ph: Dick Kratina. Mus: Gil Melle. PD: Philip Rosenberg. SpVisFX: Albert Whitlock. SpMkp: Dick Smith, Bob Laden. Ref: MFB'77:51-2. TV. V(d) 2/11/77. with Chris Sarandon, Cristina Raines, Martin Balsam, John Carradine, Jose Ferrer, Ava Gardner, Arthur Kennedy, Burgess Meredith, Sylvia Miles, Deborah Raffin, Eli Wallach, Christopher Walken, Jerry Orbach, Jeff Goldblum.

Would-be suicides become sentinels (with new ID's) at "entrance to hell" (i.e., they keep people _in_); reincarnated damned souls (with bodies of freaks) try to sabotage this operation. One of the silliest of the big-budget shockers. Award, Most Ludicrous Use of Cross in climactic sequence of a horror movie. Don't ask how, but "Paradise Lost" is indirectly responsible for the movie's lone line-to-remember: (hero to heroine) "Jesus, Alison, you really _are_ seeing Latin!" The script takes evil and corruption seriously; this does not mean, however, that one can take _it_ seriously.

The SERPENT'S EGG (W.G.-U.S.) UA/Rialto-De Laurentiis 1977 color 119m. (Das SCHLANGENEI) SP,D: Ingmar Bergman. Ph: Sven Nykvist. Mus: Rolf Wilhelm. PD: Rolf Zehetbauer. Sp FX: Karl Baumgartner, D. Ortmaier, W. Hormandinger. Ref: MFB '78:141: "mythic horror." V 11/2/77: "horror picture." with Liv Ullmann, David Carradine, Gert Froebe, James Whitmore, Heinz Bennett, Charles Regnier, Glynn Turman.

Berlin, 1923. Aristocrat conducting "cruel behavioural experiments" in underground lab "in the name of a future, scientifically ordered totalitarian society." (MFB)

SESSO DELLA STREGA see WITCH'S SEX, The

SETTE CADAVERI PER SCOTLAND YARD see JACK THE RIPPER(1971)

SETTE NOTE IN NERO see PSYCHIC, The

SETTE SCIALLI DI SETA GIALLA see CRIMES OF THE BLACK CAT

SEVEN AI/Simon 1979 color 101m. Story,D,P: Andy Sidaris. SP: W. Driskill, R. Baird. Ph: Quito. SpFX: SpFX Unltd. Ref: MFB'79:153. TV. AMPAS. with William Smith, Guich Koock, Barbara Leigh, Art Metrano, Little Egypt, Reggie Nalder, Ed Parker, Nick Georgiade.

Professor's "long-range lasergun" used to kill (MFB); combine out to wreck Hawaii economically. Push-button verbal and visual bravado--lots of "_hard dudes_" and "_bad asses_" and cool, "kicky" sadism. The first half-hour is one big, not-wholly-disguised chunk of exposition. There's also a rehearsal (with samurai sword and pistol) of the scimitar-and-pistol bit in RAIDERS OF THE LOST ARK.

The 7 BROTHERS MEET DRACULA (B-H.K.) Dynamite Ent./Hammer & Shaw 1974('79-U.S.) color/scope 89m. (The LEGEND OF THE 7 GOLDEN VAMPIRES-B. DRACULA AND THE 7 GOLDEN VAMPIRES-Far East) D: Roy Ward Baker. SP: Don Houghton. Ph: J. Wilcox, R. Ford. Mus: James Bernard. AD: J. Tsau. SpFX: Les Bowie. Mkp: Wu Hsu Ching. Ref: MFB'74:202. AMPAS. Willis/SW. V 12/24/75:6 (rated): Cannon. 6/4/75. with Peter Cushing, David Chiang, Julie Ege, Robin Stewart, John Forbes-Robertson(Dracula).
Dracula uses disciple's body "to walk the Earth again"; bats that become vampires. (MFB)

7 CITIES TO ATLANTIS see WARLORDS OF ATLANTIS

SEVEN DEAD IN THE CAT'S EYES (I-F-W.G.) Starkiss & Capitol & Roxy 1972 color/scope 96m. (La MORTE NEGLI OCCHI DEL GATTO) SP,D: Antonio Margheriti. SP: also G. Simonelli. From Peter Bryan's novel. Ph: Carlo Carlini. Mus: Riz Ortolani. Ref: Bianco Index'73. Lee. with Jane Birkin, Hiram Keller, V. Venantini, Anton Diffring, Dana Ghia.
"Vampirism in Scottish castle." (Lee)

*7 KEYS TO BALDPATE (UA-TV) 1947 Also based on George M. Cohan's play. Ref: TV. V 6/4/47. TVFFSB. LC.
Secret panel & passages; black cat; screams; snowstorm; weird shadows; creepy music; author (Phillip Terry) describing projected book about "an old house with ghosts"; loony hermit (Jimmy Conlin) who likes "comin' through windows." Slightly amusing, until the plot resolves itself into a tired crook-melodrama.

The 7 LITTLE FLAMES (Yugos) Zagreb 1975? anim short D: Stalter. Ref: IFG'76:475.
Witch "who prowls as a black knight after dark."

SEVEN WOMEN FOR SATAN (F) Daunou-Lemoine 1974 80m. (Les WEEKENDS MALEFIQUES DU COMTE ZAROFF) D: Michel Lemoine. From Richard Connell's story "The Most Dangerous Game." Ph: P. Theandiere. Mus: Guy Bonnet. Ref: MFB'76:260. V 10/26/77: 28: at Sitges. with Nathalie Zeiger, Joel Coeur, H. Vernon.
Haunting visions; son of Count Zaroff; torture dungeon; woman who turns into skeleton.

*The SEVENTH VICTIM 1943 Story: Val Lewton. AD: Albert S. D'Agostino, Walter E. Keller. Ref: screen. TV. Siegel/VL. MFB'79:82-3. V 8/18/43.
The face of Jean Brooks, as Jacqueline, in Val Lewton's The SEVENTH VICTIM--see her "haunted eyes" in the frontispiece to Siegel's book--is one of our more memorable film images. Her strangely spellbound eyes are a visual approximation of the Donne couplet that opens and closes the film: "I run to death and death meets me as fast, and all my pleasures are like yesterday." Her Jacqueline (an eventual suicide as the title's "seventh victim") is an unusual mixture of morbidity and vitality. She seems at once abnormally _life_-sensitive and

abnormally death-sensitive, as if some protective emotional insulation had been worn away inside her. She seems to see too far into herself, into her past and future; to be possessed not by another, but by her own, cold spirit. The film, as a whole, is less-finely-calibrated than Jean Brooks' characterization. Where it takes only a detail (e.g., Jacqueline's insistent drumming of her finger on the arm of her chair, as the Palladists wait for her to drink the glass of poison) to suggest Jacqueline's still, small life-force, it takes crude, character-condensing strokes of action (e.g., Jacqueline's friend Frances (Isabel Jewell) urging her to take/not to take the poison) to suggest the alternating current (optimism/pessimism) of the other characters. Kim Hunter as Jacqueline's sister Mary is the film's crucial failure. If Jacqueline is the morbid sister with a surprising spark of life, Mary is the sweet young thing who unwittingly sends a detective to his death and alienates her sister's husband's affections. Jean Brooks (and Lewton) make sense of the paradox in her case. But Kim Hunter seems stuck trying to suggest mere sweetness--let alone the ironic, attendant sourness-of-effect which Lewton apparently intended with her.

The SEVERED ARM Media Cinema/Media Trend 1973 color 92m. SP,D: Thomas S. Alderman. SP: also D. Presnell. Story: L. Alexander, M. Ray. Dial: K. Estill. Ph: B. Maxwell. Elec Mus: Phillan Bishop. Mkp: Carol Alderman;(prosth) Gordon Freed. SdFxEd: Martin Varno. Ref: TV. MFB'74:207. TVFFSB. TVG. with Deborah Walley, Paul Carr, Ray Dannis, Marvin Kaplan, David G. Cannon, John Crawford.

Abortive cannibalism-for-survival incident serves as pretext for routine revenge-with-ax story. Low-low-budgeter is a shoo-in for a "dismemberment" cross-reference in the AFI catalog for the Seventies. The psychological-Grand Guignol ending rates at least a "nice try."

SEX DEMON JDG 1975 color 70m. Ref: V 7/23/75. with Steve Spahn, Jeff Fuller, Max Scott.

"Gay young men possessed by the Devil" commit brutal murders; "cursed medallion."

SEX EXPRESS (B) Blackwater 1975 color 50m. SP,D: Derek Ford. Ph: G. Glover. Mus: De Wolfe. AD: E. Konkel. Ref: MFB'75:243. with Heather Deeley, James Lister(vampire).

Four fantasies, one involving a vampire; another, ghosts.

SEX MACHINE (I) Borde/Clesi 1975('76-U.S.) color 101m. (CONVIENE FAR BENE L'AMORE) SP,D: P.F. Campanile. SP: also O. Jemma. From Campanile's novel "Si Tratera di Far Bene L'Amore." Ph: F. Di Giacomo. Mus: F. Bongusto. AD: Ezio Altieri. Ref: MFB'76:248-9. FFacts. V 3/3/76:34(rated). 4/9/75. with Luigi Proietti, Agostina Belli, Adriana Asti.

In the year 2000, Professor Coppola develops a "new form of power" based on Wilhelm Reich's theories re: "the generation of bio-electric current during copulation." (MFB)

SEX ODYSSEY Distribpix 1970? color 60m. Ref: AFI.
Earthman becomes model for artificial male bodies on planet of bodiless minds.

SEX ODYSSEY see 2069: A SEX ODYSSEY

SEX ON THE GROOVE TUBE see CASE OF THE FULL MOON MURDERS

SEX VAMPIRES see CRAZED VAMPIRE

The SEX VICTIMS (B) Derek Robbins 1973 color 40m. SP,D: Robbins. Ref: MFB'73:106. with Ben Howard, Jane Cardew.
"Day-time ghost story."

SEX WORLD Thornberg 1980? color 70m. SP,D: Anthony Spinelli. SP: also Dean Rogers. Mus: Berry Lipman. Ref: poster. J. Shapiro: robots. with Annette Haven, John Leslie, Leslie Bovee, Sharon Thorpe, Desiree West, Amber Hunt, Johnny Keyes.

SEXORCIST, The see EERIE MIDNIGHT HORROR SHOW, The

The SEXORCISTS Cougar/Capital 1974? color D: Louis Garfinkle. Mus: Lex De Azevedo. Ref: V 5/17/78:188(ad). 5/11/77:205 (ad): the Devil. 1/16/74:1.

SEXPLORER, The see GIRL FROM STARSHIP VENUS

SEXUAL WITCHCRAFT see HIGH PRIESTESS OF SEXUAL WITCHCRAFT

SHADA KALO see BLACK AND WHITE

The SHADOW OF CHIKARA Manson Int'l/Fairwinds 1977 SP,D,P: Earl E. Smith. Ph: James Roberson. Mus: Jaime Mendoza-Nava. Ref: V 10/19/77:15(ad). with Joe Don Baker, Sondra Locke, Ted Neeley, Joy Houck Jr., Slim Pickens, John Chandler.
"The chilling Indian legend of Chikara and the Mountain of Demons."

SHADOW OF THE HAWK (Can.) Col/ICC-CFDC-Odeon Theatres 1976 color 92m. D: George McCowan. SP: N.T. Vane, H.J. Wright, Peter Jensen, L. Cahill. Ph: J. Holbrook, R. Morris. Mus: Robert McMullin. AD: K. Pepper. SpFX: Dick Albain, John Thomas. SdFxEd: Ralph Brunjes. Ref: MFB'77:198. Willis/SW. V 7/14/76. TV. with Jan-Michael Vincent, Marilyn Hassett, Chief Dan George, Marianne Jones(Dsonoqua), Pia Shandel.
Indian medicine man vs. 200-year-old sorceress (who at end assumes form of heroine, then dog); magic wall. The poor-man's MANITOU. All Dsonoqua can conjure up is an "evil car," a bear, a snake, and a self-destructing rope-bridge. The dialogue is equally pathetic.

SHADOW OF THE WEREWOLF see WEREWOLF VS.THE VAMPIRE WOMAN

SHADOWMAN (F-I) New Line/Terra & SOAT 1973('75-U.S.) color 105m. (NUITS ROUGES. L'HOMME SANS VISAGE) D & Mus: Georges

Franju. SP: Jacques Champreux. Ph: G.R. Bertoni. AD: R. Luchaire, C. Finelli. Ref: MFB'77:48-9. Willis/SW. V 7/30/75: 44: feature & 8 1-hour TV shows. 5/21/75:30(rated). 6/26/74. with Gayle Hunnicutt, Gert Froebe, Josephine Chaplin, Raymond Bussieres, Ugo Pagliai, Clement Harari, Champreux.
Criminal mastermind's mad-doctor ally develops a race of killer-zombies.

The SHAME OF THE JUNGLE (F-Belg) Int'l Harmony/SND & Valisa 1975('79-U.S.) color 85m. (La HONTE DE LA JUNGLE. JUNGLE BURGER-B. TARZOON, SHAME OF THE JUNGLE. TARZAN--SHAME OF THE JUNGLE--int ts) SP,D: Picha, Boris Szulzinger. Parody of Burroughs' "Tarzan" stories. Ph: Burlet. SP & Lyrics: M. O'Donoghue, A. Beatts. Des: Picha. Ref: MFB'80:111. AMPAS. V 12/15/76:30. 9/24/75. 1/29/75:38. Willis/SW. Voices: Johnny Weissmuller Jr., John Belushi, Bill Murray.
Two-headed man, spaceship, "zombits," "molar men."

SHAN-CHUNG CH'UAN-CH'I see LEGEND OF THE MOUNTAIN

SHANKS Para 1974 color 93m. (SHOCK-orig t) D & Exec P: William Castle. SP: Ranald Graham. Ph: Joseph Biroc. Mus: Alex North. AD: Boris Leven. SpFX: Dick Albain. Mkp: Jack Young. Puppets: Bob Baker. Ref: Lee. Willis/SW. V 10/9/74. 8/8/73: 6. Cinef IV:3:36. with Marcel Marceau, Tsilla Chelton, Cindy Eilbacher, Helena Kallianiotes, Phil Adams, Philippe Clay.
Mad puppeteer's "puppets" are dead bodies.

SHAPE OF THINGS TO COME, The see H.G.WELLS' THE SHAPE OF THINGS TO COME. THINGS TO COME.

The SHAPE OF TIME Brandon 197-? color 28m. D: Donald Paonessa. Ref: Brandon: subterranean future-world.

The SHARKS' CAVE (I-Sp-Venez) Koala(Track) & Amanecer(Comas/Alianza) & Empresa(Ulivi) 1978 color 90m. (BERMUDE: LA FOSSA MALEDETTA. BERMUDAS: LA CUEVA DE LOS TIBURONES. The CAVE OF THE SHARKS-ad t) SP,D: Teodoro Ricci. SP: also F. Galiana, Melchiorre. Ph: J. Jurado;(sp) Blasco Giurato. Mus: S. Cipriani. SpFX: Cineaudio FX. Ref: MFB'79:39: "a trifle ridiculous." V 5/9/79:487. 5/17/78:388. 11/9/77:28. with Andres Garcia, Janet Agren, Arthur Kennedy, Pino Colizzi.
Mysterious figure commands sharks in cave in the Bermuda Triangle.

*SHE 1935 Mus D: Max Steiner. AD: Van Nest Polglase. SpFX: Vernon L. Walker. Ref: screen. Lee.
Merian C. Cooper's SHE has scattered thrills and some spectacular moments--e.g., the discovery of a sabre-toothed tiger embedded in ice; an avalanche; She (Helen Gahagan) first seen in mist; a swing on a rope across a huge ceremonial chamber. But this long-lost, epic fantasy is for the most part static; the actors are wooden, and the plot is "developed" in the dialogue.

SHE GETS HER MAN Univ 1945 70m. D: Erle C. Kenton. SP,P: Warren Wilson. SP: also Clyde Bruckman. Ph: Jerry Ash. Ref: V 1/10/45. LC. Maltin/TVM: "hilarious slapstick whodunit." with Joan Davis, William Gargan, Leon Errol, Russell Hicks, Vivian Austin, Donald MacBride, Emmett Vogan.
"Series of fiendish murders....Mysterious killer who uses a gun which shoots needles into his victims." (V)

SHE WAITS CBS-TV/Metromedia 1972 color 73m. D,P: Delbert Mann. SP: Art Wallace. Ph: Charles Wheeler. Mus: Morton Stevens. Ref: TV. no Lee. V 9/13/72:62. with Patty Duke, David McCallum, Dorothy McGuire, Lew Ayres, Beulah Bondi.
"Vicious spirit" of dead woman seems to be at large in L.A. home. You may, however, tire of its touching music-box theme, and eventually not even care if it's the dead Elaine, or just the wind.

The SHE-WOLF OF DEVIL'S MOOR (Austrian) Odelga-Star-Wien 1978 (aka The DEVIL'S BED. Die WOLFIN VOM TEUFELSMOOR) SP,D: Helmut Pfandler. SP: also K.H. Willschrei. Ph: Matula, Holscher. Mus: Gerhard Heinz. Ref: IFG'80:68. with John Philip Law, Florinda Bolkan, S. Wischnewski.
Countryside's inhabitants are "under the influence of some bizarre, para-psychological phenomena...."

*SHE-WOLF OF LONDON 1946 Ref: TV. V 4/10/46. and with Clara Blandick, Jan Wiley.
The script quotes from "The Merchant of Venice," but this is still a candidate for dullest horror movie of the Forties. (See also DEAD MEN WALK.) And all those rather impressive "wolf" snarls are never explained.

SHE'LL FOLLOW YOU ANYWHERE (B) Paragon/Glendale 1971('73-U.S.) color 96m. SP,D: David C. Rea. SP: also Theo Martin. Ph: Ted Moore. Mus: Gordon Rose. AD: A. Chapkis. Ref: Lee(MFB '71:225). V 8/16/72:6. with Keith Barron, Richard Vernon.
Chemists' new shaving lotion makes them irresistible to women.

SHEN-KU CH'I-T'AN (H.K.?) 1971 Based on two stories in the "Liao-Chai Chih-I." Ref: Eberhard: snake spirit entices men.

SHEN-WEI SAN MENG-LUNG see CLONES OF BRUCE LEE

SHEPHERDESS AND THE CHIMNEY SWEEP,The(by H.C.Andersen) see KING AND THE MOCKINGBIRD,The

The SHERIFF AND THE SATELLITE KID (I) Leone 1979 Ref: V 5/13/81:160: "moppet from outer space." with Cary Guffey.
Sequel: EVERYTHING HAPPENS TO ME.

SHERLOCK HOLMES Fox 1932 71m. D: William K. Howard. SP: Bertram Millhauser, from the play by William Gillette & the stories by Arthur Conan Doyle. Ph: George Barnes. Mus D:

George Lipschultz. AD: John Hughes. Ref: screen. Everson/ TDIF. B.Warren. NYT. LC. with Clive Brook, Reginald Owen, Ernest Torrence, Stanley Fields, Herbert Mundin, Alan Mowbray, Miriam Jordan, Montague Shaw, Roy D'Arcy, B. Hurst, L. Prival.

Electro-magnetic, motor-wrecking ray which heats and burns ignition coil of model car; bulb which, screwed into socket, opens secret panel. Clive Brook as Sherlock Holmes is strangely subdued, and Brook subdued is just another actor. The script, with its weak-tea conceits, is certainly no help. If Holmes is always a step ahead of Moriarty, the audience is always a step ahead of Holmes. The movie is a gallery of non-characters--only Torrence as Moriarty seems to belong to Doyle's (or anybody's) world.

SHERLOCK HOLMES AND SAUCY JACK see MURDER BY DECREE

SHERLOCK HOLMES AND THE SPIDER WOMAN see SPIDER WOMAN, The

SHERLOCK HOLMES GROSSTER FALL see STUDY IN TERROR, A

SHERLOCK HOLMES: MURDER BY DECREE see MURDER BY DECREE

The SHINING WB 1980 color 146m. SP,D,P: Stanley Kubrick. SP: also Diane Johnson. From Stephen King's novel. Ph: John Alcott. Mus: W. Carlos; Bartok, Penderecki, Ligeti. PD: Roy Walker. Mkp: Tom Smith. Ref: screen. V 5/28/80. MFB'80:221-222. Jim Shapiro. with Jack Nicholson, Shelley Duvall, Danny Lloyd, Scatman Crothers, Barry Nelson, Anne Jackson.

Ghosts of violence past seem to possess caretaker of isolated, off-season Colorado hotel; drive him to attempt re-creation of brutal murders; his son has precognitive powers (i.e., "the shining"). Effective as a vehicle for Nicholson and for Kubrick's camera, The SHINING is finally disappointingly thin, both psychologically and philosophically. All those psychological and/or supernatural forces seem, in the end, to have been marshaled about simply to whip up a bit of suspense and to explain one writer's block. But if Kubrick makes little of the King story--the boy's ESP seems more intrusive than illuminative--he makes the hotel a ghostly Disneyland. He peoples the place with all sorts of phantoms and visions, and makes his implacably tracking camera as much a presence as Nicholson's frighteningly/hilariously-detached madman....If the hotel-Nicholson-Duvall relationship gives you a sense of _deja vu_, you've probably seen The AMITYVILLE HORROR (with its house-Brolin-Kidder triangle) or BURNT OFFERINGS (with its house-Reed-Black triangle).

SHIRLEY THOMPSON VS. THE ALIENS (Austral.) Kolossal 1972 104m. SP,D,P: Jim Sharman. SP: also H. Bakaitis. Ph: D. Sanderson. Mus: Ralph Tyrell. Ref: Lee. V 6/28/72. 5/5/76: 98. with Jane Harders, John Ivkovitch, Tim Eliott.

Alien invasion of Earth.

SHIVERING SPOOKS Pathe-Roach 1926 6m. Ref: screen. LC.

Flat "Our Gang" comedy set in a "haunted" house.

SHIVERS see THEY CAME FROM WITHIN

SHOCK see BEYOND THE DOOR II. SHANKS. SHOCK TREATMENT(1973).

SHOCK TRANSFERT-SUSPENCE-HYPNOS see BEYOND THE DOOR II

SHOCK TREATMENT (F-I) New Line/Lira & A.J. 1973('74-U.S.) color 91m. (TRAITEMENT DE CHOC. The DOCTOR IN THE NUDE-B. SHOCK-U.S.) SP,D,Mus: Alain Jessua. SP: also Jacques Curel. Ph: Jacques Robinson. Mus: also Rene Koering. AD: Yannis Kokkos. SpFX: Andre Pierdel. Ref: MFB'75:64: "vampire yarn." V 2/14/73. Willis/SW. with Alain Delon, Annie Girardot, Michel Duchaussoy, Robert Hirsch.

Doctor's rejuvenation serum contains boys' blood and organs.

SHOCK WAVES Cinema Shares Int'l. & Brenner/Friedricks/Zopix 1975(1977) color 86m. (DEATH CORPS-orig t. ALMOST HUMAN-B) SP,D: Ken Wiederhorn. SP: also John Harrison. Ph: R. Trane;(underwater) Irving Pare. Mus: Richard Einhorn. PD: Jessica Sack. SpMkpDes: Alan Ormsby. Opt: EUE. Ref: MFB'79: 116. V 5/17/78:74(ad). 10/8/80. 8/6/75: shooting. TV. with Peter Cushing, John Carradine, Brooke Adams, Fred Buch, Luke Halpin, Gary Levinson.

Ship of Nazi zombie death-troops from World War II reactivated (somehow). Okay vehicle for a quite picturesque menace. Functional continuity, but the be-goggled SS zombies seem always to be rising photogenically--singly or en masse--from sea, swamp, or swimming pool. They sleep, or rest, in shallow water, where a sixth sense seems to alert them to the presence of human prey. Cushing is around simply to explain their origin (but not why they perish without their goggles).

A SHOT IN THE DARK Chesterfield 1935 65m. D: Charles Lamont. SP: Charles Belden, from Clifford Orr's novel "The Dartmouth Murders." Ph: M.A. Anderson. Mus D: Abe Meyer. AD: Edward C. Jewell. Ref: Turner/Price. LC. with Charles Starrett, Robert Warwick, Edward Van Sloan, Marion Shilling, Doris Lloyd, Helen Jerome Eddy, James Bush, John Davidson.

"Masked killer"; "deserted house";murder weapon: cattle-slaughtering compressed-air gun. (T/P)

The SHOUT (B) Films Inc./NFFC-Rank/RPC 1978 color 86m. SP, D: Jerzy Skolimowski. SP: also M. Austin, from Robert Graves' short story. Ph: Mike Molloy. Elec Mus: Rupert Hine. AD: Simon Holland. Ref: MFB'78:142-3: "the intellectual's EXORCIST." V 5/24/78. AMPAS. with Alan Bates, Susannah York, John Hurt, Robert Stephens, Tim Curry, Julian Hough.

Charles Crossley possesses the secret of the aborigines' "death-dealing terror shout." (MFB)

*A SHRIEK IN THE NIGHT (Classic Int'l-TV) 1933 Mus D: Abe Meyer. AD: Gene Hornbostel. Ref: TV. TVFFSB. Turner/Price.

Horror scene in dark cellar, with killer cackling and preparing furnace for heroine Ginger Rogers; maid who reads "creepy" detective stories about "green faces floating up to windows." Everybody tries to get into the act: cops, reporters, and maids all try to be funny (and fail). Very talky mystery, with a plot only its mother could love, or follow.

SHRIEK OF THE MUTILATED (Cinema Shares Int'l-TV)/American Films 1974 color 92m. (MUTILATED-orig t) D: Michael Findlay. SP: Ed Adlum, Ed Kelleher. Ph: Roberta Findlay. Ref: TVFFSB. V 12/13/78:36(ad). Lee(p). CineFan 2:28. V 2/27/74:7(rated). with Alan Brock, Jennifer Stock, Tawm Ellis, Darcy Brown.
Cannibal cult; fake Yeti.

SHRINKING MAN,The(by R.Matheson) see INCREDIBLE SHRINKING WOMAN

SHUDDER see KISS OF THE TARANTULA

SI TRATERA DI FAR BENE L'AMORE(by Campanile) see SEX MACHINE

SIEGFRIED UND DAS SAGENHAFTE LIEBESLEBEN DER NIBELUNGEN see LONG, SWIFT SWORD OF SIEGFRIED, The

SILENCE OF DR. IVENS see MOLCHANIYE DOKTORA IVENSA

SILENT FLUTE see CIRCLE OF IRON

SILENT NIGHT, BLOODY NIGHT Cannon 1972 color 88m. (ZORA-orig t. NIGHT OF THE DARK FULL MOON-orig rel.t) SP,D: Theodore Gershuny. SP: also Jeffrey Konvitz et al. Ph: Adam Giffard. Mus: Gershon Kingsley. Ref: TVFFSB. Lee. Willis/SW. Cinef F '73:35. V 12/13/72:6(rated). with Patrick O'Neal, James Patterson, Mary Woronov, John Carradine, Walter Abel, Candy Darling, Ondine, Tally Brown.
Asylum inmates who kill keepers; ax murders.

SILENT NIGHT, EVIL NIGHT see BLACK CHRISTMAS

SILENT RUNNING Univ/Gruskoff 1972 color 89m. (RUNNING SILENT-orig t) D & SpPhFX: Douglas Trumbull. SP: Deric Washburn, Michael Cimino, Steve Bochco. Ph: C.F. Wheeler. Mus: Peter Schickele. Sets: F. Lombardo. SpPhFX: also Jon Dykstra, Richard Yuricich. SpFX: Richard O. Helmer et al. Ref: MFB '72:218. screen. Lee. V 3/8/72. VV 5/4/72. with Bruce Dern, Cliff Potts, Ron Rifkin, Jesse Vint.
In the year 2001, an astronaut and his three robot companions tend an experimental ecological station in space. Leftovers from 2001: A SPACE ODYSSEY. Effects scenes alternate with close-ups of the principals, and the themes of solitude-vs.-companionship and man-vs.-nature drift through the movie as aimlessly as the spaceships drift through space. The robots have some cute schtiks.
See also: MAKING OF "SILENT RUNNING," The(P).

SILENT SCREAM American Cinema 1980 color 87m. D: Denny Harris. SP: Ken & Jim Wheat, W.C. Bennett. Ph: M.D. Murphy, D.

Shore. Mus: Roger Kellaway. PD: Christopher Henry. SpFX: Steve Karkus. Ref: V 1/30/80. ad. Boxo 4/14/80. with Rebecca Balding, Cameron Mitchell, Avery Schreiber, Barbara Steele, Yvonne De Carlo, Juli Andelman.

Kids at mercy of "homicidal maniac in a spooky old house." (V)

SIMON WB/Orion 1980 color 97m. SP,D: Marshall Brickman. Ph: Adam Holender. Mus:(sup) S. Silverman; Mozart, Stravinsky, Ravel et al. PD: Stuart Wurtzel. SpFX: Ed Drohan. SpVisFX: Werner Koopman. Min: E. Sprott. Ref: screen. MFB'80:199. V 2/27/80. with Alan Arkin, Austin Pendleton, Judy Graubart, William Finley, Fred Gwynne, Madeline Kahn, Wallace Shawn.

"Think tank" intellectuals subject professor to 197 hours of sensory-deprivation (i.e., 500 million years of evolutionary regression); bring him back through the apeman-stage (nod here to 2001) and re-program him to believe that he is an alien from the nebula Orion (visualized "memories" here of his mother, a spaceship). Also: sex scene with supercomputer; "church of TV"; gas which halves victims' IQ's; Nielsen-jamming laser device. Occasionally amusing, more-generally pointless satire. One fears the worst from an "alien" spokesman for Earthmen (remember RED PLANET MARS); but SIMON is at least not pretentious--it is, rather, frustratingly unpretentious. Much ingenuity goes into establishing a premise, then nothing much is done with it.

SIN IN THE VESTRY (Braz) Borges 1975 color 88m. (PECADO NA SACRISTIA) SP,D,Ed: Miguel Borges. Ph: R. Nunes. Mus: Remo Usai. Ref: Brasil. with Mauricio do Valle, Itala Nandi.

Woman who "becomes the mule-without-a-head during some special nights"; ghost; "Water-Nymph, another apparition."

SINBAD AND THE EYE OF THE TIGER (U.S.-B) Col/Andor 1977 color 112m. (SINBAD AT THE WORLD'S END-orig t) D: Sam Wanamaker. SP: Beverley Cross. SpVisFX,Co-Story & Co-P: Ray Harryhausen. Story: also B. Cross. Ph: Ted Moore. Mus: Roy Budd. PD: G. Drake. Mkp: Colin Arthur. Ref: V(d) 5/25/77. MFB'77:174: "lacklustre." Meyers. V 9/4/74:6. with Patrick Wayne, Taryn Power, Margaret Whiting, Jane Seymour, Patrick Troughton.

Evil sorceress whose spell turns prince into baboon; giant bee; giant walrus; skeletons; mechanical monster; troglodyte.

SINBAD'S GOLDEN VOYAGE see GOLDEN VOYAGE OF SINBAD

The SINFUL DWARF (B) Boxo Int'l/Poole 1973 color 92m. D: Vidal Raski. SP: William Mayo. Mus: Ole Orsed. Ref: Indep. Film Jnl.12/24/73:88(ad). Willis/SW. V 12/12/73: "repulsive sado-exploiter." with Anne Sparrow, Tony Eades, Torben(the dwarf), Clara Keller.

Dwarf rents drugged, kidnapped women to men.

SINGAPORE, SINGAPORE (F-I) Ben Barry/Number One-Poste Parisien & Riganti 1967('69-U.S.) color 95m. (CINQUE MARINES PER

SINGAPORE) SP,D: B. Toublanc-Michel. SP: also Pierre Kalfon, Sergio Amidei. From Jean Bruce's book "Cinq Gars pour Singapour." Mus: Antoine Duhamel. Ref: AFI. with Sean Flynn.
U.S. Marines kept in "frozen hibernation."

SINGIN' IN THE CORN Col 1946 64m. D: Del Lord. SP: I. Dawn, M. Brice. Story: R. Weil. Ph: G.B. Meehan. Mus D: George Duning. Ref: V 11/20/46. LC. with Judy Canova, Allen Jenkins, Guinn Williams, Charles Halton, Al Bridge, G. Chesebro.
"The uncle's ghost comes to (the protagonists') aid through celestial wireless"; mind reader; ghost town; inherited estate. (V)

SINTHIA THE DEVIL'S DOLL Sun Art 1970 color 80m. (aka The DEVIL'S DOLL) D & Ph: Ray Dennis Steckler. SP: Herb Robins. Mus: Henri Price. AD: David Miles. Ref: AFI. Lee. with Shula Roan, Diane Webber, Maria Lease.
"Sinthia becomes possessed by the Devil...." (AFI)

*SIR ARNE'S TREASURE 1919 (SNOWS OF DESTINY-B) Ref: screen. MFB'77:267-68. and with Mary Johnson, Hjalmar Selander.
Cursed treasure-chest; prophetic vision of dead girl; man "followed" by dead-girl's image; woman who "sees" men (miles away). Some strong "epic" scenes; but not quite successful, either as romantic fiction or as moral drama. The plot rests, very shakily, on <u>four</u> key overheard conversations. (The Mauritz Stiller films to see: EROTIKON, JOHAN, THOMAS GRAALS' BEST CHILD, GUNNAR HEDES' SAGA.)

*SIREN OF ATLANTIS Atlantic 1948 D: also (uncredited) Arthur Ripley, Douglas Sirk, John Brahm. Add'l Dial: Thomas Job. Mus sc: Michel Michelet. SpFX: Rocky Cline. Ref: screen. V 12/15/48.
Generally assumed to be a lost camp classic--Atlantis, the Foreign Legion, Maria Montez, and sand--SIREN OF ATLANTIS is, actually, a wry, insinuating vision of obsessive-love-as-oblivion-as-death. Henry Daniell's sterling performance--as a cast-off ex-lover of the cruel Queen Antinea (Montez)--sets the tone. Greeting newcomers to her kingdom, with a mock-civilized "Atlantis; I bid you welcome," he's like a crazy, mocking mirror of his will-be rivals. The story itself proceeds with a Sternberg-like air of insolent inevitability, and ends with Jean-Pierre Aumont (as another in the thrall of Antinea) lost in a sandstorm, still vainly searching for the heaven-hell of Atlantis. As a metaphor for obsessive, unquenchable love, the final images are impeccable: Montez waiting for Aumont; his pursuers losing him; Aumont dying and dead.

SISTERS AI/Pressman-Williams 1973 color 92m. (BLOOD SISTERS-B) SP,D: Brian De Palma. SP: also Louisa Rose. Ph: Gregory Sandor. Mus: Bernard Herrmann. PD: Gary Weist. Ref: screen. MFB'74:121. V 3/21/73. with Margot Kidder, Jennifer Salt, Charles Durning, Bill Finley, Barnard Hughes.

Siamese twin assumes dead sister's personality, becomes homicidal whenever approached by a man. De Palma bolsters a limp narrative with split-screen, Bernard Herrmann, and references to Hitchcock,winds up with a kernel-less shell of a thriller. The climactic shock scenes would be more shocking if it were clearer who's who and what's what. Good thing they weren't triplets.

See also: CRIME DOCTOR'S MANHUNT. MORE THAN SISTERS.

SISTERS OF CORRUPTION see CORRUPTION OF CHRIS MILLER, The

SISTERS OF SATAN (I-F) Brandon/PAC-Splendida/Leitienne-IMP 1973 color 91m. (Le MONACHE DI SANT'ARCHANGELO. The NUN AND THE DEVIL-B) SP,D: Paolo Dominici, from a story by Stendhal. SP: also Tonino Cervi. Ph: G. Ruzzolini. Mus: Piero Piccioni. AD: Wayne Finkelman. Ref: Brandon: "occult chiller." Bianco Index'73: 1972? V 3/14/73: torture. 11/8/72:9(ad). MFB'74: 181-2: "flurry of horror overtones." with Anne Heywood, Martine Brochard, Muriel Catall, Duilio Del Prete, Ornella Muti, Luc Merenda, Claudio Gora.

16th-century Spain. "Unholy ceremonies" in convent. (Br)

SITTER, The see WHEN A STRANGER CALLS

The SIX MILLION DOLLAR MAN ABC-TV/Univ-TV 1973 color 75m. D,P: Richard Irving. SP: Henri Simoun. Ph: E. Oster. Mus: Gil Melle. AD: R. Beal. Ref: Lee: pilot for TV series(aka CYBORG). V 3/21/73:52. with Lee Majors, Barbara Anderson, Martin Balsam, Darren McGavin, Robert Cornthwaite, O. Soule.

Injured pilot mechanically-rebuilt as a super-man.

The SIX ULTRA BROTHERS VS. THE MONSTER ARMY (J-Thai) Fuji Eiga/ Tsuburaya-TV 1979(1974) (URUTORA ROKUKYODAI TAI KAIJU GUNDAN) Ref: JFFJ 13:30: Ultraman film.

SKADUWEES OOR BRUGPLAAS see DOCTOR MANIAC

SKLAVENSCHIFF, Das see DIAMOND SHIP, The

SKRACKEN HAR TUSEN OGON see FEAR HAS 1,000 EYES

SKYRIDER 1977? anim short Ref: IFG'78:482: "space spoof."

SLAUGHTER HOTEL (I) Hallmark(AI)/Dunia 70 1971('73-U.S.) color/scope 97m. (La BESTIA UCCIDE A SANGUE FREDDO. COLD BLOODED BEAST-B. ASYLUM EROTICA-alt U.S.t) SP,D: Fernando Di Leo. SP: also Nino Latino. Mus: Silvano Spadaccino. Ref: MFB'73:4-5: "meretricious." Lee. with Klaus Kinski, Margaret Lee, Monica Strebel, Rosalba Neri, John Karlsen.

Cloaked killer; brutal murders; isolated clinic.

SLAUGHTERHOUSE-FIVE Univ/Vanadas 1972 color 103m. D: George Roy Hill. SP: Stephen Geller, from the novel "Slaughterhouse-Five or The Children's Crusade" by Kurt Vonnegut Jr. Ph:

Miroslav Ondricek;(sp cons) Enzo Martinelli. Mus:(d) Glen Gould; Bach. PD: Henry Bumstead. OptFX: Univ.Title. Mkp: Mark Reedall, John Chambers. Ref: MFB'72:171. screen. FFacts. Lee. V 3/22/72. with Michael Sacks, Valerie Perrine, Eugene Roche, Ron Leibman, Roberts Blossom, Sorrell Booke, John Dehner, F. Ledebur, Lucille Benson, S. Gans, Perry King, H. Near.

Optometrist Billy Pilgrim becomes "unstuck in time," journeys back and forth in time and space, from Earth to the planet Tralfamadore. Alternately flip and sentimental, Geller's script uses Vonnegut's fantasy gimmick as a solution to all problems of plot, character, and structure. It's also inconsistent--we see things that Billy couldn't have seen or (probably) wouldn't have noticed (e.g., the German soldier tossing away the figurine). Tralfamadore is apparently intended as a comment on Billy's lack of imagination.

SLAVES see BLACKSNAKE

SLEEPER UA/Rollins-Joffe 1973 color 88m. SP,D & with: Woody Allen. SP: also Marshall Brickman. Ph: D.M. Walsh. Mus: W. Allen & the Preservation Hall Jazz Band. PD: Dale Hennesy. SpFX: A.D. Flowers. Cost: Joel Schumacher. Opt: H. Plastric. Mkp: Del Acevedo. Ref: screen. MFB'74:135. V 12/12/73. with Diane Keaton, John Beck, Mary Gregory, Don Keefer, Don McLiam.

A musician from 1973 is defrosted in a totalitarian world-state after 200 years in suspended animation; cloning project; scientifically-grown giant vegetables; plastic robots; HAL-voiced computer; Orgasmatron; computerized dog; monstrous instant pudding; clothes-designing machine; orbs, or "high" balls; McDonald's _still_; brain-washing machine. Mildly amusing Allen comedy. The one-liners and slapstick generally fall a bit flat, but his crazy, flailing helplessness after defrosting/Orgasmatroning/orbing is very winning pantomime. The gags, the characters, and the plot seem to be out of synch with one another, and the Allen-Keaton teaming "takes" only very occasionally.

*The SLIME PEOPLE 1963 SP: also Blair Robertson. SpFX: Harry Woolman. Ref: TV. AFI.

Hapless, pathetic imitation of Paul Blaisdell-type monster-movies would be a camp icon but for its flat action and chase sequences, which alternate with dialogue treasures: "They're huge, covered with scales, covered with slime...." "The _slime people_!" "They came at him, from the _sewers_!" "We've got to find their trail--footprints, slime, _anything_!" With Les Tremayne (and a goat) doing a tragicomic turn.

SLIPUP Slip-Art 1975 color 80m. Ref: V 5/7/75. with Darby Lloyd Rains, Jamie Gillis, Marc Stevens, Eric Edwards.

"Machine designed to produce national sexual frenzy."

SLITHIS Davis/Fabtrax 1978 color 90m. (SPAWN OF THE SLITHIS-cr t) SP,D,P: Stephen Traxler. Mus: Steve Zuckerman. Ref: SFC 9/17/78. 9/15/78. AMPAS. V 3/23/77:30. with Hy Pyke, Win

Condict(monster), Alan Blanchard, Judy Motulsky.
Radioactivity from energy plant combines with "organic mud" to create man-eating humanoid monster.

SMOKING GUNS Univ 1934 62m. D: Alan James. SP: Nate Gatzert. Story & with: Ken Maynard. Ref: LC. "Shoot-em-ups." "Great Western Pictures," p.xv: "haunted house" sequence. with Gloria Shea, Walter Miller, Harold Goodwin, Jack Rockwell, Wally Wales, Blue Washington, William Gould, Edmund Cobb.

The SNAKE PRINCE (H.K.-Mandarin) Shaw 1976 color 96m. D: Lo Chen. SP: Yi Kuang. Ph: K. Han-le. Mus: Wang Fu-ling. Mkp: Wu Hsu-ching. Ref: V 9/22/76. with Ti Lung(Prince), Lin Chen-chi, Wang Yu(Yellow Snake), Wu Hang-sheng(Black Snake).
The Snake Prince is "able to take human form at will."

SNEZHNAYA KOROLEVA see SNOW QUEEN,The(1966)

SNIFFLES AND THE BOOKWORM WB 1939 anim 8m. D: Chuck Jones. SP: Rich Hogan. Anim: Bob McKimson. Ref: Glut/TFL. Lee. LC.
Frankenstein's monster.

SNOOP SISTERS, The see DEVIL MADE ME DO IT, The

SNOW DOG Monogram 1950 62m. D: Frank McDonald. SP: Bill Raynor, from James Oliver Curwood's novel "Tentacles of the North." Ph: W. Sickner. Mus D: Edward Kay. AD: Dave Milton. Ref: V 7/19/50. FDY. LC. with Kirby Grant, Elena Verdugo, Rick Vallin, Milburn Stone, Duke York.
Superstitious natives attribute north-woods killings to a "snow-white killer wolf," but a Mountie "suspects a human is directing the killings...." (V)

The SNOW QUEEN (Russ) Lenfilm 1966 color/scope 83m. (SNEZHNAYA KOROLEVA) D: Guenady Kazonsky. SP: Eugueni Schwartz, from the tale by Hans C. Andersen. Ph: S. Ivanov. Mus: N. Simonian. AD: Burnistrov, Borovkov. SpPhFX: Prokovsky. Ref: MFB'76:10-11. no AFI. WorldF'67. with Natalya Klimova(Snow Queen), V. Nikitieako, L. Proklova.
"The malevolent Snow Queen...turns Kay's heart to ice."(MFB)

SNOWBEAST NBC-TV/Cramer 1977 color 93m. D: Herb Wallerstein. SP: Joseph Stefano. Ph: F. Stanley. Mus: Robert Prince. AD: Steven Sardanis. SpFX: Marlowe Newkirk. Ref: TV. TV Season. TVG: "Bigfoot." TVFFSB: ski resort terrorized by "some sort of inhuman creature." with Bo Svenson, Yvette Mimieux, Clint Walker, Robert Logan, Sylvia Sidney.
The "snowbeast" proves to be that most elusive of movie monsters--the subjective-camera monster. Invisible to the (viewer's) naked eye, it can be seen only by the characters, and only described to us by them. (Is it possibly a plot to bring back radio?) At the end, only the handle of a ski pole bobbing around in the air before us tells us that the monster--or the cameraman--has been speared, and is dying, and dead.

SNOWS OF DESTINY see SIR ARNE'S TREASURE(1919)

SO DARK THE NIGHT Col/Ted Richmond 1946 71m. D: Joseph H. Lewis. SP: Martin Berkeley, Dwight V. Babcock. Story: Aubrey Wisberg. Ph: Burnett Guffey. Mus: Hugo Friedhofer. Ref: V 9/18/46. LC. with Steven Geray, Micheline Cheirel, Eugene Borden, Egon Breecher, Theodore Gottlieb, Gregory Gay.

"Story about a schizophrenic Paris police inspector who becomes an insane killer at night...." (V)

SOBRENATURAL: EL REGRESO DE LA MUERTE (Sp) Kalendar 1981 color 89m. Co-Story,Co-SP,D: Eugenio Martin. Ph: Antonio Cuevas Jr. Mus: Carlos Vizziello. AD: E.T. de la Fuente. SpOptFX: Moro. Ref: V 8/9/81: spirit, psychic forces. 7/15/81: 40. 7/30/80:44. 12/3/80:36. with Cristina Galbo, Maximo Valverde, Gerardo Maya.

SOIS DA ILHA DE PASCOA see SOLEILS DE L'ILE DE PAQUES

SOLARIS (Russ) Magna/Mosfilm 1972('76-U.S.) tinted & b&w & color/scope 165m. SP,D: Andrei Tarkovsky. SP: also Friedrich Gorenstein. From the novel by Stanislaw Lem. Ph: Vadim Yusov. Mus: Eduard Artemyev; Bach. AD: Mikhail Romadin. Ref: screen. MFB'73:130-31. Soviet Film 2/73. V 9/15/76:6. 5/24/72. NYT 10/7/76: 240m. version? S&S Smr'81:153: 165m.-full version. with Natalya Bondarchuk, Donatas Banionis, Yuri Jarvet, Anatoli Solonitsin, Nikolai Grinko.

Psychologist Chris Kelvin is assigned to investigate mysterious events on a space station orbiting the remote planet Solaris. He finds that the planet's seas summon up and concretize memories of those on board. ("It has something to do with one's conscience.") SOLARIS is an sf-comedy-drama about squaring one's life morally, about being and not being where one ought (morally) to be. Quite wryly, it acknowledges that total moral reconciliation of one's life, and of the people in one's life, is impossible--there's always a corner of it that won't stay tucked in. The passing of time insures that every act or state of moral reconciliation is temporary, relative; the Solaris effect is one of time-lapse photography, of _speeding up_ this process, this moral cycle. Life on Solaris is an aggravation of life on Earth. The film is a series of sometimes-comically-agonizing interpersonal reconciliations and ruptures--the former as jarring as the latter (or as Snouth confesses, "I can't take these resurrections")--as the past (Chris's concretized memory of his dead wife Hari) erupts in the present. Snouth tells Chris not to "turn a scientific problem into a bedroom farce," but that's exactly what it does become, if a rather-more-resonant-than-average bedroom farce. Chris can't live with or without Hari (or, rather, his Solaris-stimulated reconstruction of Hari). When, finally, he finds that _he_ can accept this Hari (or these Haris), _she_ can't accept _herself_. In the scenes of the literally-inseparable-from-Chris Hari (his "living conscience") being shredded by the metal cabin-door (which he vainly tries to put between them), and the post-suicide Hari jerking back to life (a corpse-in-reverse), SOLARIS concretizes, objectifies the disaster of human relationships. To be human means (in the film) to be a mess, both physically (on its visual level) and psychically (on its narrative level). At one point the pre-shredded Hari tells Chris that he looks "rumpled, like Snouth"; and the space-station corridors and rooms are littered with the debris of living. The film is a poignantly funny spectacle, far more engaging than the rather dry (if philosophically intriguing) book by Lem on which it's based. All of Lem's books lack certain human dimensions (the fascinating "The Chain of Chance" misses them least)--Rheya, the Hari figure in "Solaris" the book, is less a character than, simply, a philosophical problem; the film's Chris-Hari interaction seems more tangled, more-thoroughly-nerved-and-veined, both comically and dramatically, than the book's Kris-Rheya relationship. The film's human spectacle is most sharply vivified in terms of past-present. One can live (however uneasily) with past and present. (As the space-pilot Burton, Chris, and Hari do.) But one can't live in both past and present--in (in effect) two different moral worlds--try as one might: if Chris, in a fever, can "return" to his mother in his dreams, the fever soon passes. The ocean of Solaris seems only to heighten this moral-temporal dilemma, to juxtapose, tantalizingly, present orientation and past obligation--until the film's last shot, which situates Chris and his father (or, as Tarkovsky has suggested, simulacra of Chris and his father) on an island in the planet's sea, in (in effect) the past-present tense: Chris is (morally and temporally) in two places at once. This family reunion is not simply a returning to the past (as in his delirium), but a restoring of the past, a temporal reconciliation, leaving Chris no longer a "boat against the current" of the film.

Les SOLEILS DE L'ILE DE PAQUES (F-Braz-Chilean) Alexandra & Barreto & THS 1971 color 106m. (Os SOIS DE ILHA DE PASCOA) SP,D,P: Pierre Kast. Ph: S. Caiozzi et al. Mus: Bernard Parmeggiani. AD: V. di Girolamo. SpFX: Claude Copin. Ref: Lee. V 6/28/72. IFG'72:138. Cinef F'73:43. with Norma Bengell, Jacques Charrier, Alexandra Stewart, Ruy Guerra, F. Brion.

Star-like extraterrestrials draw six people to Easter Island.

SOME MUST WATCH(by E.L.White) see SPIRAL STAIRCASE, The

SOMEONE AT THE TOP OF THE STAIRS (B) ABC-TV/ITC-TV 1973 color 73m. D,P: John Sichel. SP: Brian Clemens. Ph: M. Whitcutt, T. Mander. Mus: Laurie Johnson. PD: T. Waller. Mkp: Sheila Mann. Title Seq: Film-Rite & Creative. Ref: TV. TVFFSB. with Donna Mills, Judy Carne, David De Keyser(Cartney).

Inhabitants of musty Victorian mansion prove to be illusions, dead people given "life" by satanic old man, Cartney, in attic, who has absorbed their life-force. Thoroughly routine mystery, except of course for these climactic revelations--it's as if

H.P. Lovecraft had written the last page of an Erle Stanley Gardner mystery. A little-boy voyeur is the only tip-off that very strange game is afoot. Complete with clumsily-managed final "frisson."

SOMETHING IS OUT THERE 197-? Ref: SFC 5/5/80: at Embassy thea. Bob Moore(poster). with Christopher George.

SOMETHING WITH CLAWS see DARK INTRUDER

SOMEWHERE IN TIME Univ/Rastar-Deutsch 1980 color 103m. D: Jeannot Szwarc. SP: Richard Matheson, from his novel "Bid Time Return." Ph: I. Mankofsky. Mus: John Barry; Rachmaninov. PD: S. Klate. SpFX: Jack Faggard. Ref: screen. MFB' 81:9-10. V 9/24/80. with Christopher Reeve, Jane Seymour, Christopher Plummer, Teresa Wright, G. Voskovec, B. Erwin.

1980. A playwright wills himself back to the year 1912, to a past-and-future rendezvous with a noted stage actress. Philosophical-science-fantasy, as it were, as the hero goes not to a scientist, but to his ex-philosophy prof, and employs not a time machine, but self-hypnosis. The script is, for the most part, as one-dimensional (dramatically) as one of Matheson's "Twilight Zone" teleplays. It's single-mindedly romantic, and the romantic couple at the center of the time-spanning apparatus seems rather dwarfed by the latter. But (also like a Matheson teleplay) there _are_ those few memorable scenes: the actress interrupting the play which she's performing to "think out loud" and formally to sort out her life from her art; the playwright (in 1912) "inspiring" her look for the photo of her which he sees/saw (in 1980). The "show-stopping" scene recalls moments in The GOLDEN COACH in its life/art/life prestidigitations. But life and art lose out to love, as _she_ goes into seclusion in 1912, _he_ (separated from her) goes into terminal shock in 1980, and they meet in a lovers' heaven.

SON OF BLOB Jack Harris 1972(1971) color 81m. (HERE COMES THE BLOB-orig t. BEWARE OF THE BLOB. BEWARE! THE BLOB-int ts) D: Larry Hagman. SP: Jack Woods, Anthony Harris. Sequel to The BLOB. Story: R. Clair, J. Harris. Ph: Al Hamm. Mus: Mort Garson. SpFX: Tim Barr. Ref: MFB'74:185. Lee(V 6/7/72). screen. with Robert Walker Jr., Richard Webb, Godfrey Cambridge, Carol Lynley, Shelley Berman, Burgess Meredith.

The Blob is brought back from the Arctic. Unmemorable comedy.

*SON OF DRACULA 1943 Ref: TV. V 11/3/43. FM 165:38-9.

Vampirism in the Siodmaks' SON OF DRACULA seems intended to represent, variously, elitism, paganism, Naziism, selfishness, eccentricity, and anti-social behavior. The sins of the vampires here are closer to complacency or self-indulgence than they are to bloodsucking. Heroine Kay's (Louise Allbritton) vampiric morbidity--her longing for immortality--seems, for instance, like indulgent exoticism. When her sweetheart

Frank (Robert Paige) scoffs "There's no magic in dried lizards and dead chickens," she might be thinking, contentedly, "Magic is where you find it." Unfortunately, the movie divides into a sterile doctor-professor-sheriff vampire-lore-and-history "commentary" and the at-least-more-promising Kay-Alucard(Lon Chaney Jr.)-Frank triangle, which the highly erratic acting and dialogue effectively render harmless camp. Paige, however, is good, and Allbritton has moments; Chaney sounds as if he's auditioning for a role which is just not for him. The movie's campiest moments: the other actors starting in horror at the sight of this "imposing" Alucard/Dracula. Top-notch mist effects, and one oddly evocative tracking shot, back from a crowded dance-floor, past Alucard standing alone outside on the patio. (He seems here an emissary from another world.)

SON OF DRACULA (B?) Cinemation/Apple 1974 color 90m. (COUNT DOWNE-orig t. YOUNG DRACULA-re-r t) D: Freddie Francis. SP: Jay Fairbank. Mus: Harry Nilsson. Ref: Willis/SW. Glut/CMM: with the Wolf Man & the mummy. Cinef Smr'73:46. with Nilsson, Ringo Starr, Dennis Price, Freddie Jones(Dr.Frankenstein), Suzanna Leigh, Peter Frampton, Keith Moon.

*SON OF FRANKENSTEIN 1939 Mus sc: also H.J. Salter. Mkp: Jack Pierce. Elec FX: Kenneth Strickfaden. Ref: TV. Borst. Lee. Jim Shapiro. Glut/TFL.

"It's magnificent!" cries Baron Wolf von Frankenstein (Basil Rathbone), taking in the spectacle of the violent thunderstorm which rages outside the family castle. Obviously, he's taking possession here of much more than a piece of property--he's also appropriating the spirit of dark, high endeavor of his father, as SON OF FRANKENSTEIN appropriates the adventurous spirit of FRANKENSTEIN(1931) and BRIDE OF FRANKENSTEIN(1935). It should be noted, however, that Wolf is inside looking out, through a shielding window, from which vantage-point dark forces appear more manageable--even a son of the house of Frankenstein is finally limited in his traditional role of god/devil. (Next in line: Wolf's son Peter, who admits that he "likes lightning.") But until Wolf is forced (by the script)to realize his limitations, SON OF FRANKENSTEIN is an exuberant, exciting, good-humored horror film, revelling in a sense of re-discovery of the themes and ideas which fueled previous Universal shockers (and which were, later, to fuel yet other Universal, RKO, and Hammer horrors). The first part of the film is solidly constructed: we witness the Baron's discovery of his father's castle, his lab, his monster (Boris Karloff), the monster's keeper Ygor (Bela Lugosi, in a fine serio-comic performance), and the physical composition of the monster. The bringing-the-monster-out-of-drydock scenes are the equivalent--both in their narrative function and in their fascination of visual detail--of the creation scenes in FRANKENSTEIN and BRIDE. The movie, with its augmented sounds, gung-ho scoring, florid lighting effects, and breathtakingly-elaborate, people-dwarfing sets, invites you to share the Baron's zest for monster-making, or monster re-making. Unfortunately, the Willis Cooper script is better in theory than in actuality at showing Wolf--in later scenes--losing not only his zest, but his control--of Ygor, of the monster, of his house, of himself. His disintegration is detailed in a series of shouting matches with, alternately, Ygor and Inspector Krogh (Lionel Atwill), which behavior makes him seem simply very "difficult." And Rathbone is less successful than Atwill at carrying on at fever pitch--it seems as much the actor as the character who's out of control. Only Atwill successfully sees the hyperbolic spirit of the film through to the very end. Lugosi's nettling Ygor dies along the way, and Karloff more or less recapitulates his performance in FRANKENSTEIN. It's not the monster's story at all here; he's simply an extension of the Baron's delusions of grandeur, a tool, if a formidable one....But lightning proves less manageable indoors.

*SON OF KONG 1933 Sequel to KING KONG(1933). AD: Van Nest Polglase, Al Herman. Models: Marcel Delgado. SdFX: Murray Spivack. Ref: screen. TV. MFB'79:259-60. Glut/CMM.

Max Steiner brings you the first two-thirds of SON OF KONG; Willis O'Brien, the last third. Steiner's enchanting score actually makes the movie's amiable tackiness seem substantial at times, and frozen-faced Helen Mack is appealingly awful as our heroine. The final third is nonstop monsters, a mixture of stopmo-animated menace and comedy. There's no attempt by SON to rival dad (where's mom?) for spectacle, and this alternate tack proves rather satisfying. The amused, exasperated Robert Armstrong and the simpering ape make a good comedy team. This SON is an unassuming comic-romantic idyll--it's as if the makers were happily toasting their success with the original KONG.

SONG OF THE SUCCUBUS ABC-TV/Landsburg-Kirshner 1975 color 74m. D: Glenn Jordan. Ref: TVFFSB. with Kim Milford, Stash Wagner.

Rock star haunted by ghost of dead woman.

SONS OF SATAN Blue & Brooks 1973 color D: Lancer Brooks. Ph: N. Kent. Ref: Lee: horror-movie satire. with Robert McKay (vampire), Tom Payne, Ned Burke.

SORATOBU YUREISEN (J) Toei 1969 anim color/scope 60m. D: H. Ikeda. SP: M. Tsuji. Anim: Y. Otabe. Ref: Lee.

Giant robots; giant crabs and lobsters.

*The SORCERER Mage/Moulin D'Or 1944('47-U.S.) (The BELLMAN-U.S.) Ref: V 4/9/47. and with Lucien Coedel, Madeleine Robinson, Sinoel.

"Horror meller"; "murderous Bellman...fanatical character (with a) half-belief in witchcraft."

SOUL CATCHING BLACK MAGIC see BLACK MAGIC 2

The SOUL SNATCHER American Film 1965 color 68m. D: H.L. Zimmer. Ph: H. Schmidt. Ref: AFI. no LC. with Diane Webster, Hilda Goring, Scott Peters, Valerie-Ann.
The Devil claims the souls of three women.

SOYLENT GREEN MGM 1973 color/scope 97m. D: Richard Fleischer. SP: Stanley R. Greenberg, from Harry Harrison's novel "Make Room! Make Room!" Ph: R.H. Kline. Mus: Fred Myrow. AD: Edward Carfagno. SpFX: A.J. Lohman. SpSeqs: Braverman. Sp PhFX: R.R. Hoag, M. Yuricich. Ref: MFB'73:154. V 4/18/73. screen. with Charlton Heston, Leigh Taylor-Young, Edward G. Robinson, Chuck Connors, Joseph Cotten, Brock Peters, Paula Kelly, Whit Bissell, Celia Lovsky, C. Delevanti, John Dennis.
The population of New York City in the year 2022 is dependent on the Soylent Company's synthetic foods--which turn out to be recycled people. Fairish, with some clever future-tense twists. Rather loose, disjointed script.

SPACE CRUISER (J) Toei 1977 anim color 101m. (UCHUSENKAN YAMATO. STAR BLAZER-ad t) D,P & Co-SP: Yoshinobu Nishizaki. Story & AD: Reiji Matsumoto. Mus: Yasushi Miyagawa. SpFX: Mitsuru Kashiwabara. Ref: MFB'78:31-2. V 4/16/80:150: also a TV series. 10/17/79:248. 12/21/77: "less than animated." Voices: Marvin Miller, Rex Knolls, Mercy Goldman.
Year 2199. Radioactive contamination is poisoning Earth; enemy planet Gorgon; robots; Jupiter's Sea of Methane.
Sequels: BE FOREVER, YAMATO. SPACE CRUISER YAMATO PART II.

SPACE CRUISER YAMATO PART II (J) Toei 1979 anim color 151m. (SARABA UCHU SENKAN YAMATAO. GOODBYE, SPACESHIP YAMATO-ad t) SP,D: Toshio Masuda. Sequel to SPACE CRUISER. Ref: JFFJ 13: 34: from TV-series footage. V 5/9/79:374,381,389(ad).

SPACE FIREBIRD see PHOENIX 2772

SPACE MISSION TO THE LOST PLANET see HORROR OF THE BLOOD MONSTERS

SPACE 1999 (B-I) ITC-RAI/Anderson 1973-74 color 115m. D: Lee H. Katzin et al. SP: George Bellak et al. Ph: F. Watts. Mus: Ennio Morricone. Cost: Rudi Gernreich. Ref: Bianco Index'75: Ital.feature from 3 TV-series eps. V 11/28/73:33-4 (ad). with Martin Landau, Barry Morse, Roy Dotrice, J.Geeson.

SPACE PATROL see WORLD BEYOND THE MOON

The SPACE-WATCH MURDERS ABC-TV/Para-TV 1978 color 74m. Ref: TVFFSB. with Sam Groom, Tisha Sterling, Barbara Steele.
Spaceship's crew on distant planet mysteriously murdered.

SPACED OUT Miramax 1980 Ref: V 9/3/80:16: "sci-fi." 3/14/81: 4(rated). "Sneak Previews"(Dog of the Week): aliens, computer.

SPACEMAN AND KING ARTHUR see UNIDENTIFIED FLYING ODDBALL

SPAWN OF THE SLITHIS see SLITHIS

SPECIAL EDITION: CLOSE ENCOUNTERS OF THE THIRD KIND see CLOSE ENCOUNTERS OF THE THIRD KIND

SPECTRE (B-U.S.) NBC-TV/Fox-TV & Norway 1977 color 92m. D: Clive Donner. SP: Gene Roddenberry, Samuel Peeples. Ph: A. Ibbetson. Mus: John Cameron. AD: Albert Witherick. Mkp: Stuart Freeborn. Ref: TV. TVFFSB. IFG'78:125. Meyers. TVG. TV Season. with Robert Culp, Gig Young, John Hurt, Ann Bell, Majel Barrett, Gordon Jackson, Jenny Runacre, James Villiers.

Succubi; mummified body; "minor demon"; Asmodeus cult; lizard-like Asmodeus; anti-demon invocation which shatters wine glasses; disciple in monster-form. Juvenile demonology. Lotsa fantasy, but indiscriminately-dished-out.

The SPECTRE OF EDGAR ALLAN POE (TV Cinema Sales)/Cinerama/Cintel 1973 color 86m. SP,D,P: Mohy Quandour. Story: K. Hartford, D. Foxx. Ph: R. Birchall. Mus: Allen D. Allen. AD: Michael Milgrom. SpFX & Mkp: Byrd Holland. Props: Chuck Hazeldine. Ref: MFB'74:14. V 5/8/74. screen. with Robert Walker(Poe), Mary Grover, Cesar Romero, Tom Drake, Carol Ohmart, Marcia Mae Jones, Dennis Fimple.

Premature burial; snake pit; beast-man; psychopath; Poe's beloved Lenore butchered. Very, very poor horror movie. (Hi, Chuck! Hi, Carol!)

SPECTREMAN Blackhawk 1980 color 4-episode series(42m.each) 1. The Uncommon Enemy. 2. The Threat of Zeron. 3. The Air We Breathe. 4. Killer Smog. Ref: Blackhawk catalog.

Alien cyborg vs. pollution on Earth; Hedron, pollution-monster; ape-like giant; gorilla-asst.; giant cockroach.

SPEEDTRAP First Artists/Interamar 1978 color 101m. D: Earl Bellamy. SP: W.M. Spear, S.A. Segal. Ph: D. Dalzell. Mus: Anthony Harris. AD: Fred Hope. SpFX: Phil Cory. Ref: TVG. TV. MFB'79:12. with Joe Don Baker, Tyne Daly, Richard Jaeckel, Robert Loggia, Lana Wood, James Griffith, Timothy Carey.

Electronic invention which opens locked car-doors, starts engines, and jams police radios (with "weird whine") by remote control; psychic (Wood) who has vision of medallion; but mainly cars, in this 101-minute demolition derby. Lotsa slow-motion soaring, rolling, and smashing. All very "cinematic," but rather episodic.

The SPELL NBC-TV/Fries-Stonehenge 1977 color 74m. D: Lee Philips. SP: Brian Taggart. Ph: M.T. Leonetti. Mus: Gerald Fried. SpFX: Larry Roberts. Ref: TV. TV Season. TVFFSB. with Lee Grant, James Olson, Susan Myers, Lelia Goldoni.

"There's a power loose" in "the most (telekinetically) powerful area in North America," and a woman suspects her daughter of being the "sensitive" who psychically burns a woman to death and breaks a girl's neck. Sober and serious on the surface, mawkish at heart, this wake-of-CARRIE supernatural soaper adds to the usual mother-daughter bonds that of telekinesis. Parody possibilities here, none of them mined.

SPELL OF EVIL (B) ABC-TV/ITC-TV 1974 color 74m. D,P: John Sichel. SP: Terence Feely. Story: Brian Clemens. Mus: L. Johnson. Anim: Dolphin. Mkp: Dianne Joyce. Ref: TV. TVFFSB. with Diane Cilento(witch), Jennifer Daniel, Edward De Souza.
16th-century witch Carla turns up now as Clara, now using voodoo magic to marry and dispose of rich husbands; ritual-burning of hair from her brush, plus woodcut of Carla, disposes of her. One word--trite--disposes of film.

SPERMULA (F) Film & Co. 1975 color/scope 88m. SP,D,AD: Charles Matton. Ph: Jean-Jacques Flori. Mus: Jose Bartel. Ref: Bianco #4/78. V 6/23/76. with Dayle Haddon(Spermula), Udo Kier, Georges Geret, Ginette Leclerc, Isabelle Mercanton.
Vampire virgins from outer space live on sperm.

SPHINX,The(by E.A.Poe) see EVENING OF EDGAR ALLAN POE,An

SPIDER-MAN CBS-TV/Danchuck 1977 color 92m. (The AMAZING SPIDER MAN-alt t) D: E.W. Swackhammer. SP: Alvin Boretz. Based on Stan Lee's comic-strip character. Pilot for "The Amazing Spider-Man" TV series. Ph: Fred Jackman. Mus: J. Spence;(elec) Greg Hundley. AD: J. Hulsey. SpFX: Don Courtney. Ref: MFB'78:72. V 9/21/77:62. TVG. TV. with Nicholas Hammond, Lisa Eilbacher, Michael Pataki, Jeff Donnell.
Spider bite turns student (Hammond) into super-powered "Spider-Man"; villain with hypnotized minions. The usual.
See also: the following titles and SUPAIDAMAN.

SPIDER-MAN STRIKES BACK CBS-TV/Danchuck 1978 color 93m. D: Ron Satlof. SP: Robert Jones(sp?). Feature version of "The Amazing Spider-Man" 2-part TV show. Ph: J. Whitman. Mus: Stu Phillips. AD: B. McAllister. SpFX: Don Courtney. Ref: MFB'79:101. V 4/12/78:78. TVG. with Nicholas Hammond, Robert F. Simon, Michael Pataki, Robert Alda, Chip Fields.
Spider-Man vs. criminal who steals students' makeshift atom bomb. (aka DEADLY DUST)

SPIDER-MAN: THE DRAGON'S CHALLENGE CBS-TV/Danchuck 1979 color 96m. D: Don McDougall. SP,P: L.E. Siegel. Feature from "The Amazing Spider-Man" TV series. Ph: V. Martinelli. Mus: Dana Kaproff. AD: J. Sacks. SpFX: William Schirmer. Ref: MFB'80: 180. with Nicholas Hammond, Myron Healey, Benson Fong.
Spider-Man vs. kung-fu "dragons." (aka The CHINESE WEB)

*The SPIDER WOMAN (Gutman-TV) 1944 (SHERLOCK HOLMES AND THE SPIDER WOMAN-ad t) Ref: TV. V 1/12/44. and with V. Downing.
Deadly spider behind London's "pyjama suicides" is the lycosa carnivora, whose venom causes the victim such agony that he's driven to suicide; pygmy used to fetch spider; deadly "devil's foot" smoke-from-powder. Another Holmes film

stolen by Watson (Nigel Bruce), that remarkably well-detailed caricature. He's not so much "comic relief" here as "human relief." Not that the mystery story is without interest (it's a bit better than usual for the series), but the intended center of the movie (Gale Sondergaard's spider woman) is far from the actual center (Bruce).

SPIDERS, The or SPINNEN, Die see DIAMOND SHIP, The. GOLDEN SEA, The.

The SPIRAL STAIRCASE (B) WB/Raven 1975 color 89m. D: Peter Collinson. SP: Andrew Meredith, from Ethel Lina White's novel "Some Must Watch." Ph: Ken Hodges. Mus: David Lindup. AD: Disley Jones. Ref: MFB'75:63. TV. with Jacqueline Bisset, Christopher Plummer, Sam Wanamaker, Mildred Dunnock, Gayle Hunnicutt, Elaine Stritch, John Philip Law.

Isolated country house; storm; murders by madman who can't tolerate imperfection. Love that thunderstorm--but, oh those eyes! (Instead of seeing through the killer's eyes--as in the original film version--we simply see the killer's eyes, in big, shock close-ups.) Primitive suspense; prehistoric psychology. One by one, every character in the house (except killer and heroine) is eliminated (i.e., drugged, drunk, locked away, or dead)--the progression of the suspense plot is ridiculously neat. Stritch and Bisset do good work in a lost cause.

The SPIRIT (H.K.) Shaw 1977? (YU-LING) SP,D: Li Han-hsiang. Ref: IFG'78:181,185: "horror film."

The SPIRIT OF THE BEEHIVE (Sp) Janus/Beverly/Elias Querejeta 1973('76-U.S.) color 95m. (El ESPIRITU DE LA COLMENA. FRANKENSTEIN-orig t) SP,D: Victor Erice. SP: also A.F. Santos. Ph: Luis Cuadrado. Mus: Luis de Pablo. Ref: screen. Lee. V 10/3/73. 2/28/73:28. 2/14/73:32. Willis/SW. with F. F. Gomez, Teresa Gimpera, Jose Villasante(monster), A.Torrent.

Two little girls see El DOCTOR FRANKENSTEIN (the 1931 FRANKENSTEIN, dubbed; Van Sloan intro and girl's drowning shown); later, one of them imagines she glimpses the monster. Exquisite photography conveys the surface of a child's world; but the script contains very few incidents, very finely spun out into almost nothing. Winning sequence with the girls shrieking happily in mock-terror into their house, after seeing the movie.

SPIRITS FREE OF DUTY (B) Horseshoe 1915 14m. Ref: BFC. "Suitor poses as ghost to scare farmer...."

SPIRITS OF THE DEAD 1968 scope (*TALES OF MYSTERY AND IMAGINATION. TROIS HISTOIRES EXTRAORDINAIRES D'EDGAR POE. TALES OF MYSTERY-B. STORIE STRAORDINARIE) Narr: ("Metz.") Donald Sutherland? Ref: screen. Lee. MFB'73:76-77. AFI.

Confused and confusing as it may be, the Fellini "Toby Dammit" third of this Poe-inspired omnibus film is still easily the best segment (the competition is not fierce), a whirlwind of bizarre images which leaves behind scant trace of possible meaning. It's like a wild, indecipherable fragment of 8½, with a quite chilling (if still confusing) conclusion. The Malle "William Wilson" and Vadim "Metzengerstein" sections are virtually worthless, with Jane Fonda rather grotesquely miscast in the latter.

The SPOILED WEDDING (Cz) 1970? anim color 12m.
See also: DEADLY ODOR, The.

SPOILERS OF THE PLAINS Rep 1951 66m. D: William Witney. SP: Sloan Nibley. Ph: Jack Marta. Ref: V 2/7/51. MPH 2/10/51. LC. with Roy Rogers, Penny Edwards, Gordon Jones, Grant Withers, Fred Kohler Jr., House Peters Jr., Foy Willing and the Riders of the Purple Sage, George Meeker, Don Haggerty.

"Long-range weather forecasting instrument being developed at a desert rocket-launching site" (V); time-bomb substituted for timing device on experimental rocket. (MPH)

*SPOOK BUSTERS 1946 (GHOST BUSTERS-orig t) Mkp: Harry Ross. Narr: Leo Gorcey. Ref: TV. V 12/11/46. Lee. and with Maurice Cass, Chester Clute, Tanis Chandler.

Psychiatrist planning "cerebral transfer" of Bowery Boy Satch's (Huntz Hall) brain to gorilla; Menlo Estate haunted by "ghosts"; TV-spy apparatus; flip-top tombstones; "spooky" props left by dead magician Menlo the Great in estate's "Magic Room." Another challenging Bowery Boys comedy--just _try_ sitting through it. Equally unfunny scenes in fast, slow, and regular motion. On-the-verge-of-being-funny: Hall pretending that the "ghost" of the doctor's first victim is attacking him.

*SPOOK CHASERS 1957 Ref: TV. LC.

House haunted by ghost of widow's husband; two fake ghosts in skull-masks, sheets, and gorilla suits; real ghost at end (in same get-up) that walks through wall; "apparitions" of blowing bugle and glowing-eyed skull; thunderstorm; secret panels. Very late Bowery Boys comedy, with Percy Helton taking Bernard Gorcey's place and Stanley Clements taking _Leo_ Gorcey's. But Huntz Hall continues through thin and thin.

The SPOOK WHO SAT BY THE DOOR UA/Bokari 1973 color 102m. D, P: Ivan Dixon. SP,P: Sam Greenlee, from his novel. SP: also Melvin Clay. Ph: Michel Hugo. Mus: Herbie Hancock. AD: L. Thomas. Ref: Lee. V 10/3/73. with Lawrence Cook, Paula Kelly.

Black revolution in the U.S.

The SPOOKY BUNCH (H.K.-Cant.) Unique & Hi-Pitch 1980 color 97m. (CHUANG TAO CHENG) D: Hsu An-hua. SP: Joyce Chan. Ph: Tony Hope. Mus: Tang Boon-Kei. AD: Lee Lok-See. SdFX: Ng Kwok-Wah. Ref: IFG'81:162. HKFFest. with Siao Fong-Fong, Kenny Bee, Kwan Chung, Tina Lui(Catshit, ghost).

Curse; "whole army of ghosts." (HKFF)

The SPY WHO LOVED ME (B) UA/Eon 1977 color/scope 125m. D: Lewis Gilbert. SP: Christopher Wood, Richard Maibaum. From Ian Fleming's book. Ph: Claude Renoir. Mus: Marvin Hamlisch. PD: Ken Adam. SpFX: Derek Meddings, John Evans;(ph) Alan Maley. Ref: V(d) 7/7/77. MFB'77:176. with Roger Moore(James Bond), Barbara Bach, Curt Jurgens, Richard Kiel(Jaws), Caroline Munro, Bernard Lee, Shane Rimmer, Geoffrey Keene, Milton Reid.
"Submersible science-fiction craft"; "monster human known as "Jaws" because of his steel teeth" (V); "submarine Atlantis"; "shipping magnate who dreams of destroying the world and creating a new civilization beneath the sea." (MFB)

SQUIRM AI/The Squirm Co. 1976 color 92m. SP,D: Jeff Lieberman. Ph: J. Mangine. Mus: Robert Prince. AD: Henry Shrady. SpFX: Bill Milling et al. MkpDes: Rick Baker. Ref: MFB'76: 199. Willis/SW. V 8/11/76. with John Scardino, Patricia Pearcy, R.A. Dow, Jean Sullivan.
Electricity from broken cable turns worms into man-eaters.(A)

SREDNI VASHTAR(by Saki) see ORPHAN, The

SSSSSSS Univ/Zanuck-Brown 1973 color 99m. (SSSSNAKE-B) D: Bernard Kowalski. SP: Hal Dresner. Story,P: Dan Striepeke. Ph: G.P. Finnerman. Mus: Pat Williams. AD: J.T. McCormack. SpMkp: John Chambers, Nick Marcellino. SpMontage: John Neuhart. Ref: MFB'73:232. TV. V 7/18/73. with Strother Martin, Dirk Benedict, Heather Menzies, R.B. Shull, J. Ging,Reb Brown.
Ophiologist intent on creating a race of hardy, pollution-resistant snake-people turns assistant into giant king cobra; snakes-and-hellfire nightmares. Lousy horror movie is just a showcase for some jim-dandy "yucchh!" makeup effects. Film trades blatantly on bad feelings about snakes. Low-key but essentially idiotic.

STALKER (Russ-W.G.) Mosfilm & ZDF 1979 color 160m. SP,D, PD: Andrei Tarkovsky. SP: also the Strugatskys, based on their book "Picnic on the Road." Ph: Alexander Knyazhinsky. Mus: Eduard Artemev. Ref: V 9/19/79. S&S'80:152-3. MFB'81: 10-11: film's "Zone"=Bermuda triangle=mystery. with Alexander Kaidanovsky, Anatoly Solonitsyn, Alisa Freindlich, N. Grinko.
Meteorite's fall causes "mutations" in landscape.

STANLEY (Gold Key-TV)/Crown Int'l/Stanley 1972 color 96m. Story,D,P: William Grefe. SP: Gary Crutcher. Ph: C. Poland. Mus: Post Assoc. AD: Don Ivey. Ref: screen. MFB'73:132. Lee. TVFFSB. with Chris Robinson, Alex Rocco, Steve Alaimo.
Idealistic, snake-loving Seminole Indian's pet rattlesnake disposes of evil hunters and other riffraff. It must have sounded stupid at the script stage, but that obviously didn't stop them. Robinson's mumbled misanthropy, however, is effective. Once-in-a-lifetime line: (stripper) "Do you realize that with 7 shows a week and two on Friday and Saturday, I'll be biting the heads off of 9 snakes a week!?"

STAR BLAZER see SPACE CRUISER

STAR INSPECTOR (Russ) Mosfilm 1980 color/scope 82m. (ZVYOZDNYI INSPECTOR) SP,D: Mark Kovalyov. D: also Vladimir Polin. SP: also V. Smirnov, B. Travkin. Ph: V. Fastenko. Mus: Boris Rychkov. AD: Victor Gladnikov. Ref: Soviet Film 7/80. with Vladimir Ivashov, Yuri Gusev, Valentina Titova.
Futuristic mystery re: an international inspection-team investigating the destruction of a space station.

STAR MAIDENS PART I (Teleworld-TV)/Gatward 1976 color 71m. D: Wolfgang Storch, James Gatward. Ref: TVFFSB. with Judy Geeson, Christiane Kruger, Pierre Brice, Norman Warwick.
Women rule the planet Medusa.

STAR MAIDENS PART II (Teleworld-TV)/Gatward 1976 color 71m. Ref: TVFFSB: same cast as Part I.

STAR ODYSSEY (I) (Gold Key-TV)/Bless Int'l/Nais 1978 color 97m. D: Alfonso Brescia(aka Al Bradley). Ref: V 10/18/78(ad). 5/17/78:242. GKey: with Sharon Baker, Chris Avran? with Gianni Garko, Nino Castelnuovo, Yanti Somer, M. Longo.
Alien robots vs. Earth robots.

The STAR PACKER Lone Star(Mono)/Malvern 1934 54m. SP,D: R.N. Bradbury. Ph: Archie Stout. Mus D: Abe Meyer. Tech D: E.R. Hickson. Ref: TV. Turner/Price. with John Wayne, Verna Hillie, George Hayes(The Shadow), Yakima Canutt, George Cleveland.
The mysterious "Shadow" kills and seems to vanish in a puff of smoke; "ghosts" lurk about ranch. ("Strange things happen here at night.") Western begins with an invigorating open-air sequence and a few nice touches of mystery; then a bad case of dialogue sets in. Particularly telling exchange: Hayes: "A most ruthless bunch." Wayne: "How do you know?" Hayes: "Why, the cold-blooded way in which they operate." Wayne: "Oh, I see."

STAR PILOT see 2+5: MISSION HYDRA

STAR SHIP EROS 1980 color 65m. Ref: ad. J.Shapiro. with Lori Rogers(alien).
1995. Robot; Venusian spaceship with teleporter; ray gun.

STAR TREK--THE MOTION PICTURE Para/Roddenberry 1979 color/scope 132m. D: Robert Wise. SP: Harold Livingstone. Story: Alan Dean Foster. Based on the Gene Roddenberry TV series. Ph: R.H. Kline, Richard Yuricich;(mattes) Matthew Yuricich. Mus: Jerry Goldsmith. PD: Harold Michelson. SpPhFX: Douglas Trumbull, J. Dykstra. PhFX: Dave Stewart;(min) Don Baker. SpVis FX: Richard Taylor; Robert Abel. SpAnimFX: Robert Swarthe. SpSciCons: Isaac Asimov. Opt: BIG. Ref: screen. MFB'80:29. V 12/12/79. with William Shatner, Leonard Nimoy, DeForest Kelley, Persis Khambatta, Nichelle Nichols, James Doohan, George Takei.

In the 23rd Century, the Starship Enterprise discovers an alien mechanical intelligence in the heart of a gigantic cloud-like formation; stored worlds of data; tractor beam; plasma energy; electrical and humanoid (Khambatta) probes. Probably the most elaborate boy-meets-girl story ever filmed. ST-TMP's mating-of-man-and-machine ending itself mates the man-machine interdependence of 2001: A SPACE ODYSSEY with the "boomerang" twist at the end of PLANET OF THE APES. (This time, however, the object which comes back to haunt us is only an Earth-artifact, not the whole planet.) Hundreds of wonderful effects--and a cosmic-mystery plot--prove to be dependent on the plain, dumb fact that the highly-advanced machine-planet people at the far end of a black hole couldn't dust off a Voyager's logo. (It takes William Shatner a few seconds to wipe it clean, and that's that.) ST-TMP is another sf-film case of visual splendiferousness and dramatic atrophy. There are lots of cosmic signs here, but little meaning. In the movie's own visual terms, Captain Kirk's (Shatner) reunion with the Enterprise counts for immeasurably more than does the launching of a new life-form. The former sequence is a marvel of music, effects, and moving camera; the latter hinges on a soulful exchange of looks between two lovers. The score and the effects require no suspension of disbelief; those longing glances do. As spectacle, ST-TMP is a feast; as philosophical food-for-thought, it's on the level of Twinkies.

STAR WARS Fox/Gary Kurtz 1977 color/scope 121m. SP,D: George Lucas. Ph: Gilbert Taylor. Mus: John Williams. PD: John Barry. SpPhFxSup: John Dykstra. SpMechFxSup: John Stears. Anim:(stopmo) Jon Berg, Phil Tippett;(computer) Dan O'Bannon. Mkp: Stuart Freeborn;(sp) Rick Baker, Doug Beswick. SdFX: Ben Burtt. Mattes: P.S. Ellenshaw. Planets: Ralph McQuarrie. FxDes: Joseph Johnston, Colin Cantwell. Roto: Adam Beckett. Explosions: Joe Viskocil, Greg Auer. Other FX: Ray Mercer, Van Der Veer, DePatie-Freleng. Ref: MFB'77:243-44. screen. V(d) 5/20/77. with Mark Hamill, Harrison Ford, Carrie Fisher, Peter Cushing, Alec Guinness, David Prowse(Darth Vader; voice: James Earl Jones), Peter Mayhew(Chewbacca), Anthony Daniels (C-3PO), Kenny Baker(R2-D2), Phil Brown.

A long time ago...there was an evil Empire and its super-weapon, the Death Star....Plus: robots; an ape-wolf-man(Mayhew); a mystical "Force"; and a wide assortment of other fantastic creatures. In science-fiction films, the Seventies was of course the decade of STAR WARS, one of our more benign recent phenomena, featuring the most congenial theatre queues ("How many times have you seen it?" "Oh, let's see, about five."), and constituting a possibly-unending source of film lore and mythology. What inspired it?--movie serials and comic books and other sf films/books/art and adventure/action movies. But while equal or superior to many of its cultural cross-references, STAR WARS does not so much transcend them as fuse them. It's like a giant, technologically-intimidating hommage or valentine to our pulp past (and present), to the best and the worst in Hollywood and pulp art--and, appropriately, it partakes of the best and the worst. A succession of near-throwaway wonders (e.g., the holograph game, the funny-voiced denizens of the space bar, the scavenger-truck gizmos, the pink and green explosions) makes colorless main characters and bland dialogue endurable, if it doesn't quite quell the suspicion that "the Force" is supposed to be taken more or less seriously. If STAR WARS the motion picture doesn't quite live up to STAR WARS the trailer--that first exciting, tantalizing glimpse we had of the saga--well, then, what could?

Sequel: The EMPIRE STRIKES BACK. See also: HARDWARE WARS.

STAR WOMAN see MAGNIFICENT MS.

STARBEAST see ALIEN

STARCRASH (U.S.-I) New World 1979 color 91m. SP,D: Luigi Cozzi(aka Lewis Coates). SP: also Nat Wachsberger; R.A. Dillon. Ph: Paul Beeson, R. D'Ettorre. Mus: John Barry. PD: Aurelio Crugnolla. ElecVisFxSup: Ron Hays. SpPhFX: Studio Quattro. SpFxD: Armando Valcauda. MechFxD: G. Natali. Sd FX: Anzelotti. Ref: screen. MFB'79:155. V 3/28/79. with Marjoe Gortner, Caroline Munro, Christopher Plummer, David Hasselhoff, Joe Spinell(Count), Nadia Cassini.

Evil Count plotting to take over the universe with his Doom Machine; robot cop; Amazons; giant Guardian; frozen planet; floating city; insect-like robots; suspended animation; energy-shield mask; prescience; Count's Phantom Planet guarded by computer-generated, mind-blowing "Red Monsters" and by Troglodytes; time stopped by Emperor of the First Circle of the Universe(Plummer). Operating on the principle of the Christmas tree, STARCRASH is decorated, brightly, with stars and planets of all colors (or at least red, yellow, blue, and white), spaceships of all sizes (inc. one dubbed Murray Leinster), ray guns and rifles, robots, monsters, and Ms. Munro (the latter as Stella Star, the choicest ornament of all). Some of the decorations seem to have been added a bit hastily, but with tree-trimming (as with movies), it's the festive spirit that counts. Fun fluff.

STARLIGHT SLAUGHTER see DEATH TRAP

STARSHIP INVASIONS WB/Roach 1978 color 89m. (ALIEN ENCOUNTER-orig t? WAR OF THE ALIENS-int t?) SP,D: Ed Hunt. Ph: Mark Irwin. Mus: Gil Melle. AD: Karen Bromley. SpFX: Warren Keillor;(ph) Dennis Pike. SpMkp: Maureen Sweeney? Ref: V 5/17/78:98(ad). 10/19/77. Meyers. AMPAS. with Robert Vaughn, Christopher Lee, Daniel Pilon, Victoria Johnson.

Aliens from space vs. the League of Races, headquartered in the Bermuda Triangle.

START HAV see EMPTY SEA

STARZINGER (J) Toei-Matsumoto-Asahi Comm. 1979 24m. (S.F. SAIYUKI--SUTA JINGA) D: Anzai, Shigeki. Based on the Chinese

fairy tale "Saiyuki." Ref: JFFJ 13:34.
"Interstellar human civilization" vs. aliens; from TV series.

The STEPFORD WIVES (Viacom-TV)/Col/Palomar-Fadsin 1975 color 115m. D: Bryan Forbes. SP: William Goldman, from Ira Levin's novel. Ph: Owen Roizman. Mus: Michael Small. PD: Gene Callahan. Sequel: REVENGE OF THE STEPFORD WIVES. Ref: MFB'78: 143. TV. V 2/12/75. with Katharine Ross, Paula Prentiss, Peter Masterson, Nanette Newman, Patrick O'Neal, Tina Louise.
Small-town men's association's idea of utopia: a town (theirs) of subservient robot-wives (created in the image of the real wives). Or "Invasion of the Wife Snatchers." A one-joke horror movie, or rather a one-frisson comedy, on sexual conformity. What, supposedly, every woman thinks every man wants: a pod-mate. A sort of inverse BURN, WITCH, BURN--it's all for the good of the husbands, but this time it's a conspiracy by the men themselves rather than their wives. Contentment reigns: "I know I shouldn't say this, but--I _love_ my brownies!" Ross _knows_ Prentiss has gone over to the other side: "Her kitchen was _sparkling_!" At least the fact that Paula Prentiss is in the film means that there _is_ a difference between the women and the robots.

STEREO (Can.) Emergent 1969 65m. SP,D,P,Ph,Ed: David Cronenberg. See also: SCANNERS. Ref: Lee(MFB'71:204). PFA: "telepathic rape." with Ronald Mlodzik, Iain Ewing, C. Mayer.
Experiments with telepathists in the future.

STILL LIFE,The(by D.Chase) see GRAVE OF THE VAMPIRE

STONES see HORROR AT 37,000 FEET

STORIE STRAORDINARIE see SPIRITS OF THE DEAD

STORY OF A LITTLE GIRL WHO WANTED TO BECOME A PRINCESS see MAGIC CLOCK, The

The STORY OF CHINESE GODS (H.K.-Chinese) Chang Ying 1976 anim color 90m. D: Tang Chow Lup. SP: Chan Kong. Mus: Wong Koy Shin. Anim D: Chang Che Fai. Ref: V 5/19/76.
"The screen gets cluttered with bizarre monsters."

The STORY OF LOVE (Rum.) Romaniafilm-Four Film 1981 color 80m. (POVESTEA DRAGOSTEI) SP,D,Mus: Ion Popescu-Gopo. From Ion Creanga's story "The Tale of the Pig." Ph: Ionescu, Horvath. Mus: also Cornel Popescu. Sets & Cost: Adriana Paun. Ref: V 4/1/81. with Eugenia Popovici, M. Bogdan, N. Ifrim.
"Trip through space" to a "scifi beehive" kingdom; spaceship which leaves "little creature" behind on Earth.

The STORY OF PERSEUS (Russ) Soyuzmultfilm 1973 color anim 20m. (PERSEY) D: A.S.-Blotskaya. SP: Simukov. Ref: MFB'76:40.
Perseus vs. the Gorgon; Medusa; sea monster.

The STORY OF THE DRAGON AND THE LION HUNCHBACK (H.K.) 1962
Ref: HKFFest: inspired by The HUNCHBACK OF NOTRE DAME films.

A STORY OF TUTANKHAMUN (B-Egy) Ginger 1976(1973) color 52m. D: Kevin Scott. SP: Yusuf Idris. Ph: L. McLeod. Mus: Ron Grainer. AD: M. Nashedi. Ref: MFB'76:63. with Domini Blyth, E. Elalaily, Barbara Bolton.

Curse on discoverers of pharaoh's tomb proves to be visions engendered to keep his memory alive.

STRAIGHT ON TILL MORNING (B) (TV Cinema Sales)/Int'l Co-Prods/ Hammer 1972('74-U.S.) color 96m. D: Peter Collinson. SP: Michael Peacock. Ph: B. Probyn. Mus: Roland Shaw. AD: Scott MacGregor. Ref: MFB'72:172. TV. TVFFSB. Willis/SW. with Rita Tushingham, Shane Briant, Tom Bell, Katya Wyeth, A.Ross.

"Drab" heroine and her "Prince Charming" (a psychopathic killer) both translate their experiences into fairy-tale form. The translation is pathetic in her case; macabre in his, but not particularly resonant in either case. This is still your basic routine thriller, with a few fancy fairy-tale and editing effects. Only Rita Tushingham's face seems to suggest something of <u>both</u> real and fairy-tale worlds. The script--which says she's <u>not</u> beautiful--is overruled by the camera.

STRANA ORCHIDEA... see THEY'RE COMING TO GET YOU!

STRANDED see STRANGER,The(1973)

*STRANGE ADVENTURE (WGE-TV) 1933 (The WAYNE MURDER CASE-TV) Dial: Hampton Del Ruth. Ref: TV. TVFFSB. FQ Smr'80:54.

The basic family-will, cloaked-killer thunderstorm mystery, and just about the feeblest of them all. Dwight Frye is wasted in a small role, and the servant (Snowflake) disappears after about 20 minutes. (Isn't it the script-girl's job to <u>catch</u> things like that?)

The STRANGE AND DEADLY OCCURRENCE Alpine(Fries)-TV 1974 color 72m. D: John L. Moxey. SP: Sandor Stern, Lane Slate. Ph: Jack Woolf. Mus: Robert Prince. AD: Peter Wooley. SdFxEd: Ray Alba. Opt: Modern. Ref: TV. TV Season. Scheuer/MOTV. with Robert Stack, Vera Miles, L.Q. Jones, Herb Edelman, Dena Dietrich, Margaret Willock, Bill McKinney.

The heavy-breathing, subjective-camera creature strikes again! But behind it lies an even older cliche: it's no monster "haunting" the house, just a hood playing ghost and looking for buried loot. The HAUNTING turns into CAPE FEAR, as a Mitchum-styled creep terrorizes Stack's family (with loud noises and ambulatory dummies), and even subjects them to manual labor. ("Dig!") Patchwork.

STRANGE BEHAVIOR see DEAD KIDS

STRANGE CASE OF DR.JEKYLL AND MISS OSBOURN see DR. JEKYLL ET LES FEMMES

STRANGE CASE OF DR. JEKYLL AND MR. HYDE, The(by R.L.Stevenson) see ADULT VERSION OF JEKYLL AND HIDE,The. BETTY BOOP, M.D. BLACK AND WHITE. BOOKWORM,The. BOOKWORM TURNS,The. CHERE PE CHERA. COMIC,The(P). COUNTESS DRACULA. DR. BLACK MR. HYDE. DR. HECKYL AND MR. HYPE. DR. JEKYLL AND MR. HYDE. DR. JEKYLL AND SISTER HYDE. DOCTOR JEKYLL AND THE WOLFMAN. DR. JEKYLL ET LES FEMMES. DR. JEKYLL JR. DR. JEKYLL'S DUNGEON OF DEATH. DR. SEXUAL AND MR. HYDE. DUALITY OF MAN, The. EROTIC DR. JEKYLL. HAPPY HOOLIGAN IN DR. JEKYL AND MR. ZIP. HAVE YOU GOT ANY CASTLES. HELTER SKELTER. HYDE AND HARE. I, MONSTER. IMPATIENT PATIENT. JEKYLL AND HYDE PORTFOLIO,The. MAN WITH TWO HEADS. MOTOR MANIA. MYSTERY!(P). OVERSEXED. PEPITO Y CHABELO... SELTSAMER FALL,Ein(P). THREE'S A CROWD. TWISTED BRAIN.

The STRANGE CASE OF MR. TODMORDEN (B) Central 1935 20m. D, P: Walter Tennyson. Ref: BFC: sleepwalker commits murder.

*The STRANGE DOOR 1951 Mkp: Bud Westmore. Ref: TV. V 10/31/51. and with William Cottrell, Morgan Farley.

Universal horror-library sets and music; diminishing room; storm, shadows, fog. Dreary costume adventure, with Boris Karloff in a thankless role which gets _really_ out-of-hand climax-wards. ("Master! The key, the key!" he cries, as, wounded by gun and knife and just barely alive, he crawls towards the protagonists' cell.) Charles Laughton is another, much happier story--he invests even his scenes of rather-conventional villainy with wit and dramatic nuance. And _his_ climactic scenes are quite moving, as--caught between revenge and recollection of his lost love--his mind begins to go. He's an oasis of life--to the film's desert.

The STRANGE EXORCISM OF LYNN HART Classic 1974(1976) (LYNN HART, THE STRANGE LOVE EXORCIST-alt t) D: Marc Lawrence. SP: F.A. Foss. Ref: Aros(HR). Meyers.

The STRANGE FETISHES OF THE GO-GO GIRLS Americana 1967 66m. D,P: Enrico Blancocello. Ref: AFI. with Sammy Arena, Sandy O'Hara, Taylor March.

Missing TV-horror-show host and undead phantom strangler prove to be one and the same.

*STRANGE HOLIDAY PRC/General Motors 1946(1940) (The DAY AFTER TOMORROW-B) SpFX: Howard Anderson, Ray Mercer. Ref: V 10/24/45. 11/6/46. Lee.

Commercial film originally made to boost morale of GM workers; later, property of MGM, then Elite, finally PRC.

STRANGE NEW WORLD ABC-TV/WB-TV 1975 color 74m. D: Robert Butler. Sp & Exec P: Walon Green, R.F. Graham. SP: also Al Ramrus. Ph: M. Margulies. Ref: TV. TV Season. TVFFSB. with John Saxon, Kathleen Miller, James Olson, Martine Beswick, Gerrit Graham, Ford Rainey, Reb Brown, Keene Curtis.

Eterna (Earth, 200 years in the future). Suspended animation; eternal-life treatment that revives the dead; "collec-

tive womb" clones; savages; refs. to "Pax." Heavy-handed, hard-to-watch sf.
See also: GENESIS II. PLANET EARTH.

The STRANGE POSSESSION OF MRS. OLIVER NBC-TV/Shpetner 1977 color 75m. D: Gordon Hessler. SP: Richard Matheson. Ph: Frank Stanley. Mus: Morton Stevens. Ref: TV. TVFFSB. TV Season. with Karen Black, George Hamilton, Robert F. Lyons, Lucille Benson.
Housewife seems possessed by spirit of dead girl.

The STRANGER NBC-TV/Crosby-Cox 1973 color 93m. (STRANDED-orig t) D: Lee H. Katzin. SP: Gerald Sanford. Ph: K.C. Smith. Mus: Richard Markowitz. AD: Paul Sylos. Ref: TV. V 3/7/73:47. Lee. with Glenn Corbett, Sharon Acker, Lew Ayres, Cameron Mitchell, George Coulouris, Steve Franken, Dean Jagger.
Astronaut lands on parallel world on far side of sun.

STRANGER IN OUR HOUSE Finnegan & Inter Planetary 1978 color 93m. D: Wes Craven. SP: Glenn M. Benest, Max A. Keller. From Lois Duncan's book "Summer of Fear." Ph: W.K. Jurgensen. Mus: Michael Lloyd, John D'Andrea. AD: Joe Aubel. SpFX: John Frazier. Ref: TV. MFB'80:95-6. with Linda Blair, Lee Purcell, Carol Lawrence, Jeff East, Macdonald Carey, Jeremy Slate.
Mysterious events at California ranch-house traced to witch. Muddled thriller.

STRANGER IN THE HOUSE see BLACK CHRISTMAS

*STRANGER ON THE THIRD FLOOR 1940 SP: also Nathanael West? Ref: screen. TV. MFB'81:165-66.
A must-see "B", thanks principally to Peter Lorre's brilliant cameo performance as a psychopathic killer whose attention wanders very mysteriously--you can sense each successive emotion taking hold of him, then slowly drifting away, leaving him, basically, an intimidating blank. His psychic presence varies from "intense" to "hardly-even-there"....Seven minutes of genius in an uneven film, which is also, however, distinguished by Roy Webb's music--evoking precarious-night-life-in-big-city impressions--and by a bravura comic-horrific nightmare sequence.

The STRANGER WITHIN ABC-TV/Lorimar 1974 color 74m. D: Lee Philips. SP: Richard Matheson. Ref: TV Season. TVFFSB. with Barbara Eden, George Grizzard, Nehemiah Persoff, J. Van Patten.
Expectant-mother's baby "controls" her.

STRANGERS OF THE EVENING Tiffany 1932 71m. (The HIDDEN CORPSE-TV) D: H.Bruce Humberstone. SP: Stuart Anthony, Warren B. Duff, from Tiffany Thayer's book "The Illustrious Corpse." Ph: Arthur Edeson. Mus D: Val Burton. Sets: Ralph M. DeLacy. Ref: Turner/Price. TVFFSB. with ZaSu Pitts, Eugene Pallette, Lucien Littlefield, Tully Marshall, Miriam Seegar, Theodor von Eltz, Alan Roscoe, Hal Price.

"Horrible apparition" in funeral parlor (T/P); "horror and hilarity"; "capering corpses."(ad)

STRASNAJA MEST' see VIJ,The(1914)

STRATOSTARS see WAR OF THE ROBOTS

STRIGANZA see BLOOD ORGY OF THE SHE DEVILS

The STRONGEST MAN IN THE WORLD BV 1975 color 92m. D: Vincent McEveety. SP: J.L. McEveety, H. Groves. Sequel to The COMPUTER WORE TENNIS SHOES. Ph: A. Jackson. Mus: R.F. Brunner. AD: Mansbridge, Senter. SpFX: Cruickshank, Lee. Ref: MFB'76:175. V 2/5/75. Glut/CMM: title bit with King Kong. with Kurt Russell, Joe Flynn, Eve Arden, Cesar Romero, Phil Silvers, William Schallert, Benson Fong, Fritz Feld et al.

Cereal coated with student's chemical solution gives fellow student superhuman strength.

STUDENT BODIES Para/Universal Southwest 1981 color 80m. SP, D: Mickey Rose. Ph: Robert Ebinger. Mus: Gene Hobson. PD: Donald Nunley. Opt: Modern. Mkp: Lynn Wolverton. Ref: V 8/12/81. screen. with Kristen Riter, Matt Goldsby, Richard Brando(The Breather), Mimi Weddell.

Parody of HALLOWEEN-type shockers; death by paper clips, chalk eraser, horsehead bookend; students-and-faculty-as ghouls seq.; all-a-nightmare ending, with clutching-hand-from-grave coda. Unsubtle but occasionally very funny. FRIDAY THE 13TH and its ilk get what they deserve--a comedy that's a _bit_, but not _too much_ better than _they_ are. It's just as impersonal, but at least clever about it. (Graphics like "important plot point" and "big mistake" mark the most-often-taken narrative turns.) The Breather is perhaps the most ingratiating mad skulker since his counterpart in NIGHT OF TERROR(1933), and he shares his thoughts (re: occupational hazards etc.)--as well as his peccadilloes--with us.

*The STUDENT OF PRAGUE 1913 70m. P: Paul Wegener. Ref: screen. V 8/21/74:36.

The spectacle of Wegener as Baldwin the student, plagued by his omnipresent double, is amusing; if it's not especially _evocative_, the mere trick (or mirror trick) of "being double" also dominates Poe's "William Wilson," the source of the film. (Hawthorne's charming "M. du Miroir" might have proved a more profitable source for a film about mirror-images.) And what on Earth is Lyda Salmonova doing creeping around in the background in every other scene? (No point is ever made of _her_ odd near-omnipresence.)

*A STUDY IN TERROR (B-W.G.) Planet 1965 (SHERLOCK HOLMES GROSSTER FALL) Ref: TV. AFI.

Fair, rather dry period shocker. Engaging moments with Sherlock and Mycroft Holmes (John Neville and Robert Morley, resp.) and with Watson (Donald Houston), and a beauty of a fadeout shot. The Jack-the-Ripper plot fails to intrigue. See also: MURDER BY DECREE.

SUBMERSION OF JAPAN see TIDAL WAVE

A SUBSTANTIAL GHOST (B) Gaumont 1903 1m. Ref: BFC.
"Ghost" scares tramps playing cards in cemetery.

SUCCUBUS see SATANIST, The

SUCK ME VAMPIRE (F) Off 1975 D: Maxime Debest. Ref: V 5/12/76:278: "horror-pic-cum-porno."

SUGAR HILL AI 1974 color 91m. (VOODOO GIRL-B) D: Paul Maslansky. SP: T. Kelley, A. Kazak, M. Jules. Ph: Robert Jessup. Mus: Nick Zesses, Dino Fekaris. SpFX: Roy Downey. Ref: MFB'75:118. Willis/SW. V 2/6/74. with Marki Bey, Robert Quarry, Don Pedro Colley, Richard Lawson, Betty Ann Rees.
Deserted mansion; voodoo mamaloi; zombies; "lord of the netherworld." (MFB)

The SUICIDE CLUB ABC-TV/Univ-TV 1973 color 73m. D: Bill Glenn. SP: Philip Reisman Jr., from Robert Louis Stevenson's story. Mus: Michael Lang. Sets: Ralph Holmes. Ref: TVFFSB. Lee. Cinef F'73:37. with Peter Haskell, Margot Kidder, Joseph Wiseman, George Coulouris, Logan Ramsey, Ron Rifkin.

The SUICIDE CLUB (B) Thames-TV 1971 Ref: TVFFSB. with Alan Dobie, Bernard Archard, H. Neil.

SUMMER OF FEAR(by L.Duncan) see STRANGER IN OUR HOUSE

SUMMER OF SECRETS (Austral.) Secret 1976 color 100m. D: Jim Sharman. SP: John Aitken. Ph: R. Boyd. Mus: Cameron Allen. AD: Jane Norris. Ref: V(d) 1/4/77. with Arthur Dignam, Rufus Collins, Nell Campbell, Kate Fitzpatrick.
Doctor's "revolutionary brain surgery" brings wife back from the dead.

*SUMURUN 1920 60m. Mus: Victor Hollander. Cost: Ali Hubert. Ref: screen. Weinberg/TLT.
Ernst Lubitsch, as the pathetic hunchback Yeggar, spends half of SUMURUN as a body (thanks to a dose of death-semblance serum). The script is elementary pathos (Lubitsch) and passion (everyone else). Surpassingly silly melodramatics--lots of hugging-of-knees and kissing-of-feet.

SUN WIND (Finnish) 1980 D: Timo Linnasalo. Ref: V 5/13/81: 307: "scifi"; scientist frozen, resuscitated.

SUN-WU-K'UNG TA-CHAN CH'UN YAO (H.K.) 196-? From the novel "Hsi-Yu Chi." Ref: Eberhard.
Men turned into animals; dragon king.

The SUNKEN SUBMARINE (Cz) 1972? anim color 12m. See also: DEADLY ODOR, The. Ref: IFG'73:469.

SUPAIDAMAN (J) Toei 1978 scope 24m. D: K. Takemoto. SP: S. Takahisa. Ref: JFFJ 13:35: based on TV series (and on Stan Lee's "Spider-Man" character?).V 5/9/79:381.

SUPER INFRAMAN see INFRAMAN

SUPER KONG see APE(1976)

SUPER MONSTER GAMERA (J) Daiei 1980 color (SUPER MONSTER-ad t. UCHU KAIJU GAMERA) D: Noriaki Yuasa. SP: Niisan Takahashi. Ph: Akira Kitazaki. Ref: V 5/7/80:449,463. 10/15/80: 230. JFFJ 13:33. with Mach Fumiake.
Mostly old footage of Gamera, Jiger, Virus, etc.; parodies of STAR WARS, JAWS, CLOSE ENCOUNTERS, SUPERMAN.

SUPER VAN Empire/Capra-Cohen 1977 color 91m. D: Lamar Card. SP: N. Friedenn, R. Easter. Mus: Andy DeMartino et al. SpFX: Harry Woolman. Ref: V 4/13/77:20. with Mark Schneider, Katie Saylor, Morgan Woodward, Len Lesser.
Solar-powered van with laser-beam weapon.

SUPERBEAST UA/A&S 1972 color 93m. (EVIL EYE-orig t) SP,D,P: George Schenck. Ph: Nonong Rasca. Mus: Richard La Salle. AD: Hernando Balon. SpMkp: John Chambers. SpFX: Jeffrey Bushelman. Ref: MFB'73:16: "imaginative." CineFan 2:18-20. Willis/SW. Lee(p). V 10/4/72. with Antoinette Bower, Craig Littler, Harry Lauter, Vic Diaz, Bruno Punzalan, John Garwood.
Mad doctor's serum regresses men into ape-men, who are then hunted for sport by financier.

El SUPERLOCO (Mex) PCE 1936 65m. SP,D: Juan J. Segura. Story: J.A. Cardena. Ph: Jack Draper. Mus: D.P. Castaneda, C. Monge. AD: J.R. Granada. Ref: "Hist.Doc.Cine Mex.," I: 135: mad doctor; monster; a la Mary Shelley & RLS. with Leopoldo Ortin, Carlos Villarias, Consuelo Frank, Raul Urquijo(monster).

SUPERMAN (U.S.-B) WB/Int'l. Film Production(Dovemead) 1978 color/scope 138m. D: Richard Donner. SP: Mario Puzo, David & Leslie Newman, Robert Benton. Based on characters created by Jerry Siegel & Joe Schuster. Story: Puzo. Add'l Mat'l: Norman Enfield. Ph: Geoffrey Unsworth;(process) Denys Coop. Mus: John Williams;(lyrics) Leslie Bricusse. PD: John Barry. SpFX:(d) Colin Chilvers;(technicians) Roy Spencer, T. Schubert et al. OptVisFxSup: Roy Field. Mattes: Les Bowie. ModelFX: Derek Meddings. SpVisFxDes: Denis Rich. SpSeqs: Howard A. Anderson Co., CCS. Flying:(systems) Wally Veevers;(fx) Derek Botell, Bob Harman. ShipDes: Ed Gimmel. SpFX: John Richardson, Bob MacDonald. Ref: MFB'79:33-34. TV. V 12/13/78. with Christopher Reeve(Superman/Clark Kent), Margot Kidder,

Gene Hackman, Valerie Perrine, Ned Beatty, Jackie Cooper, Marlon Brando, Susannah York, Trevor Howard, Glenn Ford, Phyllis Thaxter, Jeff East, Phil Brown, Maria Schell.

Boy sent by parents to Earth from distant, doomed planet Krypton grows, uses superhuman powers for good. Country-boy Reeve and city-girl Kidder are an ideal Superman-Clark Kent/Lois Lane match/mismatch ("C-r-i...?" "K-r-y...")--the movie has a core. (But John Hamilton is still *the* Perry White.) Their comic scenes are expertly timed and played--and they succeed in establishing Reeve as both human and more-than-human, emotionally vulnerable and physically *invulnerable*. But the film as a whole coheres about as well as any five episodes of "The Adventures of Superman." The determinedly-epic early scenes, the light-comic scenes with hero and heroine, the weightless comic scenes with the villains, and the super-stunt scenes do not so much inform as simply supersede one another. The script asks us to venture with it from the feeblest of quips to the mightiest of feats, and to accept a Superman who is glibber (as well as stronger) than the villains, and who has heart as well as wit. But the script itself fails to correlate the disparate elements of its plot and its hero--only the Williams score gives it some structural underpinning.

Sequel: SUPERMAN II. See also: IT'S A BIRD, IT'S A PLANE, IT'S SUPERMAN.

SUPERMAN II (U.S.-B) WB/IFP-Salkind(Dovemead) 1980 color 127m. D: Richard Lester. SP: Mario Puzo, David & Leslie Newman. Sequel to SUPERMAN(1978). Ph: Geoffrey Unsworth, Robert Paynter. Mus: Ken Thorne; John Williams. PD: John Barry, Peter Murton. SpFxD: Colin Chilvers. Opt&VisFxSup: Roy Field. MinFX: Derek Meddings;(ph) Paul Wilson. Flying FX: Zoran Perisic, Bob Harman;(ph) Denys Coop. SpLightingFX: Lightflex. Matte Illus: Ivor Beddoes. Titles: Camera FX. Ref: V 12/3/80. VV 6/10/81. screen. MFB'81:79-80. with Gene Hackman, Christopher Reeve, Margot Kidder; Terence Stamp, Sarah Douglas, Jack O'Halloran(aliens); Jackie Cooper, Ned Beatty, Susannah York, E.G. Marshall, Marc McClure, V.Perrine.

A nuclear explosion in space releases three criminals from Krypton from their mirror-like "phantom zone" prison; they fly to Earth, ultimately to do battle with Superman with their own super-powers. More spectacle, comedy, and drama, and slightly-more-successfully blended than in SUPERMAN I. The spectacle--culminating in a spirited super-battle a la Godzilla and Gamera movies (with New York City, though, not Tokyo, as the playground)--suffers least from the multifariousness of the movie; the effects stunts require less narrative care and feeding than does the Clark-Lois-Superman triangle, which is developed in admittedly-rather-charming fits and starts, but fits and starts nonetheless. Nothing (except a loose sense of agreeableness) is sustained for more than two or three scenes--which at that puts this one-up on a *lot* of movies.

SUPERSONIC MAN (Sp) (Gold Key-TV)/Almena 1979 color/Dinavision 85m. SP,D: Juan Piquer. SP: also S. Moi. Ph: Juan Marine. Mus: Gino Peguri et al. SpFX & Sets: Emilio Ruiz, Francisco Prosper. OptFX: Jack Elkubi, Miguel Villa. Ref: V 8/29/79. 2/25/81:75(ad). Cinef X:1:12. MFB'79:255. with Michael Coby, Cameron Mitchell, Diana Polakov, Frank Brana, Richard Yesteran.
Super-hero from a distant galaxy; rocket-shooting robot.

SUPERWOMAN see MAGNIFICENT MS.

SUPERZAN Y EL NINO DEL ESPACIO (Mex) Tikal 1972 color 128m. SP,D: Rafael Lanuza. Ph: A. Ruiz. Mus: G.C. Carrion. Ref: Lee: robots. with "Superzan," G. Lanuza(alien boy).

The SURVIVOR (Austral.) Tuesday 1981 color 84m. D: David Hemmings. SP: David Ambrose, from James Herbert's novel. Ph: John Seale. Mus: Brian May. PD: Bernard Hides. Ref: V 9/23/81. 9/2/81:6:at Sitges. with Robert Powell, Jenny Agutter, Joseph Cotten.
"Zombie-like" survivor of plane crash; "creepy moments."

SUSPENSE see BEYOND THE DOOR II

SUSPIRIA (I) Int'l Classics(Fox)/Seda-S.Argento 1977 color/ Technovision 97m. SP,D: Dario Argento. SP: also D.Nicolodi. Ph: Luciano Tovoli. Mus: Goblin, D. Argento. PD: Giuseppe Bassan. SpFX: Germano Natali. Ref: MFB'77:215-16. FM 165:4. V 3/9/77. Cinef VI:3:21. with Jessica Harper, Stefania Casini, Flavio Bucci, Udo Kier, Alida Valli, Joan Bennett.
Invisible spirit of witch, "The Black Widow," haunts dance academy, animates corpse.

SUSSURI NEL BUIO or SUSSURRO NEL BUIO see WHISPERS IN THE DARK

*SVENGALI 1931 79m. AD: Anton Grot. Chor: Busby Berkeley. Ref: screen. TV. LC. Kit Parker.
Maestro Svengali's hypnotic powers enable his protegee Trilby (Marian Marsh) to sing beautifully; but the resultant strain on his own heart is slowly killing him. John Barrymore's Polish accent as Svengali may be a bit thin, but he seems to draw on an inexhaustible fund of expressive tics and gestures, and his comic impishness in the early scenes is effective counterpoint to the gaunt, wraith-like Svengali of the later scenes. The story turns Svengali's chronic exploitation of others back upon himself: Trilby's "manufactured love" for him draws its strength from <u>his</u> heart, not hers, which is simply dormant. ("But it is only Svengali talking to himself again.") Illusion fades, and Svengali dies. Marsh's pert, symmetrical, blond sweetness seems the perfect non-conductor for Svengali's romantic aspirations.
See also: TWENTIETH CENTURY(P).

SWAMP OF THE BLOOD LEECHES see ALIEN DEAD, The

SWAMP THING Avco Embassy 1982 D: Wes Craven. Mus: Harry Manfredini. SpMkp: Bill Munns. Ref: V 9/16/81:28: 3/82 release. Cinef XI:4. with Adrienne Barbeau, Louis Jourdan, Nicholas Worth, David Hess.
Chemical turns man into half-plant creature.

SWAMY AIYYAPPAN (India-Malayalam) Neela 1975 color 152m. SP,D: Subramaniam. Mus: Devarajan. Ref: Dharap: Tamil vers. by City Theatres; 1976 Telugu vers.by Prakash Prods. with Gemini Ganesh, Hari, Raghavan.
Tale of Mahishi, "the buffalo beast," and Aiyyappan, "the demon-killer."

The SWARM WB 1978 color/scope 116m. D,P: Irwin Allen. SP: Stirling Silliphant, from Arthur Herzog's novel. Ph: Fred Koenekamp. Mus: Jerry Goldsmith. PD: Stan Jolley. SpPhFX: L.B. Abbott, Van Der Veer. SpFX: Howard Jensen. Ref: MFB'78: 183: "rudimentary." V 7/19/78: "tired." with Michael Caine, Katharine Ross, Richard Widmark, Richard Chamberlain, Olivia de Havilland, Lee Grant, Fred MacMurray, Henry Fonda, Ben Johnson, Don "Red" Barry, Cameron Mitchell, Arthur Space, Slim Pickens, Jose Ferrer, Patty Duke Astin, Bradford Dillman.
Swarm of African killer-bees penetrates Texas missile base.

SWEDISH NYMPHO SLAVES (Swiss) Elite 1980? color 74m. (Die TEUFLISCHEN SCHWESTERN) D: Jesus Franco. SP: Manfred Gregor. Ph: Peter Baumgartner. Mus: Walter Baumgartner. Ref: MFB '80:222-23: "stray elements of DIABOLIQUE." with Pamela Scanford, Korine Gambier, Jack Taylor.
Plot to have man "return from the dead" to scare heroine.

SWEENEY TODD (B) Taffner-TV/Thames-TV 1971 color 76m. Ref: TVFFSB: from the Pitt-Hazelton play. with Freddie Jones.

SWEET SUGAR Crest/Dimension 1972 color 86m. D: Michel Levesque. SP: Donald Spencer. Story: R.Z. Samuel. Mus: Don Gere. Ref: MFB'76:34-5. LAT 6/16/72. with Phyllis E. Davis, Ella Edwards, Timothy Brown, Cliff Osmond, Pamela Collins.
Voodoo priest; "mass grave of murdered workers" (MFB); mad doctor's "aphrodisiacal shock treatment"; drug that turns cats into "mini-jaguars"; "cannibalistic torture expert."(LAT)

SWEET SUZY see BLACKSNAKE

SWIAT GROZY see WORLD OF HORROR

SYMPTOMS (B) Bryanston/Finiton 1974('76-U.S.) color 91m. (The BLOOD VIRGIN-B) SP,D: Joseph Larraz. SP: also Stanley Miller. Ph: Trevor Wrenn. Mus: John Scott. AD: K. Bridgeman. Ref: MFB'76:132,153. '77:249. V 4/7/76:16(ad). with Angela Pleasence, Peter Vaughan, Lorna Heilbron, R. Huntley.
Mad "spectral heroine....REPULSION territory." (MFB)

SYNTHETISCHER FILM, ODER WIE DAS MONSTER KING KONG VON FANTASIE & PRAEZISION GEZEUGT WURDE (W.G.) Herbst-SDK 1975 color

86m. SP,D: Helmut Herbst. Ph: R. Deppe, J. Hergersberg. Graphics: Michael Ruediger. Ref: V 10/3/75.
A history of special effects in films; Cohl, Melies, O'Brien, etc.

SYSTEM OF DR. TARR AND PROFESSOR FETHER,The(by E.A.Poe) see DR. TARR'S TORTURE DUNGEON. SYSTEME, Le.

Le SYSTEME (Pol) 1971 D: Janusz Majewski. From Edgar Allan Poe's story "The System of Dr. Tarr and Professor Fether." Ref: Daisne. Cinef Smr'73:37. with Jerzy Przybylski, Irena Szczurowska.

TV OF TOMORROW MGM 1953 anim color 7m. D: Tex Avery. SP: Heck Allen. Anim: Michael Lah et al. Ref: MFB'76:115. LC. Adamson/TA: stock with Dave O'Brien. J.Shapiro: broadcast from Mars.

TAGO (Swed) SFI 1977 anim color 16m. D: G. Ekholm. Ref: Zagreb 78: alien lands on Earth.

TAKE OFF Mature 1978 color 104m. SP,D,P: Armand Weston. SP: also Daria Price. From Oscar Wilde's book "The Picture of Dorian Gray." Ph: Joao Fernandez. Mus: Elephant's Memory. AD: J. Lawless. OptFX: Videart. Ref: MFB'79:155. screen. with Wade Nichols(Darrin Blue), Georgina Spelvin, Leslie Bovee, Annette Haven, Holly Woodlawn; Vanessa Del Rio?
Man remains young while his film-image ages; he finally ages, and young woman takes his non-aging place. Blue un-ages gracefully as Cagney (in the 30s), Bogart (40s), and Brando (50s), and there's some amusement in the Bogart (CASABLANCA/ TO HAVE AND HAVE NOT) section, little elsewhere.

TALE OF THE PIG(by Creanga) see STORY OF LOVE

TALES FROM BEYOND THE GRAVE or TALES FROM THE BEYOND see FROM BEYOND THE GRAVE

TALES FROM THE CRYPT (U.S.-B) Cinerama/Metromedia-Amicus 1972 color 92m. D: Freddie Francis. SP: Milton Subotsky. From comic-book stories by Al Feldstein, Johnny Craig, William Gaines. Ph: Norman Warwick. Mus: Douglas Gamley. AD: Tony Curtis. Mkp: Roy Ashton. Ref: MFB'72:196. screen. Lee. VV 3/30/72. V 3/8/72. with Ralph Richardson, Joan Collins, Ian Hendry, Chloe Franks, Frank Forsyth, Peter Cushing, Robert Hutton, Richard Greene, Barbara Murray, Patrick Magee.
Five stories (plus framing story re: hell) involving a murderous "Santa," premonitions, a living dead man, a man wished back to life (after being injected with embalming fluid), and vengeful blind men. The first two stories and the framing story are vapid; and all five are just punch-line stories. But punch line #3 is funny, #4 is ghoulishly amusing,

and #5 is well-contrived. Roughly 20 salvageable minutes.

TALES OF MYSTERY AND IMAGINATION see SPIRITS OF THE DEAD

TALES OF PILOT PIRX(by S.Lem) see TEST PILOT PIRX

TALES OF THE HAUNTED: EVIL STALKS THIS HOUSE Barry & Enright/ Global-TV/Gaylord 1981 color 120m. D: Gordon Hessler. SP: Louis M. Heyward. Ph: John Whyle et al. AD: Dan Yarhi. Sp FX: Warren Keillor. Mkp: Leslie Haynes. Host: Christopher Lee. Ref: TV. V 12/31/80:28-9(ad): avail. as 5-part mini-series or as TV-movie. with Jack Palance, Frances Hyland, Helen Hughes.

Witches' coven; evil-exorcising sacrifice which leaves man mindless; quicksand. Drab, humorless melodrama.

TALES THAT WITNESS MADNESS (B) Para/World Film 1973 color 90m. (WITNESS MADNESS-B) D: Freddie Francis. SP: Jennifer Jayne (aka Jay Fairbank). Ph: N. Warwick. Mus: B. Ebbinghouse. AD: Roy Walker. Ref: Lee. NYT 11/1/73. VV 11/22/73. no MFB. V 10/31/73. Brit.Film & TV Ybk. with Kim Novak, Joan Collins, Jack Hawkins, Donald Houston, Georgia Brown, Donald Pleasence.

Four stories, re: cannibalism; imaginary (or real) tiger; evil portrait; "shapely tree stump."

TALL SHADOWS OF THE WIND (Iran.) Telfilm-IBFC 1978? 110m. (SAIEHAIEN BOLANDE BAD) SP,D: Bahman Farmanara. SP: also Hushang Golshiri, from his novel "The First Innocent." Ph: A. Zarindast. Mus: Ahmad Pejman. Ref: IFG'80:189. V 5/16/79. with F. Gharibian, S. Nikpour, H. Kasbian.

"Scarecrow seems to stomp around town at night." (V)

TAM LIN (B) (NTA-TV)/AI/Winkast 1971 color/scope 106m. (The DEVIL'S WIDOW-alt t. The DEVIL'S WOMAN-ad t) D: Roddy McDowall. SP: William Spier, from the poem "The Ballad of Tam Lin" by Robert Burns. Ph: Billy Williams. Mus: Stanley Myers. PD: Don Ashton. Ref: TVFFSB. MFB'77:121-22: "a horror film definitely to be seen." with Ava Gardner, Ian McShane, Richard Wattis, Cyril Cusack, Stephanie Beacham, Sinead Cusack.

"An ending not unworthy of The HOUNDS OF ZAROFF (aka The MOST DANGEROUS GAME) with Ian McShane being pursued through a misty forest by a pack of hell-hounds conjured by his own imagination." (MFB)

TAME RE CHAMPO NE AME KEL (India-Gujarati) Kanodia 1978 color 160m. D: Chandrakant Sangani. SP: Ramesh Mehta. Story: N. Sevak. Mus: Mahesh Naresh. Ref: Dharap. with Naresh Kumar, Snehalata, A. Joshi, Rajanibala.

"Vampire woman" marries man "on condition that they will never sleep together"; later, she lures potentate to "old palace where she burns him to death," then reveals her identity to her husband, "promising him to be his partner in the next birth."

TANGO THROUGH GERMANY (W.G.) Mommartz-ZDF 1980 color 90m. (TANGO DURCH DEUTSCHLAND) D,P: Lutz Mommartz. Ref: V 10/29/80. with Eddie Constantine, Maya Farber-Jansen.
"Film idol...Lemmy Caution...leaves a kind of museum as a resurrected mummy."

TANYA'S ISLAND (Can.) IFEX/Baker 1981 color 82m. D: Alfred Sole. SP,P: Pierre Brousseau. Ph: Mark Irwin. Mus: Jean Musy. AD: Angelo Stea. SpMkp: Rick Baker, Rob Bottin. Ref: V 5/13/81. Cinef Smr'80:24-31. with D.D. Winters, Richard Sargent, Mariette Levesque, Don McCleod(ape).
Model's erotic nightmare of rape-by-ape on remote island; clips from MIGHTY JOE YOUNG.

TARANTOLA DAL VENTRE NERO see BLACK BELLY OF THE TARANTULA

TARANTULAS: THE DEADLY CARGO CBS-TV/Landsburg 1977 color 94m. D: Stuart Hagmann. SP: J. Groves, G. Trueblood. Ph: Robert Morrison. Mus: Mundell Lowe. AD: Raymond Beal. SpFX: Roy Downey. Mkp: Mike Germaine. Ref: TV. TVG. with Claude Akins, Charles Frank, Deborah Winters, Bert Remsen, Pat Hingle, Howard Hesseman.
Plane crash unleashes hoard of deadly Ecuadorian wandering, or banana, spiders ("the most aggressive and venemous in the world"); they hie to an orange-processing warehouse in search of insects, then are lured out of the orange crates, immobilized by the amplified sounds of spider-wasps, and drowned in alcohol. A long way to go for pickled arachnid. At one point an expert insists that these are not tarantulas; hence the title (like the movie) is a mistake. The strain to turn a rather peculiar ecological problem into a horror/disaster movie shows.

*TARGET EARTH 1954 Story: James Nicholson, Wyott Ordung. Mus: Paul Dunlap. SpFX: David Koehler. SpPhFX: Howard Anderson. Ref: TV. and with Mort Marshall, Robert Roark, Jim Drake.
Handful of people faces ray-shooting Venusian robots (operating on "electromagnetic impulses") in evacuated city; sound waves destroy robots' cathode-ray tubes. Likably tawdry sf-melodrama--familiar melo characters confront a very existential situation, yet keep their melo identities intact. Complete with the slightly worldly, expendable supporting couple (Richard Reeves and Virginia Grey), who represent an ideal of love-as-bickering.

TARGET...EARTH? Gold Key-TV/Film Farm 1980? color 90m. D,P, Ed: Joost van Rees. SP,P,Ed: Iris van Rees. Mus: Joe Levine. SpFX: Patrick Filos(sp?), Claudia Hagayanagi(sp?). Other FX: Ray Trail. Models: Rick Overton. Laser: Laservision. Ref: TV. GKey. with Victor Buono, Overton(Ino, the computer); Isaac Asimov, Carl Sagan.
Some guy in a space station and a garrulous computer hash over human response to the great Siberian meteorite explosion of 1908; female aliens. Not easy to watch.

TARGET EARTH see UFO TARGET EARTH

TARTS, The see WORST CRIME OF ALL, The

TARZAN AND KING KONG (India-Hindi) Amrit 1965 D: Shamsheer. Mus: Robin Banerji. Ref: "Indian Filmography." Lee: 1963? with Mumtaz, Randhwa, Bela Bose.

TARZAN AND THE GREEN GODDESS see NEW ADVENTURES OF TARZAN

TARZAN AND THE LEOPARD WOMAN RKO 1946 75m. D,P: Kurt Neumann. SP: Carroll Young. Ph: Karl Struss. Mus: Paul Sawtell. PD: Phil Paradise. Ref: TV. Lee. V 2/13/46: natives who "dress up in leopard skins with iron claws." with Johnny Weissmuller, Brenda Joyce, Johnny Sheffield, Acquanetta, Edgar Barrier, Dennis Hoey, Anthony Caruso, Tommy Cook, Doris Lloyd.

Caravans attacked by "something like leopard that isn't leopard"; attempted sacrifice of "living hearts" of maidens to leopard god; native boy plotting to cut out Jane's heart. Despite the horrific overtones, this is a typical Hollywood-and-vines actioner. Joyce is bland as Jane; but Acquanetta!--so beautiful, but so unconvincing a leopard person! That charmer Cheetah actually has a bigger role than she does. And, well, he is more convincing (if not as pretty).

TARZAN AND THE LOST GODDESS or TARZAN IN GUATEMALA see NEW ADVENTURES OF TARZAN

TARZAN--SHAME OF THE JUNGLE see SHAME OF THE JUNGLE

TARZAN THE TIGER Univ 1929 serial 15 episodes silent D: Henry McRae. SP: Ian Heath, from Edgar Rice Burroughs' novel "Tarzan and the Jewels of Opar." Ph: Wilfred Cline. Ref: LC. Lee. with Frank Merrill, Sheldon Lewis, Natalie Kingston.

Lost city "populated by ugly beastmen." (Lee)

TARZAN'S NEW ADVENTURE see NEW ADVENTURES OF TARZAN

TARZOON, SHAME OF THE JUNGLE see SHAME OF THE JUNGLE

*TASTE THE BLOOD OF DRACULA 1970 95m. SP: Anthony Hinds(aka J. Elder). AD: Scott MacGregor. SpFX: Brian Johncock. Mkp: Gerry Fletcher. Ref: TV. Glut/TDB. Lee. and with Anthony Korlan, Linda Hayden, Isla Blair(vampire).

Hinds does to Dracula what he did to Frankenstein in FRANKENSTEIN CREATED WOMAN. The latter's witless, supernatural-revenge plot is recapitulated here, as Dracula (imitating the young woman in the Frankenstein) takes on a mere-mortal gang of three--insert, periodically, close-ups of Christopher Lee helpfully announcing "The first!", "The second!", "The Third!" (as, one by one, he dispatches them). Thank heavens there weren't 87. Just about the dimmest in the long line of generally-dim Hammer Draculas.

TECHNO-CRACKED MGM 1933 anim 6m. Ref: Maltin/OMAM. LC. "Flip the Frog builds a robot...." (Blackhawk)

TEDDY see PIT,The(1980)

TEEN KANYA see THREE DAUGHTERS

TELEFON UA/MGM/James B.Harris 1977 color 103m. D: Don Siegel. SP: Peter Hyams, Stirling Silliphant, from Walter Wager's novel. Ph: Michael Butler. Mus: Lalo Schifrin. PD: Ted Haworth. SpFX: Joe Day. Ref: MFB'78:54-5. V 12/14/77. TV. with Charles Bronson, Lee Remick, Donald Pleasence, Tyne Daly, Alan Badel, Patrick Magee, Sheree North, John Hambrick.

Remote-control Russian saboteurs are activated by phone, their mission implanted by drug-induced hypnosis many years ago. Limp spy-suspense intrigue is really just a few premises in search of a plot. Siegel apparently hasn't heard of ellipsis (i.e., storytelling)--he shows each phone-activation sequence (not just the first one) in complete, superfluous detail. Daly has a small but pleasing role as a CIA computer whiz. Remick has her moments too, but someone should have placed a wake-up call to Bronson.

TELEPATHY 2000 see SCANNERS

TELEVISION see MAGIE MODERNE

The TELL-TALE HEART (B) Film Alliance 1953 20m. SP,D: J.B. Williams. From Edgar Allan Poe's story. Ph: Basil Emmett. Mus: Hans May. Ref: BFC: "horror." with Stanley Baker(Poe).

See also: EVENING OF EDGAR ALLAN POE,An. HEARTBEAT. LEGEND OF HORROR. VERRATERISCHE HERZ,Das.

TEMNE SLUNCE see BLACK SUN

TEMPTER, The see ANTI-CHRIST, The

TEN LITTLE INDIANS (B-Sp-G-I-F) Avco Embassy/Filibuster & Talia & Corona & Oceania & Comeci 1975 color 98m. D: Peter Collinson. SP,P: Harry Alan Towers. From Agatha Christie's novel. Ph: F. Arribas. Mus: Bruno Nicolai. Ref: MFB'76:23. Willis/SW. V 2/26/75. 5/7/75:243. with Oliver Reed, Richard Attenborough, Elke Sommer, Gert Froebe, Stephane Audran, Herbert Lom, Orson Welles(voice), C. Aznavour, A. Celi, M. Rohm.

Eight strangers isolated and threatened with death by mysterious host/voice at Persian hotel.

The TENANT (F & Eng.-lang.versions) Para/Marianne(Para) 1976 color 126m. (Le LOCATAIRE) SP,D: Roman Polanski. SP: also Gerard Brach. From Roland Topor's novel "Le Locataire Chimerique." Ph: Sven Nykvist. Mus: Philippe Sarde. PD: Pierre Guffroy. SpPh: Louma. SpPhFX: Jean Fouche. Ref: screen. V 6/2/76. 5/12/76:278. PFA. MFB'76:193: "distorting lenses and clutching hands emerging from the decor...make The TENANT and REPULSION look like the His and Hers of mental derangement." with Polanski, Isabelle Adjani, Shelley Winters, Melvyn Douglas, Jo Van Fleet, Lila Kedrova, Claude Dauphin.

It's not surprising that Polanski would want to re-work REPULSION as a starring vehicle for himself--as a director he's quite adept at capturing the dream-like inextricability of paranoia. His hero here is in a horrible mental mess which just gets worse and worse. And while the overall conception of the film may be unremarkable, many of Polanki's scenes and images are fresh, imaginative, comically pointed--e.g., the "opera" finale; the nightmare sequence (with the man pushing the Marlboro pack at him); the mysteriously missing pieces of spilled garbage. The extra 20 minutes simply make The TENANT a sort of diluted REPULSION.

TENDER DRACULA, Or THE CONFESSIONS OF A BLOOD DRINKER (F) Scotia American/Renn-FCF-VM-AMLF 1974('75-U.S.) color 98m. (TENDRE DRACULA, Ou LES CONFESSIONS D'UN BUVEUR DE SANG. La GRANDE TROUILLE. FRANKENSTEIN'S DRACULA-ad t?) D: Pierre Grunstein. SP: Justin Lenoir. Ph: Jean-Jacques Tarbes. Ref: Glut/TDB. Murphy. J.Shapiro. V 9/21/77:6. 8/28/74. Willis/SW. with Peter Cushing, Alida Valli, Bernard Menez, Miou-Miou.

Vampire-movie actor (Cushing) lives like vampire in old castle.

TENDER FLESH see WELCOME TO ARROW BEACH

TENDERNESS OF THE DAMNED (Sp?) 1981? anim D: J.-M. Costa. Ref: V 7/1/81:30: from Hugo's "Notre Dame de Paris"?

Post-holocaust future; gargoyle; skeletons.

TENDERNESS OF THE WOLVES (W.G.) Monument/Tango 1973('77-U.S.) color 83m. (ZARTLICHKEIT DER WOLFE) D: Ulli Lommel. SP & AD: Kurt Raab. Ph: Jurgen Jurges. Mus: Bach et al. P & with: R.W. Fassbinder. Ref: MFB'76:133. V 7/18/73. Willis/SW. with Raab, Jeff Roden, Margit Carstensen, Brigitte Mira, Ingrid Caven, Irm Hermann, Jurgen Prochnow.

The Depression. Police informer Fritz Haarmann secretly seduces and vampirizes boys and sells their remains as meat.

TENDRE DRACULA see TENDER DRACULA

TENTACLES (U.S.-I) AI/A.Esse(O.Assonitis) 1977 color/Technovision 102m. (TENTACOLI) D: Sonia Assonitis(aka O.Hellman). SP: Jerome Max et al. Ph: Roberto D'E. Piazzoli;(underwater) N. Ungaro;(fx) G.K. Major. Mus: S.W. Cipriani. AD: M. Spring. Mkp: J.L. Mecacci. Ref: TV. MFB'77:129-130. V(d) 6/15/77. Bianco #2/77:163-4. with John Huston, Shelley Winters, Henry Fonda, Bo Hopkins, Delia Boccardo, Cesare Danova, Claude Akins.

Monster-octopus terrorizes inhabitants of Southern California coastal towns. Interminable "suspense," as false alarms alternate with real ones. The next-best-thing-to-non-existent script has all it can handle simply establishing, (a) the mere presence of the octopus and, (b) the imminence of a sailboat race--(c), or suspense, does not, it transpires, automatically result.

TENTACLES OF THE NORTH(by J.O.Curwood) see SNOW DOG

The TERMINAL MAN WB 1974 color 104m. SP,D,P: Mike Hodges. From Michael Crichton's novel. Ph: R.H. Kline. Mus: Bach. AD: Fred Harpman. Mkp: Leo Lotito Jr., Fred Williams. Ref: V 5/29/74. TV: THEM! on TV. with George Segal, Joan Hackett, Richard Dysart, M.C. Gwynne, Jill Clayburgh, Ian Wolfe.

In order to quell his uncontrollable rages, doctors implant a set of 40 electrodes in the brain of a man (Segal) suffering from para-epilepsy; his body adapts by forcing "continuous stimulations," or repetitions, of the seizure-sensation cycle, making him act "like he was some kind of machine" that periodically erupts in violence. Or, A Clockwork Banana. The dry, low-key, Bach-backed approach is right; but the script is, polemically, simplistic. It makes an open-and-shut case against science's tampering in the brain's domain--the grim, grim ending, in particular, plays like an approximation of the sound of a prosecuting-attorney's briefcase loudly snapping shut. And the absorbingly methodical, "scientific" presentation of the operation is too glibly undercut by anti-science details of characterization and dialogue.

TERMITES FROM MARS Univ/Lantz 1953 anim color 6m. D: Paul Smith. Ref: TV. LC. Lee.

Woody Woodpecker besieged by alien insects.

TERRA HE (J) Toei 1980 anim 119m. SP,D: Hideo Onchi. Ref: JFFJ 13:35: space opera. V 5/13/81:258.

TERRIBLE THREE,The(by C.A.Robbins) see UNHOLY THREE,The

The TERRIBLE TWO IN LUCK (B) Phoenix 1914 13m. SP,D: James Read. Ref: BFC. no Lee. with Joe Evans, Read.

"Ghosts" and treasure.

TERRIBLE VENGEANCE, The see VIJ,The(1914)

TERRIBLY STRANGE BED,A(by W.W.Collins) see WORLD OF HORROR

TERROR (B) Crown Int'l/Crystal-Bowerg(r)ange 1978 color 86m. D: Norman J. Warren. SP: David McGillivray. Story & Ph: Les Young. Story: also Moira Young. Mus: Ivor Slaney. AD: Hayden Pearce. Mkp: Robin Grantham. Ref: Boxo 7/16/79:15. FM 165:4. V 12/19/79. MFB'79:102. with Carolyn Courage, John Nolan, Sarah Keller, James Aubrey, Milton Reid.

Filmmaker's film tells family history of witch burned 300 years ago; her curse lingers into the present.

TERROR AT RED WOLF INN see TERROR HOUSE(1972)

TERROR BEYOND THE STARS Wellig Int'l.-Kyowa 1978 SP: Burr Middleton. Ref: V 5/17/78:112. HR. B.Warren. with John Lawrence, Carol Byron.

TERROR CASTLE see FRANKENSTEIN'S CASTLE OF FREAKS

TERROR CIRCUS Enter Media/CMC-Pacific 1973 color 86m. (BARN OF THE NAKED DEAD-'76 Twin World t) D: Alan Rudolph. SP: Roman Valenti, Ralph Harolde. Story,P: Gerald Cormier. Ph: E. Lynn. Mus: Tommy Vig. AD: Bill Conway. SpFX & Mkp: Byrd Holland, Douglas White. Ref: screen. Willis/SW. V 8/15/73: 17(rated). 4/25/73. with Andrew Prine, Manuella Thiess, Sherry Alberoni, Gil Lamb.

Nevada. Mad young man whose mother left him keeps women chained as "circus animals" in his barn; keeps his father--turned into a "monster" by H-bomb testing--in outhouse. Embarrassingly cheesy horror flick never recovers from its outre premises. Horror and pathos on or about the level of TEENAGE MONSTER. The monster-father slashes half the cast to death yet still seems rather extraneous.

TERROR EYES (B?) 1981 (NIGHT SCHOOL-alt t) D: Ken Hughes. Ref: V 5/27/81:38: "chiller." 8/26/81:18.

TERROR FROM WITHIN (B) ABC-TV/ITC-TV 1974 color 74m. (WON'T WRITE HOME, MOM--I'M DEAD-orig t) D: James Ormerod. SP: Dennis Spooner. Story: Brian Clemens. Mus: Laurie Johnson. Ref: TV. TVG. TVFFSB. with Pamela Franklin, Ian Bannen, Suzanne Neve, Oliver Tobias, Dallas Adams.

Young woman (Franklin) has telepathic link with dead man, nightmare-vision of his death. The usual nothing-happens-till-the-last-10-minutes ITC un-thriller.

TERROR HOUSE Intercontinental/Red Wolf(Macready) 1972(1976) color 83m. (The FOLKS AT RED WOLF INN-orig t. TERROR AT RED WOLF INN-alt t) D: Bud Townsend. SP: Allen J. Actor. Ph: John McNichol. Mus: Bill Marx, AD: Mike Townsend. Opt: Modern. SdFX: Richard Harrison. Ref: TV. TVFFSB. Willis/SW. V 7/14/76:3. 11/22/72. 3/31/76:24. with Linda Gillin, John Nielson, Mary Jackson, Arthur Space, Janet Wood, M.Macready.

Cannibalism; severed-heads-in-freezer in old house run as halfway house by elderly couple. The air is thick--too thick--with irony, in this effectless variation on "Arsenic and Old Lace." This tale of two sweet old cannibals isn't funny, scary, or even-vaguely resonant, just glibly ironic, right down to the twist ending. A couple cute moments, and Gillin is very good at "sweet and naive"--too good to make the tables-turned ending credible.

TERROR IN THE WAX MUSEUM Cinerama/Crosby-Fenady 1973 color 94m. D: Georg Fenady. SP: Jameson Brewer. Story: A.J. Fenady. Ph: W. Jurgensen. Mus: George Duning. PD: Stan Jolley. Mkp: Jack H. Young. Ref: MFB'74:55. screen. V 5/23/73. with Ray Milland, Elsa Lanchester, Broderick Crawford, Maurice Evans,

John Carradine, Louis Hayward, Patric Knowles, Don Herbert (Jack the Ripper), George Farina(Bluebeard), Steven Marlo (Karkoff, hunchback), Lisa Lu, Peggy Stewart, Shani Wallis.

Ripper model in Victorian London wax museum/chamber of horrors appears to come to life and kill (ex-actor with life-like masks behind it all); wax-models-to-life in nightmare seqs. Flat-footed, plot-heavy mystery-horror. Interesting only as a sort of "curtain call" for several venerable actors who have, at one time or another, appeared in a horror movie (or, in the case of Carradine, it seems, every horror movie).

TERROR OF DR. CHANEY see MANSION OF THE DOOMED

TERROR OF FRANKENSTEIN see VICTOR FRANKENSTEIN

TERROR OF GODZILLA see GODZILLA'S REVENGE

TERROR OF MECHAGODZILLA (J) UPA & The Mechagodzilla Co./Toho Eizo 1975 color/scope 83m. (MEKAGOJIRA NO GYAKUSHU. aka REVENGE OF MECHAGODZILLA. MONSTERS FROM AN UNKNOWN PLANET-B) D: Ishiro Honda. SP: Yukiko Takayama. Sequel to GODZILLA VS. THE COSMIC MONSTER. See also: GODZILLA. Ph: M. Tomioka. Mus: Akira Ifukube. AD: Y. Honda. SpFX: T. Nakano. OptFX: Y. Manoda. MechFX: T. Watanabe. Ref: TV. MFB'76:128,222. Glut/CMM. V 10/22/75:115. with K. Sasaki, Tomoko Ai, Akihiko Hirata, Kenji Sahara.

Alien-built Mechagodzilla; remote-controlled Titanosaurus; supersonic wave oscillator; woman restored to life as cyborg; flashback montage (by Bansbach & McCann) with Spiega, Ebirah, Ghidrah; flying saucer. Despite a welter of past-and-present-tense monsters (inc. a split-screen flashback to Rodan & co.) and some outre details (e.g., the aliens install Mechagodzilla's brain in the cyborg's stomach), this is one of the less-delightful Godzillas. The dubbing ("Damned Earthmen!" "Go, Titanosaurus!") is actually more amusing than the monster battles. (Highlight of latter: Godzilla decapitating Mechagodzilla.) There's also pathos, of a sort: "Katsura, you're a cyborg, but I still love you!"

TERROR OF SHEBA (B-U.S.) Blueberry Hill/Tyburn & Fanfare 1974 ('75-U.S.) color 96m. (PERSECUTION-B) D: Don Chaffey. SP: R.B. Hutton & Rosemary Wootten, from their story "I Hate You Cat!" Ph: Ken Talbot. Mus: Paul Ferris. AD: Jack Shampan. Ref: MFB'74:227: "tawdry & tedious." CineFan 2:42. Willis/SW. V 4/9/75:21(rated). 11/13/74. with Lana Turner, Ralph Bates, Trevor Howard, Olga Georges-Picot, Suzan Farmer, Ronald Howard.

"Does the cat Sheba, one wonders, possess devilish powers, and is Carrie a kind of Cat Person?" (MFB)

TERROR OF THE KIRGHIZ see HERCULES, PRISONER OF EVIL

TERROR OUT OF THE SKY CBS-TV/Landsburg-Kirshner 1978 color 94m. D: Lee H. Katzin. SP: Guerdon Trueblood, Doris Silverton. Ph: Michel Hugo. Mus: William Goldstein. AD: Alan Panser. SpFX:

Allen L. Hall. Mkp: Dee Manges. Opt: Westheimer. Sequel to The SAVAGE BEES. Ref: TV. Maltin/TVM. with Efrem Zimbalist Jr., Tovah Feldshuh, Dan Haggerty, Ike Eisenmann, Steve Franken.

Ploys and strategies by National Bee Center officials, and bee counter-strategies, all culminating in a "suspense-filled" climax involving a killer-bee-plastered bus-full of boy scouts, a man in a queen-bee-scented diving-suit dangling from a helicopter, an abandoned missile base, and cannisters of anti-bee nerve gas. Ingenuity run amok.

TERROR TRAIN (Can.-U.S.) Fox/ABPP-Howard-Grodnik 1980 color 97m. D: Roger Spottiswoode. SP: T.Y. Drake. Ph: John Alcott. Mus: John Mills-Cock(r)ell. PD: Glenn Bydwell. SpFX: Josef Elsner. SpMkpCons: Alan Friedman. Ref: V 10/1/80. screen. MFB'80:244-45. with Ben Johnson, Jamie Lee Curtis, Timothy Webber, David Copperfield, D.D. Winters, Hart Bochner.

Mad, unkillable killer stalks masqueraders at graduation party on excursion train. Only the production gloss here helps to obscure the flimsiness of the script, which amounts to little more than "hommages" to The 39 STEPS, PSYCHO, HOMICIDAL, HALLOWEEN, etc. Logic is, perhaps, not of the essence, but when (in the latter half of the film) every narrative step seems false....A bit less random mystification and a bit more explanation might have been in order.

TERRORS (B) Smith 1930 47m. SP,D,P: Erle O. Smith. Ref: BFC. with Erle Smith Jr., Ronald Smith.

Boys tunnel to Australia, scare dinosaurs with bagpipes.

TEST PILOT PIRX (Pol) Zespoly Filmowe-Tallinnfilm 1979 color 104m. (TEST PILOTA PIRXA) SP,D: Marek Piestrak, based on the story collection "Tales of Pilot Pirx" or "Opowiescio Pilocie Pirxie" by Stanislaw Lem. Ph: Janusz Pawlowski. Mus: Arvo Part. AD: J. Sniezawski, W. Zilko. Ref: V 8/15/79:"beautifully done." IFG'79:274. with Sergei Desnitsky, Boleslaw Abart, Vladimir Ivashov, Zbigniew Lesien.

"Finite non-linears," more-human-than-human robots, tested in space flight.

*The TESTAMENT OF DR. CORDELIER 1959 Ref: screen.

A case could be made for Jean Renoir's film as the best Mr. Hyde film--and, unfortunately, the worst Dr. Jekyll. While Jean-Louis Barrault's monstrous Opale seems an at-times-inspired creation, the non-Opale scenes are slack and static, just noise, hapless victims of Renoir's experiments with multiple mikes and cameras. Execution of course is all, but conception counts for something too: the Jekyll and Hyde characters here seem, at least, explicable--and believable--as one tormented soul. Renoir the scriptwriter underscores the continuity between doctor and monster, Cordelier's accountability for Opale's actions. The "liberated" Opale is really the inextricably-bound Opale-Cordelier; each is the despair of the other. The film is a failure, yet the script is true to the spirit of Stevenson's Jekyll, a man nastily thwarted in his attempts to liberate his dual "selves," to find "a solution of the bonds of obligation."

TEUFLISCHEN SCHWESTERN see SWEDISH NYMPHO SLAVES

The TEXAS CHAIN SAW MASSACRE New Line/Bryanston/Vortex 1974 color/scope 81m. SP,D,Mus: Tobe Hooper. SP: also Kim Henkel. Ph: Daniel Pearl. Mus: also Wayne Bell. AD: Robert A. Burns. SpMkp: W.E. Barnes. Ref: screen. MFB'76:258: based on the PSYCHO material. V 11/6/74. Willis/SW. Photon 26:47-8(RVB). with Marilyn Burns, Allen Danziger, Gunnar Hanse(Leatherface), Paul A. Partain, William Vail.

A *reductio ad absurdum* of a horror movie which manages to keep a lady constantly in distress--at the mercy of a ghoulish, chain-saw-and-sledgehammer-wielding family--for over an hour (our time), with no diversions (for her or for the viewer). "Unrelenting" is a good word to use here....And yet the film *could* have been *more* harrowing: as it stands, there's surprisingly little blood-and-gore evident. Hooper's film has a weird sort of tact. The director trusts to his title and his hardware: you don't *see* what the awful chain saw does. You don't need to--all you need to know is how one works. *Hearing* is believing *here*. And yet this is still not exactly a *likable* movie. If there's such an animal as second-degree (implied) gore, this is it. Even the occasionally amusing, Clegg-like antics of the crazy family are really no relief--the film is informed by a pristine viciousness.

THAT ETERNAL PING-PONG (B) Hepworth 1902? D: Percy Stow. Ref: BFC. with May Clark.

Boy and girl playing table tennis in 1900 are still playing (as skeletons) in the year 2000.

THEATER OF BLOOD (B) UA/Cineman 1973 color 102m. (MUCH ADO ABOUT MURDER-orig t. THEATRE OF BLOOD-ad t) D: Douglas Hickox. SP: Anthony Greville-Bell. Ph: W. Suschitzky. Mus: Michael J. Lewis. PD: Michael Seymour. SpFX: John Stears. Mkp: George Blackler. Ref: MFB'73:132. screen. Lee. V 4/25/73. with Vincent Price, Diana Rigg, Ian Hendry, Harry Andrews, Robert Coote, Jack Hawkins, Robert Morley, Diana Dors, Milo O'Shea, Renee Asherson, Dennis Price, Michael Hordern.

Supposedly-dead Shakespearean actor (V.Price) wreaks brutal revenge on enemy critics. Determinedly grisly murders, bad double entendres (e.g., "one large cut"), and a perfunctory "grand finale." Sub-Phibes horror "fun."

THEN THE SCREAMING STARTS see --AND NOW THE SCREAMING STARTS!

*THERE ARE DEAD THAT *ARE SILENT* 1946 (HAY MUERTOS QUE NO HACEN *RUIDO*) Ref: Lee. "Hist.Cine Mex.": horror-comedy.

THERE IS A NAME FOR EVIL see NAME FOR EVIL, A

THERE ONCE WAS A WOMAN see REVENGE!

THERE SHALL BE NO DARKNESS(by J.Blish) see BEAST MUST DIE, The

THERE WAS ONCE A CHILD see SCARED TO DEATH(1980)

THERESE(by R.Matheson) see TRILOGY OF TERROR(1975)

THEY CAME FROM WITHIN (Can.) AI(Trans-American)/Cinepix-CFDC 1974('76-U.S.) color 87m. (The PARASITE MURDERS-Can. SHIVERS-B) SP,D: David Cronenberg. Ph: Robert Saad. Mus & P: Ivan Reitman. AD: Erla Gliserman. SpMkp: Joe Blasco. Ref: screen. MFB'76:62. V 3/24/76. with Paul Hampton, Lynn Lowry, Joe Silver, Barbara Steele.

"Experiments in the implantation of parasites...to correct bodily imbalances"; "parasite...a combination of aphrodisiac and venereal disease." (MFB) Funnier, thankfully, than Cronenberg's (similar) RABID, but, basically, just as hollowly efficient. He has a definite flair for the revolting detail, but it seems a rather minor talent, and one that he leans on too often, at least in this film and in RABID. He seems content, merely, with inventing new, indelicate ways for the sex parasites to enter and exit the human body. An aphrodisiac monster would seem, thematically, to be a promising subject; but the whole of THEY CAME FROM WITHIN hasn't the resonance of the one shot of the men filing into the female "monster" Mouna, in Fellini's CASANOVA. Victims accrue here; meaning doesn't. Nice, muted, downbeat ending, though.

**THEY DRIVE BY NIGHT (B) WB-FN 1938 84m. D: Arthur Woods. SP: Derek Twist, Paul Gangelin, James Curtis, from Curtis's novel (source also of 1940 THEY DRIVE BY NIGHT). Ref: BFC. screen. Everson. MFB. with Emlyn Williams, Ernest Thesiger, Anna Konstam, Allan Jeayes, Ronald Shiner.

The latter half of the first THEY DRIVE BY NIGHT is an engaging study in abnormal psychology, with Thesiger as a balmy killer exulting in his "researches into the crepuscular recesses of the mind." For his own amusement and edification, he holds a man (Williams) captive in an old house. The first half of the movie is familiar crime-chase melodrama. But both halves are well-acted and directed. Thesiger brings a Pretorius-like sense of dotty, fey malevolence to his delivery of such disarming lines as "Come and help me feed the kittens."

THEY SHALL OVERCOME Savage 1974 color 70m. D,P: Peter Savage. Mus: Bruce Roberts. Ref: V 1/22/75:41(ad). 1/1/75: footage from LOVELAND. with Linda Lovemore, Jennifer Jordan.

Doctor's remote-control pills turn takers into "hot human animals."

THEY'RE COMING TO GET YOU! (I-Sp) Indep.-Int'l./Lea & C.C. Astro 1972('76-U.S.) color 90m. (sfa Una STRANA ORCHIDEA CON CINQUE GOCCE DI SANGUE?) D: Sergio Martino. SP: Gastaldi, Scavolini. Ph: M.F. Mila. Mus: Bruno Nicolai. AD: Galicia, Cubero. Ref: Meyers: demon cult; sanitarium. Willis/SW. Lee(p). Bianco Index'73: sfa TUTTI I COLORI DEL BUIO? V 5/3/72:

175: TODOS LOS COLORES DE LA OSCURIDAD. with Edwige Fenech, George Hilton, Susan Scott, Paola Quattrini, Ivan Rassimov, Marina Malfatti, Julian Ugarte, Alan Collins, G. Rigaud.

*The THIEF OF BAGDAD UA 1924 120m. Mus: Mortimer Wilson. AD: also Irvin J. Martin. MechFX: Hampton Del Ruth. Cost: Mitchell Leisen. Ref: screen. AFI. and with Julanne Johnston, Noble Johnson.

Dragon; giant bat; giant water-spider; living tree; "magic army"; magic life-restoring apple; prophetic sands; cloak of invisibility. Florid, occasionally amusing, but mainly long. Douglas Fairbanks' stunts and feats of ingenuity comprise the light and lively first third; romance clogs the middle; and episodic flights of fantasy round out the movie. Scheherazade would have been dispatched after half an hour of such storytelling. There is, however, one nice, romantic strophe (apart from the lovely flying-carpet finale): the thief's double reaction to his first glimpse of the princess--a dismissive laugh, then a more considered, puzzled look.

The THIEF OF BAGDAD (B-F) Palm & Victorine 1978 color 102m. D: Clive Donner. SP: A.J. Carothers. Adap: Andrew Birkin. Ph: D. Lewiston. Mus: John Cameron. AD: Edward Marshall. VisFX: John Stears, Dick Hewitt. Mattes: Ray Caple. SpFX Sup: Allan Bryce. Ref: MFB'79:102-3. TVG: TV-movie in U.S. with Roddy McDowall, Peter Ustinov, Terence Stamp, Kabir Bedi, Frank Finlay, Marina Vlady, Ian Holm, D. Emilfork.

The evil Wazir Jaudur keeps his soul hidden in a crystal guarded by a monster-bird and is thus invincible.

THING IN THE ATTIC, The see GHOUL,The(1975)

The THING WITH TWO HEADS AI/Saber 1972 color 86m. (MAN WITH TWO HEADS-orig t. BEAST WITH TWO HEADS-int t) SP,D: Lee Frost. SP,P: Wes Bishop. SP: also J.G. White. Ph: J. Steely. Mus: R.O. Ragland. SpMkp: Dan Striepeke, Tom Burman et al. Ref: MFB'74:285. screen. Lee. Medved/TGTA. V 7/19/72. with Ray Milland & Rosey Grier(the thing), Don Marshall, Roger Perry, Chelsea Brown, Roger Gentry, Rick Baker(gorilla), Phil Hoover.

Head of bigot doctor transplanted to black man's neck. Film is amusing when treating its patently ludicrous situation lightly; less successful when trying straight comedy.

*THINGS TO COME (B) UA/London 1936 113m. (The SHAPE OF THINGS TO COME-orig t) SpFX:(ph) Edward Cohen;(asst) Lawrence Butler. Ref: TV. Lee.

See also: H.G.WELLS' THE SHAPE OF THINGS TO COME.

THIRD FROM THE SUN (Bulg.) Brandon/Bulgarfilm 1973 color 124m. (TRETJA OT SONTSA) D: Georgi Stoyanov. SP: Pavel Vezhinov. Ph: I. Trenchev. Mus: Kiril Dontchev. Ref: Brandon. Ecran 73(Jan.,p23). V 7/25/73: at Trieste. with Dobrinka Stnakova, Ivan Mikolaitchuk, Iziak Fintzi.

Three stories. "Eden": "beneficent aliens." "The Stranger":

"alien who can control matter." "My First Day": "future society"; time travel. (Brandon)

THIRST (Austral.) New Line/F.G. 1979 color 98m. D: Rod Hardy. SP: John Pinkney. Ph: V. Monton(sp?). Mus: Brian May. AD: J. Dowding, J. Eden. SpFX: Conrad Rothman. Ref: IFG'80:61. Boxo 12/31/79:29. V 12/26/79: from "Instant Terror" series. with David Hemmings, Henry Silva, Chantal Contouri.
  Dairy-farm-like vampire cult.

THIRST OF BARON BLOOD, The see BARON BLOOD

The THIRSTY DEAD Rochelle/Int'l.Amusements 1974(1979) color 96m. (The BLOOD CULT OF SHANGRI-LA-orig t) D: Terry Becker. Ph: Nonong Rasca. Ref: Boxo 7/23/79:21. Willis/SW. pr. V 11/13/74:12(ad). 8/1/73:25. 4/18/73:18(rated). B.Warren. with John Considine, Jennifer Billingsley, Tani Gutherie, Judith McConnell.
  "Vampire" cult that subsists on blood; "crones," disfigured victims whose blood has been drained; rat pit; man's head kept alive by blood 500 years; man who ages and dies instantly.

THIS HOUSE POSSESSED ABC-TV/Mandy 1981 color 95m. D: William Wiard. SP,P: David Levinson. Mus: Billy Goldenberg. SpFX: Art Brewer, David Blitstein. OdFX: Cohn. Ref: TV. TVG. with Parker Stevenson, Lisa Eilbacher, Shelley Smith, Joan Bennett, Slim Pickens, K.Callan, John Dukakis.
  A neurotic, ultra-modern, solar-powered house stops at nothing to keep the woman it loves snugly inside it; bleeding shower, exploding mirror and fireplace, overheated pool, crushing gates. This strangely sentient house is rather over-protective of its beloved (Eilbacher). In fact it's sick--it murders half-a-dozen people. And it has better closed-circuit-camera coverage than George Burns did--love is at least not _blind_ here, just dumb.

THOSE CRUEL AND BLOODY VAMPIRES see ALEGRES VAMPIROS DE VOGEL

THREE DAUGHTERS (India-Bengali) Janus/Kino Int'l/Chhayabani 1962 165m. (TEEN KANYA. aka THREE WOMEN. ***MONIHARA-segment shown separately. TWO DAUGHTERS-U.S., 114m., sans "Monihara") From three stories by R. Tagore.
  "Monihara, or the Lost Jewels" 51m. SP,D,P,Mus: Satyajit Ray. Ph: Soumendu Roy. AD: B.C. Gupta. Ref: screen. Seton/SR. TVFFSB. AFI. with Kali Bannerjee, Kanika Mazumdar, K.Roy.
  Near the haunted Saha mansion, a schoolmaster tells the 30-year-old story of Monihara, a mad woman, returning from the dead to claim (with skeletal hand) her necklace. Enjoyable, deliberately-paced ghost story. If it's a bit long for an anecdote, its high points are worth waiting for: the paranoid wife opening her sari to reveal inside her entire store of jewelry ("Now they'll have to kill me to get them"); the husband asking the mysterious figure approaching his bed at midnight, "Moni, have you come back?" (a headshake, _no_).

THREE FREAKS,The(by C.A.Robbins) see UNHOLY THREE,The

3 ON A MEATHOOK see MAD BUTCHER,The

THREE WOMEN see THREE DAUGHTERS

THREE'S A CROWD WB 1933 anim 7m. D: R. Ising. Ref: Glut/ CMM: March's Jekyll-and-Hyde aped. LC. Maltin/OMAM.

THRESHOLD (Can.) Paragon 1981 color 106m. D: Richard Pearce. SP: James Salter. Ph: Michel Brault. Mus: M. Erbe,M. Solomon. SpDes: Dr.Robert Jarvis. Ref: V 9/23/81. with Donald Sutherland, John Marley, Sharon Ackerman, Jeff Goldblum, Mare Winningham, Michael C. Gwynne.

Mechanical-heart transplant; "graphically illustrated" operation; "mad scientist."

THUNDERBIRD 6 (B) A.P.-Century 21 1968 marionettes color/ scope 90m. D: David Lane. SP,P: Gerry & Sylvia Anderson. Sequel to THUNDERBIRDS ARE GO. Mus: Barry Gray. AD: Bob Bell. SpFX: Derek Meddings. Ref: BFC: "new skyship." Lee(MFB'68: 122). Voices: Peter Dyneley, Shane Rimmer, John Carson.

***THUNDERBIRDS ARE GO A.P. 1966 marionettes color/scope 94m. D: David Lane. SP: G. & S. Anderson. Mus: Barry Gray. SpFX: Derek Meddings, S. Whittaker-Cooke. Ref: Lee. Voices: P. Dyneley, Neil McCallum, S. Rimmer.

Sequels: REVENGE OF THE MYSTERONS FROM MARS? THUNDERBIRD 6. THUNDERBIRDS TO THE RESCUE.

THUNDERBIRDS TO THE RESCUE (B) (HBO-TV)/ITC 1980 marionettes color 91m. D: Alan Pattillo, Desmond Saunders. SP: G. & S. Anderson, Martin Crump. Sequel to THUNDERBIRDS ARE GO. Ph: John Read. Mus: Barry Gray. AD: Bob Bell. SpFX:(sup) Derek Meddings;(d) Brian Johnson;(ph) Michael Wilson. Ref: TV. TVG. Voices: Peter Dyneley, Shane Rimmer.

Sabotage on Fireflash, atomic aircraft; space station; thorium beam converter; moon base; stilted dialogue. ("And however it turns out, thanks!")

THUNDERCRACK Thomas Bros. 1976 150m. D,Story,Ph,SpFX,Ed: Curt McDowell. SpFX,SP,Mkp,with: George Kuchar. Story,Mus,SpSd FX: Mark Ellinger. Ref: V 4/7/76. VV 12/31/80. MFB'80:245. with Marion Eaton, Melinda McDowell, Mookie Blodgett.

"Old dark house"; gorilla; "the horror is funny" (VV); revamping of HOUSE ON HAUNTED HILL; storm; "monstrously swollen genitalia"; man's remains pickled. (MFB)

La TIA ALEJANDRA (Mex) Conacine 1980? color SP,D: Arturo Ripstein. SP: also D. Careaga et al. Ph: J.O. Ramos. Mus: L.H. Breton. Ref: IFG'81:220. with D. Bracho, I. Corona.

"Story of witchcraft and satanism."

TICKLE ME AA 1965 color/scope 90m. D: Norman Taurog. SP: E. Ullman, E. Bernds. AD: Pereira, Lonergan. Ref: TV. AFI. LC.

TVG. with Elvis Presley, Julie Adams, Bill Williams, John Dennis, Francine York, Grady Sutton, Allison Hayes.
Sequence set in restored ghost-town's old hotel, which is "haunted" by "ghost" in rocking chair, one man in skull-mask, another in werewolf-type mask. "Bowery Boys"-level comedy.

TIDAL WAVE (J) New World/Toho 1974('75-U.S.) color/scope 93m. (113m.) (NIPPON CHINBOTSU. The SUBMERSION OF JAPAN-ad t) D: Shiro Moritani;(U.S.) Andrew Meyer. SP: Shinobu Hashimoto; (U.S.) Meyer. From Sakyo Komatsu's book. Ph: H. Murai, D. Kimura;(U.S.) Eric Saarinen. Mus: Masaru Sato. AD: Y. Muraki. SpFX: Teruyoshi Nakano;(seqs) T. Watanabe. OptFxPh: T. Miyanishi. Ref: TV. V 5/22/74. LAT. NYT 9/16/75. Bianco Index'74: 1973? with Keiju Kobayashi, Tetsuro Tamba, Lorne Greene, Rhonda Leigh Hopkins, Marvin Miller, Susan Sennett.
Continental drift/growth in the Earth's core/shifts in the Earth's crust in the Japan Trench (choose one or all of the above) sink Japan; 34 million evacuated; undersea quakes unleash tidal wave. "Why is this happening to Tokyo?" Good question; bad movie. This is like a compilation of the dullest parts of Godzilla movies--mass destruction, panic, evacuation plans. But (sigh!) no monsters....Note: the original Japanese version is reported to be somewhat more coherent.

TIEH PIEN See BUTTERFLY MURDERS, The

T'IEH-SHAN KUNG-CHU SHEN-HUO P'O T'IEN-MEN (H.K.?) 1961? Based on "Hsi-Yu Chi." Ref: Eberhard.
Spider ghost and four girl-ghosts.

TIEMPOS DUROS PARA DRACULA (Sp-Arg) Aitor & Espacio 1976 D: Jorge M. Darnell. Ref: V 5/11/77:420,114. 3/31/76:47. IFG '77:66. with Jose Ruiz Lifante, Miguel Ligero, Maria Noel, Adolfo Linvel, Alfonso De Grazia.
The Count's grandson "returns to his native land." (IFG)

TIGER FANGS (Picturmedia-TV)/PRC 1943 58m. D: Sam Newfield. SP: Arthur St. Claire. Ph: Ira Morgan. Mus: Lee Zahler. AD: Paul Palmentola. Ref: TV. TVFFSB. Bill Warren. MPH 9/25/43. V 12/1/43. FD. LC. with Frank Buck, June Duprez, Duncan Renaldo, Howard Banks, J.Farrell MacDonald, Pedro Regas.
Rubber-plantation workers in the Far East attribute a series of 27 killings to "T'jindaks." (Heroine: "It's so horrible! And all this talk about T'jindaks--humans taking on tiger forms with a lust for blood like werewolves or vampires!") In reality, the culprits are just plain old tigers, driven mad by a synthetic, blow-dart-delivered drug concocted by mad Nazi toxicologist Dr. Lang (Arno Frey), who is trying to slow down production. In perhaps the first Lewton-imitation sequence in a horror movie, a panther (at one point) menaces June Duprez in her (shadow-filled) bedroom. One villain (Dan Seymour) is trampled to death by a herd of maddened stock-footage elephants. (Very rare species except in "B" movies--this may, in fact, be the same herd that turns up in

The WHITE GORILLA.) And Dr. Lang is killed by one of his own darts. (Fitting, isn't it?) (See FQ Fall'77:66 for a note on the use of the freeze-frame in the latter scene.)

'TIL DEATH DO US PART see BLOOD SPATTERED BRIDE, The

TILL DEATH Cinema Shares Int'l/Cougar(Pamstock) 1978 color 80m. D,P: Walter Stocker. SP: Gregory Dana. Mus: Chuck Rains, Jim Ed Norman? Ref: TVFFSB: "horror....bizarre chain of events." V 5/17/78:188(ad): "terrifying secret." Willis/SW. with Keith Atkinson, Belinda Balaski, Bert Freed.

TIME AFTER TIME WB/Orion(Jaffe) 1979 color/scope 112m. SP,D: Nicholas Meyer. Story: K. Alexander, S. Hayes. Ph: Paul Lohmann. Mus: Miklos Rozsa. PD: E.C. Carfagno. SpFX: Larry Fuentes, Jim Blount. Opt: Pacific. Ref: MFB'80:13. TV. V 9/5/79. with Malcolm McDowell, David Warner(Stevenson, aka Jack the Ripper), Mary Steenburgen, Charles Cioffi, Patti D'Arbanville, Clete Roberts, Shelley Hack.

H.G. Wells (McDowell) follows Jack the Ripper--through the former's solar-powered time machine--from the London of 1893 to the San Francisco of 1979. Big thoughts on violence (Jack in '79: "Today I'm an amateur"--echoing Chaplin's Verdoux in '47) and love (H.G. in '79: "Every age is the same--it's only love that makes any of them bearable"), and small jokes on Hari Krishna, McDonald's, and current slang. Oh, it's not all bad--Steenburgen's quiet aggressiveness is very taking, and Rozsa provides a better score than the movie deserves. But, boy, is some of it bad.

TIME BANDITS (B) Avco Embassy/HandMade 1981 color 113m. SP, D,P: Terry Gilliam. SP & with: Michael Palin. Ph: Peter Biziou. Mus: Mike Moran;(songs) George Harrison. PD: Millie Burns. SpFX:(sup) John Bunker;(tech) Ross King. Models: Val Charlton;(ph) J. Doyle. OptFX: Kent Houston et al. Mattes: Ray Caple. Trolls: Ray Scott. Ref: MFB'81:163. V 7/22/81. with John Cleese, Sean Connery, Shelley Duvall, Ian Holm, Ralph Richardson, Peter Vaughan(ogre), David Warner(evil genius), Ian Muir(giant).

Minotaur; invisible wall; Castle of Ultimate Darkness; "spectres"; dwarf-into-pig; "time holes." (A)

TIME KILLER, The see NIGHT STRANGLER, The

The TIME MACHINE NBC-TV 1978 color 94m. From H.G. Wells' novel. Ref: TVG. with John Beck, Priscilla Barnes, John Hansen, Rosemary De Camp, Whit Bissell, A.Duggan, Parley Baer.

Witch-burning; future war between Elois and Morlocks.

TIME OF THE EAGLE Easy 1977 (cf The DEVIL'S CLONE(P)) D: Bill Dial. Ref: V 4/13/77:30. 12/8/76:40.

"A plot by Nazis to return to power through the use of black magic and the occult."

The TIME OF THE VAMPIRE (Yugos) Film Images/Zagreb-Dunav 1970 color 9m. (VRIJEME VAMPIRA) SP,D: Nikola Majdek. SP: also R. Munitic. Mus: V. Kostic. Ref: FI News #1. Murphy. Lee. IFG'72:388,397.
Vampires make "midnight visits" to graveyard. (IFG)

TIME SLIP (J) Toei/Kadokawa 1981 color 139m. (SENGOKU JIEITAI) D: Kosei Saito. SP: Toshio Kaneda, from Ryo Hanmura's book. Ph: Isayama. Mus: Kentaro Haneda. SpFX: H. Suzuki. Ref: V 2/4/81. 5/7/80:451(ad). JFFJ 13:34: Toho? with Sonny Chiba, Isao Natsuki, Miyuki Ono.
Japanese soldiers transported to 16th Century; "graphic bloodletting." (V)

TIME TRAVELERS ABC-TV/Fox-TV & Irwin Allen 1976 color 74m. D: Alex Singer. SP: Jackson Gillis. Story: Allen, Rod Serling. Mus: Morton Stevens. AD: Eugene Lourie. Ref: TV. TV Season. TVFFSB. V 3/24/76:54. with Sam Groom, Tom Hallick, Richard Basehart, Francine York, Baynes Barron, Walter Burke.
Time travel from 1976 to 1871, the time of the Chicago fire.

TIMEWARP see DAY TIME ENDED, The

TINTIN ET LE LAC AUX REQUINS (F-Belg) Dargaud & Leblanc 1972 anim color 80m. D,P: Raymond Leblanc. Based on the Herge characters. Ref: V 1/10/73. Lee.
"Machine that duplicates anything"; "underwater empire."(Lee)

TINTORERA (B-Mex) United Film/Hemdale & Tint-Mex, Conacine 1977 color 88m. SP,D: Rene Cardona Jr. SP: also Ramon Bravo, from his novel. Adap: C. Schuch. Ph: L. Sanchez. Mus: Basil Poledouris. Sets: J. Rodriguez, J. Saenz. SpFX: Miguel Vazquez. Ref: MFB'77:199: "JAWS with sex." AMPAS. with Susan George, Hugo Stiglitz, Andres Garcia, Fiona Lewis.

TIYU WU-MEN see WE'RE GOING TO EAT YOU

TO KILL A CLOWN (B) Fox/Palomar 1972 color 82m. SP,D: George Bloomfield. SP: also I.C. Rapoport. From Algis Budrys' story "Master of the Hounds." Ph: Walter Lassally. Mus: R. Hill, J. Hawkins. AD: Trevor Williams. Titles: T. Taylor. Ref: MFB'72:260. TVG. with Alan Alda, Blythe Danner, Heath Lamberts, Eric Clavering.
Crippled Vietnam war veteran's "Prison Game" (involving two horrific Dobermans and a kookie young couple) is played in earnest. Basically pointless study of complementary quirks of couple and cripple. Amusing at times as a sort of "get the guests" comedy, but no "Virginia Woolf." Alda and his snarling dogs make a pretty scary act.

TO LET (B) Harma 1919 22m. D: James Reardon. SP: Reuben Gillmer. Ref: BFC.
"Retired conjuror tries to scare couple from his house."

TO THE DEVIL A DAUGHTER (B-W.G.) Cine Artists/EMI/Hammer & Terra Filmkunst 1976 color 93m. D: Peter Sykes. SP: Christopher Wicking, from Dennis Wheatley's novel. Adap: John Peacock. Ph: David Watkin. Mus: Paul Glass. AD: Don Picton. SpFX: Les Bowie. Mkp: E. Allwright, G. Blackler. Ref: MFB'76:64. V 3/10/76. TV. with Richard Widmark, Christopher Lee, Honor Blackman, Denholm Elliott, Michael Goodliffe, Nastassia Kinski.

Eighteen-year-old girl (Kinski) proves to be daughter of god Astaroth, needing only baptism in the god's blood to become "Astaroth incarnate on Earth." (MFB) Fairly exciting black-magic thriller recalls Hammer's earlier Wheatley adaptation The DEVIL'S BRIDE. This one centers on "the absolute capability of man"--catastrophe, and is unoriginal but fun. It's Widmark (as occult-novel writer John Verney) and friends vs. heretical priest Lee and disciples, and an ugly little critter which is apparently Astaroth.

TOD DE FLOHZIRKUSDIREKTORS see DEATH OF THE FLEA CIRCUS DIRECTOR

TODESMAGAZIN see DEATH MAGAZINE

TODOS LOS COLORES DE LA OBSCURIDAD see THEY'RE COMING TO GET YOU

The TOM MACHINE (B) NFS 1981 color 47m. SP,D: Paul Bamborough. Ph: S. Radwanski. Mus: Benedict Mason. AD: Eric Parry. Ref: V 4/29/81. with Donald Sumpter, Pamela Moiseiwitsch, John Cleese(robot's voice).

"Robot maid....mechanized future."

TOM THUMB (F) Mannic-UP-Parc-Francos 1972 color 80m. (Le PETIT POUCET) D: Michel Boisrond. SP: Marcel Julian, from Perrault's fairy tale. Ph: D. Gaudry. Mus: Francis Lai. AD: R. Giordani. SpFX: Marc Geffrault. Ref: V 12/27/72. 5/9/73: 110. Cinef Smr'73:39. with J.-P. Marielle(ogre), Jean-Luc Bideau, Marie Laforet, Titoyo.

Ogre tricked into eating his own children.

TOMB OF THE UNDEAD see GARDEN OF THE DEAD

TOMBS OF THE BLIND DEAD (Sp-Port.) Hallmark(AI)/Plata & Interfilme 1972('73-U.S.) color 86m. (La NOCHE DEL TERROR CIEGO. CRYPT OF THE BLIND DEAD-ad t? The BLIND DEAD-alt t) SP,D: Amando De Ossorio. Ph: P. Ripoll. Mus: A.G. Abril. AD: J.D. de Brito. SpFX: J.G. Soria. Mkp: J.L. Campos. Ref: MFB'73:150. Cinef III:2:31. Lee. Willis/SW. V 11/15/72:31(ad). 7/19/72:5(rated, as NIGHT OF THE BLIND DEAD). with Lone Fleming, Cesar Burner, Joseph Thelman, Rufino Ingles.

Mummified, blood-drinking Knights Templar return from the dead.

Sequels: HORROR OF THE ZOMBIES. NIGHT OF THE SEAGULLS. RETURN OF THE EVIL DEAD.

TOMBSTONE CANYON World Wide(KBS) 1932 62m. D: Alan James. SP: Claude Rister, Earle Snell. Ph: Ted McCord. Mus D: Val Burton.

Ralph M. DeLacy, Eddie Boyle. Ref: Turner/Price. FQ Smr'80: 54. LC. with Ken Maynard, Cecilia Parker, Sheldon Lewis(the phantom), Frank Brownlee, Bob Burns, Lafe McKee, G. Chesebro.
"Weird cry" of "grotesque Phantom" haunts Tombstone Canyon.

TOMEI NINGEN--OKASE see LUSTY TRANSPARENT MAN

The TOMORROW MAN (Can.) Mega-Media 1980 color 78m. (Through the Eyes of Tomorrow series) D: Tibor Takacs. SP: S. Zoller, P. Chapman. Ref: Boxo 1/21/80. FM 161:77. V 10/17/79:182(ad). with Don Francks, Stephen Markle, Gail Dahms, David Clement.
Futuristic North American New Regime.

**TONIGHT'S THE NIGHT (B) Anglofilm 1954 color 91m. (HAPPY EVER AFTER-B) D,P: Mario Zampi. SP: M. Pertwee, J. Davis. Ph: S. Pavey. Mus: Stanley Black. AD: Ivan King. Ref: SFC. BFC. TV. J.Shapiro. Lee. with David Niven, Yvonne de Carlo, Barry Fitzgerald, George Cole, Robert Urquhart, Liam Redmond.
Haunted Irish castle with two fake ghosts and one real one.

The TOOLBOX MURDERS Cal-Am 1977 color 95m. D: Dennis Donnelly. SP: Neva Friedenn et al. Ph: Gary Graver. Mus: George Deaton. PD: D.J. Bruno. Ref: MFB'80:53: "shabby affair." V 5/17/78:114(ad). with Cameron Mitchell, Pamelyn Ferdin, Wesley Eure, Tim Donnelly, Aneta Corsaut.
Series of murders with power drill, hammer, nail-gun, etc.

*TOOMORROW Sweet Music 1970 scope AD: Archer, Davey. SpFx Ph: Ray Caple, Cliff Culley. Ref: Lee(MFB). & with R.Dotrice.

TORE NG DIYABLO (Fili) Santiago 1969 D: Lauro Pacheco. SP: Jose F. Sibal, from the comic by Nela Morales. Mus: Pablo Vergara. Ref: Lee. Glut/TDB/CMM. with Jimmy Morato, Pilar Pilapil, Rodolfo Garcia(werewolf), Ramon D'Salva(vampire).

TORMENTED, The see EERIE MIDNIGHT HORROR SHOW, The

TORSO (I) Brenner/CCC 1973 color 90m. (I CORPI PRESENTANO TRACCE DI VIOLENZA CARNALE) SP,D: Sergio Martino. SP: also E. Gastaldi. Ph: G. Ferrando. Mus: M.& G.De Angelis. AD: G. Burchiellaro. Ref: MFB'75:132. Willis/SW. V 11/13/74. with Suzy Kendall, Tina Aumont, John Richardson, Luc Meranda.
"Horror opus": masked killer; dismembered bodies. (MFB)

TORTURE CHAMBER OF BARON BLOOD see BARON BLOOD

TOSHO DAIMOSU (J) Toei-Y&K-TV Asahi 1979 23m. D: Y. Takanami. Ref: JFFJ 13:34: based on TV show; "robot superhero."

TOURIST TRAP Compass Int'l/Manson Int'l(Band) 1979 color 85m. SP,D: David Schmoeller. SP: also J.L. Carroll. Ph: Nicholas Von Sternberg. Mus: Pino Donaggio. AD: Robert Burns. SpFX: Richard O. Helmer. SpMasks: Ve Neill et al. SpSdFX: Joel Goldsmith. Ref: V 3/21/79. MFB'81:36: telekinesis. with Chuck

Connors, Joe Van Ness, Jocelyn Jones, Robin Sherwood.
"Dummy"-creatures terrorize teenagers at country museum.

TOWARDS ANDROMEDA (J) Toei 1981 anim feature Ref: V 10/14/81:195: "sci-fi."

TOWER OF EVIL see HORROR ON SNAPE ISLAND

*TOWER OF LONDON 1939 92m. Mkp: Jack Pierce. Ref: TV. Lee. with Donnie Dunagan, C. Montague Shaw, Walter Tetley.
Not really a horror movie, though it sounds like one: the score is lifted (largely) from SON OF FRANKENSTEIN. Boris Karloff's imposing presence as the executioner also suggests horror. And Basil Rathbone (as Richard III) and Ian Hunter are a good, rather sinister sibling team. (Rathbone's unsmiling implacability and Vincent Price's drunken exaltation make the cask-of-malmsey sequence the film's one fine one.) But Hunter dies early, Rathbone is often offscreen, and Karloff is just punctuation. That leaves only actors like (God forbid) John Sutton, Barbara O'Neil, and Nan Grey. And much of the movie is simply a dull procession of deaths and marriages.

*TOWER OF LONDON 1962 Mus: Michael Andersen. AD: Daniel Haller. SpFX: Modern. Mkp: Ted Coodley. Dial D: F.F. Coppola. Narr: Paul Frees. Ref: TV. AFI. Lee. and with Sandra Knight, Eugene Martin, Morris Ankrum.
Richard III (Vincent Price) haunted by ghosts of victims, hallucinations; fiery oracle; premonitions; torture by rat and rack. "B"-movie Shakespeare. Roger Corman certainly maintains as busy a stage as the Bard, if not as elevated a plane of speech. (Richard: "You talk of e-vil?!") No sooner do the bodies of his victims fall than they rise again, as accusing ghosts. The two best scenes: the boy-ghosts beckoning Richard to join them...beyond the castle parapets. And Richard's "I am the King!" counterpointing the ghostly laughter assailing him as he asserts himself on the throne. A bit less music and a bit more wit would have helped immeasurably.

The TOWN THAT DREADED SUNDOWN AI 1977 color/scope 90m. D,P & with: Charles B. Pierce. SP & with: Earl E. Smith. Ph: Jim Roberson. Mus: Jaime Mendoza-Nava. AD: M. Teeter, G. Sinclair. SpFX: Joe Catalanatto. Ref: V(d) 1/19/77. MFB'77: 130: "script that founders hopelessly on the simplest pieces of exposition." with Ben Johnson, Andrew Prine, Dawn Wells.
Hooded phantom (Bud Davis) terrorizes town of Texarkana.

*The TOY BOX 1971 AD: Nelson Cooper. Mkp: Dennis March. Ref: screen. FFacts. Lee. with Evan Steele, Marsha Jordan, Lisa Goodman, Deborah Osborne, Ann Myers.
Outre, bizarre, etc., but to no end--weird for weird's sake. Music effects lifted from INVADERS FROM MARS.

TOY FACTORY, The see NECROMANCY(1972)

TOYLAND PREMIERE Univ/Lantz 1934 anim color 6m. Ref: Glut/TFL. LC. Maltin/OMAM.
Frankenstein-monster toy comes to life.

TRACK OF THE MOONBEAST Brandon/Derio 1976(1972) color 90m. SP: William Finger, Charles Sinclair. Ref: Brandon. TVFFSB. Lee(p). with Chase Cordell, Donna Leigh Drake, Patrick Wright.
Exposure to lunar-fragment shower causes mineralogist to transform into "lizard-like beast each night at moonrise." (Brandon)

TRAIN RIDE TO HOLLYWOOD Arista/CJFC(Billy Jack) 1975 color 85m. (NIGHT TRAIN-orig t) D: Charles Rondeau. SP: Dan Gordon. Mus: Pip Williams. Ref: V 1/8/75:74. 11/5/75. 10/14/81:41(ad). with "Bloodstone," Jay Lawrence, Roberta Collins, Jay Robinson, Tracy Reed.
"Funeral with Count Dracula dancing in a deserted western street."

TRAITEMENT DE CHOC see SHOCK TREATMENT

TRANSPLANTE A LA ITALIANA see MAN WITH THE BRAIN GRAFT

TRAPALHOES NA GUERRA DOS PLANETAS (Braz) 1978 Ref: V 3/25/81: 75.

TREACHERY AND GREED ON THE PLANET OF THE APES see NEW PLANET OF THE APES, The

TREASURE OF THE PIRANHA see KILLER FISH

TRETJA OT SONTSA see THIRD FROM THE SUN

TRIANGLE...THE BERMUDA MYSTERY or TRIANGOLO DELLE BERMUDE or TRIANGULO DIABOLICO DE LAS BERMUDAS see BERMUDA TRIANGLE, The(1978, I-Mex)

The TRIBE ABC-TV/Univ-TV 1974 color 74m. D: Richard A. Colla. SP: Lane Slate. Mus: David Shire. Narr: Paul Richards. Ref: TVFFSB. V 12/18/74:48. TV Season. with Victor French, Henry Wilcoxon, Adriana Shaw.
Cro-Magnon Man vs Neanderthal Man.

*TRILBY Republic 1915 60m. SP: James Young. AD: Ben Carre. Ref: screen. S&S'80:49.
Feeble version of the Svengali saga is simply blandly-illustrated titles. Funny bit: Trilby lapsing into her natural, God-awful singing voice, after Svengali (Wilton Lackaye) dies. Lackaye's melo-villain posing for the camera gets to be more than a bit much.

TRILBY BY PIMPLE & CO. see ADVENTURES OF PIMPLE--TRILBY

TRILOGY OF TERROR ABC-TV/Curtis-ABC Circle 1975 color 72m. D,P: Dan Curtis. SP: "Julie" by William F. Nolan, from Richard

Matheson's short story "The Likeness of Julie." "Millicent and Therese" by Nolan, from Matheson's short story "Therese." "Amelia" by Matheson, from his short story "Prey." Ph: Paul Lohmann. Mus: Robert Cobert. Puppet Master: Erik M. Von Buelow. Ref: TV. TV Season. Cinef III:2:17: shot for TV series (unsold) "Dead of Night." with Karen Black(all four story-title roles), Robert Burton, John Karlin, George Gaynes.

"Julie": "witch" possesses student's mind; vampire movie at drive-in; ref. to Jonathan Harker. "Millicent and Therese": very advanced case of schizophrenia. "Amelia": hideous Zuni spirit-doll comes to life, attacks young woman, finally possesses her. The first two stories are, at best, negligible, all hackneyed themes and predictable twists. The Matheson-scripted "Amelia," however, is a funny-scary joy. The tiny terror--in the tradition of the 1936 DEVIL DOLL and BEAST WITH FIVE FINGERS--makes sounds like cat-screeches run backwards, and covers ground in Amelia's apartment like a possessed squirrel, or a malefic Speedy Gonzales. It has monster-teeth and a sour disposition--and it doesn't believe in time-out. (The last shot--of the possessed Amelia--is both colossally silly and strangely eerie. It seems half-miscalculated.) Kinetic excitement!

TRIO INFERNAL see INFERNAL TRIO

TROIS HISTOIRES EXTRAORDINAIRES D'EDGAR POE see SPIRITS OF THE DEAD

Le TROISIEME CRI (Swiss) Niddam 1974 color 90m. SP,D,Ph: Igaal Niddam. Ref: V 8/28/74. 7/31/74:34. with Jacques Denis, Leyla Aubert, Roland Mahandan.

Survivors of atomic war hide in "gigantic bomb shelter."

The TROUBLE WITH 2B (B) CFF/Balfour 1972 color 6-film series (c.18m. each) D: P.K. Smith. SP: David Ash. Sequel to *JUNKET 89. Mus: J. Hodge. Ref: MFB'72:173-4. with John Blundell, Stephen Brassett, Linda Robson.

School science-master invents "instant happiness spray," strength potion, truth elixir, youth elixir, growth spray.

The TROUBLESOME DOUBLE (B) (JED-TV)/CFF/Interfilm 1971 color 57m. D: Milo Lewis. SP: Leif Saxon, Brigit. Sequel to *EGGHEAD'S ROBOT. Mus: Gordon Langford. Ref: MFB'72:196-7. TVFFSB. with Keith Chegwin, Julie Collins, Richard Wattis.

Electronics whiz-kid makes robot double of his sister.

The TROUBLESOME FLY Biog 1902 1m. Ref: LC. Lee.

Giant fly bites man.

TRUE LIFE OF DRACULA see VLAD TEPES

TSEKLOPUT see CYCLOPS(1976)

TUMBA DE LA ISLA MALDITA see CRYPT OF THE LIVING DEAD

TUNNELVISION Worldwide/Int'l Harmony-Woodpecker Music 1976 color 75m. SP,D: Neil Israel. D: also B. Swirnoff. SP: also M. Mislove. Ph: Don Knight. Mus: D. Lambert, B. Potter. AD & Anim: C.D. Taylor. Ref: Filmex'76. V 4/7/76. with Chevy Chase, William Schallert, Phil Proctor, Howard Hesseman.
Satire of TV, set in 1985.

TUO VIZIO E UNA STANZA CHIUSA... see EXCITE ME

The TURN OF THE SCREW ABC-TV/Dan Curtis 1974 color 136m. D: Curtis. From Henry James' novella. Ref: TVFFSB. with Lynn Redgrave, Megs Jenkins, Eva Griffith, Jasper Jacob.
See also: OTHERS, The.

TUT-TUT AND HIS TERRIBLE TOMB (B) Butcher 1923 25m. D: Bertram Phillips. SP: Frank Miller. Ref: BFC. with Queenie Thomas, Frank Stanmore.

TUTTI I COLORI DEL BUIO see THEY'RE COMING TO GET YOU!

TUYUL see LITTLE DEVIL

The TWELVE TASKS OF ASTERIX (F) Dargaud-Goscinny-Idefix 1976 color anim 82m. (Les DOUZE TRAVAUX D'ASTERIX) SP,D: Rene Goscinny, A. Uderzo. Mus: Calvi, Nicolas. Ref: MFB'78:43-4. V 11/17/76.
Gaul, 50 B.C. Magician's spell; Cave of the Beast; Plain of Departed Spirits; Madhouse of Bureaucracy.

2076 OLYMPIAD Aragon 1977(1975) color 90m. SP,D,P: James R. Martin. Ph: M. Whitaker. Mus: L.J. Ponzak. AD: S.M. Steiner. Anim: Fierlinger, Voisicy. Ref: V(d) 6/14/77. 4/30/75:6 (rated). with Jerry Zafer, Sandy Martin, Dean Bennett.
Comedy. The Olympics, year 2076.

2069: A SEX ODYSSEY (Austrian-W.G.) Burbank Int'l/Kopf & TIT 1974('77-U.S.) color 85m. (SEX ODYSSEY-B. ACH JODEL MIR NOCH EINEN--STOSS TRUPP VENUS BLAST ZUM ANGRIFF) D: H.G. Keil. SP: Willi Frisch. Ph: Marsalek, Mondi. Mus: Hans Hammerschmid. Ref: MFB'76:187. Meyers. with Nina Frederic, Catherina Conti, Heidrun Hankammer.
Space women from Venus arrive on Earth to collect "supply of male sperm to help repopulate their dying planet." (MFB)

20,000 LEAGUES UNDER THE SEA(by J.Verne) see AMAZING CAPTAIN NEMO, The

TWILIGHT PEOPLE (U.S.-Fili) (Worldvision-TV)/Dimension/New World-Four Assoc. 1972 color 84m. (ISLAND OF THE TWILIGHT PEOPLE-orig t) SP,D: Eddie Romero. SP: also Jerome Small. Ph: F. Conde. Mus: Avelino, Arevalo. PD: R.A. Formoso. Opt FX & Sets: R. Abelardo. Ref: screen. TVFFSB. Lee(V). TVG. with John Ashley, Pat Woodell, Pam Grier(panther woman), Eddie Garcia, Jan Merlin, Charles Macaulay, Ken Metcalfe.

Mad doc attempting to create super-race turns humans into half-animal creatures; Ape Man, Bat Man, Wolf Woman, etc. Silly sf-monster-movie, though the monsters are amusing to behold.

TWILIGHT TRAVELERS (I-Sp) Juppiter 1979 color D: Ugo Tognazzi. Ref: V 5/7/80:412. with Ornella Vanoni, C. Clery.
"Future world where youth dominates."

TWINS OF EVIL (B) Univ/Hammer 1972 color 87m. (The GEMINI TWINS-orig t. VIRGIN VAMPIRES-int t. TWINS OF DRACULA-Austral. t. DRACULA Y LAS MELLIZAS-Sp) D: John Hough. SP: Tudor Gates. Based on LeFanu's Carmilla character; sequel to The VAMPIRE LOVERS. Ph: Dick Bush. Mus: Harry Robinson. AD: Roy Stannard. SpFX: Bert Luxford;(ph) Jack Mills. Ref: TV. Glut/TDB. Lee(MFB'71:226). VV 8/10/72. with Peter Cushing, Katya Wyeth (Mircalla), Mary & Madelaine Collinson, Dennis Price, Isobel Black, Damien Thomas(Count Karnstein).

Blood-revived vampire-spirit Mircalla turns count into vampire; he in turn vampirizes one of set of psychically-bound twins; witch-hunting Brotherhood. Vampirism treated as a form of hedonism, or as an answer to boredom. The cast's uniformly over-exuberant acting gets to be a bit much. (Sample Cushing line: "The Devil has sent me <u>twins of evil</u>!") In an <u>old</u> Universal (HOUSE OF FRANKENSTEIN), a young lady with a morbid bent confesses "The darkness beckons to me"; here, the morbid twin Frieda confides to her sister "The storm is beautiful." The Lewtons, however, are better than either Universal at accounting for the Lure of Darkness.

TWISTED BRAIN (Gold Key-TV)/Crown Int'l/Jami(e)son/Horror High 1974 color 90m. (HORROR HIGH-orig t) D: Larry N. Stouffer. SP: Jack Fowler, from "The Strange Case of Dr.Jekyll and Mr. Hyde" by RLS. Ph: Janis Valtenberg. Mus: Don Hulette. AD: Joe Thompkin. SpFX: Jack Bennett. Ref: TV: J&H filmstrip. TVFFSB. Lee(p). Willis/SW. V 6/5/74:26. 1/23/74:3(rated). with Pat Cardi, John Niland, Austin Stoker, Joy Hash, J.Greene.

High-school lab-assistant's formula turns him into bowlegged monster; he slices up teacher who sliced up his biology report; in gym shoes, he stomps coach to death. Is this <u>supposed</u> to be funny? Boring-to-unwatchable.

TWITCH OF THE DEATH NERVE (I) Hallmark(AI)/NLC 1971('73-U.S.) color 90m. (ANTEFATTO. CARNAGE. **The ECOLOGY OF A CRIME-ad ts? BLOODBATH-B) SP,D,Ph: Mario Bava. SP: also McLee, Ottoni. Story: Sacchetti, Barberi. Mus: S. Cipriani. AD: S. Canevari. Ref: MFB'80:88: "mechanical in the extreme." Lee. Willis/SW. with Claudine Auger, Claudio Volonte, Luigi Pistilli, Leopoldo Trieste, Isa Miranda, B. Skay, Laura Betti.

Decapitation; mutilation; "assorted lurkers armed with axes, spears and billhooks." (MFB)

TWO DAUGHTERS see THREE DAUGHTERS

The TWO DEATHS OF SEAN DOOLITTLE ABC-TV/Clovis 1975 color 74m. D: Lela Swift. Ref: TVFFSB. with George Grizzard, G. Hall.
Doctor claims he can raise the dead.

The TWO FACES (India-Hindi) Film Finance/Kaul 1973('75-U.S.) color 82m. (DUVIDHA. TWO ROADS-alt t) SP,D: Mani Kaul. From a folk tale. Ph: Navrose Contractor. Mus: Ramzan Hammu et al. Ref: screen. PFA notes 11/20/77. Dharap. V 11/19/75. with Revi Menon, Raisa Padansee, Shambhudan, Hardan.
Ghost impersonates bridegroom while latter is away. Agonizingly-slow ghost story, though the core anecdote seems like it might be interesting.

TWO GOOFS IN OUTER SPACE see LIANG SHA TA-NAO T'AI-K'UNG

*TWO LOST WORLDS Sterling 1951 SP:(narration) Bill Shaw? Mus sc: Alex Alexander. SpFX: Jack Glass. Ref: V 1/31/51. TV. TVG. Lee. LC. and with Fred Kohler Jr., Pierre Watkin.
A Yankee sea captain (James Arness) and settlers from Queensland--hiding in a crevice on an island in the Dutch East Indies--watch the two "dinosaurs" from ONE MILLION B.C. fight; one woman systematically loses her clothes, the better to match the B.C. shot in which the cavewoman is engulfed by lava (for this film's own volcano sequence): Fate as a stock shot. Laughably ambitious shoestring "B" charms in its determined efforts to create everything--period romance, high-seas adventure, prehistoric epic--out of nothing. Bonus: a "lyrical" narration: "Grimly his eyes surveyed the glowering, desolate landscape." Or: "Children know no danger--the world is their playground."

The TWO MRS. CARROLLS WB-FN/Hellinger 1947(1945) 99m. D: Peter Godfrey. SP: Thomas Job, from Martin Vale's play. Ph: P. Marley. Mus: Franz Waxman. AD: Anton Grot. SpFX: Robert Burks. Ref: "WB Story." screen. NYT 4/7/47. LC. with Barbara Stanwyck, Humphrey Bogart, Alexis Smith, Nigel Bruce, Isobel Elsom, Ann Carter, Creighton Hale.
Psychopathic artist--who can get "nothing more" from his wife after painting her portrait as the ("creepy...frightening") "Angel of Death"--poisons her, plots to poison his second wife. (Though a "Yorkshire Strangler" newspaper headline gives him other ideas.) The Warners version of SECRET BEYOND THE DOOR..., but too tame to make it even as camp. Bogart and Stanwyck each get a nice exit shot, and he at least gets to warm up for TREASURE OF THE SIERRA MADRE, IN A LONELY PLACE, and The CAINE MUTINY, though here his mental disintegration is simply grist for pulp suspense (and thus seems more silly than sad or frightening).

*2+5: MISSION HYDRA (Gold Key-TV)/Monarch 1966('77-U.S.) color 90m. (STAR PILOT-U.S.) AD: G. Ramacci. Tech D: Ralph Zucker. Mkp: E. Santoli. Cost: Ditta Peruzzi. Ref: V 2/14/79:71(ad). 11/2/77:4,28. TV. TVG.
Hibernating robots; aliens with incinerating rays; photon

shower; planet of ape-monsters; spaceship of skeletons; spaceflight to constellation Hydra, polluted by Earth's post-holocaust radioactivity. Tights, bikinis, and miniskirts are the fashion for women for inter-galactic travel here. And it's hard to take the more serious aspects of this hodge-podge--a combination of sf, romance, action, and social comment--any more seriously than the women's clothes.

TWO ROADS see TWO FACES, The

***2,000 B.C. Educ 1931 Ref: LC. Maltin/OMAM.

TWO TOWERS,The(by J.R.R.Tolkien) see LORD OF THE RINGS

UFO--EXCLUSIVE! Gold Key-TV 1979? color 95m. (aka UFOMANIA?) Narr: Robert Morgan. Ref: TV. TVG. GKey.
Speculation re: UFOs and extraterrestrial life; simulated manned-voyage to Mars.

The UFO INCIDENT NBC-TV/Univ-TV 1975 color 93m. D & Exec P: Richard A. Colla. SP: S.Lee Pogostin, Hesper Anderson, from John G. Fuller's book "Interrupted Journey." Ph: Rexford Metz. Mus: Billy Goldenberg. AD: Peter Wooley. OptFX: Magicam. Ref: TV. TV Season. TVFFSB. with James Earl Jones, Estelle Parsons, Beeson Carroll, Lou Wagner.
Barney and Betty Hill undergo hypnotic psychoanalysis, recall being taken aboard an alien spacecraft in 1961. A pre-CLOSE ENCOUNTERS attempt to fuse scientific speculation and human drama. The question here, however, is "_Did_ it happen?" rather than "_Could_ it happen?" and is intriguing enough, but overshadowed by the personal story. Jones and Parsons are strong, intense, almost alarmingly so--they overwhelm one. Emotional acuteness finally becomes indistinguishable from emotional overkill--there's no dramatic balance. The two just take these Martians too _seriously_. Metaphysics becomes, simply, grist for the psychoanalytic mill. Some engaging, lighter moments.

UFO JOURNALS Gold Key-TV 197-? color 92m. Ref: GKey.
Flying-saucer data examined.

UFO SYNDROME Gold Key-TV/Transworld 1980 color 92m. D,P: Richard Martin. SP,P: Herbert L. Strock. SP: also Donna Ashbrook. Mus: Aminadav Aloni. Narr: Tony Eisley. Ref:TV. GKey.
Speculation re: flying saucers, government conspiracies.

UFO TARGET EARTH (Group IV-TV)/Centrum Int'l 1974 color 90m. (TARGET EARTH-orig t) SP,D,P: Michael A.de Gaetano. Ph: J. Crowder. SpFxD: Michael Elliston. Ref: TV. TVFFSB. Willis/SW. V 10/2/74:27(ad). 9/11/74:5. 7/31/74:5. 2/27/74:7: footage of Comet Kohoutek. 1/2/74:4. with Nick Plakias, Cynthia Cline,

LaVerne Light, Phil Erickson.
   Insufferably schlocky-serious, psychic-scientific investigation into energy forces that have "waited over 1,000 years" to accept our hero (Plakias) into their time stratum (he's only the fourth person to be accepted, it seems), in a 2001-influenced climactic sequence. I'm sure we all wish him well.

UFOS ARE REAL Group 1 1979 (ALIEN ENCOUNTER-alt t) SP,D: Ed Hunt. SP: also S.T. Friedman. Ref: B.Warren. V 12/5/79(rated). 5/7/80:336. (d) 5/1/79. Willis/SW.
   Semi-documentary. Sightings, pictures of aliens.

UFOS: IT HAS BEGUN Gold Key-TV/Sandler Institutional 1976 color 93m. (UFO'S, PAST, PRESENT AND FUTURE-orig t) D: Ray Rivas. SP,Mus: Robert Emenegger. Ph: Stan Lazar, Don Peterman. Narr: Rod Serling. SpFX: Robert Abel. Ref: TV. TVG. V 3/26/75:42. GKey. with Burgess Meredith, Jose Ferrer, Dr. Jacques Vallee.
   Reports and re-creations of UFO sightings.

UCHU KAIJU GAMERA see SUPER MONSTER GAMERA

UCHU KAIZOKU KYAPUTEN HAROKKU (J) Toie-TV & Asahi-TV 1978 anim scope 34m. D: Taro Rin. Story: Leiji Matsumoto (from his TV series). Ref: JFFJ 13:33.
   The adventures of Space Pirate Captain Harlock (guest star in GALAXY EXPRESS 999).

UCHU KARA NO MESSEEJI see MESSAGE FROM SPACE

UCHUSENKAN YAMATO see SPACE CRUISER

UDOLI VCEL see VALLEY OF BEES

*UGETSU MONOGATARI Janus 1953 From the stories "Asaji Ga Yado" ("The House in the Broken Reeds") & "Jasei No In" ("The Lewdness of the Female Viper"), as collected by Uyeda. Ref: screen. Sadoul-Morris/DOF. TVFFSB.
   UGETSU is a strange mix of the ghostly and the human, the poetic ("The best of silk, of choicest hue, does change and fade/as does my life") and the platitudinous ("War twisted all our ambitions"). And it's the living characters who are the more platitudinous--dead, they add extra dimensions (thematically as well as ectoplasmically) of loss and evanescence. It's almost as if director Kenji Mizoguchi and his writers required the perspective of a lost past,the better to vivify the poignance of the present--and through the characterizations of the phantom Lady Wakasa (Machiko Kyo) and the dead Miyagi (Kinuyo Tanaka) they gain it. Ideas blandly expressed in dialogue earlier ("The worth of things and people changes") are incarnated and _felt_ in the sequence in which the dead Miyagi sits quietly by her sleeping husband. (He does not yet realize that she's a ghost, like Lady Wakasa.) The film's themes of human transitoriness and blindness find resonance, finally, in Miyagi's sorrow and Lady Wakasa's desperation.

The UGLY LITTLE BOY (Can.) Highgate 1977? color 26m. D: Don Thompson, Barry Morse. From Isaac Asimov's story. Ref: PFA (Trieste pr). with Morse, Kate Reid.
Scientists resurrect Neanderthal boy.

The ULTIMATE IMPOSTOR CBS-TV/Univ-TV 1979 color 93m. D: Paul Stanley. SP & Exec P: Lionel Siegel. Ph: V.A. Martinelli. Mus: Dana Kaproff. AD: Lou Montejano. Ref: TV. V 5/16/79:98. TVG. with Joseph Hacker, Keith Andes, Macon McCalman, Erin Gray, Bobby Riggs, John van Dreelan.
The Red Chinese biochemically erase 90% of the memory of a captured American agent; his superiors then re-program him with an artificial memory (via electrical conversion of reels of computer data into "brain language"). Any super-hero fantasy which takes half its length just to establish its premise is in real trouble. Insipid.

The ULTIMATE WARRIOR WB 1975 color 94m. SP,D: Robert Clouse. Ph: G. Hirschfeld. Mus: Gil Melle. AD: W. Simonds. SpFX: Gene Grigg. SpPhFX: Van Der Veer. Ref: MFB'76:12. Meyers. Bianco Index'75. with Yul Brynner, Max von Sydow, Joanna Miles, William Smith, Richard Kelton.
2012 A.D., a world devastated by ecological disasters.

ULTIMO MONDO CANNIBALE see LAST SURVIVOR

ULTRA FLESH 1980 Ref: Cheri 3/80:57. J.Shapiro. with Seka, Jamie Gillis, John Leslie, Serena.
"Cold" alien being (Gillis) renders Earthmen impotent; "hot" alien, Ultra Flesh (Seka), unfreezes them, with vaginal rays; spaceship with alien monsters.

ULTRAMAN (J) Fuji Eiga/Tsuburaya-TV 1979 (UROTORUMAN) Ref: JFFJ 13:30: from TV-series footage.
See also: the following title, and KAETTEKITA ULTRA MAN. SIX ULTRA BROTHERS VS.THE MONSTER ARMY,Tne.

ULTRAMAN--MONSTER BIG BATTLE (J) Fuji Eiga/Tsuburaya-TV 1979 (UROTORUMAN--KAIJI DAIKESSEN) Ref: V 8/22/79:46: sf. JFFJ 13:30: from TV-series footage.

UMANOIDE, L' see HUMANOID, The

El UMBRACLE (Sp) 1970 short D: Pedro Portabella. Ref: Lee. Glut/TDB: vampire scene. with Christopher Lee, J. Mestres.

The UNCANNY (Can.-B) Cinevideo & Tor 1977 color 85m. (BRRR!-orig t) D: Denis Heroux. SP: Michel Parry; M. Subotsky? Ph: H. Waxman, J. Bawden. Mus: Wilfred Josephs. PD: W. Kroeger, H. Pottle. SpFX: Michael Albrechtsen. Ref: MFB'77:154: "drearily routine." V 5/19/76:56. with Peter Cushing, Susan Penhaligon, Ray Milland, Joan Greenwood, Roland Culver, Chloe Franks, Alexandra Stewart, Donald Pleasence(Valentine De'ath), Samantha Eggar, John Vernon.

Three stories "documenting a feline conspiracy," and involving a horror-movie star filming "The Pit and the Pendulum," hypnosis, black magic, killer-cats.

UNCLE SILAS (B) Taffner-TV/Thames-TV 1971 color 90m. Based on Le Fanu's book. Ref: TVFFSB: "horror-drama." with Lucy Fleming, Robert Eddison.

UNDEAD, The see FROM BEYOND THE GRAVE

*UNDER THE MOON OF MOROCCO 1931 Dial: Duvivier. From the book by Andre Reuze. Ph: Thirard, Moreau. AD: Lazare Meerson. Ref: Chirat. and with Georges Peclet, Mady Berry, M. Dantzer.
See also: FIVE DOOMED GENTLEMEN.

UNDER THE SIGN OF CAPRICORN Gold Key-TV("Zodiac" series) 1971? color 93m. Ref: TVFFSB: sf; curse. with Barry Sullivan, Martin Landau, Chuck Connors, Stella Stevens.

The UNDERTAKER (Yugos.) Zagreb 1980? anim short From the story by Pushkin. Ref: IFG'81:379.
"Ugly casket-maker who scares other people to death" meets Death.

*The UNDYING MONSTER 1942 SP: Michel Jacoby. Ref: V 10/21/42.
Man cursed to become werewolf "on frosty nights." Generally juvenile blend of horror, mystery, and comedy has, however, several redeeming features: the identity and appearance of the werewolf are kept under wraps until the climactic scenes; a rocking, semi-subjective camera "is" the creature as it traps a victim in the rocks; and--the most tantalizing bit--a wolf-hair disappears as it's being projected on a spectrum. There's also a creepy-looking dog-creature statue standing guard in a crypt....When I was 11 this was a scary movie. (A long time ago....)

The UNFAITHFUL WIVES (F) Hustaix 1975 color 62m. (Les JOUISSEUSES) SP,D: Lucien Hustaix. Ph: Fattori. Mus: Eddie Warner. Ref: MFB'78:220-21. with Vivianne Guy, Claudine Beccarie, Jacques Marbeuf.
Scientist's pill produces "instant euphoria and sexual stimulation."

The UNFINISHED WEEKEND (Cz) Brandon 1971? anim color 12m. (NEDOKONCENY WEEKEND) Ref: Brandon. Lee. IFG'72:383.
See also: DEADLY ODOR, The.

UNHEIMLICHE GESCHICTEN see HISTOIRES EXTRAORDINAIRES(1932)

The UNHOLY QUEST (B) Newman-Wyer-Hopkins 1934 56m. D: R.W. Lotinga. SP: Widgey Newman. Ref: BFC. with Claude Bailey, Terence de Marney, Cristine Adrien, John Milton.
Doctor uses murdered blackmailer to revive embalmed Crusader.

*The UNHOLY THREE 1925 & 1930 versions based on the story "The Terrible Three" (aka "The Unholy Three" or "The Three Freaks") by C.A."Tod" Robbins. Ref: MFB'79:59. screen. FM 66:20. and with (1925 version) Charles Gemora(ape).

The silent version: an offbeat caper movie, cleverly plotted, which turns into a rather sweet love-story.

The sound version: faster and lighter but dramatically less substantial.

UNIDENTIFIED FLYING ODDBALL (U.S.-B) BV 1979 color 93m. (The SPACEMAN AND KING ARTHUR-B) D: Russ Mayberry. SP: Don Tait, from Mark Twain's story "A Connecticut Yankee in King Arthur's Court." Ph: Paul Beeson. Mus: Ron Goodwin. AD: A. Witherick. SpFX: Ron Ballanger, Michael Collins;(ph) Cliff Culley. Ref: MFB'79:154-55. V 7/18/79. with Dennis Dugan, Jim Dale, Ron Moody(Merlin), Kenneth More, John Le Mesurier.

Robotics engineer and humanoid robot launched by freak accident in space and time to court of King Arthur.

The UNSEEN World Northal/Triune 1981 color/scope D: Peter Foleg. SP: M.L. Grace. Story: Foleg, Grace, Kim Henkel, N. Rifkin. Mus: Michael J. Lewis. Mkp: Craig Reardon. Ref: B. Warren. V 6/10/81:4(rated). 9/16/81:13: in Chi. HR 11/18/80 (ad): "unspeakable terror." with Barbara Bach, Sydney Lassick, Stephen Furst, Lelia Goldoni, Karen Lamm.

Unseen mute proves to be murderer.

UNSICHTBARE GEGNER see INVISIBLE ADVERSARIES

UNSLEEPING EYE,The(by D.Compton) see DEATHWATCH

UP FRANKENSTEIN see ANDY WARHOL'S FRANKENSTEIN

UP FROM THE DEEP(by R.Bradbury) see BEAST FROM 20,000 FATHOMS

UP FROM THE DEPTHS (U.S.-Fili) New World/Atienza 1979 color 75m. D: Charles B. Griffith. SP: Alfred Sweeney; Anne Dyer? Ph: Rick Remington. Mus: Russell O'Malley. AD: Ben Otico. Ref: V 6/27/79. AMPAS. with Sam Bottoms, Susanne Reed, Virgil Frye, Kedric Wolfe, Charles Doherty.

Monster wreaks havoc at seaside resort.

The UPSTATE MURDERS Upstate Murder Co. 1978 color 83m. (SAVAGE WEEKEND-B) SP,D: David Paulsen. Ph: Zoli Vidor. Mus: Dov Seltzer. Ref: MFB'79:127-8: "scores low on suspense and nothing on wit." V 12/29/76:13. with Christopher Allport, James Doerr, Marilyn Hamlin, Kathleen Heaney, David Gale.

"Ghoulishly masked, crazed killer" employs "the entire tool-box of domestic technology (cars, fishing hooks, bench-saws, light-switches, chainsaws)" in series of murders. (MFB)

URLO DALLE TENEBRE see NAKED EXORCISM

URUTORA ROKUKYODAI TAI KAIJU GUNDAN see SIX ULTRA BROTHERS...

URUTORUMAN see ULTRAMAN

VAARWEL (Dutch) Cinema Film 1973 color 85m. (The ROMANTIC AGONY-B) SP,D: Guido Pieters. SP: also Ton Ruys. Ph: Theo van de Sande. Mus: Ennio Morricone. Ref: MFB'74:290,257. with Pieke Dassen, Nettie Blanken(vampire), Rik Bravenboer.
Near-immortal man travels from the Stone Age to the 29th Century; vampire episode.

The VACUUM CLEANER NIGHTMARE (B) Urban 1906 4m. Ref: BFC.
"Salesman sucked into cleaner and turned into rubbish."

The VALLEY OF BEES (Cz) Barrandov 1968 97m. (UDOLI VCEL) SP,D: Frantisek Vlacil. SP: also Koerner, Masa. Ph: F. Uldrych. Mus: Zdenek Liska. PD: J. Goetz. Ref: MFB'74:160. with Petr Cepek, Jan Kacer(werewolf), Vera Galatikova.
"The image of the werewolf haunts the film, suggested... in the presence of the hounds with a taste for human flesh"; man who turns into "werewolf."

VALLEY OF GHOSTS (India-Mal.) Anupama 1973 164m. (PRETHANGALUDE THAZVARA) SP,D,P: Venu. Ph: V. Das. Mus: G. Devarajan. Ref: Dharap. with Raghavan, Bhasi, Bahadoor.
"A horror-cum-spy thriller."

VALLEY OF THE HEADLESS HORSEMAN see CURSE OF THE HEADLESS HORSEMAN

VAMPEER Film-makers' Coop 1972 color silent 10m. D: David Devensky. Ref: F-MC cat.: Gothic (a la Webber-Watson FALL OF THE HOUSE OF USHER).

VAMPIR see OLD DRACULA

VAMPIR VON SCHLOSS FRANKENSTEIN see HORRIBLE SEXY VAMPIRE,The

VAMPIRA see OLD DRACULA

VAMPIRA'S ALL NIGHT ORGY see VAMPIRE'S ALL NIGHT ORGY

The VAMPIRE (Austrian) 1976 short D: Karin Brand(a)ner. Ref: V 7/28/76:32.
"An intelligent satire on horror pix."

VAMPIRE ABC-TV/MTM 1979 color 94m. D: E.W. Swackhammer. SP: Steven Bochco, Michael Kozoll. Ph: D. Dalzell. Mus: Fred Karlin. AD: Jim Hulsey. SpFX: Wayne Beauchamp. Mkp: Bob Mills. Opt: Pacific. Ref: TV. CineFan 2:67. with Jason Miller, E.G. Marshall, Richard Lynch(vampire), Kathryn Harrold, Jessica Walter, Jonelle Allen, David Hooks, Joe Spinell.
Wealthy, charismatic "golden vampire" (dating from 13th-

century Hungary) turns up in 20th-century San Francisco. The script tries to have it both ways: women swoon when caught in this vampire's gaze--away from him, they're entirely self-possessed, sexually and supernaturally unimplicated, innocent. Crosses here burn, steam, scorch, and shock--they do everything but pan-fry. How-to-track-down-a-vampire Dept.: (hero) "Start checking casket companies in the morning." Inessential vampirology.

VAMPIRE see OLD DRACULA

*The VAMPIRE BAT (Medallion-TV) 1933 Mus: Meyer. Ref: TV. screen. TVFFSB. Turner/Price.

Doctor (Lionel Atwill) who creates life ("Life!--that moves, pulsates, and demands food for its continued growth--I have created life!") and has semi-hypnotic power over assistant, Borst (Robert Frazer). Tired mystery and comedy, though Atwill is amusing springing his climactic revelations, and Dwight Frye as Herman ("Seems strange that a human would want to play with bats") is, as usual, winning: "You give Herman apple. Herman give you nice soft bat."

VAMPIRE CASTLE see CAPTAIN KRONOS--VAMPIRE HUNTER

VAMPIRE CIRCUS (B) Fox/Hammer 1972 color 87m. D: Robert Young. SP: Judson Kinberg. Story: George Baxt, Wilbur Stark. Ph: Moray Grant. Mus: David Whitaker. AD: Scott MacGregor. SpFX: Les Bowie. Mkp: Jill Carpenter. Animal Adv: Mary Chipperfield. Ref: MFB'72:124. TV. TVG. CineFan 2:5-7. Cinef Smr'73:31-2. with Adrienne Corri, Laurence Payne, Thorley Walters, John Moulder-Brown, Lynne Frederick, Skip Martin, Dave Prowse; Anthony Corlan, Robert Tayman, Domini Blythe (vampires).

The travelling Circus of Nights ("A hundred delights!") features vampires who can transform into bats and leopards; its Mirror of Life conjures up visions of the vampire world. A highly unusual Hammer film, at once far-removed from their usual stillborn horrors and yet ultra-Hammer in its fang-happy robustness. At times, in fact, VAMPIRE CIRCUS plays like a near-parodic exaggeration of their unsubtle brand of horror--Hammer crude gushing high and red....And the movie's odd mating of vampire and circus-film sub-genres "takes" uncannily well--e.g., through the Wonders of Editing, circus audiences seem to be gasping (with delight)...at the sight of vampires puncturing the necks of their victims. The movie has some "A" acts in and out of the ring--the on-screen audiences indeed must assume that the supernatural transformations which they are witnessing are mere trickery, "acts." (The off-screen audience knows that they're not mere trickery--cinematically, yes; dramatically, no.) If we have to suspend disbelief to enjoy the spectacle of the vampire acro-bats, the circus crowds must suspend belief--like children with their first, too-real horror-movie experiences--either that or flee in terror. We're as enchanted by the show as they are, just as willingly deceived. Our applause echoes theirs, though the nature of that applause differs: if they admire, first, the surprising realistic stroke, we admire the imaginative stroke. VAMPIRE CIRCUS imaginatively plays on, sharpens our double sense of horror films as narrative/spectacle, the sense that "it's only/it's not only" a movie. We seem to be watching a part of ourselves watching a horror movie....At its most wondrous, the film conjures up a through-the-looking-glass-darkly sequence (with two children and two vampires) that's at once chilling and Cocteau-ishly entrancing. It proposes that if, or since, vampires cannot be seen in mirrors, they can be in mirrors. Supernatural logic....

VAMPIRE DE LA AUTOPISTA see HORRIBLE SEXY VAMPIRE, The

VAMPIRE DRACULA COMES TO KOBE: EVIL MAKES WOMEN BEAUTIFUL (J) Toei-TV & Asahi Comm. 1979 (KYUKETSUKI DORAKYURA KOBE NI ARAWARU: AKUMA WA ONNA WO UTSUKUSHIKU SURU) D: Hajime Sato. Ref: JFFJ 13:34: TV-movie. with Masumi Okada(Dracula), Kei Taguchi.

"Dracula learns that the reincarnation of his lost love now lives in Kobe...."

VAMPIRE HOOKERS (U.S.-Fili) Caprican Three/Cosa Nueva 1978 D: Cirio H. Santiago. SP: Howard Cohen. Mus: Jaime Mendoza-Nava. Ref: V 5/9/79:232(ad). 5/17/78:112. Willis/SW. with John Carradine, Bruce Fairbairn, Trey Wilson, Karen Stride.

*The VAMPIRE LOVERS 1970 AD: Scott MacGregor. Mkp: Tom Smith. Ref: AFI. Lee. and with Dawn Addams, Jon Finch, John Forbes-Robertson, Madeline Smith.

See also: LUST FOR A VAMPIRE. TWINS OF EVIL.

VAMPIRE LUST Pacific Coast/Roger Wald 197-? D: "Vladimir." SP: "Al Hazrad." Ref: poster: vampire-man. with John Leslie, Alexandra, Luda Diva.

VAMPIRE MEN OF THE LOST PLANET see HORROR OF THE BLOOD MONSTERS

VAMPIRE OF DR. DRACULA see MARK OF THE WOLFMAN

VAMPIRE WOMEN see CRYPT OF THE LIVING DEAD

VAMPIRELLA see OLD DRACULA

VAMPIRES, and vampire bats See also: ALABAMA'S GHOST. ALEGRES VAMPIROS DE VOGEL. ANGELES Y QUERUBINES. BEDTIME WITH ROSIE. BLACK SUNDAY(1960). BLOOD(1971). BLOOD PIE. BLOOD-RELATIONS. BLOODLUST(1976). BRIDES. BUTTERFLY MURDERS,The. CAPULINA VS.LOS MONSTRUOUS. titles under CARMILLA. CASE OF THE FULL MOON MURDERS. CHANOC CONTRA EL TIGRE Y EL VAMPIRO. CHINESE MAGIC. CHINESE RED. CHOSEN SURVIVORS. CLOCKWORK ORANGE,A. CONFESSIONS OF A MALE ESCORT. CRAZED VAMPIRE. CREATURE OF THE WALKING DEAD. CRYPT OF THE LIVING DEAD. CULTE DU VAMPIRE.

DEAD OF NIGHT(1977). DEATH MAGAZINE. DEATHDREAM. DEATHMASTER. titles under DRACULA. DRAKULITA. EMOTION. EVIL EYE,The(1937). FASCINATION. GANJA AND HESS. GRAVE OF THE VAMPIRE. HUA-KUANG CHIU-MU. HUELLA MACABRA,La. HYOCHO NO BIJO. INTER-PLANETARY REVOLUTION. JAWS OF THE JUNGLE. KILLING GAME,The. LEMON GROVE KIDS...,The. LEMORA. LEONOR. LEVRES DE SANG. LIPS OF BLOOD. MACABRO DR.SCIVANO. MADHOUSE. MAGIA. MARTIN. MARY,MARY,BLOODY MARY. MONSTER CLUB,The. MYSTERIOUS ISLAND (1929). NAKED WITCH. NIGHT OF THE SEAGULLS. NIGHT STALKER. NIGHT STRANGLER. NIGHTMARE IN BLOOD. NIGHTWING. NOCHE DE LOS VAMPIROS. NORLISS TAPES,The. ORLAK. OTHER SMILE,The. PEOPLE(1979). PHARAOH'S CURSE. PLAN 9 FROM OUTER SPACE. RABID. RETORNO DE LOS VAMPIROS. RETURN OF DR.X. REVAMP. RIDER OF THE SKULLS. SADIQUE AUX DENTS ROUGES. SANTO EN LA VENGANZA DE LAS MUJERES VAMPIROS. SECRETS OF HOUSE NO.5. SENSUOUS VAMPIRES. SEVEN DEAD IN THE CAT'S EYES. SEX EXPRESS. SHOCK TREATMENT(1973). SONS OF SATAN. SUCK ME VAMPIRE. TAME RE CHAMPO NE AME KEL. TENDERNESS OF THE WOLVES. THIRST. THIRSTY DEAD,The. TIME OF THE VAMPIRE. TOMBS OF THE BLIND DEAD. TORE NG DIYABLO. TRILOGY OF TERROR(1975). UMBRACLE, El. VAARWEL. VAMPYRES. VAULT OF HORROR. VEIL OF BLOOD. VIJ(1967). VOODOO HEARTBEAT. WEB OF THE SPIDER. WEREWOLF VS.THE VAMPIRE WOMAN. WINTER SONGS(P). ZSARNOK SZIVA,A.

VAMPIRE'S ALL NIGHT ORGY (Sp) Int'l.Amusements/Atlantida(Frade) 1975 color 85m. (La NOCHE DE LAS ORGIAS DE LOS VAMPIROS. cf.La NOCHE DE LOS VAMPIROS. The VAMPIRE'S NIGHT ORGY-ad t) D: Leon Klimovsky. Ref: Bianco Index'76. Willis/SW. V 5/7/75:252(ad). 1/16/74:26(rated): sfa VAMPIRA'S NIGHT ORGY? with Dianik Zurakowska, Helga Line, Jack Taylor, C. Soriano.

VAMPIRES EN ONT RAS DE BOL see BLOOD-RELATIONS

VAMPIRES OF HARLEM see GANJA AND HESS

VAMPIRES OVER LONDON see RETURN OF THE VAMPIRE

**VAMPIRE'S TOMB, The see PLAN 9 FROM OUTER SPACE

Los VAMPIROS DE COYOACAN (Mex) Agrasanchez 1973 D: Arturo Martinez. Ref: V 5/8/74:238.

VAMPYRES (B) Cambist/Essay 1974 color 84m. (DAUGHTERS OF DRACULA. VAMPYRES,DAUGHTERS OF DARKNESS) D: Joseph Larraz. SP: D. Daubeney. Ph: Harry Waxman. Mus: James Clarke. AD: Ken Bridgeman. Ref: MFB'76:132. Meyers. V 11/20/74. with Marianne Morris, Anulka, Murray Brown, Bessie Love.

"Sex-horror film about lesbian vampires." (MFB)

VANADEVATHA (India-Mal.) Anjana 1976 color 132m. D & Dial: Y.A. Kachery. SP: R. Ghatak. Mus: Devarajan. Ref: Dharap. with Prem, Nazir, N.G. Kutty, K.A. Aziz, Nagan.

Ghost of murdered girl "punishes" murderer.

Le VAUDOU: ENTRE VIVANTS ET MORTS, LE SANG (F) Camera One 1972 color 95m. (VOODOO-ad t. Le CULTE VAUDOU AU DAHOMEY-orig t) D: J. Magneron. Mus: Francois Rabbath. Ref: V 5/9/73:106,131(ad). 11/29/72.
"Documentary on voodoo cult in Africa"; blood-drinking ceremonies.

VAULT OF HORROR (B) Cinerama/Metromedia-Amicus 1973 color 86m. (FURTHER TALES FROM THE CRYPT-orig t) D: Roy Ward Baker. SP: Milton Subotsky, from comic book stories by Al Feldstein, William Gaines. Ph: Denys Coop. Mus: Douglas Gamley. AD: Tony Curtis. Ref: MFB'73:234. Lee(p): sfa The HAUNT OF FEAR? V 3/21/73. 10/11/72:22. with Daniel and Anna Massey, Erik Chitty, Terry-Thomas, Glynis Johns, Curt Jurgens, Dawn Addams, Michael Craig, Edward Judd, Tom Baker, Denholm Elliott, Frank Forsyth.
Five men trapped in strange room relate stories of five recurring dreams, involving vampires, magic rope, "pickled" groom, death-semblance serum, voodoo; 4 of the 5 men prove to be dead; the room is a cemetery.

VAYANADAN THAMPAN (India-Mal.) Sri Vigneswara 1978 color 159m. Story,D: A. Vincent. SP: Nandakumar. Mus: Devarajan. Ref: Dharap. with Kamalahasan, P.K. Abraham, Balan, Gupta.
Man who ages and dies instantly; evil spirit.

The VEIL Medallion-TV/Pathe-Alpha(Roach)-TV 1958 97m. D: Herbert L. Strock. SP: Fred Schiller. Ph: Howard Schwartz. Mus: Leon Klatskin. PhFX: Jack R. Glass. Host & with: Boris Karloff. Ref: TVFFSB. TV. TVG. with Patrick Macnee, Robert Griffin, Jennifer Raine, Ray Montgomery, Terence De Marney.
Four stories, involving vision of death, crystal ball, precognition of death, phantom double of doctor(Karloff). Blandly-related stories; passable climactic frissons. Composed of episodes from the unsold TV series "The Veil."
See also: DESTINATION NIGHTMARE. JACK THE RIPPER(1958).

VEIL, The see HAUNTS

VEIL OF BLOOD (Swiss; Eng.-lang.) Leisure Time/Monarex 1973 ('78-U.S.) color 88m. (The DEVIL'S PLAYTHING-B) SP,D: Joe Sarno. Ph: S. Silverman. Mus: Rolf-Sans Mueller. AD: Cleo Nora, A. Ryf. Ref: MFB'74:174: "strong & bizarre atmosphere." V 5/31/78:38(rated). with Nadia Senkowa, Untel Syring, Ulrike Butz, Nico Wolf, Flavia Reyt.
Vampire-baroness is reincarnated in descendant.

VELA PARA EL DIABLO see NIGHTMARE HOTEL

VELVET HOUSE see CRUCIBLE OF HORROR

VENETIAN BLACK (I) 3B 1978(1977) color 95m. (NERO VENEZIANO. DAMNED IN VENICE-ad t) SP,D: Ugo Liberatore. SP: also Gandus, Alessi, Rafele. Ph: A. Contini. Mus: Pino Donaggio.

AD: S. Canevari. Ref: Bianco #4/78. V 5/11/77:288. 5/17/78: 262(ad). with Renato Cestie, Rena Niehaus, Yorgo Voyagis. "Satan and black magic." (V)

VENGANZA DE LA MOMIA see MUMMY'S REVENGE, The

VENGANZA DE LAS MUJERES VAMPIROS see SANTO EN LA VENGANZA DE LAS MUJERES VAMPIROS

VENGANZA DEL SEXO see CURIOUS DR.HUMPP

*The VENGEANCE OF EDGAR POE 1912 (Une VENGEANCE D'EDGAR POE) SP,D: Gerard Bourgeois. SP: also Abel Gance. Ref: Ecran 12/77:28.

VENGEANCE OF THE MUMMY see MUMMY'S REVENGE, The

VENGEANCE OF THE ZOMBIES (Sp) Brandon & Int'l Amusements/Profilmes 1972('75-U.S.) color 90m. (La REBELION DE LAS MUERTAS) D: Leon Klimovsky. Ref: Brandon. Lee. CineFan 2: 25. Willis/SW. V 5/9/73:144. with Paul Naschy(aka Jacinto Molina), Romy, Mirta Miller, Vic Winner, Luis Ciges.
London. "Mysterious shadow" kills robbers of the grave of Gloria Irving, who subsequently returns to life. (Brandon)

VENGEANCE OF VIRGO Gold Key-TV("Zodiac" series) 1972 color 91m. Ref: TVFFSB. with Joan Blackman, Dana Wynter, C. Lee.
Icy planet Virgo; unisexual inhabitants; oracle.

VENOM see LEGEND OF SPIDER FOREST

Das VERRATERISCHE HERZ (W.G.) Axel-Jahn 1968 color short D: Paul Anczykowski. From Edgar Allan Poe's story "The Tell-Tale Heart." Ref: Daisne. Lee.

VERY CLOSE ENCOUNTERS OF THE FOURTH KIND (I) 1978 D: Mario Gariazzo(aka Roy Garrett). Ref: V 10/18/78:176: "sex comedy in space." with Maria Baxa.

VIAJE AL CENTRO DE LA TIERRA see WHERE TIME BEGAN

VIAJE AL MAS ALLA (Sp) 1981 Ref: V 7/29/81:6: at Trieste.
Parapsychological case histories.

VICTOR FRANKENSTEIN (Irish-Swed.) NFS & Aspekt 1977 color 92m. (TERROR OF FRANKENSTEIN-TV) SP,D: Calvin Floyd. SP: also Y. Floyd, from Mary Shelley's novel "Frankenstein." Ph: Tony Forsberg, John Wilcox. Mus: Gerard Victory. Ref: Limbacher '79. IFG'78:293. Daisne. V 5/25/77. Maltin/TVM. with Leon Vitali(Dr.Frankenstein), Per Oscarsson(the monster), Nicholas Clay, Stacey Dorning, Jan Ohlsson.

VIENNA STRANGLER, The see MAD BUTCHER, The

Une VIERGE CHEZ LES MORTS-VIVANTS (F) Eurocine 1980? Ref: V 5/13/81:283: horror.

VIERGES ET VAMPIRES see CRAZED VAMPIRE

The VIJ (Russ) Khanzhonkov 1914 82m. (STRASNAJA MEST'. The TERRIBLE VENGEANCE-alt t) SP,D,Ph: Ladislas Starevitch. From Gogol's story. Ref: DDC IV:338. Lee. with Ivan Mosjoukine (witch), Olga Obolenskaya, V. Turzhansky.

VIJ (Russ) Mosfilm 1967 color 70m. (VII. VAMPIRES-ad t) SP,D: Erchov, Kropatchov. SP,AD,SpFX: Alexander Ptouchko. From Gogol's story. Ref: Lee: witch; monsters. WorldF'67. with Natalia Varlei, Leonid Kouraviliev.

VILLAGE OF THE EIGHT TOMBS (J) Shochiku 1977 color 151m. (YATSU HAKAMURA) D: Yoshitaro Nomura. SP: Shinobu Hashimoto, from S. Yokomizo's novel. Ph: A. Kawamata. Mus: Y. Akutagawa. PD: K. Morita. Ref: AMPAS. V 12/14/77: "stylized horror." with Kenichi Hagiwara, Kiyoshi Atsumi, M. Ogawa.
400-year-old family curse.

VIRGIN AND THE MONSTER, The see BEAUTY AND THE BEAST(1979)

VIRGIN VAMPIRES see TWINS OF EVIL

VIRGIN WITCH (B) Brenner/Tigon-Univista 1970 color 89m. D: Ray Austin. SP: Klaus Vogel, from his novel. Ph: G. Moss. Mus: Ted Dicks. AD: Paul Barnard. Ref: BFC. MFB'72:60. '73: 239. V 6/21/78: "tired, dated." 10/25/72:17. Willis/SW: '72-U.S. Bianco Index'73. with Ann Michelle, Vicky Michelle, Keith Buckley, Patricia Haines.
"Psychic lesbian tries to make her girl-friend a witch."(BFC)

VIRGINS AND THE VAMPIRES see CRAZED VAMPIRE

VIRUS (J) Toho/Kadokawa-TBS 1980 color/scope? 100m.(150m.) (FUKKATSU NO HI) SP,D: Kinji Fukasaku. SP: also K. Takada, G. Knapp. From Sakyo Komatsu's novel. Ph: D. Kimura. Mus: Teo Macero;(song) Janis Ian. Min: Greg Jein. Ref: V 4/9/80: 25(ad). 5/28/80. 8/20/80:45. JFFJ 13:15. with Masao Kusakari, Sonny Chiba, Chuck Connors, Glenn Ford, Olivia Hussey, George Kennedy, Henry Silva, Bo Svenson, Robert Vaughn, Cecil Linder.
In 1982 survivors of a world-wide plague and nuclear devastation attempt to start a new world in Antarctica.

VISIT FROM A DEAD MAN (B?) ABC-TV/Clovis 1974 color 90m. D: Lela Swift. Ref: TVFFSB: "story of the occult." with Alfred Drake, Heather MacRae, Stephen Collins.

The VISITOR (I-U.S.) Int'l.Picture Show(Assonitis) 1980 color 90m. (Il VISITATORE) Story,D: Giulio Paradisi. SP: Comici, Mundy. Story: also Ovidio Assonitis. Ph: Guarnieri. Mus: Franco Micalizzi. AD: F. Venorio. Anim: Bozzetto. Ref: V

3/26/80: "preposterous." with Mel Ferrer, Glenn Ford, John Huston, Sam Peckinpah, Shelley Winters.
"Fright effects"; "child monster"; "demonic force."

VISITORS FROM THE GALAXY (Yugos-Cz) Zagreb-Jadran-KZ & Barrandov 1981 color 90m. (GOSTI IZ GALAKSIJE) SP,D: Dusan Vukotic. SP: also Milos Macourek. Ph: Jiri Macak. Mus: T. Simovic. Ref: V 8/12/81. 7/1/81:21. with Zarko Potocnjak, Ljubisa Samardzic.
Spacewoman-robot, doll-monster, etc. in writer's work come to life; laser rays, time-turned-back.

VLAD TEPES (Rum.) Romaniafilm 1978 color 147m. (The TRUE LIFE OF DRACULA. VLAD THE IMPALER,THE TRUE LIFE OF DRACULA. COUNT DRACULA,THE TRUE STORY-ad ts) D: Doru Nastase. SP: Mircea Mohor. Ph: Aurel Kostrakiewicz. Mus: Tiberiu Olah. Sets: Guta Stirbu. Ref: IFG'80:265-66. Murphy. V 1/30/80:92. 5/30/79. 1/3/79:53(ad). HKFFest. with Stefan Sileanu, George Constantin, Teofil Vilcu.
The story of the real Dracula, a Rumanian prince of the 15th Century.
See also: HISTORICAL DRACULA,The(P).

VLIEGEN ZONDER VLEUGELS see FLYING WITHOUT WINGS

VOICES (B) Warden 1973 color 91m. D: Kevin Billington. SP: George Kirgo, Robert Enders, from Richard Lortz's play. Ph: Geoffrey Unsworth. Mus: Richard Rodney Bennett. AD: Len Townsend. Ref: MFB'73:177: "calcified." with David Hemmings, Gayle Hunnicutt, Lynn Farleigh, Peggy Ann Clifford(medium).
Couple who encounter "long-dead family" in "large, mouldering mansion" turn out to be dead themselves.

VOLTUS V (J) IPC/Toei-TV 1978 anim 93m. D: T. Nagahama. Ref: JFFJ 13:35: giant robot.
Feature from TV-series footage.

VOODOO see VAUDOU

VOODOO BABY Santo Domingo Universal 1979 color D: Joe D'Amato. Ref: V 10/17/79:188(ad): "sex & black magic." with Susan Scott, Richard Harrison, Lucia Ramirez.

VOODOO BLACK EXORCIST Horizon 1974? color/scope 90m. D: Manuel Cano. Ref: Willis/SW. V 5/8/74:33(rated). with Aldo Sambrel, Eva Leon.

VOODOO GIRL see SUGAR HILL

VOODOO HEARTBEAT TWI/Molina 1972(1975) color 88m. SP,D: Charles Nizet. Ref: screen. Willis/SW. Lee(V 4/19/72). with Ray Molina, Philip Ahn, Ern Dugo, Forrest Duke, Mary Martinez.
"Curse of the voodoo" turns man into blood-drinking monster. Film itself is an aural monstrosity, featuring a wretched

score, jarringly "wrong" dialogue, and actors speaking the unspeakable ("You talk like he's a...a monster!") very slowly and carefully, as if some subtle nuances might otherwise be lost. One of the worst (and funniest) of 1972.

VOODOO IN THE CARIBBEAN (F) Francos 1980 D: Philippe Monnier. Ref: V 8/13/80:37. 5/13/81:285: "Brigade Mondaine thriller series #3." FM 170.

*VOODOO ISLAND 1957 AD: Jack T. Collis. Mkp: Ted Coodley. Ref: TV. and with Jean Engstrom, Glenn Dixon.

Zombie who dies, "scared to death"; plants, phones, radios, boat engines all killed by voodoo; voodoo dolls, ouanga bag. Standard adventure-movie dialogue; comically formulaic characterizations. Rhodes Reason's mechanically Bogartian bitterness is the inverted highlight. Boris Karloff seems shut off from his talent in the tired role of skeptic (and last-minute believer)--the familiar Karloffian intonations just hang effectlessly in the air.

*VOODOO MAN (Gold Key-TV) 1944 Ref: screen. TVFFSB. V 3/8/44. Lennig/TC. and with Ethelreda Leopold, Claire James, and Dorothy Bailer(zombies).

Mad doctor (Bela Lugosi) attempts, through voodoo, to transfer the life-force of young women into his zombified wife (Ellen Hall); but they too become zombies. Perfunctorily plotted, right down to the doctor's electrical tube (which knocks out car motors), a borrowing from the 1932 SHERLOCK HOLMES. Lugosi is oddly restrained, but John Carradine as Job, Lugosi's assistant, persists in drawing attention to himself, fidgeting crazily and running in place, in a role in which probably any other actor would have preferred to go unnoticed. George Zucco, chanting and occasionally glancing up at the camera, looks as if he's as embarrassed as Carradine should have been.

VORTEX see DAY TIME ENDED, The

A VOYAGE TO ARCTURUS Brandon 1971 color 85m. SP,D,Ph,Ed: B.J. Holloway. SP: also Sally Holloway. Ref: Lee. with David Eldred, Tom Hastings, Susan Junge.

Aliens; dragons; interplanetary travel.

VRIJEME VAMPIRA see TIME OF THE VAMPIRE

VUELVEN LOS CAMPEONES JUSTICIEROS (Mex) Agrasanchez 1972 color 90m. D: Federico Curiel. SP: Ramon Obon. Story: R. Agrasanchez. Ph: A. Ruiz. Mus: G.C. Carreon. Ref: Lee. with Blue Demon, Mil Mascaras, Yolanda Lievana.

Mad scientist turns rats into monsters.

*The VULTURE 1967 (not, I repeat not The VYNALEZ) Mkp: Geoffrey Rodway. Ref: TV. Lee.

"Nuclear transmutation" of dead witch and vulture in "the

ether" yields vulture-monster (Akim Tamiroff). ("Stay away from open spaces and windows at night.") Skimpy continuity and silly mystery-elements--a feather, a sheep's leg, gold coins, and a white-haired woman. ("The only thing left to account for now is the woman's hair growing white overnight.") A very-carefully-unplanned comedy.

WAKUSEI DAISENSO see WAR IN SPACE,The(Toho,1977)

WAKUSEI ROBO DANGADO ESU--UCHU DAIKAISEN (J) Toei-Asahi Comm. 1978 anim color/scope 26m. D: M. Akebi. Sequel to ROBOT RUMPUS. Ref: JFFJ 13:34.

*The WALKING DEAD 1936 Story: E. Adamson, Joseph Fields. Mus: Rubinstein. AD: Hugh Reticker. Dial D: Irving Rapper. Ref: screen. Lee. J.Shapiro. and with Milton Kibbee, Wade Boteler, Paul Harvey, Robert Strange.

A generally awkward sf-horror-gangster thriller, with some incidental but tantalizing metaphysical speculation: the executed-and-revived John Ellman (Boris Karloff) feels "peace and..." during his minutes of death. The script goes on to link music, the subconscious, and Ellman's memories of death, as, perhaps, conduits of the soul. Unfortunately, this speculation is only a minor feature of an incredibly-contrived plot, in which the revived Ellman confronts the gangsters who framed him and makes them gulp and sweat (instant guilt) and more or less kill themselves. Metaphysics-as-corn. In his punctuating appearances, Karloff is alternately menacing, witty, and campy.

WANTED: SON-IN-LAW SALE (India-Marathi) Balaji 1973 (JAWAI VIKAT GHENE AAHE) D: Raja Thakur. Mus: S. Phadke. Ref: Dharap. with S. Talwakar, Raja Bapat, Baby Roza.

The year 1983. In order to check population growth, an ordinance is passed prohibiting marriages for 10 years.

WAR IN SPACE (I) Nais 1977 color 100m. (ANNA ZERO GUERRA NELLO SPAZIO) SP,D: Alfonso Brescia(aka Al Bradley). SP: also Aldo Crudo. Ph: Silvio Fraschetti. Mus: Marcello Giombini. AD: Mimmo Scavia. Ref: V 5/17/78:242. 2/25/81:75(ad). 8/17/77:30: sfa COSMO 2000--PLANET WITHOUT A NAME? Bianco #5-6/77:228. with John Richardson, Malisa Longo, Y. Somer, West Buchanan, Charles Borromel, Massimo Bonetti.

The WAR IN SPACE (J) (Gold Key-TV)/Toho 1977 color 85m. (WAKUSEI DAISENSO. WAR OF THE PLANETS-alt t) D: Jun Fukuda. SP: Ryuzo Nakahishi, Hideichi Nagahara. Story: H. Jinguji. Ph: Aizawa. Mus: Toshiaki Tsushima. SpFX: Teruyoshi Nakano. Ref: V 5/17/78:420. 10/18/78. Bianco #4/78. GKey. IFG'79:218. JFFJ 13:32: aliens invade Earth. with Kensaku Morita, Yuko Asano, Hiroshi Miyauchi, Ryo Ikebe, William Ross.

WAR OF THE ALIENS see STARSHIP INVASIONS

WAR OF THE MONSTERS see GODZILLA ON MONSTER ISLAND

WAR OF THE PLANETS see WAR IN SPACE,The(Toho,1977)

WAR OF THE ROBOTS (I) (Gold Key-TV)/Bless Int'l/Nais 1978 color 96m. (La GUERRA DEI ROBOTS. STRATOSTARS. ROBOTS-ad ts) D: Alfonso Brescia(aka Al Bradley). Ref: V 10/18/78(ad): sf. 5/7/80:167(ad). 5/17/78:242. 1/25/78:42. GKey: with J.R. Stuart, M. Longo, P. Gore. with Antonio Sabato, Yanti Somer, West Buchanan, Ines Pellegrini.
"Secret of eternal life"; "gigantic atomic reactor." (GK)

WAR OF THE WORLDS--NEXT CENTURY (Pol) 1981 100m. D: Peter Szulkin. From H.G. Wells' novel. Ref: SFFFest. SFC 10/26/81.
Government stages "Martian invasion" to repress citizens. See also: NIGHT THAT PANICKED AMERICA.

WAR WITH THE NEWTS(by K.Capek) see PANIK

WAR WIZARDS see WIZARDS

WARHOL'S FRANKENSTEIN see ANDY WARHOL'S FRANKENSTEIN

WARLOCK MOON ECU/CW 1974 color 85m. D,P,Ed: William Herbert. SP: John Sykes. Ph: Larry Secrist. Mus: Charles R. Blaker. PD: Douglas Saunders. SpFX: J.D.& Dan U. Dudhet. Ref: TV. V 2/20/74:5(rated). with Laurie Walters, Joe Spano, Edna Macafee, Steve Solinsky(ax-man), Ray Goman, Michael Herbert.
Apparent ghosts seek girl for midnight sacrifice at isolated spa, 40 years after <u>another</u> girl was served as the main course at her wedding party. Not nearly as jolly as it sounds. In fact downright interminable. One perverse pleasantry about "hunter's stew." Contrived shock-downbeat ending. More loopholes than plot.

WARLORDS OF ATLANTIS (B) Col/EMI 1978 color 96m. (7 CITIES TO ATLANTIS-orig t) D: Kevin Connor. SP: Brian Hayles. Ph: Alan Hume. Mus: Mike Vickers. PD: Elliot Scott. SpFX: George Gibbs;(sup) John Richardson. Models: Roger Dicken. Mkp: R. Grantham. Matte FX: Cliff Culley. Ref: MFB'78:145. V 7/26/78. 3/1/78(rated). 12/14/77. with Doug McClure, Peter Gilmore, Shane Rimmer, Lea Brodie, M. Gothard, Cyd Charisse.
Giant octopus; "fish-headed soldiers"; lost, subterranean fourth city of Atlantis, whose inhabitants are from Mars; Zaargs ("immense dinosaurs"). (MFB)

WARNING, The see IT CAME...WITHOUT WARNING

The WATCHER IN THE WOODS (B) BV 1980 color 100m. D: John Hough. SP: Brian Clemens, Harry Spalding, R.A. Sisson, from Florence E. Randall's novel "A Watcher in the Woods." Ph: Alan Hume. Mus: Stanley Myers. PD: Elliot Scott. SpFX:

John Richardson. Ref: V 4/23/80. FM 161:12: "spooker." with Bette Davis, Carroll Baker, David McCallum, Ian Bannen, Lynn-Holly Johnson, Kyle Richards, Richard Pasco, G. Hale.
"Hints of black magic." (V)

The WATER BABIES (B-Pol) (Showtime-TV)/Ariadne & Studio Miniatur Filmowych 1978 anim & live color 85m. D: Lionel Jeffries. SP: Michael Robson; Jeffries; Denis Norden. From the book by Charles Kingsley. Ph: Ted Scaife. Mus: Phil Coulter. AD: Herbert Westbrook. Anim: Tony Cuthbert; M. Kijowicz. Ref: TV. MFB'79:81. V 4/25/79. with James Mason, Billie Whitelaw, Bernard Cribbins, Joan Greenwood, David Tomlinson; (voices) Mason(Shark), Jon Pertwee, Olive Gregg.
Boy enters (animated) underwater fantasy-realm populated by eerie sea-bed creatures, sea-horse pretending to be monster haunting wrecks, sinister Shark and his eel aide, "terrifying" Kraken, Lord of the Oceans. The animated portion of the movie is lively and jolly, a collection of diverse and eccentric characters, with an atmosphere halfway between a party and a quest. The live half is unremarkable--except for a nigh-magical concluding scene in which fairy tale and reality seem, momentarily, to become one in the summer-evening air, in the little girl's exclamations of delighted belief in the boy's water world.

WATER, WATER EVERY HARE WB 1952 anim color 7m. (Bugs Bunny) D: Chuck Jones. Ref: Glut/TFL. LC. Maltin/OMAM.
Giant robot (which eventually shrinks).

WATTS MONSTER, The see DR.BLACK MR. HYDE

WAVES OF LUST (I) TDL 1975 color 92m. (Una ONDATA DI PIACERE) D: Ruggero Deodato. SP: F. Bottari, F. Pittoru. Ph: M. Capriotti. Mus: M. Giombini. PD: F. Bottari. Ref: MFB'77:49. with Al Cliver, Silvia Dionisio, John Steiner.
Painting "transformed into ominous skeleton"; blood-stained "apparition."

WAYNE MURDER CASE, The see STRANGE ADVENTURE

WE ARE ALL DEMONS! (Dan-Swed-Norw) Nordisk-Carlsen & Sandrews & Teamfilm 1969 102m. (KLABAUTERMANDEN) SP,D: Henning Carlsen. SP: also Poul Borum, from Axel Sandemose's novel. Ph: J. Skov. Mus: Finn Savery. AD: H. Bahs. Ref: IFG'80. with Lise Fjeldstad, Hans Stormoen, Claus Nissen, M.Carlquist.
Woman's presence on ship, "The Ariel," drives men to "apocalyptic mass suicide....a phantasmagoria that has been likened to "The Flying Dutchman"...."

WEB OF THE SPIDER (I-F-W.G.) Cinema Shares Int'l/DC7 & Paris-Cannes & Terra Filmkunst 1971 color/scope 93m. (NELLA STRETTA MORSA DEL RAGNO. E VENNE L'ALBA...MA TINTA DIROSSO. DRACULA IM SCHLOSS DES SCHRECKENS. PRISONNIER DE L'ARAIGNEE. EDGAR POE CHEZ LES MORTS-VIVANTS) SP,D: Antonio Margheriti.

SP: also G. Addessi; B. Corbucci? From Edgar Allan Poe's "Danse Macabre." Remake of CASTLE OF BLOOD. Ph: S. Mancori. Mus: Riz Ortolani. Ref: Bianco Index'71. Ecran 12/77:30. Lee. TVG. TVFFSB. Daisne. with Anthony Franciosa(Allen Foster), Michele Mercier, Karin Field, Klaus Kinski(Poe), P. Carsten.

Edgar Allan Poe challenges a man to stay the night in Blackwood Villa, a castle haunted by blood-sucking ghosts.

The WEDDING MARCH (I?) Brandon 1966 97m. (MARCIA NUZIALE) SP,D: Marco Ferreri. SP: also Fabbri, Azcona. Ref: PFA notes 4/6/79. no AFI. no Lee. with Ugo Tognazzi, Shirley Anne Field, Alexandra Stewart.

One of four sequences: "sex in a future when ideal partners are inflatable, life-sized dolls."

The WEEKEND MURDERS (I) Metro/Jupiter 1970('72-U.S.) color 98m. (CONCERTO PER PISTOLA SOLISTA) D: Michele Lupo. SP: Sergio Donati et al. Ph: G. Mancori. Mus: F. De Masi. AD: Ugo Sterpini. Ref: V 5/10/72. FFacts. with Anna Moffo, Lance Percival, Gastone Moschin, Evelyn Stewart, Peter Baldwin, Giacomo Rossi Stuart.

"Sex-horror-crime-comedy....gore...ghoulish pranks." (V)

WEEKENDS MALEFIQUES DU COMTE ZAROFF see SEVEN WOMEN FOR SATAN

The WEIRD ONES Crescent Int'l. 1962 76m. Ref: AFI. with Mike Braden, Rudy Duran, Lee Morgan.

Space creature lands on Earth, terrorizes women.

WEIRD TAILOR,The(by R.Bloch) see ASYLUM

WELCOME TO ARROW BEACH WB/Brut 1974 color 99m. (TENDER FLESH-orig t) D & with: Laurence Harvey. SP: Wallace C. Bennett, Jack Gross Jr. Ph: G.P. Finnerman. Mus: Tony Camillo. Ref: MFB'76:65. TVG 2/16/80. Willis/SW. TV. V 5/15/74. with John Hart, Joanna Pettet, Stuart Whitman, Altovise Gore, J. Vint.

American soldier "forced to eat three of his comrades after their bomber had crashed on a Pacific island...has suffered an insatiable craving for human flesh." (MFB)

WELCOME TO BLOOD CITY (Can.-B) BCP & EMI 1977 color/scope 96m. (BLOOD CITY-Can.?) D: Peter Sasdy. SP: S. Schenck, M. Winder. Ph: Reginald Morris. Mus: Roy Budd. PD: J. McAdam. OptFX: Rank. Ref: MFB'77:245: "unremitting plot confusion." Cinef VI:3:28. Meyers. V 10/26/77. with Jack Palance, Keir Dullea, Samantha Eggar, Barry Morse, Hollis McLaren.

Research team "programmes" subjects into fantasy-city-of-the-mind in order to determine the most promising assassins.

WELCOME WIFE,A(by Thompson & Paulton) see LET'S LOVE AND LAUGH

WE'RE GOING TO EAT YOU (H.K.) Seasonal-Yuen 1980 color 92m. (TIYU WU-MEN) D: Tsui Hark. Ref: V 5/7/80:10,454: "ill-conceived...horror-comedy." IFG'81:163. with Tsui Siu-Chang,

Cheung Mu-Lian, Han Kuo-Tsai, Kao Shiung.
Island town with cannibalistic inhabitants.

WEREWOLF AND THE YETI see NIGHT OF THE HOWLING BEAST

*WEREWOLF OF LONDON 1935 Mus: Karl Hajos. AD: Albert S. D'Agostino. Mkp: Jack Pierce. Ref: TV. Lee. FM 24:38-57.

Two werewolves (plus reports of a Yucatan werewolf); TV device; anti-lycanthropic "moon flower," the *mariphasa lumina lupina*; "artificial moonlight" machine; invisible force in Tibetan valley. The establishing scenes in Tibet and London are promisingly atmospheric, and Henry Hull, Warner Oland (as Yogami, the *other* werewolf), and the score are enjoyably florid. But the later shock scenes are undistinguished; the characters are one-note, and the London atmosphere is a bit thick, finally, with "comic relief." The script ineffectively characterizes lycanthropy as an extension of violent jealousy.

The WEREWOLF OF WASHINGTON Diplomat/Millco 1973 color 85m. (The WHITE HOUSE HORRORS-alt t) SP,D,Ed: Milton Moses Ginsberg. Ph: Bob Baldwin. Mus: Arnold Freed. AD: Nancy Miller-Corwin. Mkp: Bob O'Bradovich. Opt: Opt.Group. Ref: screen. MFB'76:237-8. CineFan 2:29. V 10/10/73. with Dean Stockwell, Biff McGuire, John Carson(werewolves), Clifton James, Beeson Carroll, Jane House, Michael Dunn, Thayer David.

Gypsy werewolf's bite turns reporter into werewolf (a la 1941 WOLF MAN); monster-making scientist. The juxtaposition of politics and lycanthropy sounds promisingly absurd, but it's not automatically *funny*. The characters here confuse "pentagram" with "Pentagon," and the President uses the phrase "perfectly clear." In any reasonably-incisive political satire, *they* probably wouldn't and *he* definitely wouldn't. (The Nixon administration lent *itself* all too easily to parody.) Stockwell has droll moments in the Lon Chaney Jr. role, but Rich Little is still *the* Nixon.

The WEREWOLF OF WOODSTOCK ABC-TV/Dick Clark 1975 color 74m. D: John Moffitt. Ref: TVFFSB. with Tige Andrews, Meredith MacRae, Michael Parks, Ann Doran, Harold J. Stone.

Electrical discharge transforms farmer into wolf-man.

The WEREWOLF VS. THE VAMPIRE WOMAN (W.G.-Sp) (Greenfield-TV)/Ellman/HiFi Stereo 70 & Plata 1970('72-U.S.) color 86m. (NACHT DER VAMPIRE. La NOCHE DE WALPURGIS. SHADOW OF THE WEREWOLF-B. WEREWOLF'S SHADOW-ad t. Le MESSE NERE DELLA CONTESSA DRACULA-I) D: Leon Klimovsky. SP: Jacinto Molina, Hans Munkel. Ph: L. Villasenor. Mus: A.G. Abril. AD: L. Orni. SpFX: Antonio Molina. Mkp: J.L. Morales. Ref: MFB'73:150. Bianco Index'71. Glut/TDB. Willis/SW. Lee. Murphy. TVFFSB. V 5/10/72: 18(ad). with Paul Naschy(Waldemar, werewolf), Patty Shepard (Countess de Nadasdy, vampire), Gaby Fuchs, Andres Resino, Julio Pena, Barbara Capell.

Sequel to MARK OF THE WOLFMAN. See also: COUNTESS DRACULA.

WEREWOLF WOMAN see LEGEND OF THE WOLF WOMAN

WEREWOLF'S SHADOW see WEREWOLF VS.THE VAMPIRE WOMAN

WEREWOLVES (and other were-animals), see also AMERICAN WEREWOLF IN LONDON. ATTACK OF THE PHANTOMS. BAT PEOPLE. BEAST MUST DIE,The. BLOOD(1974). BOY WHO CRIED WEREWOLF. COLONEL AND THE WOLFMAN,The. CRY WOLF. CRYPT OF THE LIVING DEAD. CURSE OF THE BLACK WIDOW. DARK,The. DARWAZA. DEATH IN THE SUN(P). DEATH MOON. DEVATHALARA DEEVINCHANDI. DRACULA VS.DR.FRANKENSTEIN. FROM THE CLOUD TO THE RESISTANCE. GREAT PIGGY BANK ROBBERY. HARI DARSHAN. HEBA THE SNAKE WOMAN. HOMEM LOBO,O. HOUSE OF THE BLACK DEATH. HOWLING,The. IDLE ROOMERS. LEGACY, The. LEGEND OF THE WEREWOLF. LEGEND OF THE WOLF WOMAN. LOVE IN THE CITY(P). titles under MARK OF THE WOLFMAN. MILAP. MUNSTERS' REVENGE,The. NAGIN. NAZARENO CRUZ Y EL LOBO. NIGHT OF THE COBRA WOMAN. NO-CH'A NAO TUNG-HAI. PAUK. PEPITO Y CHABELO... POODLE. PROVIDENCE. RATS ARE COMING...,The! SANTO Y BLUE DEMON CONTRA DRACULA Y EL HOMBRE LOBO. SCREAM OF THE WOLF. SHADOW OF THE HAWK. SIN IN THE VESTRY. SNAKE PRINCE,The. SON OF DRACULA(1974). TICKLE ME. TIGER FANGS. TORE NG DIYABLO. TRACK OF THE MOONBEAST. VALLEY OF BEES,The. VAMPIRE CIRCUS. WHEN THE SCREAMING STOPS. WHO'S AFRAID OF THE WEREWOLF? WOLFEN. WOLFMAN(1978).

The WEST CASE (B) 1923 25m. Ref: BFC. Lee.
See also: Mystery of Dr. Fu-Manchu series.

WESTWORLD MGM/Lazarus 1973 color/scope 88m. SP,D: Michael Crichton. Sequel: FUTUREWORLD. Ph: Gene Polito. Mus: Fred Karlin. PD: Herman Blumenthal. SpFX: Charles Schulthies. VisFX: Brent Sellstrom; Info.Int'l., John Whitney Jr. Ref: MFB'74:56. TV. Lee. VV 12/13/73. V 8/15/73. with Yul Brynner (android), Richard Benjamin, James Brolin, Victoria Shaw, Dick Van Patten, Steve Franken, Linda Scott, Alan Oppenheimer.

In the android-stocked amusement park of Delos, Western World, Medieval World, and Roman World offer tourists the chance to realize their fantasies--until the androids go berserk. An above-average, expanded "Twilight Zone," in effect. (It would have made an ideal 60-minute "TZ.") The film has two ideas--the New Old West (for the amateur Westerner), and the unstoppable, haywire robot--enough ideas, that is, for a beginning and an ending, if not a middle. (HALLOWEEN borrowed the unstoppable monster for its one-idea plot.) Effective as a horror movie, if not quite as enchanting a Western-about-Westerns as MY NAME IS NOBODY(1974). Unique-opportunity-seized Dept.: the dawn-in-the-park sequence, with robots (and roosters) "magically" activated.

WHAT A FLASH (F) Marquise 1972 D: J.-M. Barjol. Ref: V 8/16/72:25: "sci-fi"; "space capsule." 5/3/72:100.

WHAT A NIGHT! (B) BIP 1931 58m. D: Monty Banks. SP: Syd Courtenay, Lola Harvey. Ref: BFC. with Frank Stanmore.

"Traveller catches burglar during night at "haunted" inn."

WHAT BECKONING GHOST(by H.Lawlor) see DOMINIQUE

WHAT THE SWEDISH BUTLER SAW see GROOVE ROOM, The

WHAT'S COOKIN', DOC? WB 1944 anim color 7m. D: Bob Clampett. SP: M. Sasanoff. Ref: Glut/TFL. Maltin/OMAM. LC.
Bugs Bunny as "the Karloff (Frankenstein) monster." (TFL)

WHAT'S THE WORLD COMING TO? Pathe/Roach 1926 20m. Ref: PFA notes 7/20/80. LC. Everson.
"Futuristic look at a world dominated by women." (PFA)

WHEELS see CAR, The

WHEN A STRANGER CALLS Col/Krost 1979 color 97m. SP,D: Fred Walton. SP,Co-P: Steve Feke. Based on the short film "The Sitter." Ph: Don Peterman. Mus: Dana Kaproff. PD: E.B. Ceder. SpFX: B&D. Ref: MFB'80:116. V 9/5/79: "standard." with Carol Kane, Charles Durning, Colleen Dewhurst, Tony Beckley, Rachel Roberts, Ron O'Neal.
Babysitter at mercy of madman in darkened house.

WHEN EAST MEETS WEST (B) Clarendon 1915 50m. D: Wilfred Noy. SP: Marchioness of Townshend. Ref: BFC. with Dorothy Bellew.
"Indian fakir hypnotises officer's daughter and explodes gas bulbs from afar with electric rays."

WHEN IT WAS DARK (B) Windsor-Walturdaw 1919 84m. D: Arrigo Bocchi. SP: Kenelm Foss, from Guy Thorne's novel. Ref: BFC. with Manora Thew, Hayford Hobbs, George Butler, Charles Vane.
"Atheist millionaire forces professor to destroy Christianity by discovering fake sepulchre."

WHEN MICHAEL CALLS ABC-TV/Fox-TV & Palomar 1972 color 75m. D: Philip Leacock. SP: James Bridges, from John Farris's novel. Ph: Reg Morris, Don Wilder. Mus: Lionel Newman. FxEd: Evelyn Rutledge, John Newman. Mkp: Ken Brooke. Opt: Modern. Ref: TV. Lee(Warren). with Ben Gazzara, Elizabeth Ashley, Michael Douglas, Marian Waldman, Albert S.Waxman, Karen Pearson.
Bee-venom-irritated bees kill beekeeper; visions and calls from "ghost" (i.e., boy hypnotized by psychotic); thunderstorm; stage-full-of-jack-o'-lanterns sequence. Vapid, humorless thriller, with one lone, chilly telephone-bit. (The "ghost"'s "I'm dead!")

*WHEN THE DEVIL COMMANDS see DEVIL COMMANDS, The

WHEN THE SCREAMING STOPS (Sp) Independent Artists/C.C.Astro-Profilmes 1973('80-U.S.) color 94m. (Las GARRAS DE LORELEI) SP,D: Amando De Ossorio. Ph: M.F. Mila. Mus: A.G. Abril. AD: Alfonso de Lucas. SpFX: Alfredo Segoviono(sp?). Mkp: Lolita Merlo. Ref: screen. V 5/9/73:137. 10/11/78:5.

CineFan 2:24. with Luciano Stella(aka Tony Kendall), Helga Line, Silvia Tortesa, "Peter Lawrence," Lolita Tovar,L.Induni.

According to the Curse of the 7 Full Moons, the siren Lorelei, Wotan's daughter, rises from the Rhine and devours human hearts, in order to prolong her "dream of centuries" guarding the treasure of the Nibelungen; moon's rays periodically turn her into "obscene creature"; hero kills her with the sword of Siegfried. Plus!--Prof. Van Lander's "analytic spectrum" acts like moonlight on human hand, causes it to return to its "original species"; prof.'s face eaten away by acid during attack by Lorelei and aide ("I am Alberic." "Any relation to the Nibelungen?"); finally, a spirit, she rides away to Valhalla. An awful movie, yes, but hellishly ambitious. Its very lack of sophistication is part of its occasional terrible charm, though the intermittent goriness mitigates, somewhat, enjoyment of the nonsense. There's even a song, "Evil Eyes," and a "romantic" theme for Lorelei. The English dubbing is very approximate. The screen flashes red before each installment of gore, but there is--be warned--no defense against lines like those quoted above.

*WHEN WOMEN HAD TAILS FVI 1970('73-U.S.) Sequel: WHEN WOMEN LOST THEIR TAILS. SpFX: Walfrido Traversari. Mkp: G. de Rossi. Ref: Willis/SW. Lee. V 1/31/73:6(rated).

WHEN WOMEN LOST THEIR TAILS (I-W.G.) FVI/Clesi & Terra 1971 ('74-U.S.) color 100m. (QUANDO LE DONNE PERSERO LA CODA) D: P.F. Campanile. SP: M. Coscia et al. Story: Lina Wertmuller. Sequel to WHEN WOMEN HAD TAILS. Ph: S. Ippoliti. Mus: Ennio Morricone. AD & Cost: E. Job. Ref: Lee(Ital P). V 3/6/74:4(rated). with Senta Berger, Lando Buzzanca, Frank Wolff, Mario Adorf.

Comedy set in prehistoric times.

WHEN WOMEN WANT...AND MEN DON'T... (Braz) Procitel 1975 color 101m. (QUANDO ELAS QUEREM...E ELES NAO...) SP,D: Ary Fernandes. Mus: S. Curvelo. Ref: Brasil. with Cazarre,S.Lopes.

Chemical added to soup makes men impotent and women "overexcited."

WHERE HAVE ALL THE PEOPLE GONE NBC-TV/MPC(Metromedia-Alpine-Jozak) 1974 color 74m. D: John L. Moxey. SP: Lewis John Carlino, Sandor Stern. Ph: M. Margulies. Mus: Robert Prince. SpFX: Roger Bellowes(sp?). Mkp: Louis Lane. Ref: TV Season. TV. TVFFSB. with Peter Graves, Verna Bloom, George O'Hanlon Jr., Kathleen Quinlan.

A huge solar flare proves responsible for the "virus" which is sweeping the Earth and making its victims die, then disintegrate. It's no Picnic in Year Zero, as the few survivors begin acting as if this is ON THE BEACH, and dogs act as if it's DOGS or The PACK. From this downbeat situation the characters wrest an upbeat, let's-start-over ending. Awww!

WHERE TIME BEGAN (Sp) IPS/Almena 1977('78-U.S.) color 90m. (VIAJE AL CENTRO DE LA TIERRA. FABULOUS JOURNEY TO THE CENTER

OF THE EARTH-ad t) SP,D: Juan Piquer. SP: also Carlos Puerto. From Jules Verne's novel "Journey To The Center of The Earth." Ph: Andres Berenguer. Mus: J.J.G. Caffi. Sets: Emilio Ruiz. SpFX: Francisco Prosper, Ruiz. Ref: V 9/28/77: "feeble." 12/22/76:34. Boxo 2/25/80:37. Bianco #4/78. Willis/SW. with Kenneth More, P. Munne, Ivonne Sentis, Frank Brana, Jack Taylor, Lone Fleming.

"Dinosaurs, carnivorous giant turtles, lake monsters and a ludicrous imitation of King Kong." (V)

WHERE'S JOHNNY? (B) CFF/Eady-Barnes 1974 color 59m. D: David Eady. SP: M.G. Barnes. Ph: Jo Jago. Mus: Harry Robinson. SpFX: John Poyner. Ref: MFB'74:111. with Raymond Boal.

Prof. accidentally creates invisibility formula.

WHICH IS WITCH? (B) Martin 1915 9m. Ref: BFC.

Landowner cursed by old hag.

WHILE THE PATIENT SLEPT (UA-TV)/WB-FN 1935 66m. (Clue Club Mystery) D: Ray Enright. SP: Robert N. Lee, Eugene Solow; Brown Holmes. From Mignon G. Eberhart's novel "Nurse Keate." Ph: Arthur Edeson. Ref: TVFFSB: "gloomy family mansion." LC. NYT 3/2/35. "WB Story": "inferior thriller set in an old house." V 2/27/35: "as many winding staircases as a castle." with Aline MacMahon, Lyle Talbot, Guy Kibbee, Allen Jenkins, Robert Barrat, Dorothy Tree, Russell Hicks, Brandon Hurst.

Bickering family gathers at estate of apparently dying old man.

The WHIP HAND (UA-TV)/RKO 1951 82m. D & PD: William Cameron Menzies. SP: George Bricker, Frank L. Moss. Story: Roy Hamilton. Ph: Nicholas Musuraca. Mus: Paul Sawtell. AD: Albert S. D'Agostino, Carroll Clark. Ref: TV. V 10/24/51. TVFFSB. Lee. with Carla Balenda, Elliott Reid, Edgar Barrier, Raymond Burr, Lurene Tuttle, Olive Carey, Frank Darien, Otto Waldis.

Mad Nazi doctor working for U.S.S.R. in small Wisconsin town subjects party traitors and volunteers to germ-warfare experiments ("What are these characters trying to do--drop an iron curtain around Winnoga?"); at the end, his "creations" kill him. If the climax of The WHIP HAND recalls monsters-turn-on-master horror movies like REVENGE OF THE ZOMBIES, the premise--man trapped in town taken over by "aliens"--anticipates movies like INVASION OF THE BODY SNATCHERS. The movie plays like an sf-melodrama with a horror graft; the wild revelations of the latter comprise the most entertaining part of the film. The first hour or so is all "ominousness" and no story, though Menzies uses hard close-shots cannily, in a half-successful attempt to foster an atmosphere of psychological menace.

*WHISPERING GHOSTS 1942 Mus: David Raksin, Leigh Harline. Ref: TV.

"Haunted" ship; "ghostly slaves"; non-drying bloodstains. John Carradine (as radio's "Frog Man") is funny; but Milton Berle (as a radio horror-show host) isn't, and he takes up a lot more of your time.

WHISPERS IN THE DARK (I) Cinemondial 1976 color (SUSSURI NEL BUIO. Un SUSSURRO NEL BUIO-orig t) D: Marcello Aliprandi. SP: Nicolo Rienzi, Maria Teresa Carrelli. Ph: Claudio Cirillo. Mus: Pino Donaggio. Ref: V 5/12/76:211(ad),181: "extra sensory suspenser." 4/7/76:46. Bianco Index'76. with John Philip Law, Nathalie Delon, Joseph Cotten, Olga Bissera, Lucretia Love.

WHISPERS OF FEAR (B) Sideline 1974 color/scope 73m. D & Mus: H.B. Davenport. Ph: J. Mangine. Ref: MFB'76:110. with Ika Hindley, Charles Seely.

Strange noises, visions assault young woman in isolated house, drive her to murder.

WHISTLING HILLS Monogram(Frontier) 1951 59m. D: Derwin Abrahams. SP: Jack Lewis. Ph: E. Miller. Ref: V 12/26/51. LC. "Shoot-Em-Ups": SP: Fred Myton? with Johnny Mack Brown, Noel Neill, Jimmy Ellison, Lee Roberts, Stan Jolley, Bud Osborne.

"Costumed" stagecoach robber employs old legend of "whistling hills" to signal pals with "weird whistle." (V)

**The WHITE GORILLA Special Attractions(Weiss) 1947(1945) D: Harry L. Fraser. SP: Monro Talbot. Ph: Bob Cline. Mus: Lee Zahler. Set(s): Thomas Connoly. Ref: screen. LC: c.1945. V(d) 12/3/47. Lee. Everson: footage from '27 PERIL OF THE JUNGLE. with Ray Corrigan, Lorraine Miller.

White gorilla which hates, attacks men; black gorilla which battles white gorilla; Cave of the Cyclops (a one-eyed idol). The mother of invention strikes again! The WHITE GORILLA is sound-film footage "ingeniously" spliced into silent-film footage: two movies, two heroes. But oddly--and, economically-speaking, conveniently--the "sound" hero never quite catches up with his "silent" counterpart. (The story "cleverly" accounts for this non-contact.) Thus the two films, and their respective heroes, like parallel lines, never really meet--although some words and sounds (e.g., a tiger's weird roar) are dubbed onto the silent footage. The effect of this intergenerational graft lies somewhere between camp and modernism. The "epic" gorilla battles are curiously dainty.

WHITE HOUSE HORRORS, The see WEREWOLF OF WASHINGTON

*WHITE ZOMBIE (Manbeck-TV) 1932 D: also Bela Lugosi? Mus: also Guy B. Williams, Xavier Cugat. AD: also C. Tritschler. SpFX: Howard Anderson. Ref: TV. Turner/Price. TVFFSB.

WHITE ZOMBIE is by turns imaginative and embarrassing, exhilarating and campy--a horror-film fan's delight and despair. It employs augmented sounds, "majestic" long shots, glass shots, wipes, and split screen--it's one of the most atmospheric horror movies of the Thirties. One example of its aural-visual ingenuity: the subjective torment of the hero (John Harron)--haunted by (double-exposure) visions of his lost love (Madge Bellamy)--counterpointed by the objective sound of happy chatter in the tavern about him. The over-lavish musical scoring is perhaps a source of both exhilaration and embarrassment, as is Lugosi's performance. At his worst here, however, he's still hokily enjoyable. At his best, he wittily underplays his menace, and is rather magnificent. The other actors succumb to a kind of slow-motion stylization that's closer to catalepsy than to acting....WHITE ZOMBIE, MURDERS IN THE RUE MORGUE, and CHANDU made 1932 quite a year for Bela Lugosi--perhaps his finest, barring revelations from the silent era.

WHO? (B) AA/British Lion-Hemisphere 1974 color 93m. D: Jack Gold. SP: John Gould, from Algis Budrys' novel. Ph: P. Schloemp. Mus: John Cameron. AD: Peter Scharff. SpFX: Richard Richtsfeld. SpMkp: Colin Arthur. Ref: MFB'79:12-13. TVFFSB. V 6/12/74:5(rated). with Elliott Gould, Trevor Howard, Joseph Bova(Martino), Ed Grover, Ivan Desny.

"Nuclear miracle" operation turns badly-injured doctor (Bova) into "android figure," his face "an expressionless metal mask in which only the eyes and mouth can move." (MFB)

WHO? see BEYOND THE DOOR

WHO FEARS THE DEVIL?(by M.W.Wellman) see LEGEND OF HILLBILLY JOHN, The

WHO KILLED WHO? MGM 1943 anim color 7m. Ref: screen. LC.

Very funny Tex Avery parody of horror and mystery movies ("Spooky, isn't it?"); ghost.

WHO SLEW AUNTIE ROO? (U.S.-B) AI/Hemdale 1971 color 91m. (GINGERBREAD HOUSE-orig t. WHOEVER SLEW AUNTIE ROO?-cr t) D: Curtis Harrington. SP: James Sangster, Robert Blees, Gavin Lambert. Story: David Osborn. Ph: Desmond Dickinson. Mus: Kenneth V. Jones. AD: George Provis. Ref: TV. MFB'72:82. Lee(V 12/22/71). VV 3/30/72. with Shelley Winters, Mark Lester, Ralph Richardson, Judy Cornwell, Michael Gothard, Chloe Franks, Hugh Griffith, Lionel Jeffries, Rosalie Crutchley.

Suffocating mixture of pathos, "Hansel and Gretel," children, Christmas, corpses, seances, Shelley Winters, magic props, and teddy bears--the ingredients blend together all-too-disgustingly well. Only Ralph Richardson and the music let in an occasional bit of fresh air. Suffice it to say that this film deserves that title.

WHO'S AFRAID OF THE WEREWOLF? (Braz) Embrafilme 1975 D: Reginaldo Faria. Ref: V 3/31/76:71(ad): "mock-horror tale."

WICKED, WICKED MGM/UNP 1973 color/split screen 95m. SP,D: Richard L. Bare. Ph: Frederick Gately. Mus: Philip Springer; organ music from '25 PHANTOM OF THE OPERA. AD: Walter McKeegar. Ref: MFB'73:234-35: "reasonably entertaining." VV 7/12/73. V 4/18/73. with David Bailey, Tiffany Bolling, Edd Byrnes, Scott Brady, Diane McBain, Arthur O'Connell, Randolph Roberts, Robert Nichols.

Grotesquely-masked killer has victims' bodies stuffed.

The WICKER MAN (B) Larry Gordon/British Lion/Summerisle 1973 color 93m. D: Robin Hardy. SP: Anthony Shaffer. Ph: Harry Waxman. Mus: Paul Giovanni. AD: Seamus Flannery. Ref: pr. screen. MFB'74:16. V 5/15/74. Cinef VI:3. with Christopher Lee, Edward Woodward, Diane Cilento, Britt Ekland, Ingrid Pitt, Aubrey Morris, Ian Campbell.

When the crops fail, the pagan inhabitants of a Scottish island prepare a West Highland policeman for sacrifice to their gods. Touted as "the CITIZEN KANE of horror films," The WICKER MAN is closer (at least in theme) to being the I KNOW WHERE I'M GOING of socio-sexual fantasies. Like that gently didactic film, The WICKER MAN sets its strait-laced protagonist down on a Scottish isle, allowing him (or her, in the case of the older film) to observe the ways of its earthy folk. This slight premise seems even slighter in the _new_ film. Policeman and pagans are too rigidly set in their respective ways; they're at once too broadly contrasted and too simply compared--likened as they ultimately are in their dependence on deities. Pagan and Christian are _both_ supposed to seem somewhat foolish in their blind faith, but they're so thinly-characterized that they seem _only_ foolish....The most regenerating of the pagan's "regenerative influences": Ingrid Pitt, one of the foxes of horror.

WIDDERBURN HORROR,The(by L.Crozetti) see HOUSE OF THE BLACK DEATH

WILD ASS'S SKIN,The(by Balzac) see DESIRE. PIEL DE ZAPA, La.

The WILD WILD WEST REVISITED CBS-TV/Bernstein 1979 color 93m. D: Burt Kennedy. SP: William Bowers. Based on "The Wild Wild West" TV series. See also: MORE WILD WILD WEST. Ph: R.B. Hauser. Mus: Jeff Alexander. AD: A. Heschong. Ref: TV. V 5/16/79:98. with Robert Conrad, Ross Martin, Jo Ann Harris, Paul Williams, Harry Morgan, Rene Auberjonois, Joyce Jameson, Shields & Yarnell, Skip Homeier.

19th-century atom bomb; cloned duplicates of VIP's.

WILDERNESS JOURNEY Gold Key-TV 1970? color 92m. Ref: TVFFSB.

"Demons of ancient legends"; set in Alaska.

*WILLARD 1971 Sequel: BEN. SpFX: Bud David. PhFX: Howard A. Anderson. SdFX: J.L. Klinger. Mkp: Gus Norin. Ref: TV. Cinef Fall'71:39. and with Alan Baxter.

Rat and human pathos, all leading up to justifiable ratricide (i.e., murder-by-rats). Unpleasant stock characters except for the rats, who are stronger on "cute" than on "menace." (Which fact kind of throws off the horror-in-numbers climactic sequences.)

WILLI TOBLER UND DER UNTERGANG DER 6-FLOTTE (W.G.) Unipro 1972 D,P: Alexander Kluge. Ref: Lee. with Alfred Edel, Hark Bohm, Curt Jurgens.

Interplanetary warfare.

WINDS OF CHANGE Sanrio 1980(1978) anim color/scope 89m. SP, D,P: Takashi. From Ovid's "Metamorphoses." Ph: Bill Millar. Mus: Alec R. Costandinos. Anim: Amby Paliwoda et al;(ph) Dickson/Vasu. AD: Paul Julian et al. Titles: F-Stop. Narr: Peter Ustinov;(writer) Norman Corwin. Ref: screen. JFFJ 13: 10-11. V 5/17/78. SFC 11/24/80.

The Stygian witches; Cerberus; Pluto; Medusa and her two sisters; gryphon; dragons; hideous Goddess of Envy; Orpheus and Perseus. Classical mythology for easy listening, easy watching, easy forgetting. Leave your ears at the box office unless you actually want to hear misbegotten songs like "Where Are You Going, Perseus?" Your eyes will offend you somewhat less grievously. (This is still not an endorsement.) Disco mythology.

*WITCHCRAFT THROUGH THE AGES Janus 1921(1969) 80m. 1969 (English-language) version: Mus: Daniel Humair; Jean-Luc Ponty. P: Antony Balch. Narr: William Burroughs. Ref: screen. Lee. no AFI.

An investigation into the roots of superstition. Celestial hell; Black Masses with Devil (Ben Christensen), witches, and demons; stopmo-anim. goat demon; woman giving birth to Satan's children; witch transforming into cat; skeletal, horse-like creature; possessed nuns; inquisitions. HAXAN contains some of the most convincing scenes of witchcraft and black rites on film. They're at once sufficiently ungodly and lightly amusing--serious in subject but not over-serious in treatment. They make a Black Mass seem the place to be to indulge one's baser instincts. Unfortunately, the goal of the movie is to debunk such institutions--this should have been titled "Psychoanalyzing Witchcraft through the Ages." Christensen creates, only glibly to explain away, his unearthly wonders, as merely psychological and sociological phenomena. He proves to be the psychoanalyst's advocate.

WITCHES (Norw.) A/S Fotfilm 1977 (HEKSENE FRA DEN FORSTENEDE SKOG) SP,D: Bredo Greve. Ph: Svein Krovel. Ref: IFG'78:258. with Edith Roger, Ulrikke Greve.

"Underground, low-budget film about witches."

WITCHES BREW Merritt-White 1981(1978) SpFX: David Allen. Sp SeqsD: Herbert L. Strock. Ref: V 6/3/81:4(rated). B.Warren. with Lana Turner, Richard Benjamin, Teri Garr.

WITCHES MOUNTAIN (Sp) (Avco Embassy-TV)/Azor(Para) 1972 color 98m. (El MONTE DE LAS BRUJAS) D: Raul Artigot. Ref: TVFFSB. V 5/9/73. 6/28/72:22: at Sitges. with Patty Shepard, John Caffari, Monica Randall.

News photographer at the mercy of strange forces at legendary Witches Mountain.

*The WITCHING HOUR 1934 From the play, based on the novel "Caleb Powers." Ref: TV. Lee.

Romantic ghost; telepathy. For the most part pretty silly.

Furtive traces of wit, however, plus the novelty of the fantasy gimmick in an unlikely dramatic context.

The WITCH'S NECKLACE Solax 1912 short Ref: AF-Index. Lee.
Woman dreams that necklace which she saw in witch's cave is strangling her.

The WITCH'S SEX (I) Universalia 1973 (Il SESSO DELLA STREGA) SP,D: Angelo Pannaccio. SP: also F. Brocani. Ph: G.La Rosa. Ref: Lee: witchcraft?; "brutal murders." Bianco Index'74. with Susan Levi, Jessica Dullin, Camille Keaton, A. Liemezza.

WITHOUT WARNING see IT CAME...WITHOUT WARNING

WITNESS MADNESS see TALES THAT WITNESS MADNESS

The WIZ Univ/Motown 1978 color 134m. D: Sidney Lumet. SP: Joel Schumacher, from William Brown & Charlie Smalls' play, adapted from L.Frank Baum's book "The Wonderful Wizard of Oz." Ph: Oswald Morris. Mus: Smalls, Quincy Jones. PD: Tony Walton. SpVisFX: Albert Whitlock. SpMkp: Stan Winston. Sp Props: Eoin Sprott, Richard Tautkus. Ref: MFB'79:57. TV. V 10/4/78. with Diana Ross, Michael Jackson, Nipsey Russell, Mabel King(Evillene), Lena Horne, Richard Pryor, Ted Ross.
In the land of Oz, Evillene, the Wicked Witch of the West commands a squad of flying monkeys on motorcycles, and sweatshop workers who shed monstrous skins; mechanical tinman; living monster-pillars; dolls which grow to giant-size; giant TV and "mike." Musical-fantasy alternates between the effortless uplift of (some of) the tunes and the dancing and the strained uplift of (some of) the lyrics and the dialogue. At its best The WIZ has an air of genial abandon; at its worst it takes itself <u>seriously</u>. Primarily, you want to avoid the opening and closing sequences, and any scene in which only lips are moving.

*The WIZARD OF MARS Karston-Hewitt(Borealis) 1964 81m. SP (also) & AD: Armando Busick. Ph: Austin McKinney. SpFX: Cinema Research. ElecFX: Frank Coe. Mkp: Jean Lister. Ref: TV. AFI. and with Vic McGee, Eve Bernhardt.
Lily-pad-like creatures; volcano; yellow brick road ("the golden road"); ancient race inhabiting "city out of time." Oddly ambitious cheapie. Its main thought re: death (there's no new life without it) is almost...metaphysical! The production itself is somewhat less sublime. Typical she-he exchange (re: Mars): "Beautiful, isn't it?" "In its own alien way, I guess it is--it's another world, all right."

*The WIZARD OF OZ MGM 1939 color & b&w AD: Cedric Gibbons. SpFX: Arnold Gillespie. Mkp: Jack Dawn. Ref: Lee.
Sequel: JOURNEY BACK TO OZ. See also: WIZ, The.

WIZARDS Fox 1977 anim color 80m. (WAR WIZARDS-orig t) SP, D,P: Ralph Bakshi. Ph: T.C. Bemiller. Mus: Andrew Belling.

Bkgd Des: Ian Miller. AnimFX: Tasia Williams. Ref: screen. V(d) 1/25/77. 2/22/76:4. MFB'77:14.

Earth, two million years after nuclear devastation. Black Wolf, evil wizard with armies of frog-goblins, demons and mutant men; giant spider-creature; mind possession; Larry, sycophantic lizard-creature. Good-against-evil again (or love-vs.-technology), not as well-done as it has on occasion been done. But flashily-animated at least, and punctuated with humor. Bakshi has hardly mustered up a serviceable mythology of his own, though, before he's assimilating *Nazi* mythology into his limited vision of evil. WIZARDS is both an *anti-technological* work dependent on *technology*, and a *film* decrying the *power of film*. (Black Wolf stirs up his forces by running them Nazi newsreels.) These large ironies seem intentional, but are essentially stingless: within the narrative, film and technology are defined too simply to connect with their extra-narrative referents.

WOHI RAAT WOHI AWAAZ see SAME NIGHT, THE SAME VOICE, The

WOLF BOY see LEGEND OF THE WEREWOLF

*The WOLF MAN 1941 Mus sc: Hans J. Salter, Frank Skinner. Assoc AD: Robert Boyle. SpFX: John P. Fulton. Ref: TV. J.Shapiro.

"The way you walked was thorny, through no fault of your own"--the sound of "B"-movie tragedy, and an essential part of our pulp heritage. The Universal production gloss--terrific lighting for the village sets, and an "A" musical score--is appreciated. But psychology and lycanthropy seem at odds here, as characters offer psychological explanations for Larry Talbot's black-outs, and the film offers no-doubt-about-it werewolf scenes. Among the actors, only Claude Rains and Evelyn Ankers at times start to bring the meaning of the film into focus--Lon Chaney Jr. invariably whacks it out again. And when (or if) you recall faces from The WOLF MAN, you don't recall Ralph Bellamy, Warren William, or Patric Knowles, and for good reason--they have all the presence of paper napkins. Maria Ouspenskaya is her (fortunately) inimitable self, and Bela Lugosi is wasted as Wolf Man #1. Done better as CAT PEOPLE.

Sequel: FRANKENSTEIN MEETS THE WOLF MAN. See also: HOWLING, The. WEREWOLF OF WASHINGTON.

WOLF MAN, The see HOMEM LOBO, O. WOLFMAN.

WOLF MAN'S CURE, The see HOUSE OF DRACULA

WOLF WOMAN, The see LEGEND OF THE WOLF WOMAN

WOLFEN WB/Orion(Alan King) 1981 color/scope 114m. SP,D,P: Michael Wadleigh. SP: also David Eyre. From Whitley Streiber's novel. Ph: Gerry Fisher;(Steadicam) Garrett Brown. Mus: James Horner;(song) Tom Waits. PD: Paul Sylbert. SpVisFX: Robert Blalack; Betsy Bromberg et al;(ad) Eoin Sprott. SpFx

Mkp: Carl Fullerton. SpFX: Ronnie Otteson, Conrad Brink. Sd FxSup: A. London, R. Grieve. SpEquip: Sanyo. Ref: screen. V 7/22/81. VV 7/29/81. J.Willis. SFC 7/24/81. with Albert Finney, Edward James Olmos, Gregory Hines, Diane Venora, Tom Noonan, Dick O'Neill.

God-like super-wolves--evolved from wolves over 20,000 years--find new hunting-grounds in urban slums, where they prey on the diseased and the neglected; shape-shifting as red herring. Ambitious, technically-sophisticated shocker never quite resolves esthetic tensions among its disparate shock, sociological, and mythic elements. If it's not "just" a horror movie, neither is it quite myth--the wolfen don't come equipped with enough mythic paraphernalia to <u>begin</u> to replace or rival werewolves in pop folklore. And the comparison/contrast between nature and technology (wolfen-eye view vs. computer-eye view) is intriguing, but undeveloped. The Steadicam and sight-and-sound effects, however, make the wolfen-eye scenes more-interesting-than-usual monster's-eye-view sequences, and the dialogue is occasionally surprisingly good.

WOLFIN VOM TEUFELSMOOR see SHE-WOLF OF DEVIL'S MOOR

WOLFMAN--A LYCANTHROPE Omni/EOC 1978 color 101m. SP,D: Worth Keeter III. Ph: Darrell Cathcart. Mus: Arthur Smith, David Floyd. AD: Gunther Foster. Ref: Boxo 7/30/79:22. 2/25/80: 30. V 12/6/78:26(ad). 1/18/78:31(ad). with Earl Owensby, Kristina Reynolds, Ed L.Grady, Maggie Lauterer, Richard Dedmon.

Werewolf terrorizes small Southern town.

WOLFMAN OF COUNT DRACULA see MARK OF THE WOLFMAN

A WOMAN OF DESIRE (Braz) Christensen 1975 color 87m. (A MULHER DO DESEJO) SP,D: Carlos Hugo Christensen. Ph: A. Goncalves. Mus: Wagner. Ref: Brasil. with Jose Mayer, Vera Fajardo, Palmira Barbosa.

House "seems to come to life"; spirit of dead man possesses nephew.

*The WOMAN WHO CAME BACK (NTA-TV) 1945 Ed: John Link. Ref: screen. TVFFSB. V 12/19/45: "phantom dog."

Woman fears she harbors transmigrated soul of witch dead 300 years. Nothing supernatural about this horror-movie cheat--just a crazy old lady, New England history, and a tormented heroine (who seems related to Irena in CAT PEOPLE). Overwrought acting and music; crude horror scenes. However, there <u>are</u> some stunningly-conceived editing effects--e.g., a dissolve from a shot of clouds to a shot of Nancy Kelly lying in bed: the transition makes it look, eerily, as if she's lolling on a cushion of billowy white clouds. But what the hell are such sophisticated--and even thematically justifiable--effects doing in <u>this</u> movie?

The WOMANHUNT (U.S.-Fili) New World/Four Associates 1972 color 82m. D: Eddie Romero. Ph: Justo Paulino. Ref: Lee. CineFan

2:18. with John Ashley, Pat Woodell, Lisa Todd, Sid Haig. Mad hunter uses women as game on private island.

WOMEN IN THE NIGHT Film Classics/Southern Calif.(Ansell) 1948 (1947) 90m. Story,D: William Rowland. SP: Robert St.Clair, Edwin Westry, based on a U.N. Information Office report. Ed: Dan Milner. Ref: V 1/14/48. LC: c.1947. with Tala Birell, William Henry, Virginia Christine, Richard Loo, Benson Fong, Philip Ahn.
"'Cosmic ray' weapon." (V)

WOMEN OF TRANSPLANT ISLAND see WONDER WOMEN

WONDER WOMAN ABC-TV/WB-TV 1974 color 75m. D: Vincent McEveety. SP & Exec P: John D.F. Black. Based on the Charles Moulton comic-book characters. Ph: Joe Biroc. Mus: Artie Butler. AD: Philip Bennett. SpFX: George Peckham. Ref: TV. Lee. V 3/20/74:46. with Cathy Lee Crosby, Ricardo Montalban, Andrew Prine, Kaz Garas, Anitra Ford, R.X. Slattery, Charlene Holt.
Super-heroine from lost-island tribe of women with super-skills; invisible plane. Low-key super-heroics, with more comedy than fantasy. Crosby as Wonder Woman is winningly wry, but her vitality seems undermatched by her material.
See also: NEW, ORIGINAL WONDER WOMAN, The.

WONDER WOMEN (U.S.-Fili) General/Central 1973 color 81m. (WOMEN OF TRANSPLANT ISLAND-orig t) D & Adap: Robert O'Neil. SP: Lou Whitehill. Ph: R.M. David. Mus: Carson Whitsett. AD: Ben Otico. SpFX: Jessie Santo Domingo. Ref: MFB'73:235: "amateur dramatics." TVFFSB. V 1/24/73:6(rated). with Nancy Kwan, Ross Hagen, Maria de Aragon, Roberta Collins, Vic Diaz, Gail Hansen, Sid Haig.
Mad scientist (who "vanishes in a puff of smoke") conducts "monstrous transplant experiments" on remote volcanic island; her "failures" are freaks. (MFB)

WONDERFUL WIZARD OF OZ,The(by L.F.Baum) see JOURNEY BACK TO OZ. WIZ,The. WIZARD OF MARS. ZARDOZ.

WON'T WRITE HOME, MOM--I'M DEAD see TERROR FROM WITHIN

WORLD BEYOND THE MOON ABC-TV 1952 65m. Story: Mike Moser. FX: Cameron Pierce. Ref: Lee(Warren). "Directory...TV Shows." no LC. with Ed Kemmer, Lyn Osborn, Virginia Hewitt, Marvin Miller.
30th Century; time travel; feature from episodes of "Space Patrol" TV series.

WORLD OF DISNEY see MYSTERY IN DRACULA'S CASTLE

WORLD OF HORROR (Pol) Film Polski/ZRF 1968 color 89m. (SWIAT GROZY) Ref: WorldF'68: feature from three made-for-TV stories.
1) "Lord Arthur Savile's Crime." SP,D: Witold Lesiewicz. From Oscar Wilde's story. Mus: Baird. with Andrzej Lapicki.

2) "The Canterville Ghost." D: Ewa & C. Petelski. SP: Z. Skowronski, from Wilde's story. Mus: J. Maksymiuk. with C. Wollejko(ghost). 3) "A Terribly Strange Bed." SP,D: W. Lesiewicz. From W.W. Collins' story. Mus: Baird. with A. Karzynska.

WORLD WAR III WWT 1981? D: David Greene. SP: R.L. Joseph. Mus: Gil Melle. Ref: V 10/14/81:33(ad). with David Soul, Brian Keith, Cathy Lee Crosby, Rock Hudson.

The WORST CRIME OF ALL! Ajay/Horizon 1966 78m. (aka MONDO KEYHOLE. MONDO KEY. The TARTS. R---!) D: John Lamb. Ref: AFI. with Cathy Crowfoot, Pluto Felix(Dracula), V. Wren.
Woman seeking escape through drugs finds herself conducted on a tour of the Inferno by Dracula.

WOULD YOU KILL A CHILD? (Sp) AI/Penta 1975 color/scope 112m. (Los NINOS. QUIEN PUEDE MATAR A UN NINO? DEATH IS CHILD'S PLAY-orig B.t. ISLAND OF DEATH-B. ISLAND OF THE DAMNED-U.S.) SP,D: Narciso Ibanez Serrador. SP: also Luis Penafiel. From Juan Jose Plans' novel "El Juego." Ph: J.L. Alcaine. Mus: Waldo de los Rios. AD: R. Gomez, J.L.del Barco. SpPhFX: Sixto Rincoin. Ref: MFB'77:127-8. '79:138. V 2/2/77:30. 5/5/76. with Lewis Fiander, Prunella Ransome, Carlos Parra.
Children on island band together, murder adults "for the suffering of innocent children through centuries...." (MFB)

WUNDERUHR, Die see MAGIC CLOCK, The

WURDALAK, The(by A.Tolstoy) see NIGHT OF THE DEVILS

Y A PLUS QU'A(by P.Knack) see Q

YAKSHA GAANAM (India-Mal.) Aspara 1976 142m. D: Sheela. SP: Medhavi. Mus: Viswanathan. Ref: Dharap. with Madhu.
A suicide "enters the body of her lover's wife" and makes him kill himself so that they can be united.

YAMATO TOWA NI see BE FOREVER, YAMATO

YANG PA-MEI CH'U CHIN TAO (H.K.?) 1961? Based on the novel "Yang-chia-chiang." Ref: Eberhard: "fight with ghosts."

YASHAGA IKE see DEMON POND

YATSU HAKAMURA see VILLAGE OF THE EIGHT TOMBS

YEAR OF THE ANGRY RABBIT(by R.Braddon) see NIGHT OF THE LEPUS

YELLOW PERIL see CHINESE MAGIC

YETI (I) Stefano/Futuranik 1977 color 105m. (BIG FOOT-ad t. YETI--L'ABOMINEVOLE UOMO DELLE NEVI) SP,D: Gianfranco Panolini(aka Frank Kramer). SP: also Mario Di Nardo, Marcello Coscia. Ph: Sandro Mancori. Mus: S.M. Romitelli. AD: C. De Santis. SpFX: Ermanno Biamonte. Ref: Meyers. Bianco #2/78:163. V 1/18/78. 10/19/77:135,143. 4/13/77:34. with Mimmo Crau(the yeti), Phoenix Grant, Jim Sullivan,Tony Kendall.
"A snowman without snow trapped in the summer sun of a major city." (V)

YIN-YANG CHIEH see BLOOD REINCARNATION

YOU BETTER WATCH OUT Pressman 1980 color 100m. SP,D: Lewis Jackson. Ph: R. Aronovich. PD: L.J. Harris. Ref: V 12/3/80. with Brandon Maggart, Dianne Hull, Scott McKay, Joe Jamrog.
"A murdering Santa Claus....many horrific moments."

YOUNG DRACULA see SON OF DRACULA(1974)

YOUNG FRANKENSTEIN Fox/Gruskoff 1974 108m. (FRANKENSTEIN JUNIOR-I) SP,D: Mel Brooks. SP: also Gene Wilder. Ph: Gerald Hirschfeld. Mus: John Morris. AD: Dale Hennesy. Sp FX: Hal Millar, Henry Millar Jr. Mkp: William Tuttle. Sp Props: Kenneth Strickfaden. Graphics: Anthony Goldschmidt. Ref: screen. MFB'75:90. V 12/18/74. Bianco Index'75. with Wilder, Peter Boyle, Marty Feldman(Igor), Madeline Kahn, Teri Garr, Cloris Leachman, Kenneth Mars, Gene Hackman, Richard Haydn, Oscar Beregi, John Dennis, N. Schiller, Lou Cutell.
Engaging parody of old Universal horror movies ("_Dead is dead!_"), with direct narrative and visual references to FRANKENSTEIN(1931), BRIDE OF FRANKENSTEIN, and SON OF FRANKENSTEIN. This is basically the same old, workable doctor-and-monster plot, with each step marked off by a gag or two--some of them dandies, all of them deliberately telegraphed. (Thus even if the punchline fails you can enjoy the set-up.) The highlights: the monster's "Puttin' on the Ritz" number and his encounter with the hermit--two fully-developed routines, not just hit-and-miss gags. (In its cheerful misanthropy, the latter sequence is an hilarious "correction" of the corresponding sequence in BRIDE.) Wilder's more serious moments (as Victor Frankenstein's grandson) are rather ponderous--the movie is better at parodying than recapitulating its forebears. Only Boyle both convinces _and_ amuses--he uses just his _eyes_ as comic counterpoint to his monster-body-and-movements.

YOUNG GOODMAN BROWN Pyramid/CPB-AFI 1972 color 20m. SP,D, Ed,SpFX: Donald Fox. From Nathaniel Hawthorne's story. Ph: Richard Robertson. Ref: Lee: the Devil; Black Mass.

YOUNG HANNAH, QUEEN OF THE VAMPIRES see CRYPT OF THE LIVING DEAD

YSANI THE PRIESTESS (B) Int'l. 1934 32m. D: Gordon Sherry. SP: Raven Wood. Ref: BFC. with Vivienne Bell, Charles Hay.

"Mummified priestess tells audience's fortune with aid of live actor on stage."

YU-HUO FEN CH'IN see HOUSE OF THE LUTE

YU-LING see SPIRIT,The(1977?)

Z.P.G. (U.S.-B) Para/Sagittarius 1972 color 96m. (ZERO POPULATION GROWTH-B. The FIRST OF JANUARY-orig t. EDICT-int t) D: Michael Campus. SP: Max Ehrlich, Frank De Felitta. Ph: Michael Reed. Mus: Jonathan Hodge. PD: Tony Masters. SpFX: Derek Meddings. Ref: MFB'72:125: "highly sentimental." Lee. VV 7/6/72. V 4/26/72. with Oliver Reed, Geraldine Chaplin, Diane Cilento, Don Gordon, Bill Nagy.

21st Century. World government bans babies for 30 years; robot-doll child-substitutes.

ZAAT see BLOOD WATERS OF DR. Z

ZAP see INVOCATION OF MY DEMON BROTHER

ZARDOZ (B) Fox/Boorman 1974 color/scope 105m. SP,D,P: John Boorman. Story & Des:(asst) Bill Stair. Ph: Geoffrey Unsworth;(process) Charles Staffell. Mus: David Munrow; Beethoven. PD: Anthony Pratt. SpFX: Gerry Johnson. Mkp: Basil Newall. Ref: screen. MFB'74:83-4. V 1/30/74. with Sean Connery, Charlotte Rampling, Sara Kestelman, Sally Anne Newton.

In the year 2293 the tribes of Brutals who inhabit the wastelands of Earth worship Zardoz, a giant flying, stone godhead operating on the principle of the Wizard of Oz; they are forbidden to enter the Vortex, home of the Elite (whose secret is stored in the Tabernacle). Joint award (with The MAN WHO FELL TO EARTH) for most tortuous, arduous sf-movie experience of the Seventies. Its yellow brick road leads through a labyrinth of immortals-made-mortal, senile "renegades," "apathetics," etc. The movie is a ridiculously elaborate, fantasy-world house-of-cards, with occasional mitigating visual and comic felicities.

ZARKOFF--HALF MAN, HALF BEAST see MONSTER STRIKES, The

ZARTLICHEKEIT DER WOLFE see TENDERNESS OF THE WOLVES

ZERO POPULATION GROWTH see Z.P.G.

ZHONGGUO CHAOREN see INFRAMAN

ZIPSTONES (Dutch) Brandon 1976 anim color 10m. SP,D: Rob Bongers. Ref: Brandon.

"Giant machines...suck in trees, mountains," etc. to make building blocks.

Ze ZIVOTA DETI (Cz) Kratky 1977 anim color 9m. SP,D: Milos Macourek et al. Ref: Zagreb'78.
"Child's game turns into a Golem who destroys everything."

ZOLTAN...HOUND OF DRACULA see DRACULA'S DOG

ZOMBIE (I) Jerry Gross/Variety 1979 color/scope 91m. (ZOMBI 2-Eur. The ISLAND OF THE LIVING DEAD-ad t. ZOMBIE FLESH EATERS-alt t?) D: Lucio Fulci. SP: Elisa Briganti. Ph: S. Salvati. Mus: F. Frizzi, G. Tucci. PD: W. Patriarca. SpMkpFX: Giannetto De Rossi. SpFX: Corridori. Ref: screen. MFB'80:55. V 5/9/79:279(ad). 7/30/80. FM 169:44-47. with Tisa Farrow, Ian McCulloch, Richard Johnson, Al Cliver, Auretta Gay.
An undiagnosable disease kills and transforms the inhabitants of a Caribbean island into carnivorous zombies. ZOMBIE is neither notably dull nor silly, and it's not badly photographed. It's quite functional--a success on its own terms. It brings the gore, and that's it--entrail delight. The most painstakingly-revolting effect--a punctured eyeball--seems an accidental reference to the Bunuel of CHIEN ANDALOU. For Bunuel, though,the slitting of the eyeball was a means, not an end. ZOMBIE succeeds only in making one want (literally) to close, not (figuratively) to open one's eyes. It's functionally repellent.

ZOMBIES see DAWN OF THE DEAD

ZOMBIES ATOMICOS (Mex-Sp) Televicine & Lotus 1980 (El ATAQUE DE LOS ZOMBIES ATOMICOS) D: Umberto Lenzi. Ref: V 10/1/80: 65. 3/25/81:46. with Hugo Stiglitz, Lili Carati, F. Rabal.

The ZOO ROBBERY (B) CFF/Cine-Lingual 1973 color 64m. SP,D, P: Matt McCarthy, John Black. Ph: T. Imi. Mus: De Wolfe. AD: M. Pickwoad. Ref: MFB'73:136. with Paul & Denise Gyngell, Karen Lucas, Richard Willis.
The London Zoo acquires an orange-coated yeti.

ZORA see SILENT NIGHT, BLOODY NIGHT

ZREAKS see CHILDREN SHOULDN'T PLAY WITH DEAD THINGS

A ZSARNOK SZIVA, AVAGY BOCCACCIO MAGYARORSZAGON (Hung.-I) Mafilm & Radiotelevision Italiana-Leone 1981 color 88m. D: Miklos Jancso. SP: Giovanna Gagliardo, from stories by Boccaccio. Ph: Janos Kende. Ref: V 9/9/81. with Ninetto Davoli, Laszlo Galffy, Theresa-Ann Savoy.
Woman appears to remain young by drinking the blood of virgins.

ZVYOZDNYI INSPECTOR see STAR INSPECTOR

PERIPHERAL AND PROBLEM FILMS

*A-HAUNTING WE WILL GO 1942 Ref: TV: no ghosts, fake or real (apart from a drawing of one behind the end-title).

AADIYUG (India-Hindi) 1978 Ref: Dharap: "early man."

ACT OF MURDER (B) 1962 Ref: TVFFSB: "weird events" at estate.

ADAVI MANUSHULU (India-Tel.) 1978 Ref: Dharap: "early man."

ADI MANAVA (India-Kan.) 1977 Ref: Dharap: "early stages" of man.

ADI MANAVULU (India-Tel.) 1976 Ref: Dharap: caveman story.

ADVENTURES OF A PRIVATE EYE (B) 1977 Ref: MFB'77:163: psychic; "Grimsdyke Manor."

ADVENTURES OF CAPTAIN FABIAN 1951 Ref: TVFFSB: "witchcraft in New Orleans." NYT 12/14/51. V 9/26/51: Agnes Moorehead as "weird companion" to M. Presle.

The ADVENTURES OF ENRIQUE AND ANA (Sp) 1981 Ref: V 9/30/81: 53(ad): sf?

AEGGET AR LOST 1975 Ref: V 4/16/75: eggs marketed as anti-itch "gadgets."

The AFFAIRS OF APHRODITE 1970 Ref: AFI: goddess, spell,torture.

The AFFAIRS OF CAPPY RICKS 1937 Ref: V 6/30/37: "builder of electrically controlled boats." B.Warren: not sf. J.Dante.

AFTER DARK (Austral) 1975 semi-docu. Ref: MFB'77:255: "town where evidence has been found of visitors from outer space"; male witch and his coven; "Boris Karloff imitation."

AGENCY (Can.) 1980 Ref: V 1/21/81: firm which uses subliminal TV messages to affect elections.

AGRAHARATHIL KAZHUTHAI (India-Tamil) 1977 Ref: Dharap: donkey seems to have supernatural powers.

L'AIGLE ET LA COLOMBE (F) 1977 Ref: V 3/23/77: "man being groomed as a new Hitler" for neo-Nazi group; torture.

AIRPORT '80 THE CONCORDE 1979 Ref: MFB'79:207: new rocket.

AIRPORT '77 1977 Ref: TVG. TV: plane goes floppo in the Bermuda Triangle.

AL OTRO LADO DEL ESPEJO (Sp) Ref: V 5/8/74:208(ad): "call from beyond the grave."

ALICE, or THE LAST ESCAPADE (F) 1977 Ref: V(d) 1/17/77: "nightmare-like....occult....old dark house....no horror."

ALIEN TERROR Aricorn 1977 D: C. McNeill. Ref: V 6/22/77:32: shooting. with Kathi Carey, John Woods, Caroline Brown.

ALIENS FROM SPACESHIP EARTH 1978 Ref: TV: the quest for "higher consciousness."

ALIVE BY NIGHT Ref: F.O.Ray.

ALL NIGHT LONG 1981 Ref: NYorker 3/9/81: reverse-mirror invention. MFB'81:107.

ALL THE KIND STRANGERS 1974 Ref: TV. Scheuer/MOTV. Orphaned farm kids trap travellers, vote on whether to keep them as parents or kill them; vicious watchdogs; thunderstorm.
ALLA RICERCA DEL PIACERE (I) 1971 Ref: MFB'73:23: trance.
ALMOST HUMAN (I) 1974('80-U.S.) (MILANO ODIA: LA POLIZIA NON PUO' SPARARE) Ref: V 7/30/80: "orgy of...carnage."
ALWAYS ON SATURDAY (B) 1972 short Ref: MFB'72:263: clips from GHOSTS AND GHOULIES.
L'AMANTE DEL DEMONIO (I) Nova 1971 Ref: Bianco Index'76:4. with E. Purdom, R. Neri.
AMAR SUHAGIN (India) 1978 Ref: Dharap: ghost.
The AMAZING EQUAL PAY SHOW (B) 1974 Ref: MFB'75:215: "Equal Pay legislation potion" prepared in "horror-film" lab.
AMONG THE LIVING DEAD (Egy) 1967 Ref: V 7/8/81:6.
El AMOR BRUJO (Sp) 1967('72-U.S.) Ref: Lee: fake ghost. Willis/SW. WorldF'67.
AMOR, CARNAVAL E SONHO (Braz) 1973 Ref: V 2/28/73: segment with voodoo god and goddess.
AMRIT MANTHAN (India) 1934 Ref: Lee: devils.
O AMULETO DE OGUM (Braz) 1975 Ref: V 5/28/75: amulet makes wearer invulnerable.
...AND MILLIONS WILL DIE AA 1973 color 96m. Ref: TVFFSB: "unknown source that causes the deaths of several thousand people." With R. Basehart, S. Strasberg, L. Nielsen.
AND NOW MY LOVE (F-I) 1974 (TOUTE UNE VIE) Ref: V 5/29/74: talk of pollution-engendered monsters. MFB'75:145.
AND TOMORROW (F) 1974 D: Pierre Carpenter. Ref: V 5/7/75: 208: future world problems.
ANDREI ROUBLEV (Russ) 1966 Ref: screen. MFB'73:203-4. Spirit of monk; torture scenes.
L'ANGE ET LA FEMME (Can.) 1978 Ref: V 2/1/78: youth "reanimates" murdered woman "by breathing on her wounds."
The ANGRY GOD (U.S.-Mex?) 1948 Ref: V 10/27/48: fire god makes volcano erupt.
Los ANIMALES NO SE MIRAN AL ESPEJO (Sp) Tecno-fantasy 1974 anim & live D: F.M. Blasco. Ref: V 8/25/76:34: "futuristic."
ANIMALYMPICS 1979 Ref: MFB'80:63-4: 1980 Animal Olympics.
ANIMATION PIE 1974 short Ref: MFB'75:249: "plasticine dinosaur...a diplodocus plays the King Kong role." L.Artel.
ANNA KARENINA (B) 1948 Ref: TV. V 1/28/48. B.Warren. Nightmare figure appears to Anna.
ANNABELLE LEE 1972? D: H. Daniels. Ref: Lee. Completed?
Die ANSTALT (W.G.) 1979 Ref: V 1/17/79: a la Poe's "Tarr & Fether."
ANTICLOCK (B) 1978? Ref: IFG'78:125: sf? V 9/17/80: man's mind "programmed." FM 169:8: "sci-fi."
ANTROPOPHAGOUS (I) 1980 Ref: V 3/4/81:36: "chiller."
APE AND SUPER-APE (U.S.-Dutch) 1972 Ref: MFB'74:3-4: "bloody."
APPOINTMENT WITH LUST 1971? Ref: Lee(p). with H.Vernon.
ARCANA (I) 1971? D: Questi. Ref: Lee: ESP, black magic.
Les ARDENTES (F) 1973 Ref: MFB'75:5: "community of women."
ARETINO'S BLUE STORIES (I) 1972 Ref: MFB'74:79-80: ecstasies of love passed off as "demonic possession."
ARMAGUEDON (I-F) 1977 Ref: SFC: plot to take over the world.

ARWAH PENASARAN (Indon.) Ref: V 9/21/77:6: at Sitges.
ASH WEDNESDAY 1973 Ref: MFB'74:68: "morbid" plastic-surgery scenes; woman's beauty restored. V 11/21/73.
ASSO (I) 1981 Ref: V 5/6/81: ghost comedy.
ASTRAL STRANGLER Worldwide 1976 Ref: V 5/26/76:4(rated).
The ASTROLOGER 1975 Ref: V 12/17/75: child's mystical powers.
ASYLUM OF THE INSANE Regal Int'l 1971 Ref: Lee(V 12/29/71:7).
ATMA SHAKTHI (India) 1978 Ref: Dharap: witch doctor hypnotizes girl.
AU LONG DE LA RIVIERE FANGO (F) 1975 Ref: V 2/5/75:futuristic?
AUTOPSY (Sp) 1973 Ref: V 11/28/73: "autopsy in totum."
AUTOSTOP ROSSO SANGUE (I) 1976 (DEATH DRIVE-B) Ref: MFB'78: 153: seq. with DUEL-like "giant truck" terrorizing driver.
The AVENGERS: The RETURN OF THE CYBERNAUTS (B) Ref: TV. TVG: robots; shown as "CBS Late Movie" 7/18/80.
Le AVVENTURE DI PINOCCHIO (I) 1971 Ref: Bianco Index'72.
AXE 1977 Ref: AMPAS. Willis/SW.

The BABY 1972 Ref: TV. MFB'73:72: "sick joke."
BABY CART ON RIVER STYX (J) 1972 Ref: screen: dismemberment. V 11/19/80: aka SHOGUN ASSASSIN. 3/31/76:24: at Paris sf-fest.
BABY KONG (I) 1976? Ref: V. FM 170:46. Completed?
BABY ROSEMARY Essex 1977 color 80m. Ref: Willis/SW.
The BABYSITTER 1980 Ref: TVG 11/22/80: "chills." SFE 11/28/80.
BADDEGAMA (Sri L.) Ref: V 6/3/81: "witch"; "demons."
BADMAN'S GOLD 1951 Ref: V 10/24/51: professor develops "new way to melt down" gold bricks.
BALAK AUR JANWAR (India) 1975 Ref: Dharap: priest's curse.
The BALLAD OF TARA (Iran.) 1980 Ref: V 5/28/80:ghost. IFG'81.
BAMBOO GODS AND IRON MEN (Fili-U.S.) 1973 Ref: MFB'74:196: "powerful substance" proves to be gunpowder. V 1/23/74.
BANASANKARI (India) 1977 Ref: Dharap: goddess destroys man.
BARE KNUCKLES 1978 Ref: V 2/8/78: maniac with butcher knife.
The BARRIER (Bulg.) Ref: IFG'80:83: "fantastic cinema"?
BASKETBALL JONES 1976 Ref: Glut/CMM: King Kong bit.
The BATTLE WIZARD (H.K.) 1977 Ref: IFG'78:178(ad): witch?
The BEAST FVI 1981 Ref: V 6/10/81:4(rated).
The BEASTS ARE IN THE STREETS 1978 Ref: Maltin/TVM: animals from animal park terrorize community.
BED HOSTESSES (Swiss) 1975 Ref: MFB'76:168: "Satanic cult"?
BEHIND THE HEADLINES 1937 TVFFSB:"pocket-size short-wave transmitters enable reporters to broadcast news from the spot as it happens." LC. V 6/9/37.
BELLADONNA (J) 1973 anim Ref: V 2/12/75:34: "medieval witch."
BELLS OF AUTUMN (Russ) 1980 Ref: V 3/26/80: Snow White?
Die BERGKATZE (G) 1921 (The WILDCAT) Ref: screen: dream: man removes his heart, gives to woman, who bites off a piece.
La BESTIA DESNUDA (Mex) 1969 Ref: Lee. Sfa*BLOODY PLEASURE?
BESTIJE (Yugos) Ref: V 8/17/77: "a sort of Walpurgis Night."
BEYOND AND BACK 1978 Ref: V 2/8/78: semi-docu.re:life-after-death. AMPAS.
BEYOND BELIEF 1976 Ref: TVFFSB: docu. re: ESP, reincarnation, "other mysteries."

BEYOND DEATH'S DOOR 1979 Ref: Boxo 8/20/79:18: "supposedly true accounts" of people who have returned from the dead. Willis/SW.
BEYOND GOOD AND EVIL (I-F-W.G.) 1977 Ref: V 10/12/77: "hallucinations of the Devil."
BEYOND THE FOG Ref: V 3/4/81:8: in Miami.
BEYOND THE REEF Ref: V 5/20/81: man's spirit enters shark.
BHAKTHI MAIN BHAGWAN (India) 1975 Ref: Dharap: dead revived.
BHAYANKARA MANDRAVADHI (India) 1976 Ref: Dharap: mother destroys evil, "immortal" son by destroying his talisman.
BIG BOY RIDES AGAIN 1935 Ref: TVFFSB: "strange mystery...sinister adversary." G.E.Turner. no LC. HR 2/28/35. B.Warren.
BIG JACK Ref: HR & V(d) 4/8/49: grave-robbing doctor.NYT 5/23/49.
BIG SNUFF (Arg) 1975 Ref: V 5/30/79:42: woman dismembered.
BIG THUMBS Ref: V 8/17/77: "freak elevator accident" turns woman into nymphomaniac.
BILBAO (Sp) Ref: V 5/24/78: woman-into-sausages at pork factory.
The BIONIC BOY (Fili) Ref: V 5/4/77:78.
BIRTH OF THE HAUNTED (Can.) 1976 non-theat.short Ref: LC Films '78: "ghost story" docu-drama.
BIRTH OF THE WITCH (W.G.) Ref: V 9/2/81:6: at Sitges.
BISEXUAL (F-I) 1975 (Les ONZE MILLE VERGES) Ref: MFB'76:87: "curse of the 11,000 bangs."
**The BISHOP MURDER CASE 1930 Ref: TV: killer driven mad by "diabolic hatred"; secret formula; fog; storm; "remote stethoscope" which checks patient's heartbeat from distance.
BIZARRE-BIZARRE (F) 1937 Ref: screen: man ("the Butcher" or "the Ripper") who butchers butchers; prophetic dream.
The BLACK BANANA (Israeli) 1977 Ref: V 12/7/77: "Dybbuk"spoofed.
The BLACK BOX MURDERS 1975 Ref: TVFFSB: stormy country night.
The BLACK GESTAPO Ref: V 4/16/75: "extremely brutal."
BLACK INFERNO 1956? short amateur? Ref: Lee: vampires?
BLACK JACK Ref: V 12/12/73: Ft.Knox nuked.
BLACK MAGIC SEX (J) 1972? (KUNOICHI-KESHO) Ref: screen: women-into-skeletons bit; "echo"-of-pain weapon; insect-swarm weapon.
BLACK MOON (F;Eng.-lang.) Ref: V 9/24/75: "future war" between men and women. 2/19/75:32: "sort of scifi." PFA notes 11/6/80: "futuristic France." A.McMillan: Carroll-like fantasy.
The BLACK PEARL Ref: V 8/24/77:29(ad): "demon of the deep."
BLACK SHADOWS (F) Ref: V 10/5/49: "leopard men" prepare brew from eyes, heart, and lungs of victim.
BLACK SUNDAY 1977 Ref: MFB'77:140-1: dart device. V 3/30/77.
BLACKOUT (Can.-F) 1978 Ref: V 5/31/78: "comedy and terror"as four psychotics terrorize high-rise residents during blackout.
BLADE Ref: V 12/5/73: Jack the Ripper updated.
BLANCHE (F) 1971 Ref: MFB'73:120: "terrifying ballad."
BLIND GIRL AND THE DOG (Taiw.) Ref: V 6/10/81: ghost; suspense.
BLONDE ICE 1948 Ref: V 7/28/48: "weird conglomeration"; female Bluebeard.
BLOOD FREAK Variety Fair 1975 Ref: V 12/24/75:6(rated). Sfa BLOOD FREAK (Preacher Man Co.), rated 12/6/72:22?
BLOOD MONSTER Nevada Int'l Ref: V 5/3/72:26. Lee.
BLOOD RELATIONS (I) Intelefilm 1972? D: Avati. Ref: Lee: black magic. Sfa DEVIL'S HEARSE (I) Stefano '73? D: Avati.Ref: Lee.
BLOOD RELATIONS Filmcorp Ref: V 8/12/81:4(rated).

BLOOD VOYAGE 1976? Ref: MFB'80:5: brutal murders-at-sea.
BLOODLINE (U.S.-W.G.) Ref: MFB'79:193-4: anti-aging drug.
BLOODY BIRTHDAY Ref: V 9/30/81:32(ad).
BLOODY FISTS (H.K.) 1972 Ref: MFB'74:144: herbal plague-cure.
BLOW OUT (PERSONAL EFFECTS-orig t) Ref: Time: horror movie being shot. V 7/29/81.
The BLUE BIRD 1940 Ref: J.Shapiro: cat-into-woman; land of dead.
The BLUE BIRD (U.S.-Russ) Ref: V 5/12/76.
BLUE BLOOD (B) 1973 Ref: MFB'75:5: black magic.
BLUES BUSTERS 1950 Ref: TV: tonsillectomy gives Bowery Boy Satch voice like Crosby's (actually John Lorenz'). V 10/25/50.
BON VOYAGE, CHARLIE BROWN anim Ref: TV: storm, shadows. TVG: spooky chateau. V 5/28/80.
BONO BASAR (India) 1978 Ref: Dharap: curse?
The BOOGENS Farley/Taft Int'l. Ref: V 4/15/81:28(rated).
BOTTLENECK (I-F-Sp-W.G.) (L'INGORGO) Ref: V 5/16/79. pr: not sf.
The BOY IN THE PLASTIC BUBBLE 1976 Ref: TV Season. B.Warren.
The BOY WHO TURNED YELLOW (B) 1972 Ref: MFB'72:208: alien?
BRAIN LEECHES Ref: F.O.Ray.
BRANCALEONE AT THE CRUSADES (I-Alg) 1971 Ref: Lee: witch.
The BRIDES WORE BLOOD Ref: F.O. Ray.
BROTHER, CAN YOU SPARE A DIME? (B) Ref: MFB'75:76: KONG clip.
BRUCE LEE, WE MISS YOU (H.K.) 1976 Ref: MFB'79:225: spirit.
BRUCE VS. THE RED-EYED MONSTER Ref: poster: "demon for hire."
The BRUTE (B) 1976 Ref: MFB'77:64: part-"shock-thriller."
BUCK PRIVATES COME HOME 1947 Ref: TV: flying race-car bit.
BUG VAUDEVILLE 1917 anim short Ref: screen: spider eats hobo.
BUNNY LAKE IS MISSING 1965 Ref: J.Shapiro: nightmarish. TV: landlord who owns De Sade's skull; "Zombies" group. AFI.
BURNING OF THE RED LOTUS MONASTERY (H.K.) 1928 serial Ref: HKF Fest: "sonic power"; "tornado palm power."
BURNING OF THE RED LOTUS MONASTERY (H.K.) 1963 Ref: HKFFest: spirit-control.
BUSHKHUGIN ULGER (Mong.) Ref: V 7/30/80: enchanted princess.
BYE BYE MONKEY (I-F) (REVE DE SINGE) Ref: V 5/24/78: "giant carcass of a sort of King Kong mannequin."

CADDYSHACK Ref: V 7/23/80: JAWS-parody sequence.
CAGED HEAT 1974 Ref: screen. MFB'75:258: experimental brain-surgery. with Barbara Steele, Leslie Otis.
CALLAN (B) Ref: MFB'74:144: govt. section to kill "undesirables."
CALLING BULLDOG DRUMMOND (B) Ref: V 7/11/51. TV: truck with radar screen. TVFFSB: "devastating military radar."
The CAMERONS (B) Ref: MFB'74:93-4: pilotless plane with silent engine.
CAMPUS CARNAGE (Can.) 1974 non-theat.short Ref: LC Films'78: spoof of horror and beach-party movies.
CAN ELLEN BE SAVED 1974 Ref: TVFFSB: hypnosis; strange sect.
CAN I COME TOO? (B) Ref: MFB'79:69-70: theatre running KING KONG MEETS EMANUELLE.
CANNIBAL TERROR (F) Eurocine 1979 D: Alan Steeve. Ref: V 5/7/80:475.
CANNONBALL (U.S.-H.K.) Ref: MFB'77:65: Trans-American Grand Prix.

The CANTERBURY TALES (I-F) Ref: V 7/12/72: giant devils.
The CANTERVILLE GHOST (B) 1940 Ref: Limbacher'79. no BFC.
The CANTERVILLE GHOST 1975 Ref: TV Season: 60m. TV-"movie."
CAPRICORN ONE Ref: V 6/7/78. MFB'78:131: faked Mars flight.
CAPTAIN ELECTRIC (I) Ref: V 10/22/75(ad). Made?
CARAVAN TO VACCARES (B-F) Ref: MFB'74:170: "fuel substitute."
CARDIAC ARREST Ref: V 8/1/79(rated). 5/2/79: heart-thefts for transplants. B.Warren.
The CARNATION KILLER (B) 1973 Ref: TV: strangler, old mansion.
CARNIVAL OF BLOOD Monarch (DEATH RIDES A CAROUSEL) SP,D: Leonard Kirtman. Ref: V 5/12/71:203. Willis/SW. with J. Resnick.
The CASSANDRA CROSSING (B-I-W.G.) Ref: MFB'77:142: plague virus.
CASTLE OF CRIMES (B) Ref: V 4/4/45: sequel to '39 HOUSE OF MYSTERY? Spinster's relatives wait for her to die.
CAT AND MOUSE (B) 1974 Ref: MFB'74:122-23: murder with scalpel.
CHAC Ref: V 3/12/75: "diviner"; "shock ending."
CHAIN REACTION (Austral) Ref: V 4/23/80: nuclear-waste accident.
The CHALLENGE Ref: V 2/18/48: Bulldog Drummond; battle among heirs to "hidden fortune."
CHANDAN MALYAGIRI (India) 1978 Ref: Dharap: family curse.
CHARLIE CHAN AND THE CURSE OF THE DRAGON QUEEN Ref: V 2/18/81. MFB'81:109: bizarre murders; "curse" on Chan clan.
**CHARLIE CHAN IN HONOLULU 1938 Ref: Pitts/HFS: brain kept alive. B.Warren: phony story. V 12/21/38. MFB'39:15. HR: "living human brain." NYT 12/31/38. LC. "Great Movie Series."
Les CHARNELLES (F) Ref: MFB'74:270: similar to PEEPING TOM.
CHAUSSETTE SURPRISE (F) Ref: V 6/21/78: man ingests TV; device.
The CHECKERED COAT Ref: V 7/21/48: "gruesome touches"; "psychopathic killer" Creepy (Hurd Hatfield).
CHEECH AND CHONG'S NICE DREAMS Ref: V 6/3/81: man-into-lizard.
CHEN-CHU LEI (H.K.?) 196-? Ref: Eberhard: spirit.
CHERRY HILL HIGH 1976 Ref: MFB'81:37: "haunted" house; "alien."
CHHOTI BAHEN (India) 1977 Ref: Dharap: spirit.
Les CHIENNES (F) Ref: MFB'74:189: "macabre"elements.
Les CHIENS (F) Ref: V 5/2/79: murder by guard dog; horrific.
The CHIFFY KIDS (B) 1976 Ref: MFB'77:66: girl plays ghost.
CHILD'S PLAY 1972 Ref: MFB'74:246: Devil? FFacts. Scheuer/MOTV.
The CHINA SYNDROME Ref: MFB'79:194: nuclear-power-plant accident.
CHOR KE GHAR CHOR (India) 1978 Ref: Dharap: cursed idol.
CHOTTANIKARA AMMA (India) 1976 Ref: Dharap: spirit possession?
CHRISTIANA, MONACA INDEMONIATA (I) MGB 1972 Ref: V 7/26/72: 26. with M. Konopka, K. Vassilli.
CHRISTMAS EVE (Russ) 1913 Starevitch Ref: Lee: Devil.
CHUNDADI ODHI TARA NAAMNI (India) 1978 Ref: Dharap: curse.
CIRCUMSTANTIAL EVIDENCE 1935 Ref: Turner/Price: "Jekyll-Hyde" character who "keeps skeletons & mummies in his study."
The CIRCUS OF MONSTROUS LOVES (F) Ref: V 5/7/75:206.
CIRCUS SHADOWS 1935 Ref: TVFFSB: "mystic parlor" racket. no LC. B.Warren. FD 5/3/35: fortune teller. V(d): "fake astrologist."
Le CIRCUIT DE SANG (F) 1972 Ref: Glut/TDB: vampires.
CITY OF WOMEN (I?) 1980 Ref: screen: Frankenstein-monster-masked-woman bit.
The CLONES Premiere Int'l Ref: V 5/9/79:100(ad).
CLOSED MONDAYS 1974 short Ref: Glut/CMM: tiny Kong-like gorilla.

Le CLUB DES SUICIDES (I) 1922 D: E.Ghione. Ref: Daisne: from RLS? with Ghione, K. Sambucini.

A COFFIN FOR THE BRIDE 1974 Ref: TVFFSB: Bluebeard-type.

COLLEGE SCANDAL 1935 Ref: TV: student tied to headstone, scared to death in hazing.

COME BACK CHARLESTON BLUE 1972 Ref: MFB'73:190: dead man alive?

The COMIC 1969 Ref: Lee: "Jekyll and Hyde" bit.

COMIN' AT YA Ref: V 7/29/81: torture-by-bats.

COMIN' ROUND THE MOUNTAIN 1951 Ref: V 6/20/51. TV: witch; voodoo dolls; love potion; motorized, flying broom.

COMING ATTRACTIONS Ref: V 6/15/77:30: Joel Chernoff. screen: "Skateborders(sic) from Hell" seq.; "Billy Jerk Goes To Oz."

CONFESSIONS OF A POP PERFORMER (B) Ref: MFB'75:196: character named Zombie.

CONSPIRACY OF TERROR (B?) 1975 Ref: TVFFSB: man scared to death.

CORKY OF GASOLINE ALLEY Ref: V 9/12/51: "chemical pills" intended to triple "octane rating" of gas.

The CORPSE WHICH DIDN'T WANT TO DIE (I-G) Romano-Phoenix 1972 D: E. Miraglia. Ref: Lee. with B.Bouchet, M.Malfatti.

COUNT DRACULA (B) BBC-TV/WNET-TV 1978 color 180m. D: Philip Saville. SP: Sally Heal. Ph: P.Hall. Mus: K. Emrys-Roberts. Ref: TVG: "drama." Murphy: "film." TV Season: "special." with Louis Jourdan(Dracula), Frank Finlay, Judi Bowker.

COUNT EROTICA VAMPIRE 1972? Ref: Lee. Glut/TDB. Made?

The COUNTERPART OF DEATH (Braz) 1975 Ref: Brasil: doppelganger.

COUNTERSPY MEETS SCOTLAND YARD Ref: V 11/15/50: hypnosis.

Le COUPLE TEMOIN (F) Ref: V 4/6/77: Ministry of the Future.

COUSTEAU SEARCHING FOR ATLANTIS IN THE AEGEAN SEA Ref:V 1/23/80:30.

The CREEPER Coast Ref: V 12/10/80:25: in Minneap.

CRIA CUERVOS (Sp) 1975 Ref: MFB'78:173-4: dead man returns.

CRIES AND WHISPERS (Swed) Ref: V 12/20/72. screen. Lee. MFB'73: 61. NYorker 1/6/73: dead woman returns (in dream).

Le CRIME DE LORD ARTHUR SAVILLE (F) 1921 Ref: Limbacher'79.

Los CRIMENES DE PETIOT (Sp) Ref: V 10/25/72: "horror scenes."

CRIMINALLY INSANE 1976 Ref: Cinef V:3: "psycho horror film."

CROCODILE ADVENTURE STC Ref: V 10/18/78:161.

CRUEL PASSION (B) Ref: MFB'78:64: vicious dogs; grave-robbing.

CRUISING 1980 Ref: Time: "demon"?

The CURSE OF KILIMANJARO CFS Ref: V 12/15/76:30(rated).

The CUT-THROAT MAN (India) 1974 Ref: Dharap: "atomic" formula.

The DAIN CURSE 1978 Ref: TV: family "blood curse" of violence.

DANGER--LOVE AT WORK 1937 Ref: TV: bit with inventor's giant, mechanical, ambulatory teddy bear.

DANGEROUS MILLIONS Ref: V 12/4/46: murder among heirs to fortune.

DANGEROUSLY THEY LIVE 1941 Ref: TV: drug in coffee unlocks heroine's subconscious.

DARK ALIBI 1946 Ref: FM 21("Mystery Photo"). TV: M.Moreland sees lizard-headed-monster statue in costume warehouse.

DARNA VS. GIANTS (Fili) Ref: SFC 5/12/80. V 2/13/74:22: Batman-like super-heroine with winged crash-helmet.

The DAY AFTER HALLOWEEN (Austral) (SNAP-SHOT-orig t) Ref: V 10/22/80:12. 2/25/81: "horror"?

The DAY OF THE DOLPHIN Ref: V 12/12/73. MFB'74:25-6: "futuristic thriller" in which dolphins learn to speak. NYT 12/20/73.

The DAY THAT BATTERSEA POWER STATION FLEW AWAY (B) 1974 short Ref: MFB'78:166: station just ups and flies into sky.

DEADLY FATHOMS Ref: V 5/11/77:205(ad): "ghostly battalion."

DEADLY STRANGERS (B) Ref: MFB'75:102: "psychopathic killer."

DEATH AT LOVE HOUSE 1976 Ref: TV Season: "satanic influence."

DEATH HAS BLUE EYES (Greek) 1975 Ref: MFB'77:4-5:"psychic stare."

DEATH IN SPACE 1974 Ref: TVFFSB: astronaut lost in space.

DEATH IN THE SUN (W.G.-So.Afr.) 1976('78-U.S.) (NIGHT OF THE ASKARI-U.S.) Ref: MFB'77:97-8: quasi-"werewolf." B.Warren.

DEATH IS NOT THE END 1976 Ref: Willis/SW: reincarnation, etc.

DEATH ON A BARGE 1973? Ref: Murphy: vampire. TVG: "Night Gallery" episode with Lesley Warren.

The DEATH RAY 1933 amateur short fea. SP,D,P: Ray L. Maker. Ref: KTVU-TV("Friday Night Frights"),S.F., 2/16/79: scenes shown. Death ray; man-into-monster; dead revived.

DEATH VALLEY 1946 Ref: TVFFSB: Jekyll-&-Hyde? "The Western": remake of '27 Western re: sun-fried madman; "bizarre" end.

The DECAMERON (I-F-W.G.) 1971 Ref: Lee: ghost, visions.

The DEEP (U.S.-B) Ref: TVG & MFB'77:257-8: "giant moray"; voodoo. A.McMillan. B.Warren: large (but not gigantic) eel.

DEEP JAWS Ref: Willis/SW. V 5/5/76: "space shot" being filmed.

DEFIANCE Ref: V 11/27/74: "horrorific...sadistic."

DELINQUENT SCHOOL GIRLS Ref: MFB'76:129: hypnosis.

DELIRIUM (I) Ref: V 7/25/79: "fearsome" killer; bloody. CineFan 2:25(J.Duvoli). Willis/SW: with Mike Kalist(specter).

DELIVERANCE Ref: MFB'72:187: "dead hand" from river in dream.

DEMAIN, LA PETITE FILLE SERA EN RETARD A L'ECOLE (F) Ref: MFB'79: 14: bit with "ugly, bald monster." short

The DEMI-PARADISE (B) Ref: V 12/8/43: "new-type propellor."

DEMON LOVER DIARY Ref: V 2/13/80: re: making DEMON LOVER(M).

Les DEMONIAQUES (F-Belg) 1973('77-U.S.) Rollin Ref: Bianco #3/ 77:168. V 1/12/77:4(rated):IFA, DEMONIACS. with J. Couer.

DENMARK CLOSED DOWN (Dan.) Ref: V 10/15/80: D.as atom-test area.

DERANGED Sunburst Ref: V 2/7/73:24.

DESERT LEGION Ref: Limbacher: Atlantis? V 3/18/53: Utopia. NYT.

DESPERATE LIVING Ref: V 10/26/77. MFB'78:132-33: cannibalism.

The DESTROYING ANGEL 1976 Ref: Ecran 12/77:32: from "W.Wilson"?

DETRUIRE, DIT-ELLE (F) 1969 Ref: screen: invis."Godzilla"?

DEUX VIERGES POUR SATAN (Belg) 1973 Rollin Ref: V 5/12/76:422.

The DEVIL AND MAX DEVLIN Ref: MFB'81:47:deal with Devil's aide.

The DEVIL AND MR.JONES 1975 Ref: V 3/19/75: man to hell & back.

The DEVIL AND SAM SILVERSTEIN Key Whole 1975 Ref: V 9/17/75:5.

The DEVIL AND THE DIABOLICAL MISTRESS MJL Ref:V 6/19/74:28(r.).

The DEVIL CROWS (Taiw) 1974 D:W.S.Loy. Ref: V 3/31/76:24: sf?

The DEVIL GOD (aka DEAD TO RITES) Ref: F.O.Ray.

The DEVIL IN MISS JONES Ref: V 2/21/73: woman in hell.

The DEVIL INSIDE HER Leisure Time 1977 color 74m. SP,D: Z. Colt. Ref: Meyers: Satan. SFC 3/13/81. Willis/SW.with T.Hall.

The DEVIL'S CLONE Omni/Easy (cf.TIME OF THE EAGLE(M)) SP,D: W. Dial. Ref: V 3/7/79:27(ad). with S.Culpepper,J.Colbert.

DEVIL'S LOTTERY 1932 Ref: screen: bit with "haunted" room.

The DEVIL'S MISTRESS 1973 Ref: B.Warren: "horror-suspense."

The DEVIL'S SAINT (Sp) (FLOR DE SANTIDAD) Ref: V(d) 4/3/73: exorcism, "witchcraft." B.Warren. IFG'74:299.
El DIABLO NO ES TAN DIABLO (Mex?) c1960? Ref: TV: anim.mosquito that talks("Buenos noches!") & razzes the Devil; alarm-clock-gun; cartoon sun and moon.
DIABOLIC WEDDING 1972 Ref: Lee. Willis/SW: '75? M.O'Brien.
DIAL A DEADLY NUMBER (B) 1975 Ref: TVFFSB: dreams of violence.
DIE LAUGHING Ref: Boxo 4/7/80:21: "new nuclear weapon" formula.
DIE SCREAMING, MARIANNE 1973 Ref: TVFFSB. S.George, L.Genn.
DIE SISTER DIE! 1978 Ref: Willis/SW. with J.Ging, E.Atwater.
DISCREET CHARM OF THE BOURGEOISIE (F) 1972 Ref:screen:nightmares.
DISNEY'S GREATEST VILLAINS 1977 anim Ref: TVFFSB:inc.Mme.Medusa.
DITES-LE AVEC DES FLEURS (F) Ref: V 9/11/74:"weird tale."
The DOBERMAN GANG 1972 Ref:MFB'74:174:dobermans attack men.
DOBERMAN PATROL 1973 (aka TRAPPED) Ref: MFB'74:147-8: man trapped in store with "vicious doberman guard dogs." TVG.
DR.JEKYLL AND MR.HYDE Edison 1913 Ref: Limbacher'79.
DR.JEKYLL AND MR.HYDE Vitascope 1913 D:M.Mack. Ref:Glut/CMM.
*DR.JEKYLL AND MR.HYDE 1925 Sfa *DR.PYCKLE AND MR.PRIDE.
DR.JEKYLL AND MR.HYDE 1929 short Ref: Glut/CMM: edited, sound version of 1920 S. Lewis version?
DR.SCORPION 1978 Ref: TVG 2/18/78. V 3/1/78:80.
La DOLCE VITA (I) 1959 Ref: screen: "haunted" villa.
The DOLL SQUAD Ref: MFB'74:46: "new bubonic plague virus."
DON GIOVANNI (I-F-W.G.) 1979 Ref:MFB'80:175: ghost; hell.
DON JUAN 1973 Ou SI DON JUAN ETAIT UNE FEMME (F-I) 1973 Ref:MFB '74:124: D.Juan reincarnated as "vampiristic seductress."
DONA FLOR AND HER TWO HUSBANDS (Braz) Ref: V 9/14/77: ghost.
DONALD AND PLUTO 1936 anim short Ref: screen:Pluto magnetized.
DON'T GO NEAR THE PARK Ref: V 7/8/81:5(rated).9/23/81:in Miami.
DOOMSDAY 2000 Picturmedia Ref: V 10/18/78: docu.?
DORA ET LA LANTERNE MAGIQUE (F) Ref: V 3/1/78.Trieste:witchcraft.
DORELLIK (I) 1967 Ref: Lee: vampire?
DOUBLE AGENT 73 Ref: MFB'75:103: time-bomb in woman's breast.
DOUBLE TROUBLE 1967 Ref: Glut/CMM/TDB: men in opera-phantom, Dracula, and Frankenstein-monster masks.
DRACULA GOES TO RP (Fili) 1974 Ref: Glut/TDB.
DRACULA'S BLOOD Cannon Ref: V 1/16/74:5. with Naschy, T.Sainz.
DRACULIN (W.G.) Ref: V 5/17/78:369(ad).
DREAM NO EVIL Boxo Int'l 1976 Ref:Meyers: mad girl; ghost?
DREAMSPEAKER (Can.) Ref: V 2/2/77:68: shaman exorcises spirits.
DUELLE (F) Ref: V 6/2/76. NYT 10/13/76: dangerous "spirits."

ESP Sandler Ref: V 3/26/75:58: Serling.
EARTH IS A SINFUL SONG (Finn) 1973 Ref:MFB'75:200: "horrific."
The ECCENTRICS (Russ) Ref: V 12/18/74.screen: flying machine.
An ECHO OF THERESA 1973 Ref: TVFFSB: man with split personality.
ECSTASY OF THE MACUMBA 1975 Ref: Willis/SW.
EDDIE CAPRA MYSTERIES:NIGHTMARE AT PENDRAGON'S CASTLE 1978 Ref: V 9/13/78:56. TVG: TV show later shown as TV-movie.
EGGPLANTS FROM BEYOND TIME Ref: V 1/14/76:38. B.Warren:not made.
The EIGHTH DAY OF CREATION (Russ) Ref: V 7/1/81:21: Bradbury.
EL (Mex) 1952 Ref: Lee: "psy-horror." screen.

EMMANUELLE E GLI ULTIMI CANNIBALI (I) Ref:MFB'78:133.V 1/25/78:42.
EMBRACE (India) 1974 Ref: Dharap: curse haunts family.
EMERGENCY LANDING 1941 Ref: TV: remote-cont.model plane.TVFFSB.
L'ENFANT DE LA NUIT (F-I) Ref: V 11/22/78: phantom boy?
ENTER THE DRAGON (U.S.-H.K.) Ref:MFB'74:5-7:automatons?B.Warren.
EQUUS (B) Ref: MFB'77:232-33: nightmares, rituals.
ERDGEIST (G) 1923 Ref: Lee(RVB): Jack the Ripper? NYorker 6/9/80.
EROTIC EVA (I) Ref: MFB'77:122: murder with mambas.
ESCAPE TO GLORY 1940 Ref: TV: "diatherm machine,"directional beam.
Los ESPECTROS (Sp) D:M.Siciliano. Ref: V 5/7/75:242. R.Conte.
Los ESPECTROS DE TOLNIA (Sp) Frade D: Klimovsky. Ref: V 5/9/73: 137. with Jack Taylor, Luis Ciges, Charo Soriano.
El ESPEJO (Arg) Ref: V 7/14/43: magic(?) mirror "evokes" past.
El ESPIRITISTA (Sp) D: A.Gonzalves. Ref: V 5/12/76:406.
L'ETRANGLEUR (F) Ref: Cinef F'73:43: man kills unhappy women.
EVENING LAND (Dan) Ref: V(d) 3/7/77: "near future."
EXCALIBUR (U.S.-B) Ref: MFB'81:112: sorceress, necromancer.
EXECUTIVE ACTION Ref: MFB'74:26-7: conspiracy theory for John F. Kennedy's assassination. V 11/7/73.
Les EXPERIENCES EROTIQUES DE FRANKENSTEIN (F-Sp?) 1973? D: J. Franco. Ref: Glut/TDB: sequel to DRAC.VS.DR.FRANKENSTEIN?
The EXTERMINATOR Ref: MFB'81:24-5: Ghouls gang; brutal murders.

F 1980? Ref: J.Shapiro: alien?; giant vagina.
F FOR FAKE (F-Iran.-W.G.) V 11/21/73. screen. J.Shapiro. MFB'77: 12. Brief "re-creation" of "War of the Worlds" radio broadcast; clips from EARTH VS.THE FLYING SAUCERS.
FACE TO FACE (Swed) Ref: MFB'76:247: "monstrous"woman in dreams.
FACE OF THE PHANTOM Ref: F.O.Ray.
FACES OF DEATH Ref: V 5/7/80:144: flesh-eating cult.
FAHRMANN MARIA (G) 1935 Ref: Lee: Death; remade as *STRANGLER OF THE SWAMP. FIR'64.
FALSE FACE (aka SCALPEL) Ref: V(d) 12/17/76: super-plastic-surg.
La FAMILIA UNIDA ESPERANDO LA LLEGADA DE HALLEWYN (Arg) Ref: V 8/30/72: "strange parties." Cahiers de la Cinematheque #27: 38,41: "in the style of the classic horror films."
FAMILY PLOT Ref: MFB'76:146: medium, seance. V 3/24/76.J.Shapiro.
The FAMILY THAT DWELT APART (Can.) 197-? anim short Ref: Glut/CMM: Kong cameo. screen.
The FAN Ref: V 5/20/81. screen: murder with razor. MFB'81:112.
FANTAISIE NO.1 (F) 1976 short Ref:Ecran 12/77:32:Poe's "Raven."
FANTASM (Austral) Ref:MFB'78:134: "Blood Orgy" Black Mass.
FANTOMA--APPOINTMENT IN ISTANBUL (Turk) Ref:Limbacher: Batman. WorldF'67.
The FARMER Ref: V 3/2/77: "bloodbath" of violence.
FARMER ALFALFA'S APE GIRL 1932 anim short Ref: Maltin/OMAM.
FAUSTA,THE NAZI WONDER WOMAN 1976 Ref: TV Season: 60m. TV-movie or premiere show of "The New, Original Wonder Woman"?
FEDERAL FUGITIVES 1941 Ref: TVFFSB: "plane invention."B.Warren.
FEDORA (W.G.) Ref: MFB'79:172-3: messy plastic-surgery.
FELICITE (F) Ref: V 5/23/79: "haunting" nightmares.
FELLINI'S CASANOVA (I) 1976 Ref: screen. MFB'77:164-5. Necromancer; mechanical doll; "The Great Mouna."

FEMMES FATALES (F) Ref: SFC 4/19/79: giant woman.
The FIGHTING 69½TH 1941 Ref: TV: "camouflage corps" bit with invisible soldiers & horses. Correct title? M.Melodies. LC.
La FILLE DE L'EAU (F) 1924 Ref: Durgnat/JR: dragon in dream.
FINGER OF GUILT (B) 1956 Ref:screen:"Return of the Ghost"filming.
FIRATIN CINLERI (Turk) Ref: V 8/2/78: spirit possession? IFG'80.
FIRST FAMILY Ref: V 12/31/80: KONG spoof bit; super-fertilizer.
FIVE SUMMER STORIES Ref: MFB'74:175-6: end-of-the-world segment.
FLYGNIVA 450 (Swed) Ref: V 4/30/80: terrorism; "near future."
FLYING-MAN VS. "KILLING" (Turk) Ref: WorldF'67: "fantastic" f.m.
FOR YOUR EYES ONLY (B) Ref: SFC 6/26/81: one-man submersible.
The FORCE OF EVIL 1977 Ref: TVFFSB: sf? with Lloyd Bridges.
FORFOELGELSEN (Norw-Swed) Ref: V 9/9/81: witch-hunting.
The FORMULA Ref: V 12/10/80: f. for synthetic fuel. MFB'81:6.
FOUR PHASES OF THE DEVIL (Sp) Ref: V 11/21/79:36: at sf-fest.
FOXBAT (H.K.) Ref: V 12/21/77: agent with "bionic-styled eye."
FOXY BROWN Ref: MFB'75:56: plastic surgery, sadism.
FRANKENSTEIN (B) 1968(1971?) Ref: TVG. Glut/TFL: TV drama.I.Holm.
FRANKENSTEIN CRIES OUT! 1977 short non-theat. Ref: LC Films'78.
FRANKENSTEIN OF SUNNYBROOK FARM 1971 Ref:Glut/TFL: no monster.
FRAUEN-GEFANGNIS (Swiss) D:J.Franco. Ref:MFB'77:torture,sadism.
FRENZY (B) Ref:MFB'72:113.screen. V 5/31/72. Psychopathic killer.
FRIENDLY MONSTERS OF THE DEEP 1978 Ref: TVG: eels, mantas, etc.
FUNNY AMERICA Ref: V 5/7/80:34-5(ad): doomsday ending?

GAWAIN AND THE GREEN KNIGHT (B) Ref: MFB'73:168: castle "frozen" in time; corpse which "regains its severed head."
A GHOST OF A CHANCE 1973 Ref: Lee: ghost comedy.
GHOST OF CYPRESS SWAMP 1977 Ref: TVFFSB: "half-crazed hermit."
GHOST THAT NEVER RETURNS (Russ) 1929 Ref:MFB'76:14: ape-creature?
The GHOST TRAIN MURDER (B) 1959 short Ref: BFC: crime drama.
GHOSTKEEPER Ref: V 9/30/81:32(ad).
GIFT OF TERROR ABC-TV 1973 Ref: TVFFSB: "mysterious power."
GINGA TAISEN (J) anim (GALAXY WAR) D:M.Yamada.Ref:V 5/9/79:381.
The GIRL AND THE TIGER Daxx Ref: V 3/19/80:37(ad): future-beast.
The GIRL,THE GOLD WATCH,AND EVERYTHING D:W.Wiard Ref: TV. V 6/18/80:59: TV special. Watch makes time stand still.
GLOOSKAP 1972 short Ref: Lee: land of giant animals.
GLOSY (Pol) Ref: V 4/22/81: "impulses from...space."
The GODMONSTER Ellman 1973 Ref: Cinef III:2:33.
GODSPELL Ref: MFB'73:148: Pharisees as "jokey machine-monster."
The GOLDEN EYE Ref: V 9/22/48. TV: two "spooky" cave sequences.
Der GOLDENE ABGRUND (G) 1927 (ATLANTIS) Ref:Bianco. H.Albers.
GOLDENGIRL Ref: SFC 9/14/79: genetically-made super-athlete.
GOLIATHON Ref: B.Warren: sfa MIGHTY PEKING MAN? E.Kraft.
GORILLA SAFARI 1968? Ref: TVFFSB: huge killer-gorilla. G.Galley.
GRAND TOUR--MANNED EXPLORATION OF THE OUTER PLANETS 1973 Ref:Lee.
The GRAPES OF DEATH (F) Ref: V 8/23/78:7: at Sitges. D:J.Rollin.
GRAY LADY DOWN Ref: MFB'78:114: JAWS clip; experimental mini-sub.
The GREAT HOUDINI 1976 Ref: TVFFSB: the occult. with P.Cushing.
The GREATEST AMERICAN HERO Ref: TVG'81: 2-hour premiere. Aliens.
GREEN EYES 1934 Ref: Turner/Price: "weird" glowing-eyed mask.
GREEN THUMB non-theat.short Ref: LC Films'76: "horror tale."

GRENDEL GRENDEL GRENDEL (Austral) anim Ref: IFG'80:63.
GRITOS A MEDIANOCHE (Sp) Ancla-Gregor 1976 D:Klimovsky. Ref: V. with M. Martin, T. Isbert.
The GROOVE TUBE Ref: MFB'75:57: 2001 bit with first TV set.
GROUND ZERO 1973 Ref: TVG. MFB'81:156-7: nuclear bomb on Golden Gate Bridge explodes.
La GUERRA DEL CERDO (Arg) Ref: V 8/27/75: youths gang up on aged.
GUIDE TO SCIENCE FICTION (I) Ref: V 7/1/81:21: film clips.
GUNNAR HEDES SAGA (Swed) 1922 Ref: screen: vision, premonition.
GUYANA: CULT OF THE DAMNED (Mex-Sp-Pan.) Ref: V 1/30/80.

H.O.T.S. 1979 Ref: TV: robot? TVG.
HAIL! Ref: V 5/24/72: concentration camps for dissenters in U.S.
HALF WOMAN,HALF WOLF (Thai) (SAO MA PA) Ref: V 1/19/77:50.
Die HAMBURGER KRANKHEIT (W.G.-F) Ref: V 10/31/79: strange plague in northern Germany. PFA notes 5/12/81: sf/"eco-disaster."
HANGMAN'S HOUSE 1928 Ref: screen: haunting visions in fireplace.
HANSEL AND GRETEL, AN APPALACHIAN VERSION 1975 short Ref: PFA.
HAPPY GO LUCKY 1943 Ref: TV: voodoo-love-potion in spray gun.
HARE CONDITIONED 1945 anim short Ref: Glut/TFL: bit with Bugs Bunny as the "Frankincense monster."
The HATCHET MAN 1932 Ref: TV: Grand Guignol ending with hatchet.
HAUNTED Ref: V 5/11/77:185. B.Warren. with V.Mayo, A.Ray.
HAUNTED HOUSE (Thai) (KUAN TA KIAN) Ref: V 1/10/79: planned.
HAVE A NICE WEEKEND Ref: V 9/24/75: "psycho suspense tale."
HAWK THE SLAYER (B) Ref: MFB'81:7: giant; mind-sword; good witch.
HE IS MY BROTHER Ref: P.LePage: black-magic overtones; shaman. V 7/30/75:27(ad): "supernatural powers." A.McMillan.
HEART OF GLASS (W.G.) Ref: V 12/1/76. MFB'77:193: "invisible bear."
HEAT WAVE 1977 Ref: screen: satanic figure. J.Shapiro: Herrmann music (giant bird) from MYSTERIOUS ISLAND. AMPAS.
HELL OF THE LIVING DEAD (I?) Ref: V 9/16/81:5.
HERE COME THE CO-EDS 1945 Ref: TV: blow on head turns Lou Costello into super-basketball-player, "Daisy."
HERE WE GO AGAIN Ref: V 8/26/42: thread-from-cocoons formula.
HERZOG FILMS NOSFERATU WETV-Atlanta 1979 short (NEW GERMAN CINEMA: WERNER HERZOG'S NOSFERATU:THE VAMPYRE-cr t) Ref: TV.
HIGH ANXIETY Ref: V 12/21/77. TV: doc plays werewolf. MFB'78:91: sendups of The BIRDS, PSYCHO. J.Shapiro: Bond "Jaws" bit.
HILLBILLY BLITZKRIEG Ref: MPH 8/8/42:"robot aerial torpedo."
HIPS HIPS HOORAY 1934 Ref: TV: in climactic race, a) cyclone, b) skis, & c) overinflated tires make car "fly" cross-country.
The HISTORICAL DRACULA (Rum.) short Ref:Brandon: from VLAD TEPES?
HOLLYWOOD BOULEVARD 1976 Ref: screen: "Mutilated Maidens of Mora Tau" filming/later, marquee t.: "Machete Maidens"; ape-masked actor in helmet (a la ROBOT MONSTER); FJA; Dick Miller as Paisley; "Godzina as herself"; The TERROR clips; Bela's star.
HOLLYWOOD HORROR HOUSE Avco Emb 1975 Ref: V 1/15/75:5(rated):aka?
HOLLYWOOD 90028 1974 Ref: TVFFSB: psychotic killer.
El HOMBRE QUE SUPO AMAR (Sp) Ref: V 9/29/76: "gore...torture."
The HORROR SHOW 1979 Ref: TV. V 5/7/80:215: TV special avail. to theatres. Clips from PSYCHO, FRANKENSTEIN,etc. Cahiers 315.
HORRORITUAL short Ref: Lee: ad for DRACULA A.D.1972. Glut/TDB.

The HOSTAGE TOWER Ref: MFB'80:194: "little used" laser weapons.
HOT CHANNELS Ref: V 5/23/73: "Sensulator," futuristic device.
The HOT GIRLS (B) Ref: MFB'74:148 model poses as vampire victim.
HOTEL MACABRE (B) 1976? Ref: Murphy: Dracula. Made? Price.
HOUSE OF PSYCHOTIC WOMEN (Sp) D:Aured. Ref: V 1/16/74:26: sfa HOUSE OF INSANE WOMEN(Espana)? Willis/SW. Naschy, Perschy.
HOUSE OF TERROR Gamalex 1972 (The FIVE AT THE FUNERAL) Ref: Boxo 1/27/73: dead-woman's twin. V 9/13/72:26(rated). MFB'75:83.
HOUSE ON STRAW MOUNTAIN (B) Ref: CineFan 2:26: "horror."L.Hayden.
HOW TO DROWN DR.MRACEK (Cz) Ref: V 7/28/76:12: sf?
A HOWLING IN THE WOODS 1971 Ref: TV: nightmares; community murder.
The HUMAN COMEDY 1943 Ref: TV: man's spirit appears to wife.

IF MAX IS SO SMART WHY DOESN'T HE TELL US WHERE HE IS? 1973 Ref: TVFFSB: super-computer.
ILLICIT INTERLUDE (Swed) 1951 Ref: screen: anim. ghost bit.
ILS SONT FOUS CES SORCIERS (F) Ref: V 8/2/78: occult comedy.
ILS SONT GRANDS CES PETITS (F) Ref: V 4/4/79: electronic war-toys.
IN THE NAME OF THE FATHER (I) 1971 Ref: screen: dial.ref. to DAY THE EARTH STOOD STILL. MFB'77:104: ref.to planet Krel.
INN OF THE DAMNED (Austral) Ref: V 8/28/74: "Gothic horror."
The INNERVIEW 1973 Ref: screen. Clips from '31 DRACULA.
INQUISICION (Sp) D & with: J.Molina. Ref: V 5/11/77:420.
L'INSATISFAITE (F) Ref: MFB'72:164-5: super-plastic-surgery.
INSTITUTE FOR REVENGE 1979 Ref: TV: super-computer.
The INTRUDER (Can.?) Ref: V 9/3/80:48(ad): alien?
Les INTRUS (F) 1971 Ref: MFB'74:48: sadism; "horrific."
IS THERE SEX AFTER DEATH? 1971 Ref: MFB'75:176: seance, spirit.
The ISLAND AT THE TOP OF THE WORLD Ref: V 11/27/74. MFB'75:10. Experimental airship; killer-whale attack; Vikings.
The IVORY APE Ref: TV. J.Shapiro. Pregnant albino gorilla, Rangi.

JABBERWALK 1976 Ref: MFB'79:4: docu.; cryogenics; devil cult.
JACOB TWO-TWO MEETS THE HOODED FANG (Can.) Ref: V 3/14/79: concentration camp for kids.
JAI AMBE MAA (India) 1977 Ref: Dharap: curse on man.
JAI MAHAKALI (India) 1978 Ref: Dharap: curse.
JAIT RE JAIT (India) 1977 Ref: Dharap: superstition; torture.
JARDIN DES SUPPLICES (F) 1976 Ref:MFB'77:260: mutilation.
JET PILOT 1957 Ref: TV: idiocy drug.
La JEUNE FILLE ASSASSINEE (F) Ref: V 11/20/74: "necrological love scene"; brutal murder.
La JEUNE FOLLE (F) Ref: V 10/8/52: premonitions haunt girl.
JOE PANTHER Ref: V(d) 10/29/76: "kiddie version of JAWS."
JOHN BOY MEETS THE TEXAS CHAINSAW KILLER 1977 amat. short Ref: CineFan 2:51: splicing "The Waltons" to TTCSM.
JOSEPH ANDREWS (B) Ref: MFB'77:74: necromancer, Black Mass.
JUGGERNAUT (B) 1974 Ref: screen. Glut/TDB: costume-ball Dracula.

KAGEMUSHA (J-U.S.) Ref: S&S: nightmare seq. with ghost. 1980
KAJA,I'LL KILL YOU (Yug.) 1968 Ref: Brandon: "primordial forces."

KANNA MOOCHI (India) 1978 Ref: Dharap: genii under spell.
KASEKI (J) 1974 Ref: MFB'75:138: "spectral female figure."
KASPER IN DE ONDERWERELD (Belg) 1973 Ref: V 2/7/79: Orpheus.
KEEP 'EM FLYING 1941 Ref: TV: Lou-on-torpedo ride; live shadow.
KEEP MY GRAVE OPEN Wells Ref: Boxo 7/28/80:10: horror.
KENTUCKY FRIED MOVIE Ref: V 8/3/77: R.Baker as Dino the gorilla.
KENTUCKY MOONSHINE 1938 Ref: TV: Snow White-witch-dwarfs bit.
KID MILLIONS 1934 Ref: TV: mummies in "mummy room" ("They all died standing up?") do "Let My People Go" number.
The KIDNAPPING OF THE PRESIDENT Ref: V 8/13/80: by terrorists.
A KILLER IN EVERY CORNER (B) 1975 Ref: TVFFSB: scientist experiments in psych. controlling potential mass murderers.
The KILLER INSIDE ME Ref: V(d) 10/15/76: "Gothic." MFB'77:124-5.
KILLER SNAKES (H.K.?) Ref: V 9/24/75:28(rated). Willis/SW.
KING CARNIVAL (B) 1973 Ref: MFB'77:149: voodoo ceremony.
KING,QUEEN,KNAVE (W.G.-U.S.) Ref: V 5/24/72. MFB'73:250: inventor's lifelike model made of artificial skin. J.Shapiro.
The KLEEGARS 1976 Ref: Glut/CMM: A&C MEET THE MUMMY clip.
KUMMATY (India) 1979? Ref: IFG'80:185. PFA notes 4/17/80: "frightening bogeyman."
KUNTILANAK (Indon.) (The VAMPIRE) Ref: IFG'76:230.

LAC FIVE 1976 non-theat.short Ref: LC Films'78: flying saucer.
A LAD AN' A LAMP 1932 short Ref: Turner/Price: ref to INGAGI.
LADY FREAKS de Renzy Ref: SFC 4/11/80.
LADY FROM CHUNGKING 1942 Ref: TV: ghost bit at end. V 1/20/43.
**LADY IN THE DEATH HOUSE Ref: V 4/5/44. TV: doctor experimenting in resuscitation of the dead.
The LADY WITH RED BOOTS (Sp-F-I) Ref: V 10/23/74: woman with psychic powers disappears into painting. TVFFSB: "witch."
LANDLORDS OF DEATH Ref: Boxo 12/31/79:14: horror. J.Carradine.
LASH OF THE PENITENTES 1937 Ref: Turner/Price: torture cult.
The LAST GENERATION 1972? Ref: Lee: futuristic. Released?
LAST STOP ON THE NIGHT TRAIN D,P: E.Isle. Ref: V 4/7/76:15(ad): horror? with Kay Beal. Sfa NEW HOUSE ON THE LEFT?
LEGEND OF BLACK THUNDER MOUNTAIN Ref: Boxo 3/31/80(rated).
LEGEND OF DINOSAURS AND MONSTER BIRDS (J) Toei Ref: V 5/4/77:84.
LEGEND OF JIMMY BLUE EYES 1964 short Ref: Lee: deal with Devil.
LEGEND OF LIZZIE BORDEN Ref: V 2/12/75:62: "explicit gore."
LEGEND OF WITCH HOLLOW Alexander 1975 Ref: V 4/23/75:22(rated).
LETTER FROM SIBERIA 1957 Ref: screen: anim. mammoths bit; cred. for "Gorgo Herself."
LIFE OF BRIAN (B) Ref: V 8/22/79: space trip. A.McMillan: aliens.
LIFESIZE (Sp-F-I) 1973('76-U.S.) (LOVE DOLL) Ref: MFB'75:240. Willis/SW. Dentist takes life-size doll as lover.
The LITTLE GREEN DOLL (Russ) Ref: V 7/1/81:21: sf? from Bradbury.
The LITTLE MATCH GIRL (F) 1928 Ref: screen: dream of Death.
LITTLE ORBIT THE ASTRODOG J.Image anim Ref: V 2/4/81:122.
The LITTLE PRINCE AND HIS FRIENDS Ref: UC Theatre pr.
LJUBAV I BIJES (Yug.) Ref: V 8/16/78: demon possession?
La LLAMADA DEL VAMPIRO (Sp) 1971 D:Elorietta. Ref:Murphy. D.Sorel.
LOCUSTS 1974 Ref: TVFFSB: locust swarms. Scheuer/MOTV.
LOGAN'S RUN Ref: V 9/21/77:60: 90m. "debut" for TV series.

LORD SHANGO Ref: V 2/5/75:19(ad): "blood ritual."
LOST IN ALASKA Ref: V 7/30/52. TV: bit with sled-size crab.
LOST SOULS (H.K.) Ref: V 1/7/81: "unspeakable tortures."
LOVE AND DEATH Ref: MFB'75:241: visions of Death.
The LOVE BOX (B) 1972 Ref: Lee: futuristic segment.
LOVE IN THE CITY (I) 1953 Ref: screen: Fellini "Love Cheerfully Arranged" segment: reporter seeks match for (imaginary) friend who, "with the full moon, becomes a werewolf...."
LUDWIG--REQUIEM FOR A VIRGIN KING (W.G.) 1972 Ref: MFB'77:46-7: "curse of Lola Montes"; nightmare visions.
LUST FLIGHT 2000 1978 Ref: Boxo 2/25/80:16: "the unknown."
The LUST OF DRACULA 1971? Ref: Lee. Glut/TDB.

MAA AVRET JIVRAT (India) 1977 Ref: Dharap: prediction of death.
MACABRE (I) Medusa-Ama D: L.Bava. Ref: V 5/7/80:359: "thriller."
The MAD BOMBER MYSTERY 1977 Ref: TVFFSB: "Future Cop" pilot.
MADMAN Farley Ref: V 9/23/81:34:"thriller." 9/30/81:4(rated).
The MADONNA'S SECRET Ref: V 2/20/46: "macabre touches....painter tortured by hallucinations."
Il MAESTRO E MARGHERITA (Yug-I) Ref: V 9/13/72. Lee: the Devil.
The MAFU CAGE (BIZARRE. DON'T ANSWER THE DOORBELL) Ref: MFB'79: 178: "BABY JANE territory." FM 169:47. V 8/17/77:26:sfa CLOUDS?
The MAGICIAN OF LUBLIN Ref: V 5/23/79.
MAITRESSE (F) Ref: V 2/11/76: vision in slaughterhouse.
The MAKING OF "SILENT RUNNING" 49m. Ref: V 7/31/74:24.
MAKO,JAWS OF DEATH 1976 (aka JAWS OF DEATH) Ref: L.Wolf: madman who sics sharks on enemies. TVFFSB.
MAN WHO SAW TOMORROW Ref: V 3/4/81: Nostradamus; semi-docu.
MANAK (Thai) (The VAMPIRE) Ref: V 12/25/74:21: horror; planned.
MANEATER 1973 Ref: TVFFSB: tigers unleashed on young couples.
MANSION OF EVIL Mayberry-Montez Ref: V 10/4/72:24: shooting. with Leonard Barr, J. Armond.
MARS MEN (Chin.-J) Shochiku 1976 c./s. 100m. D:S.Den. SP:J.Lin. Ref: Bianco #2/78:158: aka GLI UOMINI DI MARTE. with Y.Hsiao.
MASSACRE AT BLOOD BATH DRIVE-IN D: Harrington. Ref: V 5/12/76: 275. with Kim Novak. Filmed? French?
MATER AMATISIMA (Sp) Ref: V 6/11/80: "tv scenes of Frankenstein."
MAYA (F) Ref: V 12/21/49: "eerie" Hindu, "incarnation of illusion."
McMILLAN AND WIFE: NIGHT OF THE WIZARD 1972 D:R.M.Lewis. SP:Steve Fisher. Ref: TV: CBS Late Movie 1/29/81; seance, "ghost."
McMILLAN AND WIFE: THE DEVIL,YOU SAY 1973 Ref: Scheuer: satanists.
MEAN STREETS 1973 Ref: Ecran 12/77:30: TOMB OF LIGEIA clips.
The MECHANIC 1972 Ref: Glut/TDB: wax museum Dracula.
MEDUSA Rossanne 1974 Ref: TVFFSB: "bizarre." with G.Hamilton.
MEET NERO WOLFE 1936 Ref: screen: golf-club, needle-shooting gun.
MERCY PLANE 1940 Ref: "'B'Movies": "new-fangled" airplane.
MESSAGE FROM THE FUTURE Ref: V 9/30/81:33(ad).
METAL MENACE 1963 short amat. Ref: screen: people-into-robots.
METAL MESSIAH (Can.) D:T.Takacs. Ref: V 5/17/78:400. J.-P.Young.
METAMORPHOSIS (Swed) Ref: V 5/12/76:345: from Kafka. 10/8/75.
MEXICAN HAYRIDE Ref: V 12/1/48. TV: enchilada "grenade"; elixir of contentment; handcuffs burned in half by hot sauce.
MILAREPA (I) Ref: V 4/17/74: "black magic."

MIND OVER MURDER 1979 Ref: CineFan 2:63: psychic visions.
MISBEHAVIN' Ref: Cinema-X Rev.1/80: the Devil.
MISSILE-X:THE NEUTRON BOMB INCIDENT (G-Sp-I) Ref: V 5/17/78:365.
MR.MIKE'S MONDO VIDEO Ref: V 10/3/79: "laser-firing brassiere."
MR.WONG AND BIONIC WOMEN (Fili) Ref: SFC.
The MISTRESS OF PARADISE 1981 Ref: TV: madwoman; voodoo dolls.
MODERN ROMANCE Ref: SFE 4/3/81: hero editing sf-movie. V 3/11/81.
The MONKEY'S PAW non-theat.short Ref: LC Films'78.
MONSTERS! MYSTERIES OR MYTHS? Ref: V 11/27/74:67. TV: TV special.
MONTANA DESPERADO Ref: V 11/14/51: "mysterious masked" killer.
MONTEZUMA'S LOST GOLD 1977 Ref: TV: "invisible presence."
MOOL-DORI VILLAGE (Kor.) Ref: V 7/25/79: "horror fantasy."
MORBO (Sp) Ref: V 8/2/72: sinister blind-woman in old house.
MORGIANA (Cz) Ref: V 8/9/72: cat spirit.
MORITZ,LIEBER MORITZ (W.G.) Ref: V 3/29/78: "ghoulish" fantasies.
MOSS ROSE Ref: V 5/21/47. PFA notes 8/19/80: killer; old house.
The MOVIE MURDERER 1971 Ref: TV: Oland-as-Fu-Manchu clip.
The MUCKER (Braz-W.G.) Ref: V 3/5/80: religious-cult murders.
El MUERTO HACE LAS MALETAS Ref: Cinef Smr'73:36: fake spirits.
Los MUERTOS (Sp) D:J.Aliveira. Ref: V 5/30/73:28: sf; shooting. with E. Redonda, C. Estrada.
MUKKUVANE SNEHICHA BHOOTHAM (India) 1978 Ref: Dharap: curse.
MULUNGU (Swiss) Ref: V 8/28/74: "goat girl haunts" man; god.
**MURDER AT THE BASKERVILLES 1938 (SILVER BLAZE TV) Ref: TV: powerful, silent air-gun; ref. to "Hound of the Baskervilles."
MURDER BY NATURAL CAUSES 1979 Ref: TV: man "returns from death."
MURDER CAN HURT YOU! 1980 Ref: TV(5/21/80): spaceship?
MURDER IMPOSSIBLE 1974 Ref: TVFFSB: invention translates English.
MURDER IN MIND 1973 Ref: TVFFSB: "eerie mystery."
MURDER IN TIMES SQUARE Ref: V 6/2/43: snake-venom-filled hypo.
MURDER ON THE BLACKBOARD 1934 Ref:MFB'79:216-17:"spooky scenes."
MURDER ON THE WATERFRONT Ref: V 3/10/43: The NAVY GETS ROUGH-orig t. 7/28/43: thermostat device. "WB Story."
The MURDERER IS 1 OF 13 (Sp) Ref: V 4/25/73:28: "terror item."
MY FAVORITE BRUNETTE Ref: V 2/19/47: "keyhole camera" invention.
MY GRANDMOTHER (Russ) 1929 Ref: screen: stopmo-anim toys; time stopped; bureaucrat speared with giant fountain-pen.
MYSTERIES OF THE MIND Ref: V 2/13/80:51. GKey: psychic phenomena.
The MYSTERIOUS DESPERADO Ref: V 8/17/49: "thriller-suspense mood"; heirs to Arizona ranch killed off; "mysterious doings."
MYSTERY!: DR.JEKYLL AND MR.HYDE (B-U.S.-Austral) 1981 D: A. Reid. SP: G.Savory. SpFX: Ian Scoones. Ref: TV: TV show.
MYSTERY OF KASPAR HAUSER (W.G.) 1974 Ref: screen:dreams of Death.
MYSTERY OF THE THIRD PLANET (Russ) anim Ref: V 7/1/81:21: sf?

NAGA POOJA MAHIMA (India) 1975 Ref: Dharap: king-cobra curse.
The NAKED WYTCHE Sunset Int'l Ref: V 5/17/72:26(rated).
Il NANO E LA STREGA (I) anim Ref: MFB'79:127: spells.
NARAYANA (F) 1921 Ref: Limbacher: From Balzac's "Magic Skin"?
NAUGHTY DR.JEKYLL 1973? (DIRTY DR.JEKYLL) Ref: Lee.
La NAVE DE LOS BRUJOS (Peruv) D:J.Volkert. Ref: V 9/21/77:6:Sitges.
NECROMANCY 1972 Ref: Medved/TGTA: Ed Wood as a wizard.
NETWORK Ref: MFB'77:9: "fantasy"; Finch-as-"God"-to-millions.

The NEW AVENGERS: GNAWS (B) Ref: TV: CBS Late Movie; monster.
The NEW AVENGERS: THE LAST OF THE CYBERNAUTS...?? (B) Ref: TV: CBS Late Movie 2/16/81; cybernetic monsters; bionic man.
The NEW AVENGERS: THREE-HANDED GAME (B) Ref: TV:brain-draining.
The NEWSPAPER GAME 1976 Ref: TVG: nuclear-power-plant scheme.
The NEXT SCREAM YOU HEAR 1974 Ref: TVFFSB: mystery.
The NEXT VICTIM (B) 1975 Ref: TV. TVFFSB: psychotic killer.
NICHOLAS NICKLEBY (B) 1947 Ref: V 3/26/47. screen: Gothic atmos.
NICHT ALLES WAS FLIEGT, IST EIN VOGEL (W.G.) anim Ref: V 4/25/79: nightmare seq. with giant crow; quote from Poe's "The Raven."
The NIGHT DANIEL DIED Creative Ref: V 7/9/75:34. 6/30/76:34.
NIGHT FERRY (B) Ref: MFB'77:104-5: boy plays mummy's "ghost."
NIGHT HAIR CHILD (B) 1971 Ref: Lee: sexual psychopath. MFB'73.
NIGHT 'N' GALES 1937 short Ref: TV: nightmare: "devils." LC.
NIGHT OF THE STRANGLER 1975 Ref: Willis/SW.
NIGHT OF THE VAMPIRE 196-? amat.? short Ref: Lee: "Miss Dracula."
NIGHT OF THE ZOMBIES NMD 90m. Ref: Boxo 7/28/80:9. aka?
The NIGHT STALKER: THE RIPPER 1974 Ref: TVG: CBS Late Movie.
NIGHT UNTO NIGHT 1949(1947) Ref: NYT 6/11/49:ghostly voice. V 4/20/49. "WB Story." Lee: "haunted" house?
NIGHTINGALE (Russ) (SOLOVEI) Ref: Soviet Film 4/80: robots?
NIGHTMARE 21st Century/Goldmine D: Scavolini. Ref: V 9/23/81:7.
La NOCHE DE LOS ASESINOS (F-Sp) 1972 SP,D:J.Franco. From "The Black Cat"? Ref: [illegible] 10/77:00. with L.Romay,W.Berger,Dalbes.
La NONA (Arg) Ref: V 5/23/79. IFG'80: "horrifying crescendo."
NONE SHALL ESCAPE Ref: B.Warren. NYT 4/7/44: post-war fantasy?
The NORTHVILLE CEMETERY MASSACRE 1976 Ref: Willis/SW. D.Hyry.
Le NOSFERAT (Belg) D: M.Rabinowicz. Ref: V 10/27/76:5:at Sitges. 5/12/76:422. IFG'76:110. with Martine Bertrand.
NUCLEAR TERROR (Can.) Ref: V 9/2/81:6: at Sitges.
NUIT D'OR (F) Ref: V 12/15/76: "hexed dolls...mystical sect."
NUMBER SEVENTEEN (B) 1932 Ref: screen: odd doings in old house.
The NUN AND THE MONSTER Ref: V 5/30/79:42: "horror."
The NUTCRACKER (Russ) 1973 anim short Ref: MFB'76:40: rat king.

O LUCKY MAN! (B) 1973 Ref: Lee: boy's head grafted onto pig.
OSS (Norw) Ref: IFG'77:231: "near future."
The OBSESSED ONE 21st Century 1981 Ref: Boxo: horror. with Sally Savalas, M. Panday, Tracy Parrish.
The ODESSA FILE Ref: V 10/9/74: planned '63 "germ bombing" of Israel by neo-Nazis. TVG.
ONE HOUR TO ZERO (B) Ref: MFB'77:76: nuclear-power-plant explos.?
1 2 3 MONSTER EXPRESS (Thai) Ref: V 6/22/77:16: murders on train.
ONLY A SCREAM AWAY (B) 1974 Ref: TV: psychopathic killer.
OPEN SEASON (Sp-Swiss) Ref: V 8/21/74: hunters use couple as prey.
OPIUM (F?) 1977 (L'HISTOIRE D'ANNABEL LEE. PAMELA) D: P.-H.Mathis. Ref: Ecran 12/77:32: from "Morella," "Ligeia," "A.Lee," and "The Oval Portrait." with Pamela Stanford, Howard Vernon.
ORDERS ARE ORDERS (B) 1954 Ref:BFC: sf-film being shot.
ORE THANTHAI (India) 1976 Ref: Dharap: man with dual personality.
L'ORFEO (G-Swiss) Ref: V 10/18/78: from Monteverdi's opera.
OUR HITLER--A FILM FROM GERMANY (W.G.) Ref: V 11/30/77. screen. SFC 7/20/79. Hitler-as-Frankenstein bit; spirit-of-Hitler.

OUTLAW COUNTRY 1948 Ref: TVFFSB: "Frontier Phantom." LC. no V.
The OVAL PORTRAIT Maple Leaf Ref: V 5/3/72:28: shooting. with W. Hendrix, B. Coe.

PAIS PORTATIL (Venez) Ref: V 10/10/79:man's ancestors reappear.
La PALOMA Ref: V 5/15/74: "dose of the occult"; body preserved.
PAMULU PENCHINA PASIVADU (India) 1976 Ref: Dharap: prince turned into snake; his parents "turned into inanimate objects."
PANIC (Can.) Ref: V 10/5/77:37(ad): city's water supply poisoned.
PARADA 88 (Braz) Ref: V 5/9/79:508: pollution's consequences.
The PARALLAX VIEW Ref: V 6/19/74: assassination organization.
PARAPSYCHO (W.G.) Ref: V 3/31/76: at sf-fest. 7/30/75: TV show?
PASCUAL DUARTE (Sp) Ref: V 5/19/76: mass murderer.
The PASSION OF DRACULA 1980? Ref: TV: TV special; filmed play.
PATRIOTS (Russ) 1933 Ref: screen: soldier returns to life.
PEDRO PARAMO (Mex) Ref: V 9/28/77: "horror film" trappings.
La PELLE (I-F) Ref: V 6/3/81: "creepshow...ghoul-glow...horror."
PEPPINO E LA VERGINE MARIA (I) Ref: V 10/29/75: premature burial?
PERCHE QUELLE STRANE GOCCE DI SANGUE SUL CORPE DI JENNIFER? (I) Ref: MFB'73:81: psychopathic killer.
The PERFUMED NIGHTMARE (Fili) Ref: V 12/10/80: "space trip."
PERIPHERAL AND PROBLEM FILM (F-Arg-Kor-Egy?) 1982? (OUT-orig t?) Ref: Willis/HASFFT: carnivorous time-machine? Completed? Begun? Even considered?
PETER AND INVISIBILITY (Hung.) Ref: MFB'74:61.
PETER AND THE ROBOT (Hung.) Ref: MFB'74:61.
PETE'S DRAGON 1977 Ref: TV: dragon that feigns ferociousness.
PETROLE,PETROLE (F) Ref: V 7/29/81: airliner with tennis court and swimming pool.
PHANTOM OF LIBERTY (F) Ref: MFB'75:30-1. screen: phone call from the grave.
PHANTOM OF TERROR 21st Century Ref: Boxo 7/28/80:10: horror-mystery. with Suzy Kendall, Robert Hoffman.
The PHYNX 1970 Ref: Lee: plot to conquer world. J.Shapiro. AFI.
PINK FLAMINGOS 1974? Ref: MFB'78:11-12: cannibalism. V 12/11/74.
PINOCCHIO'S STORYBOOK ADVENTURES 1979 Ref: Willis/SW.
PIRANHA,PIRANHA 1972 Ref: TVFFSB: "hunters hunted." TV:adventure.
PITFALL Ref: V 8/4/48. TV: Dick Powell frets re: son Jimmy Hunt's passion for comic books: "I'm getting terribly worried about that trash he's reading--torturing women, men from Mars." Five years later that trash gives Jimmy a bad dream. (See INVADERS FROM MARS.)
PLANET OF THE SLAVE GIRLS Ref: V 10/3/79:46: 2-hour premiere show of "Buck Rogers in the 25th Century."
PLAY MISTY FOR ME 1971 Ref: screen: psychotic woman. Cinef W'73.
*PLAYTIME 1966 Ref: screen: not sf.
PLEASE STAND BY 1972 Ref: Lee: network-TV-jamming device.
The PLUTONIUM INCIDENT Ref: TVG 3/11/80: "nuclear-age nightmare."
POINT OF TERROR 1972 Ref: Lee: prophetic dreams of murder?
PONTIANAK (Malaysian) MFD D,P: Roger Sutton. SP: A.Razak. Ref: V 5/4/77:54. 10/22/75:115. with Jennifer Kaur, Sharif Medan.
POOR DEVIL Ref: V 2/21/73:38: comedy; deal with the Devil.
The POSSESSION OF VIRGINIA (Can.) Ref: V 10/16/74:26: at Sitges.

POT LUCK (B) Gainsborough Ref: MFB'36:62: abbey with trap doors, secret entrances. W.K.Everson: spooky. with Ralph Lynn.
PRATYUSHA (India) Ref: V 2/27/80: "possessed woman."
PRESAGIO (Mex) Ref: V 10/9/74: "evil omen" seems to come true.
PRIVATE COLLECTION (Austral) Ref: V 6/28/72. Lee: sur-H.
El PROFETA MIMI (Mex) 1972 Ref: Lee: mad strangler.
The PUBLIC EYE (B) 1972 Ref: Glut/TDB: BRIDES OF DRACULA clips.
PURANA PURUSH (India) 1978 Ref: Dharap: caveman story.

QUANDO OS DEUSES ADORMECEM (Braz) 1972 D:Marins.Ref:Lee:"evil rules."
QUIET PLEASE MURDER Ref: V 12/16/42. TV: psych. thriller based on our "unconscious impulse to punish ourselves." (G.Sanders to Gail Patrick: "Hello, Lady Dracula....We're really a couple of walking horror stories.")

RABBIT TEST Ref: V 2/22/78: pregnant man.
The RACER (B) Ref: MFB'75:242-3: "vaguely futuristic."
Das RAETSEL DES SILBERNEN HALBMONDS (WG-I) Ref: V 8/23/72: "psycho thriller."
RAINMAKERS 1935 Ref: TV: KING KONG-poster gag; magic truth-tree.
RAISE THE TITANIC! Ref: SFC 8/5/80: project to r.t.T. V 8/6/80.
RAISING THE ROOF 197-? Ref: TVFFSB: "strange creature"?
RANGE BUSTERS Ref: TVFFSB: "phantom killer." HR 8/22/40. V: "phantom." B.Warren. LC.
RANI AUR LALPARI (India) 1975 Ref: Dharap: "stories of Heaven, Hell, God, under-water creatures, brave Gulliver, etc."
REACHING FOR THE MOON 1931 Ref: TV: strength potion.
REAL LIFE Ref: V 3/7/79. screen: space-helmet-like head-camera.
The REBEL NUN (I-F) Ref: MFB'75:174: "gore and perversions."
RED ALERT Ref: V 10/19/77:99. TV Season: "nuclear holocaust?"
RED SNOW Ref: V 6/25/52: "secret weapon." TV: heat-bomb with electronic firing-pin.
REDNECK (I-B) 1972 Ref: MFB'76:106: mad princess, psychopath.
REFLECTIONS OF MURDER 1974 Ref: TVFFSB: DIABOLIQUE remake.
REMEMBER LAST NIGHT Ref: Lee(V 11/27/35): hypnotism. PFA notes 12/30/80: "weirdly lit hypnosis sequence in a thunderstorm...."
REMEMBER MY NAME Ref: V 10/11/78: "chiller"?
RENDEZVOUS 1973 Ref: Glut/CMM: horror-film clips.
El RETORNO DE LA DUQUESA DRACULA (Sp) D:J.Aguirre. Ref: Glut/TDB. V 9/13/72:32.
The RETURN OF A MAN CALLED HORSE Ref: MFB'76:234: evil spirit.
RETURN OF DRACULA (Swed) 1972 Ref: Limbacher'79.
RETURN OF THE BEVERLY HILLBILLIES 1981 Ref: TV: "white lightning" solution to U.S. energy woes?
RETURN OF THE PINK PANTHER (B) 1974 Ref: B.Hill. TV: credit-seq. bit with P.P. doing Frankenstein-monster's lumbering walk.
RETURN OF THE WITCH (J) (YOMIGAERE MAJO) Ref: V 10/15/80:222.
The RETURN OF WONDER WOMAN 1977? Ref: TV(KBHK,S.F.): undisguised, 2-part "New Adventures of Wonder Woman" run as TV-movie.
RETURN TO FANTASY ISLAND Ref: TVG 1/14/78: "spookery."
RHEINGOLD (W.G.) Ref: V 2/22/78: eerie; Death Angel.

RHINOCEROS Ref: V 1/23/74: humans turning into conformist rhinos.
RICHARD Ref: V 7/26/72: plastic surgery, brainwashing.
RICHARD PRYOR 1979 short Ref: Teleg.Cinema pr: "Dracula" routine.
The RIDDLE OF THE SANDS (B) Ref: MFB'79:51: trial German invasion of England, 1901. V 5/2/79.
RIDIN' THE LONE TRAIL Ref: TVFFSB: "masked terror." B.Warren. V 11/3/37: "anachronisms such as fast trains." pb. LC.
The RIPPER 1958? Ref: TVFFSB: "vicious murderer." with H.Albers.
The RISE AND FALL OF IDI AMIN (Kenyan) Ref: V 9/2/81: "gory."
The RIVER (Cz) 1933 Ref: screen: caveman in dream.
ROAD GAMES (Austral) Ref: V 2/18/81: "suspenser."
ROCAMBOLE (Mex) Ref: "Hist.Cine Mex.," III:101: catalepsy.
ROCK 'N' ROLL HIGH SCHOOL Ref:MFB'80:26: "mad-scientist" bit.
ROGER CORMAN: HOLLYWOOD'S 'WILD ANGEL' docu. Ref: V 6/28/78: refs. to HOUSE OF USHER, etc.
ROOMMATES 1972 Ref: MFB'74:184: transvestite-killer.
ROSELAND Ref: MFB'78:52: ghostly visions.
ROUND-UP TIME IN TEXAS Ref: V 8/4/37: "voodoo drums." B.Warren.
The RULING CLASS (B) Ref: Lee(MFB'72): man who believes he's Jack the Ripper; imagines he sees walking corpses.

SAAT BHAI CHAMPA (India) 1978 Ref: Dharap: 6 evil,childless queens have sons of the 7th "turned into champak flowers."
The SABINA 1979 Ref: Oakland Trib.3/21/80: "unseen monster"?
The SAINT: THE CONVENIENT MONSTER (B) Ref: TV: "CBS Late Movie"; plesiosaur-like Loch Ness Monster behind "uncanny" events?
The SAINT STRIKES BACK 1939 Ref: TV: lobsters-driving-trucks in nightmare sequence.
The SAINT'S VACATION (B) 1941 Ref: TV: new "sound detector."
SALO (I-F) Ref: V 12/3/75. MFB'79:200: sadism; torture.
The SAND MERCHANT 1913 Ref: Ecran 12/77:28: from "Wm.Wilson"?
SANDCASTLES 1972 Ref: TVG: "dead boy's ghost." Lee. TVFFSB.
SANTO CONTRA EL DR.MUERTE (Sp-Mex) Pelimex D:R.R.-Marchant. Ref: V 5/8/74:207. with H. Line, R. Guzman.
SATANICO PANDEMONIUM (Mex?) Hollywood (NOVIZIA INDEMONIATA-I) SP,D: "Gilbert Martin." M: G.C.Carreon. Ref: Bianco Index'75.
SATORI (J) Ref: Lee. V 1/2/74: "demon...modernized."
SATURDAY SUPERSTAR MOVIE: MAD,MAD,MAD MONSTERS 1972 anim Ref: Glut/TDB: Dracula; Frank.monster; MAD MONSTER PARTY "sequel."
SAVAGE HARVEST Ref: V 5/27/81: lions stalks family in Kenya.
SAVAGE MAN...SAVAGE BEAST (I) Ref: MFB'76: docu.; cannibalism.
The SAVIOUR (H.K.) Ref: V 8/13/80: "makes the flesh creep."
The SCARECROW (N.Z.) Ref: V 9/2/81:6: at Sitges.
SCHOOLING (Yug.) 1973 anim Ref: Glut/TFL: Frank. monster.
SCREAM BLOODY MURDER APC 1973 (aka MY BROTHER HAS BAD DREAMS) SP,D,P: R.J.Emery. Ref: V 12/12/73:28(rated). F.O.Ray. Lee (Boxo 11/27/72). with Paul Vincent, Marlena Lustik.
SEASON'S GREETINGS Ref: Boxo 12/31/79:14: multiple murder.
The SECOND WOMAN Ref: V 1/24/51: "dimly lighted mansion."
SECRET HORROR short Ref: PFA notes 4/12/81: ghostly figures.
SECRETS OF THE GODS FVI 1976 Ref: Willis/SW.
The SEEDING OF SARAH BURNS 1979 Ref: TVG: "embryo transplant."
El SEGUNDO PODER (Sp) Ref: V 3/16/77: the Inquisition.

Ein SELTSAMER FALL (G) 1914? D:Max Mack. Ref: Daisne: sfa DR. JEKYLL AND MR.HYDE(1909)? with A.Neuss,H.Weisse,L.Neumann.
SERAIL (F) Ref: V 5/26/76: ghost? MFB'77:241: house "closes up."
SGT.PEPPER'S LONELY HEARTS CLUB BAND (U.S.-W.G.) Ref: MFB'79:32: girl revived from dead; mass-brainwashing plot.
SERIE NOIRE (F) Ref: V 5/2/79: "atmosphere of...nightmare."
**SEVEN DOORS TO DEATH Ref: V 8/23/44. TV: balmy antique dealer who wants to "make a mummy" with embalming fluid.
El SEXTO SENTIDO (Sp) 1926 Ref: Aranda/LB:108: magician's film projector shows people their futures.
The SEXUAL LIFE OF FRANKENSTEIN 1970? Ref: Glut/TFL. no AFI.
SHADOW OF A WOMAN Ref: V 8/14/46: "terror"; bride's husb. killer.
SHADOW OF DRACULA (Can.) 1973 Ref: Murphy. Made?
SHADOWS OF THE NIGHT Danny Vail Ref: Boxo 11/12/79:18:horror.
SHADOWS OVER CHINATOWN Ref: V 9/18/46. TV: curio-shop horror-bit.
SHAG S KRISHI (Russ) Ref: Cinef W'73:38: prehistoric sequence.
SHARK KILL Ref: V 5/26/76:58: "JAWS-inspired." TV Season.
S*H*E 1980 Ref: TVG: plot to wreck world's oil production.
SHE WOLF OF STILLBERG (F) Ref: V 5/17/78:290.
SHOCK TREATMENT Ref: V 8/26/81:20: follow-up to ROCKY HORROR PICTURE SHOW; town-as-TV-production.
SHORT WALK TO DAYLIGHT 1972 Ref: TV: terrorist bombs cripple Wall Street; subway riders think they're in an earthquake.
Un SILENCIA DE TUMBA (Sp) D:J.Franco. Ref: V 5/8/74:207. Dalbes.
The SILENT ENEMY 1930 Ref: screen: medicine man's incantations revive dead chief, summon up snowstorm; Canoe of the Dead.
SILENTLY I SCREAM Nova 1974 Ref: V 5/8/74:33(rated).
SINGAPORE WOMAN 1941 Ref: TV: run of bad luck due to coincidence not "curse"; David Bruce: "I don't believe in voodoo." Scheuer.
SIR HENRY AT RAWLINSON END (B) Ref: V 7/16/80: ghost comedy.
SIVAPPU ROJAKKAL (India) 1978 Ref: Dharap: "nightmarish."
SLAVE OF THE CANNIBAL GOD 1979 Ref: Willis/SW.
SLEEP,MY LOVE Ref: V 1/14/48: man uses hypnosis, drugs trying to kill wife.
SLEEPING DOGS (N.Z.) Ref: V 10/19/77: "near future";police state.
SLEEPWALKER (B) 1975 Ref: TV: hints of psychic phenomena. TVG.
SLEUTH (B) Ref: V 12/13/72: "gadgetry." FFacts: "robots." TV.
The SLIGHTLY PREGNANT MAN (F-I) Ref: MFB'74:274: s.p.m.
The SNOOP SISTERS: BLACK DAY FOR BLUEBEARD 1974 Ref: Glut/TDB: TV-movie?; horror-film star masquerades as Dracula.
SNUFF (Arg-U.S.) (The SLAUGHTER) Ref: V 3/25/76: gory murders.
SO SAD ABOUT GLORIA 1973 Ref: V 8/15/73:17(rated). Lee: horror?
SODOM AND GOMORRAH--THE LAST SEVEN DAYS 1975 Ref: screen. V 3/3/76:39: "zombie"? Willis/SW. Alien destroys S.& G.
SOMEONE'S WATCHING ME! 1978 (HIGH RISE) Ref: TV: mad strangler.
SOMETHING IN THE WIND Ref: V 7/23/47: "I Love a Mystery" number.
SOMEWHERE IN THE NIGHT Ref: V 5/8/46. TV: psych. thriller; line: "Stop talking like Bela Lugosi."
SONATA OVER THE LAKE (Russ) Ref: V(d) 1/21/77: "haunted" house.
SONG AT MIDNIGHT (Chin.) 1935 Ref: Limbacher'79: based on G. Leroux's "The Phantom of the Opera"??
SORRY,WRONG NUMBER Ref: V 7/28/48: "horror...spine-tingling."
SOUTH OF HELL MOUNTAIN 1971? Ref: TVFFSB: horror-drama. with Anna Stewart, Martin J. Kelly.

SPACE LOVE 1972 Ref: Lee(Boxo): Distribpix.
The SPACE ORGAN Marketta SP,D,P: W.A.Levey. Ref: V 11/5/75: started 9/5. with M.Begelieson,J.Ireland Jr., Anne Gaybis.
SPACEBOY 1972 short Ref: Lee: space siren?
SPHINX 1980 Ref: "Sneak Previews": bat attack;mummy finds.
The SPIRITUALIST (Sp?) D:A.Fernando. Ref: V 2/5/75:35:shooting. with V. Parra, N. Kastell.
SREE RAMA RAKSHA (India) 1978 Ref: Dharap: spirit of dead twin enters body of the other.
SREE SREE MA LAKSHMI (India) 1976 Ref: Dharap: "Devil incarnate."
STAND UP AND CHEER! 1934 Ref: TV: U.S.Secretary of Amusement appointed and "Poverty is wiped out! The Depression is over!"
STAR GODZILLA (H.K.) Ref: V 5/7/80:458(ad). Completed?
STAR TREK (Blooper Reel) short Ref: screen: TV series out-takes.
STAR TREK--THE MENAGERIE Ref: SFE 8/14/81:A7(ad): videodisc.
STAR VIRGIN Gail Ref: V 5/21/80(rated).
STARDUST MEMORIES Ref: MFB'80:242: imagined visit by aliens.
STEPPENWOLF 1974 Ref: MFB'76:63: "half man & half wolf"?
STEPSISTERS Ref: V 5/11/77:205(ad): "Moonhill Mansion."
STONE COLD DEAD (Can.) Ref: V 2/27/80: sniper shoots women.
The STORY OF JOANNA 1975 Ref: MFB'77:153: horror-movie atmos.
STOWAWAY TO THE MOON 1975 Ref: TV: boy aboard moon rocket.
STRANGE THINGS HAPPEN AT NIGHT (F) Clark Ref: V 1/12/77:70(rated). with S. Julien. Sfa *VAMPIRE THRILLS? Willis/SW. F.O.Ray.
STREET GANGS OF HONG KONG Ref: V 3/20/74: "incessant gore."
The STREETFIGHTER (J) Ref: V 2/5/75: "gory."
SUBMARINE ALERT Ref: TV. V 6/23/43: "shortwave portable transmitter" which baffles the FBI; steam-torture chamber.
SUICIDE CULT Ref: Boxo 2/4/80:sf-horror. V 5/7/80:286:released. with Bob Byrd, Monica Tidwell. 21st Century.
SUPER MANCHU Ref: Willis/SW: 1975?
SUPERMAN VS.THE AMAZONS AI Ref: V 5/15/74:52(rated).
SURVIVE! (Mex) Ref: MFB'76:257: cannibalism.
SWEET KILL 1972 (The AROUSERS) Ref: Cinef W'73:37: "Son of PSYCHO." MFB'76:64: "sexual psychosis...necrophilia."
SYBIL 1976 Ref: MFB'79:255: "horrific flashbacks"; woman with multiple personality. TVG.

A TALENT FOR LOVING 1969 Ref: TV: Aztec priest curses family with unquenchable lust.
The TEMPEST (B) Ref: V 9/12/79. Monstrous Caliban; spells.
TERMINAL ISLAND 1973 Ref: Lee: "near future."
TERROR FROM UNDER THE HOUSE (B) (aka REVENGE) D:S.Hayers. Ref: Willis/SW: 1976? no MFB. with Joan Collins, James Booth.
TERRORE (I) Filman D:F.Prosperi. Ref: V 10/19/77:143,109(ad): "bloodchilling";hallucinatory effects. F.Bolkan,R.Lovelock.
THAT CURSED HOUSE CLOSE TO THE MUSHROOM-BED (I) 1972? Ref: Lee: "dead man" haunts widow. with I.Demick,A.Celi,R.Hoffmann.
THEMROC (F) Ref: V 2/21/73: man reverts to cannibalistic caveman.
THEY MET IN THE DARK (B) Ref: MFB'43:88:spies. V 5/23/45:"hypnotist who strangles his victims"; illusionist. no NYT. LC.
THIS IS THE WAY THE WORLD WILL END 1978 Ref: TVFFSB:speculation.
THREE TALES DARK AND DANGEROUS Ref: TV: 2nd story sf? By Asimov.

The THREE WEIRD SISTERS (B) Ref: V 3/10/48: "horror story... rackety Welsh mansion...sinister murder mystery." MFB'48:30.
THREE WOMEN Ref: MFB'77:198: bizarre murals. Meyers.
THRESHOLD 1971 amat.short Ref: Lee: J.Carradine as Death.
THROUGH THE LOOKING GLASS 1976 Ref:MFB'78:55: "demonic lover."
THUNDER IN THE CITY (B) 1937 Ref: TV: "Magnelite," "miracle metal" combining aluminum's lightness with steel's strength.
TIMBUKTU 1959 Ref: TV: torture-by-tarantulas.
The TIN DRUM (W.G.-F-Yug-Pol) Ref: P.Lyman: boy whose screams shatter glass thinks he's responsible for series of deaths.
TIYANAK (Fili) Gonzales Ref: V 11/29/78:36: "sci-fi" filming.
TO LOVE,PERHAPS TO DIE 1975 Ref: Cinef IV:3:39: "futuristic."
TODO MODO (I) 1976('79-U.S.) Ref: SFC 4/30/80: "near future"; Italy's politicians murdered. Bianco Index'76. V 3/26/80.
TOO EASY TO KILL 1975 Ref: TVFFSB: nurse into the occult.
TOO HOT TO HANDLE 1976 Ref: MFB'78:96: paralyzing drug;torture.
El TOPO (Mex) 1971 Ref: MFB'74:247: freaks, violence. screen.
TOWER OF TERROR 1972? Ref: TVFFSB: horror; maniac.
TOYS ARE NOT FOR CHILDREN 1972 Ref: CineFan 2:28: strange girl.
TRAUMSTADT (G) Ref: V 10/9/74: "sci-fi and medieval imagery."
TRAVELLING COMPANION (Venez) Ref: IFG'80:326: "ancient myth."
TRE RAGAZZI IN GAMBA ALL'ATTACCO DI UFO (Braz) 1973 Ref: Bianco Index'76:70.
The TRIAL OF BILLY JACK 1974 Ref:screen: spirit; dead revived.
TRILOGY FROM THE PRIMEVAL AGES (Cz) 1977 D:J.Schmidt. Ref: IFG '80:104: Settlement of Crows;Calling of the Tribe;On the Great River.
TRIPLE TROUBLE 1918 Ref: screen: "wireless explosive" tested.
TROLL (Swed) Ref:MFB'74:108:"diabolic rabbit"possesses woman?
TROMPE L'OEIL (F) Ref: V 3/19/75: "birdman"; nightmarish.
I TVILLINGERNES TEGN (Dan) 1975 Ref: MFB'79:209: "elaborate House of Horror props." Cont.Film Rev.5/80: "ogre."
*The TWELFTH HOUR 1930 Ref: E.Patalas: sound version of NOSFERATU(1922), with some alternate shots.
TWENTIETH CENTURY 1934 Ref: Willis/FOHH: J.Barrymore Svengali bit.
TWILIGHT'S LAST GLEAMING (US-G) Ref: V(d) 1/28/77: set in 1981.
TWIN DETECTIVES Ref: V 5/5/76: "phony medium."
TWINKLE,TWINKLE,"KILLER"KANE 1980 Ref: screen: Frank.-monster-masked man; refs.to Dracula; split personality; allegory.
TWO GIRLS AND A SAILOR 1943 Ref: TV: "haunted"-warehouse scene.
200 MOTELS 1971 Ref: Glut/CMM: "Dr.Jekyll" bit.
The TWO WORLDS OF JENNIE LOGAN 1979 Ref:TVG:woman returns in time.

The UFO MAN (Finn) Ref: IFG'75:174.
UBU (B) anim short Ref: MFB'78:253: ghostly knight; monster?
ULTRATUMBA(Sp) D:J.Franco. Ref: V 5/8/74:207. E.Cohen, R.Wood.
UNCONSCIOUS Ref: V 9/30/81:17(ad): horror?
UNDERCURRENT Ref: V 10/2/46: "chills & thrills";animals fear man.
UNDSKYLD VI ER HER (Dan) Ref: V 12/16/80: "futuristic experiment."
UNION CITY V 9/10/80. SFC 8/10/81:42: "horror-comedy." Fear drives killer to suicide. From "The Tell-Tale Heart"?
UNKNOWN POWERS 1978 Ref: TV: psychics, faith healers, etc.
UP! 1976 Ref: MFB'81:98: Hitler in Redwood County; sadism. V(d).

UTAH TRAIL Ref: "Filming of the West": "ghost train." B.Warren. V 10/12/38: "private railroad to hijack beef." TVFFSB. no LC.

VAMPIRE Ref: Glut/TDB. Prob.sfa NAKED WORLD OF HARRISON MARKS.
VAMPIRE PLAYGIRLS MPM/Schart Ref: V 11/26/80:9.
The VAMPIRES (Sp) D:J.Franco. Ref: V 10/31/73:6.
VAMPIRES OF POVERTY (Col) (AGARRANDO PUEBLO) Ref:V 1/17/79:34.
O VAMPIRO DE COPACABANA (Braz) Ref: V 5/11/77:119.
Los VAMPIROS LOS PREFIEREN GORDITOS (Arg) Ref: V 9/10/75:32.
VARNEY,THE VAMPIRE 1975? Ref: Murphy. Made? R.D.Steckler.
VELVET HANDS (I) Ref: V 2/20/80: "bazooka-proof plate glass."
Una VEZ UN HOMBRE (Arg?) Ref: TV: Fate as 3 women (with scissors) at moviola; alchemist's glass which allows hero to see people they dispatch; "film library" (each reel of film a life).
Los VIERNES DE LA ETERNIDAD (Arg) Ref: V 6/17/81: ghost comedy.
VIGILANTE HIDEOUT Ref: V 8/9/50: inventor's gadgets foil crooks.
VIOLANTA (Swiss) Ref: V 9/28/77: "incest, ghosts, and murder."
VIOLENCE IN THE CINEMA PART I (Austral) Ref:MFB'73:236: torture.
VIR MANGDAVALO (India) 1976 Ref: Dharap: ghost.
A VIRGIN'S SEXUAL NIGHTMARE (Braz) 1975 Ref:Brasil: cavewoman.
I VITELLONI (I) 1953 Ref: screen: Frank.-monster-masked reveler.
The VOICE FROM THE SKY 1930 serial Ref: Turner/Price: anti-energy force? Parish-Pitts/TGSFP: not released?
VOODOO DEVIL DRUMS 1944? Ref: Lee: witchcraft. Aka?
The VOODOOIST Cannon 90m. Ref: V 1/16/74:5. Cinef III:2:33.
Les VOYAGES DE TORTILLARD (Can.) Ref: IFG'80:89: time travel?

WALK OF THE DEAD IAP Ref: V 8/13/80:9. 6/10/81:15: in Miami.
WAM BAM, THANK YOU SPACE MAN Ref: SFE 6/81.
WATERSHIP DOWN (B) Ref: MFB'78:208: nasty rats, etc. screen.
WE ARE NOT ALONE IN THE UNIVERSE (Sp) Iries-Gonzalez (EXISTIO OTRA HUMANIDAD) Ref: V 5/9/79:484(ad): dinosaurs?
The WEDDING (Pol) Ref: screen: straw-men menaces. V 10/3/73.
The WEDNESDAY CHILDREN Ref: V 6/20/73. Lee. The Devil; spell.
WELCOME TO MY NIGHTMARE 1975 Ref: TVFFSB: "demonic visions."
WERWOELFE (W.G.) Ref: V 5/8/74:194.
WHACKS MUSEUM 1933 anim short Ref: Maltin/OMAM.
WHAT A CRAZY WORLD (B) 1963 Ref: BFC: CURSE OF FRANKENSTEIN clip.
WHAT BECAME OF JACK AND JILL (B) 1972 Ref:TVFFSB:horror. Lee.
WHAT NEXT? (B) Ref: MFB'74:286: "Ghost Train" ride; boy who can foretell events. V 2/26/75: WHAT'S NEXT.
WHEN WOMEN PLAYED DING DONG (I) 1971 Ref: Lee: prehistory.
WHIFFS Ref: V 10/1/75. Chemicals make man impotent.
WHISKY AND GHOSTS (Sp-I) Ref: V 5/7/75:242.
The WHISPERER IN DARKNESS 1975 amat.short Ref: CineFan 2:21-23.
The WHITE BUFFALO Ref: V 9/21/77. MFB'78:32: nightmare-premon.
The WHITE DAWN 1974 Ref: screen: harpooned shaman returns without wound; fishing line "to hell."
WHO DONE IT? Ref: V 11/4/42. TV: 200,000 volts electrifies Lou.
WHO IS KILLING THE GREAT CHEFS OF EUROPE? (U.S.-W.G.) Ref: MFB'79:34-5: bizarre murders.
WIDOWS' NEST (U.S.-Sp) Ref: V 12/14/77: "gothic"; "witch."

WILD STRAWBERRIES (Swed) 1958 Ref: screen: corpse's-clutching-hand nightmare-seq.
The WILD,WILD WORLD OF JAYNE MANSFIELD 1968 Ref: J.Shapiro: monster scenes from *LOVES OF HERCULES.
WINTER SONGS 1969 short Ref: Lee: vampire-like "transfusion"seq.
WINTER WITH DRACULA (B) short Ref: MFB'72:docu.;ref. to Dracula.
WITCH'S SISTER Ref: TVG 7/20/80: scenes on "Big Blue Marble."
A WOMAN'S FACE 1941 Ref:screen: mad-dr.-like Veidt; Frank. ref.
WONDER WOMAN MEETS BARONESS VON GUNTHER 1975 Ref: TV Season.
The WORLD OF DARKNESS 1977 Ref: TV Season: pilot-film?;"occult."
The WORLD'S GREATEST ATHLETE Ref:MFB'73:156:witch dr.;voodoo dolls.
The WORM EATERS Genini Ref: V 5/11/77:405(ad). 4/27/77:32. with Nancy Kapner, Herbert Robins. Made?
The WORMS (Cuban) Ref: V 2/13/80: "nerve-jangling tale of horror."
WOYZECK (W.G.) Ref: V 5/16/79: doctor's experiments reduce orderly to "a sort of group of reflexes...."
The WRATH OF GOD 1972 Ref: MFB'73:39: "mayhem and gore... bizarrely sadistic climax."

YASEI NO SHOMEI (J) Ref: V 11/15/78: set in 1980; secret organization.
Les YEUX DU DRAGON (F) 1925 object anim & live D,P: Starevitch. Ref: Lee.
YOU'LL LIKE MY MOTHER Ref: V 10/11/72: "suspense-shock." MFB '73:39: sadist.
YUME,YUME NO ATO (J-F) Ref: V 4/22/81: "enchanted" women turn into birds.
YUPPY DU (I) 1975 Ref: Bianco Index'75: sf?

The ZEBRA KILLER 1974 (PANIC CITY-B) Ref: MFB'76:195-6: mass murderer.
ZEE BOOM BA (India) 1977 Ref: Dharap: "kind-hearted ghost."
La ZIZANIE (F) Ref: V 4/5/78: anti-pollution invention.
ZORRO'S FIGHTING LEGION 1939 serial Ref: TV: man masquerading as Yaqui god, Don Del Oro.

PRINCIPAL REFERENCES

Dates given are for editions and issues consulted

Books, Annuals, Catalogs

Academy of Motion Picture Arts and Sciences. Annual Index to Motion Picture Credits, 1978; 1979. Westport, Conn.: Greenwood Press, 1979, 1980. Two volumes.

The American Film Institute Catalog of Motion Pictures: Feature Films 1961-1970. New York: R.R. Bowker Co., 1976.

Aros, Andrew A. A Title Guide to the Talkies: 1964-1974. Metuchen, N.J.: Scarecrow Press, 1977.

Audio Brandon Films. Mt. Vernon, N.Y.: Audio Brandon Films, 1978.

Brasil Cinema 1975 (No. 10). Rio de Janiero: Embrafilme, 1977.

Chirat, Raymond. Catalogue des Films Francais de Long Metrage (1929-1939). Brussels: Cinematheque Royale de Belgique, 1975.

Cowie, Peter, ed. International Film Guide. Cranbury, N.J.: A.S. Barnes & Co., 1972-1981. Ten volumes.

Cowie, Peter, gen.ed. World Filmography 1967; 1968. So. Brunswick & N.Y.: A.S. Barnes, 1977. Two volumes.

Daisne, Johan. Dictionnaire Filmographique de La Litterature Mondiale. Ghent: Editions Scientifiques, 1971, 1975; 1978 (supplement).

David, Nina. TV Season 74-75; 75-76; 76-77; 77-78. Phoenix, Ariz.: The Oryx Press, 1976, 1977, 1978, 1979.

Dharap, B.V. Indian Films: 1972; 1973; 1974; 1975; 1977-78. Poona, India: Motion Picture Enterprises, 1973-1980.

Eberhard, Wolfram. The Chinese Silver Screen: Hong Kong and Taiwanese Motion Pictures in the 1960's. Taipei, Formosa: The Orient Cultural Service, 1972.

Gifford, Denis. The British Film Catalog 1895-1970. N.Y.: McGraw-Hill, 1973.

Glut, Don. Classic Movie Monsters. Metuchen, N.J.: Scarecrow Press, 1978.

________. The Dracula Book. Metuchen, N.J.: Scarecrow Press, 1975.

________. The Frankenstein Legend. Metuchen, N.J.: Scarecrow Press, 1973.

Lee, Walt. Reference Guide to Fantastic Films. Los Angeles: Chelsea-Lee, 1972, 1973, 1974. Three volumes.

Lennig, Arthur. The Count: The Life and Films of Bela "Dracula" Lugosi. N.Y.: G.P. Putnam's Sons, 1974.

Limbacher, James L. Haven't I Seen You Somewhere Before? Ann Arbor, Mich.: The Pierian Press, 1979.

Maltin, Leonard. Of Mice and Magic. N.Y.: McGraw-Hill Book Co., 1980.

________. TV Movies. N.Y.: New American Library, 1974.

Meyers, Richard. The World of Fantasy Films. So. Brunswick & N.Y.: A.S. Barnes, 1980.

Motion Pictures: 1912-1939; 1940-1949; 1950-1959; 1960-1969. Washington, D.C.: Library of Congress Register of Copyrights, 1951, 1953, 1960, 1971.

Murphy, Michael J. The Celluloid Vampires. Ann Arbor, Mich.: The Pierian Press, 1979.

The New York Times Film Reviews: 1913-1976. N.Y.: The New York Times & Arno Press, 1970, 1971, 1973, 1975, 1977. Ten volumes.

Scheuer, Steven H. Movies on TV. N.Y.: Bantam Books, 1977.

Television Feature Film Source Book. N.Y.: Broadcast Information Bureau, 1978.

Turner, George E. and Michael H. Price. Forgotten Horrors. So. Brunswick & N.Y.: A.S. Barnes, 1979.

Willis, John A. Screen World. N.Y.: Crown Publishers, 1972-1981. Ten volumes.

Periodicals

Bianco e Nero. Rome: Centro Sperimentale di Cinematografia, 1972-.

Boxoffice. N.Y.: Associated Publications, 1979-.

CineFan. Los Altos, Calif.: Fandom Unlimited, 1980.

Cinefantastique. Oak Park, Ill.: Frederick S. Clarke, 1970-.

Ecran 72-. Paris: Editions de l'Atalante, 1972-.

Famous Monsters. N.Y.: Warren Publishing Co., 1971-.

Film Facts. N.Y.: American Film Institute, 1971-1977.

Film Notes. Berkeley: University Art Museum/Pacific Film Archive, 1975-.

Film Quarterly. Berkeley: University of California Press, 1975-.

The Japanese Fantasy Film Journal. Toledo, Ohio: Greg Shoemaker, 1981.

The Monthly Film Bulletin. London: British Film Institute, 1972-.

Motion Picture Herald. N.Y.: Quigley, 1934-1940.

San Francisco Chronicle. S.F.: The Chronicle Publishing Co., 1975-.

Sight and Sound. London: British Film Institute, 1972-.

TV Guide. Radnor, Pa.: Triangle Publications, 1972-.

Variety. N.Y.: Variety, Inc., 1942-1953; 1972-.

The Village Voice. N.Y.: Village Voice, Inc., 1972-.

ADDENDA

(M) BLUE SUNSHINE 1977 Mkp: Norman Page. Puppet Master: Steve Stegman. Ref: TV. and with Ray Young(madman).

Well-done, but is it worth doing? Script essentially just comes up with a new type of bizarre killer--these psychos don't just kill; their eyes go funny and they suddenly lose their hair. Closest cross-references: DEMON, RABID, Yul Brynner. Some good, strange visual touches, but, basically, a formula horror-mystery.

CHINESE WEB, The see SPIDER-MAN: THE DRAGON'S CHALLENGE(M)

(M) CLASH OF THE TITANS Titan(Schneer) 1981 Ph:(aerial) E.S. Woxholt. SpVisFX:(asst) Jim Danforth, Steven Archer. OptFX: Van Der Veer, Roy Field. Models: Cliff Culley. Masks: Colin Arthur. Ref: screen.

Carrier-vulture which fetches caged spirit of Andromeda to monstrous Calibos; Stygian witches; helmet of invisibility; giant-scorpions-from-blood-of-Medusa; mechanical owl; Greek gods. The Harryhausen spectacular proves to be little-better-than-usual on continuity--the script is essentially mythology-as-exposition. But there are quite a few delightful effects-moments, and even a couple near-whole sequences which properly exhilarate--e.g., the Pegasus-mounted Perseus following the vulture-and-its-charge through the skies. (Not your everyday-type effect....) Perhaps the most striking moment: the shadow of the chess-piece representing Calibos-the-man transmogrifying into Calibos-the-monster.

DEAD PEOPLE see MESSIAH OF EVIL(M)

DEADLY DUST see SPIDER-MAN STRIKES BACK(M)

A FIRE IN THE SKY Col-TV & Bill Driskill 1978 color 135m. D: Jerry Jameson. SP: Dennis Nemec, Michael Blankfort. Story: Paul Gallico. Ph: M.F. Leonetti. Mus: Paul Chihara. PD: Dale Hennesy. SpFX: Joseph A. Unsinn. Ref: TV. TVG. with Richard Crenna, Elizabeth Ashley, David Dukes, Joanna Miles, Lloyd Bochner, Andrew Duggan, Cynthia Eilbacher, John Larch, Kip Niven, Merlin Olsen, Bill Williams.

Comet has a date with Phoenix, Ariz., keeps it. "Meteor, Jr.," with similar dramatic problems.

HALLOWEEN II Univ/Akkad-De Laurentiis 1981 color/scope 95m. D: Rick Rosenthal. SP,P: John Carpenter, Debra Hill. Sequel to HALLOWEEN(M). Ph: Dean Cundey. Mus: Carpenter; Alan Howarth. PD: Michael Riva. SpFX:(sup) Larry Cavanaugh; Frank Munoz. Masks: Don Post. Title Seq: Jamie Shourt. Ref: screen. V 9/9/81:4(rated). with Jamie Lee Curtis, Donald Pleasence, Charles Cyphers(Leigh Brackett), Dick Warlock(The Shape), Lance Guest, Pamela Shoop, Ford Rainey.

"Why *me*?" asks our heroine (Curtis); *because* (it transpires) she's the unkillable killer's half-sister; murder by butcher knife, hatchet, scalpel, hydrotherapy pool, hypo, transfusion-tube; NIGHT OF THE LIVING DEAD on TV. Less a sequel than a redundancy. This should have been called HALLOWEEN 1.01 it adds so little to the original. HALLOWEEN may have been fairly mechanical, but HALLOWEEN II demonstrates that there's mechanical and there's mechanical. It makes "I" look positively organic. A new nadir for Carpenter & co.

LEGACY OF MAGGIE WALSH, The see LEGACY,The(M)

MAGAZINE RACK see I LIKE MOUNTAIN MUSIC(M)

*The MONSTER AND THE GIRL 1941 Mus D: S. Krumgold. AD: Hans Dreier, H. Douglas. Ref: TV. and with Abner Biberman, Edward Van Sloan.

A bizarre fusing of MARKED WOMAN (small-town-girl Ellen Drew becomes big-town "hostess") and The WALKING DEAD (her unjustly-executed brother, Phillip Terry, returns from the dead--as a brain in the skull of a gorilla--to wreak revenge on those who framed him for murder). A basically-routine revenge story (with a ludicrous sf twist), MONSTER AND THE GIRL is, nevertheless, occasionally compelling as a weird sort of brief against injustice. (The latter represented, principally, by Robert Paige's creepily-smooth cad-con-man.) "Pathos" too gets a new wrinkle, in the scene in which the brother (now a gorilla) slips into sis's room and tenderly watches over her for a moment as she sleeps. The latter scene should be *anything* but touching, yet somehow....Maybe it's the way the *light* hits the *gorilla's eyes*; or perhaps it's simply the sheer, lovely, loony improbability of the scene.

PANIC OFFSHORE see INTRUDER WITHIN,The(M)

(M) PLANET OF DINOSAURS 85m. Ph: Henning Schellerup. SpDes: S. Wathen. Mattes: Jim Danforth. SpProps: Bill Malone. Titles: Freeze Frame. Ref: screen. "Encyc.Brit." and with Derna Wylde, Louie Lawless.

To wit: tyrannosaurs, stegosaurs, brontosaur, sea monster, styracosaur, spider, ornitholestes-types; laser rifles. Another dinosaur yawner. The characters here wax Darwinian while the monsters go through their usual stop-motions. But the animation does afford scattered redeeming moments--one huge carnosaur suddenly bending down into frame to gobble up a smaller one; the ornitholestes-types lending their scene a bit of sleek, ostrichy elegance; the spider scampering out of a crevice (only to be summarily batted away by the heroine).

(M) PLANET OF HORRORS UA 81m. Mus: Barry Schrader. PD: James Cameron. SpMkpFX: Thom Shouse. SpElecFX: Steve Barncard. SpVisFX: Tom Campbell. GraphicAnimDes: Ernest D. Farino. Opt FX: Jack Rabin. Ref: screen. V 10/21/81. and with Zalman King, Sid Haig.

"Master" of the universe (and his replacement); fear-bred monsters (inc. cat-like creature, giant worm, lash-like constrictors); monsters and creators/victims returning to face hero. The look and feel is ALIEN; the premise goes back to such mind-generated-monster movies as FORBIDDEN PLANET and JOURNEY TO THE SEVENTH PLANET. But it all boils down to miscellaneous zapping (by monsters) and yapping (by characters). _Some_ of the former is fun.

PSYCHOPATH Larry Brown 1974 color 84m. Story,D,P: Brown. SP: W.C. Dallenbach. Ph: Jack Beckett. Mus: Al Ross. Opt: CFI. Ref: MFB'81:159. TVFFSB: "horror." with Tom Basham (Tommy), Gene Carlson, Gretchen Kanne.

Madman (Basham) dispatches child-abusers with garden shears, lawnmowers, etc.

*RED PLANET MARS Hyde-Veiller 1952 Source play also by John Hoare. Mus: _Mahlon Merrick_. Elec Tech D: Vern Stineman. Mkp: Don Cash. Ref: TV. V 5/14/52. Baxter/SFITC. with W. Bouchey.

Circa 1957. God, speaking from Mars, turns swords of Earth into ploughshares. For-the-most-part facile and jerrybuilt, this sf-religious-fantasy features an insidiously-inveigling climactic sequence in which spiritual faith, doubt, and satanic defiance vie for dramatic supremacy. Not that this section is any less outlandish than the rest of the movie--it's arguably even _more_ so. But it's also (unlike the rest) very cannily engineered, and it has a certain screwy power to it. It raises hope, only to dash it, then raise it again: one moment, it seems, God certifiably exists, the next He doesn't, the next He does--the movie is a metaphysical rollercoaster. Even the Devil (in the form of Herbert Berghof's Nazi genius) receives his due here, or at least his say. But God--in the form of scanning lines on the television-set-like hydrogen tube--has the last Word. ("Ye have done well...."). And It comes _just in time_, one moment before a beneficent explosion dispatches the Devil-Nazi and makes the world safe for faith. (It also makes the husband-and-wife-scientist-team (Peter Graves and Andrea King) heroic martyrs--and their two so-proud, "lucky" children orphans.) This is--God forbid--the American version of DIARY OF A COUNTRY PRIEST; home-grown, transcendental kitsch with sights set as high as the latter's art--and if the thematic reach of RED PLANET MARS perceptibly exceeds its dramatic grasp, well, what's a camp-heaven _for_?

SOMETHING EVIL 1972 color 73m. D: Steven Spielberg. Ref: Scheuer/MOTV. no Lee. Maltin/TVM. with Sandy Dennis, Darren

McGavin, Ralph Bellamy, Jeff Corey, John Rubinstein.
"The Devil occupies a Pennsylvania farmhouse...." (MOTV)

(M) SQUIRM Lansbury-Beruh 1976 Asst AD: Neal De Luca. Ref:TV.
Not bad--until the worms start doing their turns. The people here are decidedly pleasanter to watch. The worm scenes are "hyped" by music, mandibular close-ups, worm "shrieks," and masses-and-masses-of-worms effects....The word "overkill" comes to mind.

(M) TIME BANDITS 1981 SpFX:(exec) Ross King; Chris Verner, Andy Thompson. Ref: screen: bovine monsters serving Evil.
Loads of action, effects, fantasy; scattered laughs. Fun for kids, probably. Adults will be grateful for the (too-brief) appearances of John Cleese as Robin Hood and Ralph Richardson as the Supreme Being; they give their scenes a comic point and clarity which the film as a whole rather lacks.